RETAIL ADVERTISING
AND SELLING

BY THE SAME AUTHOR

THE ADVERTISING HANDBOOK
Pocket Size, Flexible Cover,
735 pp., more than 400 illustrations

THE HANDBOOK OF BUSINESS CORRESPONDENCE
Pocket Size, Flexible Cover,
1048 pp., more than 260 illustrations

THE HANDBOOK OF SALES MANAGEMENT
Pocket Size, Flexible Cover,
950 pp., more than 250 illustrations

RETAIL ADVERTISING AND SELLING

ADVERTISING, MERCHANDISE DISPLAY, SALES-PLANNING, SALESMANSHIP, TURNOVER AND PROFIT-FIGURING IN MODERN RETAILING

Including "Principles of Typography as Applied to Retail Advertising," by RICHARD M. BOREN

BY

S. ROLAND HALL

ADVERTISING COUNSELOR; FORMERLY ADVERTISING MANAGER, ALPHA PORTLAND CEMENT COMPANY AND THE VICTOR TALKING MACHINE COMPANY; FORMERLY DIRECTOR OF THE INTERNATIONAL CORRESPONDENCE SCHOOLS OF ADVERTISING AND SALESMANSHIP; AUTHOR, "THE ADVERTISING HANDBOOK," "THE HANDBOOK OF BUSINESS CORRESPONDENCE" AND "THE HANDBOOK OF SALES MANAGEMENT."

FIRST EDITION

HF
5429
H27

McGRAW-HILL BOOK COMPANY, INC.
NEW YORK: 370 SEVENTH AVENUE
LONDON: 6 & 8 BOUVERIE ST., E.C. 4
1924

Copyright, 1924, by the
McGraw-Hill Book Company, Inc.

PRINTED IN THE UNITED STATES OF AMERICA

THE MAPLE PRESS COMPANY, YORK, PA.

THE DAY OF BETTER RETAILING

There are doubtless many communities in which the retail store, even in this day, serves merely as a depot of supply for those purchasers who have a definite idea of what they want and who are interested enough to seek the merchandise or service with little or no encouragement from the merchant.

But retailing, in its rapid advance of the past score of years, has gone far past the stage of the local warehouse with a proprietor or a "clerk" in charge. "Clerks," by the way, are not named in this volume unless the author has been obliged to do so by reason of quoting the phraseology of others.

The improvement of transportation and of mail facilities, the growth of population, the vast circulation of periodicals of many kinds, the multiplication of kinds and styles of goods, the spread of house-to-house salesmanship and the establishment of the chain-store, have laid upon retailers generally the necessity for using every available expedient of good merchandising. The retail merchant's personal acquaintance and his standing in his community still mean much, but they are no longer the whole, or even the greater part, of retailing success.

"Better retailing" is not a subject of interest only to the retailer. Those manufacturers who sell their products through independent retail stores, or their own retail agencies, are as keenly interested today in good retail merchandising as is the local merchant. For no matter how superior may be the goods or service or how effectively such goods may be exploited to the public by the manufacturer, the wholesaler or other selling agent, at the last the retailer or his assistant stands before the customer as the interpreter of that product. Its success will depend largely on the retailer's interpretation or presentation.

There seems to have been in the past a general belief that any young man or young woman could step behind a counter and sell goods efficiently. It is far from the truth. Retail selling, like any other kind of selling, is a fine art. It can be a real service. Much space in this volume has accordingly been devoted to scientific salesmanship and methods of training for it.

Better retailing can hardly be covered comprehensively in any one volume of the size of the present one. Therefore, the treatment has been confined to those phases of retailing that have to do directly with advertising and selling, the training of assistants for such work, and the fundamentals of good store layout and merchandise display.

In preparing this review the author has been very materially assisted by the publishers of *Retail Ledger, Good Hardware, Dry Goods Economist, Talking Machine World, Progressive Grocer, New York Times, Grand Rapids Furniture Record, System, Automobile Trade Journal, Business, Printers' Ink, Marketing, Shoe Retailer, Burroughs Clearing House, National Builder, Permanent Builder, Building Materials, Advertising & Selling, Merchandising Advertising, Sample Case, American Builder* and still others, whose names are given in the various Sections of the volume.

The courtesy of these enterprising publishers and of many business acquaintances who answered questions and gave freely of their experiences has made possible a definiteness to the text that otherwise could not have been attained. This cooperation is gratefully acknowledged.

S. ROLAND HALL

COLLEGE HILL, EASTON, PA.
October, 1923

CONTENTS

	PAGE
THE DAY OF BETTER RETAILING	v

SECTION
I.	GETTING READY TO SELL	1
II.	COSTS OF SELLING	34
III.	TURNOVER AND PRICE-FIGURING	42
IV.	COMPENSATION PLANS	78
V.	STORE EQUIPMENT AND LAYOUT	90
VI.	WINDOW-DISPLAY MERCHANDISING	118
VII.	PLANNING AND MANAGING NEWSPAPER ADVERTISING	139

Including "Principles of Typography as Applied to Retail Advertising," by Richard M. Boren.

VIII.	MANUFACTURERS' SYNDICATED AND COOPERATIVE ADVERTISING	186
IX.	DIRECT ADVERTISING METHODS	202
X.	STREET-CAR, OUTDOOR, AND SPECIALTY ADVERTISING	257
XI.	THE WRITING OF COPY	272
XII.	TRAINING THE SALES FORCE	331
XIII.	MANUALS AND COURSES	361
XIV.	TALKS ON BETTER SELLING	389
XV.	SALES IDEAS, PLANS AND EXPERIENCES	497
INDEX		567

RETAIL ADVERTISING AND SELLING

SECTION I

GETTING READY TO SELL

"Retail," like many other simple words, is of broad scope. Strictly speaking, any merchandise or service that is sold direct to the consumer may be said to be sold at retail, though the merchant may be a great, centrally located mail-order concern serving the consumer living five hundred miles away. A manufacturer who operates his own system of retail outlets, whether these be stores or sales agents, may perform the function of a retailer.

For practical purposes, however, it seems best to confine the scope of this work largely to those business enterprises that serve a restricted section of the country rather than the entire nation and that deal with the public through a local office or store. Stores, from large department- and dry-goods stores down to the small specialty store, have come in for attention. Such special undertakings as those dealing with home-building, banking, automobiles, and other businesses of distinctive character in which goods or services are delivered direct to users have been studied with a view to uncovering sound fundamental ideas.

The principal purpose has been to draw attention to sound advertising practice, to stimulate efficient sales-planning and to encourage training for better salesmanship rather than to record clerical and accounting practice, financing or shipping methods.

Value of Adaptation.—One who happens to be in the harness business, the jewelry business, the ice cream business, the laundry business, or in any other of a score of businesses of special types, who expects to find in this volume a "ready-to-wear," worked-out solution of his particular problems or a precise list of the appeals that he should use in his advertising copy or his oral salesmanship will be disappointed. No book can specialize to that extent and be of service to a large number of readers. Even in one class of retail business, problems will differ materially. The small jeweler cannot always follow in the footsteps of the large jeweler.

One of the most valuable lessons to be learned in business is the lesson of adaptation. Even if the author and the publisher of a business book could provide much in the way of business plans and sales appeals that a reader could safely follow, word for word, they would do the reader an injustice. The successful business man is not a copyist or a slavish imitator. He keeps eyes and ears open for all successful ideas, principles and experiences, weighs them carefully and then asks the question: "How far can they be adapted and adopted by me?"

A sampling method used originally by a cigar store might, in modified form, be a profitable plan for a bakery. Package-advertising as carried out by a laundry might illustrate a principle that an automobile-supplies store would do well to employ. A successful appeal that is used by a hundred or more savings banks today had its origin in a "baby letter" sent out by department stores. Probably few bank men would have seen in the description of the department store's plans anything that seemed like a sound idea for a financial institution. The man who saw and used this plan had learned the lesson of adaptation. Such a man, when he receives a good solicitation in the form of a letter, a folder, a booklet or a catalogue, or when he observes some distinctive sales plan or sales tactic, analyzes it to see if it can be adapted in any way to his own business. Probably in the form in which it is finally used by him—if he does use it—the details are far from the details of the original plan or idea; only the fundamental principle remains.

The plan of exploiting a special savings account as a means of buying an automobile, promoted generally by the Ford Motor Company in 1923, was merely an adaptation of an idea that had been in use by banks and other concerns for many years. The club idea has, likewise, been applied to a wide range of purchases. Essentially, it is only the instalment plan of payment in a more appealing form.

There is not a great deal under the sun that is absolutely new. Effective methods are to a large extent adaptations and improvements of other men's experiences.

Importance of Survey and Outlook Departments to Retailers.—A great many manufacturers have made good use of surveys as a means of determining sales possibilities and also as a means of improving their advertising and sales efforts. The survey method has not apparently been used to any large extent in the retail field—possibly because of the amount of work involved—and yet, undoubtedly, it is often worth what the adoption of it would cost.

Reports by Government or Educational Institutions.—Sometimes surveys that have been made by the Federal Government, the State Government, some educational institution, or some social organization can be used by a merchant and a great deal of his time saved. For example, the State University of Iowa undertook some years ago to gather information that would answer such questions as:

Who are the customers of the retail stores?

Where do they live?

How do they live?

How far will they drive to buy certain goods?

What appeals can be made to induce them to buy?

Some extracts from the report of this institution, published originally in the *Dry Goods Economist*, follow:

It has been found that no analysis is adequate which does not take into consideration the fact that nearly all people will shop for some things, but will not shop for others.

The survey under discussion shows two territories—one for "convenience goods" and the other for "shopping lines." Groceries, drugs and hardware come under the head of "convenience goods," while clothing, furniture and other goods are "shopping lines."

The territory for "convenience goods," as may be inferred from the term, is confined to a comparatively small area, determined by distance or convenience of location. "Shopping" territory often includes "convenience" territory but extends as far as each individual merchant can extend it by advertising, service, satisfying stocks and any other factor that will attract people to his store. Train service and good roads influence to a great extent the area of "shopping" territory.

In the survey referred to, the influences in buying merchandise were indicated in their order, as follows, by city and country women:

How Customers Are Influenced

	City	Country
Window-displays	1	3
Newspaper advertisements	2	4
Shopping from store to store	3	1
Recommendations of friends	4	2
Recommendations of the merchant	5	5
Samples	6	7
National magazine advertisements	7	10
Demonstrations	8	9
Circulars through the mail	9	8
Mail-order catalogues	10	6
Billboards	11	11
Street-car signs	12	12

Strength of Certain Appeals.—To determine the strength of certain appeals used in advertising women's apparel, this question was asked in the survey carried on by the State University of Iowa, "In buying a dress or a suit for yourself, which of the following characteristics do you consider most important? List them by number in the order of their importance." The result was:

Appeals	City	Country
Perfect fit of garment	1	1
Excellent materials	2	3
Comfort to the wearer	3	2
Durable garments	4	5
Up-to-date style	5	4
Merchant's guarantee	6	8
Low price	7	6
New goods	8	9
Money back if not satisfied	9	7
Manufacturer's guarantee	10	10
Fine hand-tailoring	11	11
Made by union labor	12	12

Such surveys as these, in addition to bringing out many interesting reasons for certain purchases, also yield considerable constructive criticism from purchasers of the stores of various localities.

Value of Special Survey to a Merchant.—The *Dry Goods Economist* says, on the subject of surveys for retail merchants:

Experience has shown, too, that some retail stores can afford to make personal surveys. A large store in a western New York center made that kind of an investigation a few years ago in order to ascertain whether the strong and easy-selling lines of merchandise were being pushed by the concern, to the neglect of those in which the store was weak.

It was that part of the suburban public who could afford to visit the store frequently, by auto or by rail, toward whom the inquiry was directed. The work was carried on by an unusually bright woman, one who had the personality and ability to talk effectively to well-to-do people. She would visit a family or home, ostensibly for the purpose of telling of improvements made in the store. She would show photographs of various departments and would explain that she was there for the purpose of answering questions regarding the store. What she really did was to study the family and their abode, note the number of children, their ages and various other particulars. The information thus gained showed just how to approach the various families by letter, the kind of merchandise in which they would be most interested and the way in which they would best be handled on coming to the store.

This work did not, as might be supposed, involve a house-to-house canvass. In some of the suburbs visited, or sections thereof, the class or position and living conditions of many families were obviously so similar that it was necessary to call on only one family in ten, while in some other instances even a smaller percentage was sufficient.

Questionnaire Methods as Aids to Buying.—Returns from a questionnaire may serve to aid a buyer in selecting merchandise on his trip to market. For instance, a questionnaire sent to women customers of a store, asking them what garments they expect to purchase during the coming season, and giving a list of apparel, with means for checking off items, would, if carefully and tactfully prepared, be given attention by a fair proportion of the women addressed and prove of great help to the buyer. Such a questionnaire should be sent with return postage enclosed; should be made as easy as possible to fill out; and should contain an introduction or footnote explaining that the return exacts no obligation but that it will be of invaluable assistance to the store in selecting stocks for the coming season. This explanation can be worded so as to make the woman feel complimented to be asked for her views on the kind of garments that will be worn by careful buyers. In addition to gaining much buying information, the store will have on hand a classified list of people desiring certain articles and can use it to advantage in mailing letters or circulars regarding special purchases.

Questionnaire on Reading Habits and Influence of Different Media.—The information under this heading is taken from a survey made by the Women's Advertising Club, of Los Angeles. As a very large proportion of retail buying is done by women, this club decided that it could do an important work by determining, as far as possible, the attention given by women to various kinds of advertising and the effect of this attention.

Speakers from the Advertising Club appeared before various organizations of women, clubs, parent teacher-associations, and similar organizations. The object of the survey was explained and the questionnaires were distributed, the speaker urging that the questions be given careful consideration before the answers were written. It is stated by Mrs. Lula E. Eckles, publicity director of A. Hamburger & Son, that the information was secured as far as possible without coercion or bias and that various classes of women were included— the well-to-do club woman, the wage-earner in moderate circumstances, teachers, housewives generally, workers in factories, stores and offices, and professional women. The summary was made up from the answers given on a thousand of the questionnaire sheets.

Do you read:	Yes Per Cent	No Per Cent
1. Newspaper advertisements?	83	6*
2. Circular letters?	33	40*
3. Announcement cards?	64	17*
4. Booklets and pamphlets?	32	35*
5. Magazine advertisements?	72	10*
6. Program advertisements?	65	14*
7. Street car advertisements?	75	11*
8. Billboards?	54	23*

9. Which of the above advertising media influence you most?

	Per Cent
Newspapers?	36
Circular letters?	1
Announcement cards?	4
Booklets and pamphlets?	1.7
Magazine advertisements?	22.7
Program advertisements?	3
Street car advertisements?	4.2
Billboards?	4.4
Did not answer—could not decide	2.3

10. Do you prefer advertisements with illustrations?	64	16*
11. Do you like chatty, conversational advertisements?	34	41*
12. Do you like more statement of facts and prices?	60	20*
13. Have you faith in comparative prices?	35	30*
14. Have you sometimes found that merchandise is not as represented in advertisement?	78	8*
15. Where possible, do you specify "home products?"	42	21*
16. Have you confidence in advertising generally?	73	10*

* Balance represents percentage who read only occasionally or who did not answer.

The review is very favorable to newspaper advertising. These findings were reproduced in a document of the American Newspaper Publishers' Association entitled "Advertising Costs and National Selling."

The reader should always be on his guard, however, against forming fixed opinions from researches of this character. No matter how carefully people attempt to answer questions, they often do not know just what they give most attention to or just what influences them most. A person, for example, may have some prejudice against circularizing methods or house-to-house salesmanship and give an answer decidedly derogatory to these methods while at the same time being influenced to a much greater degree by them than is realized. For instance, it is common to have people insist that they do not read long letters or that they pay no attention to mail received under 1-cent postage, and yet the experiences of various concerns show that it is often profitable to use long letters and 1-cent stamps. It is not the purpose of the author to discredit such findings as those assembled under this heading, but merely to warn readers against accepting them as the last word on the subject.

Another Research to Determine Aid of Advertising.—Another research that contains something of value to retailers is that conducted by the National Retailers' Association for the purpose of determining how far the advertised article is preferred over unadvertised goods of similar class.

The findings were these: when two similar articles are offered for sale at the same time and on the same conditions, one a well advertised commodity and the other an unadvertised article, in 87.6 times out of 100, the customer preferred the advertised article; in 3.6 cases the unadvertised article was preferred; and in 8.8 cases the customer seemed to have no preference.

When there was a price difference in favor of the unadvertised article, the customer preferred that in 24.2 out of 100 sales. The well advertised article, however, was the choice of 60.6 per cent of the people who bought. In 15.2 times, the customer seemed to have no preference.

It is not stated how many sales were included in arriving at these figures.

Becoming Acquainted with Motives.—No merchant's copy or sales talk will hit the mark unless he becomes acquainted with the motives that impel purchases.

Research work and questionnaires are often conducted with the hope of getting at the underlying motives, but, after all, one of the best sources of information is through the advertiser's daily contact with customers and in his talk with people generally.

Consider, for example, the state of mind of heads of families today where it is extremely difficult to secure capable household assistants. Under such conditions, the offering of children's clothing that does not soil easily, or that is easy to wash and iron, means more than the usual bargain-price appeal. Likewise, women, as a rule, are much more interested in the time-saving and freedom acquired through the use of mechanical devices in the home than they are in other features. The merchant who advertises that he has a gas range with a fireless cooker attachment that enables the housewife to start her dinner cooking and then go off and enjoy a church service, an automobile trip, a card party or a visit with neighbors, makes a direct appeal that is hard to resist.

There is hardly a man who takes care of his own furnace who does not dread to get up early on cold winter mornings and go down to stoke up the fire. The furnace-regulator dealer can appeal to this motive more effectively even than he can to the coal-saving feature of the regulator.

Suppose, for example, the copy-writer has the job of helping to sell a familiar type of automobile. What are the real family discussions on the automobile subject? People are probably saying, "Would it be an extravagance for us to own a machine?" "We can't buy a car this year, but maybe we can next," "I wonder if I would be too nervous to drive an automobile—if it would be a real pleasure, or just an added burden," and so on.

Familiarity with these reflections and conversations makes it easier for the copy-writer to get into the heart of his subject and score with his argument in favor of acquiring an automobile.

And this information can be gained in no better way than through direct contact with the people of the community served by the advertiser.

Miscellaneous Suggestions on Surveys.—In finding out what people will buy, it is a good plan for the buyer to consult salespeople and to mingle freely with customers in the store, overhearing comments on the merchandise on display or perhaps such questions as, "Why don't you have so-and-so?" In this way he learns at first-hand what appeals to people or what they would like to have. Should a customer leave without purchasing an article she has looked at, the buyer should ascertain from the salesman the reasons for the failure to sell. A little observation of this sort would soon show him why people will buy certain brands of merchandise in preference to others and give him the customer's viewpoint, without which he cannot be a successful buyer.

Surveys along restricted lines have been conducted by various merchants, not only for the purposes already outlined but to determine the extent of mail-order buying, to gage the probable chance for success for a new department being considered by the merchant, and so on. The following paragraphs from the *Talking Machine World* describe the work of an enterprising saleswoman engaged in the talking-machine business. These paragraphs describe not only house-to-house work of a survey nature but also similar work from the office.

The people of our section are Saturday-spenders—men who wear working shirts most of the week and on Sunday dress up. You can spend a lot of time during the week going after them. I sold children's books for three years, rang door-bells, and in that way came to know people. I made more money then than I probably ever will again.

During the last month I have made a house-to-house canvass of certain sections. I have charge of our store and have to be there a great deal of the time. But I gave half an hour a day to canvassing, and it has brought me three sales of instruments. This may not be much, but just now it is worth going after, and it shows the possibilities in this field. I have directly traced the selling of these

GETTING READY TO SELL 11

instruments to this campaign. When I call at the house I address the woman by her name and say, "We would like to put you on our mailing-list. Do you receive the supplements from any other store?" If she does, she is a prospective customer for records, and if she doesn't, she is a good prospective purchaser for an instrument.

I am also interested in doing work for schools. You can do that sort of thing in every community. I gained access by getting in touch with the principal and explained that it was for the good of the school. I talked to her on nationality in music and asked her to let me try it. After permission was granted, I brought some records to entertain the children. I started down South. Then we heard Indians, went to Hawaii and heard Hawaiian music, then Japanese and Chinese music. I showed them how there is a rowing rhythm to Italy's music. The children entered right into the spirit of it. I told them the name of the record, let them repeat it, had them sing it, made them pronounce it. We then went to Ireland and came home, all the children singing "Home, Sweet Home."

We call ten people every day on the telephone. On rainy days we manage to keep the operators busy. I think it is best to have a girl call, as she will always talk more graciously to another woman. The usual form of address is: "I am Miss.........., from .... shop. We are just considering your name for our mailing-list. We will be pleased to mail you our supplements if you do not receive these from another store. If you are in our neighborhood and need anything in our merchandise, stop in. Ask for me. I would like to wait on you myself. My name is .... Have you an instrument?"

If she says she hasn't, of course there is a chance for us to make a sale. If she says they have an old instrument, tell her that you can put this old instrument in first-class condition. I have traced fifteen direct sales to our telephone this past month. I find very few people are rude; in fact, most of them thank us for calling up.

Special-appeal Effort Was Combined with Survey.— Donahoe & Donahoe, Victor dealers, Fort Dodge, Iowa, conducted a musical census of their community and obtained results far beyond their expectations, reporting it very profitable and successful in every way. A brief description of the plan appeared in the house organ of Mickel Bros. Company, a Nebraska distributor of musical merchandise.

The company secured a number of salespeople, gave them each six phonograph records, one late roll for player-pianos, and full instructions on how to proceed with the census. Each was assigned to certain territory and instructed to use, as the opening talk, the argument that they were making a musical census for the store in order to find out what make of piano, talking machine or player-piano was in use at the present time, so that the store could properly equip its service department to give expert repair service when needed. This argument usually resulted in the salesman's being invited in to see the instrument, where there was one, and the chance for a trial of the record or roll. Customers for rolls and records were thus secured and where there was no instrument, a name was added to the mailing-list for future solicitation. In cases where information was refused it was easily obtained from neighbors.

The salespeople were paid at the rate of $1 a day, 10 cents for each item in a sale, and 3 cents for all cards fully and correctly filled out. For each talking machine sold within 5 days to these prospective customers, $1 to $10 was paid, according to size; $5 on new pianos and from $7.50 to $10 on player-pianos. To prevent any temptation to dishonesty, salespeople were informed that their work would be verified by telephone.

Organizing for Advertising and Selling.—The Namm Store, Brooklyn, N. Y., affords a good example of functional organization. The two branches that are directly responsible to the board of directors are known as the administration branch and the merchandise branch. The first has to do with financial matters and with general store service. All questions in this domain come to the consideration of several executives, including the president of the company, the store manager, and the comptroller. Service in connection with this administration branch has to do with the receiving of goods and delivery, but not with sales service.

The jurisdiction of the merchandise branch covers the buying and selling of the store and the policies and practices relating to these two branches of effort. The executives in this division include the secretary of the company, a merchandise manager and a sales manager.

GETTING READY TO SELL

The administration branch has charge of store planning, equipment, making of budgets, accounting, credit, health service department, paying of employes, and so on.

The merchandise branch, in addition to active selling, controls the research work and the advertising. It is also responsible for keeping the right stocks of goods on hand and in proper selling condition.

The sales manager controls both the selling and the advertising. Directly responsible to the sales manager is the superintendent of each floor, to whom all salespeople are directly responsible.

In this large store, provision is made for an employes' committee, made up from all the principal divisions of the store. This committee is charged with the responsibility of making suggestions regularly for the betterment of the business and of individual employes.

Other interesting features of this large retail organization are the following:

1. Every employe is made to understand that he is not only responsible for the most efficient performance in his position but is expected to *study the job ahead, as well as train an understudy*.

2. The store slogan: "It can't be done! But here it is!"

Organization Chart of the Duffy-Powers Company.—The chart of this Rochester, N. Y., organization, shown in Exhibit 1, affords an interesting comparison with a manufacturing organization. As will be observed, the Duffy-Powers Company regards sales promotion, merchandising, research, operation, and finance and statistics as subjects of major importance.

On the theory that plans for the sale of merchandise should be made before the merchandise is bought, the sales promotion department and the merchandising department were merged, under the direction of the general manager. As is usual, the buyers for the various departments are under the direction of a merchandise manager. There are three merchandise managers. One supervises the ready-to-wear departments, including the basement; another has charge of most of the main-floor departments—the notions, toilet goods, gloves,

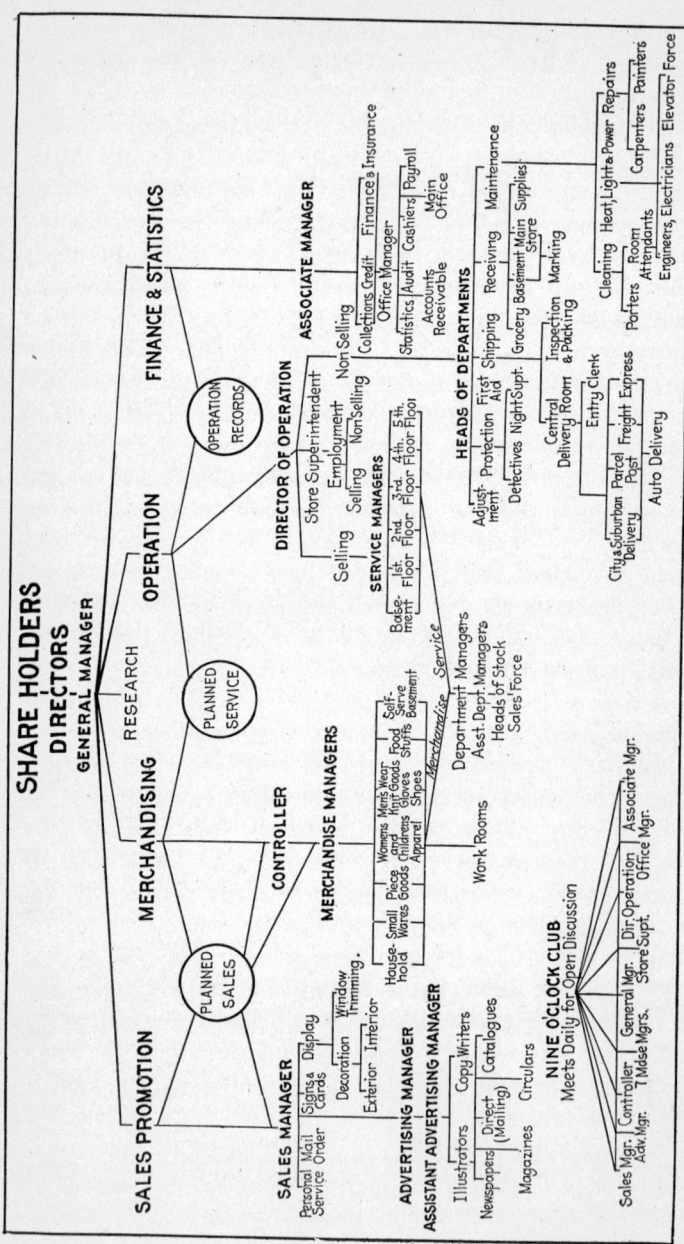

Exhibit 1.—Chart of organization of a large department store.

and neckwear departments—and the third, who is also the comptroller of the company, has charge of the remaining departments.

The policy of the store requires that these merchandise managers shall be able at any time to discharge the duties of buyer for any department under their supervision. Every purchase made by a buyer is supervised by the merchandise manager of that division, who also passes on all questions of marking up or marking down. Before purchases are actually made, the sales manager is consulted, but all buying requisitions are O. K.'d by the comptroller. This policy gives all of these various executives an intimate knowledge of just what is being bought and what selling effort is being planned. While nothing is done to take away from the initiative of any part of the buying and selling work, the system followed makes possible a better understanding and better teamwork.

Since this chart was made up, the "Nine o'Clock Club" has been discontinued, but for several years this was a feature that made possible a daily exchange of opinions among the executives of the Duffy-Powers store.

In a large department store such as the one here charted, it is highly important that in the employment office, receiving and delivery departments, the marking room, show-card writing room, and so on, extra facilities be provided for unusual events. Through the teamwork indicated by this chart, it is possible for every department to be notified of any extra effort that is likely to be required. Thus, the big store becomes like a big machine with every part of the mechanism doing its work efficiently.

A View of the Retail Sales Manager of the Future.—The former sales manager of a large retail store, now managing editor of the *Dry Goods Economist*, thus describes the trend of the times with respect to the responsibilities of the department store manager:

The functions of a department-store sales manager of the future will relate completely to store and business organization. He will be consulted in the formation of selling plans, have control of advertising merchandise, be responsible for the method of selling and expense connected with selling. Such a store manager will budget for department managers the amount of monthly investment in merchandise.

He will have the say as to what shall be advertised and the prices of the merchandise. It will be his privilege to decline for advertising continually items that buyers want to close out rather than articles sought by the public. He will make a small advertisement perform what now takes a half-page. He will recommend reductions in prices in preference to spending more than the amount of the reductions in advertising. He will consult with the buyers, so as not to superimpose "quick close-outs" at the expense of departments requiring sales boosts.

Last year's record for a certain day will not be made the fetish for the same day of the current year. Supervision of salespeople will be within his province; floor-walkers will be men able to see that departments are working smoothly and shall report directly to the sales manager. Bonuses will have lifted from them the burden of responsibility of sales.

Western Merchant's Simple Platform.—A successful Midwestern retail merchant has defined the six most important things in retail selling as:

1. The right goods.
2. The right prices.
3. A good location.
4. Courteous, efficient salespeople.
5. Attention-arresting newspaper advertising.
6. Attractive window-displays.

Such a platform consists of more than organization or policies. The succeeding Sections give many helpful suggestions bearing not only on the six points listed but on all of the most essential features of successful merchandising.

Determining Advertising Appropriation.—A review of the methods of a large number of business firms reveals that the following are the methods used in determining advertising appropriation:

1. Arbitrarily fixing a yearly appropriation, according to the views of the proprietor.
2. Basing the appropriation for a new year on a percentage of sales for the preceding year.

3. Fixing a quota or estimate for a forthcoming year and basing the advertising percentage on this quota or estimate.
4. Having no yearly advertising appropriation but creating a fund for advertising month by month by the "percentage of sales" syestm.

Of the methods listed, undoubtedly No. 3 is the progressive and scientific method, although it is probably true that the larger number of concerns simply take the preceding year's business and figure on a percentage of that amount. This, however, has been aptly called "grinding with water that has passed the mill." No progressive enterprise should have anything in its program that indicates a stand-still policy. The business is likely to go either forward or backward. If all of its efforts—space for doing business, window-display merchandising, personal selling effort, advertising, and so forth—are planned merely to match a preceding year's work, the program is not likely to be a progressive one. A preceding year's work affords, in the normal condition, a good basis for calculation, but it should be used as a basis only. The retailer has as much reason as the manufacturer for establishing a standard or quota of sales and then arranging all expenditures and percentages in accordance with this quota. A large store, consisting of a number of sections or departments operated on separate accounting systems, should, of course, call on each department to make its own quota and its own percentage.

Value of the Budget.—The budget system is as useful in planning an advertising campaign as in the general operation of a business. By studying the work of previous years and the costs of the various kinds of advertising undertaken, the modern advertising manager or sales manager—if the sales manager is responsible for advertising effort—will make up a budget showing probably the following items:

General overhead expense
Newspaper advertising
Direct advertising
Booklets
Folders

Catalogue
Letters
House organ
Postal cards
Mailing cards
Outdoor advertising
Car-cards.
Posters and signs
Emergency fund

Whether or not an advertising department provides for such expense as show-cards and price-tickets will depend on the organization of the enterprise. Ordinarily, these items are grouped either under merchandise-display expense or as a part of the general selling expense.

The emergency fund is important, because unlooked-for increases may come in any one or a number of the items. Besides, special occasions for advertising come up that cannot be foreseen at the beginning of a year. One value of the budget lies in the fact that it gives a general program to be followed as consistently as possible. There should be a monthly check against it so that the expenditure for any one item will not accumulate too rapidly.

The Budget as a Barometer.—The budget plan aids in teamwork, if the various departments can be convinced that it is an efficient plan and can be induced to arrange their own activities according to some budget program. In a large store, a complete budget will cover material for window-displays, equipment for show-cases, outdoor display, street-car work, printing and plates of all kinds, drawings, photographs, goods given away or space purchased for purely goodwill purposes, direct advertising of all kinds, newspaper space.

A good feature of the budget plan is that the totals of these various departments of advertising effort may be shown year after year and comparison made by years, so that it can be seen at a glance whether one kind of effort is costing more or less than it did in a previous year. Furthermore, the budget plan permits a monthly check. This monthly showing may be arranged on a large sheet, which may serve as a barometer of activities. The form shown in Exhibit 2 is a practical one.

MONTHLY INDEX OF ADVERTISING EXPENDITURE

	Salary Expense								Newspaper Space				Direct Advertising				Street Car				Total Advertising Expense			
	Overhead				Clerical																			
	Planned	Spent	%	Last Yr.	Planned	Spent	%	Last Yr.	Planned	Spent	%	Last Yr.	Planned	Spent	%	Last Yr.	Planned	Spent	%	Last Yr.	Planned	Spent	%	Last Yr.
Jan.																									
Feb.																									
Mar.																									
Apr.																									
May																									
June																									
July																									
Aug.																									
Sept																									
Oct.																									
Nov.																									
Dec.																									
Totals																									

EXHIBIT 2.—Convenient form for a monthly tabulation of advertising expenditure, according to the various items of the budget.

Such a form should be wide enough to include all the units of the budget. The final column at the right should give the monthly totals. The same plan could be carried out on the same sheet, or a separate sheet, to show sales expense. Ordinarily, however, the advertising department does not plan or control this budget, and therefore would have no need of a monthly index of expenditures, except as a matter of general information. Most alert advertising men would prefer to have this information handy as a means of checking up constantly with the ratio of advertising and selling expense.

Distribution of Advertising Charges.—As advertising appropriations or percentages are figured separately for each section or department of large stores, it is, of course, only good accounting that all charges for advertising be distributed accurately. This can be done usually by means of a large sheet carrying such headings as those shown in Exhibit 3.

In a large retail organization there is always a considerable amount of advertising that can not be charged directly to any one class of goods or to any particular department. This applies not only to signatures, general headings, introductory talks, and the like, but also to special features such as editorials.

In describing its practice, the Wanamaker organization gives the following information:

Headings, signatures, addresses, editorials and other miscellaneous items are classified as "general advertising." At the end of the year the total amount of all such general advertising is charged proportionately to the various departments.

All other advertising is charged directly to the department for which the advertising is done, according to the number of agate lines devoted to each separate department, or the cost of some piece of direct advertising literature.

Should it happen that an advertisement is made up which cannot be charged directly to any particular department, it is charged to "general advertising" and redistributed among the various departments at the end of the year, just as the miscellaneous items are.

It is entirely practical for a retailer conducting a moderate sized shop to use just one advertising distribution sheet, charging on this sheet newspaper advertising, as well as the

THE DAYLIGHT DEPARTMENT STORE

Perryville, Ohio

Advertising Distribution Sheet

Date of adv.	Medium or method	General adv.	Coat and suit dept.	Millinery dept.	Linen dept.	Hosiery dept.	Toilet goods dept.

Exhibit 3.—Specimen advertising distribution sheet, showing how a large department store charges against each department the advertising which is done in behalf of the different departments.

cost of folders, booklets, mailing cards, car-cards, billboards or signs and any other direct advertising literature.

On the other hand, the large retailer has something to gain by having several distribution sheets—one for newspaper advertising, another for letters, folders, booklets, mailing cards, and the like, and still another for outdoor and street-car advertising. This would simplify the work, because on the newspaper advertising distribution sheet, for example, the distribution might be made each day according to the number of agate lines chargeable to each department and the total cost for each department, worked out by the week or by the month, according to the rate per agate line, instead of working out each day the proportionate cost chargeable to the various departments.

Methods of a Druggist in Apportioning Expense.—Harry Sanford, a Muskegon, Mich., druggist who operates three drug stores in a community of somewhat less than 50,000 population, has worked out an interesting system of apportioning all kinds of operating and selling expense so as to have a very accurate idea of just what each section or department produces. This merchant maintains his planning and accounting department in an office building entirely apart from his stores, so as to have plenty of room for charts and blackboards. One room is lined with large blackboards with special rulings. The object of the Sanford system is to keep close watch of all selling details and to make fair and accurate distribution of the various items that have a tendency to reduce the net profit, such as wrapping paper and twine, signs, repairs, delivery, donations to charity and even telegrams. The theory of this merchant is that every department and every article has a certain share of the advantages and should bear a proportionate part, not only of the salary of the general manager and the office expense, but of the hire of janitor, and so on.

Exhibit 4 is a reproduction of the floor layout of one of the Sanford stores. A study of this exhibit and of the following explanation, published originally in *Business*, will give a good idea of this Muskegon merchant's method.

To distribute the item of rent, each of the stores has been divided into four divisions. One division consists only of the display-windows. The three other divisions are equal cross-sections of the store—the forward one-third, the middle one-third and the rear one-third—and these cross-sections Sanford has named, respectively, A, B and C. Experiments in the Sanford stores have demonstrated that, in sales possibilities, cross-section A is worth one-third more than section B, and section B one-third more than section C.

Of the whole amount of rent for the entire store, the windows absorb 25 per cent and this 25 per cent is charged, against the various departments proportionately as their respective merchandise occupies the windows. The remaining 75 per cent is distributed over the three interior sections of the store, section A carrying 33⅓ per cent, section B 25 per cent, and section C 16⅔ per cent. Thus, if the rent of the whole store is $400 a month, the windows carry $100, section A, $133.33, section B, $100 and section C, $66.67.

Within each section this sectional quota of rent is distributed among the departments that occupy the section. By the guidance of a floor plan drawn on paper, the departments are identified as to sections and compared in area. Thus, suppose that in section A the total space occupied by departments is 352 sq. ft. and suppose that the cigar department, which stands wholly within the section, occupies 140 sq. ft. To determine the cigar department's share of the rent of section A, divide 140 by 352; the result is 39.8 and 39.8 per cent of $133.33 is $53.06.

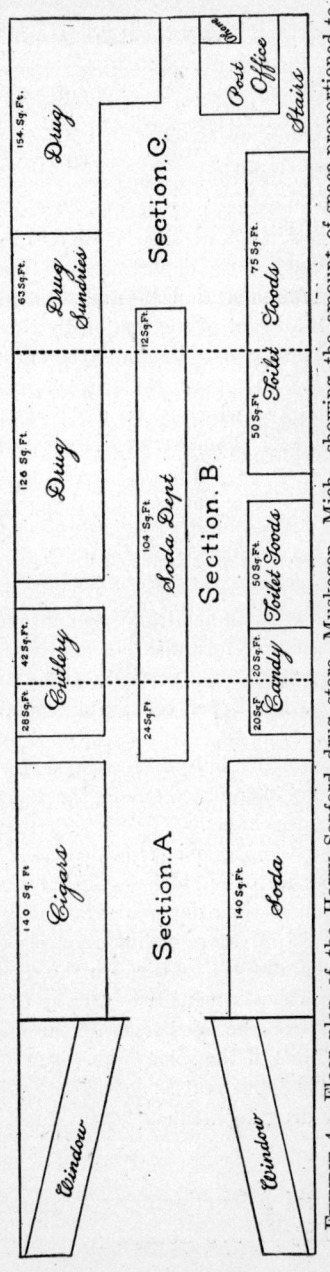

EXHBIT 4.—Floor plan of the Harry Sanford drug store, Muskegon, Mich., showing the amount of space proportioned to different articles or departments. Each of the three Sanford stores includes seven departments, and three are patterned on the same ground plan. Of the total rent the windows pay 25 per cent, Section A 33⅓ per cent, Section B 25 per cent, and Section C 16⅔ per cent.

A department may occupy space in more than one section. For instance, in each of the Sanford stores the soda department extends into all three sections and the cutlery, candy, toilet goods, and drug departments into two sections each. To figure the rent to be charged to such a section, Sanford applies the same formula, but applies the formula to different floor-space values. Thus, the cutlery department, for instance, may occupy a total of 70 sq. ft., of which 28 sq. ft. lies in section A and 42 sq. ft. in section B. To figure the rent to be charged against the department, divide 28 by 352—the total area of departments in section A—and thus arrive at a percentage. Multiply the total rent of the section by this percentage and arrive at the amount to be charged against the cutlery department for its rent in section A. In section B the total area occupied by departments is 392 sq. ft., of which the cutlery department's share is 42 sq. ft. Divide 42 by 392 and arrive at a percentage; multiply the total rental charge of the section by this percentage and arrive at the amount of rent to be charged against the department for its space in section B. Then add together the two sectional amounts and the total is the cutlery department's share of the rent of the store.

Advertising expense is apportioned among the departments in accordance with arbitrary percentages of their respective sales. In the Sanford "formulas" of figuring, these percentages are: cigars, 1 per cent; cutlery, 2 per cent, soda, 2 per cent, drugs, 1½ per cent; drug sundries, 2 per cent; toilet goods, 1½ per cent; candy, 1½ per cent.

Electric light bills and expense for janitor service and janitor supplies are distributed among the departments in proportion to their departmental areas. The rent for the public telephone, however—since the telephone is regarded as a business-builder that brings customers into the store—is distributed among the departments in proportion to their departmental sales.

The Sanford store policy requires every department to display its merchandise, in its turn, in the display-windows, and the extent to which a department is to occupy the windows is regulated by the ratio between the sales of the department and the sales of the entire store. Thus, if the sales of the drug department are running at the rate of $32,000 a year as compared with $96,000 for the entire store, then the drug department is to occupy the windows one-third of the time.

Unusual Advertisement Produced by Auction Plan.—The Pettis Dry Goods Company, of Indianapolis, Ind., evolved an

GETTING READY TO SELL

unusual method of apportioning space in its advertisements to various departments of the store, to introduce a month of general sale events. The merchandising manager and the advertising manager gave a luncheon for the department buyers, at which they put up for auction various sections of the double-page advertising space in the newspapers. There was space available for only 14 out of the 64 departments and the bidding was based on the estimated business of the department for the first day of the sale. The largest space—11 by 12 inches—went to the aluminum-ware department which estimated $3,000 worth of business, and the smallest—2½ by 4¼ inches—to the electric-cleaner department on a bid of $400 estimated business. The actual cost of the space was charged against the advertising appropriation of each bidder. As to results of the plan, the advertising manager says:

The plan proved to be a success, as is shown by the fact that the sales of each of the fourteen departments more than justified the bids for space. From the merchandising standpoint the idea is a good one, inasmuch as it drives home to the individual department managers and salespeople the truth concerning the value of advertising space. The fourteen departments that bought space in the double-page spread gained much valuable information concerning the relation between advertising and sales. Furthermore, the desire to make the advertising expenditure pay the largest possible dividends inspired keen salesmanship.

(*Retail Ledger*).

INCREASING EFFECTIVENESS OF PUBLICITY AND PERSONAL SALESMANSHIP

Cooperation with Manufacturer's Advertising.—Local and retail advertisers can add much to the force of their publicity by carefully cooperating with national advertisers. It is probably true that some of the national advertisers attempt to make more capital out of their campaigns than the facts warrant. Unfortunately, it is too often the case that some manufacturer plans a campaign of advertising that in the aggregate seems to him to be a promotional effort of great power, but which is so thinly spread out that it has very little effect in a city or over a trade community of fair size. In such cases representatives of the manufacturer are inclined to claim more for their campaign than they are warranted in claiming.

On the other hand, retail advertisers must take into account that it is not possible for every national advertiser to have an intensive local campaign, however desirable this might seem from the retailer's point of view. Though it may seem to the retailer that the amount required for an intensive local campaign is not large, when this amount is multiplied by 1,000, or perhaps even a larger figure—representing the other communities in which the manufacturer, if he carried out such a plan generally, would have to deal—the total will likely represent an expenditure far beyond a figure that the manufacturer could afford.

Perhaps no advertising problem comes up oftener and is more perplexing than the question of whether a manufacturer should deal with separate communities and separate campaigns or undertake a nation-wide campaign in generally circulated mediums to give support to retailers.

When conditions warrant the expenditure, there is undoubted value to local advertising that ties the publicity up closely to the retailer of the product and gives the public the name and address of the local distributor at the time interest in the merchandise is secured. On the other hand, some manufacturers are selling to such a large number of retailers that it is impractical to attempt any form of advertising that connects directly with the names and addresses of retailers. This is a problem that must be worked out between retailers and manufacturers. Manufacturers are usually more than willing to have the views of enterprising retailers as to how money can be spent to the best advantage. Still, on their side of the case, the complaint is often made—and often justified—that retailers are lax in tying up properly with constructive advertising campaigns reaching selected groups of good size in the retailer's community. A good number of national publications are circulated so generally that an advertiser undertaking a fair-sized campaign in a well selected list of these publications is giving his retailers valuable support. The enterprising retailer should become acquainted with the advertising plans of the manufacturer whose goods he sells and should connect his own plans with the efforts of the manufacturer. If he uses the local newspapers at the very time that impressive advertisements in popular, nationally circulated mediums are reaching thousands of local readers, he has a much better chance to crystallize or concentrate interest than he would ordinarily. Even such a reference as the following may be very effective:

The all-enamel kitchen cabinet—the last word for the modern kitchen—advertised in the current numbers of the *A. B. C. and D.* Magazines, is on display in our north window. Be sure to see it and to come in for an explanation of our easy-payment plan.

In those cases where national advertisers are using local mediums, the retail dealer can benefit by running his own advertisement on the page with the manufacturer's announcement. Sometimes, he can even arrange to have his own message to his readers appear alongside of or underneath the manufacturer's appeal.

It is obvious that where conditions permit the manufacturer to run his local campaign exclusively for the benefit of his local retailer or retailers and can include the names and addresses of local dealers in the main advertisement, the arrangement is close to ideal.

Resourcefulness in Exploiting Merchandise.—A merchant who found at the end of a late spring that he had a lot of rather stout shoes for women remaining unsold conceived the idea of offering them as vacation shoes for tramping, etc. This made a summer sale possible.

Another merchant, finding himself with a supply of tennis balls on hand that were lacking in liveliness, offered them as children's play balls, at a reduced price, and disposed of the stock. The balls were perfectly good for this latter purpose, though they would have been unsatisfactory at any price to tennis players.

A grocer's inventory revealed that he had a good supply of odds and ends on hand—packaged goods that had been in stock quite a while and become uninviting because of discoloration or soil. The contents of these packages were all right, and so the grocer believed it was proper to sell the goods. He made up a quantity of baskets, each containing a number of these useful articles, and offered the baskets at the attractive price of $1 each. The idea was so appealing to the public that he quickly cleared his shelves of all old stock.

These are good examples of how slow-moving goods, or goods that have proved unsalable through the ordinary means, may be converted into salable goods and truthfully advertised.

Advertising Goods of Fair Quality.—The retailer's most difficult problem is not with the first-class article that possesses distinctive selling points, but with goods of fair quality, representing neither the best workmanship nor the highest type of materials; these nevertheless, enjoy a popular sale, because they fit the purses of the masses.

There is no formula for such copy, but if a cap is produced that is a real value for $1, the resourceful copy-writer should be able to build a story around "The great dollar cap," explaining why it is a good value for $1 without, at the same time, claiming that it is the equal of caps costing $1.50 to $2.

A wonderful sale was created for the dollar watch. This article was purchased by thousands of people who could afford to buy watches costing $50 to $100, or more. Many of them owned more expensive watches as well as the dollar article. This was accomplished by constructive advertising that explained what high value was put into a low-priced article. Nobody expects a dollar watch to last a lifetime. If the advertiser had claimed that it would, he would have been put down as a liar. He exploited his watch as a great thing for boys, the right watch to take hunting, on camping trips, picnics, and so forth. Like possibilities exist for every other article of popular price, as long as the value is there for the price.

Keeping Salespeople Informed as to the Advertising.—Advertising has appropriately been called the "dress" of a business. The principles and policies of a firm are consciously or unconsciously expressed in its publicity, both through printed mediums and through the service of the people making up the business. It is well-nigh useless to build up by advertising claims that cannot be substantiated through actual performance.

Consequently, it is important that salespeople be familiar with and in harmony with the advertising of a store. The man who writes the advertising rarely has much actual contact with customers. Working with the management, he may set a standard for the store, but it is left to the salespeople to translate or reflect this standard to the customer. The salesperson is the real representative of the merchant and manufacturer; to him or to her is left the last link in the chain —the link that makes a customer or loses one.

Some stores content themselves with putting all advertisements in a frame that is placed somewhere in the store where all employes will be certain to see it and making it a store rule that all employes are expected to read the advertisements, or at least the sections of such advertisements that deal with the goods they are called on to sell. Unfortunately, however, 100 per cent of salespeople cannot be depended on to acquire this familiarity with advertised offerings, if it is left too much to their own volition. Consequently, many stores place a copy of the advertisement in each section, or have the various parts of the advertisement cut apart and placed on sheets and sent to the departments that are represented in the advertising. To be sure that each employe gets the information, he or she may be required to sign the sheet.

Booklets Bulletins and Meetings.—Good merchandising requires, of course, that the manager will go over with his helpers anything that should be made clear about the advertised offerings, coaching them properly.

One retailer has tried to solve the problem of keeping his salesmen informed not only on the policies of the store but as to the goods advertised, by getting out booklets now and then in which the salesman's relation to the advertising of the firm is treated in a chatty, newsy style—to insure reading. Such an educational service may do much to bring about the proper cooperation.

Department meetings, or general meetings, of salespeople, held early each morning, at which the day's offerings are discussed, sales arguments advanced and objections overcome is the plan followed by other retailers. This is more effective in small organizations than in large ones. It has the double advantage of informing the salespeople about the goods advertised and, at the same time, giving them good salesmanship instruction. Such meetings need not last more than half an hour or an hour. Usually, there are few customers in the store early in the morning, so that this is the best time for such a meeting. Besides, the salespeople are more likely to give attention to what is said at that time than at the end of a day, when they may be weary and restless.

Akin to the plan of getting out occasional booklets is that followed by some retailers, of inserting little business talks in the pay-envelops. Naturally, it would not do to have all of these talks about advertising, but it is possible, through this means, to accomplish something. Such talks might appropriately take the form of little letters, signed by the management. There is always danger of having such material too "preachy," but the resourceful writer can usually appeal to the self-interest of the employe. The "you" language is more resultful than the "we" language, though "we" language is not altogether out of place and may sometimes strengthen the desirable feeling that the salesperson is an important associate or helper.

Prizes for Errors found in Advertising.—Abraham & Straus, of Brooklyn, offer a prize of $1 for each error found in their advertising. This induces employes to read the advertisements carefully, and also serves as a check on the advertising department. Other stores have made use of this plan.

At the risk of making a little trouble sometimes for the advertising department, retailers might offer prizes for the best suggestions bearing on the improvement of the advertising of the store. It should be made clear, however, in making such an offer, that it will be impossible for the advertising department always to carry out the suggestions or views offered.

After trying prize-offers and many other plans, one retailer found that better cooperation was obtained by furnishing each salesperson every day with a slip containing, in condensed form, the various offerings in the advertising that particular day. With such a system working, there is really no excuse for a salesperson to be unable to answer intelligently any question that may be put to her about merchandise featured in the advertising.

Bulletins as a Means of Raising Standard.—The Dives, Pomeroy & Stewart store, of Reading, Pa., issues store bulletins. The one on "The Store's Advertisements" is reproduced in Exhibit 5, to show how this enterprising retailer puts stress on a proper knowledge of the store's advertising. This bulletin was appropriately and humorously illustrated with cartoon pictures, showing to what length the advertising manager goes in order to get people into the store, only, in some instances to have what is humorously called "Miss Wet Blanket" discourage or repel inquirers by her ungracious or unthinking attitude.

To sum up, advertising may be made to act as a real tonic to the entire organization in the way of building up its standards. The advertising man usually puts his best foot forward, so to speak, and pictures the service and ideals of the organization in the very best light. He may sometimes go beyond actual performance, because it is human to err. As the chief executive of the American Telephone & Telegraph Company once expressed it:

"A high advertising standard is like the heart of Bruce before the advancing Scots."

In other words, the writing and publishing of high standards should be an incentive to an organization to be constantly improving performance. Some business men frankly admit that they have been made to improve their standards by the advertising done by some capable, high-minded advertising man. Having seen their platforms in the limelight of publicity, they have felt more keenly the necessity of living up to these platforms than if the store had never claimed anything in the way of service.

A well known advertiser of Buffalo once spoke before a group of retailers, urging them not to employ a certain advertising man unless they were prepared to do business in a thoroughly efficient way. He said, in effect: "If you hire him, he will exploit you as doing your business the right way and then you will have to do it that way, whether you want to or not. So, don't get him on the job unless you are looking for hard work."

THE STORE'S ADVERTISEMENTS

The store's publicity methods (printed matter, window-displays, department exhibits) are your *best friends* in making sales. Stick by these "best" friends and your *sales-making ability* with us will be increased to the point where you will be a real power in our selling effort.

1. The store advertisements reflect the LIFE and ACTIVITIES of the store.
2. WIDE AWAKE PEOPLE read the newspaper to see what we are doing.
3. You must read them, too, and keep in touch with them, or you'll get OUT OF TOUCH with the store happenings.
4. You and the advertising department are WORKING TOGETHER to sell the goods.

    The advertisements and you are the *two points of contact* between the customer and the store.

5. The customer, having read our advertisement, comes in for the advertised article. The fact that she's interested in it makes her HALF SOLD. It's up to you to add the OTHER HALF and make a COMPLETE SALE.

    Advertised goods are always *easiest to sell*. Our advertisements talk to thousands of people.

6. If, when the customer asks about the goods, you KNOW which they are, PRODUCE them and use the SAME ARGUMENTS in the advertisement you have completed the contact, and you sell her.
7. If you don't follow the advertisements and don't know what's advertised, the POINT OF CONTACT IS BROKEN.

    The customer's confidence in you is *destroyed*.

    Her interest in the goods is *killed*.

    She reflects, if you didn't think the goods *worth while enough* to bother about them, they can't *amount to much*.

    The sale is *lost* and she leaves the store much *disgusted*.

    The next time she reads our advertisements, her faith in them *suffers* because she remembers *your* indifference.

8. Read our store advertisements carefully EVERY EVENING.

    You know *which goods* are half sold.

    You *broaden your knowledge* of them because you have furnished to you sales ammunition in the arguments of the advertisements.

    It makes you a part of the store *too valuable* to be dispensed with.

9. Know not only the advertisements of your own department but all that the store is advertising.

    Then you can *intelligently direct* customers to other good things in our store.

10. All this applies EQUALLY WELL to window- and department-displays.

    EXHIBIT 5.—Store bulletin of Dives, Pomeroy & Stewart.

Usefulness of Scrap-books.—An advertiser does well to have a series of large scrap-books—one to show his own advertisements, day by day or week by week, so that it forms a complete yearly record. It is well to include a form as a part of this exhibit, so that figures inserted regularly will show the cost of each advertisement, and the returns, as far as they can be figured.

Other scrap-books should show the offerings of competitors. Still another exhibit could consist of good advertisements of merchants in other sections of the country—material that offers good suggestions in the way of layout, illustration, selling plan or ideas.

The resourceful advertiser will not stunt his own mind by slavishly copying the efforts of others, but he can adapt. Something that he sees in an advertisement of a far-off city may be just the thing to start him to thinking. The result may be something quite different and more effective than the exhibit that afforded the suggestion.

A useful type of scrap-book is the loose-leaf style, into which sheets punched to fit a binder may be inserted at will. By this method, when one month's or year's sheets are removed from the binder, they can be tied up and filed away, with a label to show just what the exhibit is. Such a binder can be used for several years.

SECTION II

COSTS OF SELLING

Before any advertiser decides on his advertising appropriation or his percentage of selling expense he usually, and with good reason, wants to know what is spent by other firms in the same line of business. The tabulation in Exhibit 7 is a review of a large number of stores in different parts of the United States. It will be observed that advertising expense varies from 0.2 of 1 per cent to 2.9 per cent and that inside salary expense ranges from 4.9 per cent to 15.83 per cent.

The following list shows the position of the various types of stores on nine items of expense:

HIGHEST AND LOWEST FIGURES

	Highest	Lowest
Total expense	Jewelry	Meat stores
Net profit	Drug stores	Jewelry
Gross margin	Jewelry	Meat stores
Turnover	Groceries	Jewelry
Rental	Jewelry	Groceries
Advertising	Furniture	Groceries
Taxes	Stationery	Groceries
Interest	Jewelry	Meat stores
Supplies	Jewelry	Men's clothing
Service	Furniture	Hardware
Repairs	Stationery	Hardware and small dept. stores
Insurance	Furniture	Groceries
Bad debts	Stationery	Shoe and department stores
Depreciation	Men's clothing	Groceries

EXHIBIT 6.—Comparative position on 9 items of expense in various retail businesses.

According to these figures which were assembled by the *Retail Ledger* and published in October, 1922, the least expensive store

EXPENSE AND PROFIT FIGURES IN 15 LINES

Type of Store	Total Expense %	Net Profit	Gross Margin	Stock Turnover	Total Salaries & Wages	Exec. & Office Salaries	Inside Selling Salaries	Rental	Advertising	Taxes	Interest	Supplies	*Service	Repairs	Insurance	Bad Debts	Depreciation	Delivery	Total of General Selling
Department Stores (Aver)	27.8	0.9	28.7	3	15.4	3.2	6.6	2.4	2.4	0.6	2.3	0.8	0.6	0.2	0.4	0.2	0.5	0.9	8.7
Annual Sales To $250,000	26.6	†0.8	25.8	2.2	14.5			2.2	1.8	0.7	2.9	0.6	0.7	0.1	0.5	0.3	0.4		
Annual Sales To $500,000	27.6	0.7	28.3	2.9	15.6			2.2	2.1	0.7	2.4	0.5	0.7	0.2	0.5	0.2	0.4		
Annual Sales To $1,000,000	28.6	1.0	29.3	3.5	15.5			2.3	2.6	0.6	1.9	1.0	0.7	0.3	0.5	0.2	0.5		
Annual Sales To $2,500,000	28.7	1.5	30.2	3.3	15.8			2.9	2.9	0.5	2.0	0.9	0.6	0.2	0.3	0.2	0.6		
Over $2,500,000	28.5	3.1	31.6	4.0	16.0			2.7	2.7	0.5	1.9	1.2	0.5	0.2	0.3	0.2	0.5		
Drug Stores	27.6	6.3	34.0	2.3			12.0	2.8	0.7	0.4	3.1	.	0.8	0.2	0.4	0.3	0.6	0.1·	13.3
Shoe Stores	27.8	†1.9	25.9	1.9		3.5	10.8	3.0	2.3	0.7	3.1	0.3	0.6	0.2	0.5	0.2	0.4	0.2	13.4
Jewelry Stores	43.5	†6.6	36.9	0.8		6.2	12.8	5.4	2.5	1.3	7.0	2.3	1.1	0.3	0.8	0.5	0.9	0.2	
Groceries	16.8	2.5	19.3	8.3		2.0	4.9	1.1	0.2	0.2	1.0		0.23	0.07	0.15	0.3	0.27	2.4	5.9
Meat Stores	16.57	2.29	18.86		10.25			1.33			0.51	0.76	0.98						
Hardware	21.9	5.9	27.1	2.1	10.2	4.0	6.2	1.7		0.5·	3.3		0.4	0.1	0.4	0.5	0.3	0.7	7.0
Furniture	30.2				12.1			4.6	3.0		2.0	0.25	1.5		1.75	0.5	2.0	2.5	
Stationery	34.17	2.86	36.87	2.89		7.32	15.83	3.28	1.34	1.09	0.74	0.71	0.93	0.58	0.57	0.74	1.74	1.19	
Men's Clothing	24.03	1.13	25.16	2.1		4.99	4.49	2.64	2.07	0.58	0.64	0.46	0.56		0.47	0.64	1.83		

† Loss.
* Service means light, heat and power principally.

EXHIBIT 7.—Compilation by *Retail Ledger* showing the percentages of different kinds of expense in the experience of types of specialty stores and groups of department stores.

to run is the meat store, while the most expensive is the jewelry store. The store giving salespeople the greatest percentage as compensation for their services is the stationery store. The *Retail Ledger*, in publishing Exhibits 6 and 7, makes the following interesting comment:

The cost of conducting a retail business, within the 15 lines of trade represented, varies all the way from $16.57 out of every hundred of net sales to $43.50. This, it should be understood, is a statement which does not hold so far as the exceptional individual retail enterprise may be concerned. It is made on the basis of common or average expense figures ascertained for the lines of trade mentioned.

The purpose of the tabulation is not to show the greatest success which a store may possibly achieve in a given line, nor to sound the depths of possible losses. Exceptional cases are barred from the chart throughout and every attempt has been made to hold the figures within the limits of reasonable expectation or reasonable indication to the average merchant in the lines in which he may be interested.

A strictly average store, it should be remembered, does not actually exist, being a figment of mathematical calculation. But, since a majority of stores will run close to the average, with more or less variation in details, average figures may reasonably be assumed as standards of measurement, though common, or most usual, figures are somewhat preferable where obtainable.

The figures in the accompanying table, therefore, may be accepted as reliable for purposes of general comparison, regardless of whether they happen to be average or common.

There are a number of interesting problems in retail efficiency brought out by a comparison of the figures for the department store group embodied in the tabulation.

A glance at the second and fourth columns (Exhibit 7) reveals that there is a direct relation between the rate of stock turn and the rate of profit. As the turnover increases, the rate of net profit increases. But it is also true that as the size of the store increases, the turnover and the rate of net profit increase.

A glance down the expense column, however, is disconcerting. The general tendency of total expense is to rise along with the size of the store. The average for all department stores is $27.80 per $100 net sales. Department stores which do less than $500,000 annually range under the common figure for expense and those which do more than this amount go distinctly over it. True, the store which does more than $2,500,000 has a slightly lower expense than that which does between $1,000,000 and $2,500,000, but it is still higher than the average expense figure.

The figures in the gross margin column show that the big stores' profits lie apparently in their ability to obtain larger margins, and not in connection with lower overhead costs—all of which raises the question of whether or not there is an efficiency limit to the size of the department store, and if so, at just what point it lies.

SOME METHODS OF REDUCING GENERAL EXPENSE

Wide awake retail merchants, realizing the great amount of publicity given to selling costs, are leaving no stones unturned in their efforts to make merchandising methods more efficient and to be able to earn a proper profit while, at the same time, not incorporating a mark-up that looks excessive to the buying public. Wastes have undoubtedly been large in retail selling practice generally. Outright extravagance is all too common. When the country is prosperous and buying is very free, the additions to selling prices that come about through wasted effort and wasted material are passed without serious objection from the purchasers. But when purchasing power decreases, these wastes in selling practice come into the limelight. They are emphasized by the chain stores, by mail-order houses and by cooperative buying associations. While the most important items in a program for the reduction of selling expense are those which cover better advertising, better merchandise-display and better personal salesmanship, there are other expenses that increase alarmingly unless carefully studied. The following may be taken as indicating the trend in the direction of economical selling.

Employment of Part-time Workers.—There are certain hours in every retail store during which the salespeople do not have much to do. Many stores eliminate this waste of time by employing part-time workers to fill in during busy hours and also to come in during lunch periods, thus reducing the payroll. Other stores utilize the time of idle salespeople in the receiving and marking departments, where the busy hours come at the time when the work of the sales force is lightest.

Saving in Wrapping and Packing.—Most department stores use several grades of tissue paper for wrapping various kinds of articles. An especially high-grade of tissue is required for the wrapping of jewelry. Several weights of wrapping paper and varying weights of twine and cord are ordinarily used. The various qualities of these materials involve considerable difference in expense, and the more expensive kinds are bought with the view of special uses for them. Failure to supervise the wrapping results in the promiscuous use of these materials by employes and an unnecessary increase in the volume of expense.

Sometimes paper of a little lighter weight than that in use will answer the purpose just as well. One firm that found it could adopt this idea reported an annual saving of $2,000.

Using bags, where it is practical, instead of paper and string, saves in both time and material, and it is obviously more economical to use the bag nearest the size of the article.

Most department stores use pasteboard boxes of many different sizes—some stores carry as many as a hundred different sizes. This item makes up one of the most expensive of the delivery costs. Careful study of this end of the shipping in some stores has revealed the fact that, by folding certain articles, the number of different sizes of boxes could be cut down substantially, resulting in a large reduction in expense.

Many department stores formerly regarded a large part of the packing material and containers in which they received merchandise as refuse. Most merchants are now alive to the great value to be saved from the proper sorting of this material. One store found that all of the excelsior required to do all of its packing could be taken from cases of incoming merchandise. There was actually an excess, which the store baled and sold.

One store puts its old duplicate slips through a shredding machine and uses this instead of excelsior.

Gummed Tape.—Still another device now being used by retailers to save time, which often means more expense than supplies, is the sealing machine that provides gummed tape to be used instead of cord for fastening packages. It is possible to have tape supplied with the name of the store, the store-slogan with other advertising matter. This advertising must, however, consist of only a few words, as the amount of tape used on a package is often not more than an inch or two.

Crating and Delivering.—Delivery expense is one of the largest items in selling. Accurate sorting, routing and dis-

EXHIBIT 8.—The diagonal bracing and 3-way corners of this crate make a strong, rigid container that absorbs the bumps and protects the contents from strain.

Interior bracing holds the contents in place. Liberal use of resawed lumber for sheathing affords ample protection against damage from the outside. The dealer will receive unmarred merchandise.

Curiously enough, the new crate shows a number of savings over the old one, indicated by Exhibit 9.

This new crate is made up in sections on jigs and is delivered to the packer in sections. He is not required to do any cutting or fitting.

patching will do much to save expense and it is as important in this department as in any other that employes be carefully selected and supervised. One firm offers a bonus for all packages properly delivered, over and above a certain minimum, and the result is said to be a saving of $3,200 a year, even after the bonuses have been paid.

Such an item as poor crating and packing may enter considerably into selling costs of retailers as well as those of jobbers and manufacturers. When goods arrive poorly packed and damaged, the loss must be suffered by some one. While the loss may often be collected from a transportation company, on the ground of improper handling, even this procedure runs up a considerable total of expense if a large number of claims must be prosecuted. Many firms believe it good policy, in cases of damaged goods, to replace the shipment, though this may be done at their own loss. The duplication of shipments and extended correspondence about them may accumulate a heavy item of expense.

It is interesting to see how a large lumber company has recognized this situation and given considerable publicity to

EXHIBIT 9.—Crate made in the old way, with no plan for getting the greatest strength and protection with the smallest amount of material and labor. Such crating brings complaints and losses.

This Exhibit and Exhibit 8 are shown through courtesy of Weyerhaeuser Forest Products.

the diagrams shown in Exhibits 8 and 9 which indicate safe and unsafe crating. The approved method not only makes losses less likely but actually requires a smaller amount of lumber.

A large manufacturer of talking machines saved thousands of dollars a year in time and material by abandoning the method of packing excelsior all around his instruments. The new method is that of placing a wrapped strip of excelsior the size of a man's arm around the instrument in two ways, providing a "bumper" that holds the product securely within the case.

Cooperative Deliveries as a Reducer of Selling Expense.—Union delivery organizations are working on a successful basis in a large number of Mid-western towns, especially in the grocery trade.

The goods are picked up at the various groceries at a scheduled time and brought to an assorting station, where the packages are redistributed for delivery into various sections.

This system, which has worked out with economy to the grocers and satisfaction to the customers of these grocers, is not without a number of complex problems. Experience has shown that light delivery wagons, drawn by horses, constitute the best vehicle-equipment with possibly a few light motor-trucks to help out a broken-down wagon and for rush orders. Containers for each order, either folding wooden boxes, or, better, metal boxes, must be furnished by the delivery organizations for each customer's order, so as to avoid error in delivering. Special containers for eggs, as well as racks under the wagons for kerosene cans, are essential. Drivers must be specially trained for this type of work. Most delivery organizations of this type have worked out a system of merits for avoiding mistakes in delivery, this being used as a basis for figuring a weekly bonus.

Punctual "pick ups" and deliveries are the chief means of guarding against complaints. Orders telephoned too late for the scheduled delivery should be sent "special." A printed card giving delivery schedule and general features of the system should be provided each customer to be posted near her telephone. Much supervision and check-up of the drivers' orders and equipment are necessary, but a saving of from 25 to 50 per cent in delivery costs has been effected in more than 400 towns that have used the plan successfully.

Plans of this kind usually work out best among merchants organized for protecting local business against the inroads of mail-order houses and the merchants of larger centers. Members of such organizations are as a rule alive to the fact that closer cooperation among all handlers of merchandise is one practical way of reducing the high cost of operating.

SECTION III

TURNOVER AND PRICE-FIGURING

Simple as the principle is in its fundamentals, the principle of turnover is one that is thoroughly understood and applied too infrequently by manufacturers, wholesalers, retailers and salesmen generally.

Comparison of Small and Large Profits.—A wholesaler of long business experience has been heard to remark, "My general expense is about 12 per cent. How, then, can a manufacturer have the nerve to ask me to handle any item on a margin of 10 per cent." This comment was made with emphasis, apparently no consideration being given to the question of whether the manufacturer's goods referred to turned once a year or twelve times a year.

The simple truth is that an article with a 10 per cent mark-up could easily bring this wholesaler a fortune if it were in sufficient demand and turned often enough, while another article affording a 30 per cent mark-up might bring him an actual loss if it proved exceedingly difficult to sell and the turnover of capital invested in it occurred only at long intervals.

The 5-cent and 10-cent stores have illustrated what total profits are possible through small prices and small margins, aided by quick turnover.

Consider two extremes: 1. In the selling of fruits and vegetables, the capital must turn rapidly or not at all, for in a short time the stock is worthless. If it were possible in this business for a merchant to correctly forecast his sales and buy exactly what he could sell, his capital would be turned every few days. Putting the turn at twice a week, a turnover of one hundred times a year would be theoretically possible. If the net profit were only 2 per cent, a dollar in this business could bring a profit of 200 per cent, or two more dollars, in a year.

TURNOVER AND PRICE-FIGURING

2. Take, as the other extreme, musical instruments of the class of violins and harps, where the turnover is exceedingly slow. Some instruments remain in the retailer's hands for years before being sold. Here the mark-up must be very large or the merchant would be wrecked, unless he had other sales on which to depend for profits.

Variation of Turnover in One Business.—The sales in one business may vary greatly as to rate of turnover. A review for an entire year of the sales records of five electrical jobbing houses shows the following rates of turnover for different merchandise:

Products	Rate of Turnover
Fan motors	1.93
Bare copper wire	1.21
Electricians' tools	1.30
Washing machines and parts	6.85
Tape—rubber and friction	6.48
Dry batteries	8.18

The *average* turnover in this business of rather wide range was 2.49, and yet these merchants were handling a number of items that yielded only about half the average turnover, while other items were turning capital from two to three times as rapidly as the average.

Consideration of Trade-bringing Value of Product.—Turnover cannot be properly considered without due attention to demand or probable demand for the articles to be marketed. Goods may be classified as "trade-bringers" and "goods that must be sold." The latter class requires distinct sales effort—are not bought voluntarily by the customer, but call for the expenditure of the time of the salesman to show and demonstrate them.

The staple articles—those which people generally are accustomed to buying and which they buy regularly, according to habits that are more or less fixed as to place of buying, quantity, etc.—are trade-bringers. Among these may be listed sugar, tea, coffee, bread, meat, hosiery, gasoline, and hundreds of other items. Consumers have fixed habits in buying these. They do not, of course, always buy the same brands or purchase at the same place but their purchases will be made of some merchant. Their needs of such goods are established, the commodities have become necessities, and no sales-expense has to be incurred in creating the original demand, though various merchants, in striving for such trade, may create sales expense.

But the point is that if a merchant were deprived of the opportunity to handle these staples, these trade-bringers, his sales expense would be enormously increased. For he would then be under the necessity of providing some attraction for every customer. Few, if any, customers would come to his store voluntarily. Therefore, the trade-bringers are invaluable to the merchant. They give him daily opportunities to sell other goods, through window- and inside-displays and efficient selling work by employes. He is, therefore, a short-sighted dealer who deplores that he must sell sugar, cement, gasoline, bread or some other item on a smaller margin of profit than he makes on other goods. It is possible, of course, that he may be asked to sell even these staples on a margin that is unfairly small but before he comes to the conclusion that this is the situation he should weigh not only the annual turnover of the commodity but also its value as a trade-bringer.

Overhead and Selling Expenses.—The expenses of operating a retail selling business of any kind may be divided into two general classifications:

1. Overhead, or carrying expenses
2. Selling expenses

If one rents a store or an office, equips it and purchases a stock of goods to be resold, there are expenses that immediately accumulate, whether or not a customer ever enters the place or a cash register is ever punched. These are: rent, insurance, taxes, possibly a license, interest on investment, depreciation, salary of proprietor, and maybe other items. Whether the volume of business is large or small—$100, $1,000, $10,000 or $100,000 a year—these expenses go on.

If these expenses are, say, $2,000 a year and the sales total only $20,000, the expense becomes 10 per cent of the gross business. If, now, with the same stock and without increasing the overhead or carrying expenses, sales can be increased to

$40,000 a year, the general expense is cut to 5 per cent of the gross sales.

There are other expenses that are incurred only as goods are sold or moved and some that are incurred only when goods are sold on credit. These are salaries of helpers, advertising, delivery, wrapping, packing, office expenses, bad debts, collection expense, interest lost on outstanding debts, and kindred items. For, if the merchant has a considerable part of his own capital out on credit accounts, while he in turn has to borrow money and pay interest, or becomes unable to make additional turns of capital or to take cash discounts, there is a distinct loss to be accounted for.

If these additional expenses, chargeable directly to selling operations, total $2,000 on $20,000 of sales, there is an additional 10 per cent to be borne by the gross business. If they total $4,000 on sales of $40,000 and do not diminish, no matter how the sales increase, then this percentage must be reckoned with as a fixed expense. It may be possible, however, for the merchant, as he increases his sales, to add $5,000 extra sales in some department without increasing his costs more than $200. If so, his total cost percentage may be materially reduced.

It is evident, then, that before a merchant, or a manufacturer—for the fundamental principle applies to both—can have a clear idea of what his actual net profits are, how they come, etc., he must acquire a closer knowledge of what it costs him to handle each product sold—the space it occupies in his store and windows, the time and difficulty required in selling it, the number of times he sells it in a year, its deterioration, credit loss, and so on.

The Essentials of a Profit-maker.—Overhead items must be considered in fixing all prices. Many retail dealers, in arriving at their mark-up, add only freight, drayage and a small amount of "profit" to the invoice price of the goods and think they are making money. Various items of expense must be allowed for, even if the goods are shipped direct to the customer and do not enter the dealer's place of business at all. This, however, does not prevent the dealer from making a close price where competition makes it good strategy for him to lose part of his usual profit on some transaction. But the principle of taking account of all expenses is one that the far-seeing merchant must return to and practice generally or he is headed for failure.

In those cases where mark-down is common as a means of getting rid of goods that are slow-selling, or that deteriorate, these mark-downs must be reckoned with as a depreciation of the usual profit.

The only safe method of analyzing the business is to divide time and effort so as to charge each department or class of goods with its proper part of all expense as nearly as the expense can be determined.

Any merchandise sold must justify itself in one of three ways:

1. Large profit on infrequent sale.
2. Small profit but frequent turnover.
3. Trade-bringer and easy to sell.

Part Played by Concentration in Turnover.—The more successful a retail merchant is, the more he will be urged by salesmen and manufacturers to purchase different brands of goods. It is natural for these distributors to want the most successful retailer. But there are usually limits to the stock a retailer can carry. Unless he has an extraordinary amount of room and an unusual sales opportunity, he cannot afford to carry large stocks of competing articles. While it may be argued that he loses sales whenever he is unable to supply the particular article that the customer calls for, there are on the other side of the question the disadvantages of having a large amount of capital tied up in competing products, and of being out of sizes in some of these products. A retailer with the ordinary amount of space for a commodity like hosiery, for example, is likely to be much better off in carrying a full assortment of colors, sizes and styles of one brand rather than to carry stocks of four, five or six competing brands and to be continually out of stock on a number of these.

The manager of a well known hardware concern says, in *Good Hardware*:

I believe hardware stores should concentrate on a well known line of stoves and ranges and advertise and talk that line and at least get the business of their cash customers; also give credit on the payment or contract plan to well known reliable customers. This is our plan and we enjoy a very satisfactory stove business.

This expression undoubtedly reflects the experience of many successful merchants.

Application to Shoe Business.—A review of the shoe business by *Associated Business Papers, Inc.,* includes the following comment on the tendency of the shoe retailer to give his attention to fewer brands.

It is not an easy matter for manufacturers to get new dealers in the shoe business, for the reason that retailers know it is more profitable to carry only a few brands of shoes in stock. To have an adequate stock of the many standard sizes and styles (to say nothing of the "novelty" lines) of one brand of shoes means a heavy investment. The addition of more brands does not mean more sales, it is found. Therefore, it is the dealer's aim to have enough of a few brands to give style, size and price service, rather than to meet all calls for various brands.

Since the addition of a new brand is a matter for serious consideration by retailers, it follows that more vigorous advertising and sales effort is required to get new dealer representation than would be required for other goods of which so large and so varied a stock is not required.

From a Dry Goods Authority.—The following significant opinion appeared recently in the *Dry Goods Economist*, a leading publication of the dry goods and department-store fields:

Even after cutting down on the number of brands of an article sold, it pays to concentrate further on the particular styles or priced articles of brands. For example, if a merchant is selling an article at five different prices and finds from his sales checks that he sells the largest number of the article at the first, third and fifth price, he could discontinue handling the second and fourth grades. The loss he might have by not carrying those grades would easily be made up by the increased turnover of the other grades and probably would not equal the loss he would have by carrying too many of the slower moving articles.

An Advertising Agency's View.—N. W. Ayer & Son, a large advertising agency, whose experience covers many different businesses, thus expresses its view of concentration of effort by retailers:

A national association of wholesale merchants, planning to extend credit assistance to worthy retailers needing financial aid, investigated the causes of success or failure in thousands of retail stores.

In almost every case where a retailer was unsuccessful, investigation showed among the contributing causes:

First, that the unsuccessful retailer carried so many competitive lines of merchandise that he could not afford to carry a complete line of any one:

Second, that the bulk of his stock consisted of merchandise which possessed no known or recognized value among the trade and the public.

The Golden Rules of Turnover.—The Burroughs Adding Machine Company in the following advice, sums up the importance of having full knowledge of a business and of concentrating on fewer lines or products:

Classify your sales, costs, stock and turnovers by lines—then use this information to speed up the slow-selling goods and to cash in on paying lines. Aim to keep your stock clean, attractive and new. Buy only in quantities you know you can sell. Establish stock limits that are only high enough to take care of the demand, prevent overbuying, keep down capital investment, and remove the inclination to indulge in too many so-called "snaps."

Above all, keep before yourself the four "golden rules" of turnover:

1. Locate the fast moving lines.
2. Weed out the unprofitable lines.
3. Establish definite stock limits.
4. Concentrate buying among a few concerns, preventing duplication of orders, cutting down bookkeeping, and insuring better cooperation and less danger of overstocking.

CHART AND ILLUSTRATION OF TURNOVER

Exhibit 10 shows the principle of turnover in graphic form. The maker of this chart has assumed that there is no increase of fixed expense because of more frequent turnover, such as additional sales help, etc. This is often the case, though it is true, on the other hand, that more frequent turnover may increase sales and delivery expense and other items, though in a decreasing proportion.

TURNOVER AND PRICE-FIGURING

The Armstrong Cork Company, in using this table, adds the following comments in an editorial directed to its dealers:

Suppose you buy $100 worth of linoleum, and mark it up to sell at 50 per cent gross profit, or $150. If people aren't much interested in linoleum, it may take all year to sell that one lot—so in a year's time you have made $50 or 50 per cent, minus your fixed expense or overhead (suppose it to be about 30 per cent), and the interest on the money you have invested in linoleum (suppose it to be about 5 per

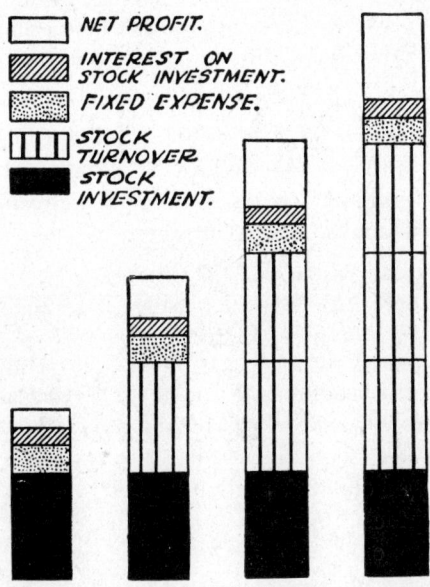

EXHIBIT 10.—Illustration of how net profit may be largely increased by multiplying turnover. The short column represents a single yearly turnover; the second, two yearly turnovers; the third, three yearly turnovers; and the fourth, four turnovers—all on the same capital.

cent). That leaves you a net profit on your year's linoleum business of 15 per cent, or $15.

Now, suppose that it doesn't take you a year to sell your whole stock of linoleum. People know that you carry linoleum, and you dispose of your $100 stock in 6 months, you reorder and sell the second lot in 6 months also. You make 50 per cent, or $50, on each lot, or a total of $100 gross profit. If your capital invested, your overhead, and your interest remain the same, your net profit on the year's business is much larger—$65, or 65 per cent of the money you have invested, in fact.

Again, suppose that you advertise linoleum, so that people buy more readily, and you sell your whole stock in 4 months, or turn it three times in a year. Then your gross profit is three times as great, and your net profit correspondingly larger. If you turn your stock still faster—speed up turnover to four or five times a year, your gross profit will be four or five times as big as it was with one turnover a year. And the net profits are bigger each time.

So that is the reason faster turnover is worth while. That is why it pays to sell advertised goods—products that people know and accept readily. That is why it pays for you to advertise your goods and get people to buy more at your store.

While the calculations in the foregoing explanation are clear, "gross profit" as used in the comment would be expressed as "mark-up" by most modern merchants.

The Other Dimension of Turnover.—Within recent years a well known manufacturer, in seeking to explain high prices to the public, gave much publicity to the fact that his average net profit on certain meat products was only 2.07 per cent. The firm neglected, however, to state the rate of turnover. On certain of its products the turnover is understood to be about 26 times a year, which means a yearly net profit of more than 53 cents on each dollar of capital, a very satisfactory profit and one that probably could be reduced and still leave the manufacturer with a comfortable margin.

"Profit," says one economist, "is like land—it is a thing of two dimensions. You can't learn the acreage of a field by knowing only its length or its breadth. Likewise, you can't learn what the profit is in handling goods by knowing only the net profit that a mark-up evidently allows. You must know the frequency with which that profit is or can be earned under normal or average conditions."

An Accountant's Explanation.—G. W. Hafner, a nationally known accountant, states the turnover principle this way in a business-magazine article:

If a dollar earns ten profits for its owner in a year, the owner can afford to take a smaller profit *each time* than on another dollar which earns him, say, only five profits during the same length of time. And yet the dollar which returns the smaller *rate* of profit will bring in the larger *volume* of profit, simply because it is so much more active.

Now, this is precisely the point that most business men seem not to understand. They do not seem to be able to grasp the fundamental principle that even though the percentage of profit on merchandise or service be but, say, 5 per cent, if it is earned often enough, say, ten times in a year, the annual turnover on money or rate of profit on investment will be 50 per cent.

Too many merchants overlook the fact that their cost of doing business of, say, 25 per cent, cannot correctly be used to demand a 15 per cent margin of profit on each and every kind of merchandise sold, because it is the percentage of profit on one sale and not on the year's investment. A larger margin of profit needs to be added to the slow-moving materials and a smaller margin to the quick-moving.

How to Determine Rate of Turnover.—In figuring turnover, it is vital that two items be determined: (1) Money invested in the business according to an average inventory, and (2) sales during the period to be figured, which is usually one year. To avoid serious error, both sets of figures must be on the same basis, that is, either cost figures or selling figures.

If the average inventory at cost prices is $5,000 and the purchase price of goods sold during the year is $12,500 then the turnover is 2.50.

The Burroughs Adding Machine Turnover Table.—Through the courtesy of the Burroughs Adding Machine Company, a table is reproduced in Exhibit 11 that facilitates calculations about turnover, how to find the amount of stock that should be carried, the amount of sales that should be made when the stock and turnovers are known, and how to find the turnover on a yearly basis when sales and stock are known. The following description makes the use of the table clear:

How To Use the Turnover Table.—To find the amount of stock that should be carried when the monthly sales and the number of turnovers are known, find the amount of sales in the "Sales per month" column and follow across the line to the given turnover column.

Example: With $5,500 sales and 4 turnovers, a stock of $16,500 should be carried.

To find the amount of sales that should be made when the stock and turnovers are known, find the amount of stock in the

Turnover Table

Sales Per Month	\multicolumn{12}{c}{TURNOVERS}	Sales Per Month
	1	2	3	4	5	6	7	8	9	10	11	12	
100	1200	600	400	300	240	200	171	150	133	120	109	100	100
150	1800	900	600	450	360	300	257	225	200	180	164	150	150
200	2400	1200	800	600	480	400	343	300	267	240	218	200	200
250	3000	1500	1000	750	600	500	429	375	333	300	273	250	250
300	3600	1800	1200	900	720	600	514	450	400	360	327	300	300
350	4200	2100	1400	1050	840	700	600	525	467	420	382	350	350
400	4800	2400	1600	1200	960	800	686	600	533	480	436	400	400
450	5400	2700	1800	1350	1080	900	771	675	600	540	491	450	450
500	6000	3000	2000	1500	1200	1000	857	750	667	600	545	500	500
550	6600	3300	2200	1650	1320	1100	943	825	733	660	600	550	550
600	7200	3600	2400	1800	1440	1200	1029	900	800	720	655	600	600
650	7800	3900	2600	1950	1560	1300	1114	975	867	780	709	650	650
700	8400	4200	2800	2100	1680	1400	1200	1050	933	840	764	700	700
750	9000	4500	3000	2250	1800	1500	1286	1125	1000	900	818	750	750
800	9600	4800	3200	2400	1920	1600	1371	1200	1067	960	873	800	800
850	10200	5100	3400	2550	2040	1700	1457	1275	1133	1020	927	850	850
900	10800	5400	3600	2700	2160	1800	1543	1350	1200	1080	982	900	900
950	11400	5700	3800	2850	2280	1900	1629	1425	1267	1140	1036	950	950
1000	12000	6000	4000	3000	2400	2000	1714	1500	1383	1200	1091	1000	1000
1500	18000	9000	6000	4500	3600	3000	2571	2250	2000	1800	1636	1500	1500
2000	24000	12000	8000	6000	4800	4000	3429	3000	2667	2400	2182	2000	2000
2500	30000	15000	10000	7500	6000	5000	4286	3750	3333	3000	2727	2500	2500
3000	36000	18000	12000	9000	7200	6000	5143	4500	4000	3600	3273	3000	3000
3500	42000	21000	14000	10500	8400	7000	6000	5250	4667	4200	3818	3500	3500
4000	48000	24000	16000	12000	9600	8000	6857	6000	5333	4800	4364	4000	4000
4500	54000	27000	18000	13500	10800	9000	7714	6750	6000	5400	4909	4500	4500
5000	60000	30000	20000	15000	12000	10000	8571	7500	6667	6000	5455	5000	5000
5500	66000	33000	22000	16500	13200	11000	9429	8250	7333	6600	6000	5500	5500
6000	72000	36000	24000	18000	14400	12000	10286	9000	8000	7200	6545	6000	6000
6500	78000	39000	26000	19500	15600	13000	11143	9750	8667	7800	7091	6500	6500
7000	84000	42000	28000	21000	16800	14000	12000	10500	9333	8400	7636	7000	7000
8000	96000	48000	32000	24000	19200	16000	13714	12000	10667	9600	8727	8000	8000
9000	108000	54000	36000	27000	21600	18000	15429	13500	12000	10800	9818	9000	9000
10000	120000	60000	40000	30000	24000	20000	17143	15000	13333	12000	10909	10000	10000
20000	240000	120000	80000	60000	48000	40000	34286	30000	26667	24000	21818	20000	20000
30000	360000	180000	120000	90000	72000	60000	51429	45000	40000	36000	32727	30000	30000
40000	480000	240000	160000	120000	96000	80000	68571	60000	53333	48000	43636	40000	40000
50000	600000	300000	200000	150000	120000	100000	85714	75000	66667	60000	54545	50000	50000
60000	720000	360000	240000	180000	144000	120000	102857	90000	80000	72000	65455	60000	60000
70000	840000	420000	280000	210000	168000	140000	120000	105000	93333	84000	76364	70000	70000
80000	960000	480000	320000	240000	192000	160000	137143	120000	106667	96000	87273	80000	80000
90000	1080000	540000	360000	270000	216000	180000	154286	135000	120000	108000	98182	90000	90000
100000	1200000	600000	400000	300000	240000	200000	171429	150000	133333	120000	109091	100000	100000
125000	1500000	750000	500000	375000	300000	250000	214286	187500	166667	150000	136364	125000	125000
150000	1800000	900000	600000	450000	360000	300000	257143	225000	200000	180000	163636	150000	150000
175000	2100000	1050000	700000	525000	420000	350000	300000	262500	233333	210000	190909	175000	175000
200000	2400000	1200000	800000	600000	480000	400000	342857	300000	266667	240000	218182	200000	200000
250000	3000000	1500000	1000000	750000	600000	500000	428571	375000	333333	300000	272727	250000	250000
300000	3600000	1800000	1200000	900000	720000	600000	514286	450000	400000	360000	327273	300000	300000
Sales Per Month	1	2	3	4	5	6	7	8	9	10	11	12	Sales Per Month

EXHIBIT 11.—Table furnished through the courtesy of the Burroughs Adding Machine Company. This may be used to readily calculate the amount of sales that should be made when the stock and turnovers are known, also the amount of stock that should be carried, and, finally, the turnover on a yearly basis when sales and stock are known.

given turnover column and follow across the line to the "Sales per month" column.

TURNOVER AND PRICE-FIGURING

Example: With 5 turnovers and carrying a $48,000 stock, the monthly sales should be $20,000.

To find the turnover expressed on a yearly basis when sales and stock are known, find the sales in the "Sales per month" column and follow across the line to the Stock Carried. The number of yearly turnovers will be at the top of the column in which the stock carried is found.

Example: With $1,500 sales and $4,500 stock, the yearly turnover is 4.

The range of monthly sales and of turnovers was curtailed to make the turnover card a reasonable size. By the following formulas other turnover problems can be figured:

Formula 1:

The stock that should be carried may be found by multiplying monthly sales by 12 and dividing by the number of turnovers.

Example: If a department's sales this month were $9,750, with 6 turnovers, what stock should be carried in this department?

Solution: $\dfrac{\$9{,}750 \text{ (Sales)} \times 12}{6 \text{ (Turnovers)}}$ equals $19,500 (Stock that should be carried)

Formula 2:

The monthly sales should equal the amount of stock on hand times the turnovers divided by 12.

Example: $\dfrac{\$18{,}600 \text{ (Stock on Hand)} \times 4 \text{ (Turnovers)}}{12}$

equals $6,200 (Required Sales)

To arrive easily and approximately at turnover expressed on a yearly basis, figure inventory at selling price December 31, add goods put in stock in January at selling price, subtracting January sales. By repeating this procedure monthly until succeeding December 31, thirteen calculated inventories are secured, which may be averaged by dividing by 13. This average, divided into yearly sales, gives rate of turnover.

In order for such a table as the one shown to cover all the various volumes of sales and stock carried by thousands of different stores, a very large card or sheet would be required. So the figures are graduated from sales of $100 to $300,000 a month and the turnovers listed from 1 to 12. With this variety of figures and the three formulas, it should be easy for any calculation to be made.

United States Chamber of Commerce Recommendation on Turnover and Stock Control.—The Chamber of Commerce of the United States in a recent bulletin, after setting forth some of the fundamental facts covered in this Section, offers the following analysis of slow turnover:

When the various expenses and wastes involved in slow turnovers are stated separately the subject becomes even more easily understood. What are the elements in which losses due to slow turnovers may be found?

1. Investment
2. Interest
3. Mark-down
4. Salaries and wages
5. Shelf or storage room
6. Prestige-reputation
7. Inefficiency

An examination of these elements shows their relation to each other.

1. Invested money is the source of profit, which in turn depends upon the amount of goods in stock and upon the length of time which these goods are carried. It is evident that to double the turnover comes to the same thing as doubling the amount of stock without increasing the investment. Or, vice versa, one half as many turnovers results in doubling the amount of money invested for the same quantity of goods.

2. Interest must be paid upon all borrowed money and most merchants are borrowers. If the turnover is reduced from a period of six months to one of three months the interest on a given loan is reduced in the same proportion.

3. Mark-downs are required for three principal reasons:
    (a) The goods have proved unsalable at the original mark-up.
    (b) Too many were bought and a change in the style or season has left some of them on the shelves—
    (c) With the result that they have been soiled, chipped, bent or otherwise defaced by frequent handling.

4. Salaries and wages must be included because every operation in every establishment costs something. When an unprofitable operation is performed it represents a loss. Roughly, these losses are due to:

(a) Waste of time by management in reaching decisions as to when and what mark-downs are to take place.

(b) Waste of time by sales force.

(c) Rewriting tickets.

(d) Rearranging goods for mark-down sales.

5. Shelf or storage room is a definite part of the expense of doing business, and that portion which is devoted to slow-selling merchandise is wasted.

6. Prestige-reputation—for the high character or timeliness of merchandise is sought by most stores. There is a distinct waste measurable in dollars and cents when the reputation of an establishment is lowered by unstylish or shop-worn goods.

7. Inefficiency always results in waste. The buyer whose judgment often is wrong usually makes the mistakes from lack of knowledge as to the stock and the speed or slowness with which it is moving. Frequent mistakes cause uncertainty in the mind of the one who makes them and tend to worse errors as time goes on, unless some measures are taken to make them improbable.

Exhibit 12 is offered by the Chamber of Commerce of the United States as an example of a simple "Control Card." The purpose of the card and the best way of using it are described as follows:

First and foremost is the necessity to divide the establishment into departments. Usually this is the case already where a large stock is carried, but small stores often have not done so and a part of their trouble comes from this neglect. An additional advantage following the practice is due to the better display which may be made of the stock. This, however, is another subject, since the discussion now relates solely to control of the stock which can be accomplished effectively only if it be arranged according to a definite departmental plan.

It may be thought at first by some readers that there would be difficulty in dividing into departments a store which, like a shoe store, might itself form one of the departments of a true department store. But on second thought it will be seen that there are several possible departments even in a small retail shoe store. For example, many shoe stores sell stockings; there are men's and women's shoes; and there are costly and cheap shoes for men and for women. Many departments are possible in hardware, groceries, jewelry and, indeed, in every wholesale or retail business, whether it be large or small. Neither need departments be separated by partitions or show-cases;

STYLE 1783		BOUGHT FROM Shipper & Co									DESCRIPTION Black Oxford Blucher													MATERIAL Calf							
Cost	S'z	Aug	1	2	3	4	5	6	7	8	9	10	11	12	13	14	15	16	17	18	19	20	21	22	23	24	25	26	27	28	29	30	31
4.50	9	Rec'd				00	0	24																								
		O.H.	19					3																								
		Sold	3	4	3	6	2		5 3																								
		O.O		24																												
4.50	9½	Rec'd				0		24																								
		O.H.	11																														
		Sold	2	2	1	3	4		6																								
		O.O		24																												
		Rec'd																															
		O.H																															
		Sold																															
		O.O.																															
		Rec'd																															
		O H																															
		Sold																															
		O.O																															
		Rec'd																															
		O.H.																															
		Sold																															
		O O																															

EXHIBIT 12.—A form of control card recommended by the United States Chamber of Commerce as being suitable for many kinds of business. It shows at any moment the condition of stock and rate at which it is selling.

TURNOVER AND PRICE-FIGURING

an imaginary division is quite enough so long as the proprietor is conscious of it and uses it on the control cards to secure are liable sales analysis.

It is the only method by which unprofitable departments may be reorganized intelligently.

After the departmental plan has been arranged, an inventory must be made on the control cards, which are designed to exhibit every necessary fact for every day in the month. A sample card is shown, but the exact shape and size will vary somewhat according to the department or kind of business involved. The idea is adapted to the most widely differing merchandise, as for example, shoes and wire nails—or canned goods and vacuum cleaners. By printing on both sides, the capacity of the cards may be doubled, and by using a card twice the size, folded in the middle, a quadrupled capacity is secured.

Many methods are practicable for indicating to which department a control card belongs. Probably the simplest is by means of tinted cards, of which there are seven standard colors: white, blue, red, green, yellow, salmon and gray. If a greater variety is needed, the name of the department may be printed faintly in large characters on the face of the card, or the upper edge of the card may be indented or clipped at the corners so that it may be identified at a glance. Whatever plan is adopted should be considered carefully beforehand, since changes are troublesome and expensive.

The row of figures at the top are the days of the month and the blank spaces below are for the quantities "Rec'd," "O.H." (on hand), "Sold" and "O.O." (on order).

According to Exhibit 12, the firm had on hand at the opening of business on August 1, 19 pairs of size 9 and 11 pairs of size 9½ black oxford blucher calf shoes, style 2783, which cost $4.50 a pair and were bought of Stevens and Company. During the first week of August, 18 pairs of size 9 were sold, 2 pairs were returned by customers (one each on the fourth and fifth) so that 3 pairs were on hand at the opening of business on Monday, August 7. On the same day 24 pairs were received which had been ordered on the second.

Certain of the figures, like "returned goods," are usually made with red ink, but the color cannot be shown in the engraving, for which reason the figures are enclosed in a circle. The figures 24, "O.O." also should be cancelled with red ink. In practice, most words are abbreviated and "Black Oxford Blucher" would be written "Blk Ox Bl."

These cards, it will be observed, constitute a perpetual inventory which displays at a glance every factor in which the management and the buyer may be interested: at what rate the goods are selling; which sizes are selling fastest; which styles are most popular; when it is time to order more; and which of the goods must be marked down. They are under the charge of one person who makes all of the entries and are mounted in an open rack. Probably the most remarkable characteristic of the control card is the fact that changes are recorded within a quarter of an hour after they take place, so that those in authority, if it is necessary, may know the precise condition of the whole stock at any hour of the day.

From this description it is evident with what certainty and rapidity judgments may be formed and policies may be altered.

HOW TO FIGURE MARK-UP AND PROFITS

Merchandising practice requires that mark-ups and profit percentages be figured on the selling prices of goods rather than on their cost. This seems contrary to early studies in pure mathematics where we learned that when we buy something for $1 and want to make 50 per cent profit we offer the article at the selling price of $1.50.

The reason for this modern practice of figuring is well expressed by an editorial in the *New York Times*, quoted below:

Several well meaning friends have written to *The Times*, expressing surprise at the statement, printed last Sunday, that profits are figured on the selling price of goods instead of on the cost. Some have quoted the authority of arithmetics of standard make on the subject of percentages, thereby showing they have not forgotten certain teachings of their youth. But all of this does not alter the situation. Dealers who are wise and who do not wish to "go broke," always calculate their profits on selling prices. Buying and selling are not one transaction. Much intervenes between the two events besides the time, which in itself is a very variable quantity, as all who are familiar with turnovers know. If everything were sold as soon as bought, without removal or change of possession, calculation of profits would be as simple a matter as the elementary arithmetics of school days indicate. But this is not the case. Very often, part of a purchase is sold at one time while the remainder may remain on the shelves for six months or a year. The sales price of each portion may be the same per yard or other unit, but no one would contend that the profit was the same. This is only one of the obvious difficulties in this matter of

TURNOVER AND PRICE-FIGURING

determining percentages of profits. Others will readily suggest themselves. They are well known to merchants, who found by experience that the only safe way to calculate profit percentages was on the amount received when an article was sold, and not on what it originally cost. This has become a settled rule.

COMMON TERMS IN FIGURING PRICES

In figuring prices it is well to follow these definitions:

Overhead, Fixed, or Carrying Expense.—This includes all such fixed charges as rent, light, heat, power, telephone, interest, taxes, insurance, deterioration, maintenance, salary for proprietors, cost of maintaining general departments of business, etc.—in fact, all expenses that would be incurred if no sales were made.

Selling Expense.—Salaries of salesmen, advertising, packing, delivery, collection, etc.

Mark-up.—Formerly this phrase was usually expressed by the word "profit," but as it represents the increase of the cost figure to the point where a selling price will cover all expense as well as a satisfactory net profit, the calculation is more properly referred to as the mark-up. Sometimes the words "Gross Profit" are used.

Mark-down.—To indicate a reduction of the original marked-up price.

Profit.—Sometimes expressed as "Net Profit" to indicate the margin or percentage remaining *after all costs have been deducted*.

Loss, or Net Loss.—Words of obvious meaning that too often have to be used, when all the facts are known.

Example of Figuring Mark-up.—Following the modern practice, the first important thing for the firm having goods to sell—whether it be a manufacturer, wholesaler or retailer—is to determine what its total cost-percentage is, this percentage to include the overhead or fixed charges as well as selling costs, the latter covering packing and delivery expense, percentage for bad debts, etc.

If this total cost is, say, 20 per cent and it is desired to have goods bring at least 10 per cent net profit, the selling price would be figured in this manner:

Percentage representing general cost of doing business 20
Net profit desired on selling price 10
———
30

Deducting 30 from 100, we get 70. *This result should be divided into the cost price of the article to obtain the selling*

MARK-UP TABLE

Overhead %	1%	2%	3%	4%	5%	6%	7%	8%	9%	10%	11%	12%	13%	Overhead %
0	1.0101	1.02041	1.03093	1.04167	1.05263	1.06383	1.07527	1.08696	1.0989	1.1111	1.1236	1.13636	1.14943	0
1	1.02041	1.03093	1.04167	1.05263	1.06383	1.07527	1.08696	1.0989	1.1111	1.1236	1.13636	1.14943	1.16279	1
2	1.03093	1.04167	1.05263	1.06383	1.07527	1.08696	1.0989	1.1111	1.1236	1.13636	1.14943	1.16279	1.17647	2
3	1.04167	1.05263	1.06383	1.07527	1.08696	1.0989	1.1111	1.1236	1.13636	1.14943	1.16279	1.17647	1.19048	3
4	1.05263	1.06383	1.07527	1.08696	1.0989	1.1111	1.1236	1.13636	1.14943	1.16279	1.17647	1.19048	1.20482	4
5	1.06383	1.07527	1.08696	1.0989	1.1111	1.1236	1.13636	1.14943	1.16279	1.17647	1.19048	1.20482	1.21951	5
6	1.07527	1.08696	1.0989	1.1111	1.1236	1.13636	1.14943	1.16279	1.17647	1.19048	1.20482	1.21951	1.23457	6
7	1.08696	1.0989	1.1111	1.1236	1.13636	1.14943	1.16279	1.17647	1.19048	1.20482	1.21951	1.23457	1.25	7
8	1.0989	1.1111	1.1236	1.13636	1.14943	1.16279	1.17647	1.19048	1.20482	1.21951	1.23457	1.25	1.26582	8
9	1.1111	1.1236	1.13636	1.14943	1.16279	1.17647	1.19048	1.20482	1.21951	1.23457	1.25	1.26582	1.28205	9
10	1.1236	1.13636	1.14943	1.16279	1.17647	1.19048	1.20482	1.21951	1.23457	1.25	1.26582	1.28205	1.2987	10
11	1.13636	1.14943	1.16279	1.17647	1.19048	1.20482	1.21951	1.23457	1.25	1.26582	1.28205	1.2987	1.31579	11
12	1.14943	1.16279	1.17647	1.19048	1.20482	1.21951	1.23457	1.25	1.26582	1.28205	1.2987	1.31579	1.33333	12
13	1.16279	1.17647	1.19048	1.20482	1.21951	1.23457	1.25	1.26582	1.28205	1.2987	1.31579	1.33333	1.35135	13
14	1.17647	1.19048	1.20482	1.21951	1.23457	1.25	1.26582	1.28205	1.2987	1.31579	1.33333	1.35135	1.36986	14
15	1.19048	1.20482	1.21951	1.23457	1.25	1.26582	1.28205	1.2987	1.31579	1.33333	1.35135	1.36986	1.38889	15
16	1.20482	1.21951	1.23457	1.25	1.26582	1.28205	1.2987	1.31579	1.33333	1.35135	1.36986	1.38889	1.40845	16
17	1.21951	1.23457	1.25	1.26582	1.28205	1.2987	1.31579	1.33333	1.35135	1.36986	1.38889	1.40845	1.42857	17
18	1.23457	1.25	1.26582	1.28205	1.2987	1.31579	1.33333	1.35135	1.36986	1.38889	1.40845	1.42857	1.44928	18
19	1.25	1.26582	1.28205	1.2987	1.31579	1.33333	1.35135	1.36986	1.38889	1.40845	1.42857	1.44928	1.47059	19
20	1.26582	1.28205	1.2987	1.31579	1.33333	1.35135	1.36986	1.38889	1.40845	1.42857	1.44928	1.47059	1.49254	20
21	1.28205	1.2987	1.31579	1.33333	1.35135	1.36986	1.38889	1.40845	1.42857	1.44928	1.47059	1.49254	1.51515	21
22	1.2987	1.31579	1.33333	1.35135	1.36986	1.38889	1.40845	1.42857	1.44928	1.47059	1.49254	1.51515	1.53846	22
23	1.31579	1.33333	1.35135	1.36986	1.38889	1.40845	1.42857	1.44928	1.47059	1.49254	1.51515	1.53846	1.5625	23
24	1.33333	1.35135	1.36986	1.38889	1.40845	1.42857	1.44928	1.47059	1.49254	1.51515	1.53846	1.5625	1.5873	24
25	1.35135	1.36986	1.38889	1.40845	1.42857	1.44928	1.47059	1.49254	1.51515	1.53846	1.5625	1.5873	1.6129	25
26	1.36986	1.38889	1.40845	1.42857	1.44928	1.47059	1.49254	1.51515	1.53846	1.5625	1.5873	1.6129	1.63934	26
27	1.38889	1.40845	1.42857	1.44928	1.47059	1.49254	1.51515	1.53846	1.5625	1.5873	1.6129	1.63934	1.66667	27
28	1.40845	1.42857	1.44928	1.47059	1.49254	1.51515	1.53846	1.5625	1.5873	1.6129	1.63934	1.66667	1.69492	28
29	1.42857	1.44928	1.47059	1.49254	1.51515	1.53846	1.5625	1.5873	1.6129	1.63934	1.66667	1.69492	1.72414	29
30	1.44928	1.47059	1.49254	1.51515	1.53846	1.5625	1.5873	1.6129	1.63934	1.66667	1.69492	1.72414	1.75439	30
31	1.47059	1.49254	1.51515	1.53846	1.5625	1.5873	1.6129	1.63934	1.66667	1.69492	1.72414	1.75439	1.78571	31
32	1.49254	1.51515	1.53846	1.5625	1.5873	1.6129	1.63934	1.66667	1.69492	1.72414	1.75439	1.78571	1.81818	32
33	1.51515	1.53846	1.5625	1.5873	1.6129	1.63934	1.66667	1.69492	1.72414	1.75439	1.78571	1.81818	1.85185	33
34	1.53846	1.5625	1.5873	1.6129	1.63934	1.66667	1.69492	1.72414	1.75439	1.78571	1.81818	1.85185	1.88679	34
35	1.5625	1.5873	1.6129	1.63934	1.66667	1.69492	1.72414	1.75439	1.78571	1.81818	1.85185	1.88679	1.92308	35
36	1.5873	1.6129	1.63934	1.66667	1.69492	1.72414	1.75439	1.78571	1.81818	1.85185	1.88679	1.92308	1.96078	36
37	1.6129	1.63934	1.66667	1.69492	1.72414	1.75439	1.78571	1.81818	1.85185	1.88679	1.92308	1.96078	2.	37
38	1.63934	1.66667	1.69492	1.72414	1.75439	1.78571	1.81818	1.85185	1.88679	1.92308	1.96078	2.	2.04082	38
39	1.66667	1.69492	1.72414	1.75439	1.78571	1.81818	1.85185	1.88679	1.92308	1.96078	2.	2.04082	2.08333	39
40	1.69492	1.72414	1.75439	1.78571	1.81818	1.85185	1.88679	1.92308	1.96078	2.	2.04082	2.08333	2.12766	40
41	1.72414	1.75439	1.78571	1.81818	1.85185	1.88679	1.92308	1.96078	2.	2.04082	2.08333	2.12766	2.17391	41
42	1.75439	1.78571	1.81818	1.85185	1.88679	1.92308	1.96078	2.	2.04082	2.08333	2.12766	2.17391	2.22222	42
43	1.78571	1.81818	1.85185	1.88679	1.92308	1.96078	2.	2.04082	2.08333	2.12766	2.17391	2.22222	2.27273	43
44	1.81818	1.85185	1.88679	1.92308	1.96078	2.	2.04082	2.08333	2.12766	2.17391	2.22222	2.27273	2.32558	44
45	1.85185	1.88679	1.92308	1.96078	2.	2.04082	2.08333	2.12766	2.17391	2.22222	2.27273	2.32558	2.38095	45
46	1.88679	1.92308	1.96078	2.	2.04082	2.08333	2.12766	2.17391	2.22222	2.27273	2.32558	2.38095	2.43902	46
47	1.92308	1.96078	2.	2.04082	2.08333	2.12766	2.17391	2.22222	2.27273	2.32558	2.38095	2.43902	2.5	47
48	1.96078	2.	2.04082	2.08333	2.12766	2.17391	2.22222	2.27273	2.32558	2.38095	2.43902	2.5	2.5641	48
49	2.	2.04082	2.08333	2.12766	2.17391	2.22222	2.27273	2.32558	2.38095	2.43902	2.5	2.5641	2.63158	49
50	2.04082	2.08333	2.12766	2.17391	2.22222	2.27273	2.32558	2.38095	2.43902	2.5	2.5641	2.63158	2.7027	50
Overhead %	1%	2%	3%	4%	5%	6%	7%	8%	9%	10%	11%	12%	13%	Overhead %

Exhibit 13.—Mark-up Table by which can be determined the proper selling price, figured on known overhead expenses and a desired net profit.

price. Thus, if the cost were $2.10, the calculation becomes: $2.10 ÷ .70 = 3. This method proves its correctness, for 20 per cent (60 cents) taken from $3 leaves a balance of $2.40, and 10 per cent taken from this (24 cents) leaves the original cost of $2.10.

Use of Burroughs Mark-up Table.—The table shown in Exhibit 13 is a time-saving method of calculating the proper mark-up when the overhead costs and the desired net profits are known. In making up this table the percentages of net profit and overhead are figured on the selling price. The selling price of goods that cost $1 may be found in the desired net profit column *at the intersection of the line opposite the required overhead per cent.*

If the overhead is 30 per cent and the desired net profit is 6 per cent, the selling price of an article that cost $3.75 may be found by multiplying $3.75 by 1.5625. The result is $5.86. To prove the operation, deduct from $5.86 the total of 36 per cent, as in trade discount.

TABLE OF PROFIT-PERCENTAGES

The following table shows at a glance the percentage of profit made on sale price when a given percentage is added to the cost price of goods.

Percentage added to cost:	Equivalent percentage on selling price:
5	4¾
6	5⅔
8	7⅖
10	9
12	10 5/7
15	13
20	16⅔
25	20
33⅓	25
40	28½
50	33½
66⅔	40
75	42¾
85	46
100	50

EXHIBIT 14.

The Burroughs Company gives this further illustration of the usefulness of the "Mark-up Table."

Marking Goods

Retail prices are sometimes fixed by the manufacturer. Competition regulates the selling price of others. Both conditions are covered in the following problem:

An incoming invoice is to be marked to cover an overhead of 35 per cent with a net profit of 5 per cent.

The first item on the invoice ($27.25) should sell for $27.25 × 1.66667, or $45.42. (See Mark-up Table.) The second item ($4.80) should be marked at $8 and the third item, $39.17.

	Cost		Selling
1 Suit	$27.25		$45.42
1 Pr. shoes	4.80		8.00
1 Coat	23.50		39.17
	$55.55	Marked up by the table..	$92.59

The manufacturer requires that the suit be sold for........	$40.00
Other merchants are selling this shoe for.................	7.00
The coat is an excellent value and can be sold for.........	47.50
The actual selling price...............................	$94.50

It will be seen that the total of the invoice has been marked to bring $1.91 more than the gross profit required.

The invoice is then returned to the office where calculations are made to secure the following information. This is shown in the form below which is put on the face or back of the invoice with a rubber stamp.

Selling price	$94.50
Cost	55.55
Mark-up	38.95
Mark-up per cent	41.2

The mark-up (gross profit) is the difference between the selling and cost price. The mark-up per cent is secured by dividing the mark-up by the selling price.

Range of Mark-up, Fixed Expense and Profit in Various Lines of Retailing.—The Dealers' Service Department of the *Retail Ledger* gives the following data as indicating the range of mark-up, fixed expense and net profit in a number of representative lines of retailing:

Shoes

Mark-up, 27 per cent is common; variation range, 10 to 45 per cent.
Net profit, 1.2 per cent is common; variation range, 0 to 20 per cent.
Wages, 10 per cent is common; variation range, 5 to 17 per cent.
Advertising, 2 per cent is common; variation range, 0 to 7 per cent.
Rent, 2.5 per cent is common; variation range, 4 to 16 per cent.
Total expense, 26 per cent is common; variation range, 12.5 to 43 per cent.

Men's Clothing

Total overhead, 22.5 per cent is common.
Wages, 12.5 per cent is common.
Rent, 2.64 per cent is common; size of town causes variations.
Advertising, 3 per cent is common.

Meats

Mark-up, 18.7 per cent is common figure.
Net profit, 2.3 per cent is common figure.
Wages, 10.3 per cent is common figure.
Rent, 1.4 per cent is common figure.
Total expenses, 16.50 per cent is common figure.

Jewelry

Mark-up, 40 per cent is common.
Net profit, 6.4 per cent is common.
Wages, 10 per cent is common; range, 8 to 20 per cent.
Rent, 4 per cent is common; range, ½ of 1 to 13 per cent.
Total expense, 32 per cent is common; range, 17 to 56 per cent.

Hardware

Mark-up, 27 per cent is common; range, 10 to 40 per cent.
Net profit, 6 per cent is common; range, loss to 15 per cent.
Wages, 6 per cent is common; range, 2.5 to 16 per cent.
Rent, 1.7 per cent is common; range, ½ of 1 to 7 per cent.
Buying, 4.5 per cent is common.
Interest, 3.3 per cent is common.
Total expenses, 21 per cent is common; range, 12 to 36 per cent.

Groceries

Mark-up, 19 per cent is common; range, 7 to 33 per cent.
Net profit, 2 per cent is common; range, loss to 20 per cent.
Wages, 5.5 per cent is common; range, 3 to 11 per cent.
Rent 2 per cent is common; range, 1 to 5 per cent.
Total expenses, 15 per cent is common; range, 7 to 30 per cent.

Department Stores

Mark-up, 33 per cent is common.
Net profit, 2.7 per cent is common.
Wages, 12 to 16 per cent is usual.
Advertising, 3 to 4 per cent is usual.
Rent, 3 per cent is usual.
Total expenses, 30 per cent is usual.

Drug Stores

Mark-up, ranges from 20 per cent to 50 per cent, with 34 per cent common.

Net profit, ranges from loss to 20 per cent, with 6 per cent common.

Wages, range from 7 to 20 per cent, with 12 per cent common.

Rent, range from 1 to 11 per cent, with 3 per cent common.

Total expenses range from 18 to 43 per cent, with 28 per cent common.

Remarks

In all lines there is to be found considerable range in profits, mark-ups and expenses, due often to location of store, widely varied class of merchandise handled, class of trade catered to and in a very great many cases owing to inaccurate records.

The foregoing figures represent what these items in ordinary locations and under ordinary conditions ought to average. They represent the reasonable standard which ought to be achieved.

Shoes: In the retail shoe trade there is a wide variation of experience, as there is a wide variation in the class of trade catered to and the styles of goods handled. The expenses on women's shoes run higher than on men's, and much higher on fad styles than on staple lines which can be held over from one season to another.

Jewelry: The common figures quoted are for stores which split their business in normal proportion between expensive and inexpensive lines. But it must be remembered that the store which specializes in precious gems and sterling ware will have much slower turnover on the average than the store which specializes in quick-moving trinkets and plated ware.

The foregoing figures, as applied to the individual store, should not be considered as absolute, but rather as indicatory.

Additional Data on the Shoe Business.—A rather extensive research made a few years ago on the shoe business showed that the average mark-up in 1919 by the retailer had reached

TURNOVER AND PRICE-FIGURING

35 per cent but had receded later to an average of about 25 per cent of factory price. The annual turnover of the average store was about $8,500. The net profit, after deducting all expenses, including salary of proprietor, ran to 2 per cent or even less. The turnover of stock was $1\frac{8}{10}$ times per year. The following table indicates the monthly variation of sales according to this same research.

	Per Cent		Per Cent
January	6.1	July	10.0
February	5.0	August	8.1
March	5.2	September	8.2
April	7.0	October	11.1
May	9.1	November	10.0
June	10.2	December	10.0

The survey made somewhat later and including more of the larger shoe stores and the country stores indicated the high peaks of business for April and May in the spring, and October and November in the fall.

Statistics from the National Retail Dry Goods Association.— Statistics compiled by the National Retail Dry Goods Association show the average sales per salesperson in 19 stores doing a basement business in a general line of merchandise amounted to $13,310 annually, or a little over $266 a week, allowing for two weeks' vacation.

The average sale in such departments was around $2.50. The average mark-up was found to be 37 per cent and the average gross profit 27.1 per cent.

One store doing a large basement business submitted the following table of gross profit and stock turn:

	Gross Profit Per Cent	Stock Turn		Gross Profit Per Cent	Stock Turn
Corsets	32.4	9.3	Skirts	27.4	11.8
Infants' wear	24.4	5.6	Women's shoes	22.6	8.7
Muslin underwear	19.3	7.4	Coats	25.4	14.4
Negligee	17.3	6.3	Misses' goods	27.5	13.3
Hosiery	20.5	7.6	Waists	20.4	11.0
Knit underwear	18.7	7.0	Furs	13.3	8.0
Women's gloves	21.9	5.7	Millinery	21.5	30.0
Boys' clothing	23.4	6.2	Dresses	24.0	17.0
Haberdashery	16.0	5.6			

The mark-down showed a wider variation, averaging a little over 8 per cent, with some running as high as 17 per cent. Expenses ran from 17½ to 31½ per cent. Sales expense alone ran from 5 to 11.7 per cent, with a general average of about 7½ per cent.

Monthly Variations in Sales Totals.—Season plays its part in turnover and in increasing or lowering the overhead and net-profit percentages. Exhibit 15 shows the busiest month of the year for a number of enterprises.

Statistics from Federal Reserve Banks.—The table shown in Exhibit 16 gives the rate of turnover as determined by the Federal Reserve Banks by districts. This information, therefore, covers the entire United States and shows the variation on twelve representative lines of goods, but the inquiry was confined to department shores. The figures given show the highest rate of turnover and the lowest on each classification, and finally the average. Naturally, there is much variation, even with the classifications themselves. The figures as given cover all kinds of furniture, for example. One kind of furniture may sell much more rapidly than another. It would hardly do to conclude that the showing of department stores is identical with that of specialty stores handling the same kind of goods. Nevertheless, the figures afford a general basis on which to figure turnover.

This table was compiled by the National Retail Dry Goods Association. In sending out this data to the trade press the National Retail Dry Goods Association offers these comments on turnover:

At the present time expenses probably cannot be reduced, and increased turnover presents the greatest and only possibilities for economy in operations. Taking the illustration of the merchant who repurchased a $100 stock four times, his purchases cost a total of $400, with sales of $600, resulting in a gross profit of $200, or $50 for each turn. Consequently, for each additional turn his gross profit would be further increased $50, while expenses will not be increased in like proportion. Executive and administrative expenses will remain constant with an increase in sales volume, as will building maintenance, rent, buying expenses, taxes, interest, light, heat, repairs and depreciation on buildings and fixtures. A very certain and con-

TURNOVER AND PRICE-FIGURING

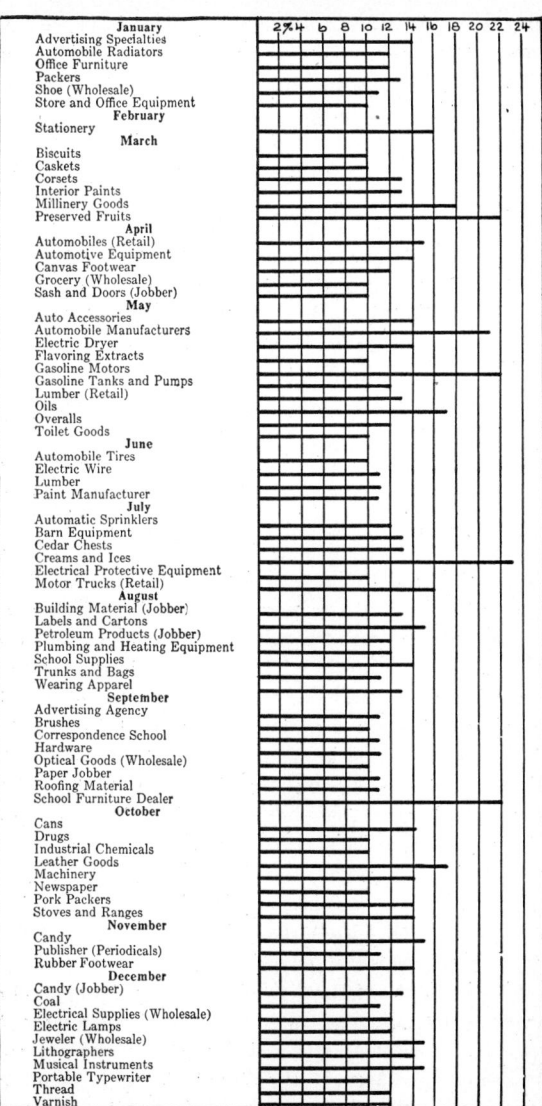

Exhibit 15.—Chart made up by Lefax, Inc., from information gathered by the Dartnell Corporation, showing the busiest month of the year for various enterprises. The length of the line in each case indicates the percentage of that month's business as compared with the yearly total. For example, February is the busiest month for the stationery business and this amounts to 16 per cent of the yearly total.

siderable saving. Other expenses, such as office and advertising, may increase to some extent but not in proportion to the increase in sales volume. This saving may mark the dividing line between failure and success. In addition to the savings in expenses, you are receiving at least 2 to 4 per cent discount on the increase in purchases.

But these savings are not the only ones, and may indeed be less than the saving through the avoidance of mark-downs. Such a department as women's shoes is many times operated at a loss because of the fact that some of the styles are out of fashion before the retailer has had the goods on the shelves for any appreciable length of time. Within a short while the stock will consist of out-of-style, discontinued numbers, and other odds and ends. Such stock, of course, cannot sell. By measuring the turnover rate in the shoe department by a reliable standard this unsatisfactory condition would have been revealed at its very inception and the merchant would have been saved from a severe loss. Besides actually saving money in this manner, the retailer will become known as a live and progressive business man, and his store referred to as a good place in which to buy. The women's ready-to-wear departments are also either profitable or not according to how well they are merchandised. It is very easily seen that, with a large number of mark-downs as were shown in the recent clearance sales in apparel goods in New York City, serious losses will result. This sale came immediately after the Christmas holidays and was due to a genuine attempt to reduce surplus stocks. For instance, coats were reduced from $95–$550 to $25–$250 in one store, and in another from $30–$225 to $15–$99.75. This indicates where careful buying with a resultant good turnover would have saved more than half the price of the garments.

"Size does not determine success," says John H. Tregoe, secretary and treasurer of the National Association of Credit Men, and, with equal certainty, it may be said that size does not determine rate of turnover. The fear that the large department store would supplant and wipe out the small retail shop in large cities has been dispelled. The larger institutions are usually better managed and good managements means not only efficient salesmanship, but much more; it means careful buying. But some small stores can be and are equally as well managed as the largest department stores. All along Forty-second Street, near Broadway, in New York City are small shops paying probably the highest rentals of stores anywhere. One such retailer of women's apparel finds it profitable to pay an annual rental of $6,800 a year, $132 a year per square foot of space occupied. How can he do it? Again the answer is "quick turnover."

	Federal Reserve District											
	(1)	(2)	(3)	(4)	(5)	(6)	(7)	(8)	(9)	(10)	(11)	(12)
Colored wash goods:												
Highest	7.30	6.60	4.80	9.60	5.18	5.20	4.60	3.16	4.19	2.70	3.66	3.75
Lowest	1.54	1.66	1.90	1.54	1.10	1.03	.74	.85	1.00	1.16	1.67	1.10
Average	3.61	3.99	3.13	3.76	4.11	3.08	3.54	3.45	3.88	2.15	3.16	3.10
Leather goods:												
Highest	5.90	11.92	4.40	7.25	7.19	7.80	8.20	4.17	7.73	4.40	6.40	4.94
Lowest	1.09	1.32	1.60	1.10	1.50	2.18	1.59	1.34	2.04	1.70	1.33	1.10
Average	4.22	3.42	2.74	2.85	3.60	3.34	2.81	2.32	3.18	2.76	4.30	3.01
Men's clothing:												
Highest	6.88	5.52	4.10	7.98	5.00	6.80	5.62	4.83	3.34	2.53	5.26	3.88
Lowest	2.00	1.33	1.49	1.16	1.40	2.20	1.16	.89	1.53	1.44	2.84	1.10
Average	4.14	3.05	2.72	2.98	2.81	2.84	2.45	3.00	2.15	2.04	3.91	2.22
Women's coats:												
Highest	17.26	14.19	11.50	14.20	13.75	14.00	12.20	9.81	14.34	10.00	8.25	12.04
Lowest	2.02	2.40	1.90	2.90	2.40	3.50	2.03	1.37	3.00	1.80	4.28	3.16
Average	5.55	5.62	4.50	5.69	5.00	4.84	5.10	5.05	5.16	3.40	5.38	5.70
Women's dresses:												
Highest	18.09	12.60	13.20	15.30	15.10	14.00	13.00	9.81	8.55	8.80	8.70	8.91
Lowest	2.02	2.57	1.90	2.88	2.90	2.74	2.03	1.37	3.48	1.80	5.22	2.06
Average	5.93	5.45	4.10	5.03	5.96	4.68	4.69	4.55	5.10	3.85	5.87	5.04
Millinery:												
Highest	11.50	20.42	23.30	12.34	12.30	18.80	20.88	8.22	15.47	8.11	12.60	13.33
Lowest	1.15	3.90	4.20	3.20	2.60	6.44	1.40	2.80	5.25	3.91	2.82	2.23
Average	5.20	6.57	5.22	6.21	6.01	6.85	5.96	6.17	5.62	4.53	5.80	5.27
Aprons and house dresses:												
Highest	7.50	8.85	6.10	8.90	6.71	5.40	8.80	4.68	5.52	4.90	7.75	4.50
Lowest	1.11	1.82	1.65	.92	1.70	1.98	1.15	.87	1.58	1.50	2.15	.94
Average	4.61	4.20	3.25	3.55	3.65	3.13	3.40	2.17	3.50	2.95	4.12	2.86
Women's shoes:												
Highest	4.54	6.69	4.00	4.09	5.26	3.13	5.60	2.02	2.46	2.90	2.85	3.21
Lowest	1.14	1.40	1.20	1.00	1.30	1.83	1.02	.78	1.12	.80	1.50	.97
Average	2.63	2.45	2.07	2.20	2.61	2.56	2.25	1.50	1.65	1.71	2.18	2.14
House furnishings:												
Highest	9.52	4.41	7.00	2.69	3.10	3.43	3.98	4.43	3.94	2.65	3.90	3.39
Lowest	1.57	.80	.90	.83	1.20	1.18	1.14	.94	1.50	1.10	2.16	1.00
Average	2.64	2.32	1.83	1.70	2.27	2.18	2.23	1.81	2.30	1.92	3.10	2.13
Domestic rugs:												
Highest	5.29	5.43	4.00	7.10	4.92	4.00	5.00	4.95	6.62	3.90	2.43	5.21
Lowest	1.10	1.08	1.10	.78	1.53	1.27	.76	.94	1.28	1.03	.89	.61
Average	2.40	2.63	2.00	1.85	2.60	2.32	2.32	1.76	2.20	1.90	1.90	2.60
Art wares:												
Highest	4.50	3.50	4.00	3.25	2.50	2.73	3.53	3.41		2.80	3.90	3.70
Lowest	.77	.60	3.00	.50	1.16	1.31	.94	.49	1.94	.96	1.41	.74
Average	2.88	1.90	3.50	1.80	1.98	2.10	2.07	1.70	1.94	1.50	2.97	1.81
Furniture:												
Highest	3.46	4.19	4.40	3.21	2.05	1.88	1.83	2.14	2.48	1.30	3.30	2.21
Lowest	*1.21	.60	.84	.70	3.30	2.80	3.48	2.14	4.37		3.30	6.50
Average	2.27	2.33	1.93	1.87	.80	1.15	.60		1.15	1.30		1.10

Exhibit 16.—Rates of turnover for 1921 in 12 departments in stores located in the different Federal Reserve Districts. This table was compiled by the National Retail Dry Goods Association.

Mark-downs and Turnover.—The Director of the Bureau of Accounting and Control of the National Retail Dry Goods Association says, on the subject of turnover, (*New York Times*, December 3, 1922):

AVOIDANCE OF MARK-DOWNS

Not only are the large mark-downs which some merchants have to make escaped by a rapid turnover, because the goods are kept moving and do not have a chance to depreciate while on the shelves, but there is practically no increase in the amount of expenses as turnover increases. The fixed operating charges of a store are the same whether the merchant sells $1,000,000 or $1,200,000, the only difference there might be occurring in the direct selling salaries. Even here the percentage to sales would be less in proportion to the larger volume. The studies made by the Harvard School of Business Research for 1921 show the total expenses to sales to be 27.9 per cent. In other words, this merchant would have a clear gain of practically 27.9 per cent of $200,000 by increasing his rate of turnover only one-fifth.

When we compare this small increase with what is possible, it is really a marvel that some merchants are still in business. It is very proper to assume that lack of attention to turnover is the cause of so many small, inefficient merchants now operating in this country. Since they are able to stay in business, it is evident that the public is supporting them, and that they are being supported at too great a cost. This is a matter in which every consumer is very much interested, as it affects his cost of living very directly.

Added to the saving in expenses by a more rapid turnover is the item of mark-downs, which average about 5 per cent in the less efficiently managed store. This figure means that the merchant with such a mark-down must add 5 cents to every dollar's worth of sales he makes in order to even up this loss, which is due very largely to defective merchandising.

It is the advantage arising from a quick turnover that enables the merchant in the large city not only to compete with, but very frequently to undersell, the stores in the smaller communities. This fact is even more remarkable when it is considered that rents are many times higher in a large city than in the smaller towns. All operating costs are, likewise, much higher, so that a store with a slow-moving stock is forced to adopt better selling methods or retire.

The question may be asked, "Can a good turnover be secured in a small town?" In answer, I will cite an actual example of a store in a town of about 15,000 people, which has an annual turnover of about seven times in its ready-to-wear departments, with the other divisions showing up equally well. The average is not much more than half this figure. What has been done in this case can be done in many another store if the right methods are pursued.

How Small Percentages Multiply.—The following table is a good reminder with respect not only to rapid turnover but

TURNOVER AND PRICE-FIGURING 71

to cash discounts, of how large a profit is represented during a year by multiplying smaller margins or profits.

½ per cent in 10 days—net 30 days—equals 9 per cent a year
1 per cent in 10 days—net 30 days—equals 18 per cent a year
1½ per cent in 10 days—net 30 days—equals 27 per cent a year
2 per cent in 30 days—net 120 days—equals 8 per cent a year
2 per cent in 10 days—net 60 days—equals 14 per cent a year
2 per cent in 30 days—net 60 days—equals 24 per cent a year
2 per cent in 10 days—net 30 days—equals 36 per cent a year
3 per cent in 10 days—net 120 days—equals 10 per cent a year
3 per cent in 30 days—net 60 days—equals 36 per cent a year
3 per cent in 10 days—net 30 days—equals 54 per cent a year

A FOE TO TURNOVER

The Idle Dollar.—The thief in the night that cuts down the profits in thousands of businesses is the "idle dollar"—the dollar that, for some reason or other, is invested in goods that do not move, that merely take up room, prevent the merchant from realizing on his investment and that actually lessen the value of the dollar, so that eventually the dollar comes back possibly with a fifth, fourth or half of its value vanished.

Idle dollars are not merely those that come back with their value lessened. If either a manufacturer or a merchant has his dollar tied up in raw material, idle plant, or goods that will not be sold for months, though the dollar eventually returns with its value unimpaired, it fails to bring a profit for the time being and thus the burden is thrown on other dollars in the meantime to earn the overhead for the firm as well as the net profit.

Only a theorist of the most dreamy type will hold that every idle dollar can be kept at work every day. That would be a business Eutopia, and such ideal conditions never exist. Trade conditions do not always permit either a manufacturer or a merchant to buy exactly what he needs for his exact period of turnover. Supplies of raw materials, manufacturing processes and shipments of finished goods from either manufacturer or wholesaler do not move with such machine-like precision as to permit this. Furthermore, buying is not an exact science.

The Unknown Quantity in Business.—Records of past experiences and surveys of present situations and of the probable future tell the business man much, but they do not enable him to know exactly how many 34 by 4 automobile tires the American public will use in a given year, nor what brands of manufacture will have the first, second and third call. The most carefully compiled statistics do not enable the dry goods department store to know exactly how many cloth-top shoes of a new style the women of its community will take during a season, nor whether white gloves will increase or decrease in popularity.

Both manufacturer and merchant have to cope with a certain unknown quantity.

Trade conditions sometimes make it absolutely necessary for a merchant to anticipate his demand for a longer period than perhaps he would prefer if he could be sure of buying quickly and exactly what he might want. Often, too, the large purchase means a much better price.

The great danger is that the extra discounts and price concessions earned by large purchases so often load a merchant up with more goods than he can sell. A small amount of unsalable stock or stock that must be sold at a great loss because of being out of style, or some other potent reason, will cut deeply into net profits. It is better that a merchant should be out of stock occasionally for a short time than to carry many loads of slow-selling goods.

It is apparent, therefore, that all that the foresighted manufacturer, wholesaler, importer or retailer can do is to make a close study of records, of reports of current tendencies—private reports or those circulated in the press—and then use his best judgment in buying. He can hardly hope to have all of his forecasts and conclusions 100 per cent accurate, but the nearer he comes to the perfect standard, the more nearly will he come to the Eutopian state of his business where he can buy at the rate that will permit the most profitable turnover of his capital.

Most employers watch the idle employe closely. They know that when an employe is on the payroll and there is little or nothing for him to do, a loss is taking place. It is just as imperative to watch the idle dollars, for their laziness or inaction may mean just as great a loss to a business.

"Making Two Blades of Grass Grow."—The National Cash Register Company, in a booklet entitled "Making Two Blades of Grass Grow Where Only One Grew Before," presents the following interesting illustration of the value of increased turnover and suggests ways and means of bringing it about:

The real salesman is quick to associate the goods the customer wants with something that the customer needs but does not think of at the moment.

The customer *buys* the goods she asks for. She is *sold* the goods she doesn't ask for. That's selling—salesmanship. And it is service.

Think what this means to the store in the way of increased business and increased profits.

Suppose you and your helpers waited on 120,000 customers last year and that you did a business of $40,000—that your merchandise cost you 66 per cent, your overhead was 28 per cent and your net profit 6 per cent.

Suppose your average amount of sale was 33⅓ cents. Now, by increasing your average amount of sale to 40 cents, your yearly business would be $48,000. Your net profit would increase from 6 per cent, or $2,400, to 10.7 per cent, or $5,120. Would pay you, wouldn't it?

Another important thing is to know what it costs to wait on a customer. Divide each salesman's salary by the number of customers he or she serves. This will give you the average cost of serving customers. If an employe serves 600 customers and you pay that helper $30 a week, then the cost of serving each customer is 5 cents. Be sure to keep a record of cost of handling customers. It's important.

If you keep a record of average amount of sales only, your helpers may be tempted to pick out the prosperous-looking customers and neglect the less prosperous-looking ones and the children. By keeping a record of the average amount of sales, employes will sell as much as they can to each customer. By keeping a record of cost of sales, your salespeople will wait on every customer they can.

So, you see, it's a matter of salesmanship. Salesmanship is a matter of training. And the merchant who neglects to teach his helpers up-to-date selling methods will never make the money he should make.

How about you? What are you doing to increase your profits? Are you holding a school for your salesmen or saleswomen? Are you showing them how to make associate sales?

Are you coaching them to suggest seasonable goods?

Are you explaining to them the quality of goods?

Are you showing them the value of increasing the average amount of sales?

Are you impressing upon them the importance of serving as many customers as possible?

Are you rewarding them properly as they become more valuable to you?

You owe it to yourself, your business and your staff of employes, to think about these things.

---

1. Buy goods in the right quantities.

2. Advertise your store.

3. Give customers the kind of service they want.

4. See that salespeople make a note of goods out of stock.

5. Display as much merchandise as possible, without crowding.

6. Arrange stock so that it will help to sell itself.

7. See that your prices are right.

EXHIBIT 17.—Advice from the National Cash Register Company to retail merchants on the problem of getting faster turnover.

How Turnover Sometimes Eliminates a Loss.—The speeding up of turnover is sometimes an effective method of overcoming what seems to be an unavoidable loss. During the days of the high-peak prices in textiles a dry goods merchant found himself in the position of selling a well known grade of dress goods at $2 a yard. It had been selling at that price for some time, but the market was falling rapidly and it seemed obvious that the price of $2 could not long be continued. Nevertheless, the store had a good-sized quantity of this material on hand.

The man in charge of sales realized that the store first coming out with an announcement of this grade of goods materially reduced in price would win the favor of the public. He did not care to take a chance on that store being a competitor, so he decided to adopt a bold remedy.

He bought a new lot of the same material and, combining this with his old stock, he offered it to the public at $1 a yard. All possible uses for the material were suggested in store advertising and displays and the stock was sold with remarkable speed. This sale brought to light a very large demand for the particular material and the store continued to aggressively go after the business in this line. Immediately further stocks of the material were laid in and sale was made with equal speed. This procedure was continued, over 16,000 yards of the material being sold within 60 days. All this time the wholesale price on the material had been dropping, but the material was still sold for $1 by the store. The margin of profit on the later purchases of the material made the sale a very profitable venture, notwithstanding the fact that a loss was taken on the original stock.

How Pelletier Store, of Topeka, Kan., Increased Turn of Stock.—A business newspaper is authority for the statement that the Pelletier Department Store of Topeka, Kan., increased its turn of ready-to-wear clothing from 7 times a year to 12 times a year by managing the department according to the following 12-plank platform:

1. New models daily
2. Two popular price groups
3. Specials, but no "job lots"
4. Nothing but first quality garments handled
5. Sales plans figured eight weeks in advance
6. Steady, constant advertising
7. Direct, descriptive copy, emphasizing price
8. Group purchases featured
9. Daily changes of displays

76 RETAIL ADVERTISING AND SELLING

10. Windows feature same goods as in rior displays
11. Weekly sales conferences
12. Prize contests for saleswomen.

It is explained that this program meant trips to the buying markets by the head of the department every four weeks;

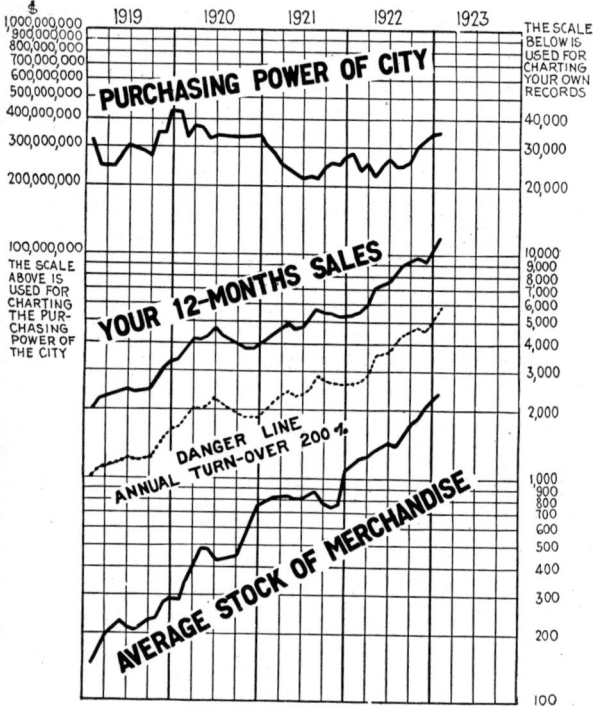

EXHIBIT 18.—Chart prepared for this volume by Babson's Statistical Organization, Inc., indicating how average stock, danger line of turnover, and the total of 12 months' sales can be shown for comparison with the purchasing power of a city.

that deliveries were so scheduled that some new suits, coats and dresses, as well as blouses, skirts and petticoats, were coming in every day—thus making the No. 1 plank of the platform a live one. Job lots were not purchased, but when good quantities meant large price concessions, these were made, though small-quantity buying was the rule. Sample lines were also purchased. Standing orders were maintained with a resident buyer in the largest market, so that attractive specials were picked up regularly and shipped in.

The prize contests were arranged in different ways: one prize would be offered to the saleswoman who sold the largest number of garments over a given price, and another prize to the saleswoman having the largest number of sales to her credit, irrespective of price. The first prize was usually $10, with second and third prizes of $5 and $2.50. The sales conferences were held at the beginning of every week.

The cost percentage for the year in which the twelve turns of stock were made was actually a little less than that of the previous year with only seven turns to its credit.

(Summarized from *Retail Ledger*).

Chart Showing Stock, Turnover, Yearly Sale and Purchasing Power of City.—The Babson's Statistical Organization's chart reproduced in Exhibit 18 illustrates the value of showing yearly sales and the rate of turnover of the average stock of the merchant for close comparison with the purchasing power of the city or other territory. It is suggested by the originator of this chart that the danger line on annual turnover be drawn parallel to the plot of sales at whatever distance below may be appropriate. In the illustration in Exhibit 18, a danger line is set at 200 per cent. If the lower line indicating the average stock touches or crosses the danger line it is an indication that the merchant is making two turns or less a year of his stock.

SECTION IV

COMPENSATION PLANS

There are undoubtedly more retail merchants following the plan of paying straight salary than have adopted any other method, but a growing number have seen the advisability of basing the salaries of their helpers either on gross sales or gross profits.

A number of well known stores that have worked out an analysis of their selling costs for each department take their salespeople into their confidence and let them see just what salary-cost the department or goods can stand. A quota or standard task is then made the basis for the weekly or monthly salary. This method often results in salespeople discovering that they were not overworked, after all, and makes them resist the introduction of new employes into their departments instead of making a plea for extra help.

Bonus on Certain Goods.—The system, familiarly known as the P. M. system, whereby retailers pay their salespeople a premium for disposing of shop-worn, out-of-style, or other slow moving goods, has its good points and also its unsatisfactory side. Many of the better stores do not use it but merely make special prices on slow moving goods, advertise them aggressively and let them sell themselves.

A variation of the bonus system is the plan of "playing up the higher-priced goods" and paying a special commission or bonus on such sales. For example, if the customer asks for $2 shirts, the salesman, instead of contenting himself with showing only $2 goods, is encouraged by the system to display higher grades. It often happens that the customer, when he sees the better goods, prefers to buy them. In general, people have a little margin beyond the limit they may set when naming the price-grade of the goods they want to see.

Fixing Salaries of Retail Salesmen According to Total of Sales.

—The growing tendency to base the compensation of retail salesmen on the amount of their sales, checked up with the sales-cost percentage, makes it desirable for every retailer to have at his command reliable data as to selling costs. Naturally, any table of this kind must be more or less general, because the locality, the size of the store, and many other factors enter into costs. Nevertheless, the table shown in Exhibit 19, made up by the *Retail Ledger* from first-hand data,

Items of expense	Kind of store							
	Grocery, per cent	Drug, per cent	Hardware, per cent	Furniture, per cent	Men's Clothing, per cent	Shoe, per cent	Jewelry, per cent	Department store, per cent
Rent..............	3.07	4.02	3.41	5.04	3.04	3.21	4.98	3.24
Salaries...........	8.46	10.95	10.11	9.73	9.49	10.51	10.96	9.65
Advertising.......	1.83	2.76	1.12	3.72	3.16	2.65	2.85	4.67
Heat and light...	.39	.69	.43	.92	.62	1.10	.61	.54
Delivery..........	2.53	.51	.91	.94	.65	.46	.09	1.02
Supplies..........	.37	.36	.60	.41	.43	.30	.89	.38
Insurance and taxes............	.58	1.21	.99	1.57	1.07	1.03	1.32	1.08
General expenses.	.45	4.49	2.01	1.10	2.31	4.36	3.95	4.15
Depreciation and shrinkage........	.76	.47	.52	2.14	2.16	.50	.95	1.11
Bad debts........	.47	.19	.31	1.94	.34	.10	.21	.21
Percentage of total expenses to sales............	18.91	25.65	20.41	27.51	23.27	24.22	26.81	26.05

(*From Retail Ledger, March 15, 1921*).

EXHIBIT 19.—Various items of expense in the principal branches of retail trade. They represent the common experience in percentage of net sales.
The National Association of Newspaper Executives issued these figures. They were compiled from data furnished by the Harvard Bureau of Business Research and other retail research organizations.

affords a general guide. The larger chart shown in Exhibit 20 saves figuring or working out just what an employe's sales cost is. While quotas and bonuses are playing an important part in sales practice, the method of fixing compensation on sales cost is, after all, a simple and an equitable one. It is a

80 RETAIL ADVERTISING AND SELLING

Clerks' Weekly Salaries

Clerk's Weekly Sales	$10	10½	11	11½	12	12½	13	13½	14	14½	15	16	17	17½	18	19	20	21	22	22½	23	24	25	26	27	27½	28	29	30	32½	35	37½	40	42½	45	47½	50
$100	10.0	10.5	11.0	11.5	12.0	12.5	13.0	13.5	14.0	14.5	15.0	16.0	17.0	17.5	18.0	19.0	20.0	21.0	22.0	22.5	23.0	24.0	25.0	26.0	27.0	27.5	28.0	29.0	30.0	32.5	35.0	37.5	40.0	42.5	45.0	47.5	50.0
110	9.1	9.6	10.0	10.5	10.9	11.4	11.8	12.3	12.7	13.2	13.6	14.5	15.5	15.9	16.4	17.3	18.2	19.1	20.0	20.5	20.9	21.8	22.7	23.6	24.6	25.0	25.5	26.4	27.3	29.6	31.8	34.1	36.4	38.6	40.9	43.2	45.5
120	8.3	8.8	9.2	9.6	10.0	10.4	10.8	11.3	11.7	12.1	12.5	13.3	14.2	14.6	15.0	15.8	16.7	17.5	18.3	18.8	19.2	20.0	20.8	21.7	22.5	22.9	23.3	24.2	25.0	27.1	29.2	31.3	33.3	35.4	37.5	39.6	41.7
130	7.7	8.1	8.5	8.9	9.2	9.6	10.0	10.4	10.8	11.2	11.5	12.3	13.1	13.5	13.9	14.6	15.4	16.2	16.9	17.3	17.7	18.5	19.2	20.0	20.8	21.2	21.5	22.3	23.1	25.0	26.9	28.9	30.8	32.7	34.6	36.5	38.5
140	7.1	7.5	7.9	8.2	8.6	8.9	9.3	9.6	10.0	10.4	10.7	11.4	12.1	12.5	12.9	13.6	14.3	15.0	15.7	16.1	16.4	17.1	17.9	18.6	19.3	19.6	20.0	20.7	21.4	23.2	25.0	26.8	28.6	30.4	32.1	33.9	35.7
150	6.7	7.0	7.3	7.7	8.0	8.3	8.7	9.0	9.3	9.7	10.0	10.7	11.3	11.7	12.0	12.7	13.3	14.0	14.7	15.0	15.3	16.0	16.7	17.3	18.0	18.3	18.7	19.3	20.0	21.7	23.3	25.0	26.7	28.3	30.0	31.7	33.3
160	6.3	6.6	6.9	7.2	7.5	7.8	8.1	8.4	8.8	9.1	9.4	10.0	10.6	10.9	11.3	11.9	12.5	13.1	13.8	14.1	14.4	15.0	15.6	16.3	16.9	17.2	17.5	18.1	18.8	20.3	21.9	23.4	25.0	26.6	28.1	29.7	31.3
170	5.9	6.2	6.5	6.8	7.1	7.4	7.7	7.9	8.2	8.5	8.8	9.4	10.0	10.3	10.6	11.2	11.8	12.4	12.9	13.2	13.5	14.1	14.7	15.3	15.9	16.2	16.5	17.1	17.7	19.1	20.6	22.1	23.5	25.0	26.5	27.9	29.4
180	5.6	5.8	6.1	6.4	6.7	6.9	7.2	7.5	7.8	8.1	8.3	8.9	9.4	9.7	10.0	10.6	11.1	11.7	12.2	12.5	12.8	13.3	13.9	14.4	15.0	15.3	15.6	16.1	16.7	18.1	19.4	20.8	22.2	23.6	25.0	26.4	27.8
190	5.3	5.5	5.8	6.1	6.3	6.6	6.8	7.1	7.4	7.6	7.9	8.4	9.0	9.2	9.5	10.0	10.5	11.1	11.6	11.8	12.1	12.6	13.2	13.7	14.2	14.5	14.7	15.3	15.8	17.1	18.4	19.7	21.1	22.4	23.7	25.0	26.3
200	5.0	5.3	5.5	5.8	6.0	6.3	6.5	6.8	7.0	7.3	7.5	8.0	8.5	8.8	9.0	9.5	10.0	10.5	11.0	11.3	11.5	12.0	12.5	13.0	13.5	13.8	14.0	14.5	15.0	16.3	17.5	18.8	20.0	21.3	22.5	23.8	25.0
210	4.8	5.0	5.2	5.5	5.7	6.0	6.2	6.4	6.7	6.9	7.1	7.6	8.1	8.3	8.6	9.1	9.5	10.0	10.5	10.7	11.0	11.4	11.9	12.4	12.9	13.1	13.3	13.8	14.3	15.5	16.7	17.9	19.1	20.2	21.4	22.6	23.8
220	4.6	4.8	5.0	5.2	5.5	5.7	5.9	6.1	6.4	6.6	6.8	7.3	7.7	8.0	8.2	8.6	9.1	9.6	10.0	10.2	10.5	10.9	11.4	11.8	12.3	12.5	12.7	13.2	13.6	14.8	15.9	17.1	18.2	19.3	20.5	21.6	22.7
230	4.4	4.6	4.8	5.0	5.2	5.4	5.7	5.9	6.1	6.3	6.5	7.0	7.4	7.6	7.8	8.3	8.7	9.1	9.6	9.8	10.0	10.4	10.9	11.3	11.7	12.0	12.2	12.6	13.0	14.1	15.2	16.3	17.4	18.5	19.6	20.7	21.7
240	4.2	4.4	4.6	4.8	5.0	5.2	5.4	5.6	5.8	6.0	6.3	6.7	7.1	7.3	7.5	7.9	8.3	8.8	9.2	9.4	9.6	10.0	10.4	10.8	11.3	11.5	11.7	12.1	12.5	13.5	14.6	15.6	16.7	17.7	18.8	19.8	20.8
250	4.0	4.2	4.4	4.6	4.8	5.0	5.2	5.4	5.6	5.8	6.0	6.4	6.8	7.0	7.2	7.6	8.0	8.4	8.8	9.0	9.2	9.6	10.0	10.4	10.8	11.0	11.2	11.6	12.0	13.0	14.0	15.0	16.0	17.0	18.0	19.0	20.0
260	3.9	4.0	4.2	4.4	4.6	4.8	5.0	5.2	5.4	5.6	5.8	6.2	6.5	6.7	6.9	7.3	7.7	8.1	8.5	8.7	8.8	9.3	9.6	10.0	10.4	10.6	10.8	11.2	11.5	12.5	13.5	14.4	15.4	16.4	17.3	18.3	19.2
270	3.7	3.9	4.1	4.3	4.4	4.6	4.8	5.0	5.2	5.4	5.6	5.9	6.3	6.5	6.7	7.0	7.4	7.8	8.1	8.3	8.5	8.9	9.3	9.6	10.0	10.2	10.4	10.7	11.1	12.0	13.0	13.9	14.8	15.7	16.7	17.6	18.5
280	3.6	3.8	3.9	4.1	4.3	4.5	4.6	4.8	5.0	5.2	5.4	5.7	6.1	6.3	6.4	6.8	7.1	7.5	7.9	8.0	8.2	8.6	8.9	9.3	9.6	9.8	10.0	10.4	10.7	11.6	12.5	13.4	14.3	15.2	16.1	17.0	17.9
290	3.5	3.6	3.8	4.0	4.1	4.3	4.5	4.7	4.8	5.0	5.2	5.5	5.9	6.0	6.2	6.6	6.9	7.2	7.6	7.8	7.9	8.3	8.6	9.0	9.3	9.5	9.7	10.0	10.3	11.2	12.1	12.9	13.8	14.7	15.5	16.4	17.2
300	3.3	3.5	3.7	3.8	4.0	4.2	4.3	4.5	4.7	4.8	5.0	5.3	5.7	5.8	6.0	6.3	6.7	7.0	7.3	7.5	7.7	8.0	8.3	8.7	9.0	9.2	9.3	9.7	10.0	10.8	11.7	12.5	13.3	14.2	15.0	15.8	16.7
325	3.1	3.2	3.4	3.5	3.7	3.9	4.0	4.2	4.3	4.5	4.6	4.9	5.2	5.4	5.5	5.9	6.2	6.5	6.8	6.9	7.1	7.4	7.7	8.0	8.3	8.5	8.6	8.9	9.2	10.0	10.8	11.5	12.3	13.1	13.9	14.6	15.4
350	2.9	3.0	3.1	3.3	3.4	3.6	3.7	3.9	4.0	4.1	4.3	4.6	4.9	5.0	5.1	5.4	5.7	6.0	6.3	6.4	6.6	6.9	7.1	7.4	7.7	7.9	8.0	8.3	8.6	9.3	10.0	10.7	11.4	12.1	12.9	13.6	14.3
375	2.7	2.8	2.9	3.1	3.2	3.3	3.5	3.6	3.7	3.9	4.0	4.3	4.5	4.7	4.8	5.1	5.3	5.6	5.9	6.0	6.1	6.4	6.7	6.9	7.2	7.3	7.5	7.7	8.0	8.7	9.3	10.0	10.7	11.3	12.0	12.7	13.3
400	2.5	2.6	2.8	2.9	3.0	3.1	3.3	3.4	3.5	3.6	3.8	4.0	4.3	4.4	4.5	4.8	5.0	5.3	5.5	5.6	5.8	6.0	6.3	6.5	6.8	6.9	7.0	7.3	7.5	8.1	8.8	9.4	10.0	10.6	11.3	11.9	12.5
425	2.4	2.5	2.6	2.7	2.8	2.9	3.1	3.2	3.3	3.4	3.5	3.8	4.0	4.1	4.2	4.5	4.7	4.9	5.2	5.3	5.4	5.6	5.9	6.1	6.4	6.5	6.6	6.8	7.1	7.6	8.2	8.8	9.4	10.0	10.6	11.2	11.8
450	2.2	2.3	2.4	2.6	2.7	2.8	2.9	3.0	3.1	3.2	3.3	3.6	3.8	3.9	4.0	4.2	4.4	4.7	4.9	5.0	5.1	5.3	5.6	5.8	6.0	6.1	6.2	6.4	6.7	7.2	7.8	8.3	8.9	9.4	10.0	10.6	11.1
475	2.1	2.2	2.3	2.4	2.5	2.6	2.7	2.8	2.9	3.1	3.2	3.4	3.6	3.7	3.8	4.0	4.2	4.4	4.6	4.7	4.8	5.1	5.3	5.5	5.7	5.8	5.9	6.1	6.3	6.8	7.4	7.9	8.4	8.9	9.5	10.0	10.5
500	2.0	2.1	2.2	2.3	2.4	2.5	2.6	2.7	2.8	2.9	3.0	3.2	3.4	3.5	3.6	3.8	4.0	4.2	4.4	4.5	4.6	4.8	5.0	5.2	5.4	5.5	5.6	5.8	6.0	6.5	7.0	7.5	8.0	8.5	9.0	9.5	10.0
525	1.9	2.0	2.1	2.2	2.3	2.4	2.5	2.6	2.7	2.8	2.9	3.0	3.2	3.3	3.4	3.6	3.8	4.0	4.2	4.3	4.4	4.6	4.8	5.0	5.1	5.2	5.3	5.5	5.7	6.2	6.7	7.1	7.6	8.1	8.6	9.0	9.5
550	1.8	1.9	1.9	2.0	2.2	2.3	2.4	2.5	2.5	2.6	2.7	2.9	3.1	3.1	3.3	3.4	3.6	3.8	4.0	4.1	4.2	4.4	4.5	4.7	4.9	5.0	5.1	5.3	5.5	5.9	6.4	6.8	7.3	7.7	8.2	8.6	9.1
575	1.7	1.8	1.9	2.0	2.1	2.2	2.3	2.4	2.4	2.5	2.6	2.8	3.0	3.0	3.1	3.3	3.5	3.7	3.8	3.9	4.0	4.3	4.3	4.5	4.7	4.8	4.9	5.0	5.2	5.7	6.1	6.5	7.0	7.4	7.8	8.3	8.7
600	1.7	1.8	1.8	1.9	2.0	2.1	2.2	2.2	2.3	2.4	2.5	2.7	2.8	2.9	3.0	3.2	3.3	3.5	3.7	3.8	3.8	4.0	4.2	4.3	4.5	4.6	4.7	4.8	5.0	5.4	5.8	6.2	6.7	7.1	7.5	7.9	8.3

EXHIBIT 20.—Chart prepared originally by the National Cash Register Company. This chart, known as the Salary Calculating Chart, affords a convenient method of checking sales expense with salary. By running the finger down the left-hand column, headed "Clerk's Weekly Sales," until the amount of the clerk's weekly total is reached and then moving across to the right to the column containing his salary figure at the top, the percentage cost of his sales is quickly determined

system that is likely to remove the feeling that an employe sometimes has that he is being discriminated against.

Suppose an employe in a grocery store, who is getting $13 a week, approaches his manager with a plea for an increase to $18. If his total sales have averaged only $150 a week, the manager can quickly show him by Exhibit 20 that his salary is already 9 per cent of his sales, and by referring to the smaller chart, illustrated in Exhibit 19, let him see that in general the salary cost of grocery stores runs to 8.46 per cent. This makes it clear that the employe is already receiving a little more money, on a percentage basis, than salesmen occupying similar positions. The manager can go further and run his pencil down the $18 column and indicate that this salary would be equitable to the store when the sales total is from $210 to $220 a week.

As the charts are nothing but the result of accurate percentage calculations, the intelligent employe can hardly quarrel with their indications. Exhibit 19 is also a good check against other expenses. It shows the proprietor whether or not a rent or advertising expense is higher than the average in his division of business.

Chain-store Practice.—The compensation plan used by most chain stores is that of paying the general manager a percentage of all sales over a specified quota. The district manager gets his percentage on the earnings of district stores.

In the Woolworth organization, employes are paid on the commission plan. At the New York headquarters the basis for compensation of executives is the earnings of the entire business. Each district manager receives his pay on the basis of his district's earnings. Likewise, the manager and assistant manager of the separate store receive compensation based on what the store earns. A cash bonus is given to every employe who has been with the company a year. A similar amount is added each year for five years. A woman leaving to marry, after having been with the company three years, receives a cash wedding present.

The method of the United Cigar Stores is that of providing extra pay, based on amount of sales—not on profits. This concern holds that its employes then have no desire to push the goods bearing the most profit.

The method of the Penney dry goods chain, operating more than 400 stores, gives the branch manager the opportunity to conduct business almost as if he were a partner and to receive his compensation on such basis.

In general, branch-store managers in the principal chain-store systems are expected to keep overhead at a minimum, and the reward for such endeavor is extra compensation. An example of this is the method of a system of drug stores paying all store managers a bonus of $25 a month for keeping down their expenses (aside from rent and advertising) to 15 per cent of sales. Rent and advertising are not regarded as factors, because these are the specific concern of the home office.

Following is the method for arriving at the 15 per cent expense permitted:

>   Salaries and commissions........10   per cent
>   Light, heat, water............... 1½ per cent
>   Contingent, renewal expenses..... 1½ per cent
>   Supplies........................ 2   per cent
>   Total.........15   per cent

A competitive spirit is engendered by this standard. Each manager strives to make a better showing for his store over that of the others in the system. While 15 per cent is laid down as the yardstick of good management, as it were, it is not impossible to outdo this percentage. Greater volume of sales and turnover, or careful watch over expenses without increase of volume, help toward the desired result.

Lord & Taylor's System.—The Lord & Taylor organization, of New York, has a regular rating system, each salesman rating monthly in personality, production and loyalty, as shown by the rating sheet reproduced in Exhibit 21.

Promotions or increases in salary are based on these ratings, and all salespeople are compensated on the straight salary basis, no commission or bonuses based on sales being paid. The only bonus paid by this organization is the Christmas bonus, which is based on length of service.

Rating Chart

If in your opinion the employe should be rated Perfect, mark 10 Excellent, mark 8 Good, mark 6 Fair, mark 4 Poor, mark 2 Deficient, mark 0	Health	Appearance	Manner	Initiative	Industry	Accuracy	Loyalty	Cooperation	Responsibility	Knowledge	Total	Dept. Date

Exhibit 21.—Employe rating chart used by Lord & Taylor, New York City.

1. HEALTH — In rating for health, consider regularity of attendance, attitude toward work and general physical condition.
2. APPEARANCE — In rating for appearance, consider neatness, cleanliness and conformity to the dress regulation.
3. MANNER — In rating for manner, consider courteous treatment of customers, and of other employes.
4. INITIATIVE — In rating for initiative, consider resourcefulness, and ability to work without continual direction.
5. INDUSTRY — In rating for industry, consider constancy of application to work.
6. ACCURACY — In rating for accuracy, consider correctness in the execution of every detail.
7. LOYALTY — In rating for loyalty, consider faithfulness to a personal ideal and to the interests of Lord & Taylor.
8. COOPERATION — In rating for cooperation, consider willingness to work with others.
9. RESPONSIBILITY — In rating for responsibility, consider reliability in the discharge of every duty.
10. KNOWLEDGE — In rating for knowledge, consider possession of necessary information.

EXHIBIT 22.—Explanation of the Lord & Taylor rating chart shown in Exhibit 21.

S. Kann Sons Company's Method.—In addition to the salary paid its employes, S. Kann Sons Company, of Washington, D. C., allows a commission on sales, as an incentive to greater effort.

Contests are also arranged at times, as an extra sales stimulant. For example, a contest was recently held in the millinery department. The salesperson responsible for the highest sales in the trimmed hat section and the salesperson showing the highest standing in the untrimmed hat section were each awarded a prize of $10, with a second prize of $5 to the next highest record in each of the sections. Experience has shown that these occasional contests stir up considerable interest and enthusiasm.

Ed. Schuster & Company's Method of Compensating.—The salespeople of this Milwaukee department store are compensated, in general, on the straight salary basis. The firm's experience has demonstrated this plan of compensation to be the most satisfactory, provided the method is properly followed up by the employment office.

The only bonus plan used by this concern is one worked out for the ready-to-wear department, and even in this department it has not proved entirely satisfactory. While the bonus plan for salespeople has not worked out well, according to reports received direct from the firm, the plan seems to yield good results as applied to the drivers. A rather elaborate Service Record sheet, Exhibit 23, is used by the firm in determining the amount of bonus salary to be paid its drivers each month. This Service Record covers such important points as courtesy, proper attention to customers' reasons for refusing to accept goods, reasons for returning goods, and so on, as well as the reporting of accidents and the requirement of properly looking after the delivery truck. These delivery men are also credited with a certain number of points toward their bonus when they bring in orders amounting to certain sums.

It seems logical, therefore, to conclude that perhaps the poor result with bonus and commission plans of payment as applied to salespeople may be charged to the adoption of an inferior plan or a failure to impress on employes the merit of a system by which compensation is gaged directly by the quality of sales effort.

Straight Commission Arrangement.—Although compensation on the straight commission basis is not customary in retail selling, a Kansas merchant has adopted the following basis of sales cost, so far as salary is concerned:

Class of Goods	Per Cent Allowed For Compensation Of Salesman
Hats and caps	$6\frac{1}{2}$
Furnishings	6
Men's clothing	5
Work clothing	5
Boy's clothing	5

P1622		SERVICE RECORD				

Driver_____ Route_____ Begun_____ Ended_____

No.	Points	DELIVERY SERVICE PENALTIES	Deductions	When Made	Checked	REMARKS
1	150	Accidents (of any kind) not reported.				
2	350	Accidents (when driver is at fault)				
3	250	False Report of Does not Want.				
4	250	" " " Not at Home.				
5	250	" " " Short Change				
6	250	" " " Will Call				
7	250	" " " Wrong Addresses				
8	100	Merchandise accepted by Driver in bad order.				
9	100	Damage to Customer's property by Driver.				
10	50	Shortage of C. O. D. Money.				
11	50	Interfering with entry clerks except on business.				
12	50	Failure to enter customer's reason on return package.				
13	50	Incomplete orders accepted.				
14	50	"Look Ups" neglected.				
15	50	Merchandise Calls neglected.				
16	50	Driver's Book forgotten.				
17	50	Smoking on Customer's Premises.				
18	50	Strangers on cars.				
19	25	Change on hand.				
20	25	Driving out of own route.				
21	25	Failure rendered complete and satisfactory at customer's request.				
22	25	Leaving parcels without obtaining customer's name.				
23	25	Packages, left in driver's bins or shelves.				
24	25	Redemption check, failed to enter name and C. O. D. number.				
25	25	Crockery baskets not returned.				
		CAR AND OPERATION PENALTIES				
26	100	Damage to Body.				
27	50	" " Chassis				
28	50	Tires not properly inflated.				
29	50	Oil not level in crank case or grease cup neglected.				
30	50	Violating road rules.				
31	50	Speeding.				
32	50	Turning corners carelessly.				
33	25	Braking too quickly and skidding tires.				
34	25	Motor not clean.				
35	25	Transmission Bands Burned.				
36	15	Windows and lamps not clean.				
37	15	Non. skid chains out of order.				
		GENERAL CREDITS—750 POINTS TO BE EARNED Total Penalties				
1	50	Economy in Gasoline Consumption.				
2	50	Customer's suggestions				
3	50	Driver's suggestions				
4	50	Courtesy				
5	50	Personal Appearance				
6	250	Driver's reclaim report of dissatisfied customers.				
7	150	Orders brought in: 20 pts. for order brought in up to $10.00, 30 pts. for orders brought in up to $20.00, 40 pts. $33.00, 50 pts. $40.00, and so on to whatever amount of orders brought in.				
8	50	Punctuality				
9	100	Special Delivery				
		Total Credits Earned				

RESULTS

Total Points Credited............750
Add Credits Earned............
Total Credits ....
Deduct Penalties Imposed ....
Net Points ....
Bonus due at 2c Per Point............

Date_____ This Record Checked by_____ Rechecked by_____ Paid_____

EXHIBIT 23.—Service record used by a Milwaukee store in figuring the compensation of its delivery men. The principle is sound, but to keep the record complete requires a tremendous amount of clerical work, to say nothing of inspection and supervision. Simplification seems desirable.

After nearly a year of experience with the new system, the merchant—Spines Clothing Company, Wichita, Kan.—reports that both the firm and its employes are well satisfied with the results attained.

Compensation Methods and Percentages in Coffee-roasting and Grocery Trades.—A report prepared originally by the Bureau of Business Research, of New York University, and summarized in *Printers' Ink* of Sept. 21, 1922, shows the following interesting facts about the compensation methods and percentages that prevail in the coffee-roasting and grocery trades. The facts are the result of three hundred questionnaires sent out to four different groups:

1. Tea and coffee dealers exclusively.
2. Tea, coffee, spices, baking powder and extract dealers.
3. Tea and coffee dealers who also handle grocery sundries, in addition to the items given under No. 2.
4. Wholesale grocers.

The first of these groups reported an average cost for salesmen of 5.7 per cent of sales; the second group, 9 per cent; the third group, 9.4 per cent; while the fourth group, comprising the wholesale grocers, gave their percentages from 2.7 up to 5 per cent. The average was around 3.3 per cent. These figures of the wholesale grocers cover all their business. Few, if any, of them know the cost of selling coffee or tea separately.

Nineteen per cent of these dealers reported that they paid all salesmen a straight salary; 23 per cent reported that they allow a drawing account and commissions; 4 per cent pay straight commissions, while 54 per cent had no uniform system of compensation.

Of the dealers who pay commissions, 56 per cent pay on the basis of sales; 16 per cent, on gross profits, less deductions; 16 per cent on net profit; and 12 per cent on gross profit.

Many of these dealers have adopted the method of paying different commissions to their salesmen on different classes of goods, or a different commission to salesmen in different territories. For example, one firm of coffee importers and manufacturers pays a commission of $7\frac{1}{2}$ per cent to city salesmen and a commission of 10 per cent to salesmen working territory outside of city limits. This variation is accounted for by the different character of the business in the two sections.

Another example of variation: a Mid-western coffee concern pays its city salesmen 8 per cent on sales, while the men working the country or rural districts get 9 per cent. Still another Mid-western wholesale grocer allows 5 per cent on sales made in territory that is close to the home city, while in distant territories he pays his salesmen as high as 8 per cent commissions.

Bonus Methods Used by the Coffee-roasting and Grocery Trades.—The seventy-five replies received by the Business Research Bureau, of New York University, showed a wide variation in the method of paying bonus. The following are the principal methods:

1. Bonus on largest tonnage.
2. Bonus for decrease in outstanding accounts.
3. One-half cent bonus on profitable brand (paid on sales above quota).
4. Five per cent bonus on all sales above quota.
5. Extra commissions on slow moving articles.
6. Bonus on special drives.
7. Bonus for largest tonnage of leading brand.
8. Bonus for seasonable specialties
9. Bonus of $\frac{1}{8}$ or $\frac{1}{4}$ cent per pound extra for sale of certain brands at certain times. (Slow moving articles, or seasonable specialties.)
10. Bonus for new customers.
11. Five dollars per month bonus for new business.
12. Prizes for new accounts.
13. Extra commissions to move slow selling items.
14. Bonus for reducing expenses. "The regular commission is 5 per cent on sales. If sales cost us less than 10 per cent, the salesman gets an extra commission or bonus."

Ninety per cent of these coffee-roasting and grocery firms pay commission to salesmen on orders received through the mails. It may be at a lower rate than on orders turned in by the salesmen but the value of thus cultivating the good-will of the salesmen seems to outweigh the amount involved.

In summing up, the Bureau says:

The fact which stands out above all others in this study of the methods of paying salesmen is the need of adequate cost-accounting methods. Probably the best way to pay salesmen is by commissions based on net profits, and net profits cannot be accurately determined except by scientific cost-accounting methods.

Research Bureau's Recommendations.—As a result of the information obtained, the Business Research Bureau, of New York University, made the following recommendations to the trade:

1. The commission basis furnishes the best method for paying salesmen.
2. The commissions should be based as nearly as possible on net profits. (There should be a full and frank understanding between company and salesmen as to the system of accounting and the details of arriving at net profits.)
3. The payment of salaries should be the exception.
4. Straight commissions are not desirable in many cases.
5. The rate of commission should differ on different lines of goods and in different territories.
6. Goods should be grouped according to the margin of profit and the rate of turnover for the purpose of paying the different rates of commission.
7. Any method of paying salesmen should be supplemented by the use of various bonuses and prizes to stimulate maximum effort.
8. An important consideration in paying salesmen is to retain control over their activities.
9. There should be a closer check on salesmen's calls and inactive accounts than most firms now have.
10. It is generally best to charge a salesman with 50 per cent of the loss on his bad accounts.

(Published originally in *Printers' Ink*).

SECTION V

STORE EQUIPMENT AND LAYOUT

The title of "Store Equipment and Layout" is comprehensive enough to include the cash register, the adding machine, the quick, accurate scales, and all the other labor- and time-saving devices that may be employed in a modern retailing business. The particular purpose of this Section, however, is to draw attention to store layouts, show-cases and allied equipment that is connected more immediately with the exhibition of goods or the ready showing and selling of them.

Profits Increased by Saving Steps.—Retail stores, like other lines of business, may be studied profitably with a view to conveniently arranging stock, proper placing of cash registers, or cash carrying system, easy access to extra stock, and the like. While such savings of time may seem small on a single sale, the saving, through efficient arrangement, in a store employing hundreds of salespeople and where during the rush hour it is difficult for customers to get attention, may be very large.

An expert in store arrangement reports instances of where a saleswoman whose work was closely studied walked several thousand feet unnecessarily in an hour or so. In this case a change of five or six feet in the position of a cash register, or some other sales-recording device, saved from a quarter of an hour to half an hour a day. This lost time may represent a number of sales.

In another store studied it was found that frequent and lengthy absences from a number of the departments were caused by trips to another part of the store for the purpose of replenishing stock. This discovery led to an immediate reorganization of the stock-keeping system.

The importance of such savings lies in the fact that there are spurts or rush hours during the day when every minute counts. Any inefficient arrangement of counters, sales-recording system, extra stock, and other necessary equipment, means impatient and departing customers and lost sales that are rarely recovered.

An entire rearrangement of a store will sometimes pay well, not only in the saving of steps, but—even more important—

EXHIBIT 24-*a*.—"Cluttered up" appearance below is too often typical of a general store. Merchandise is piled on the cases, counters and floor. Nothing is really "displayed." Such haphazard arrangement creates unfavorable impression.

EXHIBIT 24-*b*.—Orderly arrangement that permits easy inspection of a large variety of small merchandise, through use of counter-show-cases. The articles on the floor are placed neatly, so that they do not hide other merchandise.

increased facilities for showing goods. Compare the two views shown in Exhibits 24-*a* and 24-*b*.

Preliminary Steps in Remodeling a Store.—The *Good Hardware* magazine sets forth the following outline as a plan to be followed by a retail hardware merchant in remodeling his store so as to bring about the greatest improvement in selling methods. While this plan deals particularly with the rearrangement of the store, similar charts or layouts would be appropriate for reorganizing the personal sales effort, window-display, advertising, and so on.

1. Get Cooperation of Store Force:
    (a) By store meetings
    (b) By question box
    (c) By personal discussion
2. Plan Rearrangement of Store
    (a) Study other hardware stores
    (b) Departmentalize the store
    (c) Classify stock in each department
    (d) Decide on methods of sampling, stocking and pricing
3. Plan Installation of New Fixtures
    (a) Divide store into sections
    (b) Plan method of remodeling each section
    (c) Plan sequence of work on each section
4. Select and order New Fixtures
    (a) Decide on kind of fixtures:
        1. Manufactured
        2. Home-made
    (b) Decide on material of fixtures
    (c) Decide on finish of fixtures
5. Engage Extra Help:
    (a) Truckers (if necessary)
    (b) Carpenters, painters and electricians
    (c) Extra help for sampling
6. Receive and Unpack Fixtures

Remodeling may extend further than a rearrangement of the interior of a store. The store front and display-windows may be very unattractive or wasteful, in which case some slight remodeling of the outside may go far toward attracting and holding customers. In Exhibits 25 and 26 are shown, through the courtesy of *Good Hardware*, the front view of a Connecticut hardware store before and after remodeling.

Some Features of Store-front Construction.—Exhibits 27-*a*, 27-*b*, 28, 29, 30, 31 and 32, published originally in *National Builder*, show what good planning and good lighting may do to aid a store in making a good first impression, not only with respect to the window-displays but with respect to the store as a whole.

EXHIBIT 25.—View of the front of a Connecticut hardware store before it was remodeled. This uninviting appearance is unfortunately too often a feature of retail stores.

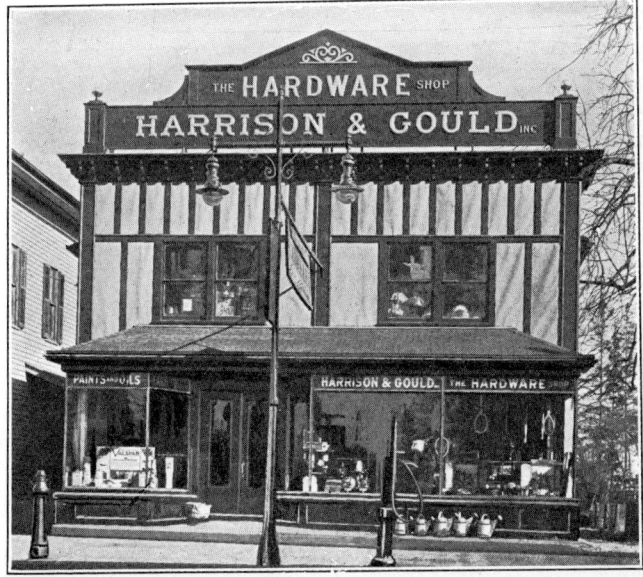

EXHIBIT 26.—Another view of the store represented in Exhibit 25. The changes were not extensive, but the store now has an effective, businesslike appearance, from the windows to the sign at the top.

Exhibit 27-a.—Food supplies do not show off to the best advantage when piled up in an old store window of this type. Compare with Exhibit 27-b.

Exhibit 27-b.—This is the "made-over" meat market illustrated in Exhibit 27-a. Observe the use of tile above the doorway, as well as around the entrance and in the windows.

Naturally, good designing requires particular consideration of the display needs of the kind of merchandise for which the store front is to be constructed. Wood, brick, tile, and metal all have their place.

Take Exhibit 27-*b* as an example. Here the clean white tile is admirably adapted to creating the idea of a thoroughly modern meat market. The merchandise is not only more sanitary in such a window but it looks more appetizing—an

EXHIBIT 28.—A terra cotta and tile store front, designed especially for a shoe store.

important consideration. Contrast this inviting looking store front with the old front illustrated in Exhibit 27-*a*.

Exhibit 28 is an example of an artistic use of terra cotta and tile, with appropriate decorations. Here the show-windows are not large but afford display room for a good variety of shoes, and there is unusual space in which prospective customers may walk around and view the offerings. In fact, one could hardly restrain the temptation to walk into such a space and look over the season's exhibit of footwear. Compare this design with Exhibit 29, where there is no need to provide an

Exhibit 29.—A brick front with steel frame windows for an automobile display room.

Exhibit 30.—While there is nothing remarkable about this store front, it shows an advantageous layout of window-display cases, while at the same time presenting to the shopper a tempting area in which to stroll around and look at new goods. The whole effect is inviting.

unusual amount of space for people to stand in the entranceway and look over the goods.

Exhibit 29, with its spacious windows extending almost to the street level, is obviously designed to give a complete view of automobiles.

Exhibit 31 affords an illustration of what may be done through a distinctive lighting system. An unusual amount of space is taken up here by the show-windows, but the space

EXHIBIT 31.—An attractive store front built especially for the display of clothing. This picture was taken at night and illustrated the pleasing effects obtainable when all illuminating units are concealed.

probably "earns its keep." All lamps are concealed, so that there is a soft lighting effect that exhibits the merchandise at its best.

The firm name of the store, inlaid at the front entrance, is an effective feature.

Good use is made of the small space between the two doors.

Exhibit 33 shows a window layout suggested by an expert in *Good Hardware* as being an ideal arrangement for a hardware store, or any other store of this general character. The entrance gives unusual opportunity for the exhibition of goods.

The so-called "island" window affords an additional exhibit-case that is ideally located. The lower diagram indicates the floor plan and the two entrances from the store into the larger windows.

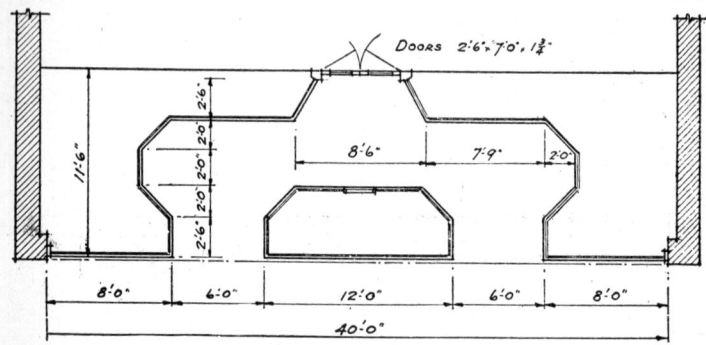

(*Courtesy of National Builder.*)

EXHIBIT 32.—Diagram of the "island arrangement," which gives a good-sized separate window immediately in front of the doorway, while having ample area for observers and a pleasing layout of the two main window spaces.

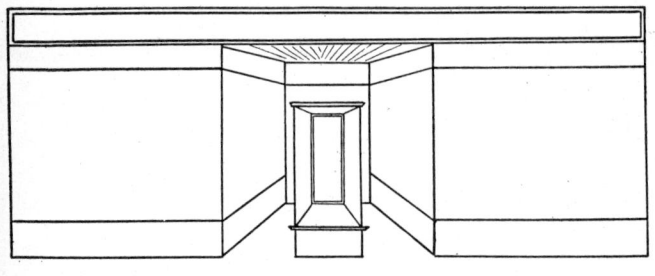

IDEAL HARDWARE WINDOWS SHOWING THE ISLAND WINDOW

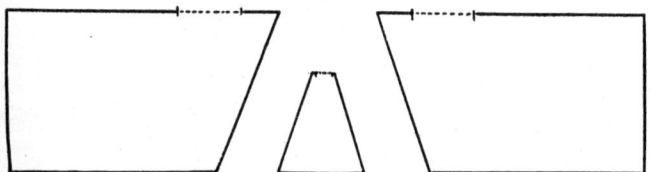

EXHIBIT 33.—An effective layout of the display space in front of a hardware or other store of general character.

Exhibit 34 shows three possible arrangements of a small store front.

STORE EQUIPMENT AND LAYOUT

Some Tendencies in the Layouts of Large Stores.—While every large store is a law unto itself in the matter of layout and business system, working its plans out in accordance with its location and its class of trade, some interesting tendencies have been revealed through a study made of a score of large stores by the Retail Research Association.

Most of the large department stores use the main floor space almost entirely for what is called "pick-up goods"—in other words, goods that can be displayed well in small space and without a great deal of light, such as jewelry, gloves hosiery, laces, handbags and purses, toilet goods, candy, and the like. The reason for this is that the demand for this class of goods is increasing, thus crowding from the main floor many of the departments that were formerly maintained there. Although the Macy store in New York has recently greatly enlarged its floor space, the management finds room on the main floor only for the men's shop, in addition to the "pick-up" goods described above. Lord & Taylor still carry silk by the yard on the ground floor, but indications are that the silk department may be moved upstairs almost any day.

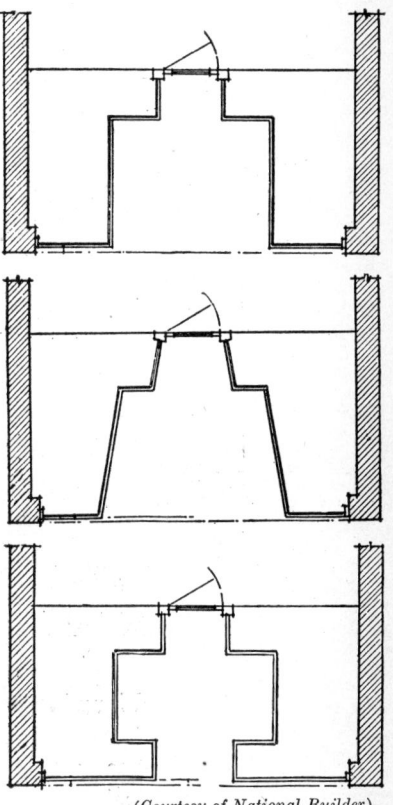

(*Courtesy of National Builder*).
EXHIBIT 34.—A suggestion on three different arrangements for show-windows and entranceways of a small and simple store front.

Formerly, yard-goods were sold almost exclusively on the main floor of the big stores. The modern tendency is to have this department of merchandise either on the second or third floor, where there is more room for display. Besides, the light is usually better here than on the main floor—another important consideration.

If there is room, retailers seem to feel that something is gained by having the millinery department on the same floor with the ready-to-wear-merchandise—women's and misses' outer apparel—so that shoppers may stroll from one department to the other, matching coats and gowns to better advantage with the millinery.

Department stores carrying house-furnishings, lamps, china, rugs, furniture, and so on, have not found that the moving of these goods to upper floors has caused any slackening in

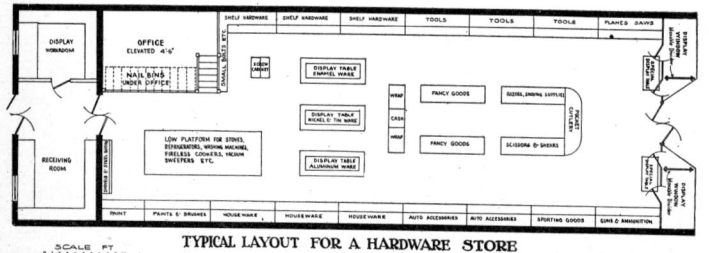

Exhibit 35.—An arrangement that gives display to a great variety of goods. The character of goods carried and personal preference will naturally modify any general plan such as this one. It, however, presents fundamental needs for a retail hardware store.

buying. Kitchen and laundry equipment is carried by many stores in the basement.

In almost every case, men's clothing is given a special department, with a special entrance, or with express elevators going to it, if it is located on an upper floor. This is catering to the dislike that most men have of mixing with women in their shopping. They like to have an exclusive shop of their own, which may be reached without too much contact with women shoppers.

Such representative stores as Bamberger's, Newark, Strawbridge & Clothier, Philadelphia, Filene's, Boston, the Emporium, San Francisco, and others, have bargain basements, which they seem to feel add considerably to the volume of sales of popularly priced goods, while at the same time raising the standard of the departments of the upper floors.

Good Hardware suggests Exhibit 35 as a floor layout for a typical hardware store, explaining at the same time that as hardware stores vary greatly in the types of goods handled, all such layouts are subject to modification.

Importance of Proper Lighting System.—Good lighting is in itself an attraction and a real pulling power. Dark corners do not invite favorable inspection of merchandise. It is a reflection on the store's lighting system if a customer has to take an article to the front door, or have it sent to her home in order to get a good idea of how it looks.

Good illumination means that the lighting system shall provide the light where it is needed—on the merchandise rather than in the eyes of the customer.

The whole subject is one that calls for the services of an expert store-planner, but some fundamental principles always apply.

Some stores need more light than others, and some classes of merchandise need direct lighting, while others look better under indirect or semi-indirect lighting systems. In a jewelry store, for example, the direct light adds to the sparkling effect of jewelry, cut glass, and so forth. Here the shadowless, indirect illumination would have a tendency to make the gems appear flat and lifeless.

In a store with counters on both sides of the main light, it is frequently the custom to have the lighting system consist of a single row of lights down the center. This is not good practice, for the reason that the lights placed in this way will throw shadows from the customer to the merchandise.

On the other hand, such a store as a shoe store, where the stock is usually brought to the center of the room for inspection and fitting, might appropriately use the central lighting arrangement. Here the indirect method of lighting gives a soft diffusion of the illumination that corresponds closely to the well appointed home. If this system is used, the customer can see shoes and hosiery in about the same way as they will look when worn, and there are no shadows to be thrown by either customer or salesman.

Such stores as confectionery and cigar stores, while not needing a brilliant type of light, call for enough illumination to bring out the clean, high-class character of the merchandise. The semi-direct system is used to advantage by many stores of this class, though the concealed system of lighting may also be used effectively.

An ample supply of switches at convenient points enables a merchant and his helpers to give a flood of light just when and where it is needed, without, at the same time, having an extravagant continuous lighting system in operation.

EXHIBIT 36.—How a Newark, N. J., store concentrates attention on some of its merchandise through an interior, well lighted show-cases display. Reproduced through courtesy of the Joint Committee for Business Development, New York City.

Interior Show-windows.—Interior cases and cabinets are nothing new but many different classes of merchandise are shown attractively behind plate glass or in cases made of wood, wallboard, or other material, with sliding doors, or some other means for the easy inspection of merchandise. These cabinets are obtainable in excellent designs and restful finishes that lend good background treatment to the goods offered for sale.

Realizing the value of concentration, some of the more resourceful merchants have gone further and arranged for lighted interior display-windows. Exhibit 36 is an example of such a window. If the entire store were brilliantly lighted, this lighted display would not stand out as it now does through contrast.

Such an interior display might be used for the exhibiting of the latest merchandise and become quite a fashion feature of a store, if some reference were made to it now and then in the store's publicity.

Show-cases as Aids to Selling.—Probably no part of store equipment, except perhaps the show-windows, plays a larger part in increasing sales, and thus reducing overhead, than the modern show-case. There is an ancient motto reading *Ignoto nullo cupido* which, interpreted liberally, means "You cannot desire what you do not know." While knowledge of merchandise is disseminated to a large extent through printed word and picture, much that is bought cannot be known by the prospective purchaser until it is seen. Obviously, a merchant cannot display all of his goods in the show-windows. He must rely a good deal on cases and cabinets that display to good advantage as well as those which make it convenient for goods to be removed. When goods are placed so far from the sight of customers that they do not come within the line of vision and cannot be reached by the salesman, except with a ladder, the chance for sales is considerably lessened. The modern display-case makes it easy for the merchant to get goods out without knocking down the display, crouching behind a low show-case, or leaving the customer. Modern display-cases make it possible for merchandise to be displayed attractively, behind good glass, and in front of a background that shows off the goods to the best advantage.

Goods such as cigars, candies, etc., must be displayed in such a way that they are kept from dust, flies, and other deteriorating influences. A single missing detail, such as the omission of the dainty candy shovel, may be fatal. Perhaps most readers of this volume can recall occasions when they were on the point of refusing a contemplated purchase of candy because none-too-clean hands were used instead of the candy shovel.

No better argument for the use of fine glass in show-cases exists than the fact that some of the great 5-cent and 10-cent

EXHIBIT 37.—Good use made of two tall show-cases in small spaces between radiators.

stores use plate glass exclusively, evidently believing that a clear, substantial-looking show-case (adds materially to the appearance of goods.) Not only does plate glass add to the appearance of goods, but it is much less likely to be broken.

STORE EQUIPMENT AND LAYOUT

The relatively small stand has grown in importance with retail stores. Exhibit 37 shows how the small stand can often be placed to advantage between radiators and make an unproductive nook produce a great many sales. Good merchandising requires that these small stands be placed, wherever possible, in close proximity to the customer's paths and stopping places. Likewise, it is important to have such cases where it is easy for a customer to request a handling of the articles or a demonstration of them. The modern merchant, in other words, aims to make his merchandise of easy access to

EXHIBIT 38.—Judicious choice and arrangement of show-cases, presenting a wealth of merchandise for the customer's inspection. Observe that the customer walks past show-cases in going to the soda fountain. The little tables are themselves miniature display-cases and are also so placed as to afford close view of goods in nearby show-cases.

customers. His policy is in direct opposition to the policy of the older type of store in which a sign "Merchandise Shown Only on Request" might have been appropriately placed.

Exhibits 38 and 39 show further the great sales value of appropriate show-cases and tables. These views and Exhibits 37, 40 and 43 are shown through the courtesy of the McLean Manufacturing Company.

Exhibits 41 and 42 show how merchandise can be displayed attractively and at the same time have it accessible to the customer. Some buyers get from touching or fondling of goods an impression and a desire that mere visual inspection does not create.

EXHIBIT 39.—A combination show-case, base and top, that shows about the limit that brings a maximum of goods within the range of the customer's vision. With such a case, eight different assortments of goods are easily within sight.

Even such equipment as tables is nowadays made up in a way that permits close display of merchandise. Exhibit 43 shows a type of table used by many drug stores and illustrates the modern tendency to utilize all available space for display

STORE EQUIPMENT AND LAYOUT

EXHIBIT 40.—Illustrating the value of a rich background for dainty merchandise.

EXHIBIT 41.—The progressive retailer arranges his goods so that they help to sell themselves.

(Courtesy of the American National Company, Toledo, Ohio).

EXHIBIT 42.—The idea in this arrangement of toys is a simple one—many of the little vehicles are exhibited on low shelves, where they can be fondled by the youngsters visiting the store or department. Keen merchants know that this often has a decided influence. When parents see the youngster's fondness for the tricycle or automobile to which he has attached himself, the sale is well along toward the close.

EXHIBIT 43.—The so-called "Snug-Seat" chairs. Many extra sales are made by displaying goods under the plate glass top of the table.

purposes. In some fixtures of this kind, the chairs are combined with the table and may be swung in and out.

Other Compact and Attractive Cases.—The case shown in Exhibit 44 is of the center-revolving wardrobe type. There is a patented fixture which permits the hanging of garments on a hang-rod, which can be pulled out of the cabinet and revolved at will.

This permits the salespeople to have easy access to every garment, thus eliminating the waste of time and lost motion

(*Courtesy of the Grand Rapids Show Case Company*).

EXHIBIT 44.—Show-cases or racks that keep clothing in good order while exhibiting it to the prospective buyer.

which accompanies the old process of going through piles of garments stacked up on tables, and also saves wear and tear on garments caused by excessive handling.

Another feature of these wardrobe cases is the fact that suits hung in this manner retain their smoothness, which eliminates the cost of frequent pressing.

The fact that clothing is kept behind disappearing glass doors, which can be opened and closed at will, insures a fresh, clean stock, free from dust and soil, making the entire stock of merchandise readily salable at all times.

Exhibit 45.—The modern show-case plan. Cases filled with several tiers of stock, yet exhibiting the merchandise attractively. (*Courtesy of the Grand Rapids Show Case Company*).

This equipment is of the sectional, interchangeable type of construction, which is standardized, so that new units may be added at any time, with uniform results in appearance and finish.

STORE EQUIPMENT AND LAYOUT

Exhibit 45 is a view of a retail store equipped with various types of modern cases that keep large quantities of merchandise clean and in good order while at the same time exhibiting it impressively.

Counter Containers for Small Goods.—Counter display-cases have been worked up in a variety of ingenious forms,

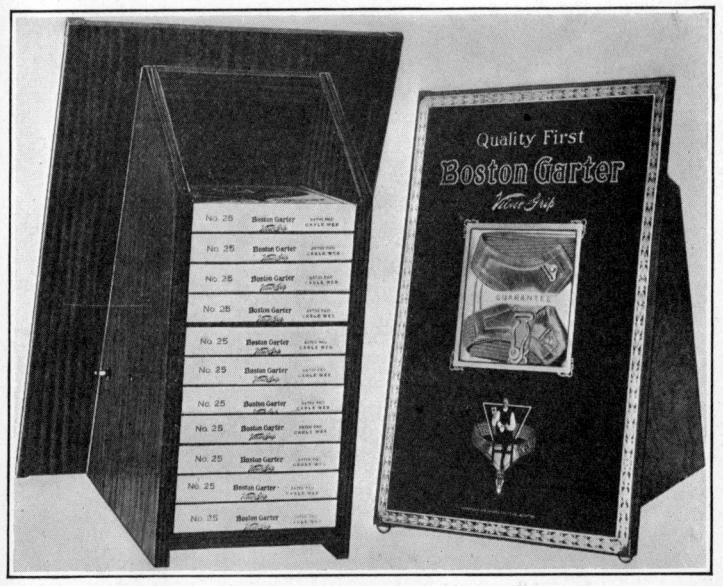

EXHIBIT 46.—Convenient counter cabinet, with sample of product under glass panel, and which carries a small stock of goods in the back, easily accessible.

many of them containing in the rear small drawers or shelves for the carrying of extra stock. Some cases of this variety, designed for 5-, 10- and 25-cent articles, are open affairs, encouraging the customer to take up a package and proffer payment. Still others show goods very attractively behind glass.

Most cabinets of this kind come from manufacturers who are interested in seeing that their goods have the best chance for sale, as well as being protected from dust, or against misplacement on large stock shelves.

It has been demonstrated time and again that goods shown in such maner sell at such an increased rate that the cost of the display-case is more than warranted. In a great many stores, there is much of what is called "impulse buying"— purchases that were not planned when the customer entered the store but which are made through seeing attractive or useful commodities. The retailer of today can hardly go

EXHIBIT 47.—An easily-constructed, home-made rack for displaying oilcloth is shown in the above illustration. The rack consists of a number of troughs designed to carry rolls of the oilcloth with the cut end hanging down. This is a convenient method for displaying a variety of patterns, and if the rack is placed in a conspicuous position in the store it serves to call the attention of customers to the product. The same kind of a rack could be used in a small dry goods store to show various colors and patterns of curtaining, ginghams, or other materials.

wrong in any effort that he may make to show goods conveniently and attractively.

Exhibit 46 is an example of such a counter-case or cabinet. It supports itself solidly on the counter, has space in the back for a small stock of garters, as well as a clear glass opening for a display of one pair of the garters. With goods of this character, actual samples look more attractive than illustrations.

STORE EQUIPMENT AND LAYOUT

OTHER MERCHANDISING AIDS

Exhibits 47 and 48, shown by courtesy of the *Good Hardware* magazine, are merely suggestive of the dozens of expedients that may be adopted by the present-day retailer to facilitate the showing and the rapid turnover of goods. Selling costs have a tendency to pile up at such an alarming rate that it

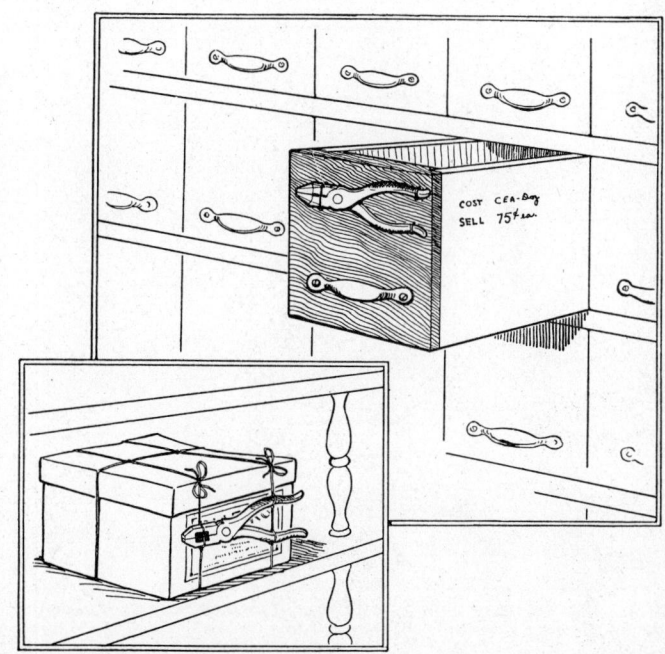

EXHIBIT 48.—The modern sample drawer. Observe cost and price data on the side. The tied-up box, shown at lower left, is the old, time-wasting way.

behooves the man who hopes to earn a comfortable living through retailing to make such aids a constant study.

Open Display of Small Tools.—Exhibit 49 is a modern interior display arrangement of small tools and supplies such as are handled by a general hardware store. Usually displays of this kind of merchandise are either behind glass frames, so that the tools are visible but may not be touched, or with a sample of the tool or other commodity fastened on the outside of the drawer as a clue to the contents. While the behind-glass form of display has the advantage of protecting the tools against handling and consequent rusting, many merchants, realizing that people like to touch articles that they are thinking of buying, prefer the display method indicated by

EXHIBIT 49.—People like to touch or handle tools. This display encourages handling and makes extra sales.

Exhibit 49. Here the background is an orange-colored Beaver Board that looked rather loud in color before tools were mounted on it but which proved to be a good contrasting background when the exhibit was complete. Simple fasteners are used, so that if a tool becomes soiled or rusty it may be easily removed and cleaned or another put in its place. A feature of this arrangement is that the stock, instead of being immediately behind the door in which the sample is shown, is behind an adjoining door. Thus, the prospective customer can continue to gratify his eyes by looking at the contemplated purchase while the salesman is taking one out of stock. This array of small merchandise is very impressive and experience shows that it makes a great many extra sales.

Merchandising Cabinets That Facilitate Selling.—In selling merchandise that consists of small parts that have to be

EXHIBIT 50.—A convenient cabinet for flashlight batteries of various kinds, including a display of flashlights and a device for testing batteries and bulbs.

refitted or renewed occasionally with extra supplies, the retailer has a big opportunity for repeat sales. Obviously, such sales are small and unless the merchant can handle the storing and selling requirements of these supplies economically the game is a losing one.

Realizing this problem, manufacturers are cooperating with retailers in furnishing merchandise cabinets, counters, fixtures and other devices that facilitate sales. Exhibit 50 is an excellent example of store equipment that makes a good display of goods. It is a convenient container for batteries for various flashlights and, at the same time, gives the sales-

Exhibit 51.—A revolving display-case that holds stock and permits different groups of knives to be displayed on all four sides. Stock-lists and order blanks are in handy pockets, ready for the merchant's use.

man opportunity to test batteries and bulbs without searching or wasting steps.

Here the stock of batteries is stored compactly; the display of flashlights at the top helps in making sales of new outfits as well as affording an excellent reminder to customers to buy needed parts; the batteries are arranged in a gravity feed so that the oldest battery is automatically sold first. On the left, at the bottom of the cabinet, is a device for the testing of bulbs. A similar device at the right is for the testing of batteries. Even the tiny lamp bulbs are stored in a specially constructed stock drawer in the bottom of the cabinet.

The cabinets are sold to the dealers at a price considerably less then the cost to the manufacturer. Possibly the manufacturer could afford to give the cabinets away to his best merchants, but experience seems to show that, in general, devices of this kind are used to better advantage when merchants either pay some part of the cost or are obligated to make good use of the selling aid.

Exhibit 51 shows a view of another very useful form of merchandise cabinet. On four sides of this cabinet are attractive displays of domestic knives of great variety. These are under glass but have a background that brings them out impressively. The open door of the cabinet forms one of the sides. There is ample space inside the cabinet for stock and on the back of the door are convenient pockets for stock-list, order blank, etc.

A Druggist's Lemonade Well.—A Wichita druggist secured a sandstone well top which he placed over a stone jug in an ice-lined box in the counter. A dipper enabled each customer to respond to the suggestion of the sign reading "Ice cold lemonade direct from the old stone well" and doubled the sales of lemonade. The counter was kept supplied with clean glasses, the customer using the old-fashioned dipper merely to fill his glass.

A Mirror Invitation.—A merchant who noticed that people looked at their reflections in his plate glass door, put up a mirror in the front part of his store and across the top placed this sentence: "This is the person we want as a customer."

SECTION VI

WINDOW-DISPLAY MERCHANDISING

Several volumes of the size of this one could be devoted to the big subject of window-display, treating the subject from the retailer's point of view and discussing manufacturers' cooperation in furnishing material for display, assisting in the arrangement of displays, and so forth. It is possible here to show just a few adaptable illustrations and to list in a brief way some of the salient points of good window-display. A number of these suggestions are drawn from excellent advice to retailers in the literature of the National Cash Register Company.

Salient Points of Good Window-display.—1. A window should be well lighted, so that the light shines on the merchandise on display and not in the eyes of the passing throng. Many people see show-windows at night, when their minds are freer from the worries of the day and more open to suggestion.

2. It is important for the display man to have a definite idea of what he wants to accomplish before beginning operations. Some expert decorators even go so far as to make a diagram before starting the window-trimming. The hit-or-miss, or conglomerate, method is rarely effective.

3. While it is not always possible, it is a good plan to conceal the fixtures, wherever they do not add to the display. In some cases, however, the fixtures really form a background for bringing out the beauty of the merchandise. Shoes, for example, look more attractive when displayed on a stand that is in harmony or in contrast to the shoe itself.

4. Window-displays should be simple in order to be effective. If more than one article of merchandise is displayed, the various exhibits should be related articles and not merely a window full of indiscriminate merchandise (see Exhibit 52) that the retailer wishes to bring to the attention of the public.

A window featuring an assortment of gowns, with the proper hats, furs, gloves, hosiery and shoes to be worn with the gowns is an example of good display.

Exhibit 53 illustrates this point, showing related articles of men's clothing.

5. Color harmony is another important thing. Nature makes no mistakes; so the brown and yellow of the sunflower or the blending of colors in ripened fruit are good examples to follow.

6. In order to create desire for the thing being displayed, show how it will look when in actual use. That is, if the display

EXHIBIT 52.—The often-observed result of crowding a window with unrelated merchandise, trusting that the passerby will see something he wants. Such a conglomeration is sadly lacking in power of attraction.

be of furniture, show how the room would look if this furniture were used in it. If the display be of kitchen cabinets, show an attractive kitchen fitted up with a kitchen cabinet (see Exhibit 54).

7. Akin to the foregoing idea is the idea of suggesting in window-displays the use of the articles displayed. This

serves to attract attention and therefore makes the display more effective. For example, if it is planned to display garden tools, the window can be turned into a miniature garden, with grass, flowers, and gravel walks forming an appropriate setting for lawn-mower, rake, sickle, garden hose and many other things that are needed to keep the garden or lawn in proper condition.

8. Make window-displays seasonable. A display of tennis rackets, nets and balls in the early spring reminds the tennis-

EXHIBIT 53.—Show one kind of goods, or goods that are used together.

fan that it is time to check up his tennis needs and lay in new supplies.

9. No display should be allowed to remain unchanged for a long time. People like variety. Besides, many articles become unsalable if left in a show-window too long.

10. Keep in mind the class of people to whom the display is intended to appeal. Costly articles should always be shown in rich settings. If the appeal is to people of moderate means,

naturally the articles on display should be those of medium, or moderate prices. It is difficult to mix two such appeals and have both effective. If they cannot be sharply separated—as in different windows, for example—display the costly goods at one time and the low-priced at another.

11. Give important things the proper place. Something is gained if a natural setting can be arranged, but if there is one

(Courtesy of Good Hardware).

EXHIBIT 54.—Fine example of a window-display by R. H. Macy & Company, New York. Everything shown is a feature of the modern kitchen —even the linoleum on the floor. Such a large, progressive store as the Macy organization may plan displays of this kind entirely of its own initiative, but such a suggestion offered by the manufacturer of a kitchen cabinet or of a modern kitchen table would be welcomed by stores handling goods of this class.

central feature, be sure to put it where the eye of the passerby will rest. Straight lines are inartistic, and therefore should be avoided.

12. Get the proper "atmosphere" for merchandise-displays. For instance, if the display is of tea from India, much is gained if the setting shows a scene in the life of India, such as women

picking tea. If the display is of cotton cloth, interest will be stimulated if the scene shows a cotton field with the colored folks picking cotton.

13. There is an attention-commanding value in human beings and in animals, also in lifelike representations of people and animals, that does not exist in merchandise. Therefore, in addition to using "living models," many firms use the figures of large dolls, to represent children, to attract the attention of lovers of children. A pointer dog standing a covey of quail will be sure to win the eye of the huntsman and quicken anew the thrills and joys of days spent in the open with a good dog and a good gun.

14. Novel displays are good only when they help to center attention on the idea that the merchant is trying to convey to the public.

15. Of course there must be show-cards. For these, fancy lettering is usually inappropriate. Select a plain style of lettering. Aside from the fact that such lettering is easy to read, there is a quiet beauty about a simply lettered message. Do not make the mistake of using too many show-cards. Usually one card bearing a pertinent selling or instructive message, correctly spelled, is all that is necessary for a small window.

16. Do not lose sight of the fact that manufacturers have studied this matter of displaying their goods to the best advantage and are usually glad to cooperate with the dealer by furnishing holders, cartons, posters, etc., in sizes suitable for windows of varying dimensions. Some dealers take advantage of the help offered by manufactures and make their displays link up with the national advertising that the manufacturer may be doing, as well as with the local advertising that the dealer himself may be doing. There is always value in concentrated effort.

Notes on Foregoing List.—Something is gained by contrast. Working on this principle, shoe displays are sometimes made up with flowers as a contrasting, decorative, or attention-attracting feature. A single large spray of dogwood blossoms in the Spring catches the eye of the passerby, and he lingers to see the attractive assortment of spring footwear.

Somewhat allied to seasonableness is the idea of linking up window-displays with local events, such as the annual football game between the local college or high school and its hated rival.

Making a display of the raw materials in connection with the finished product has an educational and interest-centering value that is often overlooked. Such an exhibit in connection with gloves or shoes might be a hide shown untanned, with the various stages of the process marked, from the tanning of the leather to the finished product.

An effective method of getting pointers is to watch the efforts of others, especially windows in other cities. Last, but not least, many good suggestions for window-display are to be found in the various trade papers, and the progressive merchant is quick to avail himself of this ready aid.

Open-backed versus Enclosed Show-windows.—The background of a window-display is almost as important as the display itself, for it must either contrast or harmonize pleasingly with the merchandise displayed in order to be effective. That the large stores realize this is indicated by the extensive use of enclosed show-windows, the back of the windows forming a substantial foundation for draperies or other background treatment.

The smaller retail merchant is often inclined to the view that an enclosed show-window cuts off light from the interior of the store, increases the lighting bills, prevents the passerby from seeing the store interior and being attracted by the activity inside. R. W. Crane, an expert on display-window construction, writing in *Good Hardware*, answers these objections by declaring that the added selling power of displays in enclosed windows more than offsets the increased electric light bills. He argues that cutting off the street view of the store interior impels the passerby to concentrate attention on the articles in the window. A background also prevents salespeople from gazing out of the window, a habit that is often annoying to passersby, especially women, and that causes them to pass the store quickly rather than remain at the window to be stared at. Another advantage of the enclosed window is that, as the display faces only one way, it need not be arranged to appear attractive from the store interior as well as from the street. The enclosed window also affords protection to displayed merchandise, keeping out flies, dust and the store cat.

Proper Background Treatment for Windows.—To make the display effective, it is important that the background of a window be such that it will harmonize with, or show off, the merchandise in a pleasing manner. Sometimes contrast is more to be desired than delicate harmony.

For example, if the merchandise to be displayed is of a dark or sombre color and the background of the window is of mahogany or dark-oak finish, there will not be enough contrast to produce a pleasing, or even an attention-attracting, display. On the other hand, if a light and inconspicuous background is used, not only will the richness and beauty of the goods be displayed to the best advantage, but the attention-drawing power of the display will be increased. There are a number of neutral colors and restful tints that do not attract attention away from the goods, look clean and cool, do not soil very easily and yet afford a suitable setting for almost any kind of merchandise except those of colors close to the colors of the backgrounds themselves.

The light background for a display of dark-colored merchandise also has the advantage of making the display visible at a much greater distance than would be possible with a dark setting. Then, too, a window of light background is more effectively and easily lighted than a dark background which absorbs light. For these reasons, many stores have had their window backgrounds painted a soft, light gray or a "pearl" white or cream, making it unnecessary ordinarily to use plush or other material as a setting. Still another advantage of the light background is that it does not cause the glass to reflect shadows. Dark, highly polished surfaces are likely to do this, making the objects in the window indistinct to the passerby unless the eye happens to focus on the article itself.

Unit Displays.—There is a growing tendency toward the unit display of merchandise. That is, if a firm has one or two large windows, these are divided into sections by means of partitions, which are usually 3 to 4 feet high. Sometimes these partitions are much higher in the background of the display than they are in the foreground, making the display more pleasing as a whole, while, at the same time, distinctly separating each unit of the exhibit.

Displays of the unit type usually have panel or screen backgrounds, as it is easier to select screens that will show off the display to advantage than it would be to drape the window or have the permanent finish of the wood changed from time to time.

This method has the advantage of allowing displays of several distinctly different types to be set up at the same time without conflict.

Manufacturers often supply retailers with very convenient panel fixtures or backgrounds that can be used in carrying out this idea of harmonious divisions of a window (see Exhibit 55).

One may go to extreme in natural wood finishes but some of the handsomest unit fixtures as well as some of the most permanently pleasing window backgrounds are in light natural wood finishes, or those consisting of attractive natural wood frames with panels of fabrics or composition board in harmonious colors.

Suggestions on the Lighting of Windows.—The National Electric Light Association makes the following suggestions as to the lighting of display-windows.

Conceal all light sources to avoid glare and resultant distraction and annoyance. In general, the only lamps that should be visible are those of very low brilliancy used for decorative purposes.

Fit all lamps with efficient reflectors to get the maximum light on the goods for the minimum expenditure of power.

Choose reflectors which distribute the light in such a manner as to illuminate the display uniformly. A high, shallow window obviously requires a different type of reflector from a low, deep one. A window likely to have a high dress should be lighted differently from one in which the material is always close to the floor.

All mechanism of lighting should be hidden from the observer by some sort of screening device.

Use a background of dull finish to prevent reflections of light sources.

A light-colored backing makes a window appear brighter with less illumination than when a mahogany, walnut or similar backing is used. Warm gray, neutral buff, cream or ivory have been very effective for this purpose.

The show-window is a miniature stage, and similar methods of lighting apply. Make use of the same color effects as the theater uses, and give every layout special attention.

Overcoming Reflections from Shiny Objects in Windows.—Displays of aluminum ware, cut glass, or other bright merchandise often reflect sunlight unpleasantly into the eyes of the passerby. The glare may be corrected by keeping one or two electric lights burning in the window, thus neutralizing the effect of the sunlight.

Miscellaneous Suggestions on Lighting.—Of late years, color lighting has come into vogue as a means of attracting customers. Merchants who have made a test find that show-windows lighted in colors command more attention than when just a white light is used.

If it is necessary or desirable to draw particular attention to some one object in a window, a spot light may be used to advantage. Spot lights are sometimes used in combination with color lighting, because the contrast is so great as to almost compel passersby to stop and take a look.

Footlights are used extensively as a means of bringing out details and eliminating shadows.

Checking Up Results from Window-displays.—The Liggett drug stores employ a method of checking sales against window-displays that gives a fair indication of results of effective window-trimming. When a special display is to go into a window, the store makes a complete inventory of the goods on hand, including those in the display. Each sale of the articles on display is credited on a sheet kept for that purpose. If a customer asks for a tooth-brush, for instance, and does not mention the brand in the window, the sale is not credited to the display. But if he inspects several kinds and finally decides on the one displayed, the sale is credited to the window-trim.

To test this system, recently the manager of a Boston store placed in his window a display of chocolates of a manufacturer whose goods had not been handled previously by the store. The sign in the window read: "One Dollar a Pound and Worth

It." In ten days more than 800 pound-boxes were sold by this store. The salespeople received no commission on sales of this candy, as they do on sales of Liggett products, yet the sales were large and the experience was later repeated at another store of the Liggett chain.

("The Store," *Times-Picayune*).

Examples of Timely Window-displays.—As already suggested, timeliness is a vital feature of many window-displays. There are almost innumerable ways of carrying out the timely feature.

A sporting goods store that received a large shipment of Babe Ruth bats secured the Pathé phonograph record giving Babe Ruth's account of how he makes home runs. A window-display was worked out with the central feature of the bats, also a card inviting the spectator to come in and listen to Babe Ruth's account of how to handle a bat so as to make home runs.

When the Disston Saw Company featured the contest based on counting the teeth in a number of saws, a hardware store featured this contest for ten days, displaying twenty-four different kinds of saws in the window and distributing coupons on which the customer's guess had to be made. The contest was also exploited by a newspaper advertisement and by the distribution of circulars. Three prizes were awarded.

When a nearby farmer was robbed at his home, a hardware store featured firearms for the following week and told under what conditions permits for the use of defensive weapons could be obtained.

On learning that a dairymen's league had looked with favor on a new sanitary dairy pail, a hardware merchant stocked the pail and featured the dairymen's league's approval of it.

When the newspapers came out in 1922 with announcements that homes must be equipped with either mail-slots in doors or windows or mail-boxes, in order that postmen might deliver without waiting for an answer to the door-bell, various stores scored a success by giving the item extra publicity and offering neat letter boxes.

A large Boston department store, recognizing the widespread interest taken by the public in D. W. Griffith's motion

(*Courtesy of White & Wyckoff Manufacturing Company, Holyoke, Mass.*)

EXHIBIT 55.—Artistic example of 3-panel window-display. Along with the central display the White & Wyckoff Manufacturing Company furnishes the retailer attractive tickets that he can insert in boxes of stationery, as indicated by the illustration. These price-tickets are made to harmonize with the 3-panel display poster. The firm sends along the above illustration, when furnishing the display material, so as to indicate to the merchant an effective arrangement

picture, "Orphans of the Storm," secured the original Normandy holiday gowns worn by the Gish sisters when the play was filmed and arranged a window-display of silks with the two gowns as the central feature. The picture at the time was receiving a great deal of publicity in the newspapers. Consequently, the timeliness and attractiveness of the display kept the sidewalk crowded in front of that particular window while the display lasted.

(Summarized in part from *Good Hardware*).

EXHIBIT 56.—Photographic view sent out by the manufacturers of Lyon Resilient Bumpers to suggest to dealers in automobile supplies the exhibition of three styles of the bumpers, together with a 3-panel display poster that illustrates the peculiar value of Resilient Bumpers in preventing accidents.

"Nature" Scenes in Windows.—Weather records have been used in an interesting way by a Colorado department store. This store featured a sale of blankets in September, placing them in a window with a back ground representing a snowy landscape. Part of a tree trunk was placed conspicuously in the window and attached to it was a sign giving the dates of the first snowfall for several years past. The record attracted the attention of numbers of passersby.

Some stores give in their newspaper advertisements the weather outlook for each day, but records such as those just referred to might also be appropriately introduced.

What Some of the Largest Stores Approve.—Some of the large department stores, those of the class of R. H. Macy & Company, New York, and Charles Stevens & Company, Chicago, for example, value their show-windows at $150,000 or more a year. Some of these popular stores attribute as high as 25, 30 or 40 per cent of certain classes of sales directly

Exhibit 57.—Interesting historical window-display planned by the Namm store of Brooklyn. The Namm is a cash store that constantly preaches economy. Therefore, this window was particularly appropriate for "Thrift Week," which included Benjamin Franklin's birthday. The large frame at the lower right edge of the view contained a number of scenes of American life about the time of Franklin. The figure of Franklin had three movements. The head rose to a natural position, the left hand was lifted to the forehead as if the figure were in deep thought. This hand lowered itself after a few seconds and the right hand then began a writing movement. A stereopticon machine on the mantel displayed sixty-five pictures of the life of Franklin.

to well trimmed windows. Therefore, it can be readily understood why manufacturers' displays must fall within reasonable requirements if they are to appear in such valuable space.

Manufacturers' display cards that are most acceptable to these large stores are of standardized sizes, 14 by 11 inches and 11 by 7 (for smaller products). Colors should be subdued and the manufacturer's name should not be obnoxiously prominent; they should be made for upright use, not for hanging. Posters and reproductions of attractively painted pictures are approved by larger stores.

Small articles are shown to the best advantage in wing frames four to six feet high; and cut-outs may be used with the screens.

(Summarized from *Printers Ink*).

EXHIBIT 58.—A page from a book of "Window Trims" sent out by the Stetson Company to the retail trade. This book is made up of fine examples of Stetson displays arranged in various parts of the country. In making up this book, the Stetson Company not only gives credit to the retail store creating the display but to the designer of the display. The good-will of the window-display man is worth while preserving. This exhibit is from a photograph of a window designed by George Hurst for Bond Brothers, Pentleton, Ore.

Value of Illustrations of Good Arrangements of Material.—Even with the largest stores, employing expert trimmers, a photograph of an attractive layout of the material furnished is welcome (see Exhibit 55).

Exhibit 56 is a photographic view of a display arranged in the offices of the manufacturer of Lyon Resilient Bumpers.

The view here shown was sent out to automobile dealers as a suggestion for an appropriate arrangement of a "Bumper Window."

Exhibits 57 and 58 are views of two different types of window-displays—one a historical feature in which motion is employed as an attention-attractor and the other a window that gains a decidedly masculine atmosphere by the employment of a saddle and a painting of Western life.

IDEAS FOR NOVEL DISPLAYS

Variation of an Old Display Idea.—"Our pillows are light as feathers," was the text on a sign in a furniture store window. Floating about in a string "cage" were three or four pillows—apparently real. "How is it done?" onlookers asked. Inside the pillows was a rubber lining filled with illuminating gas; they were kept bobbing up and down by the breeze from a cleverly concealed fan. It was merely a new form of the old balloon idea—but it drew the crowd.

(Marketing).

"Lingerie Silhouette" Attracts Attention.—A window-display arranged by the Ville de Paris, of Los Angeles, produced a novel effect. During the day the window held lingerie, corsets, and underwear placed on the floor or on forms, with a background of white oiled paper divided into window-like panels by strips of black velvet. At night, however, there appeared silhouetted against the white windows feminine figures attired in lingerie. The silhouette effect was obtained by life-size figures cut from cardboard with strong lights back of them. The display attracted much attention.

This is merely an example of the hundreds of novel ideas that may be carried out in window-display merchandising. Novelty is not always essential. Quiet, appropriate settings may often have more real selling power. But the window merchandiser studies to avoid the commonplace.

(Retail Ledger).

Making Rain to Sell Umbrellas.—A window-display at Macy's, New York City, featured a wax figure in summer apparel with raised umbrella in a shower of real drops of water from a bath-spray hung from the centre of the ceiling. The water ran off on the grass-mat floor and into a tank back of the window.

Displaying Old and New Fashions for Babies.—To promote interest and sales in the infants' goods department, Gold & Company, of Lincoln, Neb., procured pictures and clothing from citizens showing how babies were dressed in Civil War

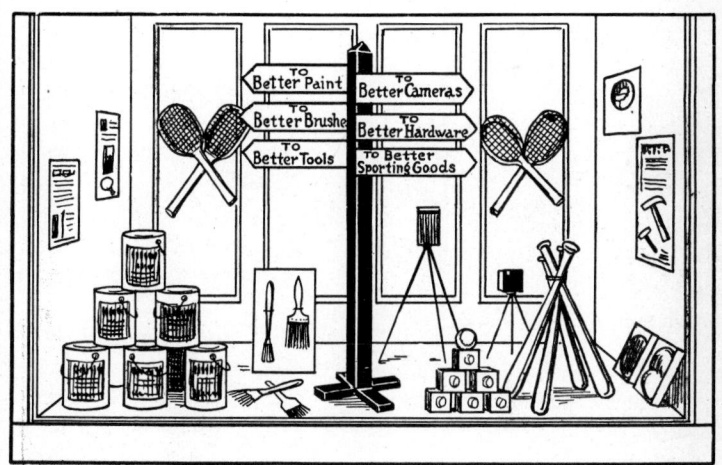

EXHIBIT 59.—Example of how a simple feature will often make a small display-window stand out well.

times. An attractive window-display was arranged, one of the features being a tintype of Lincoln's mayor at the age of five. Another display was made up of present-day outfits for babies, illustrating most conspicuously the improvement in comfort and appearance of today's styles over those of a generation ago.

Example of Simple but Effective Display.—Exhibit 59 shows a simple display in the window of a hardware store. In this case the central feature was a wooden sign-post with signs directing the attention of the passerby to various articles in the window.

Silkworm Exhibit in Windows.—The Corticelli Silk Mills, of Florence, Mass., made an effective use some years ago of an exhibit of live silkworms. As the silkworms spin their cocoons from the latter part of May through the first week of June, the shipments of exhibits had to be timed accordingly. In addition to the worms, the exhibit included a book of raw

EXHIBIT 60.—Example of window-display made with the assistance of a trade association. Illustration by courtesy of Joint Coffee Trade Publicity Committee. The streamers at the top of the window illustrate the cooperative service of the coffee roasters and wholesalers. Such an exhibit has a distinct educational value.

silk, a cabinet showing the silkworm at different stages of its existence, framed pictures, papier mâché kittens made up in the style of the Corticelli trade-mark, as well as booklets, small kitten "cut-outs" and little boxes containing two silk cocoons for free distribution.

This unique educational display was announced to dealers but they were required to fill out and send a special application blank in order to get the exhibit. On receipt of this exhibit the dealer was instructed carefully about the staging of the display and the treatment of the silkworms. The worms were forwarded by parcel post a day or two before the beginning of the spinning period and the company furnished the dealer with a fresh supply of mulberry leaves daily for feeding the worms.

According to a statement of the Corticelli Silk Company, published originally in *Printers' Ink Monthly*, this display was very successful in drawing the attention of men, women and children.

Coffee Exhibit.—Exhibit 60 shows an educational display of coffee arranged to good advantage in a grocery store window.

ADDITIONAL DATA ON WINDOW-DISPLAY MERCHANDISING

Easy Method of Making Small Window Posters.—Attractive show-cards and posters for use in window-displays can be made by utilizing cover designs and advertisements in magazines, or pictures in Sunday supplements. Almost any school bulletin board, public library, or Y.W.C.A. will show examples of this sort of poster work. As a rule these posters are crude, but, given the idea, a liberal supply of good quality pasteboard stock of various colors, a pile of magazines, a pair of scissors and a paste-pot, a person possessing a little artistic ability should be able to produce very attractive posters on which prices or advertising messages may be stenciled, or hand-lettered. A young woman in a Southern department store uses with great success this method of creating posters. Sometimes when she finds illustrations which are only partly suitable for her purpose she cuts out the sections not wanted and fills in a design of her own with paints or ink. She also paints in backgrounds to her cut-outs so that it is difficult to see where the division is. A valuable hint given by this young woman is that pictures from advertisements of a certain brand of hosiery, for example, should not be used with a window-display of a competitive brand of hosiery. Trade-marks also must be avoided. Aside from these two cautions, there is no limit to the pictures, photographs or decorative effects that can be transformed into posters.

Price Tickets on Displayed Articles.—There has been considerable discussion about the advisability of putting price tickets on articles displayed in show-windows. A window- and store-display specialist, Carl Percy, contributes this experience in an article published by *Sunset:*

The question of whether or not to mark prices on articles in show-windows has always been the subject of much discussion. An investigation was made of two stores in the same neighborhood. Store A had articles price-marked. Store B did not. Of 147 people passing store A in ten minutes, 43 stopped to look, 12 stayed for a minute or more and 3 went in. The same test applied to store B showed that just 3 people stopped to look and none went in.

It seems probable that this experience would hold good in most cases. Now and then it may happen, however, that the high price of an article repels unless the reader has opportunity to understand the worth of the article thoroughly. If, for example, a price-card were to inform the passerby that a certain type of cash register cost $500, he might "canvass himself," as salesmen say, and conclude that he could not possibly afford to pay $500 for such a store-fixture. If, however, he could be impressed by the service of the register, be induced to come inside and spend an hour or two in understanding the cash register system and seeing the machine demonstrated, and if, also, the payment plan could be presented in such a way as to appear within his reach, he might be induced to purchase.

Unless the article is clearly one of this class, the giving of prices seems desirable. While it may be argued that the absence of such a commercial feature as a price tends to exclusiveness, on the other hand there is the risk that people will walk away rather than be embarrassed by asking the price of an article admired in the window and having to admit that they cannot afford the price.

Exhibit 61 shows a display in which the price idea is foremost, making the price ticket a necessity.

Payment for Window Space.—The Liggett organization, which consists of more than two hundred chain drug stores operated throughout the United States, recently adopted the policy of charging for window-space in all of their stores. The idea is to sell to the manufacturers desiring to have displays in the Liggett chain of stores a specified unit of space at a specified price, which makes it certain that the manufacturer's

EXHIBIT 61.—There is nothing novel about this idea, but it suggests how a variety of slow-selling goods may often be assembled and offered in the window or in some inside display at an attractive average price. This idea can be used in the displaying of goods to be offered at 10 cents, 25 cents or 50 cents. The same thought may be carried out, if the store has room, by a series of tables or counters, one table containing articles at 10 cents, another at 25 cents, and so on.

goods will be simultaneously displayed in all of the Liggett stores and also makes it reasonably certain that the Liggett stores will have a sufficient quantity of the goods displayed ni stock, to supply whatever demand the display may create.

This does not mean, however, that the Liggett organization limits its buying to goods displayed in its windows by different manufacturers. It makes it clear that the buying is done independently of goods that may be displayed in the paid-for-space by other manufacturers.

The Liggett argument for selling space is that their stores are located well and that space is worth something to manufacturers who want to have their goods displayed. No goods are displayed, except Liggett goods, of course, unless the manufacturer buys the space. This gives every manufacturer a fair chance.

The Liggett organization has the trimming done by experts, but the material for the displays is all furnished by the manufacturers buying the space.

Some large department and dry goods stores have also followed the plan of charging for window-space where this is used in the particular interest of manufacturers.

In general, manufacturers have not been favorable toward plans of this kind, believing that effective window displays are for mutual benefit and that when they furnish costly material for such displays, as well as pay the cost of national advertising campaigns, they have done their share.

Furthermore, a policy of this kind is likely to result in manufacturers bidding against each other for the favor of the dealer, because however much a dealer may try to be fair, he can hardly avoid favoring the manufacturer who pays a price for the window-displays that he gets. It can be said, too, on behalf of the manufacturers, that few retailers are in a position to give such window-display service as would warrant payment for space.

SECTION VII

PLANNING AND MANAGING NEWSPAPER ADVERTISING

If every advertiser had a perfect mailing-list of the people who use his goods or service or who are likely to become users of his goods or service, the argument in favor of direct advertising methods would be complete. But in most groups of business, the man with something to sell never knows all the people who either need his article or are likely to need it.

The newspaper for such an advertiser is a broadcasting method. It goes out into the highways and byways, with some waste, of course, finding the prospective customer and fanning the small spark of interest into a flame of desire, so to speak.

Newspaper Indispensable to Most Retailers.—In a community well covered by a good newspaper or by several newspapers, it seems almost unnecessary to make the observation that newspaper space is the most valuable medium for most advertisers. News has magnetic attraction. It is not extraordinary to find a single newspaper reaching from 60 to 80 per cent of the homes in the city of its publication. In reaching such a large proportion of the reading population the newspaper enjoys the advantage of low cost per thousand as compared with other forms of advertising on which postage must be paid. Furthermore, the newspaper reaches people daily and can be used on short notice, thus permitting timely and frequent appeals. As people are in the habit of reading, the newspaper advertiser has no difficult job to get attention, that is, so far as the medium is concerned. To get attention for his own message is the problem.

Other forms of advertising are valuable as supplements and occasionally some other medium meets the needs of a local or retail advertiser better than the newspaper, but the high-class daily paper is so strongly entrenched as the leading medium for local or regional advertising that it scarcely needs the paragraphs here devoted to its power.

News, while an attracting force, is at the same time a force that the advertiser must reckon with as a distraction from what he has to say. While newspapers may be bought in some instances merely to read advertising—such, for example, as classified advertising or a favorite department-store page—in general the papers are purchased for the news. The most interesting local, state, national and international events are set forth in their columns. The amount of time given by a reader is very small, probably not more than fifteen or twenty minutes on the average. Good newspapers are filled with advertisements. Several hundred hands, as it were, are upheld, each advertiser saying, in effect, "Please give me attention." Consequently, no advertiser need deceive himself into thinking that because he uses a newspaper reaching from 10,000 to 100,000 readers he has a good chance to interest all these readers, or even a large proportion of them. He has a most difficult undertaking to command and hold the attention of even 5 or 10 per cent with an advertisement of ordinary size.

Most newspapers are popular mediums. Here and there, however, there is a paper that appeals to a more or less selected class. In cases where advertisers have to deal with very small groups, it may be necessary to resort to mailing-lists and direct forms of advertising. These conditions are discussed elsewhere in this volume.

THE JUDICIOUS USE OF SPACE

Having decided to advertise and made an appropriation, an advertiser faces these interesting and important questions:

1. How much space should be used?
2. Is it better to run a series of advertisements of the same size or to vary from small or medium-sized advertisements to large ones?
3. How frequently should the advertisement be inserted?

These, like many other questions that an advertiser must solve, cannot be decided arbitrarily by rules or formulas. What he should do, in order to get the greatest value for each

PLANNING NEWSPAPER ADVERTISING

of his dollars, can be determined wisely only after a careful study of the exact situation that is before him. Some of the factors are these:

(a) How well he is already advertised
(b) What he has to offer—its extent and timeliness
(c) The habits of the readers he is appealing to
(d) What competitors are doing
(e) The medium he is using.

The Story That Can Be Split into Chapters or Points.—Often there is a story to be told that can be divided effectively into a series of chapters or points. Suppose, for example, there are twelve good selling points about an automobile. It would hardly do to say that one advertisement, or several advertisements, might not be written that would incorporate effectively all of this information or argument, but if the papers are full of long advertisements about automobiles, the advertiser could score a hit by preparing a series of concise appeals and presenting these at intervals in spaces of uniform size.

Such a series could be summed up well in an advertisement of larger size reviewing all the good argument presented in the entire series of small, pointed appeals. There are enough advertisers using uniform spaces and running these regularly to demonstrate that this plan can be used successfully.

Varied Size Breaks Monotony.—There is some advantage in not tying an advertising schedule down to a fixed program of advertisements of one size. Some messages are much more important than others and require more space. The advertisers to whom fixed spaces are most appropriate are those who are exploiting staples—groceries and drugs, for example—commodities for which a market is well established and the announcements of which the public is likely to look for. In such cases there is some advantage in having a regular location for the advertisement, so that it serves as an index or directory of supplies.

Staples call for more frequent advertising, for they are likely to be bought daily.

Even with such commodities, however, there are occasions when an unusual list of offerings warrants the use of larger space. A principle to be remembered is that anything that the public sees regularly in much the same way runs the risk of becoming monotonous. This holds good whether the object of attention is the size of the advertisement, the display or some other feature. It is argued occasionally that "repetition makes reputation" but this principle should be applied to a name, slogan or trade-mark rather than to a fixed style for *everything* about an advertisement.

Unusual Sizes to Meet Unusual Needs.—A baker may be using newspaper advertisements running from 3 to 4 inches, hammering home a point at a time about his bread. But such advertisements will not do for an announcement of a new product of his or the opening of a fine new plant. A dealer for a popular make of automobile that, because of its position in its field, calls for regular large-space advertising may, with advantage, use smaller advertisements featuring used cars.

When competitors are using small advertisements, the large advertisement stands out well through contrast. Under different conditions, when competitors are using large advertisements, a series of smaller messages, written and set up distinctively and inserted more frequently than competitors are advertising, may be good strategy. A moving-picture theater, believing that large advertisements were being used to an extravagant extent in its town, saved money by having a series of smaller appeals designed with distinctive borders and illustrations of high-class theatrical atmosphere.

It is possible, through careful planning of space and good layout, to give a comparatively small advertisement a dominating position. To accomplish this, headlines should be simple, so they can be treated boldly, with white space around, and there should be few display lines. A small advertisement cluttered with display lines becomes a monotonous mass, with no outstanding feature.

Advertising may be likened to a battle in which various kinds of firearms and artillery are used. The rifle, revolver and machine gun do an important work but they do not take the place of the long-range, big-calibered artillery. Each has its place according to the task to be accomplished.

Reading Notice Advertising.—Many retailers make effective use of that class of advertising known as "reading notices," "telegraphic readers" and by other names. These are merely paragraphs or sentences set either in regular news type or in a smaller size and ordinarily inserted with black-faced headings or at least one black-faced word at the beginning of the text.

Some newspapers run such advertising only at the bottom of columns or with a cut-off rule. Other newspapers run reading-notice advertisements freely between items of real news. The law now requires that all such notices be marked plainly "adv." or that it be indicated in some other way that the material is advertising and not editorial or news items.

This class of advertising calls for no special comment with respect to display arrangement, for the style is a simple one and is regulated by each newspaper according to its own ideas. It may be recorded that unless the newspaper is over-run with advertising of this class, the style is usually an effective method, provided the copy is well written.

Even when the advertiser is a liberal user of display space, reading notices may serve to call attention to particular features of the display advertisement by referring to the page on which the larger advertisement appears. For example, some stores have found it profitable to scatter these "readers" throughout the local news from different sections. This form of reader is usually very simple running about as follows:

Helpful suggestions for picnic lunches are given in the grocery section of the advertisement, on Page 6, of the Thomas Store, 34 Broad Street, Newton.

As newspapers usually charge much more per line for this kind of advertising, there rests on the copy-writer the responsibility of having strong copy. As in street-car card advertising, there is no room for useless introductions or the essay style of treatment. Such messages must be succinct and forceful and in order to get the most attention, should have as much news value as possible. It is very appropriate in advertising of this kind to include in messages the names of people, provided this is agreeable to customers. For example:

Eleven Thousand Miles and Still Going.—Dr. M. V. Smithers remarked on Saturday, when he stopped for gas, that his last set of ....tires, bought from us in May, has given him so far eleven thousand miles of use with no wear-out signs in sight.

Reid Tire Company, 10 Broad Street.

THE POWER OF ILLUSTRATION

Illustration serves two purposes:
1. To draw attention.
2. To picture the service or goods advertised.

Some illustrations fulfil both purposes. If so, so much the better. A few advertisers today use the comical illustration successfully but unless the humorous treatment ties up aptly with the subject of the advertisement it is of very doubtful value. Years ago advertisers evidently believed it was good advertising to make use of all sorts of ridiculous illustrations. Even though they trick the reader into giving attention, the modern advertiser will not risk them. He has learned that unless attention is favorable it will avail him nothing. It is easily possible to get sprightly treatment without being ridiculous or making the reader feel that he was tricked into giving his attention.

If an illustration, in addition to showing the article, can demonstrate its service or its operation, that is an added advantage.

Use of Illustrations.—The free use of illustrations by the most successful department stores and the big mail-order houses is good argument for illustration in retail advertisements generally. This is not equivalent to saying that some advertisers get along very well without illustrations. While this is true, there can be no question about the fact that often the best of copy gains, not only in attention-attracting value but in clear description by the use of good illustrations.

For example, in Exhibit 62, while the copy is excellent, the illustration of the well-dressed man adds force to the thought of the text.

The various exhibits of this Section show a variety of well illustrated advertisements. Good illustrations run up a good-sized total of expense, if the advertiser has all of the

CLOTHES : IN THE NEW YORK MANNER

First Impressions

A GREAT many stock and bond salesmen buy their clothes at our stores. Their business has taught them the importance of first impressions.

In a calling where letters of introduction are not always available, they know that the best substitute is a good appearance.

And they know that our suits, even to the most casual of glances, convey a definite impression of character, dignity and breeding.

We are showing a particularly attractive group at $50, $55 and $60. Others from $35 to $75.

Thirteen Stores—8 Featuring Clothes

*241 Broadway	Broadway at 37th
345 Broadway	150 Nassau
9th and Broadway	20 Cortlandt
*28th and Broadway	*30 Broad
*44th and Broadway	*Nassau and John
*42nd and Madison	

BROOKLYN: *381 Fulton Street
Borough Hall

NEWARK: *800 Broad Street

Weber and Heilbroner
HABERDASHERS   CLOTHIERS   **HATTERS**

EXHIBIT 62.—An advertisement that excels in lifelike illustration. The man looks like a real man rather than a fashion-plate. The "first impressions" idea and the reference to the dress of stock and bond salesmen is in keeping with the general thought of the advertisement.

drawings or plates made especially for his own use. Most retailers cannot afford to do this, but content themselves with some original and individual illustrations and make effective use of a variety of plates secured either from manufacturers or from syndicates.

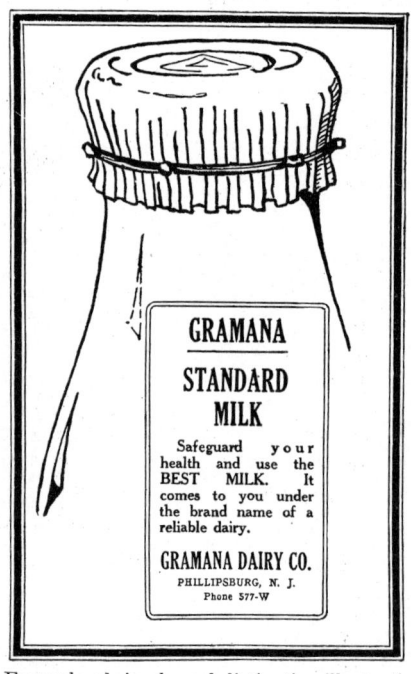

EXHIBIT 63.—Example of simple and distinctive illustration. By showing only part of the article, leaving the commonplace part of it to the imagination, the maker of the illustration has scored a success. It seems desirable, however, to have the top part of a milk bottle bring out the trade-mark or name of the advertised article more prominently.

Such an illustration as that of Exhibit 63 may be used in connection with a variety of arguments about the product, thus distributing the original cost of the drawing and plate.

VIEWS OF AN EXPERT PLANNER OF ADVERTISING

It has seemed well to the author of this volume to introduce into the discussion of relations with publishers and printers some views other than his own, covering typography, layouts and methods of getting good results.

The material that follows, up to and including page 171, is from the pen of Richard M. Boren, a former associate of the author, a man of unusual ability and experience in the planning and laying out of effective advertising. Mr. Boren's experience includes not only service as a printer, but many years as a planner and writer of advertising with a number of the largest advertising agencies.

There are likely to be some exceptions or qualifications to any set of general principles or rules that may be laid down as governing good display. Nevertheless, an advertiser can hardly fail to get good results by giving heed to the recommendations that follow.

The direct form of address is used in the greater part of this advice, just because it seems easier in this way to make pointed recommendations.

PRINCIPLES OF TYPOGRAPHY AS APPLIED TO RETAIL ADVERTISING

By Richard M. Boren

The rules of good typography are quite simple. Any merchant or advertising manager may quickly learn them in a broad, general way. In fact, most merchants already apply the same principles in the arrangement of their counters and store-windows.

A merchant selects the location for his store on the busiest street in town, near to street-cars and other forms of transportation, so that the store will be seen by and be convenient to the greatest number of people.

Over his door he places a sign to tell the name and nature of his business. He makes his show-windows and his entrance as inviting as possible; he allows liberal space for aisles so that customers may easily come and go; he arranges goods on counters and in show-cases, so that selections may readily be made.

The same motives that prompt him to arrange his store so that it will be a convenient and inviting place in which to make purchases should guide him in the typographical arrangement of his advertisements.

The advertisements are extensions of the retailer's store. They should be easy to find, easy to identify, easy to "enter," *i.e.*, to read.

The typographical display should aid readers who may be in search of specific articles, to locate their needs *quickly*. To the roving eye, traveling down the newspaper aisles, the typographical display of the merchant should invite a pause and an examination.

You can, Mr. Retail Advertiser, accomplish all of these purposes in your advertisements, just as you do in your store, if you will follow the same principles of orderly simplicity and good taste. There are obstructions that will bar readers out of your advertisements quite as effectually as a pile of packing cases in your doorway would keep them out of your store. Even in the metropolitan newspapers, where the cost of space would seemingly mean the employment of competent planners of advertising, you may see advertisements that fail to offer the reader the easy access that is such a marked characteristic of every good store.

Tools for Advertising Arrangement.—A printer thinks of the materials of an advertisement as type, rules, leads, etc. This is entirely right from his mechanical and technical point of view. But a merchant or advertising manager, in planning the typographical make-up of an advertisement, should think of the various parts as display elements. These elements for him may be enumerated as:

1. White space
2. Borders
3. Headlines
4. Sub-heads
5. Illustrations
6. Text- or body-matter
7. Price-displays
8. Signature or name-plate

Each of these elements requires careful study, if you would have your advertisements stand out distinctively, and also give them that easy-to-enter, easy-to-read quality so essential for effective selling.

Use of White Space.—How does white space help? White space is somewhat like floor-space, or it may be likened to wall- or counter-space. It may be economized or wasted; crowded or used too liberally.

White space has a powerful effect on all the other display elements, by *throwing them into contrast.*

The proper adjustment of white space to the blacks and grays[1] of display and body type is one of the most difficult tasks in the layout of an advertisement.

Heavy borders and black display lines require wider margins and more generous separation than light-faced borders and type.

Large type, likewise, requires more white space than type of smaller size.

[1] "Gray" is used as the most convenient way of describing the effect of light or medium-weight text type on the background of paper.

When you wish to throw an advertisement or any part of an advertisement into great prominence, surround it liberally with white space (see Exhibit 64). You know how a single article in a show-window stands out and attracts attention. But the article should be something worthy of such liberal treatment.

Some advertisers make effective use of white space by leaving an ample band or column of it alongside several paragraphs of text.

The Several Purposes of Borders.—1. A border may be used as a *fence* to separate your advertisement from other advertisements and reading matter surrounding it.

2. A border may be used as a *frame* to hold your advertisement together and give it unity.

3. A border may be an *ornament* to beautify your advertisement.

In retail advertising it is often advisable to use continuously a border so distinctive that it will act as an identifying *sign-board*.

After readers have seen such a border surrounding your advertisements often enough, the two will become connected in their minds and the border will attain an identifying power that will make it a valuable advertising asset.

To accomplish such a result, it is not necessary to use expensive, hand-drawn borders. Type or rule borders will do as well, if they have distinctive character, and if the one you select is used by no other advertiser in your locality.

Never use a border heavy enough to overshadow your display lines.

Never use a border the pattern of which takes the attention away from the type matter. The artist who frames a picture with a heavy ornate frame is lacking in his perception of the purpose of advertising.

Borders that are well-proportioned and pleasing in large space often become too dominant in small space.

The little Ovington advertisement, (Exhibit 65), illustrates the appropriate use of the ornamental border. Here there is harmony between the decorative effect and the subject of the advertisement—an engraved crystal jug. This example

FITTED BY CRAFTSMEN

HENNING

An Evening Sandal of irresistible beauty with the Henning touch of simplicity and charm—in black or brown satin; silver brocade; and gold and silver brocade.

Boot Shop
Custom Made
575-577 MADISON AVE. AT 57th ST.
NEW YORK

EXHIBIT 64.—A dainty setting in which a mat or background of white space is used to good advantage. Ordinarily, such heavy type would be out of place in describing women's shoes intended for evening wear but the artistic character of the lettering here is not only in harmony with the subject of the advertisement but gives unusual display. The point "Fitted by Craftsmen" is well handled, from both a copy and a display point of view. Such a fine setting deserved an illustration that printed better.

throughout is excellent. The only possible criticism is the lack of a headline, and the illustration, partly at least, meets this need. The copy is pointed, concise, and the typographical simplicity is excellent.

When there is need for departing from the use of a plain border that is used merely for contrast or to hold the various

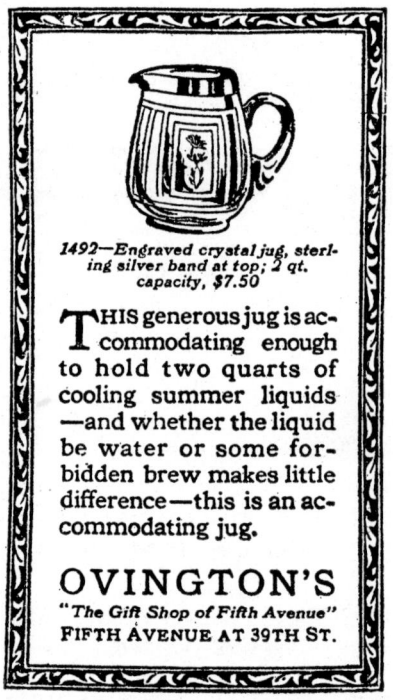

EXHIBIT 65.—Excellent example of simple typography and harmonious border. Reproduced in original size.

parts of an advertisement together, look for some border that has some harmonious relation to, or symbolism for, the commodity to be exploited.

Occasionally the subject of the advertisement is of such a distinctive character that a border such as that illustrated by Exhibit 66 can be used. Such a border as the Moffats border would be appropriate for use with all kinds of advertisements exploiting the value of the electric current.

Headlines Are the Beckoning Fingers.—The headline stands at the opening of your advertisement to invite every reader who passes that way to leave the "reading columns" and other advertisements of the paper for a study of your goods and your prices.

As the headline has the important function of ushering readers into your advertisements, it should be as attractive and as inviting as you can make it.

Short headlines deliver their messages quickly.

Exhibit 66.—Special border treatment used in an advertisement exploiting electrical goods. Ordinarily, the advertiser would not be able to find a stock border of this nature but would have to have it drawn for his particular use.

Headlines set in lower case letters are easier to read than those set in capitals. Think how few news articles you would read were you forced to decipher them in capitals instead of letting them *flow* into your consciousness as they now do.

Condensed type is type that compresses more words into a line than regular letters would permit. Because it looks so crowded, such type is less easy to read and should be avoided. Use it in emergencies only.

Liberal white space around headings makes them more prominent and more readable.

Short headings may be set on one line. Where a heading runs into more than six or seven words, better results will usually be secured by using two or more lines (see Exhibit 69).

When a heading or sub-heading occupies two or more lines, try to break the lines where there is a natural break in the sense of the words. This will make for easier reading and better understanding. Compare *a* and *b* of Exhibit 69.

Do not separate the lines of a two-line heading with a band of white space. Hold them together so that they will be read as a single unit.

Exhibit 67. (Comments on opposite page).

Do not use outline type or freakish type of any kind. Outline type will not harmonize with any other type, and when used alone it gives a blurry, undecided tone that lacks force.

The minor parts of an advertisement are always easier to adjust if the advertisement has one strongly dominating display.

Avoid having several display lines contesting for first place. Secondary displays may be given equal prominence, but there should never be any question as to which is of leading importance.

Roosevelt Military Academy
For Your Boy

Officers and Trustees:

Gen. Leonard Wood
Col. Theodore Roosevelt
Henry J. Allen
Judge Elbert H. Gary
Philip B. Stewart
Senator Walter E. Edge
Harry F. Sinclair
R. Livingston Beekman
John G. Lonsdale
Col. Henry L. Stimson
J. S. Wannamaker
Russell R. Whitman
J. P. Muller
George Leigh
J. A. Cruikshank

An ideal preparatory school for boys from ten to sixteen.

Trains American boys for practical American citizenship.

Teaches boys to be alert, obedient, and to have respect for law and the Constitution.

The Roosevelt aim: Scholarship, service, citizenship.

Splendid teaching personnel. Supervised athletics. Outdoor life. Healthy minds in healthy bodies. Teaches boys to think straight and act straight.

Finest home surroundings and atmosphere. For full information and catalogue, address

JOHN CARRINGTON, Headmaster
West Englewood, New Jersey
Phone Hackensack 2363

EXHIBIT 68.—Example of how panelling may be used to make some particular feature of copy, such as a list of officers or a list of users of a product, stand out.

Sub-heads Direct Attention to Points of Interest.—Sub-heads open a number of entrances to your advertisement.

They lead the reader down the aisles of your messages and across to the various departments in which he may be interested.

EXHIBIT 67.—Many fancy borders are less effective than plain borders. In this advertisement, however, the special border is particularly appropriate. Baker, Murray & Imbrie, Inc., have a variety of these borders for exploiting different sporting goods. The advertiser gains by confining this one message to fishing tackle. But the text would be greatly improved by leading between the various items. The sub-heads would be much more legible in upper-and-lower case setting.

Sub-heads help to tell your story quickly. Too many sub-heads, however, make an advertisement "spotty" and uninviting.

Sub-heads should be placed close enough to the text to which they relate so there can be no question as to the relationship.

If possible, avoid the use of more than two kinds of display type in one advertisement. One "face," in its various sizes, will usually be ample for both headings and sub-headings.

They shorten
the road to
your promotion

(a)

They shorten the road
to your promotion

(b)

EXHIBIT 69.—For easy comprehension, headlines consisting of more than one line should be divided with careful regard, both as to copy-thought and typography. The lower arrangement is an improvement over the upper.

Italics that correspond with the general character of straight letters offer a pleasing variation.

Illustrations and Text Should Work Together.—Place illustrations so they will help in leading the reader into the advertisement.

The best teamwork can be expected from illustrations and headings when the two are yoked together. When they refer to each other, place them close enough together so that both may be comprehended in the same "eyeful."

Captions or explanatory notes in regard to illustrations may be set in quite small type. The reader's attention is first secured by the illustration.

A little experiment with the proof of an illustration and an outline of the space your advertisement is to occupy will show you that, like a piano in a parlor, the picture can be shifted to numerous positions. The same experiment will usually show you also that there is one position where the illustration is more effective than in any other. Put it there! The other parts of your advertisement can always be made to conform to the needs of your illustration.

A little study sometimes reveals a striking arrangement of illustration with the border or the main display, without freakishness or lack of balance. There is not so much danger of "top-heaviness" as of "bottom-heaviness." In other words, an advertisement usually has better balance when the greater part of the display is above the lineal center of the space. If it becomes necessary to place the chief illustration at or near the bottom of the space, as in Exhibit 72-*b*, balance is maintained by a headline of good strength at the top.

Keep in mind that while borders may sometimes run entirely around illustration and text, so as to hold the message together, as it were, this is not always the best arrangement. Borders at top and bottom only, or borders broken at the side or at the corners may permit effective placing of illustration and headlines.

Relation of Type to Text.—Type may make text matter easy or hard to read.

Tell the most inviting story in capitals and few readers will take time to decipher it. Capitals are popular for inscriptions on tombs and for architectural lettering, but that is not an argument for using them in an advertisement. Only very rarely does the subject of an advertisement make all-capital treatment appropriate.

Freakish types, or letters that run into each other, are almost as effective as capitals in turning the reader away from your message. Leave all types that are not plain, clear and readable to the undiscerning buyer of space (see Exhibit 70-*a*). This advertisement is not crude. It just falls short of

Exhibit 70-a.—Frequently white lettering against black background is a pleasing change from ordinary type display. In this case, the advertiser's artist erred by arranging the headline words in irregular fashion. A plainer arrangement, with the little ornament at the right of the headline left out, would be more effective. This advertisement suffers by the use of too much black. Plain type-setting of the advertiser's signature would be an improvement.

a good standard. The headline, "Free music lessons," has real power. With simpler white lettering against the black background, this headline would have stood out strongly.

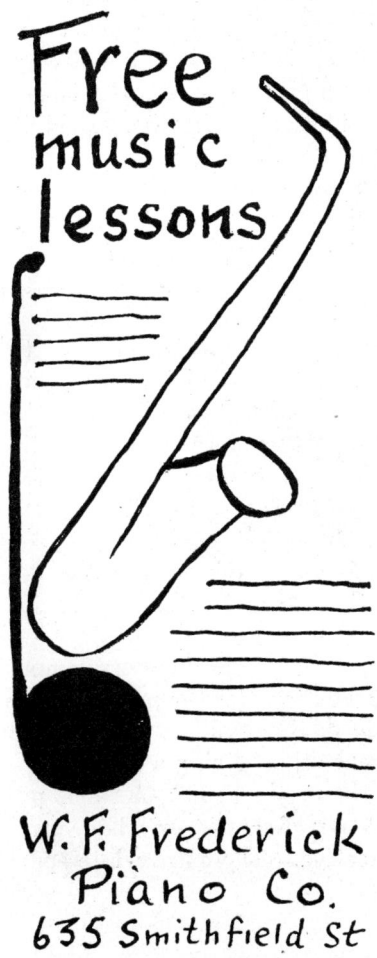

Exhibit 70-*b*.—Suggested simplification of the advertisement reproduced in Exhibit 70-*a*.

Black background is not to be recommended where the white lettering must be small, but for such a headline as that of Exhibit 70-*a*, the effect might be distinctive had the surrounding advertisements been mostly black type against white background.

In sketching Exhibit 70-*b* as a suggestion for improvement, no attempt has been made to use the black background, though —as already indicated—this treatment is not condemned. An effort has been made to simplify the display and to use the white space so as to give greater emphasis to the two principal displays and illustrative feature. Exhibit 70-*a* contains an excessive amount of border and black background, and the display effect is made worse by having all the text in black-faced type. A light-faced text type would give a pleasing contrast to the rather strong display features.

Long lines are wearisome to the eye. Short lines and short paragraphs look inviting.

Avoid the use of numerous *sizes* of body type in a single advertisement. Note how the best looking books, magazines and newspapers are set almost entirely in one size of body type. Two sizes should be enough for any one advertisement. Have at least two to four points difference when two sizes of type are used. The difference may even be as great as six points, with advantage. The contrast is more striking when there is this decided difference, such as 6-point or 8-point following 12-point, rather than where such sizes as 10-point and 9-point are used close together.

Likewise, avoid many variations of alignment. Give different sections of body matter the same indention and see how much more inviting they will be than if each maintains a different alignment, thus giving a zigzag appearance to the to the edges of the type matter. A *single* paragraph or list set in somewhat narrower measure than surrounding matter may be very effective. The extra white space on each side "sets it off."

The eye resents the constant readjustment necessary when body matter is set in many sizes of type and different lengths of line.

When a word or a sentence is to be emphasized in body matter, use italics in preference to bold face. Bold face stands out too much and mars the general pattern with unpleasant "spottiness." Italics, though useful for emphasis, are unsatisfactory where used for entire paragraphs. They put a check on the reader's speed.

Text may be made easier to read by the use of:

1. Short lines
2. Frequent paragraphs
3. Leads between lines
4. Generous indention of first lines
5. Extra space between paragraphs.

Crowding against borders or column rules makes text matter more difficult to read.

Emphasis is secured for headings by setting them in larger and bolder type. Emphasis may be secured for introductory paragraphs and other important text matter in the same manner, though usually sufficient emphasis is given by body type one or two sizes larger than that used for the remainder of the text.

Sometimes unusual prominence may be given by setting a paragraph in type several sizes *smaller* than the other matter and surrounding it liberally with white space.

In advertisements of fair size, extra attention as well as in increased legibility may be attained by *panelling* certain text that can stand apart from the other matter (see Exhibit 68).

Never use more than one face or "family" of type for text matter. Different sizes of the same face will give ample variation, and a much more pleasing ensemble.

As between extremely small type and extremely large type, when used at any length for text matter, very large type is the less readable and tempting of the two, that is, in such advertising as newspaper advertising.

Do not be afraid that people will not read your advertisement when it is set in moderate sized type. Look at the news columns of any city newspaper, and think of the millions of men and women who read thousands of columns of small type like that every day. Just look out for newsy copy, good arrangement, interesting headlines and other essentials here covered.

What Emphasis Should Be Given to Price.—Admitting that price is one of the most important factors of any retail advertisement, it does not follow that it is always, or even usually, necessary to "shout" prices in large-sized, bold face.

Equal prominence can be given to prices in a much lower tone, by setting the figures apart and surrounding them with white space.

A number of arrangements can be devised that will make prices stand out for easy reading without the use of heavy, black-faced type.

Lighter figures give all the advantages of naming low prices without forcing the reader to think of low price as the main reason for buying. Every reader senses more than the words when he reads. This is another reason for giving the typography of advertisements careful study.

Let the Signature Be Legible.—Most retail advertisements are to be answered in person.

The signature or name-plate tells the reader where to go.

Let the letters of your signature take a distinctive form, so that it may in time attain trade-mark value. But be sure that the signature of your advertisements may be read instantly and without any chance of error by any reader who sees it. Do not allow the desire for "curlicues" or fancy lettering tempt you to depart from what is clear and readable.

Include your street address, although you are *sure* that every man, woman and child within buying radius of your store knows just where it is.

Short signatures possess advantages over those of greater length. A short name like Macy's permits large display and is easy to remember.

Although the word signature suggests placing the name at the bottom, sometimes it is advisable to place the signature at the top. Some advertisers find it advisable to have a signature at both top and bottom.

Layouts as an Aid to Effective Typography.—A layout should be a help to the advertiser as well as to the printer.

A layout the exact size your advertisement is to be should prevent you from over-crowding the space as well as from calling for impossible or inappropriate arrangements.

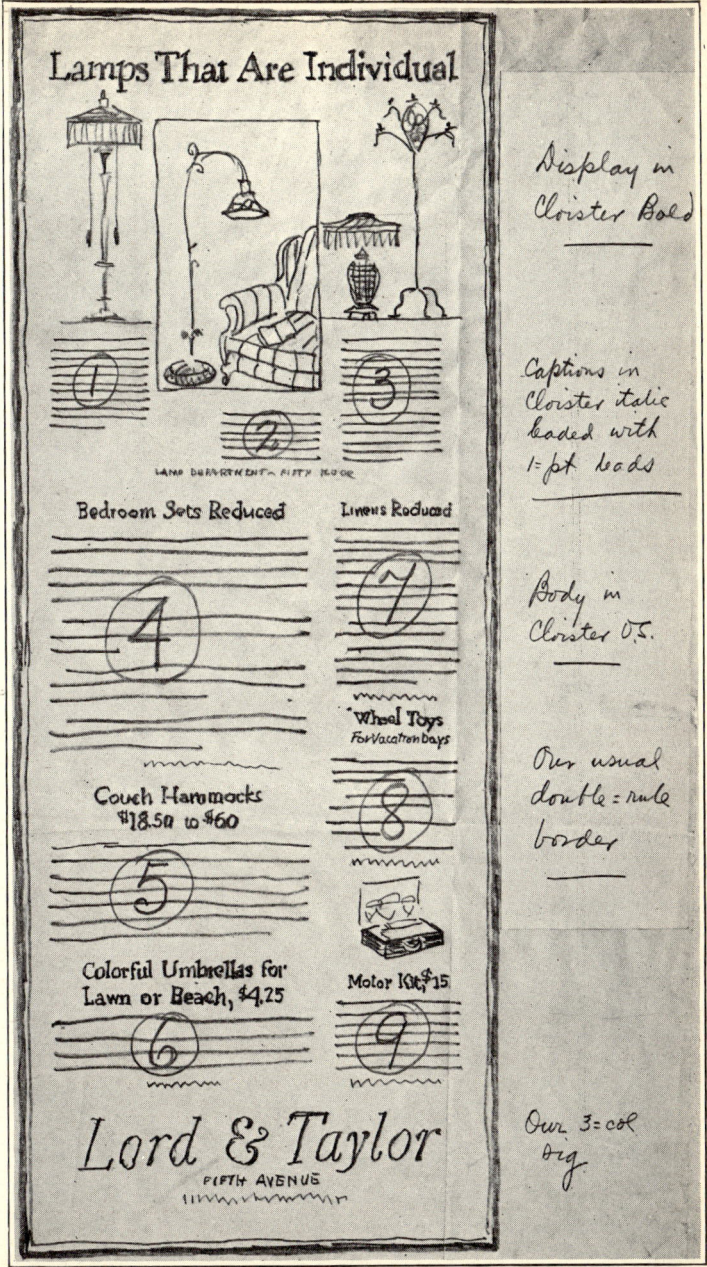

Exhibit 71-a.—Layout of a 16-inch, three-column newspaper advertisement for a large store. The various sections of the copy manuscript are lettered so as to "key" with the layout. If an advertiser of this class uses the same border regularly, time can be saved by indicating merely the corners.

Lamps That Are Individual

The junior floor lamp, above, with slender shaft of wood finished in antiqued silver and gold, tipped with an amethyst finial. The oval-shaped shade is of putty Georgette lined with rose, banded with book and black festoon and edged with silk fringe. 2 lights, $80.

Above — A wrought iron bridge lamp with adjustable shaft and socket, finished in polychrome. The shade is decorated parchment. 14 inches. $37.50

Chinese porcelain lamp, above right, ginger-jar base. Flat Empire shade is of putty Georgette lined with rose, lined with ocean blue and edged with tucking and silk fringe. 22 inches. 2 lights, $120.

Italian iron candlestick, beautifully proportioned, medallion with hand-hammered flower design. Tripod base. Five candle holders, $32.50.

LAMP DEPARTMENT — FIFTH FLOOR

Bedroom Sets Reduced

For a few days only we have reduced prices on four of our most popular bedroom sets. They are as follows:

A walnut set of Louis XVI. motif, consisting of double bed, bureau, chifferobe, dressing table, chair and bench, $350.

A Louis XVI. walnut set with double bed, dressing table, chifferobe, bureau, chair and bench, $375.

A Hepplewhite set of walnut combined with other wood, double bed, dressing table, chifferobe, bureau, bench and chair, $375.

A Louis XVI. set in two-tone walnut, consisting of double bed, dressing table, chifferobe, bureau, chair and bench, $400.

SIXTH FLOOR

Couch Hammocks
$18.50 to $60

Make your porch more livable. A happier place in which to rest. An upholstered couch hammock will add color and comfort. In our large assortment of these hammocks there is a choice of cretonne and plain striped duck coverings in various colors. All have upholstered, button-tufted backs and roll-edged mattresses. Awning and stands extra.

Colorful Umbrellas for
Lawn or Beach, $4.25

Made of heavy canvas. Variety of colors, such as orange and black, Harvard crimson and natural khaki. 6 feet in diameter. Adjustable wooden handle. Can be folded compactly to fit into your car.

FIFTH FLOOR

Linens Reduced

The following three items have just been greatly reduced, and offer exceptional opportunities for investing in the quantities you need.

Irish Linen Damask — Unbleached good weight and quality, 70 inches wide, a yard, $2

Glass Towels — Pure Irish linen weft, a dozen, $3.50.

Damask Table Cloths — All linen, splendid quality for general use, variety of designs, 2 x 2½ yards, $4.75.

SECOND FLOOR

Wheel Toys
For Vacation Days

Express Wagons — with rubber tired disk wheels with brake at $8 up to $12.75.

Velocipedes — "Iver Johnson," $16.50 to $19.50.

Bicycles — "Iver Johnson," $30 to $40.

Biplane Flyers, $4.50 and up.

SEVENTH FLOOR

Motor Kit, $15

This motor kit holds all the equipment to make six people enjoy a picnic — plates, cups, silver, 2 large sandwich boxes and space for two 1 quart Thermos bottles. Built for a strenuous outdoor life!

SEVENTH FLOOR

Lord & Taylor

FIFTH AVENUE
TELEPHONE FITZROY 1900

EXHIBIT 71-*b*.—Reproduction of the setting of the Lord & Taylor advertisement indicated by the layout in Exhibit 71-*a*.

EXHIBIT 72-a.—Pencil layout for a 10-inch, three-column newspaper advertisement.

Four Financial Hints For Travelers

1. *Care of Securities:* —All of the detail work connected with the proper care of your securities during your absence can be taken over by this Company. Our Customers' Securities Department will act practically as your financial secretary and carry out your instructions minutely. The income from your bonds, stocks, mortgages, etc., will be collected promptly and credited to your account or remitted to any address you wish. We will also notify you, whenever possible, of stock rights, called bonds, etc., and buy sell or deliver securities for you upon order. Our booklet, "Your Financial Secretary," sent upon request, gives full information concerning this service.

2. *Travel Funds:* —At each of our offices you can secure Letters of Credit and A·B·A Travelers' Cheques and thus solve your "travel money" problems.

3. *Safe-Deposit for Valuables:* —At our Fifth Avenue Office, our Fifty-seventh Street and Madison Avenue Office and our Paris Office, we have safe-deposit boxes where you can safely and conveniently leave your securities, jewelry and other similar valuables.

4. *Special Service for Holders of A·B·A Cheques and Bankers Trust Company Letters of Credit:* —If you are going to Europe, the Travel Department of our Paris Office can obtain passport vises for you, receive and forward mail and cables, supply reliable information regarding travel, shopping and residence abroad, and render many other special services.

BANKERS TRUST COMPANY

Downtown Office: Fifth Avenue Office:
16 Wall Street at 42nd Street

57th Street Office: Paris Office:
at Madison Avenue 3 & 5 Place Vendome

EXHIBIT 72-*b*.—Reproduction of setting from the layout shown in Exhibit 72-*a*. A seasonable dignified, well displayed advertisement. As the lower illustration is in a light tone, the balance of the composition is excellent.

EXHIBIT 73.—Layout of a single-column food advertisement in which the copy descriptions are confined to two lines under each of the sub-heads. With such a layout, the printer has no difficulty in setting up an effective "price-list" style of advertising.

Exhibit 74.—Layout of a small advertisement that combines a simple illustration with effective display of five attractively priced products.

Even a crude sketch will explain your ideas to the printer better than mere words and a profusion of gestures. It will save many last-minute alterations and prevent arguments as to instructions.

The layouts indicated by Exhibits 71-*a* and 72-*a* are more carefully prepared than are most layouts that come to a newspaper composing room, but they indicate a good standard of practice.

Exhibits 73 and 74 appeared originally in the *Progressive Grocer* and are shown here through the courtesy of the publishers. While the style of these two advertisements is well adapted to the grocery business, the address of the store might be an aid to some readers.

Unless the planner of the advertising letters readily, there is no need for attempting to match type styles closely. It is sufficient to indicate approximately the size and strength the display type that is to be used should be.

Exhibit 75 suggests how a regular user of newspaper space may save himself and the newspaper workers misunderstandings, labor and loss of time.

Some advertisers, by the establishing of a standard style for their advertising, have publishers and printers so familiar with the settings desired that a rough or hurried layout answers all practical purposes. In the case of the smaller advertisements, where there is not likely to be great variation in the arrangement of illustrations or sections, the advertiser can go further and establish a number of standard layouts or arrangements, numbering them or referring to certain dates of the newspaper; then all that is necessary in the way of instructions is something like the following:

"Set up by Layout A."

"Run in style of our June 14 ad."

Exhibit 76 offers some suggestions as to types that afford distinctive displays.

Foreman of Composing Room
*Publication*_____

Follow these instructions when setting advertisements for Clarke Brothers

We wish to cooperate with you in securing for our advertisements the most effective display, to the end that they may be attractive and easy to read.

To facilitate your work and to avoid misunderstandings, the copy for each of our advertisements will be accompanied by a layout that will indicate the general arrangement.

Other points which might be open to question are covered in the following suggestions. A careful study and observance of these suggestions will obviate the need for resettings, and will prevent the costly delays which so often result from alterations and revisions.

Border
In every advertisement for Clarke Brothers, large or small, use, as indicated by layout, a rule border like the one shown here.

▬▬ ▬▬ ▬▬ ▬▬ ▬▬ ▬▬ ▬▬

This border is not to be used on any other advertisement appearing in your paper.

Display Lines
Set all display lines in Caslon Bold.

Only such lines as are indicated on the layout are to be displayed.

All display lines are to be set in lower-case letters, except that the first word of each display and all proper nouns are to be capitalized.

Never under any condition use condensed type.

Wide letter-spacing is to be avoided. If normal spacing between words is not sufficient, shorten the line or use some other expedient.

Do not use punctuation marks in display lines if you can avoid it without confusing the meaning. Periods are necessary only after abbreviations.

Body Matter
Use Caslon Old Style for all body matter.

The space to be occupied by each section of text is shown on the layout. That will indicate to you the *size* of type to be used.

The width in which body matter is to be set is approximately indicated on the layout.

The maximum widths in which body type may be set are as follows:

6-point	2 inches
8-point	2½ inches
10-point	3 inches
12-point	3½ inches

Spacing
The layout is your general guide for the distribution of white space.

Use slightly less space between columns than between border and type matter.

Surround display lines generously with white, using a little less below than above.

Cuts
The location of each cut is clearly indicated on the layout. Do not change the arrangement.

Each cut is numbered on the bottom to correspond with the number on the layout.

Cuts must not be crowded against type matter.

All cuts are to be returned promptly when advertisement has been "killed."

Bold Face
Bold face is not to be used for emphasis or for any other purpose except headlines, as indicated.

Where words in the text require emphasis, use italics.

Captions
Set captions for cuts in 6-point Caslon O. S. lower case. Lead with 1-point leads and place each close to the cut to which it relates.

Name Plate
Name plates have been supplied you in 1-, 2-, 3-, 4- and 6-column widths.

In each advertisement the name plate must correspond with the width of the advertisement. That is, a 1- or 2-column name plate must not be used in a 3-column advertisement.

In 1-, 2- and 3-column advertisements, the name plate is to appear at the bottom. In larger sizes, the name plate is to appear at both top and bottom.

The Layout
Considerable time has been spent on each of the layouts sent you, to insure a typographical arrangement that will give our advertisements the maximum selling power.

At times, perhaps, the layout will ask you to do the impossible. At such times, we shall be glad to receive your suggestions. More often you will find the layout working with you to save time and get better results.

Address
The full street address must appear under the name-plate in each advertisement.

Proofs and O.K.'s
You are not authorized to run any advertisement until you have a fully O.K.'d proof.

Do not make any change or alteration from our copy and layout until you have communicated with us and received our approval.

CLARKE BROTHERS

Exhibit 75.—A "style card" or set of directions that saves time and facilitates good composition.

A selection of type faces suitable for retail advertisements

for display:

Caslon Old Style
Caslon Old Style Italic
Caslon Bold
Caslon Bold Italic
Bodoni
Bodoni Italic
Bodoni Bold
Bodoni Bold Italic
Goudy Old Style
Goudy Old Style Italic
Goudy Bold
Goudy Bold Italic
Cloister Bold
Cloister Bold Italic
Century Bold
Scotch Roman
Scotch Roman Italic
Cheltenham Bold
Cheltenham Bold Italic
Bookman Old Style

for body matter:

Caslon Old Style

Goudy Old Style

Bookman Old Style

Cloister Old Style

NOTE:

This list does not exhaust the many good type faces now available for advertising. But the types named here offer an ample selection.

Old style Roman (this type) is, of course, always in order as body-matter type but is not as distinctive as a less used face.

Some types such as Cheltenham Old Style (in which this paragraph is set) have faces so small that, in the smaller sizes, they fill easily and blur when printed on newspaper stock.

EXHIBIT 76.

ADDITIONAL SUGGESTIONS ON DISPLAY AND RELATED SUBJECTS

By S. Roland Hall

The following suggestions, while related more or less directly to the various topics discussed by Mr. Boren in preceding pages express particularly the views of the author of this volume on some phases of retail advertising. It should also be mentioned that Exhibits 64, 65, 66, 67, 68, 69, 70, *a* and *b*, 73 and 74 inserted in Mr. Boren's explanations, are selections made by the author to illustrate points brought out by Mr. Boren.

Distinctive Typography.—Advertising gains in individuality and distinctiveness when the advertiser adopts an appropriate type or other display treatment. He need not stick slavishly to such a style until it becomes commonplace or possibly boring to readers, but he can make it characteristic of all or most of his announcements.

This idea may be applied to both display and text type, as well as to the use of borders and signature, or it may include only one or two of these elements of display. Sometimes, merely a distinctive type used for a main or a sub-heading is enough to make the advertiser's offering distinctive. Such a type may be one particularly appropriate to the business represented, or to some article that is advertised. A tea room, for example, planned in Japanese style, could very appropriately have a Japanese style of lettering for its signs, as well as for its newspaper advertising. This style of display is very appropriately carried out in the Real Silk lettering reproduced in Exhibit 77.

The display "Stripes," reproduced in Exhibit 77, was used in connection with an advertisement by one of the prominent New York retailers of a fashionable offering of striped coats for women. Having the lettering such that it of itself suggests stripes made this advertisement much more distinctive and probably more effective than it would have been had the display heading been in ordinary display type.

Of the various examples shown in Exhibit 77, the three featuring Real Silk, Art Metal and Alpha Cement are the

Brick

REAL SILK

STRIPES

Art Metal

HEAT

ALPHA CEMENT

EXHIBIT 77.—These examples show how special types of hand-lettering can be used in obtaining display lines that are particularly harmonious with the subjects of the advertisements.

more simple and usable. Some lettering of this character is useful only as a main display.

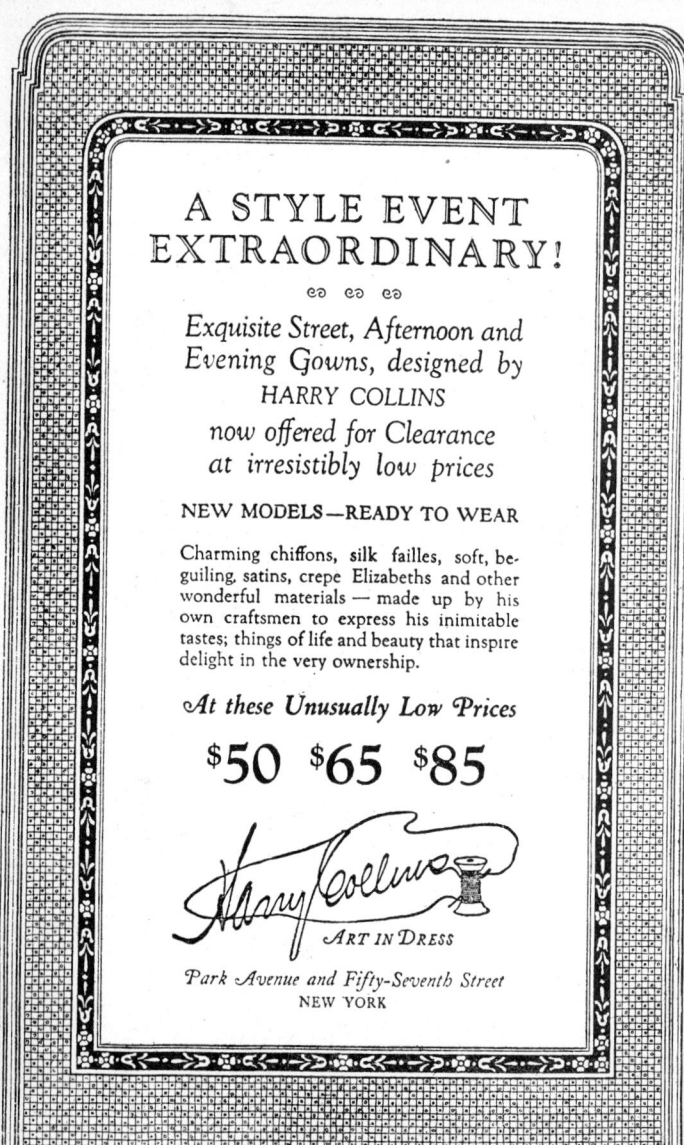

Exhibit 78.—Inappropriate border treatment that takes up much space and obscures the meaning of the headline. Originally, a three-column, 10-inch advertisement.

Excessive Display and Wasteful Borders.—Two of the most conspicuous faults of newspaper advertising are excessive use of heavy display lines and the employment of borders that have no real harmonious or illustrative application to the subject of the advertisement but merely take up costly space. Many advertisers appear to prepare their messages under the misguided notion that the more display lines inserted and the greater the use of all-capital displays, the more forceful are their appeals.

In Exhibit 78 is reproduced an advertisement that has a "different look" and yet has little in its favor. The broad border, while conspicuous enough to dominate a newspaper page, occupies much expensive space and has no apparent connection with the subject of the advertisement. The heaviness of this border and the all-capital setting of the headline obscure the meaning, unless the reader pores over the heading. "Irresistibly low prices" is an extravagant expression that good copy-writers will not use.

This advertiser would have done better had he "blue-penciled" the upper part of his copy, letting his message begin with "New Models—Ready to Wear."

With some appropriate border treatment, that would have been more suggestive of the work of a good designer, this message could have been effectively presented in about half its original space, which was 10 inches across three columns.

Position of Signature.—Some very well known stores who deem their names to be a better index or attention-commander than any merchandise they offer carry their names at the top of all, or nearly all, advertisements. The eye undoubtedly travels along the top of advertisements and pages, for the simple reason that we read from the top downward. Hence, when stores are so well known that readers look for their announcements, or are impelled to read such messages when they see a name that commands their confidence, the position of the signature at the top of the advertisement is justified. From a display point of view, however, this position of the signature is unfortunate, for it usually detracts from the power of a headline. In those cases where a headline deals with an important event or offering, the layout providing for signature at bottom gives a better opportunity for a logically presented message and well balanced typography.

Exhibit 79-a is an example of inappropriate placing of signature, as well as excessive display. In such a small advertisement as this (originally 3½ inches deep, across two columns), the headline and a bottom signature would be so close together that the eye would catch both almost immediately. As the advertisement stands, the signature at the

Exhibit 79-a.—All display and consequently poor display.

top takes away from the effectiveness of the offer of "560 new summer hats at $5.50." This thought is really the headline and is entitled to headline position.

Such explanations as the need for vacating the premises would be set more appropriately in readable, text type.

An advertiser always has much to gain by leaving out of his copy hackneyed expressions such as "for quick clearance," and so on. If his reason for a special sale is a change of location, he should make this explanation simply and believably, such as, "We move June 1 to ———. This week we offer our present stock of 560 new summer hats at just $5.50 each."

In place of the rather abrupt, "All sales final—No exchanges," which may possibly excite some suspicion as to the real value of the offering, it seems that this advertiser might do well to explain that on account of the special circumstances and the unusual price, he cannot offer the usual exchange privilege.

In remodelling such an advertisement as that shown in Exhibit 79-a, it is necessary to make a fresh start with both copy and display. After all, a change of location of this advertiser's business is not of paramount interest to the reader, unless it happened that it were a favorite store. The topic of real interest is the opportunity to get new summer hats at $5.50 because of the proposed change.

It seems well, therefore, to adopt a new headline, "Your choice of 360 new summer hats at $5.50." The original amount of space—3½ inches across two columns—gives ample room for the explanation about the move to be made in a legible text

Exhibit 79-b.—Rearrangement of the advertisement shown in Exhibit 79-a. This gives the real message of the copy a better chance.

type of good size, so that this part of the message will be caught almost as soon as the headline.

Exhibit 79-b is a suggestion for an improved arrangement. The italic display lettering is again suggested for the signature, because very likely this style of signature display is used regularly by this store as an identifying mark. The arrangement of 79-b, which is only one of a dozen or more appropriate layouts of a combination consisting of a newsy headline, the signature and a small amount of copy, encourages a reading of the advertiser's message.

Although the argument is rather against stressing the removal as the principal thought, it would be possible to make an effective layout from a display point of view by featuring "We must move" at the top of the composition, following this by a sentence or two of explanation, and then featuring in a sub-display the real message to womankind—"360 of these new summer hats to be sold at only $5.50" This arrangement is indicated by Exhibit 79-*c*.

We must move ═══

June 1 is our last day at this address, and so on—

———————————
———————————
———————————

360 of these new summer hats to be sold at only **$5.50**

The Fifth Avenue Shop
349 Fifth Avenue, at 34th St.

Exhibit 79-*c*.—Another arrangement of the advertisement reproduced in Exhibit 79-*a*.

Store Addresses.—Store addresses should be made a part of all advertising. Not only does this facilitate the work of the post-office department and is asked for by post-office officials as an aid to giving good service, but store addresses are a needed guide to many people who cannot be expected to be familiar with the location of a store, however big it may be. Some large, well known stores do not give this information in advertising and even go so far as to have no name appear on their buildings. Such merchants may possibly feel that they gain something in the way of dignity by having prospective customers inquire how they can find the store. But if the truth could be known it is probable that much more is lost than is gained by such procedure. Something is due to newcomers and visitors as well as out-of-town buyers who want to address the advertiser.

PLANNING NEWSPAPER ADVERTISING

Give Location of Goods in Large Stores.—In advertising special offerings in a large store it is usually important to give the location of the goods advertised. Unfortunately, salespeople and sometimes even the floor-walkers are not able to direct incoming customers to just the department or section of a floor where advertised goods may be found. Consequently, it is worth while adding such directions as "On sale Tuesday in the basement," "Monday in the Sporting Goods Department," "Fourth floor, opposite elevators," and so on.

Furnish Printers with Typewritten Copy.—Typewriting is more than an aid to rapid writing in preparing copy for advertising. If affords a ready method of figuring the amount of copy required to fill a certain space. For example, the usual typewritten page with 72 spaces to the line will run about 12 words to the line, or about 300 words to the letter-sized sheet of paper, having the material double-spaced.

It is comparatively easy for a copy-writer to figure out elite or any other style of typewriter type so that he knows about how many pages of typewritten matter it takes to fill a certain space in the newspaper. In this way it is easier to exactly fill a desired space.

Besides, with typewritten copy to follow, the printer or compositor is less likely to make mistakes in setting the advertisement and is able to furnish cleaner proofs.

Practice of R. H. Macy & Company.—All R. H. Macy & Company layouts are sent to the printer on regular layout paper bearing a plain rule border. This border is marked along the side in agate-line units of 20—20, 40, 60, 80—and so on, up to 280, when the division units are in multiples of 5— 280, 285, 290, 295 and 300. This division makes the layout adaptable to all newspapers, no matter whether the column happens to be 285 agate lines or 300 agate lines.

At the top, this layout form bears the printed line: "Use regular Macy border and corner name cuts." By this it will be seen that with respect to certain features, the layout is more or less of a "key layout." In all other respects, however, the Macy advertising department sketches in on each layout just what it wishes done by the newspaper setting up the advertisement.

Lord & Taylor's Method.—In order to secure uniform and distinctive arrangement for all advertising, some of the leading stores go so far as to have their copy set up in a job printing shop. The Lord & Taylor advertisement, Exhibit 71-b, is an example of this method.

Lord & Taylor give the following information:

> None of our newspaper advertisements are set by the publications themselves. The type, size and styles are standard with us. We merely indicate to the printer whether a heading is to be Roman or Italic. All notations—"Second Floor," "Fourth Floor"—are always set in the same style. We furnish the newspapers with heavily coated proofs for reproduction.

Such a plan naturally means working a little further ahead than some stores do with their advertising.

This Lord & Taylor plan is followed nowadays by a large number of New York stores. Evidently it has been found that the superior results warrant the extra cost and trouble. The newspapers make their plates by the photo-engraving method from first-class complete proofs of the advertisements.

Nevertheless, the general practice throughout the country is that of furnishing copy direct to the newspapers and having the newspaper office attend to all the details of setting up the advertisement. The various hints in this Section show how care and a little forethought will aid greatly in getting good results from publishers.

The Problem of the Small Advertisement.—The small advertisement needs careful planning, even more than the large advertisement, because it has no great expanse to draw attention. To stand out, it must be distinctive, both in the copy and display arrangement. There is great danger of its being swamped or buried unless these essentials are provided. There are a large number of advertisers that can only use small space with profit. Small advertisements call for striking headlines, concise, convincing copy and impressive displays.

There are many ways in which the principles covered in the preceding pages of this Section can be applied so as to yield distinctive treatment for the small advertisement, as well as larger space. Exhibits 80, 81, and 82 suggest three ways.

PLANNING NEWSPAPER ADVERTISING

In the next two Exhibits, Nos. 83 and 84, the author of this volume attempts to show how a little study will bring about great improvement in a simple newspaper message.

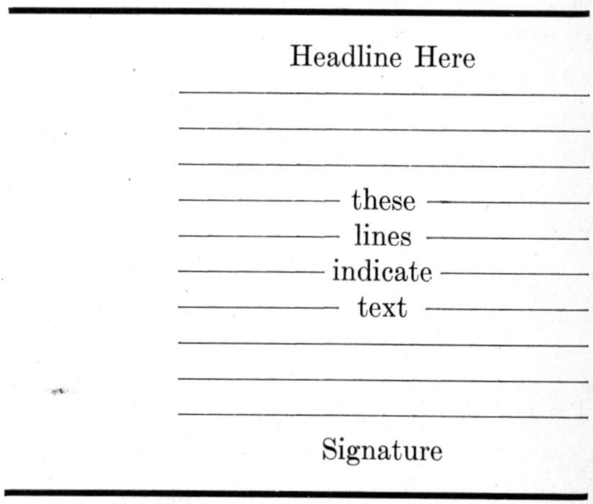

Headline Here

——————— these ———————
——————— lines ———————
——————— indicate ———————
——————— text ———————

Signature

EXHIBIT 80.—Leaving a good margin of white space on one side of a narrow column of text, as here indicated, is one good way of securing contrast and easy reading.

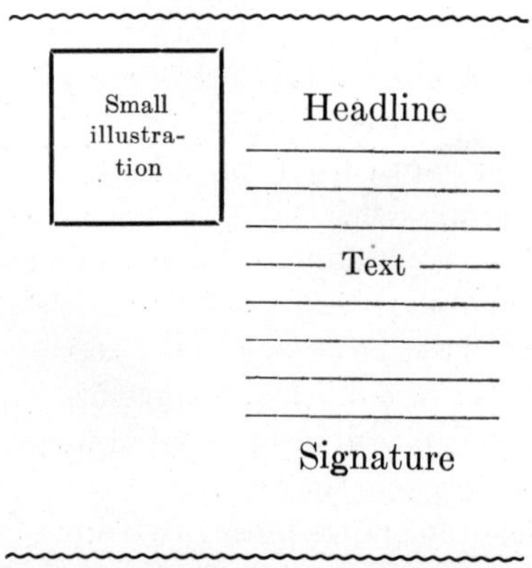

Small illustration

Headline

——— Text ———

Signature

EXHIBIT 81.—Another variation of white-space treatment.

EXHIBIT 82.—One suggestion for unusual arrangement of illustration, border and signature.

Study Exhibit 83. In the first place, the copy is mediocre. The main feature of the message is not something about the meals of the restaurant, but a "direct-command" heading of the shouting variety, to eat at the restaurant named. In this respect the advertisement resembles the "barking" salesman who might stand at the door of the restaurant and shout "Eat here." Patrons of restaurants are more interested in reasons for eating at a given place.

The first sentence of the text is the best one, but even that is too general to mean much. It at least, however, contains the headline-thought nicely buried!

The final sentence of copy is of the old, hackneyed variety that makes no impression.

By changing the copy around a little, "Old fashioned cooking" and "reasonable prices" can be made the two displays. These two displays can be placed at the top and bottom of the space and made to stand out by a little white-space treatment. A small piece of rule placed in an unusual way gives the advertisement some display distinction.

It is likely that the things most interesting to people about the restaurant are the things to eat. Therefore, it seems well to change the copy. If the advertiser hasn't some of these distinctive things about his bill of fare, he ought to have them. Otherwise, there is little need of advertising. He probably hasn't the framed bill of fare at his doorway nor the big oyster sign, but a good advertising man would encourage the advertiser to adopt some feature of this kind. So, for the sake of comparison between the old copy and the new, these features will be added. This is only another way of saying that in order to have good displays the advertiser must have a real message to convey. Exhibit 84 shows the advertisement as it was finally revised and set up.

EAT AT THE

Easton Oyster and Lunch House

Van C. Kemmerer, Mgr.

Clean, wholesome, old-fashioned cooking at reasonable prices.
Give us a trial and be convinced.

45 North 4th St.

EXHIBIT 83.—An unattractive display of commonplace copy.

Old fashioned cooking

Daily supply of fresh sea-foods and meats.

Appetizing sandwiches. Three plate-lunch specials daily.

See bill of fare at the doorway under the big oyster sign—45 North Fourth Street.

Easton Oyster and Lunch House

reasonable prices

EXHIBIT 84.—A revised appeal for the restaurant exploited in Exhibit 83.

Importance of Having a Meaty Message.—All the details of an advertisement merit careful attention and must have it if the advertiser is to get a proper return for his money. Yet it is likely that in advertising circles relatively too much importance is often given to some such detail as typography, llustration, border treatment, when the advertisement really stands or falls on the fundamental message that it conveys. Charles R. Mears, a well known advertising counselor of Cleveand, Ohio, speaking on this topic before the Associated Advertising Clubs of the World in 1923, said:

The ability to reach into the minds of people and move them toward your counters is applied art in a very high sense. But the word "art" does not here refer to your unique illustrations, "foxy" borders, outstanding type dress or those boxed-up panels that are so dear to the heart of innumerable advertising people. These are more or less valuable, but, when you calmly analyze them, it is astonishing how large a proportion of all these elements have merely an attention value.

I do not underrate the importance of attention value. I do not underrate beautiful composition and layout. To make an advertising communication inviting to the eye is to give your communication an advantage over those which are not so distinguished. And yet, I wonder if some of these good looking advertisements of ours have not been prepared and published at the expense and to the damage of other elements. Such, for instance, as ease of reading, genuine sincerity and effectiveness of appeal. Do we not often attract attention to that which is not worth attending to?

As advertisers we must stir up the emotions of readers, and readers are perfectly willing to have their emotions stirred up, but they do not like too consciously to face the machinery which is doing the stirring. The finest art is imperceptible. And an emotional appeal, unless it is tactfully and delicately handled, becomes an absurdity.

Institutional advertising can be interpreted in several ways, notwithstanding which, there is only one way in which it can be applied. To start out and say, as one great Eastern store has recently done, that "We have at last become an institution," and so on, is putting the cart before the horse and stating a fact that the public cares very little about.

You are always safe in writing from the point of view of your public rather than in writing from the point of view of the store manager or of the goods on sale in the store. Cash in on your service, on your policies, on the personality of your store, but make your cashing in certain by expressing what you have to say from such point of view and in such language that the reader will have no difficulty in saying, "That's so."

Some Other Views on Good Newspaper Advertising.—Two other well known merchandising men have, in the Data Book of the Advertising Group of the National Retail Dry Goods Association, given some earnest views on how the common faults of retail advertising may be overcome.

D. A. Garber, assistant merchandise manager of Boggs & Buhl, Pittsburgh, Pa. says:

Advertising can be attractive without losing sight of all its other qualities to make it so. Likewise, it can be forceful without being bombastic, can be impressive without being flowery, and it will embody all the major better qualities if it is simple and truthful. These comprise the real vehicle, and the less it is encumbered with flowers and ink, the smoother and more rapid will be its progress. Department store advertising is "turned out" in such volume, and so frequently, that it becomes a habit rather than a profession if it is not guarded with all the devotion an artist expresses on every canvas his brush touches. I further believe that the greatest thought should be given the copy. A fountain can rise no higher than its source. No matter how much thought and money we spend on layout, type, art, etc., the force of an advertisement *will never* rise higher than its copy.

Ralph Underwood Brett, advertising manager of James McCreery & Company, says:

One of the best methods in advertising, is to get the facts about merchandise, and truthfully present them in a simple, straightforward convincing manner. Moments of warm enthusiasm are often disastrous to the vision of the buyer who quite unintentionally overstates his merchandise. In other words, the picture he presents is out of perspective. The copy-writer absorbs it, so through the combined efforts of the three the advertising is insincere: it conveys not only facts but the strained effect of overrating and overselling the merchandise. The mind of the reader as a result is confused and direct-action is not easily obtained.

There is little danger of the under-statement of merchandising facts. I do not believe this happens as frequently as the over-statement. It is usually a result of over-construction and lack of plan. I have yet to see the time when, if buyer and advertising manager get together, the true merits of an article cannot be exploited with such convincing power, that the advertisement would not sell goods.

SECTION VIII

MANUFACTURERS' SYNDICATED AND COOPERATIVE ADVERTISING

Extent of Syndicated Services for Retailers.—While many syndicated services offered retail advertisers consist only of newspaper plates, other services are offered, both by manufacturers' advertising departments and independent creators of advertising, that deal with all the various well known forms of advertising—newspaper plates, street-car cards, posters, window-displays and cards, counter cards and fixtures, illustrated letters, mailing cards and folders, series of follow-up letters, and so on.

These services are of great variety. Some are offered only in complete form. Others consist in part of stock matter and in part of material written separately for each subscriber to the service.

Much of this material, while usually lacking the individual touch of the local advertiser, is more economical and often better than the material that the retailer has the time or facilities for producing himself.

Rug-cleaning Service.—The service to carpet and rug cleaners, issued by Landers, Frary & Clark, through their United Vacuum Appliance Division, is typical of a number of advertising services. The material offered rug-cleaning departments and establishments by this firm consists of complete newspaper advertisements, attractive folders and booklets that tell about the modern carpet-cleaning process; blotters and post cards, for personal distribution or mailing; novel posterettes, to be used in packages or sent out with statements and other correspondence; colored lantern slides, for use in local moving-picture houses, letters and copy suggestions. Many of the folders, booklets, blotters, etc., are prepared in colors.

Rolls of Dirt Carried Away
Rolls of Cleanliness Brought Back

IN most homes rugs and carpets are cleaned about as thoroughly as a boy washes his face. All dirt is removed except what remains. Shampooing is the latest improved process for thoroughly cleaning carpets and rugs. The work is done with all the care of gentle hands. Pure soap and water are scrubbed into the fabric by a soft electric brush. All dirt is loosened, all grease spots are dissolved. A vacuum cleaner removes every particle of washed-out dirt, grit and grime, leaving the rug dry, clean and bright as new.

Put Your Cleaning up to Cleaners Who Know How

NO rug is too soiled to be perfectly cleaned by our Shampoo Process. Don't discard rugs and carpets because they are old and soiled. Let us shampoo *cleanliness* into them and you'll get more wear out of them. We'll roll them up, carry them away and return them to you with everything except the dirt.

YOUR IMPRINT HERE
No. X11C

X11C

EXHIBIT 85.—Syndicate newspaper advertisement furnished rug-cleaning establishments and departments by Landers, Frary & Clark. The headline of this advertisement is likely to catch the eyes of thrifty housewives.

In Exhibit 85 is reproduced one of the complete newspaper advertisements furnished retailers by this advertiser. Exhibit 86 is a reproduction from a photograph, showing a rug that has been partly scrubbed. Such an illustration has real convincing power.

Manufacturers' Plates and Other Material.—Most manufacturers are quite ready to furnish retailers with a variety of illustrations, or even plates of complete advertisements, if they are assured of the retailer's cooperation. Some of this advertising is up to a high standard and much better than the retailer could produce for himself, except by incurring considerable expense.

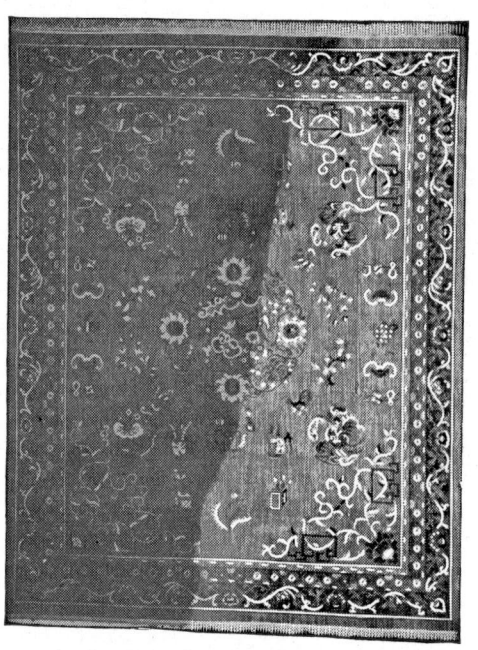

Exhibit 86.—One of the illustrations from a syndicate booklet service furnished rug cleaners. This illustration is reproduced in the booklet in the attractive natural colors of the rug, showing how the rug looks before and after cleaning. This is good "pictured salesmanship."

A common fault with manufacturers' advertising material, on the other hand, is that the manufacturer's advertising department is inclined to overlook the retailers' point of view and prepare the illustrations or plates as if they were to be inserted in space paid for by the manufacturer. That is, they over-emphasize the manufacturer's name, trade-mark, or other trade features.

It is just as difficult, in this department of advertising, to lay down a working rule as it is in other departments. The retailer may prefer to give a great deal of emphasis to such a well known name or trade-mark as that of the House of Kuppenheimer, for example. It may be good business for him to do that. In another instance, however, he may prefer

Coal That's All Coal—
Hourly Tested Cement

IF you have never heard of "clean coal", let us tell you that it's coal that is unusually free from dirt, rock or other impurities. It's the kind we buy and deliver to you.

And as for cement, we handle the well known ALPHA brand, tested hourly by the manufacturers while being made and guaranteed to run full strength to every bag.

We can give you a copy of the well illustrated ALPHA handbook on concrete building, showing how to make all sorts of concrete improvements—walks, walls, driveways, garages, foundations, tanks, etc.

Come in and get these practical helps and let us figure on your needs.

(Dealer's Name, Address and Phone Number)

EXHIBIT 87.—One of a series of double-column advertisements furnished building-material dealers by a manufacturer of cement. A pleasing feature of these plates was that they exploited other products carried by the retailer.

to use a good illustration furnished by the manufacturer but to eliminate the manufacturer's name or trade-mark.

Plates that May Be Used in Exploiting Several Commodities.—Some manufacturers have scored strongly with retail dealers by furnishing a variety of plates, some of which deal only with the manufacturer's goods and others on which ample room is left for the retailer to feature other products allied with the products of the manufacturer furnishing the plate. An example of this is indicated by Exhibit 87, which is a plate furnished by the Alpha Portland Cement Company to building-material dealers. There were half a dozen of these plates in a series of twenty double-column advertisements. A number of dealers who handle coal, feed, lime, etc., in addition to cement, were much pleased with plates that enabled them to exploit several products in one advertisement. Other dealers preferred to use the plates featuring Alpha Cement only.

A common complaint heard at retailers' conventions is that manufacturers "hog" the space in the plates they send out and sometimes hardly leave room for the dealer's signature. Retailers have been known to use the cold-chisel on plates sent out by manufacturers and use only the effective illustration.

Some manufacturers may do well to furnish plates consisting merely of good illustrations and good headlines, leaving the dealer to his own resources as to appropriate copy for text, or they may send along some proofs suggesting appropriate text but not incorporating this in the plate or finished advertisement. When this is done, retailers can use their own ideas as to changes in the text suggested. This, of course, leaves something to be done by the retailer. Where the group of retailers to which the illustrating service is sent is not very enterprising, it may be well to go to the other extreme and furnish plates that are complete in every respect, except as to signature.

The Plumb, Kodak, and Sharples examples give a good idea of the retail plates furnished by different manufacturers.

The enterprising retailer will find manufacturers generally more than willing to cooperate with him in furnishing good illustrations, if he will make his wants known. The retailer should, however, keep in mind that what he asks for should ordinarily be something that the manufacturer can, as a means of reducing expense, also supply to other retailers.

One big advantage of manufacturers' illustrations is that they show the exact goods sold by the retailer. Further-

EXHIBIT 88.—Small but pointed advertisements supplied by Fayette R. Plumb, Inc., to the retail trade.

These advertisements are designed with the view that they may either be published as separate small advertisements or made parts of the larger advertisements used by the retailer.

EXHIBIT 89.—One of the two-column advertisements supplied by Fayette R. Plumb, Inc., to the retail trade. The illustration is a fine example of simplicity, and would get attention on any page. The axe, or principal object of the advertisement, is given more prominence by showing only a part of the handle.

Painstaking Finishing

Your Kodak plus Kodak Film plus our developing and printing service—result, results.

We take pride in our finishing department—that means we take pains in our finishing.

Bring us your films— you'll like the results

EXHIBIT 90.

EXHIBIT 90.—Example of advertising supplied dealers by the Eastman Kodak Company. This advertisement not only exploits the products of the manufacturer but the service of the dealer.

Paste This In Your Hat

YOU know as well as we do that the only separator worth buying is one which *skims clean at any speed*. Then why try to get along without a Sharples Suction-feed— the only separator which, day in and day out, skims clean at any speed.

Ask some farmer who has owned a fixed-feed if he could get all the butter-fat all the time. Ask him if the bell that warns him when he is turning too slowly does any good *after* the butterfat has been lost. Then stop in and let us demonstrate the Sharples Suction-feed to you.

Other exclusive Sharples advantages are: Simple tubular bowl (no discs); knee-low supply tank; once-a-month oiling.

Sharples

SUCTION-FEED
CREAM SEPARATOR
Skims Clean at any Speed

EXHIBIT 91.

EXHIBIT 91.—Manufacturer's advertisement made up in two parts. This arrangement permits the dealer to extend his space as deeply as he needs in order to insert special copy.

more, such illustrating service usually costs the dealer nothing but his cooperation.

Sometimes, if the retailer is resourceful enough to put on a special campaign, he will find the manufacturer willing even to bear a part or the whole of the cost of the campaign in a local medium.

The style of the Sharples display, with borders merely at top and bottom, is a good style of plate for retailers, because there are no side borders to be cut and matched when the dealer wants to add copy of his own relating to the particular subject of the plate, or allied subjects. While many plates are made up by manufacturers in such a way that borders or other portions of the plate can be cut and additional matter inserted, this always means extra trouble and is an obstacle in the way of the use of the plate. Besides, local newspapers frequently make a botch of advertisements where plates have to be cut apart, through poor matching of borders, and so on.

In the case of the Sharples example, the national advertiser not having included his name at the top, naturally wishes to get it displayed at the bottom, in connection with the lower border. In general, however, it is better to have such plates made with plain lower borders, so that the aggressive local advertiser, after giving one article all the attention he wants to give in the first third or half of his copy space, may be free to devote the remainder of his space to his own copy ideas, on allied articles perhaps, without being bothered with having to incorporate a display line about the article first treated in the copy.

Some manufacturers get around the problem of appropriate illustrations and copy by furnishing plates merely of illustrations.

The Westinghouse Plan.—The advertisement reproduced in Exhibit 92 is one of a number of attractive plates furnished by the Westinghouse Electric & Manufacturing Company to its retailers. By cutting the plain border at the sides, retailers can use a plate of this kind with no expense for either illustration or plate work, and incorporate some individual advertising, either with reference to articles closely connected with the one illustrated, or with reference to the service of the store.

EXHIBIT 92.—One example of a great variety of attractive plates in the three-column, 10-inch size furnished retailers by the Westinghouse Electric & Manufacturing Company.

While the Westinghouse Company prefers to have its dealers use newspaper space three-columns wide and 10 inches deep in exploiting electrical devices, it also supplies advertisements in smaller size—two-columns wide by 6 ½ inches deep—to dealers who may believe, often with good reason, that they cannot afford to use large space for the exploiting of every specialty.

Realizing that a series of advertisements of this size runs up a considerable total, this electric manufacturer offers financial assistance to dealers and jobbers who are willing to cooperate properly in carrying out the local campaign.

Syndicated Illustrations.—There are a number of syndicated-illustration services available to retailers in every field. For a reasonable cost a retail merchant can secure weekly or monthly sheets, showing a variety of plates. If a retailer is in a position to use a reasonable amount of such advertising aids, he can usually get the exclusive right in his particular community.

Syndicated illustrations call for good judgment. Many of them are excellent value for the reasonable cost, while others are so far removed from the particular type of goods sold by the merchant or from his individual style of advertising that they are of no service. As already indicated, the resourceful merchant can often make good use of humor and sprightly treatment, but if he goes too far in this direction and makes a strained effort to tie up his argument with some cartoon series, he may attract attention temporarily, but really fail to impress the value of his goods or service in the community.

Exhibit 93 is a good example of a syndicate illustration that meets the need of the sporting goods store as well as anything it might have drawn for its own exclusive use, and the cost is much less. With a collection of plates of this kind, some featuring fishing goods, others baseball goods, others golf supplies, and so on, the advertiser of sporting goods will have no difficulty, at small cost, in giving all of his messages appropriate illustrated dress.

Exhibit 93 also illustrates how a simple, bold design, with one strong word across the top, makes an advertisement of medium size stand out. In its original size—6 inches deep

(*Courtesy, Advertising and Selling*).

EXHIBIT 93.—Example of high-class syndicate plate. The bold, single-word heading gives unusual strength.

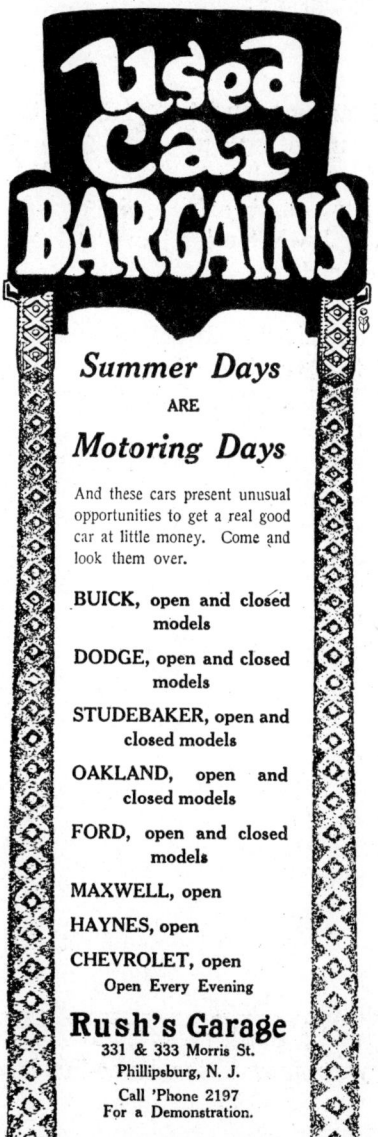

Exhibit 94.—Syndicated design that is based on an idea that is fundamentally appropriate—the subject of the advertisement. The execution of the idea, however, is poor, the decorative treatment being too heavy and the main display, "Used-Car Bargains," not readable enough.

across two columns—this plate easily had as much display strength as most advertisements of three-column width, 8 or 10 inches deep.

Exhibit 94 is an example of a syndicate headline plate and border that occupies a great deal of space without much distinctiveness. As reduced, the headline is really more readable than it was in its original size of two columns.

It is never worth while using hand-lettered headlines unless something is gained, either in legibility, good arrangement, or "atmosphere."

After studying this "used-car" advertisement for a while, it is apparent that the black background is designed as the rear of an automobile. The heavy border is a representation of the tread of the wheels of the car. The general idea of this illustration was not inappropriate. But if the background had been worked out so that at first glance it would have been identified as the back of a car and the tire border in such a way as not to take up so much space, the result would have been much better. The border as it stands robs the sub-displays of some of their effect.

Cooperative Material Furnished by Retailers' Association.— Some of the associations of retail merchants have undertaken to furnish their members advertising material and have done remarkably well.

An association of building-material dealers in New York State and New England, for example, furnishes members with attractive posters, showing a variety of neat homes; also mailing cards and folders, and an unusually effective series of illustrated letters.

Three books of plans are offered by this association—one large book to be kept by the building-material dealer in his own office, another to be sold to contractors and builders at a popular price, and a third, prepared at moderate expense, to be given away to prospective home-builders, or sold at a nominal price, according to the judgment of the local dealer. Some building-material dealers who have exploited these books aggressively have found that it is better to ask a small price for them than to give them away.

These associations realize that the large concerns selling building-material by mail and offering ready-cut homes have encroached extensively on the field of the local contractor and building-material dealer. They realize that these aggressive advertisers have used pictures and catalogues very successfully and that the day is past when the local man can sit in his office without the aid of a consistent publicity plan and expect people to come in regularly and solicit him about building a home.

The cooperative idea in such associations not only saves a great deal of money to the individual member, but provides an excellent variety of material. Furthermore, the use of such material by dealers leads to helpful discussions and exchange of experiences at the meetings of the members of the association.

Exhibit 95 is an example of cooperative advertising for home-builders, though not a specimen of the service of the association referred to. This exhibit is an example of the service provided to contractors by a technical magazine, *The Permanent Builder*. An issue of the magazine gives the contractor a blue-print plan-supplement that presents complete working drawings for an attractive, well planned house of the size and type that appeals to a large number of prospective home-builders. These plans are drawn by some well known architect. In the plan-supplement is a "quantity material survey" giving a full list of the materials required for building the house.

The cover of the particular issue of the magazine referred to showed an attractive illustration of the completed house. The magazine also contained an editorial article describing the various desirable features. As, however, the contractor cannot expect prospective home-owners to hunt him up in every case, a suitable plate for newspaper advertising is also furnished to any contractor-reader of the magazine who will ask for it. The contractor can run this advertising in the newspaper or as a direct-mail advertisement, as he prefers. This is a part of the service of the magazine and no charge is made for the electrotype. All the magazine requires of the contractor is that he send a copy of the newspaper or the circular in which the electrotype is used.

Own Your Home—But Build it *Permanent*

for Sale

This Enduringly-Built Eight-room House

A HOME you'll be proud to own—and one you'll always enjoy living in. A beautiful example of English architecture. Large light living room, library, dining room, pantry, kitchen, and two porches on the first floor, with four bedrooms and two baths on the second floor. Large attic. All rooms well-arranged and perfectly appointed with numerous built-in features.

Permanent, Fireproof
Stucco on Galvanized Steel Reinforcing Fabric

A permanently constructed, fire-resistive home like this costs you no more materially and is by far the most economical and enjoyable to live in. It minimizes repair and upkeep, depreciates but slightly, and always retains its attractive, well-conditioned appearance. We'll build it to suit your requirements.

See the complete plans at our office

"THE JACQUIS" $(Fill in Your Price)
Built ready for occupancy in 60 days

Your Name and Address Displayed Prominently Here

Numerous Other Designs to Select From

EXHIBIT 95.—One of a series of attractive syndicate advertisements furnished by *Permanent Builder* magazine to builders and contractors.

Other Kinds of Cooperative Effort.—The term "cooperative advertising" is more likely to suggest to the reader the combined efforts of a group of retailers in carrying out sales and advertising plans than the mere production of advertising material. Some suggestions on cooperative marketing efforts in overcoming outside competition and in drawing large crowds for market days, expositions, and so forth, will be found in Sections IX and XV.

SECTION IX

DIRECT ADVERTISING METHODS

WHAT DIRECT ADVERTISING IS AND DOES

Direct advertising is frequently understood as mail-order advertising. It may be that and it may not. Strictly speaking, direct advertising means merely a form of advertising in which the appeal is mailed or sent direct to the addressee or reader instead of being published in a newspaper, magazine or otherwise circulated broadcast. A great deal of the most effective direct-mail advertising is intended to bring customers to the store. Such advertising might, indeed, encourage a variety of methods of ordering—by mail or telephone or by a visit to the store.

Pointers from Retail Dry Goods Association.—Referring to direct advertising in the immediate community surrounding a large store, the following advice is offered in the Data Book of the National Retail Dry Goods Association:

A number of the larger stores say that the direct-mail offerings of lower- to medium-priced merchandise alone brought good results. Although some of the literature which these stores use presents the merchandise in appealing manner, both in illustration and text, yet the inducement offered the prospective buyer was to *shop by mail.* Accordingly, such publicity did not bring the customer into the store. In the case of other stores, classes in the community were appealed to which comprised people either having little time to shop, because of confining employment, or people too far removed from the store. Those of the latter who responded used the mails, because it would not have paid them, for the sake of the saving, to have incurred the traveling expense involved.

Our members have often questioned whether stress laid upon merchandising through mail-order solicitation encourages a healthy condition. If special or slow moving merchandise is featured exclusively, the public naturally tends to associate your store activities with those of the larger mail-order houses, and makes price comparisons as a natural consequence. Many argue that a retail department store is bound to experience no small difficulty in competing with a highly developed organization, such as the larger mail-order houses represent. Accordingly, not a few of our stores have concentrated their selling efforts by mail upon the better class of merchandise. They thereby sell the institution and the service it has to offer and eliminate from the public mind that comparison with mail-order houses which the offering of special or low-priced merchandise is bound to bring up. The direct-mail message should carry a cordial invitation to shop in your store and should stress your service. Personal contact can do more to build up the name of an organization than can any number of successive mail orders.

Analyzing the experience of stores that have successfully sold *all grades* of merchandise by direct mail, we find that these stores did not offer goods calculated to lessen the attendance of customers at the store, nor yet merchandise which the store felt would produce good attendance if advertised in the newspaper as a sales event.

The merchandise selected for direct-mail exploiting by these stores meets the following requirements:

1. It must be seasonal.

2. It must fully correspond to and be typical of the quality suggested in the publicity.

3. It must be offered to an appropriate clientele and be supported by suitable follow-up.

4. It must induce people not only to buy but to come into the store in order to buy. Usually the offerings are tied up with newspaper advertising.

5. The literature, in its physical make-up, must symbolize in the minds of those receiving it, the personality of the store and the character of the merchandise which it presents.

ORGANIZING THE MAILING-LIST WORK

A member of the National Retail Dry Goods Association, who has done enough effective direct advertising work to be convinced of the advisability of giving this type of selling effort more attention, has centralized responsibility for mailing-lists and the mechanical equipment for handling this type of advertising under the advertising manager of the store, supervised by the sales promotion manager. The compiling, correcting and organizing of mailing-lists is deemed so important that this work is placed in the hands of a capable young woman. General catalogue distribution is regarded as a separate feature. The department has specialized on multigraphed letters sent out on neat stationery, bearing the full address of the recipient. Special circulars are designed for the various departments, for package enclosures and for enclosing in daily correspondence and monthly bills. The following outline of a mailing-list of this store indicates the length to which it has gone in specializing:

Charge Account and Cash Customers (In town and out of town)
Special:
  List of Infants and Children:
    Obtained from: Birth Register
                     Infants' Department
                     Children's Shoe Department
                     Barber Shop—Register.
  List of Boys:
    Obtained from: Y. M. C. A.
                     Boy Scouts
                     Boys' Department
                     Barber Shop—Register.
  List of Girls: Ages 6 to 16:
    Obtained from: Junior Department
                     Schools
                     Girl Scouts
                     Y. W. C. A.
List of Men:
  Golf List—Obtained from Golf Clubs.
  Chauffeur List—Obtained from Social Register.
              Sent to owners of cars.
Sporting and Vacation List:
              Work up list of men who go hunting or go away for vacation annually.
University List: Faculty and Students.
Young Men Attending Out-of-Town Schools:
              General Men's and Young Men's List:
              Used for general announcements.
  Obtained from: Department Records
                 Y. M. C. A.
                 Engineers' Clubs
                 Sources mentioned above.
List of Women:
  Stout List: Compiled from all departments handling stout wear.
  Mothers' Lists: Mothers of Infants: Compiled in Infants' Department and from birth registration or birth notices.

Mothers of School Children: Compiled from School Records.
Young Women's List: Compiled from Y. W. C. A.
       High School
       Clubs.
Women Who Go to Winter and Summer Resorts:
     Compiled through society editors of newspapers and whatever sources possible.
Prominent Women: Compiled from Social Register
      College Women's Club
      All Women's Clubs.
Maids' List: Used to Sell Maids' Uniforms to Employers.
      Compiled from Social Register
      Exclusive Clubs
Nurses' List: Compiled from Hospital Lists.
General Women's List:
     Used for General Announcements.
     Compiled by combining the lists above.

Compilation of Classified Mailing-list for Bankers.—A mailing-list may be of great value to every local and retail advertiser if it is made up with care and kept up to date. Unfortunately, too often the retailer's mailing-list is one general list made up with no great care and rarely revised unless mail is returned as being undeliverable. Most mailing-lists would be much more effectively used if they were divided into groups. As an example of what might be done in this direction, the following is reviewed from some suggestions made by Mr. Edward Mott Woolley in *The Burroughs Clearing House.*

Before making any suggestions as to groups that might well make up a bank's mailing-list, Mr. Woolley cites the fact that for many years after owning a home he received regularly circular letters from the bank making the point that the beginning of a savings account was the first step toward owning a home. This was fine argument for the man who did not own a home and who had the longing to own one but it missed fire entirely with the home-owner. It showed at the outset that the bank knew little or nothing about the person addressed, which did not create a favorable impression. This personal experience suggests Mr. Woolley's first group—families that do not own homes. Names of these may be secured from lists of apartment-house dwellers and tenants of rented houses.

A second group mentioned by Mr. Woolley is the "home replacement group." This may be a list of home-owners who should be encouraged to save for additions to the home, a new set of furniture, new plumbing or any of the wants that develop after a house has been lived in for a number of years.

Lists of prospective patrons of the women's department, to be found in many banks, can be made up from the various women's clubs or organizations in any city. Some banks that have a women's department seem contented with providing a special window and a few chairs for women patrons but make no effort to help them with their investments or other financial matters unless specifically called upon.

A fourth group could be composed of children's names. Securing a small child's account usually means keeping the account after the child grows up. A special list of children of wealthy parents may be made up that will be of great value to the bank.

High-school students and pupils of private schools nearing the age of higher education constitute a group to whom a very definite appeal can be made.

The idea of saving for travel could be directed toward school teachers, college students of well-to-do families, and young men and women earning fair salaries.

In any city there are a number of organizations or societies which, though their treasuries may not boast many dollars, may well be on a bank's mailing-list. The fact that the funds of a society are deposited with a certain bank may influence members of the society to place their individual deposits with the same bank.

In the concluding paragraphs of his article Mr. Woolley suggests what he calls a list of "key" men and women. These are persons who, because of their social or business positions, would be able to influence many of their friends and acquaintances. Some of them may be found on the lists already mentioned, and they may include doctors, lawyers, teachers, nurses, welfare workers, the clergy, and city officials. In a city of large foreign population the finding of a few of these key men or women possessing influence among those of their own race would be likely to result in drawing many depositors to the bank who are not ordinarily reached.

Unusual Methods of Adding Names to Mailing-lists.— When a man has bought a hat at the store of King Brothers Company, Seattle, Wash., the salesman hands him a printed form reading:

Free! You will receive a special signature slip to go under your hat band, showing ownership of hat, by signing your name and address below. Please write plainly.

The old idea of getting something for nothing usually appeals. The store thus adds to its mailing-list, besides being able to hold customers in the store for a few more minutes, which often results in additional sales.

Firms that send out inspectors or collectors regularly have unusual opportunity to build up valuable mailing-lists and to create opportunities for immediate sales.

It has been found, for example, that collectors for the gas company are frequently asked questions about the different models of gas-stoves, gas-logs, and other gas equipment. An enterprising gas company should equip its inspectors and collectors with small circulars and train them to discuss new equipment with a householder in a helpful way.

Some of the electric light companies, following this plan, furnish their collectors with neat, attractive folders about vacuum cleaners, washing machines, and other devices, and have found that the distribution of this material is a prolific source of new business. It is by no means easy for the specialty salesman to get a hearing as he goes from house to house with the particular purpose of selling. But such employes as inspectors, collectors and service men have an open door, as it were, and an easy road to attention.

In a broad sense, every such employe is a salesman and should be given opportunity to serve as such, so far as that does not interfere with the special work he is sent out to do.

Gift shops, jewelers, and stationery stores might find it profitable to follow the plan of a successful florist who keeps a record of the birthday anniversaries of women in his town. Shortly before a birthday some one in the woman's family receives a short note reminding that "tomorrow is Mrs. Smith's birthday" and suggesting flowers as an acceptable remembrance. The method used to secure the birthday dates was an advertisement announcing that the florist would give prize chrysanthemums to each woman whose birthday was that of the greatest number of women in town. Cards were sent out to the women and almost all were returned with the birthday date. Other methods of securing names through the contest idea will be found in Section XV (Sales Ideas, Plans and Experiences).

There is a jeweler who keeps a record of wedding anniversaries, sending a note to husbands and friends a short time beforehand, suggesting appropriate gifts for the various kinds of anniversaries.

Use of Mailing-list Supplied by Salespeople.—A large Boston store used an effective method of securing names for a mailing-list to which it intended to send a special folder advertising the regular anniversary sale. A department bulletin describing the plan was sent to every salesperson. A small wooden filing box was placed conveniently in every department and each salesperson was requested to write on separate cards as many names and addresses of cash customers as could be secured. The cards were filed alphabetically so that duplicates could easily be withdrawn.

Use of Children's Mailing-list.—Children generally receive so few letters that any merchant is likely to attract favorable attention to his store by appealing directly to them. A shoe store in an Illinois city sent out 1,000 letters to children ten days before Easter. This mailing crowded the children's section of the store the entire week. Many children brought their letters with them, asking to see the man who had written to them and wondering how he had found their addresses. They carried them to school to compare with their friends' letters and the fact that all, or nearly all, had received letters seemed to give the youngsters a certain feeling of fellowship—made the shoe store "our store."

The letter itself contained a story-telling picture of two boys, apparently on a hike, one of whom seemed to be enjoying himself, while the other, with a frown on his face, was seated on a stump, pulling off his shoes. The text of the letter was based on an incident in the boyhood of the writer which tallied with the picture, ending with a few words about the store's salesmen, shoes for father and mother, and Boy Scout shoes.

This same store has made effective use of a letter of congratulation to every new mother whose name and address can be secured. Following is the part of the letter featuring the special appeal:

> Some day you will be looking forward eagerly to the time when baby will take the first step. How you will watch the tiny feet cautiously make their way to your knee! The foot comfort of the little one will be of great concern to you then, and through the years that you will have shoes to consider for your child you will want the feet to develop normally, as Nature intended they should. Foot trouble, brought on in childhood, is hard to correct and, in some cases, impossible.
>
> Siebert's fit the baby in soft comfort shoes and the older youngsters in shoes that will allow the feet to grow the natural way. The men who sell shoes at Siebert's are specialists in foot anatomy. The trend of the times has emphasized equally the importance of specialists in shoe fitting as in the treatment of the eyes or specialists in any line of public service.
>
> Bring up a child in the way that he should walk and when he is old he will not have foot trouble.

This letter was multigraphed on the firm's letterhead and contained no illustrations.

(The Shoe Retailer).

How Rug-and-carpet Cleaners Build up Mailing-lists.—Spring and fall are still popular house-cleaning times, and much of the rug-and-carpet cleaning business comes at these seasons, but the progressive rug-and-carpet cleaners are trying to build up a steady all-the-year trade. This enables them to maintain an efficient organization.

One prolific source of business is created by people's changes in living quarters. There is more or less moving going on throughout the year, and moving usually presents live possibilities of securing rugs and carpets to be cleaned, especially if the house to be entered is a new or remodeled one. A home manager naturally dislikes to take into new quarters anything that has not been thoroughly cleaned.

Fires offer another source of rug-cleaning business. Often when a fire is not very serious to the building or home, the rugs are badly soiled and water-soaked. The progressive rug-cleaner who goes out after such business usually gets it. Prospective customers in this class may be secured through cooperation with the local fire insurance companies, or by watching the local newspapers for notes about fires.

The Charge-account Mailing-list.—A ready-made mailing-list belongs to any retail store carrying charge accounts, and it is surprising that more stores do not make use of it. Three large department stores of Chicago enclose with each customer's monthly statement an attractive booklet or folder that, they hold, puts the recipient into a good humor for looking over the bill. The charge customers are thus kept in touch with the store's offerings at no extra postage expense.

Miscellaneous Mailing-list Suggestions.—Florists have found it profitable to address double postal cards to business men asking them for dates about which they would like to be reminded—anniversaries, birthdays, Mothers' Day and the like. This gives them an opportunity to send out special solicitations, either by letter or through the use of the telephone.

A jeweler has done a distinctive bit of advertising by keeping the numbers of good watches received by him for repair and sending out follow-up letters addressed to the watches themselves, the envelops, of course, being addressed to the owners' street numbers. The letter is of the cute variety, referring to the service given the watch previously, asking about its state of health, and so on. To carry out the idea still further, this dealer advertised himself as "The Watch Doctor."

A furnace and heating man, having built up a list of customers and prospective customers, sends out a card around the end of the summer, offering the services of a man to look the furnace over and find out just what is required before it is pressed into duty for winter work.

Force of Specialization.—If a general mailing-list is subdivided according to profession, interests or tastes, it is, of course, possible to make more pointed and direct appeals than could be made to a general audience. Professional men are more interested in the firm that caters to their special needs and tastes. Chevrolet owners, Ford owners, Buick owners, Cadillac owners, are more likely to pay attention to a direct appeal that mentions the make of their car than to an appeal that simply refers to "your automobile," or "your car."

The classification method may be carried to great length. There may be one list of physicians and surgeons; another of dentists, architects and contractors, school girls, college girls, business women, club women, housekeepers, mothers, and so on.

If an enterprising laundry were to get up a selected list of business women and offer a special service to them, that laundry would lift its appeal out of the ordinary and put it where it would command unusual attention and probably bring a large return in business. There are thousands of business women who are not reached through the general appeal to householders.

One well known store of Ohio has a correspondent in every populous district within a radius of twenty miles of the store. This correspondent serves much as the correspondent of a local newspaper does—giving the store information about events of the community, removals, and peculiar needs of the people.

A sporting-goods merchant has found that the prompt securing of the names of people who have been granted hunting and fishing licenses gives unusual opportunity for timely advertising.

Dealers in aluminum cooking utensils have found that mailing-lists of engaged girls are good sources of business, while lists of newly married people are not so productive. The reason given is that the young married people have spent so much that they feel they must begin to save rather than buy new outfits.

A photographer who has a good reputation as a producer of children's photographs, made an arrangement with the registrar of births in his town to furnish him with the names and addresses of babies born in the community. When the baby is two or three weeks old, a letter is sent to the parents, asking if the photographer might have the privilege of calling and taking the baby's picture.

Many of these letters bring results, and when the photographer makes his call he takes along with him an attractive baby book, showing pictures of his own little girl, taken at regular intervals. This baby book usually proves so appealing to the mothers that they immediately resolve to keep such a pictured record of their own child's progress and development.

An enterprising luggage dealer makes it his business to try to find out when his customers and prospective customers will take trips or vacations. With this information on file, he can easily send to the traveler a baggage tag, containing his or her name in plainly lettered type, so that there will be no difficulty in identifying baggage. While this might be put down as purely good-will advertising, it has proved productive of business. The arrival of the tag from the merchant with a pleasant letter often reminds the traveler that he is in need of something that can be supplied by the store. Even if his needs may not be apparent at the time, he is likely to recall the little service rendered by the merchant when he is in the market for new luggage or leather goods.

Addresses of Customers Who Have Their Purchases Mailed.— One of the large New York stores makes up a mailing-list of out-of-town customers by instructing its salespeople to keep a record of all goods that are to be mailed to customers. When a customer buys a pleated skirt, for example, and asks that it be mailed to 348 Cherry Street, Cicoville, Pa., the salesman is likely to say something like this: "You are the fourth customer I have had from Cicoville this week. Do you come to New York often? We try to give our out-of-town customers such good service that they will want to come back." Such remarks will usually bring from the customer the information that the salesman is looking for. He finds out whether the customer lives permanently in the place she has named, or whether she is just there for a few days or for the

DIRECT ADVERTISING METHODS 213

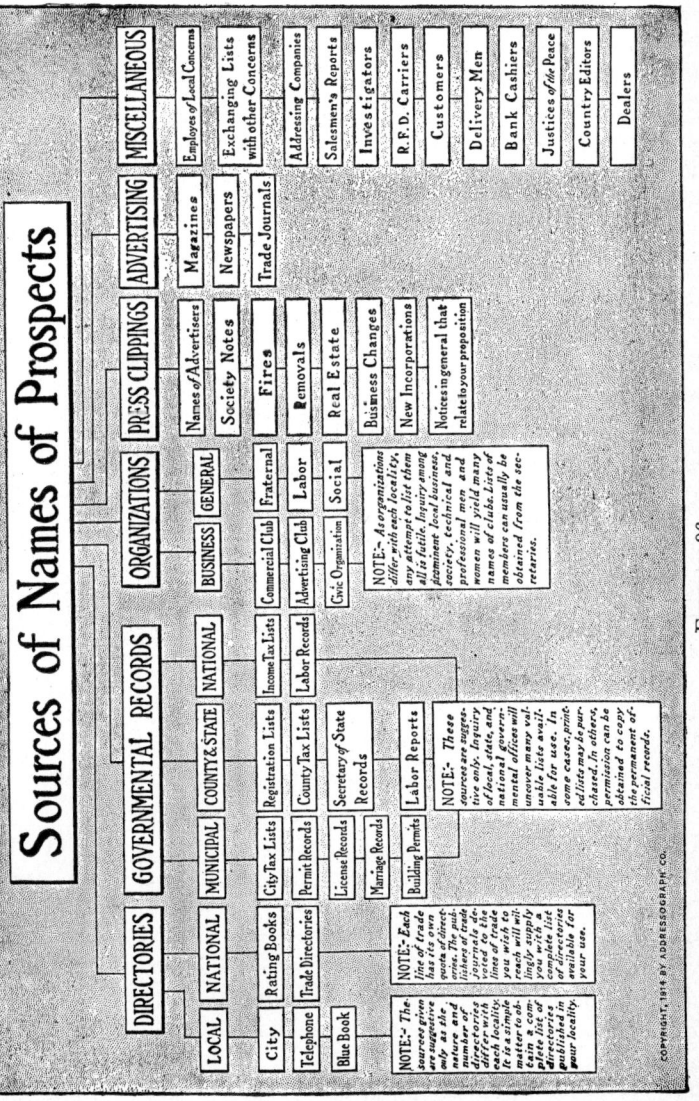

Exhibit 96.

summer. Catalogues and special folders mailed to such a list bring a good volume of mail-order business.

Appeals to Foreigners.—One successful merchant has made a specialty of appealing to foreigners. His experience has been that the foreign population of a city gets less mail, as a rule, than the native population, and that most foreign people feel complimented to get a special letter—even a letter that is obviously trying to sell something. Care would have to be exercised in compiling such a list, as the danger of getting names incorrectly spelled would be very great, and no one likes to see his name garbled. Lists of foreigners may be obtained from the offices of consuls, through cooperation with priests or pastors of churches made up largely of foreigners, from social service workers, Americanization records, employment offices, and even sometimes from industrial plants.

News Items Afford Valuable Additions.—A careful reading of the newspapers, particularly in smaller towns where there are many personal news items, will result in valuable additions to mailing-lists and important changes.

Other Sources from Which Mailing-lists Can Be Compiled.—Exhibit 96, published here through the courtesy of the Addressograph Company of Chicago, furnishes a number of different suggestions as to sources for mailing-lists. While the list covers many items given in previous pages, the review is a convenient one.

IMPORTANCE OF KEEPING MAILING-LISTS UP-TO-DATE

The greatest waste in direct advertising work comes about through the use of poor mailing-lists. Mailing-lists may be wasteful through any one of the following causes and reasons:

1. Original compilation from inaccurate sources
2. Poor handwriting in original lists
3. Changes of address
4. Changes of name through marriage
5. Deaths
6. Changes in position and need.

To avoid waste and also to avoid creating the impression on customers and prospective customers that the store is not up-to-date, there should be periodical house-cleaning with respect to mailing-lists. Some stores go so far as to make a house-to-house canvass as a means of dropping dead names and freshening up their lists. Others send out letters enclosing a return card, or use double postal cards, as a means of finding whether or not mail sent to the addressee is regularly received, whether or not the addressee would like to receive the latest catalogue, and so on. In order to get a large return from appeals of the kind here described, the return card should be so designed that the addressee can write a "Yes" or "No" or check a line, sign his or her name, and mail. The return of a mailing-piece sent out at first-class rates will, of course, indicate names to which mail cannot be delivered.

DISTINCTIVE LETTER-WRITING

So many sales and soliciting letters are received by customers nowadays that it is worth while spending time and money to have letter-appeals made distinctive in one way or another. This does not necessarily mean that they shall be sensational or freakish. Good, earnest letter-writing with pointed suggestions and interesting descriptions is often enough to command attention. The conspicuous faults of sales letter-writing are identical with the faults of advertising in general —too much broad, extravagant claim, too little definite appeal and interesting description, too much of the essay style of composition and too little of the frank, earnest appeal.

If a tailoring establishment, for example, is about to address its customers, instead of opening the message with some such appeal as "Today we are putting on display about the finest $50 and $60 suitings we have ever had in the place," the announcement would probably be, "At this season of the year it is but natural that every man who takes the pride in his personal appearance that he should take is reflecting over a choice of a summer suit."

Letter-advertising is in itself a subject large enough to fill a good-sized volume. There is room here for only a few examples of effective letters used by retailers.

The following letter from the First National Bank, Madison, Wis., is an example of an effective letter sent to newcomers:

Dear Mr. Mackesay:

We always like to be among the first to say "How-do-you-do," and "Welcome" to new arrivals in our city for we know we would appreciate a like welcome, were we to move into a new town.

To give you a glimpse of our civic activities and enable you to get in touch with things in your new home town, we're having *The Wisconsin State Journal* sent to your home every day for one month, with our compliments. This subscription is paid for and you are under no obligation to continue it.

Possibly there is some little service or information we can give you. We want you to feel free to call on us at any time and give us the opportunity of helping.

Naturally, a satisfactory banking connection is always desirable to strangers or comparative strangers and we would esteem it a favor if you would permit us to explain why this is the proper bank for you to use.

We shall be glad to see you.

EXHIBIT 97.—Welcoming letter sent out by a Madison, Wis., bank to people who have recently moved to Madison.

The Burroughs Clearing House, in which this letter originally appeared, is authority for the statement that the invitation brought fine responses from newcomers, and that the bank is frequently enabled to be of some special service to the new resident, thus establishing a valuable relationship at the very outset. *The Wisconsin State Journal* also profits by this plan, for many subscriptions are secured after the newcomers have become acquainted with the newspaper through the month's free subscription.

Exhibit 98 is a distinctive letter-appeal that, at the same time, is not so freakish as to divert the reader from the real subject of the letter. Instead of inserting the name of the addressee at the top it is placed down in the body of the letter, and the recommendation of an acquaintance is given as the reason for sending the letter. This little touch of interest and an attractive sample attached to the letter give it unusual attention-commanding value.

D'Andrea Brothers Inc.
MEN'S TAILORS

587 Fifth Avenue, New York

```
Woolens like these for

A Ready to Wear Overcoat'

Designed by the Brothers D'Andrea

Made in their own workrooms

Under their personal supervision

By skilled, custom-trained tailors.

        *    *    *    *

Suggested to Mr. Roland S. Hall

Because Mr. A. F. Ashbacker gave his name

As one who appreciates

Good taste and value in clothes.
```

EXHIBIT 98.—Distinctive type of letter sent out by a tailoring establishment. A sample of overcoat material was attached with a clip. The interest of the prospective customer is stimulated by the reference in the eighth line to an acquaintance.

218   RETAIL ADVERTISING AND SELLING

"Ask Letty the Shopper" Anything You Wish to Know She will write you fully at once

THIS LETTER IS FROM THE MAIL ORDER DEPARTMENT

LEWIS & SON
DENVER COLO

MAY
Nineteen
Twenty-two

Dear Friend:

Would YOU like to have the most up-to-the-minute information about the new modes, fashionable attire; what to wear, and what not to wear, in a HURRY?

If you would, write "Letty, the Shopper;" ask anything you wish--whether you want to buy or not, and she will write you fully at once.

No matter where you live--or what you need in the merchandise line, LEWIS & SON will send it to you, PREPAID, on approval, AT ONCE. A query from you will bring full particulars by return mail.

Free Fashion Sheets and Samples of new materials will be sent on request at any time.

Note the very latest spring styles in silk hose shown in the "Allen A" book I am enclosing, and tell me how I can help in your shopping problems.

Get the NEWEST ideas while they are new.

You'll like the Lewis one-day, prepaid shopping service.

Cordially yours,

DictLS/AAH   *Letty the Shopper*

(You May Use Other Side of This Page for Reply)

EXHIBIT. 99.—A pleasing feature of this letter, used by the A. T. Lewis & Son Dry Goods Company, Denver, Col., is the fact that it is signed "Letty the Shopper," giving the woman-customer the impression that her requirements will be looked after carefully and individually by "Letty." Suggestion is also made that the back of the letter-sheet may be used for reply.

Exhibit 99 is a style of letter-message that dry-goods stores use effectively.

Exhibit 100 is an example of the special type of letter that may bring direct returns if sent to a selected mailing-

---

YOUR NAME HERE

Slogan, Telephone, etc.

Your Town, U. S. A.

Prospect's Name
Address

Dear Sir:

When springtime comes--

And your farm becomes an oozy sea of mud--

Who is it that is inconvenienced the most?

You've guessed it right. It is the lady of the house--the housewife who already has so much to do to keep things clean.

Every time you return from the barn, the garage or the road you carry a certain amount of mud into the house. Not only is it inconvenient and disagreeable to you but it means work for the housewife.

It is such a simple matter to eliminate this condition that there is really no need to tolerate it. A concrete walk laid between the home and the barn and over other frequently used paths is a clean, attractive remedy. It keeps mud out of the house, makes walking a pleasure, enhances the beauty of your place and serves you as well as those who come after you.

Laying concrete sidewalks is such a simple proposition, too. A stretch at a time in spare moments and soon, at surprisingly low cost, there is an attractive walk wherever you want one. Or if you prefer we will recommend a good contractor to do the work for you.

To defeat this spring's mud your sidewalk should be laid the moment weather permits. Why not drop in tomorrow and talk things over so that when the time comes you will be ready to start?

Very truly yours,
YOUR NAME HERE

EXHIBIT 100.—Type of letter that is suitable for a building-material dealer. This is a suggestion from a manufacturer who offers to multigraph such letters on the dealer's letterheads and return the completed letters for mailing at the local post-office.

list. Many manufacturers offer to cooperate with their dealers in the preparation and printing of such letters. Some go so far as to offer to print the appeals on the dealers' own letterheads or on some well designed, illustrated letterhead prepared by the manufacturer. Others will even pay the postage on such solicitations, if the dealers give other valuable cooperation. A well known knitting company handles annually the mailing of about a million letters and style books to mailing-lists furnished by its dealers.

Exhibit 101 shows the first page of a four-page letter used by Wm. Filene's Sons Company, Boston, Mass., as an effective producer of business on summer wash-dresses. The idea of clipping a sample of one of the materials to the first page of this letter is a good one. The second, third and fourth pages of the letter showed illustrations of five of the attractive models offered, with a little description and the price of each. It is good selling argument to ask the patron to make her selection early while the stock is new and complete and also to shop before the weather gets hot.

It is made very easy for the customer to order from this letter, without coming to the store. As a parting shot, there is a little paneled display at the bottom of the fourth page, reading:

You can Order These Dresses by Mail

Your Money Back if You Say So

Please state sizes and colors when ordering. If you are at all dissatisfied, just return the dresses.

Free delivery anywhere in New England. Better order these great values now—Phone Beach 3800, or write MAIL SERVICE.

Filene's Boston 2, Mass.

The letter reproduced in Exhibit 102 is one that brought good results. This was a four-page affair, also, but only two pages were utilized—the first and the third. The other two pages were left white, giving distinction or "class" to the solicitation. On the third page was an illustration from a crayon sketch of three of the offerings, with the footnote on page 222.

Wm. Filene's Sons Company

WASHINGTON, SUMMER AND HAWLEY STREETS

Boston
May 2, 1923

Dear Mrs. Heartz:

For your convenience we have arranged so that you can come in and look over the merchandise before it is announced in the newspapers.

You can make your choice now leisurely from a stock that is new and complete. The difficulty that often arises later in the season, in obtaining just the size, color and style you want will not trouble you if you make your choice now. If you wish, delivery can be made at a later date.

If you cannot come to the store and see these new dresses (sixth floor), we will be glad to fill your order by mail -- telephone Beach 3800 -- or write to Filene's Mail Service, and your order will be given the same personal care and attention you yourself would receive here in the store. When ordering by mail kindly enclose picture of dress desired.

Very truly yours,

Wm. Filene's Sons Co.

N. B. The materials in these new dresses seem so good to us that we had to attach a little sample for you to see one of the many colors, and if you will just turn over the page you will get an idea of the styles.

EXHIBIT 101.—First page of a 4-page letter used by a large Boston merchant. It was an effective producer of summer business on wash dresses. The sample of material that was clipped in the lower right-hand corner of this letter gave the recipient a good idea of the quality of the materials of which the dresses were made.

L. BAMBERGER & CO.
NEWARK, N. J.

March 9, 1923

Dear Sir:

Here's news of a big sale of new Spring two-trousers
suits and top coats for men and young men.

The sale begins Monday, March 12. The suits are low
priced--$39.50--and every suit has extra trousers.
Business suits, sport suits, golf suits, in serges,
worsteds, cassimeres and cheviots.

The extra pair of trousers is a feature of this sale.

Here is the top coat event. Hundreds of fine quality
top coats for Spring wear, sale-priced in this event
at $29.50. The materials are tweeds, gabardines and
whipcords in practically all models. Also staple
silk-lined Chesterfields in gray only. All sizes
from 36 to 46 in both suits and top coats.

This is an event of events--about the biggest of
the year in men's clothing in Newark. Mark the date
again--Monday, March 12.

Very truly yours,

L. Bamberger

(See next page)

EXHIBIT 102.—First page of a 4-page letter used by L. Bamberger & Company, and reported as an effective producer of business from men.

The above illustration shows three of the models (sketched from the actual merchandise) in our Spring Clothing Sale:

  The Business Suit (with extra pair of trousers) $39.50
  The Golf Suit (knickers and long trousers).....$39.50
  The Top Coat...............................$29.50

Experience of a Shoe Dealer.—Carrying out the principle that has already been set forth with respect to sub-dividing and classifying mailing-lists, R. H. Fyfe & Company, of Detroit, has had notable success with special types of letters. According to *The Shoe Retailer*, this large concern has on its lists some 5,000 boys, about the same number of girls, 3,000 nurses and teachers, several thousand golfers and several hundred members of riding clubs. At the graduation season, it makes up special lists of high-school and college graduates. The practice of this concern is indicated by the following paragraphs giving the views of one of the executives of the firm:

Lists should by all means be specialized, because otherwise one's letters must be of the most general nature, thereby losing much of their effectiveness. There should be entirely different letters for boys and for girls, for instance, and certainly one would not send the same letter to a policeman and to the woman school-teacher. By securing specialized lists, one is enabled to adapt the tone of the letter to the particular group of addresses, and to appeal directly to the particular needs or desires of the different groups. All letters should be addressed to the prospective customers by name, as this gives them a personal touch and insures consideration that a general letter, addressed merely to "Dear Madam," or to "Dear Sir," will not receive. Similarly, we think it of very great importance to have the manager of the store or of the particular department to which the letter refers sign the letters over his title. These signatures, as a matter of fact, are multigraphed along with the rest of the letter, but they are duplicates of the men's signatures and they convey the personal touch. We find this of especial value in letters to boys and girls. They frequently come in, with the letters, or with the little folders which we send along with them, in their hands and ask by name for the signer of the letter. Then, they have the shoes they want already picked out from the illustrations and prices in the folder and they proceed to tell the supposed author of the letter that they want such and such a pair of shoes as listed and numbered in the folders.

In this connection, too, we think it well to salute boys and girls by their given names in addressing the letters to them. That is, where we follow the heading of a letter to an adult with the salutation, "Dear Mrs. ———," or "Dear Mr. ———," we say "Dear William," or "Dear Edith," in a letter to a child. This, we think, gives them a warm glow of self-satisfaction and causes them to attach greater importance to the letter. They feel that we are personal friends of theirs, and that is just the way we want them to feel.

The following are the opening paragraphs of some of the special letters:

Our spring shipments have brought a number of new low shoes so particularly adapted to the requirements of young teachers and others that we are taking the liberty of bringing a few models directly to your attention.

Dear William:

"Some time ago we decided that there ought to be something more to a boy's shoe than just good wearing quality and comfortable fit. Designers of boys' shoes apparently didn't know that such a word as "style" was in the dictionary.

Permit us to offer our assistance in opening up the new golf season. We refer, of course, to the footwear you will need.

Dear Miss Lindsey:

"We know you are very busy with the multitude of details connected with commencement preparations, so we will take but a moment to extend our congratulations, and to suggest our possible helpfulness in planning your outfits.

The "College Girls" Department on our second floor has lately received a number of interesting models for class-room, street wear, informal occasions, and for commencement itself.

Envelop Enclosures.—As the postal laws allow the sending of one ounce for 2 cents, the daily mail of a large store affords opportunity for circulating information about many different kinds of goods. Some manufacturers of such groups as office specialties have found that the enclosing of cards and folders in the daily mail brings enough sales to pay a considerable portion of the advertising campaign. The statistician who has made some calculations about the amount of daily mail and its weight figures that the present number of letters mailed daily would amount to 47 tons an hour at regular postage charges. The actual weight runs to about 23 tons an hour. The conclusion of this reasoning is that thousands of advertisers are losing an opportunity to send out additional information. It should not be assumed, however, that it is advisable for all classes of mail to carry advertising matter. It is just as easy to err in the direction of stuffing the mails with too much literature as it is in the direction of losing sight of the opportunity altogether. But all who have made a study of the situation know that hundreds of thousands of dollars are invested in attractive folders, cards and booklets of light weight that are overlooked or neglected in mailing departments. Without question, a live retailer can reap many extra thousands of dollars in sales by giving special attention to this end of his work.

It is pertinent, also, to remark, in this connection, that it costs just as much to mail a cheap letterhead, poorly printed or duplicated, as it does to mail a first-class message that bespeaks good quality of merchandising service. Granting that there are a great many solicitations that do not require expensive letterheads, any one who examines the bulk of the circular-letter material that goes into waste-baskets, the kitchen stove, or the fireplace, will conclude that the cheap or commonplace character of the material is responsible for most of the waste. Often stores that pride themselves on the freshness of their merchandise and the cleanliness of their display-windows and interiors are guilty of much cheap and slovenly looking direct advertising matter.

Exhibit 103 is a selection from a great variety of little folders, used by retail merchants either to send out to customers in packages, or to put in envelops with statements, or to be sent with some special letter solicitation.

A progressive retailer will occasionally want to prepare material of this kind himself and entirely at his own expense. He can, however, save himself a great deal of time and money by using the valuable material that most manufacturers are glad to furnish. In some cases, of course, literature of this kind furnished by manufacturers may not meet the retailer's need, but if he will make his specific needs known, the manufacturer is, more often than not, willing to cooperate in furnishing special literature.

There are several glaring weaknesses in this particular department of advertising:

1. Acceptance by the retailer of a great deal of advertising circular material that is never used. Very likely the manufacturer's or the wholesaler's salesman talks with the retailer about using such literature and sends it to him but overlooks

seeing that it is placed where customers are likely to pick up the circulars, or does not suggest to the dealer ways in which such advertising material may be used in connection with his mailing-list work.

2. The waste of such material by sending so much to a customer at one time that none of it gets attention. Circulari-

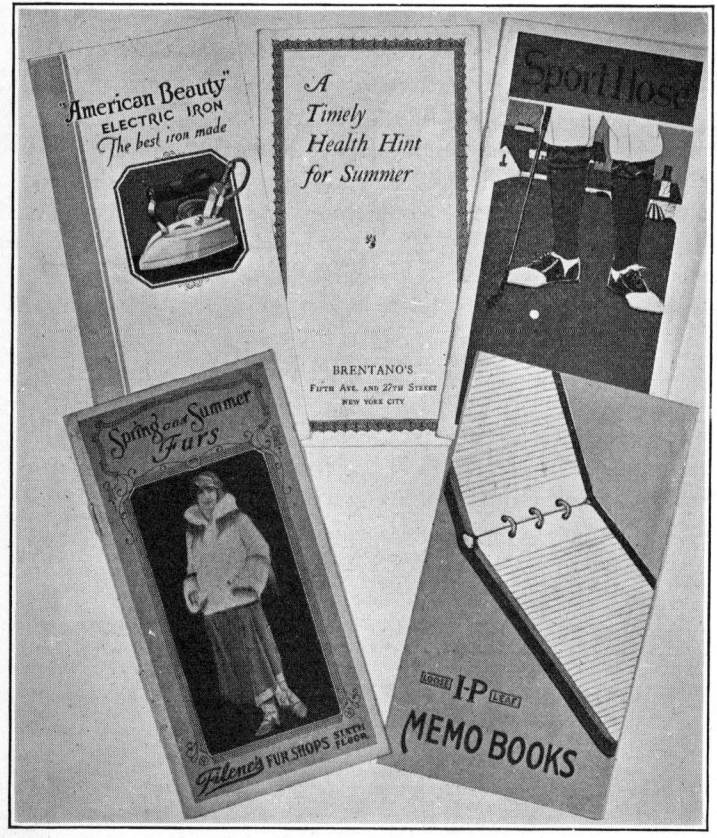

EXHIBIT 103.—Specimens of light-weight booklets and folders appropriate for use with special letters, or as enclosures with the daily mail and monthly statements.

zation is much better, as a rule, if it is specific. If half a dozen folders or booklets are enclosed, all about different things, the customer is not likely to be favorably impressed by any of it. Again, something depends on the class of goods to be promoted. A high-class food store might, in calling attention to some of its specialties, send along folders dealing with half a dozen products and still not fail in its mission. But the haberdasher who mixes up appeals on hats with those of shoes, collars, cravats and raincoats is likely to defeat his own purpose.

EXHIBIT 104.—Mailing card that brought good results. The original size was 7 by 5 inches.

Use of Single and Double Postal Cards.—An effective, though much neglected, method of advertising is the postal card in both the single and double styles. In the first place, the advertiser gets his stock free, being required by the government to pay only the postage. In the second place, postal cards come within the classification of first-class matter, are received by readers as such and are forwarded and handled just as 2-cent letters.

A thousand postal cards may be printed for a few dollars, and it is difficult to conceive of anything more effective for a mailing-list of a thousand names at a cost of some $12 to $15 for stock, printing and postage.

Postal cards, being small, encourage good copy-writing, as the street-car card does. Retailers should use them liberally in exploiting special items on either goods or service. The double postal card is particularly useful where a reply is asked for and in those cases where the advertiser invites the reader to return the card as an acceptance of his offer, or as a request to put one of the advertised articles aside for him.

Use of Mailing Cards.—Mailing cards are exceedingly useful to the retail advertiser in exploiting special offerings.

Exhibit 104 is an example of a type of card used freely by merchants who maintain classified mailing lists.

This card, in the original, was 7 by 5 inches. The unique character of the illustration commands attention. The address-side of the card was large enough to carry the following matter:

15,000 Pairs Women's
Silk Hose, $1.95

Made to sell at from $3 to $4.25 a pair

8,000 *pairs* of fine silk hosiery—some slipper heel, others square heel, others lace clox; some Marvel stripes. Reduced in price because of slight shadowings in the silk. Colors are black, white, seal brown, biege, silver gray and beaver.

4,000 *pairs* of heavy ingrain silk hose, double silk soles and heels, garter tops, lined with lisle. In black, gray and navy.

3,000 *pairs* fancy glove silk hose, all full elastic garter tops, pointed heels. Colors are black, white, beaver, seal brown and biege.

All Boxed for Christmas Giving.
Your Choice at $1.95 a pair
Also 6,000 Pairs of Men's Onyx
Silk Sox at 59¢
3 pairs, $1.65
No Mail or 'Phone Orders Filled
on the Women's Hosiery

L. BAMBERGER & CO.   "One of America's Great Stores"
NEWARK

L. Bamberger & Company, who furnished this card for reproduction, reported that it brought good results on the hosiery sale.

Selling through Catalogue.—The catalogue method is not one to be followed only by mail-order houses, though the larger mail-order organizations have made such effective use of catalogues that they have long been referred to generally as "catalogue houses."

Catalogue buying is attractive because of the interesting variety of merchandise shown through illustration and good descriptions. Most retail advertisers who are using only the daily newspapers, or letters and folders, can take a valuable lesson from the "catalogue houses." The newspaper advertiser too often contents himself with generalities that few people pay attention to or believe. Catalogue descriptions, on the other hand, are usually specific.

Retail firms that do the larger part of their business within the store frequently command much aditional patronage through the use of catalogues of different types. The catalogue may be a general mail-order catalogue of goods that can be readily ordered from the mills and shipped easily, issued perhaps quarterly, or it may be a catalogue of a special nature such as a listing of furniture, coats and suits, children's clothing, farm supplies, or other classifications of seasonable merchandise.

Unless the catalogue is of a very temporary nature, great care must be used to list only merchandise which will be kept in stock and on which prices will not change frequently.

The general use of catalogues in the encouragement of buying through the mails and through the use of the telephone also calls for some additional organization. The carrying on of a mail-order department is by no means an easy undertaking and brings about requests from customers for careful shopping in their behalf by some employe in the store, prompt attention to orders, good correspondence, liberal exchange facilities and so on.

Some specialty stores use the catalogue as a very important medium. A large tea and coffee concern, for example, selling its products by means of wagon salesmen who go out from a chain of stores in one state, uses a general catalogue of its teas, coffees, spices, baking powder, laundry supplies, flavoring extracts, and other allied goods.

One of the chief features of this form of merchandising is the profit-sharing system, carried out through the giving of premium coupons with every purchase. The premium plan, in spite of all that has been said against it, continues to be a large factor in this type of merchandising.

The concern here referred to uses also the part-cash payment plan as a means of maintaining an account with the customer and continuing her patronage.

As the wagons of such merchants are essentially stores on wheels, they have their greatest appeal in the outlying districts or in small towns where customers do not find it so easy or convenient to go to stores for the ordinary supplies needed.

Result of Questionnaire on Catalogue Advertising.—In order to determine the modern trend with respect to catalogue merchandising, a series of letters was addressed by the author of this volume to representative stores throughout the United States.

The replies received, and other data on this subject, indicate that the tendency is in the direction of special literature dealing with departmental or seasonable goods that group well together, rather than the issuing of large, bulky catalogues. A number of stores replied frankly that they did not believe in the value of general catalogues, or that their experience in this direction had been unprofitable.

It is evident that large stores, like Marshall Field & Company, Chicago, have more opportunity to realize a profit on catalogue productions. Even this concern does not issue a general catalogue but publishes a number of smaller catalogues on departmental, timely, and seasonable goods.

Marshall Field & Company has adopted a standardized page size of $9\frac{1}{2}$ by 13 inches for all of its catalogue productions, with the exception of the one on automobile accessories. The argument is that this size enables the placing of the illustrations in such a way as to give a more attractive page.

Practically all of this concern's publications are specialized, and an appropriate mailing-list is maintained for each classification.

The Duffy-Powers Company, Rochester, N. Y., does not issue a general catalogue. The only large circulars used are bulletins of gift goods, sent out at the Christmas season, and occasional sale broadsides, mailed to a selected group of customers.

In answering the questionnaire referred to, the L. S. Donaldson Company, Minneapolis, Minn., gives the following information:

> We have found it most profitable to send out catalogues each season—Spring, Early Fall, Holiday, and January White Sale.
>
> We have found that a catalogue 7½ by 10¼ inches is a convenient size for handling and reasonably satisfactory for display purposes.
>
> Our catalogues are mailed to a general list of out-of-town customers in the surrounding communities, and we usually depend on our customers for new names. These are obtained by providing new customers with blanks on which to fill in names and addresses of their friends, which they are always glad to do without cost. This type of name is almost always good, because there is no financial reward offered to encourage the sending of fictitious or useless names.
>
> Our experience in sales-results from our catalogues is fairly general —ready-to-wear goods predominate in sales, with silks, shoes, hats, gloves, hosiery, etc. following.
>
> We believe that catalogues properly merchandised and gotten up to cover a certain objective are well worth their cost. Our catalogue expense is approximately 9 per cent of the net sales of the mail-order department. This, of course, does not include the business that comes in over the counter, which it is practically impossible to compute.

Luckey, Platt & Company, Poughkeepsie, N. Y., does not send out an annual catalogue. Four or five times a year this concern sends out a direct-mail advertisement to a list of approximately 25,000 customers who buy by mail from time to time.

One of the large retailers of the far West, the A. T. Lewis & Son Dry Goods Company, Denver, Col., does not issue a general catalogue. Commenting on general catalogue-advertising, this firm goes so far as to say:

> We do not believe catalogue advertising is generally profitable for the department store, for the reason that the store cannot com-

pete with the big mail-order houses carrying enormous stocks of regular catalogue goods, either in the completeness and expertness of the descriptions and illustrations in the catalogues, or the price of the merchandise. Furthermore, the average department store would not carry the class of merchandise advertised in the mail-order catalogues.

The direct literature of this retailer is confined to "bargain bulletins," sent out about once a month, or at any time when the store has a number of seasonable or specially priced items to offer, and to a monthly booklet called *The Shopper*. This booklet is a twelve-page affair, the covers of which are in color, attractively illustrated. The inside pages are also effectively illustrated, though printed only in black on white, smooth-finished stock. The pages are $6\frac{1}{4}$ by $9\frac{1}{4}$ inches. The firm considers *The Shopper* more a means of bringing the out-of-town customer into closer relation with the store than a business-getter. It is mailed monthly to a picked list of 10,000 customers. Names and addresses for the "bargain bulletins" are secured from county telephone directories, from county clerks' offices, and other sources.

The A. T. Lewis & Son Dry Goods Company also uses circular letters to advantage, one of which is reproduced elsewhere in this Section.

A large Chicago retailer, who prefers not to be quoted by name, reports that his experience with catalogues has been very successful, orders being secured through this method of merchandising at small selling expense.

Seasonable Direct-mail Solicitations.—Most of the progressive retailers of the present day seem to find it profitable to send out departmental or seasonable booklets and folders, mailing cards, special letters, and the like.

Exhibit 105 is a reproduction of two of the inside pages of an attractive twelve-page booklet sent out by L. Bamberger & Company, Newark, N. J., containing appropriate suggestions for wedding gifts. The title of this booklet, "Here Comes the Bride," was appropriately carried out in the illustration on the front cover. A bride in all white, with her veil and wedding bouquet, was shown against a blue tinted background. The booklet was in two colors—black and delft-blue—on an antique-finished stock. In the original, this booklet measured 5 by 6½ inches.

Another effective bit of direct literature used by the Bamberger store is a booklet on the half-yearly sale of furniture and floor coverings. A page from this folder is reproduced in

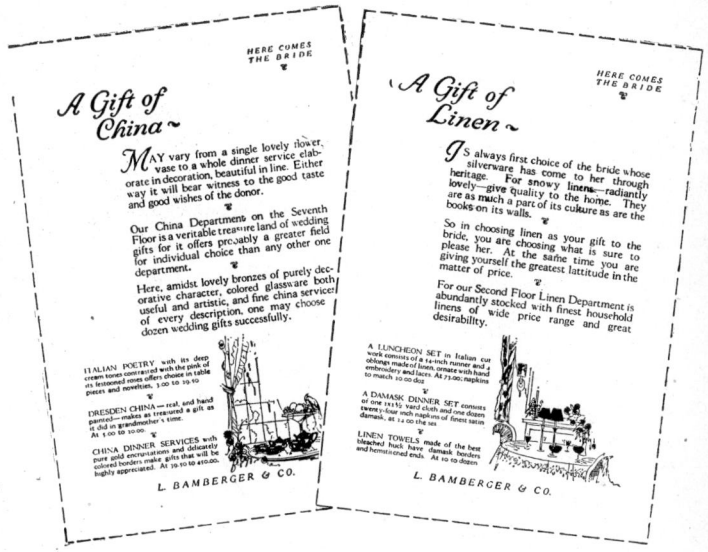

Exhibit 105.—Specimen pages from a booklet of L. Bamberger & Company, offering suggestions as to appropriate wedding gifts. In the original, this was a two-color job.

Exhibit 106. The size of this folder was 7¼ by 9¾ inches, printed on smooth, dull-finished stock in one color. There were just twelve pages.

Exhibit 107 is a page from what may be appropriately called a periodical catalogue or price list from the Mitchell-Fletcher Company, Philadelphia.

This publication is a four-page affair, issued every two weeks and sent out in an envelop under 1-cent postage. It is nothing more than a well written description of seasonable food supplies, with an occasional illustration. The issue from which this exhibit was taken was sent out the latter part of June. Therefore, it appropriately features the Fourth of July decorated cake.

L. BAMBERGER & CO. NEWARK

THREE-PIECE OVER-STUFFED LIVING ROOM SUITE—225.00

Round barrel ends and soft spring arms give unusual distinction to this over-stuffed suite which may be obtained upholstered in a choice of good grade tapestries. The loose cushions are reversible, spring filled, and rest on a full spring foundation. There is a large sofa, a graceful fireside chair and a big armchair to each set. The sketch only gives a brief idea of its beauty.

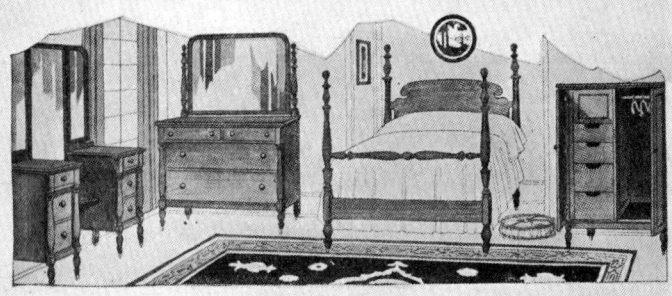

FOUR-PIECE MAHOGANY COLONIAL BEDROOM SUITE—395.00

Of Post Colonial and massive design, this roomy suite boasts a 50-inch dresser that is 24 inches deep and has a French plate mirror measuring 30 x 40 inches. It is fitted with four big drawers. The wardrobe to the set measures 40 x 22 inches and the vanity is 50 inches long by 19 inches deep. The latter has three mirrors. A full size bed is included with the set at this price or twin beds may be had in its stead for 65.00 extra. Finished in a beautiful shade of mahogany.

EXHIBIT 106.—Specimen page from a furniture folder sent out by L. Bamberger & Company, featuring its "Half-Yearly Sale of Furniture and Floor Coverings."

Suggestions

2 — Prices Subject To Change Without Notice

Reliable Picnic and House Party Supplies for the 4th

July 4th is almost here and regardless of whether you celebrate it in the city, or at the seashore, yachting or camping, the quality of the food served will either enhance or mar the pleasure of the occasion.

May we be of service to you in supplying the Foods for the Fourth?

Stuffed Luncheon Olives

22 Oz. Bot., $1.15
Small Bot., 20c.; $2.25 Doz.

Stuffed Luncheon Olives are enjoyed by many who do not care for the Plain Olives. The Spanish Sweet Red Pepper or Pimiento with which they are stuffed makes them pleasing to the eye and tempting to the palate.

Dill Pickles in Jars

40c. Jar; $4.50 Doz.

Dill Pickles packed in large glass jars in brine.
Especially suitable for the picnic and equally popular in the home.

Beechnut Peanut Paste

Large Jars, 35c.; $4.25 Doz.
Medium Jars, 24c.; $2.75 Doz.
Small Jars, 15c; $1.75 Doz.

Spread on thin crackers, it makes decidedly appetizing sandwiches.

Park Farm Baked Beans in Tomato Sauce

20c. Can; $2.25 Doz.; $4.25 Case

As popular in midsummer as in midwinter.
Each bean baker seems to have his own peculiar way of preparing baked beans, and there's a tremendous difference in quality and flavor.
Park Farm Baked Beans are very palatable and rich in nutrition.
The fine tomato sauce adds to their tastiness.
Prepared for us by a down east Bean Baker who understands our ideas of quality.

Cape Cod Cookies

30c. Lb.—Special June 18th to 23rd

The very name suggests something old fashioned and home made.
An ideal Cookie for the children—that's what Cape Cod Cookies are. They are made from the very best quality of creamery butter, selected wheat flour, sugar and the pure flavoring.
Regularly 35c. Lb.

Old Fashion Ginger Snaps

2 Lbs., 25c.—Special June 25th to 30th

Everyone wants Ginger Snaps for the 4th of July picnic.
Snappy Ginger Cakes with a fine Ginger flavor.

Crystallized Ginger

½ Lb. Tin, 50c.; 1 Lb. Tin, 90c.

Always a pleasing tid-bit.
A delightful Summer Confection. One or two pieces make an appropriate ending to the Summer meal.

"Own Baking"—Chocolate Iced Brunswick Cakes

45c. Doz —Two Weeks

Delicious Ginger Cakes, baked in muffin tins, enriched with Fancy Currants.
Iced on top and sides with a soft Cream Chocolate Icing.

"Own Baking"—Fresh Cocoanut Layer Cake

45c. Lb.—Special Two Weeks

Did you ever taste "Own Baking" Cocoanut Cake in layer sheet form?
Just as delicious as it is tempting —three layers of quality cake with a soft Cocoanut Meringue between the layers and coated on top and sides with rich Cocoanut.
Cakes weigh about 3 Lbs.

Seasonable Reminders

Nut and Raisin Bread, Loaf, 25c.
Iced Cinnamon Roll . . 40c.
French Coffee Cakes . Lb., 30c.
Breakfast Cakes . . . . Each, 30c.
Dutch Cake . . . . . . " 25c.
Moravian Cakes . . . " 15c.
Meringue Shells . . Doz., 1.00
Spiced Jumbles . . . " 20c.
Coffee Twists . . . . " 22c.
Bread Zweiback . . . Box, 18c

Hard Rolls

Crescents, Plain or Salt, Doz., 40c.
Long Rolls . . . . . . " 32c.
Short Rolls . . . . . . " 32c.
Round Kaiser Rolls . " 32c.

"Own Baking" 4th of July Decorated Cake

2½ Lb. Cake, Complete, $1.60

What a glorious Fourth this will be!
A rich golden cake, attractively decorated with American flags, will add to the occasion, especially if you're giving a children's party.

Reading Terminal Store Open Evenings

EXHIBIT 107.—Specimen page from a little 4-page folder on food suggestions, issued every two weeks by the Mitchell Fletcher Company and sent to customers and prospective customers.

The Mitchell-Fletcher Company gives the following information about the distribution of this bit of direct literature:

Suggestions is a continuation of *Acker's Weekly*, which was published over a period of more than thirty years. In 1919 the Acker business was purchased by Mitchell Fletcher Company, and on account of issuing the folder every two weeks, with the exception of the holiday season, the name was changed to *Suggestions*.

Form 40-A																							
NAME																							
ADDRESS																							

1923						1924						1925						1926					
1	2	3	4	5	6	1	2	3	4	5	6	1	2	3	4	5	6	1	2	3	4	5	6
7	8	9	10	11	12	7	8	9	10	11	12	7	8	9	10	11	12	7	8	9	10	11	12

DATE ENTERED ON LIST	BY	DATE DISCONTINUED FROM LIST
..................19........	..................19........	..................19........

EXHIBIT 108.—Card form used by the Mitchell Fletcher Company for keeping tabs on customers' buying.

Suggestions keeps our patrons posted on all that is new, seasonable and desirable in foods. More direct returns can be traced to it than to any other form of advertising which we have used.

Some years ago we made the experiment of asking customers to give us the names of their friends who might be interested in receiving the folder, but we have found better results from having our outside salesmen ask the same question of customers and then call on the prospective customer, telling her that she is called upon at the suggestion of Mrs. So. and So.

The card reproduced in Exhibit 108 shows the Mitchell-Fletcher Company's method of checking orders received from customers. This form is used for charge, c.o.d. and paid customers. The twelve months of the year are given by figures under the year. When an order comes in during the first month, or the third month, the proper figure is checked, so that at the end of the year, or at any time during the year, the record is an accurate guide as to the buying of each customer. Only orders above a certain amount are checked on this card.

Insuring Attention for the Catalogue.—As a means of insuring that his catalogue would be kept on file, a Western retailer offered a discount on orders sent to him during the period from September 1 to December 1 for goods listed in his mail-order catalogue. He made it a condition that the catalogue be returned with the order.

Another Western retailer, in attempting to check mail-order or distant-store buying, conducted a "popular customer-contest" in which a piano was given as a prize. "One vote for the most popular customer" was allowed for each purchase of a given amount.

To lend a little extra feature to his contest, this merchant offered a credit of two additional votes every time a catalogue of one of the mail-order houses was turned in. This merchant boasted of the fact that several tons of catalogues were turned in and sold as waste paper at a profit.

His procedure was very risky. In the first place, he ran the risk of action against him by the Federal Trade Commission on the ground of unfair competition, if directly or indirectly he induced customers to send to mail-order houses for catalogues to be used in the manner indicated. In the second place, he showed that he was so fearful of the effect of competition or of having mail-order catalogues in the houses of his patrons that he was willing to use an unsportsmanlike method of having them destroyed. This is small-calibered merchandising. It is likely, anyhow, that to a large extent he defeated his own purpose in that some people who had not troubled themselves to get mail-order catalogues sent for them as a means of getting more votes and then saw in these catalogues goods that they felt like ordering.

Mail for Farmers.—George B. Sharpe, formerly of the De Laval Cream Separator Company and later of the Cleveland Tractor Company, in addressing the Cleveland convention of the Direct Mail Advertising Association in 1919, said:

In the preparation of printed matter for the farmer, keep in mind that the farmer does not have an office boy to open his mail and lay it on his desk. Visualize if you can how the average farmer gets his mail. The R.F.D. man pushes it into the little tin box on the side of the road. That's one reason I have for years recommended folders not over 4 inches wide.

Good Imprints Are Worth While.—Much valuable advertising literature, in the form of folders and booklets, that comes to the retailer from manufacturers or other sources is somewhat spoiled by poor imprinting of the dealer's name and address. Rubber-stamping is a cheap-looking makeshift. It is not only crude but reveals at once that the booklet is not of the retailer's creation but material obtained elsewhere and hastily stamped by somebody. Most manufacturers will gladly imprint advertising matter for their dealers, either free of charge or at a nominal cost. If this cannot be arranged for, the dealer should either, on a press of his own or in a job shop, arrange for an imprint that is harmonious with the circular.

Store Papers.—A very large store or a chain of stores has unusual opportunity to profit by a store paper or magazine, because the high cost can be distributed over a good-sized sales total.

The variety of goods that can be offered through the display advertising in a publication of this kind gives a better opportunity to appeal to every home.

Exhibit 109 is made up of specimen pages from the *Rexall Magazine*, issued monthly by the United Drug Company. The Company gives the following information about the plan of publishing and distributing:

The *Rexall Magazine* is now entering upon its twelfth year. The magazine is sold to our Rexall store stockholder-agents in quantities of from 250 to 10,000 copies monthly, depending upon the size of the community. It is distributed by the Rexall store to the public in its own particular community. Each lot of magazines naturally carries the individual imprint of the dealer who distributes it. Distribution is accomplished in various ways, depending upon conditions and the type of people the dealer wishes to reach. I believe the greater part of it goes out on rural free delivery routes to country population, although considerable distribution is also made by mail and house to house in town, and some distribution probably in the store.

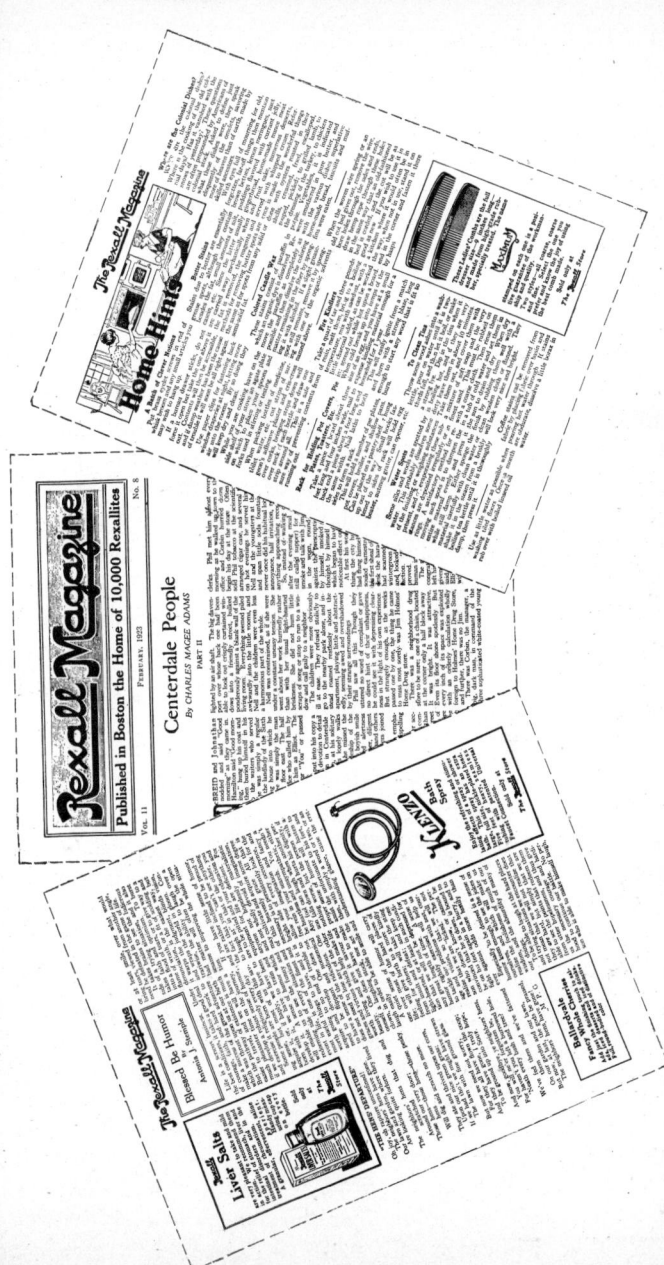

Exhibit 109.—Specimen pages from the store paper of the Rexall chain stores, issued by the United Drug Company, Boston, and distributed by Rexall dealers.

The primary purpose of the magazine is to help the Rexall dealer develop good-will and consumer-acceptance for Rexall goods in his community, and, judged on this basis, the magazine is very successful and a very good advertising investment for the dealer. In our files, we have hundreds of letters testifying to the value of the magazine for this purpose.

The circulation is now close to 1,000,000 copies monthly, and is increasing all the time.

This *Rexall Magazine* consists of sixteen pages, printed inexpensively on paper of fair grade. The size is 9 by 7 inches. Two-color printing is used on the front and back covers and there is also a double-page spread printed in two colors—orange-red and black. The name *Rexall Magazine* is printed in the orange-red on the front cover. Color is used on the back cover in a display advertisement. In the double-page spread are featured two display advertisements (all-type appeals), with the rest of the space given over to the picturing of the newsy, timely events of the day, in much the same way that the larger newspapers feature a pictorial or rotogravure section. As an illustration, one of these pictures shows Charlie Chaplin and Douglas Fairbanks having their pictures taken by the Ringling Bros. midgets, with this footnote:

An exclusive "International" photograph of the two greatest stars of the film world—Doug. Fairbanks and Charlie Chaplin—being photographed by the midgets with the Ringling Circus in Los Angeles.

Another shows a picture of a man and a strawberry plant, with the heading and footnote:

Fifty Thousand Dollars for a Strawberry Plant: Photo is of Frank E. Beatty, of Three Rivers, Mich., who has purchased the strawberry plant shown at the right for fifty thousand dollars. This plant bears gigantic fruit the year round, and represents fourteen years of untiring effort on the part of Harry Rockhill, who developed it.

Popular pictures are also used for the front cover design. Some of these are fictitious, while others are of prominent buildings or people. One number shows a view of the Woolworth building, while still another gives a picture of Constance

Talmadge. Besides display advertising and pictured news, this little publication carries serial stories, sections on "Home Hints," "Mothers' Helps," "Good Eats," a section of humor, a "puzzle page" and interesting contest features. Evidently, the idea of the publishers is to make the appeal of the magazine a broad one, so as to enlarge the attention that will be given to Rexall remedies.

Newspaper Advertisements for Direct Mailing.—A furniture store, of Lexington, Ky., uses an inexpensive and effective method of securing circulars for direct-mail advertising. An 8-page publication is made up of advertisements that will appear later in the newspapers. Newspaper publishers are glad to cooperate with the store in producing the circulars practically at cost. These circulars are mailed to families within a radius of sixty miles from Lexington before special sales. The 8-page advertisements of which the circulars are composed appear at intervals in the newspapers during the sales.

The circulars of this furniture store are distinctive in that they are made up in newspaper style, the first page containing eight columns with headlines and sub-heads, another page carrying an editorial, and the remainder display advertising, with illustrations, prices and descriptive matter.

(Grand Rapids Furniture Record).

Marshall Field & Company's Consumer House Organ.—This great company issues a house organ for its patrons, called *Fashions of the Hour*, which is mailed every other month. On the editorial page appears a panel reading:

> This magazine is published by Marshall Field & Company with the object of presenting to our customers the news of this great organization in its every branch, which is the news of a whole world of industry, of art, of fashion, of science, of progress. We shall be pleased to place on our mailing list, upon request sent to our editorial department, the name of any one desiring to receive it.

While a large part of the magazine is devoted to proper clothing for men, women and children, for the many varying and different occasions, there are sections also on linens, millinery, silverware, furniture, underwear, cooking utensils, tapestries, jewelry, luggage, hints on entertaining, and the like. One of the most attractive pages of the June, 1923, issue of *Fashions of the Hour* is entitled "Little Things Noticed on a Walk Through the Store." On this page are played up in a newsy, attractive way short items such as those reproduced below:

A place in the sun is yours—or anything else you want—if you wear a fur Deauville scarf on deck. These scarfs drape and knot over the shoulder, and the soft, vivid fabric which lines them, and folds back, may or may not show, as you like. In all summer furs.
Sixth Floor, North, Wabash Avenue.

Join him with eagerness and smart golf gloves. In chamois with half fingers, $1.25. Full chamois gloves, $2.50. Leather gauntlets with silk back and strap wrist, $4. For other occasions, there are silk gloves, in new styles, plain or embroidered, long or gauntlet. Doeskin gloves, 12-button length, washable, extremely smart, $3.50.
First Floor, South, State Street.

Keep your eye on the ball, with serenity, for your own sweater of Scotch plaid, stripes and checks of all colors and sizes, is making a very attractive and satisfactory point of focus for everyone else. There are many styles. In wool or silk. Wool, $8.75 to $18.50; silk, $25 and up.
Sports Apparel Section, Sixth Floor, South, State Street.

A sports costume is as smart as its belt, and these new belts are the smartest of all. Among the styles for this summer are white tubular belts ¾-inch wide. Sizes 28 to 44, 75 cents. White kid, braided with patent leather ¾-inch wide, black metal buckle, $1.25.
First Floor, South, State Street.

"And every dog his"—sleeping basket, blankets and pillow; for his morning bath, brushes, comb, soap, and nail clippers; and for his morning walk, a smart leash and collar. These, and other dog accessories.
Fourth Floor, Middle, Wabash Avenue.

"Natural selection"—of the gifts for the ushers, becomes a simple matter when there are distinctive match cases of leather or moire, $2.50. With gold mountings, they are priced $4.50 to $9.
First Floor, Middle, Wabash Avenue.

Tea is the reason for five o'clock, and one of the most important reasons for tea, is a brightly colored tea set for summer of Awaji pottery. In a wide assortment of colors, $10.
Second Floor, North, Wabash Avenue.

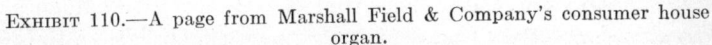

WE FOLLOW CHICAGOANS EVERYWHERE

OUR DELIVERY SYSTEM SHOWS THE WAY
OF SERVING WHENEVER SERVICE
CAN BE RENDERED

"PARCELS just arrived in good condition. Add to my order a pair of black oxfords, six triple A, arch preservers like those purchased in December," wrote a lady in Lucknow, India; for many a missionary's wife makes all her purchases here. Pins, needles, hats, blouses, and even home furnishings with the Marshall Field label above the address are found regularly on steamers bound for India, for China, and for Africa. You also—if you are going abroad for a month or two—maybe for years—can have orders delivered over-seas. Otherwise many a Chicagoan would miss her best fitting sizes and most favored brands such as are "found only at Field's."

"Package mailed to me care of the Claypool received. Your quick service is appreciated," writes a business man on his way through Indiana. His letter was directed to The Store for Men, but similar service is rendered by every department in both buildings. In the main store the candy section in particular makes a specialty of candies suitable for shipment to summer homes.

CANDIES DELIVERED TO YOUR SUMMER HOME

By taking order cards with you and mailing them each week (or whenever you see fit) you can be sure of a fresh supply of chocolates, caramels, and bonbons in one, two, or five-pound boxes. Our facilities for packing and shipping are unsurpassed and sweetmeats intended for seashore, week-end outings, and automobile trips will be sent promptly on receipt of the order.

The size of your purchase, the amount of the expenditure, has no bearing on your assurance of shipments from home. Perhaps last year in the Maine woods you needed a staunch swing under the pines and longed for the hickory swing, priced twelve dollars, that you had seen on the eighth floor. Had you written back for it, it would have been sent by the quickest route—we hope you will try writing this year.

Or maybe your country home will need a couch-hammock, new blankets, and chintzes. These can be selected and sent when you are ready. Handkerchief, hat, or china vase, if you but send a note to identify the article, the name of the salesman or a detailed description, we can assure the prompt careful service you get in the city. And conversely, you may send home apparel and drapes too sheer for the laundress and we will have them cleaned and returned expeditiously.

Bon voyage gifts, too, almost daily, go from our packing rooms direct to train or steamer. You may write and have the selection made by us, may select the gift yourself, or make your bon voyage a collection of greetings gathered by a group and sent in one huge packet. The delivery superintendents know the importance of meeting boat or train and no parcel accepted by them misses a sailing date except through dire accident.

YOUR PARCELS WILL MEET YOU AT THE TRAIN

For those who live near to Chicago—though not within regular delivery limits—just beyond the suburbs or in one of our neighbor states there is an additional service. If you wish to arrive early, shop in the morning, and spend your afternoons at the concert, your parcels will meet you at the train all ready for the "red cap." All you need do is to secure a shopping or purchase ticket of the first floorman you meet; make your purchases upon it; and exchange it, together with whatever else you wish sent, for a depot check.

Of course, nothing in the world is unbounded, but when the essential limits of a service are made to meet, overlap, and coordinate every related service, the bounds become invisible and the service continues indefinitely. Such a service—functioning wherever you go —and as far as you go—is our delivery system.

EXHIBIT 110.—A page from Marshall Field & Company's consumer house organ.

The magazine contains about twenty-four pages 13 by 9½ inches—a page large enough to permit free illustration. The cover is a gayly colored affair. The page reproduced in Exhibit 110 shows how the mail-order and delivery services are featured.

House Organ for Group of Stores.—A chain of half a dozen stores in a city of 150,000 and adjoining suburbs issued a store paper with the title of "The Money Saver." This was circulated with good results to a mailing-list of country customers.

This paper consisted of twelve to sixteen pages, the inside dimensions being 9 by 12 inches. The publication consisted of half to two-fifths of general reading matter, with the remainder of the space occupied by display advertisements.

Methods Used by Retailers to Offset Long-distance, or Mail-order Buying.—There is no need of elaborating on the loss that retail merchants in the smaller centers suffer through long-distance or mail-order buying by people of the community from the great stores of the larger cities. This has always been one of the retailer's greatest problems, and it has increased with the improvement in transportation and mailing facilities, the great spread of periodicals of all kinds, and so on.

The retailer should be on his guard against denouncing mail-order buying in general, for he may want to encourage mail-order buying for his own store. Likewise, if he is attempting to secure business from nearby towns and villages that are tributary to his own town, he should be careful how he phrases his appeals about buying at home. There is always the chance that such argument might be construed or applied by his distant customers as meaning that they should buy from their own local merchants rather than from the advertiser of the neighboring city.

The great stores of the large centers excel in their advertising work. Not only do they exploit their advertising attractively in newspapers and magazines, but they send out catalogues, circulars and letters that are usually more effective than those produced by the smaller merchants. The mail-order specialists also trade on the disposition of buyers to value more highly something that is purchased away from home. Nevertheless, the local advertiser enjoys advantages, if he will only use them. Among these advantages are the following:

1. The local advertiser often has personal acquaintance with his customers.

2. He is in a better position to determine credit.

3. He can show the actual goods rather than ask the customer to depend on mere illustration and catalogue description.

4. He can give immediate delivery, and other service.

In general, it is better to exploit these advantages than to solicit business through scolding people for the buying-away-from-home habit. Such "scolding" advertising often adds fuel to the flames, so to speak.

A local merchant can easily learn of instances where people of his community have bought from distant sources at a disadvantage. If he is a ready writer, without mentioning names he can tell of these instances in a newsy, good-natured way, so as to point his moral. A dealer in women's coats and suits once made good use of this instance: a customer came in to tell him that, after buying a suit from his store, she had been in New York, visiting a friend. While there, she had seen a suit similar in every detail to the one she had bought only the New York suit was priced $20 higher. After telling about the incident, she added, "If it had been the other way round and I had seen that I had paid you $20 more than the New York store charged, I should probably have come in and found fault, so I think it is only fair to tell you how pleased I was to find I had really saved money by buying the suit before going to New York."

Exhibit 111 is another illustration of how the buying-away-from-home habit can be treated in an advertising way.

That Delicious Allentown Ice Cream!

Two Easton ladies were shopping the other day in our sister city of Allentown. Taking their lunch in one of Allentown's largest stores, they were highly pleased with the ice cream served them.

"I wonder why," said one of the ladies, "we can't get ice cream like this in Easton. See here, waiter," she called, "Where do you get your ice cream?"

"Abel's, Easton, ma'am," was the reply.

EXHIBIT 111.—A pleasing way of dealing with out-of-town buying.

An enterprising firm of Honesdale, Pa., the Murray Company, fights long-distance buying by putting out a small catalogue that features goods that the Murray Company can sell at prices comparing favorably with those listed in the catalogues of the mail-order houses. Many of the goods in the Murray catalogue can be shipped direct from the manufacturers to the farmers by the usual mail-order plan. The catalogue is printed and illustrated in the style of that of the well known mail-order concerns. The object is not particularly to develop mail-order trade but to show patrons that if they want to buy by mail, they can be served better by the Murray Company than by the stores that are thousands of miles away.

A small retailer of Roundup, Mont., successfully combatted mail-order buying by adroit comparison of values in his advertising under the heading, "The deadly parallel." His plan was to list in one column the actual description of an article as taken from the catalogue of the mail-order house most popular in his immediate vicinity, while in a second column alongside of the first he would describe his own article. One of this merchant's advertisements ran about in this manner:

See page 423, 41-F(707)—Bib Overall, extra heavy, weight in size 38 waist 29 ounces; no union label; cost (to customer) $1.39, plus 17 cents parcel post, 3-cent money order and 2-cent stamp; cost laid down in Roundup, $1.61.	Big 3-Bib Overall union label, weight in size 38, 36 ounces, or 7 ounces more than...... (name of mail order house inserted here); sells here for $1.25 every day, or 36 cents less than mail-order house.

Exhibit 112.—Comparative advertising used by a Western retailer to offset buying from the big mail-order houses on the part of his customers.

This Roundup merchant supported his advertising by carrying in stock only standard goods of excellent value. Thus, gradually the people of the community came to realize that they could actually do better by buying at home than they could by patronizing the mail-order houses.

It is interesting to note that price is not the only point of comparison in this merchant's advertising. He, as well as many other merchants, has found that there are many ways of measuring or comparing merchandise, and that price often is not the determining factor, though it is always an important factor.

A resident merchant once scored strongly with a customer by showing that a pair of blankets from a mail-order concern was several inches shorter and a few inches narrower than his own blankets, as well as lighter in weight. The price of the resident merchant's blanket was slightly higher than the price of the mail-order blanket, but the customer was convinced that the heavier blanket of the local merchant was the best value.

Naturally, more can be accomplished if the merchants of a community will work together in a cooperative effort to overcome the mail-order or buying-away-from-home habit, but it is difficult to get a group of local merchants to cooperate harmoniously in a plan of this kind. There are always so many different viewpoints.

A cooperative effort that was very successful was carried out in Horton, Kan., where a number of merchants combined in the fight against mail-order competition through showing by comparisons of their own goods with goods of mail-order concerns that the customer is served better in the long run by patronizing home stores. The tests that these merchants made showed that the mail-order houses unquestionably undersold them on some articles, but in making up combinations of goods, the percentage in favor of the local merchants was anywhere from 17 to 22 per cent. In these tests, no specially priced merchandise of local merchants was allowed to figure.

When the public realized that buying away from home was costing it more, on the average, and that in many cases the goods bought did not compare favorably with home products, the mail-order buying fever in Horton abated considerably.

(Summarized in part from *New York Times*).

The Problem of the Neighborhood Store.—The store or other business that operates to a large extent only in one section of a good-sized city lacks the opportunity enjoyed by the centrally located store, so far as the use of newspaper advertising is concerned.

The size or peculiar character of the business may be such that even if it is a long way from the center of trade, it may still use the newspapers of the city to advantage. Its merchandise or service may be such that people will send or go a long way for it. For example, the J. B. Van Sciver Company, of Camden, N. J., right across the river from Philadelphia, is, in point of location, at a disadvantage so far as the Philadelphia trade is concerned, and yet because of its reputation and stock of furniture and the extent of merchandise it sells, it is undoubtedly just as able to profit by Philadelphia newspaper advertising as the large furniture stores of Philadelphia are.

When, however, the goods sold are of the classification known as "convenience goods"—those that people will not go a long way for—such as groceries, drugs, phonograph records, general hardware, electrical goods of a popular nature, and the like, the store that is far away from the center of trade will probably have to content itself with doing little newspaper advertising, or perhaps none, and have recourse to one of the following methods:

1. Store paper, bulletin or magazine, which may be an entirely individual affair or partly made up of syndicated matter. In a number of lines of retailing, it is possible for the local store to get an attractive 8-page publication with some space left open for individual advertising and the name and address of the firm.

A number of furniture stores use syndicated publications of this kind, sending them out to a selected mailing list at intervals of every month, or four to six times a year.

Exhibit 113 shows the cover page of a syndicated publication used by leading furniture stores. As its name "Home" indicates, it gives a number of attractive presentations of the furnishings of a modern home. Naturally, such a publication is of greater value to a retailer when it deals with the particular kind of furnishings that he is prepared to sell. For this reason, manufacturers frequently put out magazines of this kind for their retailers, showing just exactly the kind of stock carried. Even if it is not possible to prepare a magazine showing the retailer's goods exclusively, it is always possible to leave open the back page, or the two center pages, in a publication of this kind, so that a dealer who may be so disposed can feature his own merchandise in this space in such a way that it links up very well with the syndicated material contained in the rest of the publication.

For example, on the back cover of *Home*, the magazine referred to above, space was left for the dealer's imprint, and below this imprint appears the line: "We shall be pleased to quote prices on any article shown in this magazine."

2. The use of attractive folders or booklets. These are probably most often secured from the manufacturers whose goods the store handles. In other cases, the merchant may prefer to make up his own booklets, folders, mailing-cards, and other direct literature. In Exhibit 103 are reproduced a number of booklets that have been used by merchants to advantage.

EXHIBIT 113.—Cover page of an attractive syndicated publication prepared for furniture retailers. The imprint of the dealer in this case was on the back, or fourth, cover.

3. Series of letters about the goods or service of the store. Into these letters may be slipped a folder, booklet or card giving more details about certain merchandise than can be conveniently given in a letter.

4. Signs or bulletins around the front of the store or in the immediate neighborhood, or along the roads or streets leading to the place of business.

Before deciding, however, that he will use advertising methods that he can confine strictly to the particular neighborhood or community in which he does business, the proprietor of a business should give full attention to the fact that a well circulated newspaper offers him an opportunity to reach many thousands of people at small cost, and that it is often used profitably by advertisers, even when there is a chance of selling to only 10 to 20 per cent of the circulation of the medium. It is not always wise, anyhow, for a business to circumscribe its sales territory too sharply. While it is true that people cannot be expected to go miles to reach a drug store when another can be reached by walking a few blocks, the progressive merchant should seek always to be reaching out and introducing new features that will widen his selling territory.

There are many stores that can make occasional use of newspapers, even though their location may make it necessary for a large part of the advertising to be done by the direct methods indicated in the preceding paragraphs.

Miscellaneous Experiences with Direct Advertising Methods. The following reviews of experiences with mailing-list advertising, store papers and other direct advertising features are prepared from information courteously furnished by the Advertising Group, National Retail Dry Goods Association.

A store in a New England town of 20,000 population makes up its mailing-lists through cooperation with clubs, post-office officials, voting lists, heads of private schools and public school teachers. Such methods are used as distributing free rattles and booklets to mothers who call at the infants' department for them. An offer of this kind is made to a general list and the responses aid the store in classifying its list.

The store reports the following results from letters, circulars and envelop enclosures:

> Infants' Wear—Excellent
> Boys' Department—Fairly good results
> House Furnishings and Furs—Poor
> Appeals to High School Graduates—Good

An effort is made by this firm to keep in touch with local events and to advertise an article to certain groups at a time when it is most appropriate or most likely to be considered.

Announcements from Paris Increase Prestige.—A store in a New England town of 70,000, which, in addition to a farming element, has a large resort and tourist population, announces purchases made abroad through post cards mailed from Paris. The mailing-list is built up from newspaper subscribers, charge accounts and delivery records. The appeal of this store is rather institutional and prestige-building, as no special attempt is made to sell specific merchandise. The mailing of a series of filled-in multigraphed letters to its patrons direct from New York is also reported to have brought most satisfactory results.

Circularizing with Newspaper Advertisements.—A store in a farming center of 150,000 population planned a campaign on summer dresses, featuring garments of three prices. A full-page advertisement showing twenty sketches of the garments was set several days before the sale and 10,000 circulars were printed. These were enclosed in letters to charge customers, calling attention to the sale and giving them the privilege of making selections on the day before the sale. The store reports that several hundred dollars' more business resulted on the day before the sale than on the opening day. The opening day was advertised to the general public by a full-page advertisement in the three local papers.

A letter to a general list sold 3,000 boxes of stationery, and a similar letter sold 225 army blankets to a list of Boy Scouts and Y. M. C. A. members.

Use of Monthly Paper and Multigraphed Letters.—In a western city of about 100,000 population where industrial and mine workers predominate, a large general store pays more attention to a monthly store paper sent to an extensive mailing-list and to a series of multigraphed letters than to any other form of advertising. The management does not hold that the store does well to eliminate newspaper advertising altogether. It is admitted that the newspapers cover a broader field and exercise a greater publicity power than a direct campaign can give. This store, nevertheless, feels that it has established its methods of direct advertising so successfully that in a measure it is independent of the newspaper medium. The mailing-list is built up largely through rewards given employes and through customers and teachers furnishing the names of probable customers.

A number of stores have found a four-page paper of newspaper size valuable in appealing particularly to country women. Other stores have found it profitable to have a newspaper office reprint ten, fifteen or twenty thousand or more copies of a newspaper page, which is mailed direct to a selected mailing-list. Sometimes, in order to make these store papers readable, some columns are left open for household suggestions, short stories or other items.

Business Quadrupled by Use of Form Letters.—The L. A. Hudson general store, Colgate, Okla., increased its volume of business from $34,000 to $138,000 in three years by the following advertising methods, described by A. F. Hudson:

We have an addressograph, a mimeograph, a grapho-type and an electric folding machine to fold our circulars. Every week we send out a mimeographed circular to our customers and prospective customers, telling them about the bargains we are offering. We have built up a mailing-list of 3,500 names, which we got from the tax rolls of the county. These persons live in a radius of thirty-five miles from Colgate in all directions. Farmers will drive that far in their motor-cars to buy supplies and we have cultivated the farm trade and sought means of interesting it in our store and in keeping its good-will.

We do not just write form letters. We put descriptions of merchandise in them and we quote prices. They are written to sell goods, not just to make a good impression on the reader. We want their business, so we tell them just what we have to sell and how much it will cost them.

The store is run by two brothers who returned from the war in 1918 and found their father hampered by lack of help. The first thing they did was to put the business on a strictly

Exhibit 114.—Advertising forms of this kind are so useful that they are rarely wasted or thrown away.

cash basis. Then by means of hard work and the advertising already described they proceeded to turn their stock on an average of five times a year.

(*Retail Ledger*).

Winter Campaign by Service Station.—In order to keep their electric-service station busy during the winter, two brothers in Augusta, Me., purchased an addressograph, compiled a mailing-list of owners of automobiles and trucks, and began a direct-mail campaign on eight selected articles of fall and winter equipment for automobiles. In spite of the fact that many people in that section of the country put their cars in storage for the winter, enough business was secured to keep the entire force employed during the season.

The campaign consisted of "Monday Morning Messages," printed on light manila stock, 5½ by 8 inches, the color of ink varying from time to time. The campaign lasted two months. Follow-up postal cards were used and mailing-lists carefully checked. It was found that mail sent to the car-owner's home brought the best results. Following is one of the series:

ANOTHER GOOD ONE THIS WEEK

If you keep your car in a cold garage you should have it for your own protection. It saves excessive drain on the battery. It makes unnecessary the use of hot water to start.

If your car hasn't a self-starter and you have to crank it yourself; Oh, Lord, how you need it!!!!!!

The ——— Primer

Delivers an easy-to-fire mixture to the Right Place when you want it and makes starting almost instantaneous.
They do not get out of order, and this year WE INSTALL them for $——— on any car.

EXHIBIT 115.—One of a series of small direct appeals used by an automobile service station during cold weather.

At the time the campaign was being carried on, owners of cars were compelled to have lights tested and obtain licenses. This station secured an appointment as an official testing-station and immediately made glaring headlights the subject of a "Morning Message," including, of course, the service on lighting equipment. Other messages covered stop-lights, wind-shield cleaners and electric hand-warmers, the last-named as a Christmas gift suggestion. The final message referred to the former one about light-testing and reminded car owners of the necessity for renewing licenses.

(Summarized from *Automobile Trade Journal*).

Direct Advertising Forms That Are Useful to Others.— Advertising that sometimes brings a good return for the expense involved consists of forms that are useful to the recipient. For example, these might be ice cards, furnished by the ice company, bearing refrigerator advertisements; wet-paint signs, featuring the paint used on the job or the store supplying the paint; laundry lists, bearing the name of the laundry; payroll envelops bearing an advertisement of a local bank, and so on.

An ice-cream manufacturer has scored a success with drug stores, cafeterias, refreshment parlors, and the like, by furnishing them with an attractive panel (Exhibit 114) advertising his ice cream. These are made of "Crystaloid," a material resembling celluloid or oilcloth, which can be easily cleaned. There is a large display panel at the top and separate smaller panels that can be appended with metal rings, each of the smaller panels advertising just one flavor. The panels can be changed from day to day, so as to advertise the flavors the retailer is prepared to serve that day. There is also a panel labeled "Special." Customers inquiring about the "special" will be told what it is and can then be served.

SECTION X

STREET-CAR, OUTDOOR AND SPECIALTY ADVERTISING

Street-car Cards.—The street-car card affords room for only 25 to 50 words of text if it is to be set in a style that permits easy reading. The street-car card may be regarded as a small indoor poster to be read at the range of 5 to 15 or 20 feet. The points that apply to posters and painted board advertising apply in a large measure to street-car cards.

While the use of the automobile has to some extent interfered with the opportunity of street-car advertising, the street-cars, nevertheless, serve the people to such an extent that this type of advertising enjoys a broad opportunity. While no one medium such as the street-car fills the need completely for most advertisers, there are instances on record where the street-car has been used as the principal medium with marked success.

The larger concerns controlling street-car space have been of great assistance to local and retail advertisers by providing first-class designs and ideas at reasonable cost, thus permitting the advertiser in the city where only 100 or 200 street-cars are operated to have the use of colored and well illustrated designs that he could hardly afford to have prepared for his own exclusive use.

The writing of street-car cards is instructive copy-writing practice, for there is room for only a striking headline or opening sentence and perhaps an explanatory sentence. This means that all temptations to write introductions or to be verbose must be overcome.

Most good street-car advertisers place the principal display of their cards either in the center or near the bottom of the space, because of the angle at which street-car cards are usually read.

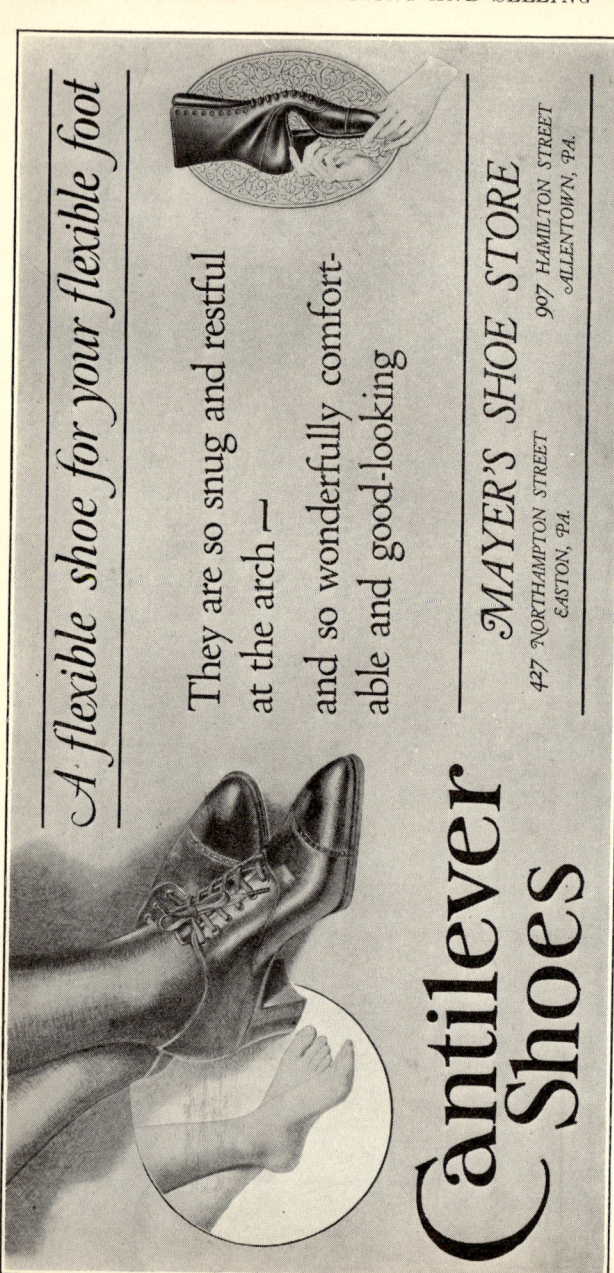

EXHIBIT 116.—An unusually well illustrated card. The double illustration of the bare feet and the shod feet show how admirably Cantilever Shoes adapt themselves to natural positions of the foot. The other illustration occupies little space but is enough to bring out the point of flexibility. The headline is well-phrased, and the principal display, "Cantilever Shoes," is effective. The only criticism of this card is that the text type should have been a little stronger, so that at a distance of 10 or 12 feet the message could have been read more easily. In the original, this card was printed in black on a very light green background.

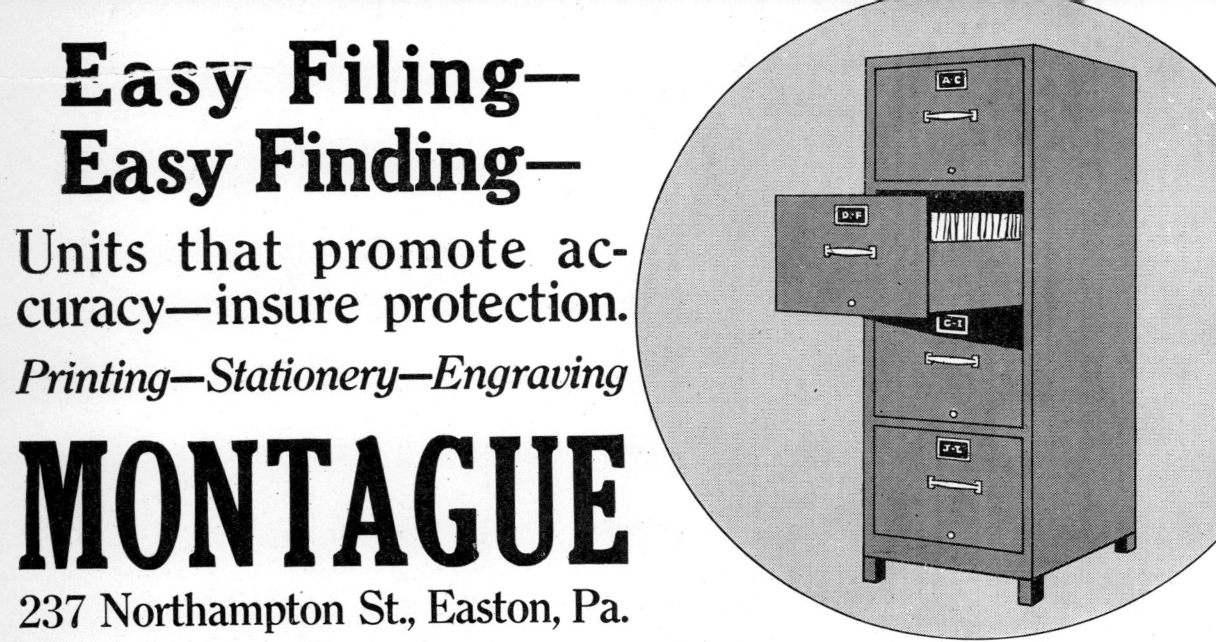

OUTDOOR AND SPECIALTY ADVERTISING 259

Easy Filing—
Easy Finding—

Units that promote accuracy—insure protection.

Printing—Stationery—Engraving

MONTAGUE

237 Northampton St., Easton, Pa.

EXHIBIT 117.—Fine example of simple, strong illustration and terse text. In the original, the metal file appeared in green against an orange background, making it stand out vividly. The double headline is right to the point. The name of the merchant here appeared in 2-inch letters.

Types for street-car card advertising should be more than ordinarily strong. Sizes below 36-point are usually ineffective. Sizes ranging from 42-point up to 72-point afford more readable messages. Main displays may carry letters 2 inches deep or deeper. The heavier types should be used unless the subject of the advertising requires light treatment.

Proof for street-car cards should never be judged at a range of a foot or two but should be placed across the room and viewed from a distance of 6 to 10 feet.

EXHIBIT 118.—The illustrator in this case, realizing the lack of space for a human figure, has wisely shown just the hat. The price being a popular one, the card gains in value by its prominent display. This card is another example of how strength is gained by simplicity. Compare with many of the cluttered-up cards seen in the street-cars.

In getting up original cards the advertiser should be on his guard against excessive color treatment. Many of the two-color combinations are far superior to cards in which three, four or more colors are used. There is great need for simplicity.

Exhibits 116, 117, 118 and 119 afford some excellent examples of street-car advertising.

Combining Street-car Advertising with Newspaper Advertising.—Street-car advertising and newspaper advertising may often be connected with advantage.

In the case of the Biltmore Hat card, for example, the street-car advertisement was reproduced in half of a double run service of the H. & S. Pogue Company, department store merchants of Cincinnati, during the week preceding Easter Sunday.

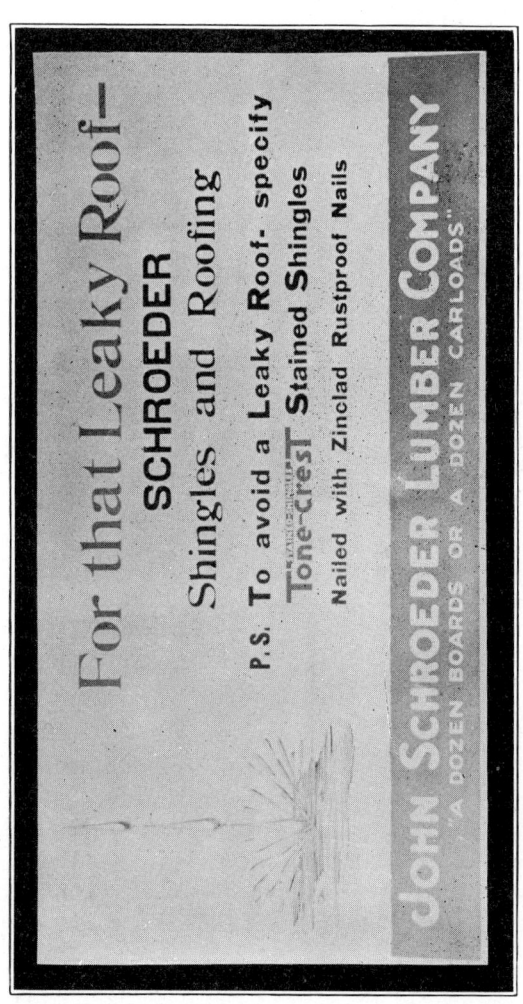

EXHIBIT 119.—The kind of street-car advertising used by a progressive lumber dealer for reaching prospective purchasers of prepared roofing. In the original, this card was 11 by 21 inches, printed in blue and black on white cardboard. The slogan is an apt one. There is too much variation in the length of the various type lines to afford easy reading.

On account of the original colors of the card, it is not possible to give a reproduction that does justice to the water-dropping illustration and background treatment.

In the two Cincinnati morning papers on the Saturday before Easter, the following copy appeared over the signature of the Pogue Company:

> ## LOOK FOR THE "BILTMORE HAT" CARD IN THE STREET CARS
>
> It will be in every car in the city of Cincinnati.
>
> The Biltmore is the greatest value in men's hats that we have ever offered, and we want every man with $3.65 to have one.
>
> *Have you wanted a hat that will wear---on and off ---for years?*
>
> *Have you wanted a hat that even your wife will like?*
>
> *Have you wanted a hat that will increase your manly beauty 100 per cent and save you 50 per cent by its low price?*
>
> ## HERE IT IS---THE BILTMORE--- $3.65---JUST IN TIME FOR EASTER!
>
> Men's Shop—Separate Entrance on Fourth Street

The writer of the copy shows his consideration of men's aversion to going into a department store by adding the information about "Separate Entrance on Fourth Street."

It is stated by the advertiser that this combination campaign produced an unusually good record in hat sales during the two weeks that the Biltmore Hat was featured in the cars.

POSTERS AND PAINTED BOARDS

While this volume does not afford space for detailed description of all outdoor forms of advertising, it is not inappropriate to point out that posters and painted boards of different sizes and styles, as well as electric signs, afford many retail advertisers an opportunity to exploit the leading selling points of their enterprises. The merchant using this form of publicity should take into account the opposition the public has to seeing signs at points where they obstruct attractive scenery or for some other reason seem not in accordance with good taste.

The poster and painted board give unusual opportunity for pictorial treatment in colors. They have the advantage of strong display that is largely a unit in itself and is not likely to be blanketed by other displays. This medium is one, however, that is suitable only for exploiting simple messages.

It is obvious that such advertising cannot give the complete information that letters, newspaper advertisements and other forms often give. On the other hand, the truth is that often an advertiser is benefited by compressing certain of his messages to a single telling sentence. Even if such a message does not tell the whole story, it may serve a valuable supplemental purpose. A large store, for example, while depending on newspaper advertising, may make use of outdoor advertising to call attention to outstanding features of the establishment or to particular departments.

The J. B. Van Sciver Company, of Camden, N. J., for example, is well known to its patrons as a store offering an

EXHIBIT 120.—Board that gives the reader a pleasing picture of the great variety of stock offered by the J. B. Van Sciver Company.

unusual stock of furniture. It is therefore good publicity for this advertiser to exploit the great variety of his stock. This is very appropriately done in the sign shown in Exhibit 120. The four words, "Ten Acres of Furniture," convey an impressive picture to the reader's mind.

This sign is posted along the tracks of the Pennsylvania Railroad, close to the Broad Street Station, Philadelphia. Camden being just across the river from Philadelphia, it can draw trade from this metropolitan territory.

Exhibit 121 illustrates two of the so-called de luxe type of signs, now seen with increasing frequency on the main highways and also on prominent streets of cities.

This form of sign, while obviously more costly, has real decorative features, and therefore escapes some of the criticism directed at the flaring or inartistic posters and signs.

(*Courtesy, R. C. Maxwell Company, Trenton, N. J.*)

EXHIBIT 121.—Two of the de luxe type of signs that are gradually replacing the cruder forms of painted boards along the main thoroughfares.

The Barlow example is something of a novelty sign. In the original the board measured 14 by 60 feet, with an added feature of a platform built out from the sign, on which was placed a dummy Bambach Baby Grand piano. The peacocks at the two ends of this sign were attractive in the original colors, and constituted appropriate decorative treatment. The lettering gains by its simplicity, and the advertiser shows his merchandising sense by giving the information that a baby grand can be had as low as $635.

The Blakely sign shows how an outdoor display may be linked up with the display on delivery wagons of the advertiser. While this sign goes further than most signs go in giving general information about finished family laundry service, it would have been better had the laundry gone still further and specifically named the different types of laundry service— Prim-Prest, Rough-Dry, Thrif-T-Service, Ho-mestic, Float-Ironed, Wet Wash, etc. Even if there was not room to explain what these terms mean, such a message would at least convey the information to the housekeeper that the laundry offered six or more types of laundry service. This would arouse interest, and at the first opportunity, the woman reader would likely inquire what the different services offered her.

Exhibits 122 and 123 indicate other possibilities of outdoor advertising in local and retail campaigns.

A well known Canadian store uses lighted billboards to portray attractive home scenes and to exploit the information that the store "Gives Time on Furniture." The attractive picture, together with this pointed bit of information, makes an effective appeal.

An argument frequently offered by salesmen of outdoor advertising—posters, painted boards and electric signs—is that not everybody reads but everybody walks and sees. There can hardly be any successful controverting of the fact that the most intelligent part of the public reads the newspapers and other printed material that is interesting enough to command attention. At the same time, it is true that any single issue of the paper may be missed by many people or a particular announcement missed. The success of the theaters in drawing crowds by means of poster advertisements demon-

EXHIBIT 122.—A poster that combines the picture of a pleased user of the article with a slogan that interprets well the name of the bread. There is also a good selling point in the line, "The large, economical loaf."

OUTDOOR AND SPECIALTY ADVERTISING 267

(*Copyright, Donaldson Lithographing Co., published by permission*).

EXHIBIT 123.—Excellent example of simple human interest design. The copy idea of middle-age and old-age "carefreeness," brought about by a bank account, though essentially sound, is not presented as definitely as it might be. The poster-story should be such that it is grasped instantly.

strates the value of this medium for announcements, especially the announcement that can be accompanied by attractive pictures. The pictures themselves, with some brief text, tell a complete story effectively. Judiciously used, the outdoor medium may be made a strong supplement to any other form of advertising. It does not meet the needs of every advertiser but has often served in successful campaigns as the principal medium.

Novel Wording on Signs.—Novelty and apt phrasing have their places in outdoor advertising as in the headlines of newspaper advertising and the titles of folders. A laundry has made effective use of the invitation to "Send Your Duds to Our Suds." Various electrical contractors have made use of the invitation, "Wire Me and I'll Wire You." A tire repairer instead of adopting commonplace phraseology uses "Invite Me to Your Next Blowout."

A Tire-dealer's Road Signs.—A tire dealer in Quincy, Ill., finds that considerable business comes to him as the result of passersby seeing his neat red-and-white varnished signs along the roads entering the city. The signs are in the form of arrows, a red one lettered "To Quincy," a larger white one with the name of the store, and another red one with the street address, all three pointing in the same direction and nailed to the same post.

Signs That Are Sales Bulletins for Farmers.—A Wisconsin merchant uses the familiar roadside sign in a new way to gain good-will from customers, as well as to direct the public in general to his store. In front of the farms of willing customers he places a well made sign with the name of the farmer at the top, followed by the number of miles to the merchant's address, his name and the kind of goods he sells. Underneath this information is a blank space in which the farmer can chalk notices of any products he may have for sale. Farmers appreciate these signs and the attention of the passing public is attracted to them because of the changing items at the bottom.

Advertising Possibilities of Trucks and Wagons.—A delivery truck or wagon can be made to serve as an effective outdoor sign for a local advertiser, especially when it is connected with efficient delivery service. The laundry wagons throughout the country are now exploiting, by means of special announcements on the sides of the wagons, the various kinds of laundry service offered—Prim-Prest, Rough-Dry, Thrif-T-Service, Ho-mestic, Float-Ironed, Wet Wash.

A music dealer of Michigan has a large white truck bearing on the front in black lettering, "Here Comes Thor," and on the back, "There Goes Thor." Other retail merchants use trucks as a means of displaying certain slogans or trademarks. Often in the case of such goods as ice cream, bread or other provisions the delivery wagon or truck affords opportunity for attractive pictorial representation. A well known local baker uses as his trade-mark a picture of an attractive small boy labeled "The Little Baker." This trade-mark appears on his delivery wagons.

Delivery Vans in Shapes That Advertise.—Another form of mobile publicity is that in which the body of the van is shaped to resemble a giant example of the product sold. Pencils, fountain pens and commodities put up in bottles or packages lend themselves to this form of advertising. Where this plan is not possible, large models of goods, such as pipes and cigars, can be placed on the roofs of vans. One firm of tea blenders combines both ideas, the body of the wagon being a package surmounted by a teapot. Another merchant has used effectively a delivery vehicle shaped like a shoe—the business being a shoe store. Still another has a mammoth Victrola back of the driver's seat.

(Marketing).

CALENDARS, NOVELTIES, SPECIALTIES AND OTHER FORMS

The retailer, like the manufacturer and other advertisers, can make good use of various direct forms of advertising such as calendars, novelties and specialties that customers and prospective customers can carry around in their pockets, use on their desks, at home, and so on; convenient or especially serviceable types of blotters; handy devices to use in practical work, such as a celluloid scale of mixtures for the cement-worker.

It is often said that such forms of advertising as calendars are overused to so great an extent that it is difficult to get the advertising placed. There is truth in this argument, and yet the advertiser who creates a calendar of unusual utility or attractiveness has a good opportunity, provided, of course, his business is one that may be reasonably expected to profit by such a concise type of standing advertisement as the calendar.

There is solid truth in the argument that advertising gets a better chance when it is tied up appropriately with something that is useful—something that the recipient will appreciate and keep. Hence the use of imprinted big-lead pencils for the mechanic, the desk utility for the office man, the novel form of eraser for the typewriter operator, the prescription blank for the physician, and the useful kitchen or household forms for the housekeeper.

The essentials in arranging for these forms of advertising are:

1. Judgment in deciding whether the willingness of customers or prospective customers to receive remembrances really produces enough of the right kind of attention and impression for the advertising to be profitable. Most people are more than willing to receive valuable and useful gifts. One who is prepared to give away good dictionaries or serviceable automobile jacks will not lack for a crowd eager to aid him in disposing of the presents. There are few, if any, advertisers who could afford to adopt such methods unless the purchases of customers are large. To a lesser degree the principle applies to many other articles given away as advertisements. Advertisers who purchase expensive novelties sometimes find that they vanish quickly and that customers and prospective customers who were not remembered feel aggrieved.

2. A selection of something that is particularly appropriate to the business to be exploited. A book on "How to Plan for a Home" would be ideal for a real-estate concern selling home building lots or marketing completed homes. A handy pressure-tester would be appropriate for a tire-dealer. The shoehorn is in order for the shoe retailer. But the baker or

restaurant-keeper who distributes pencils, pens or pen-clips is getting rather too far away from his business for the venture to show a return. The salesman for specialty goods will argue that the presentation of a useful novelty, even if its use is entirely disassociated from the business of the advertiser, creates appreciation and good-will that brings patronage. This may be true in cases, and yet it seems that the advertiser has much more to gain by putting out something that is associated with his business. If the business college is to distribute some novelty, it should select something that its students will wear as a standing advertisement—a watch-fob, for example—or something that employers will keep as a reminder of the service of the school in furnishing new employes.

3. If at all practicable, adopt some method of distribution that will induce people to ask for the novelty or call for it. Some firms adopt the plan of sending out a neat card, informing the reader that the useful article is on hand for him if he is interested in having it, or will call. In this way many advertisers have induced people to visit their establishments or have secured valuable mailing-lists. It is possible to secure mailing-lists of acquaintances of the customers by this method.

A double postal card, for example, can be used in a message of the following character:

We recently secured a limited quantity of............ This..............is a very handy little affair (give concise description). We don't want to sell them, but prefer to present them to some of our good friends. We are putting one aside for you. All you have to do is to fill out and return the attached card. You see, we are trying to enlarge our mailing-list of buyers of.................. We know you will have no difficulty in giving us several additional names for our records, so we can send these acquaintances our announcements from time to time.

ADVERTISER'S NAME

SECTION XI

THE WRITING OF COPY

No one style of copy meets all advertising needs. The breezy style that may be appropriately used in exploiting such goods as men's hats or golf clubs would be inappropriate for the advertising of cemetery lots or high-class investments.

Faults and Requirements.—The only real test that can be applied is whether or not the style of appeal fits the subject and the type of reader addressed. Advertising copy is usually faulty because of:

Commonplaceness or triteness

Wordiness and general claims

Extravagance.

An old and well known formula for good advertising is worth repeating. This formula sets forth that to be effective an advertisement:

1. Must be seen
2. Must be read
3. Must be believed
4. Must be remembered.

Such a formula requires that an advertisement must be pointed enough to command attention and interesting enough to hold that attention after attention has been drawn. Copy will not be believed unless interest is sustained and unless the statements or descriptions ring with sincerity. Finally, unless the advertisement scores impressively, through picture or through the points made in the printed language, the reader will not remember what the advertiser says long enough for the message to play its part in an immediate or a subsequent sale.

The Range from Formal to Chatty Language.—Dignity and formality are not always out of place in advertising. Some subjects require these qualities. The exclusive millinery shop may not be so well served by copy of the chatty, clever or familiar style as by language of some such tone as:

Madame C.........., the well known designer, who has just returned from a month's stay abroad, will give our patrons the benefit of her observations on Thursday afternoon of this week at 2 o'clock.

Except, however, where the occasion or the merchandise requires the conservative treatment, advertising copy is more effective when formal style is dropped and the language is earnest, direct and chatty. The day has passed when the "We announce" style of composition received a good measure of attention. The hardware man years ago would have written:

As the Spring season approaches and the need for outdoor work becomes apparent, we take pleasure in drawing attention to our very complete stock of gardening and farming implements.

Nowadays, if he is a good advertiser, he is more likely to write:

The right tools for that gardening work you are going to start next week.

Introductions.—Essays have little place in modern advertising. There is too much competition for attention and space is too costly. The writer of unusual skill, he whose ideas and words would command good attention if he elected to write editorials or stories, may now and then write a message in the essay style and put enough entertainment or good sense into it to make the message good institutional advertising for some store or business. But the increasing pace of life and the multiplication of newspapers and magazines have placed on advertisers the need for terseness. Consequently, most of the introductions that formerly required a paragraph or two are nowadays eliminated or condensed to a few sentences. This should not be construed to mean that all advertisements should be begun with a description of the goods or service offered. The word "introduction" is an elastic term. It may be good advertising to devote a paragragh, or even more, to the need for an article or the service to be derived from it before giving details of the article itself. The useless introductions are those made up of language that the copy-writer uses merely to get started in his subject, as it were. Courtesy may impel people to listen to the salesman who rambles a while before getting to his real errand, but readers of advertisements are impelled by no such motive. Unless the advertisement immediately commands their attention, the roving eye wanders to something else.

Simple Language.—Long words are not always out of order. Many long words are among those easiest to understand and may be as useful as short ones. Technical and rarely used words may be appropriate and effective in describing certain commodities to special types of audiences—engineers, chemists and doctors, for example. One who is advertising fine drawing instruments to experienced draftsmen can use terms and descriptions that would not be advisable in selling other types of drawing instruments to buyers making their first purchase of such material.

Simple language, however, has not only the usual arguments in its favor in advertising practice, but also the additional argument that it takes less space. If "It lasts" conveys the idea just as well as "It is permanent," then the shorter sentence should be used. Compare "Come in and talk it over" with "We should be much pleased indeed to have you visit our establishment and discuss your needs." Again, however, it should be taken into account that there are occasions when dignity and conservatism make good advertising.

Once in six months there may be justification for such an expression as "We are pleased to announce," but the remainder of the time this much-used phrase should be given a rest. "We announce," "We are tickled to tell you," "Good news for you," "You will be glad to know," "You've waited, and here it is," and a score of similar sentences illustrate how the "announcing" thought may be expressed simply and directly.

Essentials of Good Description.—The wise advertiser, knowing how people discount the claims of the bragging or gushy person, strives for earnestness and simplicity in his copy. Habit plays its part in writing, as in other things. Merchants for ages have been claiming that things are "incomparable," that they "excel all others," are "best in the world," and so on until these phrases roll off the pen, as it were. It is easy to write such copy without doing much thinking. Consequently, the advertising columns are full of what is appropriately called "advertising jargon." An advertiser owes it to his business and to his own personal reputation to strive for a different kind of copy. He can adopt no better rule than to sit down, close his eyes, and imagine himself addressing some customer. Written language cannot always be as familiar, nor should it be as wordy, as spoken language is; but the nearer it approaches a good conversational style, the clearer, more direct and impressive it is likely to be.

The flamboyant, extravagant style of advertising still brings its crowd, just as the street barker with his braggadocio manner and far-reaching claims still brings business from a certain type; yet the modern trend of good advertising is in the other direction.

Good description necessitates acquaintance with the article or service to be advertised and with the people to whom it is advertised. Though good copy can often be written with second-hand knowledge, and second-hand knowledge is sometimes all that the copy-writer can get, something is to be gained if the writer can secure his information from original sources and write with honest, enthusiastic conviction. Let him remember that most copy is full of general claims that create no real pictures in the readers' minds. "Safest tire on the market" means very little, but when the writer explains that the tire is made puncture-proof by overlapping metal discs imbedded in the solid rubber, and shows a picture of a tire being run over a board filled with spikes, he drives home a truth that will long be remembered.

It would be much easier for the advertisers of Campbell's Tomato Soup to write that the Campbell product is "made in the finest kitchens on earth by the most skilled cooks and with only first-grade products," but such copy does not ring with conviction. This is the way the Campbell Soup people set forth their claims:

Begin with a hot, fragrant plate of Campbell's Tomato Soup to delight the appetite with delicious flavor. Here is a soup that pleases everybody who relishes the tonic richness of pure tomato. There's health and vigor in every spoonful!

Campbell's Tomato Soup is the smooth puree of finest tomatoes, sun-ripened on the vines, plucked at their prime and made into soup the very same day. The plump, meaty parts of the tomato and the juices are strained free of all skins, seeds and core fiber. Golden butter is blended in. The best-liked soup in the world!

"Sun-ripened on the vines" draws a real picture of properly matured fruit. When the reader gets to "strained free of all skin, seeds and core fiber," the definiteness of the description encourages belief that this process is really performed. An appetizing flavor is given to the copy by "golden butter blended in." This successful advertiser does not even claim that his soup is the "best in the world." He keeps clear of this moss-covered argument by saying that his soup is "the best-liked soup in the world," which claim he can probably substantiate by actual sales.

It may not be possible to write such definite and convincing copy about every commodity, but fact-giving copy should be the standard. A copy-writer should search his mind and good reference books for the language that has the greatest picture-creating power. If he does this, he will not be under the necessity of putting into his copy obvious pleas for the purchase of the article. It is a good plan, anyhow, to keep out of copy the language that manifestly aims at selling. Of course, the reader probably realizes that the object of most advertising is to sell something, but he has no particular liking for seeing this purpose made apparent. The object of the story-writer is likewise to entertain the reader, and to make money for himself, but he does not begin or end his stories with the explanation: "I want to entertain you and I want to make a good-sized fee for myself. Therefore, I am going to tell you a story about a man who fell deeply in love with a woman fifteen years older than himself. Please give me your careful attention."

The reader likes to be entertained, and if the story-writer does his job well, both entertainment and payment for the job are brought about. In like manner, if the writer of an advertisement is interested in the pleasures, comfort and needs of his readers and if he tells about things that meet these requirements, sales will be the result.

Humor and Sprightliness.—Comparatively few people are successful as humorists, especially in print. One who is a real humorist can indulge himself freely in advertising practice and possibly score a distinct success, but humor is a tool with which writers should work very carefully. Most people do well to confine their attempts to a certain brightness or aptness which does not advertise too much of an effort to be clever and yet throws a certain entertaining quality into staid copy.

Many writers of advertising secure unusual attention for their messages by relating entertaining incidents, remarks of customers, and so on.

The Place for "Snappy" Copy.—Within the last dozen years much has been said in business circles about "snappy" advertising copy. The most frequent criticism of advertising is that it is not "snappy" enough or that it lacks "punch." Sometimes advertisers have become so much impressed with publicity such as that devoted to Prince Albert tobacco or other like subjects that they feel that vigorous, bright or slangy copy is necessary in all appeals in order to give them life. On this point the editor of *Merchandising Advertising* makes these pertinent comments:

> There are all kinds of people in the world, and not every one prefers slapstick comedy to any other dissipation on earth. Some men and women like to have people address them in a quiet and gentle tone of voice for the same reason that they prefer music to jazz, the waves of the sea to the roar of the subway and a tone of persuasion, consideration and refinement to the ravings of the Coney Island barker who yowls, "Hot Dog! Hot Dog!! Hot Dog!!!"
>
> Yes, there are a few people here and there who do not like 'em "snappy." For these people, quiet advertisements are written, modulated in their tone, but none the less interesting for all that. They are not all printed in 24-point type. Some of them are as small as 8-point, nor do the illustrations show heads bursting through the paper or gigantic hands clutching at you.

Advertising of the breezy style has undoubtedly achieved great successes for the articles referred to at the beginning of this comment. Many other commodities have been exploited successfully with chatty, conversational advertising that is not quite as vigorous or as slangy as the Prince Albert appeal. Still other commodities can be more appropriately exploited with advertising that is of the quieter or more earnest tone, so to speak. In fact, snappiness or breeziness must be graduated with due respect for the article to be advertised and the people to be addressed until the other extreme is reached—the business that really requires dignified treatment. Despite all that may be said about lively language, no good advertising man would seriously hold that this is the proper style for an appeal about will-making, the education of children, and many other subjects.

Value of Concentrating and Being Specific.—The great weakness of most retail advertising, as of other kinds of advertising, is that of generalization. The writer, knowing that he is addressing large audiences, as it were, feels that he must say something that will be of interest to a large group. The result usually is that he scatters his ammunition so broadly that he makes very little contact with the public. There are occasions when general appeals are needed, but ordinarily the advertiser has something to gain either by featuring some particular product or service or addressing himself to some special group of readers. The clothing store that daily tells the reading world that it has "all kinds of clothes for all kinds of people" gets nowhere. When it features sporting clothing for sportsmen, children's play suits, women's house dresses, blouses, evening wraps, or some other particular kind of clothing, it is more likely to command the attention of an interested group. Furthermore, a variety of such special advertising will, in the long run, create the general publicity that the store seeks. A firm can hardly exploit scores of different kinds of merchandise at different times without making the impression on the public that it has a great variety of goods.

The Langley advertisement, Exhibit 124, illustrates how a cleaning and dyeing concern can specialize. The proprietor of this Toronto firm, when he began business, believed that the chief weakness of the publicity of cleaning and dyeing establishments was that the advertiser usually attempted to cover his whole service in one advertisement. So the Langley concern wisely decided to deal with only one point or just one incident at a time.

When a very valuable Keshan rug, 300 years old and worth $12,000, came to the Langley establishment to be cleaned, a

---

About Langley Service—No. 17

Blankets for Summer Cottages

We have noticed going through our plant these days a great many blankets which are being dyed red.

Apparently, many of our customers are having their extra blankets done this color for use in their Summer homes.

For this same use, we are getting bedspreads to be dyed in fancy colors, such as yellow, rose, tans and blues.

There are really many things which are not quite good enough for your City home which could be fixed up in this way.

Suppose you phone us to call for a bundle of things you would like advice on? If we decide it would not be satisfactory or you think it would not be profitable—we are always glad to be of service to anyone.

Phone HILL. 8000

Langley's LIMITED
CLEANERS AND DYERS
OF FINE FABRICS, WEARING APPAREL, AND HOUSEHOLD GOODS, CARPET RENOVATORS

249 SPADINA RD. *Just North of Dupont*

EXHIBIT 124.—One of a series of small advertisements run by a Toronto firm. This advertisement emphasizes one special feature of Langley service and offers a seasonable suggestion to house-keepers. Incidentally, the copy is handled unusually well in the small space used.

special advertisement was written about it, telling of the pride the establishment took in the fact that people entrusted such valuable and beautiful things to its care. The result of the advertisement was a call to clean old Irish lace, heirloom wedding dresses and various other treasured garments that housekeepers ordinarily hesitate to trust to a cleaning establishment.

As illustrations of the way that the Langley cleaners and dyers feature daily incidents to their advantage, two examples are cited. The headline of one of these advertisements was: "She Left the Window Open." The text follows:

> Lace curtains just up. Also new overdrapes of an oxford blue shade. *It rained.* See what happened. The rain was blown in on the blue side curtains. The wind rubbed the lace curtains and the overdrapes together. Result—lace curtains were spotted all over with blue dye which ran from the overdrapes.
>
> A friend suggested that she get in touch with Langley's.
>
> We removed the spots from the lace curtains and dyed the overdrapes in the Sunfast shade—that color will never run again, never fade.
>
> Langley's service is available to anyone anywhere for any problem of cleaning and dyeing.

The other appeal was based on a telephone message from a man customer. This man telephoned: "You are the first cleaner I've struck who hasn't put those crazy creases down the arms of my coat. If there's anything I hate it's pant-legs for sleeves."

The attention of the fastidious man is sure to be caught by such a direct appeal, not only because of its newsiness, but because it infers that Langley's renders real, intelligent service. Such an advertisement is in striking contrast to tame generalities such as, "We clean and dye everything—suits, coats," etc., or "Expert cleaners and dyers of suits, dresses, coats," etc.

Interest Attached to Single Subjects.—One of the best ways of being specific in advertising is that of singling out some one bit of merchandise or one type of service and making it a leading topic, dealing with it as definitely and sincerely as a salesman would in oral salesmanship. The salesman, when a customer is in the store, does not with a flourish call attention in a grandiloquent way to the fact that the store carries all kinds of furniture, rugs, crockery and so on. He is aware that people have a fairly good idea of what furniture stores, jewelry stores and others carry. It is a work of supererogation to explain to the public that a coal dealer carries coal. What the public is interested in knowing is something about his coal or service, whether that be a bit of news or a selling point.

Newspapers and other mediums of advertising are full of commonplace statements such as, "For big values in electrical goods come to Wilson's," "Give us a trial—if we please you, tell others; if not, tell us." The advertisers who use this kind of copy do not heed one of the essentials of good advertising which is that advertising must be believed. They would not believe these statements themselves if they heard them uttered by others, yet they go on year after year with noisy, over-drawn appeals, forgetting that in the long run it is sincere, pointed information which makes people believe and act.

On the other hand, of course, it is true that not all advertisers can single out one article and devote a fair amount of space to a description of its virtues. The grocer cannot do this but he can at least take some

---

EXHIBIT 125.—This advertisement presents too great a variety of articles to be interesting or pointed.

The House of   100,000 Gifts

Graduation Watches

Designed for beauty and built for accuracy. A complete assortment of all the best American and finest imported movements in the new smart thin models.

A new thin model Illinois, choice of many beautiful gold filled cases, plain or decorated, with porcelain, gold or silver dial as preferred, **$25.00** only ....

Other beautiful Illinois Watches in green, yellow or white gold, round and octagon shapes, with plain or fancy dials, at
$28.50, $31.50, $40.00 to $200.00

Genuine Elgin movement, thin model open face, in 20 year gold filled case, plain or decorated
$14.00

All other Elgin models, including Streamline and Corsican, in green, yellow or white gold, at
$22.50, $25.00 to $450.00

A very fine Hamilton movement, thin model, 14 Kt. gold filled case, attractive dials
$43.00

Others at
$40, $60, $80 to $200

Smart Waltham Watches, with the better grade movements, at
$25.00, $35.00 to $325.00

Howard Watches in all their different models
$63.00, $84.00 to $200.00

SPECIAL

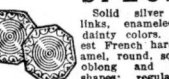

Solid silver cuff links, enameled in dainty colors. Finest French hard enamel, round, square, oblong and fancy shapes; regular at $2.50—

This week, only $1.00

Waterman's Ideal FountainPen
The complete line from
$2.50, $3 to $50

Bill Folds and Wallets, finest leather, plain or with gold corners, shield for monograms or name stamped in gold—
$2.50, $5 to $30

A deposit will reserve your selection, additional payments to suit, or entire balance when merchandise is taken. All the advantages of easy payments without contracting a debt.

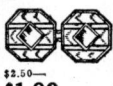

Golf, Dickens and Waldemar Watch Chains in green, yellow and white gold filled—
$2.50, $3.00 to $10.00

In solid gold, yellow or green, at
$6.50, $7.50 to $35.00

Smart designs in solid white gold—
$10, $12.50 to $50.00

Gold and platinum combinations—
$35, $40 to $100

JOHN M. ROBERTS & SON CO.
435-437 Market Street
3 Doors From Market House   Open Saturday Evening

interesting thing, make it a leader with which to get attention, and then attach brief descriptions and prices of staples that are so well established that they need little more than listing.

In the John M. Roberts & Son Company advertisement, Exhibit 125, for example, the advertiser has erred by attempting to present a great variety of things ranging from graduation watches to fountain pens and bill-folds. With a whole month in which to advertise, he would have gained much by dealing with specialties.

Frank Irving Fletcher's Views on Good Retail Copy.—One of the ablest copy-writers of America is Frank Irving Fletcher, of New York, who has excelled in the production of good advertising because of his ability in apt expression and terse treatment. Some years ago Mr. Fletcher, in addressing the League of Advertising Women of New York gave the following interesting views on the subject of good copy:

It has always seemed to me that the great desideratum in a piece of copy is that it should steer clear of the obvious and discover the unusual. The world is interested in the unusual and mortally tired of the commonplace. A murder receives more attention than a divorce, because you don't get a murder every day. It is something special. Yet, on the other hand, if a divorce announcement were headed: "Mrs. Jones is sick and tired of Mr. Jones," you would read it, not because the circumstance is unusual, but because the caption is.

We are all of us so shackled to hackneyed phrases and ideas, some of us because we have no imagination of our own, and some of us because they have no imagination higher up.

But I do believe that there never was a time when there was such need of individual, even brilliant, advertising copy as now. Particularly in newspapers, for there is such a crowding of the advertising columns these days that an advertisement has got to possess some unusual quality to attract attention.

If I were asked wherein most advertisements offend, I should say lack of brevity. There is a French proverb which says the surest way to be dull is to say it all. And another that says no souls are saved after fifteen minutes. See how the bubble of length is punctured with a phrase. "Youth is a blunder—manhood a struggle—old age a regret."

There we have a scenario of life in eleven words, embracing the vicissitudes of existence from cradle to crepe, from birth to oblivion.

There is nothing like the literature of epigram to develop brevity, clarity, felicity and strength.

Of course, some advertisements require a hundred words, some a thousand, and some could get along on a baker's dozen; but the point to remember is that brevity is the soul of a good advertisement, and that it is fatal to make a mountain of copy out of a molehill of circumstance.

This above all—give your copy the human touch.

We write like Baedeker guides, labeling our facts but illuminating none of them, throwing the commonplace and the beautiful together into a ragout of meaningless phrases, like the man with the megaphone on a sight-seeing automobile, who dismisses in one breath the New York Public Library on the right and the United Cigar Store on the left.

Advertising is literature—the literature of Supply and Demand—and if anything, it needs to possess more of the human touch than any other branch of letters, for it has infinitely more to accomplish. It has got to open both the mind and the pocket-book, and it cannot do this successfully by the dull recital of facts.

Have you ever stopped to consider how many people are acquitted at law, not by the evidence in their favor, but by the summing up of the attorneys, who appeal from the facts to the emotions, and by hanging their arguments on human, homely pleas, often obscure testimony of guilt sufficient to hang their clients?

The Advertisement-writer Is a Live Question mark.—The writer of advertisements, like a good lawyer, should be a good questioner.

When he starts out to find why a thing is made, why a service was created, why a certain price was fixed, where certain materials come from and how they are handled, why certain sizes or models are made, why people buy the article, or why they use it, he is likely to find abundant material for the creating of convincing advertising.

He is not always able to ask these questions of the actual producers or purchasers and get his information first-hand. Sometimes the answer is to be found in printed matter. But, again using the lawyer as an example, a good honest search for information often reveals interesting items that the questioner at the outset had no notion existed.

The department store writer learns that often when the heads or buyers of departments will not put down in writing good selling points for the articles they want sold, if he will sit down and chat a while with the department manager or buyer, asking a few casual questions, some very interesting information will be given. People who have interesting facts often do not regard them as such until some one who knows little or nothing about the article asks leading questions.

The News Element in Advertising.—Much use can be made of the news element in advertising. Advertising can often be connected with current news to distinct advantage. The connection should, of course, be logical. When a famous golfer comes to town, the sporting goods store can feature the kind of clubs the famous player uses. News about the coal situation makes it possible for the advertising of the coal dealer and the oil-stove man to be more than usually effective. Municipal ordinances, state laws, national news, all make it possible for the keen advertiser to call attention to some particular merchandise or special service that he offers.

The Sherman, Clay & Company advertisements, Exhibit 126, are fine examples of how musicians and concerts can be exploited as a means of selling Victor records. Here the advertiser lays hold on publicity worth hundreds of dollars, already created for his use.

Style is often good news. What other people say about their purchases may be news, if they are prominent or what they say is interesting.

The news item of real interest is something to which the eye of the reader is attracted as if by a magnet. Therefore, the advertiser has much to gain by linking up his messages with something that his public really wants to read rather than something that they must be coaxed to read.

The writer who has a "nose for news" or who cultivates this sense will find many opportunities to bring the news element into play. For example, a furniture store was awarded the contract for supplying the furniture for a new $2,000,000 hotel of its city. The advertising manager of the store wrote a special story about the new hotel and its furnishings using half-tone illustrations and detailed descriptions of the features of the new building and the furniture installed. This was all written in an entertaining, newsy way with no reference to the furniture house until the end of the story. The closing paragraph gave the advertiser an appropriate connection with the new hotel that meant so much to the city. Such an advertisement receives unusual attention because it is real home news.

Exhibit 126.—Advertising that has double force because it lines up with current events of great interest to music lovers.

Names Often Make Good News.—Nothing is more interesting to people than other people. While the advertiser must be on his guard not to introduce names into his publicity where such use would be objectionable to a customer or customers, or to friends of prospective customers, at the same time he can keep in mind that most people like to see their names in print, if the references are complimentary. A home-owner is not likely to be offended if his contractor publishes a neat picture of a new home with the information that it is "the new home of John Sanborn, on Elm Street, built by the Sanders Home Builders."

A country town dealer has gone so far as to run newspaper advertising that tells of farm implements and other supplies that his customers are buying. Caterers can make a point of the fact that their services were used in notable social affairs. The baker, the florist, the interior decorator, the ice-cream manufacturer, the photographer and many other advertisers of goods or service can make appropriate reference to the way their services have been used on social occasions, or how they have met individual needs. Some of this publicity may be inappropriate for newspaper advertising but can be circulated in better taste in the form of letters or other direct means.

An effective method of bringing in names is often that of quoting some apt remark made by a customer. This is testimonial advertising in its improved form. Though the testimonial style is sometimes said to be out of date, it can be made very effective. Suppose, for example, an automobile dealer can get a well known physician to say how he feels toward a certain make of car after having used his third machine of that make and having called on it for service under trying conditions day and night for many years.

If people are not willing to be quoted, sometimes they are more than willing to have references made to their business or affairs. For example: "Smith & Brown, who do more trucking business than any other organization in Columbia County, operate twelve of our trucks and only four of all other makes. Smith & Brown require hard service from their trucks and get it."

Other Examples of Newsiness in Advertising.—The advertising of Langley's, Limited, Toronto, Canada, cleaners and dyers, referred to previously, is likewise a good illustration of how newsy advertising pays. The Langley appeals are fresh and interest-creating because they are written in much the same way that the real news of a paper is written. That is, there is a constant striving to play up the ordinary daily happenings in the establishment in such a way that the people of the community will be informed of the usual as well as the unusual little services rendered. What is meant is best illustrated by some of the newsy headlines. For example, one advertisement was headed, "He Sent his Limousine—" Then, the writer told in an interesting way of a man who sent

EXHIBIT 127.—This advertiser takes his public into his confidence and tells frankly of the difficulties of doing certain work and of the little profit in it.

his limousine to Langley's to have the upholstery cleaned. Perhaps there would not be enough people who would send cars to a cleaning establishment to make this direct appeal effective, but the incident certainly enabled the advertiser to tell in a newsy, attractive way of the unusual services, which would no doubt set others to thinking that Langley's would be a good place to have some work done that they had been considering—that there was a wide range in the service rendered.

"One's own mother couldn't do all these little repairs any better," the remark of an appreciative bachelor, was made the subject of another advertisement telling how missing buttons, holes in pockets, or other minor mending is attended to. This example of copy not only introduces the news ele-

Exhibit 128.—How an incident in the week's work can be made the subject of an interesting advertisement. The appeal, in the original, was a two-column advertisement $6\frac{1}{4}$ inches deep.

ment, but brings in the testimonial suggestion, which is all the more effective because the testimonial is handled so adroitly that the reader hardly realizes that it is what is known as a "testimonial."

Tell the Public about Tests.—Many good retail merchants study the products of various manufacturers carefully before deciding between competing grades of goods. They usually do not regard it as good business to carry more than one line of filing equipment or more than one make of refrigerators.

Sometimes the tests or investigations that they make offer excellent advertising copy.

System tells of a merchant who considered very carefully three makes of refrigerators. All were of about the same price, so the choice came down to a question of performance. To determine which of the three makes of boxes would give the best service, ice was placed in each of them and the temperatures taken about four times daily over a period of three days. The results showed that one of the boxes had maintained an average temperature 1.5 degrees less than either of the others and that the cake of ice—the cakes of ice had each weighed 100 pounds when put into the boxes—was several pounds heavier than the other two.

The test was made accurately as far as possible. Tested thermometers were used. It was carefully noted that each of the boxes was of the same temperature when the ice was put in. Customers were informed of what the store was doing. It was a straight, honest test without any attempt to dress it up as a "stunt."

The data obtained from the test became the basis of a series of interesting advertisements and the year's business in the sale of refrigerators in the one brand retained was greater than that of the previous year when three makes were carried.

Bargain Advertising.—No kind of advertising has been more greatly abused than the bargain style. So much of exaggeration and deception has been included that many advertisers would prefer to get along without the advertising of bargains, if they could. But as long as there are slow-selling goods, odd sizes, unpopular styles, and special purchases, just so long will there be opportunity for advertisers to exploit goods at special prices. Even comparative prices can be accurately and honestly used: "$12 for the models we sold earlier in the season at $16," "The usual $1 size this week for 80 cents."

The attraction of special price is strong and there is no good reason why the advertiser should not appeal to it, but if he is running a high-grade business he owes it to his future reputation to keep clear of all suspicious and flamboyant bargain advertising. He can advertise his bargains at such intervals and in such a frank, earnest, honest style that the public will come to regard his store as one of "real bargains.' Bargain advertising should be a stimulant, a special feature rather than a regular bill of fare.

The keen advertiser, when he has to contend with much bargain advertising of the exaggerated kind, can make his announcements stand out by keeping clear of superlative statements:

No better tire was ever offered in this size, we believe, at less than $40. We ask just $35 for it.

We don't say it is the best shoe ever made, but we have never seen a better at $5.

A mighty good lawn-mower. We can't sell it at $6.75, or even $7.98. The lowest figure at which we can make a profit is $8, and you can't beat it anywhere at that figure.

Comparative Prices.—"Comparative-price" advertising is a perplexing problem to many advertisers who prefer to be truthful in their advertising and yet know the value of measuring value by means of price. There can be no objection to advertising "Was $25, now $18" or "Formerly sold at $40 to $50, now to be closed out at $38," if these figures represent the facts. In the case of "$50 Models for $38," the difficulty comes in deciding just what is a $50 model. The author has no advice to offer those advertisers who believe they are justified in advertising untruths. He is of the opinion that while untruth may temporarily bring a larger return, in the long run the policy of truthful advertising is actually a commercially profitable one as well as the only self-respecting policy that a business man can follow.

It seems better, in using comparative prices, to be more specific. The advertiser can say, "Sold all last season at $50; a few models now left to be offered at $38." Or, "Many stores expect $50 for an article of this grade. We are able to offer it at $40."

In this department of advertising, as in others, the advertiser gains by taking his readers into his confidence and giving them the real facts. "Never was such a value at $8," is not likely to be believed except by the unsophisticated. "Their slight imperfections have been repaired and they are big values at $8" rings true.

Instead of holding constant special sales, the progressive retailer does well to confine his sales events to those occasions when he can give a real reason for clearing out stock and offering prices that are unusually attractive.

The business that is continually having special sales, clearances, week-end sales, monthly sales, and the dozens of other sales events that have little or no reason for their existence may soon find itself in the position of the boy who cried wolf once too often, or of the narcotic user who becomes so afflicted with the habit of stimulating or soothing himself that he is forced to keep on with his ruinous practice, despite its injury.

Some bargain sales, unless very carefully directed, may make enemies for the store instead of friends. Defective merchandise may be sold without full explanation that it was defective. Shoes or hats may be sold when they really do not fit, thus resulting in nursed grievances.

Pledges by Retailers as to Reform in Language.—In the summer of 1923 a movement was launched by the Associated Advertising Clubs of the World, through the Division of Associated Retail Advertisers, that will probably have a good effect in freeing bargain advertising of some of its evils. These pledges follow.

We pledge ourselves to refrain from doing or saying anything which might tend to bring any accepted form of advertising into disrepute.

We pledge ourselves to a just respect and consideration for competitors, avoiding derogatory statements regarding the merchandise or advertising of others. We pledge ourselves to refrain from the use of unqualified statements in advertising copy. Such phrases as the "Greatest Sale in America," "Biggest Bargains in City," "Unmatchable Values," are to be avoided.

We pledge ourselves to construe the terms, "Value" and "Worth" to mean the reasonable retail market price the article would bring at the time of the advertisement and to be determined by what the same or similar article is selling for by other merchants at the time of the advertisement. We pledge ourselves to construe the term "formerly" to mean the last price to which the merchandise was marked in our store previous to the date of publication of the advertisement, and we further pledge ourselves to eliminate the use of the word "originally" as it is conducive to probable misrepresentation.

We pledge ourselves to construe the term "regularly" to mean price prevailing in our store immediately prior to the sale of the specific merchandise advertised, and referring in all cases to a temporary reduction. We pledge ourselves to an understanding that, when the words "up to," accompanied also by the maximum value or former price, are used, they shall be accompanied also by the minimum value or former price, and that at least 10 per cent of the merchandise so advertised shall be of a value of former price as high as the maximum price quoted.

We pledge ourselves to refrain from the use of statements of fractional reductions or savings unless these reductions or savings are based upon today's "value" or "worth," as these terms are herein defined.

We pledge ourselves to avoid unqualified comparative prices except when "value" or "worth" are inferred, for example; $20, $25 and $30 dresses at $17.50, means $20, $25 and $30 values at $17.50 in accordance with the "value" term as herein defined. We pledge ourselves to the use of "special reductions," "specially priced" and similar terms, only when merchandise is being offered at a price less than the regular or prevailing price in our store.

We pledge ourselves to avoid "never before," "elsewhere" and similar terms which cannot be proved. We pledge ourselves to avoid the use of terms "made to sell at," inasmuch as it lends itself to abuse and misrepresentation. We pledge ourselves to refrain from advertising articles as given away free unless those so advertised can be obtained without any obligation either in purchasing other merchandise or by performing a service.

We pledge ourselves to use such terms as "sample," "clearance," "remnants," "special purchase," "marked down," "reduced," etc., only when expressing exact facts. We pledge ourselves to advertise "seconds," "factory rejects," "sub-standard," etc., in a manner so prominent that it will be clearly indicated to the reader that such merchandise is not first quality. We pledge ourselves to discourage the use of trade names that, of themselves, are misleading.

We pledge ourselves to a careful use of trade names of fiber, silk and cotton, silk and wool, wool and cotton, etc., qualifying these terms to indicate the materials involved. We pledge ourselves to the use of branded names only when they shall be applied to articles made by the legal owners of such brands. We pledge ourselves to maintain names, which through proper usage, have come to mean the names of fabrics of particular content, such as pongee, taffeta, cashmere, wool, linen, etc. We pledge ourselves to a clear and honest description of finishes, materials, workmanship, quantities, qualities, sizes, dimensions, and colors, so as to avoid any possible deception or misrepresentation.

We pledge ourselves to avoid the use of illustrations which mislead regarding size, quality or appearance of merchandise advertised. We pledge ourselves to govern advertising and store signs, window-cards, etc., with the same strict supervision that we have pledged ourselves to apply to newspapers and other forms of advertising. We pledge ourselves to influence salespeople to an observance of "truth in advertising."

It may be years before these standards gain extensive adoption so that misleading bargain advertising will no longer be run. Nevertheless, the observance of such standards by leading advertisers is certain to improve the general trend toward honest statement.

Frank Announcement of Bargains.—Rogers Peet & Company, famous clothing merchants, announce frankly to their customers that certain offerings are "Tag ends and broken lots, with some mighty good selections, if you can find your size. We can't guarantee having every size or pattern, but the price is a great attraction—$11.50."

Human Element versus "Bargain" Advertising.—A furniture store in an Illinois town near Chicago was not succeeding in the way its proprietors felt it should. The usual type of newspaper advertising featuring the price appeal failed to attract customers in sufficient numbers. A change in policy seemed imperative if the store was to continue doing business. So the bargain style of advertising was discontinued and new copy was prepared by the wife of one of the proprietors who had been an instructor in art and interior decoration before her marriage. The "better home" appeal was used and the public was told in a clever feminine manner of the varieties of one kind of furniture on display in the store. One time the subject would be lovely tables or handsome mirrors that could be placed in any home with good effect. A dainty type of illustration was used consistently, in order to make the advertisements distinctive. To make a definite test of the new style of appeal before adopting it as a permanent feature, some

EXHIBIT 129.—Some advertisements of a furniture store that attained distinction through eliminating all bargain advertising and substituting the "better homes" appeal.

advertisements were run offering furniture at cost price, in the same issue in which the "better home" messages appeared. Results of the test were decidedly in favor of the human element and the artistic appeal. Exhibit 129 is an example of this advertising.

The experience of this furniture company led to the adoption of the following principles:

1. No more special sales.
2. Merchandise will be marked at fair prices that will not be cut for feature publicity.
3. Only worth-while furniture will be shown.
4. Service in its every phase will be given the customer, not only on quick delivery but in expert advice on interior decoration. Every customer must be a satisfied customer.
5. Advertising will always be distinctive and individual.

(Grand Rapids Furniture Record).

Curiosity-exciting Copy.—"Teaser" or curiosity-appeal copy may be made effective if not utilized too frequently. A store in a large Ohio city excited considerable curiosity by running every now and then in the regular newspaper advertisements a line about "Sweet Sixteen, "Sweet Sixteen is Coming," and other brief references that centered attention on "sixteen." Every package that went out from the store contained a slip on which the words "Sweet Sixteen" were printed in large letters. Posters were placed about the store picturing a dashing "flapper" with the announcement "Sweet Sixteen is Coming." People began guessing, surmises running from cosmetic to candy. The mystery was solved when a large advertisement appeared with a huge $16 in the center as the price of a lot of 4,500 fall dresses. The border of the advertisement was made up of sketches of the dresses so that the customer was enabled to form an idea of the style she wanted before entering the store, a helpful feature in a large sale.

Headline Construction.—The headline, or the opening sentence of an advertisement, is almost as important as the title of a story or play or the subject of a sermon. Not all advertisements carry headlines. An opening sentence, set out strongly, or an appropriate illustration, may suffice as an attention-attractor. But headlines play a very important part. Advertising columns and pages are full of commonplace headlines that fail to draw attention to the text that follows.

Headlines should be short enough to be grasped at a glance. The headline of four lines or more is usually difficult to read. It is better to confine the topic of the advertisement to one or

---

What is an Oculist?

An oculist is a doctor of medicine whose specialty is the eye. The law authorizes him to put M. D. after his name.

Be sure that an "M. D." oculist examines your eyes. Your eye trouble may be due to indigestion, nervous disorder or to many other causes. Only an "M. D." oculist can tell you what your eyes really need.

If he prescribes glasses, bring your prescription to us—opticians for over 50 years.

AITCHISON & CO.
OPTICIANS   FIFTH AVENUE
At No 483 ~ Opposite the Public Library

EXHIBIT 130.—An advertisement that carries a double appeal.
1. It offers information that interests the public and impresses on the reader the need for care in having the eyes treated.
2. A suitable appeal to the competent oculist who undoubtedly is inclined to favor the opticians who represent the best standards.
Note the conservatism. The copy closes with "If he prescribes glasses."
The one fault seems to be the heavy ornamental border. There seems to be no reason for this, since it has no illustrative or harmonious relation to the subject of the advertisement. Some of the lighter parallel or double-rule borders would have been more in keeping with the dignity of the appeal and would have given the display type a better chance.

two lines and when two lines are occupied to so divide the sentence that the eye is not confused.

Headlines may consist of a "direct command" statement: "Open your door to the greatest musical artists." "Do away with hard washing." "Make your own ice."

Questions often make excellent headlines: "Does ordinary typewriting bother you?" "Is your widow's comfort worth

Commas, Colons: Periods.

A slip in phrasing or punctuation may change the meaning of a whole clause in your Will,—home made Wills are therefore frequently valueless. Have this important instrument legally drawn by your lawyer,—do it today, if not already attended to,—and before signing give serious consideration to the appointment of your Executor.

This Company's experience of more than half a century as Executor and Trustee for hundreds of estates similar to yours, is a practical guarantee that, if you appoint us to act in that capacity, your testamentary wishes will be faithfully observed.

An interview with us on this subject places you under no obligation, and should be of ultimate benefit.

BROOKLYN TRUST COMPANY
BROOKLYN   AND   MANHATTAN

EXHIBIT 131.—A good illustration of how an odd heading can be made to draw attention to an important fact.

twenty cents a day?" "How many miles do your tires give you?" See also Exhibit 130.

Selling points, sometimes those that consist of only a word or so, often make excellent headings. "Healthful Milk," "Crisp and Dainty," "Delicious," "Waterproof."

The name of a product may sometimes alone be a good headline: "Lawn-mowers," "Golf Hats." Combinations of a

EXHIBIT 132.—Good example of a timely advertisement that is all the more effective because of the simplicity of the setting. The three displays stand out strongly and make a complete message in themselves. The copy is not sensational, but the writer very properly took advantage of the public's concern about coal supplies.

name with a selling point are likely to be better: "Non-rusting Fence," "Double-wear hoisery," "Ice-saving refrigerators."

In writing copy for headlines the advertising man has particular need for clear, readable language. Obscure words and awkward phrasing may mean lost opportunity.

"The Bank That Bankers Bank With" is much better than "The Bank With Which Bankers Bank," despite the fact that the latter is better grammatical form. Extracts from conversation sometimes make the best headlines because the use of quotation marks adds a little interest.

References to incidents may embody news interest.

"She just loves the little hills," says a recent Dodge buyer.
"That bumper saved my car."
"Never tasted the equal."
This customer was doubtful at first.
Saved him $125.

While the writing of headlines for advertisements presents a somewhat different problem from that handled by the writers of headlines for newspaper and magazine articles, there is much to be learned by a study of the headlines of the leading periodicals.

Novelty and Vigor versus Sensation and Deception.—Startling statements have no place in advertising, in headlines or elsewhere, unless they have a logical connection with the advertiser's message. One may get attention with "Stupendous Undertaking," but the advertising will be ineffective if the reader feels deceived when he comes to the explanation. Yet there is need for fresh, vigorous treatment, and for novel statement. "Shears that will snip a broom-handle" is more effective than "Shears that possess more than ordinary power." "Ask your wife. She Knows." is more likely to pin down the attention of the married man than "A matter of interest to heads of homes." "That boy of yours" will catch the eye of a parent more readily than "Announcement of interest to all parents."

The advertisement shown in Exhibit 133 illustrates a number of common faults.

1. There is an attempt in the headline to make a mystery of something that really is not a mystery. The reader is likely to feel that he has been tricked into giving attention.

2. The real interest-impelling item is buried under a mass of display. Such a headline as "A Real Haynes Car at $1,295," displayed at the top, with a little white space around the display to give contrast, would have drawn reasonable attention.

3. Most of the text of this advertisement should have been set in a good readable text type instead of having the composition all-display in the familiar style of centering all

---

An Un-Covered Mystery

J. R. Kiefer Motor Car Co. Inc.
121 Northampton St.
Easton, Penna.

Local Distributors of "HAYNES"
Announce
An Uncovered Mystery
Saturday Afternoon
See the Mystery UnCovered
June 16, 1923
at 2.00 P. M.

Can You Beat It? A Real Haynes Car of Latest Model at the Unprecedented Price Of

$1,295.00 F. O. B.

EXHIBIT 133.—Unwise attempt to make a mystery out of an item of real business news.

lines. Advertisements consisting of all-display may be likened to the speaker who screams at the top of his voice with every sentence.

If the advertiser had begun with the idea of making his message as difficult to read and as unconvincing as possible, he could not have succeeded more admirably. Such an advertiser will have no occasion to call in the police to protect his place of business from the rush of people who respond!

Exhibit 134.—Distinctive type of advertising used by a prominent St. Louis financial organization and inserted on news pages rather than on the financial pages of newspapers.

The real mystery is why business men will deceive themselves into believing that such announcements are good advertising.

Unexpected Style of Advertising.—Not all advertising has to be startling to be effective but there is so much of routine and commonplace in advertising generally that it pays occasionally to break away from the beaten track. A good illustration of this practice is afforded by Exhibit 134, an advertisement of the Mercantile Trust Company, of St. Louis, arranged in the style of a department-store announcement. The Mercantile Trust Company used this style for a number of months, filling a space five columns wide and 260 lines deep. The size and character of the messages were such that they easily dominated the newspaper page. These advertisements, instead of being inserted on the financial page, were run on the general and local news pages. The reason for not using the financial page was that the advertiser believed that most of the people he wanted to address were not regular readers of the financial news.

It will be observed that the different sections of this distinctive advertisement deal with various services offered by the trust company, all the way from the purchase of bonds to the making of a will and the renting of a safe-deposit box.

Usefulness of the Slogan.—Many national advertisers have made effective use of slogans.

The value of a good slogan lies in the fact that it emphasizes some of the important facts in an apt way and by constant repetition may bring valuable publicity to the article or firm to which it refers. Millions of people are familiar with such slogans as "It hasn't scratched yet" (Bon Ami), "Keep smiling with Kelly's," "Goodyear means good wear," "From mill to millions" (Real Silk Hosiery), "A skin you love to touch," or "Keep that schoolgirl complexion," "Let the Gold Dust Twins do your work," "From Larkin to family," "Best in the long run," "Had your iron today?," and so on.

The essentials of a good slogan are:

1. That it express truth in a striking way
2. That it be easily read and remembered

3. That it have some direct association with the article or firm.

The local or retail advertiser can often make good use of a slogan, but he should be on his guard against adopting or spending much money on anything that will not "wear well." The slogan of the Loft Candy Stores, "A penny a pound profit" carries with it the idea of good quality at low cost, and it is a real selling point for the candy. The Joseph Horne Company, of Pittsburgh, uses the slogan, "Best place to shop after all." A slogan of this kind for a reliable store is much better than some of the more bombastic slogans that are probably not generally believed.

Other examples of retail slogans are: "If it is hardware, we have it;" "On the square," carrying the double meaning of square treatment with the location of the store on the public square of the town; "The all-steel store," an office equipment shop making a specialty of steel equipment; "Happiness in every box," used by a chain of candy stores; "The upstairs shop with the lower price," a specialty shop that was denied the advantage of a ground floor location; "Built for beauty and double duty," the slogan of a retailer handling an attractive daybed that may be opened up and made to serve as a double bed; "Your bosom friend," used by Archer's Laundry, Baltimore, Md.; "The big homey store with the little prices," adopted by a large general store of Baltimore, Md.; "Year's wear in every pair," (Nu-Way Stretch Suspender Company) is essentially a manufacturer's slogan, and properly so, but it is a slogan used effectively by retailers in exploiting suspenders.

Getting the Viewpoint of the Reader.—Advertising is likely to be written too much from the writer's point of view, unless the copy-man makes an earnest effort to look at subjects from the viewpoint of the typical reader of his message. This does not mean having every sentence begin with "you" or any other word, but it does mean thinking of the reader's interests and needs. That the merchant has goods or service to sell is of no great interest to the world. What the reader will be interested in knowing is how the goods or service fits into his life. Instead of writing, "We have concluded to tell you of something," write "Here is an article that will save you hundreds of steps." Appeal to the reader's pleasure, comfort, or needs. He asks himself, unconsciously perhaps, "Why should I buy or investigate?" and he responds to the appeals of the advertiser who seems to have that question in mind.

It follows, therefore, that before the advertiser can write effective copy he must devote some study, or give some thought to the living, buying and reading habits of the people he wishes to reach. If they are business-office people, then he must appeal to their motives and needs. Likewise, with farmers, housekeepers, trained nurses, mechanics, automobile-owners, high-school graduates, and many other classes.

Advantage of Change of Point of View.—Every writer of advertising copy is likely to "go stale." Furthermore, unless one writer's style is unusually effective, there is something to be gained by occasionally adopting a new style of message. If rather full descriptions and closely set text has been the style for some time, an occasional advertisement of the very concise kind will be a refreshing change. Perhaps an excellent illustration can be used with only a sentence or two of text.

If the proprietor of the business has been writing the copy, he may do well to give some one else a chance to study the business or the merchandise and prepare a new series of appeals. Sometimes there are several people within an organization who are competent to prepare advertisements. Each of these is likely to have some good ideas that others have not. In fact, a number of instances are noted whereby retailers have introduced a new note into their advertising by prevailing on their wives, daughters, or some bright assistant in the store to take a hand in the advertising.

One series of advertisements that found favor with the public was written by a retailer's wife in the form of a story describing the adventures of a customer. Such advertising, however, requires real writing ability.

"Institutional" Advertisements to Help Other Advertisements.—Exhibit 135 presents examples of copy written in the "Institutional" style. Instead of exploiting an array of merchandise, these little advertisements deal with distinctive policies or features. It is the "editorial style," handled apart from the main advertising and executed in such a way that it brings increased attention, and possibly increased respect and belief, for the regular or main announcements of the stores using this method. Undoubtedly, a great deal of business gravitates to a successful store just because of the general impression of the community that the store is reliable; that it gives unusually good service, or carries attractive merchandise. Advertisements that deepen this impression

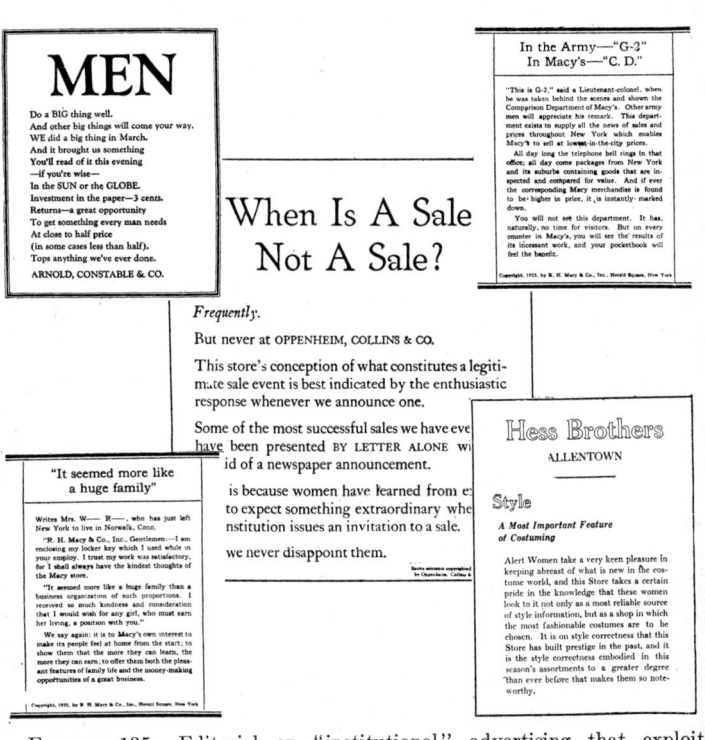

Exhibit 135.—Editorial or "institutional" advertising that exploits definite policies and increases attention for larger announcements. The Oppenheim, Collins & Company and the Macy examples are copyrighted.

are as much worth while as the announcements that feature particular merchandise and bring a direct response.

Another form of institutional advertising is that illustrated by the Corn Exchange National Bank's advertisement, Exhibit 136. Here the advertiser is not dealing primarily with his own history or policies but is devoting attention to

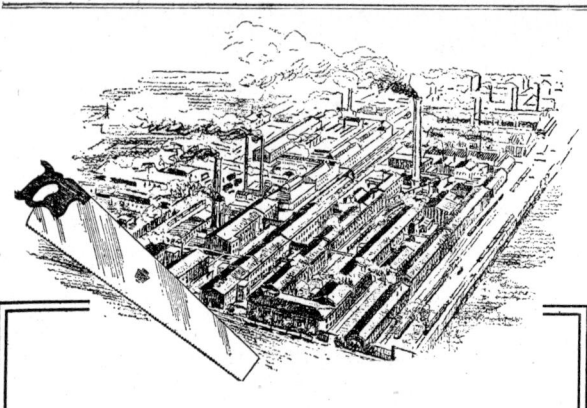

Reflecting Philadelphia's Industries

THE constant and sturdy growth of Philadelphia is strikingly reflected in its marvelous industrial concerns. More numerous and varied in their lines of output; more efficient in method and operation; and more productive now than ever before, these industries, large and small, place metropolitan Philadelphia in an enviable position.

Tools—one of the many lines in which Philadelphia has attained manufacturing pre-eminence — are made here for the markets of the world—manufactured in astonishing quantities.

To the small manufacturer who plans building his business on a quality basis, we bring this example: Disston's is the world's largest saw factory. It started in a small room, distributing its product in a basket.

Our part in the development of the future Disstons of the City is clear to us. We are here to encourage you in the upbuilding of your business. Not acting according to old-fashioned set rules of banking, but handling in a constructive way each individual case, after careful study and investigation.

Have you business problems to solve? Let us help you.

CORN EXCHANGE NATIONAL BANK
CHESTNUT AT SECOND ST.
PHILADELPHIA

EXHIBIT 136.—One of a series of distinctive and interesting advertisements featuring the basic industries of Philadelphia. Its appeal to the young or small manufacturer is strong.

the industries of his community. This style of advertising, being distinctively different from the usual type of bank publicity, undoubtedly draws a great deal of attention from the business men of the community and builds up good-will. The indirect message from such publicity—a message that the reader will probably think out for himself in most instances—is that the bank which can afford to do this broad type of advertising must be a thoroughly established institution with wide vision. It will be observed that the bank does not devote its space entirely to the industry featured but ties up its own appeal very appropriately.

A Correction

Owing to an error, we inadvertently stated in our advertisement yesterday of Men's Imported All-Wool Golf Hose at $2.69 that they were full-fashioned. This statement was incorrect. If any of our customers who purchased any of these hose, under the impression that they were full-fashioned, wish to return them, we shall be glad to accept them for exchange or refund.

R. H. Macy & Co.
Herald Square   *Inc.*   New York

Exhibit 137.—A type of "institutional advertising" that shows the advertiser's desire to make fair and accurate statements.

Such advertising as that illustrated by Exhibit 137 may not ordinarily be grouped as "institutional advertising." At the same time, it is publicity of the type that gives a merchant general prestige. It has frequently been stated that the most difficult thing in advertising is to induce readers to *believe.* Frank confession of error and an offer to rectify the error is an effective method of showing the public that a merchant means always to do the fair thing.

Service Advertising of a Building-materials Firm.—A building-materials dealer enjoys unusual opportunity to do service advertising. In the first place, the constructive instinct and the home-owning instinct are universal. Most people like to build or plan. Building-material dealers throughout the country have scored strongly in their newspaper, street-car and poster advertising by catering to the home-owning instinct in showing attractive buildings and offering estimates.

A Denver building-materials concern, McPhee & McGinnity Company, has carried out this service idea through a "home promotion" department. While, of course, the main object of the campaign is to interest people in home-building and to influence the business for the advertiser, a great deal of useful information has been put out in much the same way as a conscientious builder or home-planner would give the advice in personal conversation. The following paragraphs indicate some of the points:

Choose, if you can, lots on which the special taxes have been paid, or at least find out what such taxes will amount to.

Don't build a larger house than you have real use for, and remember that heavy cornices and purposeless brackets are things of the past.

Don't confuse costliness with beauty. The smallest home can be a gem, if carefully designed.

Start with a nestegg that is equal to at least one-fourth and preferably one-third of the cost of the house you intend to build; remember you cannot build entirely on the other fellow's money.

Think of McPhee & McGinnity Co. as "Building Headquarters" and consult our Home Promotion Department and its library of plans often and freely. You can get much valuable information on building and on financing without any charge and without placing yourself under any obligation to us.

Many people going about the building of a home are ignorant of business. One cannot doubt that the advice, under the head, "Put Everything Down on Paper," has helped a great many.

A disagreeable misunderstanding has developed between a Denver property-owner and a contractor. The former took a fancy to some terraces he had seen and gave the contractor an order to "duplicate" them. The trouble has grown out of using that word "duplicate" instead of having a complete set of plans and specifications and a list of materials.

To all home-builders we would say: "Put everything down in black and white. Never assume that others will understand exactly what you mean from verbal instructions. Never start operations before you have fully settled on your plans and specifications and have your list of materials."

Our Home Promotion Department will be very glad to help you with all the preliminary steps without charge. On all estimates furnished by us, a complete list of exactly the quantity of each material that you will need, and the cost of it, is shown.

And the less money you have, the more important are the above remarks. The builder of a small house can be just as keenly disappointed over the result of a misunderstanding as the builder of a big home, and it may pinch him harder to pay for correction.

These quotations are from the newspaper advertisements of the McPhee & McGinnity Company. The same information could, of course, be given in different form in car-cards, posters, folders or letters, or in a little house organ.

(*Building Materials*, April, 1923).

Distinctive Advertising.—A retailer bearing the firm name of Greentree uses effectively an illustration showing two pine trees, one on each side of the firm name. This distinctive treatment is also carried out in the newspaper advertising, and as little poster features on delivery wagons, signs, paper bags, sales checks, and the like. Where the character of the advertising permits color, green is used, so as to enlist the aid of color in impressing the idea of the firm name on the public mind.

A Detroit firm, operating under the name of White Brothers, uses, in like manner, a silhouette treatment of the faces of the two White brothers. These faces are outlined in white against a black background, one face appearing on each side of the signature.

Other names lend themselves to this individual treatment. If a retailer's name happens to be Katz, he could appropriately feature in his advertising and on his stationery supplies the faces of several amiable cats. The *Progressive Grocer* cites an instance of a Portland, Ore., firm by the name of Ham Brothers, which uses three hams on their signs and in their advertising, each ham bearing the name of one member of the firm of three brothers. Such a feature would naturally be more appropriate for a meat or food store than for some other class of merchandising.

As another style of distinctive copy, the *Progressive Grocer* suggests a series of advertisements under the heading, "John, Our Delivery Boy, says." Each advertisement of this series should carry the picture of a jolly delivery boy at the top, with copy something like the following:

That basket of groceries I delivered to Mrs. Smith last Saturday sure made her happy. She says to me, "John, I call this service, bringing me my things in this kind of weather, and just look at those fine bananas for only 30¢ a dozen."

Gee, I bet I'll have to go some next week, for the Boss is putting Quality Coffee on sale at 27¢ a pound, and it's regular 35¢ coffee! Boy, I bet I'll have to trundle some heavy loads. Leave it to me, though, I never miss an order.

Such a series, under the guidance of a resourceful writer, might be continued for a long time effectively. Usually, however, it is better to vary the style after a reasonable run, lest it become monotonous or the messages become strained.

The Benson advertisement, Exhibit 138, is an example from a series used by a building-material dealer, George W. Benson, of Derry, N. H. This copy is obviously written in imitation of the well known "K. C. B." talks that have become so popular as a newspaper feature. The originator of the "K. C. B." talks probably has no legal way of preventing any advertiser from adopting this abrupt and somewhat fragmentary style of composition. But some advertisers, as a mere matter of ethics, in using the style will pay tribute to the original author by a reference such as: "With apologies to 'K. C. B.,'" or "As 'K. C. B.' would say." It is usually well to do this in order to forestall any criticism that the advertiser is borrowing the method of a well known author.

As a temporary method, this kind of advertising is effective. If used year after year, the style would probably become stale and ineffective. It profits largely, in the first place, because of the popularity of the K. C. B. talks. Furthermore, the very style of the announcement encourages deliberate reading. Finally, the "fragmentary" style encourages the eliminating common-place generalities and the including of specific selling points.

THE WRITING OF COPY

DOES YOUR roof leak?

* * *

EXASPERATING, IS it not?

* * *

MAKES YOU want to say things.

* * *

NOT PROPER things either.

* * *

WHEN THE CEILINGS are stained

* * *

AND THE wallpaper ruined.

* * *

NOW WE have several perfectly good remedies.

* * *

FOR BOTH big leaks and little leaks.

* * *

SHINGLES, FOR one thing.

* * *

XXXXX RED CEDARS, a car just in

* * *

JIM DANDY'S too.

* * *

WHITE CEDARS, for those who like them better.

* * *

FOUR GRADES, so as to suit all needs.

* * *

RU-BER-OID STRIP shingles.

* * *

RU-BER-OID ROOFING with or without Wyron fasteners.

* * *

SPC STAREX roofing, three grades, made by the same reliable company.

* * *

BIRD and BARRETT roof coverings as well.

* * *

RU-BER-OID COATINGS to mend little leaks.

* * *

SWP EBONOL, the old stand-by,

* * *

AND TOCOSEAL, for the same purpose.

* * *

REMEMBER THE man who could not mend his roof when it rained, etc?

* * *

HE WAS in the same class as the foolish virgins.

* * *

IF YOU are in that class, good night.

* * *

IF NOT, look over our stock.

* * *

YOU WILL be hard put to find a better one.

* * *

............BENSON'S

Martin Street,   Phone 101

EXHIBIT 138.—This advertisement was built after the style of the popular "K. C. B." newspaper talks.

Individuality in Advertising.—In order to stamp his messages with individuality, an advertiser may adopt some such device as that of "little joe"—a sporting goods merchant of Baltimore who invariably publishes his name without capital letters.

He may adopt the letter style of message, beginning each talk with a salutation such as "Dear Folks."

Or he may adopt a general headline for a series of advertisements, such, for example, as "Cunningham Says Today," "Wilson's Good Food News," "Fitzgerald's Building Bulletin," "May's Real Estate Items," or "At the Ellsworth Store Friday."

A Colorado garage sends out daily letters to the "dear public" in its newspaper space, the character of the messages being distinctive as well as the form. Local news is used as subject matter and humorous comments are made that, as a rule, tie up with some one feature of the goods or service of the garage. The letters are printed in the style of the one given here, without punctuation and some of them with even more simplified spelling.

>
> dear public
> if the hail
> had come a day later
> we'd of thot it had
> been sent to celebrate
> decoration day
> cause it sure did
> a good job of decorating
> our roofs with holes
> which made us awful mad
> but when we think
> it might have been as
> large as footballs
> instead of baseballs and
> lasted two times as long
> as it did
> we are glad it wasn't any worse.
> THESE DAYS
> Our Trim Shop Specializes In
>   Repairing Tops Damaged By Hail.
>   WELD COUNTY GARAGE.

In the Spring Exposition

MILLINERY

Reverts to the Elegance of the Directoire and the First Empire

SUCH surprises as have been planned in the Millinery Sections—with their six great divisions, French, English, American, Debutante, Juvenile and Untrimmed! Such historic styles have been revived, such old-fashioned stuffs and trimmings! From the world-famed flower-maker—*Natalie Bourseul of Paris*—our own French designer personally chose many of her most exquisite flowers.

From days of the Directoire and the First Empire are descended; even the famed personages of those days—*Pauline Bonaparte, Josephine de Beauharnais, Madame Recamier, La Marechale Lefebre*—live again in the Names given some of the Hats created for the French Salon.

Fashion has swung from the extreme simplicity of the past few years to a splendor which yields ample opportunity to the skill and deftness of the milliner. No one can view the present displays without appreciating that Millinery—always of extreme importance in a woman's Spring plans—becomes this season of supreme importance!

Distinctive Sports Hats

AN important division of the Hats shown in the English Room are those especially made for the woman who golfs, rides, paddles a canoe, plays tennis, or spends much of her time in the great out-of-doors. Only in these Hats is the influence of the luxurious French epochs missing. For these are inspired by the American woman's own love of the practical, the comfortable, the becoming. *The Hat illustrated* shows one of the new styles—made with plant straw brim embellished with whole wool roses crocheted flatly. It is taffeta faced and taffeta scarfed, a charming Hat with pronounced practicability.

English Room, Fifth Floor, North, State.

French Salon Millinery Interprets Its Wearer's Moods

"MATERIAL is nothing" said the French designer, with a slight shrug, when we asked her about the lovely surprises she was creating for this week's Exposition. "It is the Hat. We designers like to feel we are creating—as artists, as sculptors, do. We like to feel the Hat is going to live its life as a Hat," and she turned and caught up a turban-like creation of woven cork curlings, outlined with jade velvet and accented with one eye-concealing aigrette.

"Now this I have named '*Un Flirt Serieux*'—don't you know a woman couldn't wear this Hat at a dinner without flirting a bit?" And this —"*Pensees du Matin*"—morning thoughts,' 'ecaille' colored, with its velvet pansy and its shoulder-draped veil, this is for a young woman on a Summer morning."

And so she went on through the exquisite collection. "*L'envers des roses*" names aptly a lovely Hat trimmed with the Paris-made roses turned faces down on the brim.

Turbed-he-ools, roses and taffeta from Paris shown in Debutante Section.

"*Soleil Couchant*"

describes a Hat which is the key to many a color symphony of the new showing—a gradation of tints of one color—from tan to old-rose-brown. Other Hats show a blending of lavenders—purple—blue.

"*Whispering Pine*"

names a very smart turban-shaped Hat with crown of brown mklines and green pine-needles with bronzed cones to encircle it.

French Salon, Fifth Floor, North, State.

Spring Millinery in the Salon des Debutantes

Here one finds the upturned, face-revealing shapes that Youth can wear so well, and small Hats with a carelessly smart air. On many, flowers and silks of exquisite colors are used, while others, for trotteur wear, are quill or ribbon trimmed.

Fifth Floor, North, State.

The American Room Hats

THIS Section interprets the smart prevailing modes, modified by the practical demands of the clientele. The one sees many of the exquisite fabrics now in favor—laces, changeable taffetas, sheer crepes flower printed, organdies and the like, trimmed with flowers, velvet streamers, or plumes, and yet priced moderately.

The present collection is exquisite with its old-timey flowered taffetas, its crepe-veiled leghorns, its malines, streamers, its transparent shapes. Orchid and jade colorings are to be noted.

American Room, Fifth Floor, North, State.

"*English Hats*" *for Street Wear*

BECAUSE it was the English woman who first set the example for a simplicity in walking and street dress, the Hats designed to accompany tailleurs are displayed in the "English Room."

Against the widened brims of the new season, the love of sheer laces and silks, the devotion to trimmings of plumes and flowers, the English Hats will appeal to women who prefer a tailored simplicity in their street clothes.

The present displays include trim, small-brimmed affairs, quill wing and feather trimmed; up-curling brim styles, and many variations.

English Room, Fifth Floor, North, State.

MARSHALL FIELD & COMPANY

EXHIBIT 139.—Typical example of an appropriate treatment of a spring style event. The dainty italic headings are in keeping with the general subject. The Marshall Field & Company signature is carried at the top of many of its announcements, but in this instance it is placed at the bottom, in order to give the "exposition heading" and the chief illustration a better chance.

The STORE for MEN

A Far Stride in Hat Making

ACROSS nearly three centuries the styles of headwear affected by man, the customs which governed his wearing it indoors, at table and in church, even before great personages at formal banquets, have varied no more than the methods of hat manufacture.

Amusing to us—if it were not so shockingly insanitary—was the old method of "felting" hats from beaver fur. Adriaen van der Donck, who traded at Fort Orange from 1641 to 1648 with the Indians, gives, with a description of beaver fur, the following illuminating (and unattractive) process:

> "When hats are made of the fur, the rough hairs are pulled out, for they are useless. The skins are usually first sent to Russia, where they are highly valued for their outside shining hair, and on this their greatest recommendation depends with the Russians. After the hairs have fallen out, or are worn, and the peltries become old and apparently useless, we get the article back, and convert the fur into hats, before which it cannot well be used for this purpose, for unless the beaver has been worn it will not felt properly, hence these old peltries are the most valuable."

How different is hat making today! Great reserve stocks of new peltries are thoroughly "cured" and sanitarily stored. The hair is then felted by a painstaking process and blocked into the light, modish shapes of the new season.

And yet, in those old days, "a good hat was very expensive, and important enough to be left among bequests in a will. They were borrowed and hired for many years, and, even down to the time of Queen Anne, we find the rent of a *subscription hat* to be £2.6s. per annum." Considering the marked shrinkage of the supply of fur-bearing animals in this country and the buying-power of money between the "sixteen-hundreds" and now, fine Hats of the present season are remarkable for their low cost.

Even the Ribbon Band on Your Hat Is of Ancient Lineage!

SO far back as 3500 B.C. there are indications that a band with streamers fastened the head-dress of Egyptian women. This style was retained with many peoples, through many centuries; pictures of head-dresses in the Fourteenth Century, showing its use, without streamers, when it was known as a "fillet," holding the cloth head-dress in place.

A Streamlined Head-dress of the Fourteenth Century

is somewhat reminiscent of the Scottish Highlander's cap today. To quote Alice Morse Earle: "Hat-bands were just as important for men's hats as women's—especially during the years of the reign of James I.

Endymion Porter had his wife's diamond necklace to wear on his hat in Spain. It probably looked like paste beside the gorgeousness of the Duke of Buckingham, who had 'the Mirror of France,' a great diamond, the finest in England, 'to wear alone in your hat with a little blacke feather' so the king wrote him."

A Hat is a Cap with a Brim

"Flat caps as proper are to city gownes As to armour, helmets, or to kings, their crowns"

This was written in 1630, proving again the centuries-old interest men have demonstrated in the details of dress. The cap of the ancient Greeks, Romans and Britons had acquired a small fold—first semblance of a brim—by the time of Henry VIII, and was sometimes ornamented with a small jewel or a feather. Later, with the activities of the pioneer fur-traders and the great supply of beaver-skins, beaver hats became the choice article of dress and went through many amusing forms—"bell" and "steeple" crowned, cocked and straight of brim.

The Small Bow Inside Your Hat

even hails from the day when hunting-hats were greatly worn, and in a time when hats could not easily be got to fit their wearers. Then, the leather inside band, laced with a narrow ribbon terminating in a bow, was a "buffer" for fallen horsemen, some writers even claiming that the small device saved many a life. As for its adopting the ill-fitting hat to its prospective wearer—so far removed from London shops as across the sea, maybe—there can be little doubt of its efficacy. It is a proof of the curious manner in which fashions persist — even after the need which caused their creation has gone — that men will still find in their hats of today a small bow on the inside band!

A World of Good Things For Spring Offered All Men

THE STORE *for* MEN stands high in this—that each Section is captained by a merchandising expert who has power to make selections from the whole wide world of Things-for-Men.

The newest and the finest—without limit—are accessible to him, and those styles, fabrics, shapes, patterns, colors and qualities are chosen which daily personal acquaintance with Chicago men has taught him will give the greatest satisfaction to the greatest number.

Wherever an improvement can be effected, our ideas are carried through in every detail of the merchandise. It is a perfect system of service, and the exclusive advantages it offers are open wide to every man who steps within these doors.

Speaking of Hats—
You Never Saw a Finer Display

Every resource of our world-wide organization has been taxed to offer Chicago often and young men the widest variety in Spring Headwear. When a man buys a Hat here, he buys not merely labor and materials, but the brains and service of the most efficient organization of its kind. No Spring display has brought more style—more value than now. These Hats are made in all fabrics, imported and domestic, in the season's most exclusive colorings and designs. The soul and substance of that elusive thing called style have been put into our Headwear. The Spring note in Men's Hats is gayer and jauntier, breaking away from the seriousness of war-time days. The length to which a man can go in selecting a Hat that is out of the ordinary for him—and yet be in good taste—is disclosed in our display

The Hat which All Chicago Will Talk About—$25

A Hat fit for the most fastidious dresser; a Hat which will give the wearer assurance and comfort; a Hat which is the supreme achievement of modern hat making—such is the latest acquisition to our stock. Made of the finest materials available, trimmed and worked to our exacting specifications, this Hat, either stiff or soft, is without question the best ever produced.

And There are Caps Here for Every Purpose and Every Need
For the man who prefers a Cap to a Hat this season of the year; and for the golfer or tourist, our display includes headwear that will fit every head and every whim.

MARSHALL FIELD & COMPANY

EXHIBIT 140.—The simplicity of this Marshall Field & Company appeal, the general spirit of the copy and the illustrations are such as to set the announcement apart from the usual appeals to men by dry goods and department stores.

Cards

— *all colors*
— *all sizes*
— *all prices*

Even low-priced L.B. Pacific grade cards for temporary records have the same rotary cut edge, the same uniformity of size as Library Standard cards used for permanent records. You'll find the cards you want, at the right price, at 910 Chestnut Street.

LibraryBureau

M. W. MONTGOMERY, Manager

910 Chestnut Street

Telephones: Main 7394 and Walnut 3394

EXHIBIT 141.—By giving unusual display to a single letter and a single word, a local Library Bureau office has secured an unusual display effect.

The individuality of these advertisements has created good-will and general interest in the garage.

(*Automobile Trade Journal*).

Dominant Note in Advertising.—There should be some dominant note. If this does not exist, then the advertising

EXHIBIT 142.—The advertiser in this case has saved much space by using a small silhouette illustration. This affords contrast in an issue of the paper in which there are many advertisements with large human-figure illustrations. The general effect is high-grade.

is more than likely to be commonplace. The dominant note may be goods of superior quality, unusual assortment, or finely organized store service. This dominant note may sometimes be expressed by a slogan, such as that used by the

Terminal Barber Shops of New York, "Where the Promise is Performed." In order to make this feature more than a slogan, all of the barbers in these shops are trained to perform systematically, for and before each customer, the outstanding features of Terminal Barber service, such as the barber washing his hands before serving the new customer, taking a brush out of a sealed envelope, and so on.

Exhibits 139, 140, 141, 142, 143, 144 and 145 are examples of distinctive newspaper advertisements.

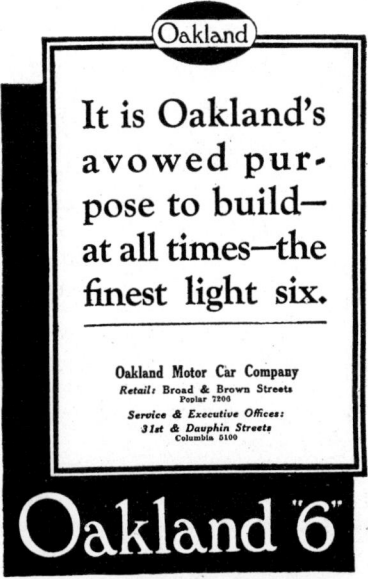

EXHIBIT 143.—Local automobile advertising that is a good example of the brief style of copy. This appeal stands out with unusual prominence because of the distinctive border arrangement.

Distinctive, Timely Advertising of a Coal Dealer.—That a coal dealer can win the respect and admiration of the public in a time of great stress, through frank, timely advertising, has been proved by the George B. Newton Coal Company, of Philadelphia, one of the largest retailers of coal in the country. This has been brought about largely through the use of "service advertising" rather than "product advertising." In other words, the whole policy of this big retailer, ever since

Exhibit 144.—An instance of how an advertiser in a difficult field—that of men's clothing—gets away from the commonplace by using an illustration of fabric rather than of a complete suit.

early in 1922, when the coal strike loomed large in the public mind, has been one that has stressed the fact that a coal dealer is a commercial house in business to give fair and adequate distribution of coal, or, to put it another way, to

Let's think back— and then ahead!

Trace back in your mind the past winter. Did you find it easy to get coal?

Go back farther still. Do you remember when the coal strike started? Don't you recall our advising you, long before the strike, to put in enough coal to protect yourself?

Did you do it? Or were you one of those who took a chance, and were still taking their chances when winter came around?

Are you going to repeat it all over again this year? Don't think for a minute that the coal strike is settled. The temporary agreement between miners and operators runs only until August 31st.

Experiences like the past winter are bitter but practical teachers. Some never will get the point. Our advice to you, just as it was our warning last year is to plan ahead now, to get your coal in just as soon as you can when Spring comes. Don't forget this winter! Put in your coal early and you can forget about next winter.

Now you can be assured of a full supply of real Newton Coal, the coal that sets a nation's standard for fuel value and cleanliness, the coal that keeps a million people warm.

GEO. B. NEWTON COAL CO.
Everywhere in Philadelphia

EXHIBIT 145.—A distinctive type of advertising run by a coal dealer, giving timely, helpful information to the public on a subject that was vitally interesting, because of abnormal conditions in the coal industry.

give genuine service without preference or favor in order to fulfil his public obligation. This, in the words of the Newton Coal Company, means "giving the customer the full benefit of the dealer's knowledge of coal quality, coal conditions, heating problems and the like."

Before the coal strike in 1922 the Newton Company had been running an advertising campaign designed to educate the public. This had been done through telling of some of the difficulties of a retailer and informing the consumer as to the economic use of various sizes of coal. As an illustration of one attractive way this concern had of conserving as well as making the best of its opportunities, it put out what was called the "Newton range coal." This was merely a combination of nut and pea, and was described as that in all advertising, but by giving the mixture a definite name or purpose, the public was induced to order "Newton range coal" instead of ordering all chestnut, as most people would be inclined to do.

That the advertising was effective in gaining the public confidence and good-will is evidenced by the fact that the company received something like 80,000 letters of appreciation and commendation. It is true that most of these letters were received when coal was exceedingly hard to get and also contained orders, but it is also true that the greater proportion of the customers of the Newton Coal Company showed by their letters that they were willing to have the company act as their agents, believing that the company would do what was fair.

Even after every pound of coal in the twenty-seven yards of the Newton Company had been sold and there was no immediate prospect of getting a further supply, the company continued its advertising, with the result that when the coal strike ended, there were thousands of orders on its books. Then, with a limited supply in prospect, which would have to be distributed as fairly as possible, the company announced that its general deliveries would be limited to one ton. At the same time, it explained that these smaller deliveries were much more expensive to the firm than capacity-truck deliveries would be.

The newspaper advertising was supported by more than 40,000 letters sent to people whose orders were on file and could be only partly filled. These letters asked the customers to tell just how much coal each had on hand, how long the supply would last them and so on. This was done so that an intelligent delivery schedule might be worked out. Practically every one replied to this letter, giving the desired information—another evidence of the confidence the Newton establishment had built up. About a month after the first lot of letters went out, a second lot was mailed, so that an accurate check might be kept on the situation.

During the summer of 1923 when coal was again plentiful, the advertising appeals of the Newton Company were devoted to copy that urged the public to put in the winter's supply ahead of time.

It is a plan of the Newton Company to follow up the newspaper advertising by a regular plan of direct mailings. One piece of direct literature that is bringing excellent results is a little folder or house organ, entitled *Coalogic*. In this little publication the public is reminded of the recent shortage and urged not to be caught napping a second time. In Exhibit 145 is reproduced one of the advertisements of the Newton Company. It is through advertisements of this character that the firm expects to build up the largest summer business in its history, as well as keep the confidence and good-will of its large patronage.

Some full-page newspaper space was used, but, in the main, the advertising was confined to from 75 to 150 lines.

The slogan of this retailer, "Newton coal answers the burning question," is unusually apt.

"Shopper" Advertising.—A form of retail advertising that has been used effectively in a number of cities during the last ten years is that which may be referred to generally as "shopper columns" or "shopper style."

Examples of this form of advertising are afforded by Exhibits 146, 147 and 148.

Exhibit 146 is a part of an advertisement of the Cotrell & Leonard store, Albany, N. Y., showing how the "Peggy Schuyler" column is made a part of the regular display advertisement. Some stores follow the plan of making a column, or part of a column of this kind of material, a special feature of their display advertising. Other columns of this kind are either made up by an independent writer or by a writer employed by a group of retailers, or a retailers' association.

Established 1832
COTRELL and LEONARD
472-478 Broadway ALBANY 15 James Street

When Fashion Speaks of Sports Clothes

Fashion says that sports clothes are clothes for Springtime. That beige leads, pleats lead. That hats are little, overblouses smart, hose light and shoes colored!

Wraps for Motoring
$39.75

Soft-pile wraps and capes for motoring, long of line, silk lined and hand tailored, are fashioned from beautiful Geronas, Fashionas and Marvellas.

Soft greys, tan, beige, navy and black, $39.75, $59.75 and $79.50.

from Peggy's notebook

I never can keep them in pairs.

For every time I wear earrings the right one departs to glory.

I've a pink one, and a pearl dangle, and a shiny bit of jet, and one lone vampy green jade; left over, left alone, left hand earrings!

But list and hear how sweet are the uses of adversity.

Not twins

Word comes that the smartest of earrings for the same pair of ears are no longer twins. They needn't even look alike. Different lengths, different colors. And the right ear no longer knoweth what the left ear weareth.

But tell me one thing! How shall I know which ear is to be pink and which green?

Versatile

One must be well armed with versatile bracelets to be well dressed. For they are with us more and more so, and the more so the merrier.

The newest ones are blown glass that tinkle when they jingle against each other. In blues, greens and reds. Down by the Broadway door. 49c.

Little Hats Add Piquant Brims

$7.95

Ribbon trimmed straws, with little whirls of shirring, quaint pokes to be tilted to the right. Dark colors for formal wear, beige and grey for sports. Special selling at $7.95.

$10

Embroidered felt hats have just arrived! Gay, colorful and vastly becoming. Whites, greens and tans, stitched with silken flowers, or weighed down by a sudden pompom of slashed felt. $10.

Hose News

Black silk hose has lost favor and in its place come greys and tans and the nude shades. With colored shoes wear either beige or silver stockings for daytime, but match the shoes at night. McCallum pure silk hose, all colors, $1.95.

Smart Sweaters Take to Monograms, $13.50

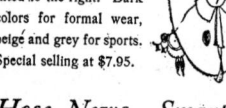

Monograms as they grow in popularity grow in new places. They embroider the left sleeves of Iceland pullovers in colors to match the silk and wool hip bands. White and black, blue and white, green and white, $13.50.

Up

And the best place for a bracelet for many bare arms now is up, just above the elbow. Remember that. It's important.

Peggy Schuyler

EXHIBIT 146.—Part of a display advertisement, showing how the "Peggy Schuyler" column is made a part of the Cotrell and Leonard publicity.

In the Eyes of the Observing Shopper

FOR about a week there has been on display a very striking window exhibit by the Merrill Millinery Shop, 516 Northampton Street. This exhibit is so pretty and unusually distinctive looking that one cannot pass the window without involuntarily stopping to gaze at the beautiful little turbans in their gay colors of tangerine, pheasant, and sunset.

I was wandering aimlessly up Northampton Street when I spied this window. My first thought was "Oh, how beautiful!"

The outside display was so attractive that I was sure there must be hats inside that were equally pretty. I wasn't a bit disappointed in my inside look. The little salesgirl seemed glad to show me around and to tell me about the new hats, and there were many lovely ones.

Most of the models seemed to be made of silk, or silk and straw combined. Some were gayly trimmed, while a number were without trimming of any kind, the soft beauty of the silk being quite sufficient in itself.

EVERY afternoon about 5.15, pans of steaming hot cinnamon buns come from the great gas oven in the window of Felver's Bakery on North Third Street. They are baked in bread pans, made six to the pan, which retain the heat until you break them at your dinner table. They are made of raised dough, very light and delicious, and slightly sweetened with a cinnamon syrup. Easton people have been quick to show their approval of this experiment. If you would like to try some of these appetizing buns for your evening meal, be on hand when they come from the oven for there is always a crowd waiting to carry off the good things. Orders are taken during the day, so you can have some laid aside if you cannot get there on time.

SURELY the Spring blouses are quite the daintiest and most attractive that any season has yet produced. The tie-on and over-blouse models are equally popular. O. S. saw quite a rare combination of the two styles in a blouse at Grollman Brothers' Shop on 'East Northampton Street. It is made up in georgette-crepe of the softest quality in a delicate shade of bisque. A youthful round collar is edged with finest lace and finished with a bit of brown ribbon. An inverted V, raised from the waist line, is outlined with hemstitching covered with graduated rows of lace which continue, forming the overblouse. It isn't a bit fussy—just one of those simple, pretty things suitable for so many occasions. This is only one of a large assortment at Grollman's that happened to attract my attention. You can't help but find several blouses that will suit your fancy in the attractive stock of this shop.

ABEL'S have been making elaborate preparations for St. Valentine's Day. An almost unbelievable variety of heart-shaped favors, place-cards, candies and novelties supply just a wealth of material to make pretty Valentine table for those who make much of celebrating this holiday. They also carry a very attractive variation of the old-time Valentine. This is an envelope, appropriately designed with cupids, arrows, hearts, etc., containing a piece of sweet chocolate. This, wrapped in a piece of cardboard to protect the chocolate and enclosed in another envelope, can be mailed anywhere and makes a greeting pleasingly different from those we have been accustomed to send. I can hear many saying "How sweet of you" when they receive their Abel Valentines.

CHILDREN'S Shoes! What mother hasn't said it during the last year or so with a shiver, especially if she were talking about boys' shoes. But the Observing Shopper got a new light on this the other day in the Heiberger Store. Mr. Heiberger said: "An old customer came in not long ago and said she wanted to make a confession. She said when shoes began to cost more than they did before the war, she concluded she could save money by going elsewhere and buying a low grade of children's shoes that looked fairly well. 'But,' she declared, 'they lasted only a week or two, and I've come back to get a shoe that you can assure me will give good service.'" And then Mr. Heiberger showed me the type of boys' and girls' shoe that he is recommending these days—real leather soles—not paper—and with substantial leather tops made for wear, not mere looks. The Observing Shopper was so impressed with the soundness of that argument that she bought a pair right on the spot.

O YES, the Observing Shopper knows a lot about typewriters for she has written millions of words on them. Hence, she is always attracted when she sees the handy little Corona typewriter on display, as it is regularly in the Nixon Store, Northampton Street, near Circle. When the Coronas first came out, they were regarded by many as toys, but nowadays they sell so rapidly that the factory has a hard time keeping up. The Corona is very light and comes in a neat traveling case. It takes up little room in baggage or on the desk or table. It has the full keyboard and, despite its lightness, stands very exacting service. It is a visible writer with an easy touch. It would be hard to imagine a more appropriate present for a son or a daughter or for any relative or friend who travels or who has reports, correspondence, manuscript, etc., to get out. And the cost is only $50 with case.

EXHIBIT 147.—Reproduction of one of the "Observing Shopper" advertisements, showing how a group of merchants is represented by an independent writer.

Exhibit 147 is an example of the "Observing Shopper" series as carried out by an independent writer. The advertising office giving this service had a working agreement with each merchant that a specific amount would be paid each week that a paragraph appeared in the "Observing Shopper"

PROMENADES with JOAN DALE

WHEREIN the case of the one who goes to market and the wiser one who stays at home, receives our attention.

This fair stay-at-home it is by no means to be confounded with Mother Hubbard. For while her cupboards are bare, it's because she has not yet put away her newly canned fruit. It was the Basement fruit jar sale that inspired her. Pint mason jars, 89c a dozen.

No properly minded sister will admit for a moment that a woman's place is in the home. But—now we've the vote and can do as we please—we are willing to ascribe a certain amount of truth to that masculine adage. (Especially in hot weather!)

Just balance the account of the man who plays golf all morning against the woman's who stays home, f'instance: Man—something to talk about.

Woman—well, here are just a few of the things that she might be accomplishing.

Original

The parchment shade has proven itself the simplest and most effective covering for most lamps—be they iron, bronze or china.

You will be interested to know you can buy uncolored parchment shades in the Lamp Department (basement). These you may tint or decorate yourself to blend with your color-scheme.

Of course, unpainted shades are much cheaper! 69c to $3.85. The latter are 18 inches in diameter.

A comfortable tweed coat and a pair of gabardine riding breeches—in a good mousey-tan color—make one of those fashionably careless riding costumes! Breeches, in tan, gray, also khaki, $6. Men's department.

The resignation of Dr. Joseph Swain, after twenty years' service as president of Swarthmore College, brings to mind the many things he has done for the education of women at Swarthmore. Swarthmore's ideal woman is the practical woman who can manage her home as well as achieve distinction in other lines. It is this type of woman who patronizes the Chestnut Street Shops.

Deborah Logan

TODAY I am going to introduce to you the Emery Vacuum Cleaner, which is on exhibition this week at the store of J. Franklin Miller, 1612 Chestnut Street. It is made here in Philadelphia, and that means prompt and efficient service for the Philadelphia housewife. The Emery has the carpet-sweeper type brush, which picks up all thread, hairs, lint, etc., from the rugs, yet does not wear the nap. The powerful air suction removes all surface dirt, leaving bright, clean rugs. These two features insure the best possible method of cleaning rugs and carpets. The cleaner is light and easy to handle, and requires no other attention than oiling once in six weeks. You will appreciate the fact, too, that it is most reasonably priced.

ALL the genius of the artists who create those exquisite settings for the most precious of stones at the store of Bailey, Banks & Biddle Company, finds expression in a wonderfully beautiful dinner ring. It bears a Polished Girdle Diamond—a diamond cut and polished according to a special patented process which brings out all the hidden beauties of the stone—in a platinum setting, whose delicate, fairy-like traceries enhance the beauty of the diamond. What a wonderful Christmas gift it would make! Then, there are pearls perfectly matched and of that rare color and luster that only the Oriental pearl itself possesses. There are many rare and exquisitely lovely things in that department devoted to the one-of-a-kind jewels.

ONE can see so much time when a shopping trip if one knows beforehand just which stores one is going to visit. Many out-of-town people have formed the habit of buying at Oppenheim, Collins & Company's stores at Twelfth and Chestnut Streets, because they are certain of finding there the very newest things in wraps, gowns, blouses, etc. Now, take the matter of wraps. You really must not miss seeing their luxurious dolmans and wrappy coats. If you are tall and slender, you will want one, for it will make you look stouter, and if you happen to be stout, you will find at Oppenheim, Collins' just the right one to make you look slender. For "it's all in the lines," you know, and these clothes really have the right lines.

WHAT is quite so satisfying as the feeling that one is well-dressed? A well-tailored, comfortable sports shirt adds immeasurably to the joy of an autumn ride through country lanes. It is not generally known that MacDonald & Campbell, 1334-36 Chestnut Street, are making custom-tailored shirts for women, but they have really earned a reputation for the excellence of their workmanship—they are tailored as carefully, of course, as their custom shirts for men—and for their remarkably reasonable prices. One has the advantage, too, of selecting from a varied assortment of patterns and an excellent range of colors. Many women like them for business as well as sports wear, and I'm sure you will want not only one, but several of them.

"WHERE did you buy those good-looking new shoes, if I'm not too inquisitive?" asked the Main Line lady.

"I wouldn't call them new, said the other. "I've been wearing them for two months, but they have held their shape remarkably well. I bought them at Del Mar & Company's. The shop is on the second floor at 1311 Chestnut Street."

"Do you know whether they have any bronze slippers? I'd like to have a pair to wear with this suit—the kind with crossed straps if I can get them at anything like a reasonable price."

"Why, yes. I saw a pair there last week, and their prices really are reasonable. I want a pair of brogues, myself, so I'll go with you."

THE CHESTNUT STREET ASSOCIATION

EXHIBIT 148.—Two more examples of the shopper style of advertising, one from the Chestnut Street Association, Philadelphia, and the other an independent effort formerly conducted by Bloomingdale Brothers, New York.

columns about the merchant's store. To make a plan of this kind successful, a large number of stores should be represented, so that the public would not become wearied by seeing too much attention given any one store. In other words, the success of the advertising depends primarily on its newsiness. A good-sized list and a variety of stores increase the possibilities for interesting treatment.

Cases are on record where customers were so much interested in this chatty, newsy style that they have asked whether it was advertising, or just some one's review of interesting merchandise.

Exhibit 148 shows two forms of "shopper advertising." One is a reproduction of the column type of advertising as conducted by the Chestnut Street Association, Philadelphia, while the other is a reproduction of the "Promenades with Joan Dale," formerly an independent effort on the part of Bloomingdale Brothers, New York, but now discontinued.

Argument for Column Style of Advertising.—Helen Landon Cass, a well known writer of column advertisement, the "Peggy Schuyler" of the Cotrell and Leonard advertisement (Exhibit 146), has given the following argument for advertising of the class that deals with human desires. This argument is good not only for advertising of the kind Miss Cass refers to particularly but for advertising copy in general.

Earrings we buy, not as twinkling bits of jeweled metal, but because they will give us youth or age, sophistication, piquancy or romance. We are trying to buy the gifts of the gods, two for 59 cents. Furs mean luxury and the flattery of deep color against soft cheeks. People don't buy things to have things; they buy things that will work for them. They buy hope, hope of what your merchandise will do for them.

Most advertisements sell things—dresses, earrings, soap. The column sells hope, luxury and the whirl of parties. A column sells because it shows merchandise in action. It shows merchandise in relation to the reader. It tells what to do to be beautiful and what to wear to be fashionable. It flatters, and a little flattery goeth deeper into the human soul than much shrieking of prices.

Event Advertising.—At various seasons of the year the minds of different groups of buyers turn to events that are more or less fixed. The enterprising retailer can take advantage of this trend of mind and make his appeals more than ordinarily effective by exploiting goods that are particularly useful or appropriate in connection with such events. Among these events may be listed the following:

Graduation season, affording opportunity not only for appropriate clothing but also for graduation presents of great variety. This occasion also affords opportunity to the advertiser of tours, business college courses, and many other enterprises having special attraction for graduates of schools and colleges.

Vacation season, affording an opportunity for clothing, trunks, suitcases, etc., in addition to the regular vacation goods of camping outfits and sporting goods of various kinds.

Thanksgiving, Christmas and other national holidays are so generally exploited that it is hardly necessary to mention them. Exhibit 149 is an excellent example of a wedding-season appeal.

The paragraphs below illustrate the type of advertising appeal made by an Illinois music dealer. The copy here given is simply the general thought, the details as to instruments being omitted:

COMPLETE HER HOME WITH A VICTROLA

You cannot choose a more substantial and useful wedding present for the June bride than a Victrola. For what is more welcome than music in the home of the newly married?

A Victrola, with appropriate Victor records, is the sort of a gift that remains a joy forever. Choose your gift from our complete selection of Victrolas. We will deliver it on the day desired.

A Wedding Gift that Carries Happiness with It
THE VICTROLA

A wedding! Two hopeful young souls starting down life's long road—together. Music will smooth the road—will make the hills less steep. It will dull the edge of sorrow—and impart to joy a brighter glow. The home where music dwells is a more contented home. The home that starts with music gets a better start.

So there's hardly any wedding gift that can bring so much happiness as the Victrola—nor will any other gift be more cherished through the years.

The Final Purpose of Advertising.—It is frequently stated that the ultimate object of all good advertising is to sell. Usually the man who makes this statement goes further and

Who is seeking gifts in silver?

Here are Avenues of Good Gifts for any Bride

RIPPLING with a thousand highlights, the Silver Shop is ablaze with good gifts. And every ripple and every highlight is a delightful silver something!

Some eyes may find their delight in the quaint lines of Colonial candlesticks; others prefer the intricate design of an old Dutch box; again it is the clean cut outline of a tea service that cajoles.

The things that will fascinate you are many. In their opulent array they provide many answers to many questions, for there seems to be, at Ovington's, a piece of silver that slips into your idea of a wedding gift as neatly as the ring on the bride's fourth finger!

And there's one thing you will promptly discover about the Silver Shop when you come — the prices are reasonable — reasonable, sensible and just.

OVINGTON'S
"The Gift Shop of Fifth Avenue"
FIFTH AVENUE AT 39TH STREET

For serving after-dinner coffee, the bride will find this set attractive. The Colonial design is good looking; of heavy silver plate. Set with tray, $25.

EXHIBIT 149.—A seasonable advertisement that carries two illustrations pleasingly. The simple scene at the top, with the flying cupids, is just enough to give the proper atmosphere to a message about weddings.

The lower illustration, with equal simplicity, portrays the attractiveness of a gift of silver plate. There is just enough display to be effective and the well written text in 2-column setting invites complete reading. The border is ornamental enough to give a pleasing finish to the entire composition.

This advertiser found a way to combine simplicity and dignity with a price quotation on one article illustrated—a combination that most advertisers find it hard to achieve.

derides the advertisement that does not "actually sell goods." Very likely he adds that, because of his own remarkably rich experience in actual selling, the copy that he writes has the selling quality so often lacking in the efforts of others, and so on.

Whether an advertisement can actually complete a sale depends on conditions. Some who have no physical merchandise to sell advertise to increase appreciation of the service they offer. Others, knowing that it would be futile to attempt an immediate sale through advertising, use printed word and picture to pave the way for future selling, to induce people to think of them as the proper person or source for certain goods or service. As an extreme example, consider the undertaker: Few people nowadays buy their coffins while they are living, and when they are dead they are beyond the reach of the most effective earthly medium! The undertaker can hardly, therefore, time his advertising for immediate sales. All he can do is to create the impression or conviction that he is the proper man for the service he renders, so that he will be called on in due season.

Exhibit 150 does its work well if it creates merely the impression that Tetley's tea makes an unusually fine drink.

A large volume of advertising, on the other hand, can either complete sales or put into motion a procedure that ends in an early sale. Mail-order advertisements often complete the transaction by giving information about terms, price, guarantee, and other details, and calling on the reader to send his money. Sometimes, however, the nature of the article is such that the advertisement, instead of being planned for a complete sale, offers a catalogue or a circular, or offers, maybe, to send the article on approval to responsible people.

Under other conditions, it may be more expedient for the advertisement to close with some such admonition as:

"Call us on the telephone and let us put one of these aside for you."

"Be at our store early tomorrow and get your pick."

"Just sign and mail the enclosed card and we will deliver one of these washing machines to your home, entirely on approval, with free use for a whole week."

The third offer is appropriate for direct advertising literature. In a newspaper advertisement such an offer could be changed to "Mail the coupon below."

The important principle to remember is that there should be some tangible purpose to an advertisement. Too many printed messages close in a vague way that means lost opportunity. If the conditions are such that all an advertisement can do is to impress some point or quality strongly, then the

TETLEY'S
Makes good TEA a certainty

A TALL, frosty glass—full of clinking ice and Tetley's Orange Pekoe—is one of summer's true delights. Refreshing — fragrant — delicious—it is the incomparable hot-weather drink.

EXHIBIT 150.—This advertisement as it stands is one of a manufacturer rather than a retailer, but it affords an excellent lesson of strong display in small space, as well as a lesson in seasonable and convincing copy-writing. The display is as strong as most advertisers get in a space three columns wide and 8 or 10 inches deep. In the original, the appeal measured 4 inches wide by 3½ inches deep. The border arrangement is effective, without being freaky or difficult for the printers to handle. The advertisement appeared in June.

writer should aim to do that. He should ask himself this question: "What can I, in this solicitation, probably induce the reader to do?" Having commanded attention by his headline or illustration, interested and convinced the reader by his good description and argument, he should close his message in the most impressive manner possible, whether that means inducing a call at the store or over the telephone, a written reply or merely a preference for some article or service when the reader is in a position or the humor to buy.

In this part of his message the advertiser has opportunity to exercise his knowledge of psychology. Suppose, for example, the advertisement is about accident insurance. The closing may be:

Tomorrow, or next week, that unlooked-for accident may come. You, or some other member of your family may be driving. How gratifying it will be if you are protected by one of our policies costing only a few cents a day.

The following may be appropriate closing arguments for some other commodity:

Don't deprive yourself of the enjoyment of............a day longer. Our plan makes it possible for you to have the real pleasure of a............during this hot weather. A telephone call will bring our demonstrator at whatever hour suits you.

Admonitions may be brief:

Order for Sunday morning breakfast.

Just call Main 64 and our delivery wagon will serve you promptly.

You need all of the service that the De Laval Separator gives. Don't be satisfied with less.

SECTION XII

TRAINING THE SALES FORCE

Both merchants and manufacturers have made marked progress in the last dozen years in the formulating and carrying out of plans that build better retail salesmanship. Jobbers, wholesalers' associations, retailers' associations and other trade organizations have taken part. The undertaking is one of tremendous scope, made all the more difficult because the retailer, as a rule, is not in a position to pay as large a wage as the employer of traveling salesmen and therefore must deal with helpers of less aptitude and experience.

The following review is based on a study of the business press of recent years and correspondence with representative retail merchants and business organizations.

State Movement in the Direction of Schools for Salespeople.—For many years private schools of salesmanship have enjoyed fair success. For the most part, however, these schools aimed at preparation for traveling, or special kinds of salesmanship such as insurance, real estate, etc.—rather than retail salesmanship. One school, conducted by Lucinda Prince, of Boston, has, however, seemingly been successful in turning out good retail saleswomen, many of whom have become instructors in stores.

It is significant that public educators are now recognizing the need.

The National Society for Vocational Education is responsible for the statement that in the state of Ohio there are ten cities which employ sixteen directors for the purpose of giving instruction in retail merchandising. Approximately 1,000 students have enrolled in these ten cities, giving an average of 100 students to each city.

The instruction is provided for two classes—salespeople who are already employed, and for students in high school who anticipate entering the merchandising business when their high-school training has been completed.

How One Association's Educational Plan Is Conducted.—Retail instruction on a large scale, covering all parts of the country, has been undertaken by a number of trade associations. The following is an outline of the work of the Retail Shoe Salesmen's Institute, of Boston, Mass.

This Institute was established in 1917 by the National Shoe Retailers' Association. Membership is not restricted to retailers, many manufacturers being numbered among the fifty-odd members.

The first three years of this Association's existence were taken up in the preparation of textbooks and organizing the work, which is entirely self-supporting. The text is in eight parts, made up as follows:

1. Retail Shoe Salesmanship
2. Correct Fitting
3. Materials of Which Shoes Are Made
4. Shoemaking
5. Footwear Merchandising
6. Stockkeeping
7. Window- and Store-displays
8. Introduction to Shoe Store Management.

The work of the Institute is carried on mainly by correspondence, although not confined strictly to the correspondence method. Wherever it is possible to do so, it is the object of the Institute to enroll a number of members of a given store and give them actual classroom instruction. This has been done for the Jordan Marsh Company, Boston; Cammeyer, New York; Strawbridge & Clothier, Philadelphia; and for many other large employers.

Six weeks are allotted to each division of the course, making a forty-eight weeks' course in all.

Before a student is allowed to undertake the study of any of the eight units of the course, he or she is supplied with a pamphlet in which is outlined the practical importance of the points covered in the unit and the value to be gained from an actual testing of the principles in the student's daily work. Eight problems are given for solution by the student—one at the end of each unit of study—these being prepared so as to give a correct ideal of just how far the student has been able to master the different units of the course. These test problems are reviewed and criticised at the Institute, after which they are returned to the student, together with a model solution as prepared by the Institute, which may be compared with the student's own work in such a way as to reveal weaknesses or strong points. At any time during the course, a student has the privilege of submitting problems from his daily work for suggestions and guidance in solution.

To cover the actual cost of conducting the work of the Institute, a fee of $36 is charged each student.

Enrolments are obtained both by personal solicitation and direct advertising. The cost of selling the course has been about 25 per cent.

Trade Bulletins of Retail Shoe Salesmen's Institute.—In addition to the regular course of instruction, the Retail Shoe Salesmen's Institute issues bulletins on current conditions. These consist mainly of printed circulars of eight pages. The page shown in Exhibit 151 suggests answers to four of the following eight questions:

1. "I read in the papers that shoes would be cheaper this fall. How much cheaper?"
2. "I read in the papers that hides and leather were much lower. Why are shoes not much lower also?"
3. "Will shoes ever be lower? When?"
4. "Since shoes sold this past summer so much cheaper, why not this fall?"
5. "Why do not high shoes sell at the same price as low shoes?"
6. "Why are shoe prices so high this fall?"
7. "How about children's and boys' shoes?"
8. "What's good in shoe styles this fall?"

At the time this bulletin was issued, these were the questions most likely to be asked shoe salesmen.

sickness is over the patient cannot of course continue that way, but gets back to his regular order of life as soon as possible. One good thing—these cut-price sales tended to show how little real "profiteering" there was in the shoe business.

Question No. 5. High shoes do not sell as cheaply as low shoes for the simple reason that they require more leather, more linings, more of this and that to produce, and more labor, more room, more everything. A good many people do not understand this simple thing; it needs to be explained carefully. It takes nearly twice as much upper leather to make a pair of ten inch boots as to make a pair of oxfords. This is not a serious question, but when it comes up should be met fully and clearly.

Question No. 6. Shoes are as high in cost as they are this fall because it is possible to produce, ship and market them only at the prevailing cost of doing business that applies to all industries. The only possibility of lowering prices comes from cheaper leather and some other minor materials, only a fraction of the cost of actually making and selling shoes, and by a reduction of profits.

Whatever reduction there has been in the price of hides and leather came largely after the manufacturers had already made up shoes from leather bought at the higher prices. Offsetting whatever gain could thus possibly be made, there is the increase in other directions, as referred to above several times. The customer, from his own experience in many ways knows that this is so—that his expenses in many directions have mounted in the past six months. The shoe merchant and manufacturer are powerless to prevent such increases any more than the customer himself can.

You can suggest to the customer that there is a likelihood of improvement in this respect when excess profit taxes, income taxes, war taxes, etc., are modified, when the enormous cost of government on a war basis are reduced, when the general financial condition of the whole world improves, when the dollar gets to have a larger purchasing power. He knows that this takes time, and that shoe prices have to wait on the general run of improvement.

Question No. 7. The high cost of children's and boys' shoes have occasioned as much complaint as anything else in the shoe line. With some substantial reduction in men's and women's shoes, the public is quite likely to expect the same numerical reduction in children's shoes. For instance if a certain style of men's welt calfskin boots is reduced $2 in its public price, the purchaser is apt to expect that a pair of welt calfskin shoes for his boy ought to be $2 cheaper. Explain to him that it takes as many mechanical operations to produce the smaller shoes as the larger, that it takes a pair of lasts that cost just as much, a set of patterns just as expensive and in general there are many items in the production of the boys' shoes that parallel the men's shoes. While there would be some reduction in the price of the boys' shoes, you can as above suggested, show him convincingly that it is impossible to show the same reduction in dollars and cents. This is only right and fair both to the store handling little shoes as well as the manufacturer who produces them.

Question No. 8. It is safe to answer this question by saying that whatever you have on your shelves, as your customers come in, is "good style this fall." This can be said in all sincerity because there is no radical change in style such as would nullify or seriously impair the sales-and-style-utility of the average stock as it will be constituted this fall.

In each and every case, the salesman reading this Current Conditions Bulletin should consult with his employer on this question and secure his complete answer. It is, of course, impossible in a Bulletin of this sort to make a statement on fall styles that will fully cover every store. The salesman is perforce concerned only with the stock in his particular store.

Ascertain, therefore, all the facts, as

(6)

EXHIBIT 151.—Page from a current 8-page bulletin issued regularly by the Retail Shoe Salesmen's Institute, suggesting answers to timely questions.

TRAINING THE SALES FORCE

National Commercial Gas Association's Experience.—The National Commercial Gas Association in 1910 prepared a Gas Salesmanship Course on a cooperative basis. An educational director was secured from New York University to take active charge of the big job of making employes of the gas companies better salesmen.

Ten lectures were issued and the plan followed of sending out one each month. The following shows the scope of the course:

		No. of Pages
1.	The Real-salesman and the Near-salesman	16
2.	Practical and Personal Elements in Selling Gas	20
3.	Four Steps in Selling	16
4.	The Customer's Attitude Toward a Sale	18
5.	Building a Selling Talk	22
6.	Building a Selling Talk (continued)	23
7.	Turning Technical Matter into Selling Points	16
8.	Selling Gas on a Large Scale Part I—Factory Illumination	16
9.	Selling Gas on a Large Scale Part II—The Factory and the Store	23
10.	Selling Gas on a Large Scale Part III—Gas for Industrial Purposes	19

On the last page of each pamphlet were test questions to be answered by the student in writing and sent to Association headquarters for review and grading. The cost of the course was $5, payable in two instalments of $2.50 each, and only members of the National Commercial Gas Association were enrolled.

Of the first enrolment of 725 students, 110, or a percentage of 15, completed the course. When the course was repeated the following season 200 students enrolled and 67, or 28 per cent, completed the list of subjects.

In 1912 a second course was undertaken. This also consisted of ten sections:

1. The Salesman and the Corporation
2. The Sales Department and the Organization
3. The Basis of Departmental Organization

4. Elements of Gas Manufacture for Salesmen and Commercial Men
5. What the Commercial Man Should Know About Distribution
6. Elements of Gas Accounting and Purchasing
7. Orders and Dispatch
8. Organization of the Sales Department
9. Advertising and Special Campaigns
10. Company Policy and Public Relations

This course was sold on the same terms as the original course except that, if paid for on the instalment plan, the price was $1 a month for six months. Seven hundred students were enrolled, and 119, or a percentage of 17, completed the course. The secretary of the National Commercial Gas Association visited sixteen of the larger cities to present this course to managers and members of gas companies.

A third course was presented in 1914, entitled "The Utilization of Gas Appliances." This was also a 10-lesson program. It was sold for $5 on the cash plan to members of the N.C.G.A., or at $6 on a dollar-a-month plan. To others, the price of the course was $10 in advance. There were 3,850 students enrolled and 1,081, or a percentage of 28, completed it.

Finally a three-year course was planned. This was intended to be much more than a Salesmanship Course. It included an introductory division affording the student references and reviews of the manufacture and distribution of gas, generation and distribution of electrical energy, also arithmetic, chemistry, magnetism, mechanics, algebra, geometry, heat, light and sound.

At the outset there was a lecture on "Starting Right." There were suggestions on how to study, and side talks on arithmetic, business English and the manufacture of gas, also a self-analysis chart.

Then followed the major sections of the instruction: Business English, Industrial Fuel, Illumination, Salesmanship, Commercial Management and Accounting.

Students were allowed to select subjects, according to the nature of their work, being counselled in their selections by those in charge of the educational bureau. The introductory material and the first four lessons in Business English were the same for all courses.

The cost of these 3-year courses ranged from $25 to $30, on the cash plan, and from $36 to $43.20, on the monthly-payment plan.

Within a period of four years 2,300 students were enrolled, and 6,405 lessons were received. Of the total work done, 3,722 covered the four introductory lessons and the self-analysis chart, while 2,683 covered special lessons in five different courses.

This extensive educational work by the gas companies, was abandoned during the Great War but enough good was accomplished to make the new association, known as the American Gas Association, favorable toward a resumption of the undertaking.

This experience shows that the longer courses in business subjects are, the greater the difficulty of getting out-of-school people to complete them. The better plan, if it be possible, is to plan short courses that may be completed in a month or two. If desirable, a number of short courses may be planned to follow each other, and thus get through a longer course of study without appalling the spare-hour student by letting him know at the outset that it will require a year or two years to complete the program.

Those who are interested in the training of large groups of business workers, retail salespeople, or others, must be prepared to find that the average amount of work done will not be large where the students are left to their own volition. This sometimes seems discouraging, but, after all, the proportion of ambitious people is not a large one. It is easy to make a resolution or to start something new and useful, but diversions and natural laziness will soon sidetrack the mass of "starters."

The manufacturer or merchant behind the program must have some one in charge who will introduce interesting features and stimulations, such as contests, marks of honor, or rewards. He cannot get 100 per cent of his group to receive solid instruction in any useful subject. If the proportion that does receive this instruction warrants the expense of his program, he should continue it, despite the average low percentage of work done.

The situation is, of course, different where the group receiving the instruction is made up of employes of one organization, where company-time can be used and certain studying and examination work compelled.

---

1. Hold a school for salespeople regularly.

2. Make them responsible for their part in the business.

3. Show them the value of courtesy to customers.

4. Show them how to make sales by suggesting additional things for customers to buy.

5. Show them the importance of stopping waste.

6. Give them an incentive to make more and better sales.

EXHIBIT 152.—Six pointers from the National Cash Register Company on the training of retail salespeople.

Exhibit 152 is a program advised by a manufacturing concern that has been unusually successful in training for better retail salesmanship.

PLANS OF REPRESENTATIVE LARGE STORES

Lord & Taylor's Method.—This well known New York store has a regular course in salesmanship for its employes, which consists of five lessons, the course being given about twice a month, except in the fall when it is scheduled for every week. The class meets at 10 o'clock and is in charge of a woman director of training. The lecture method is used entirely, supplemented by demonstration sales, which visualize to the class just how a certain sale should be handled and leave a more lasting impression on the minds of the salespeople than any amount of mere talk would do.

This instruction is supplemented by a system manual which is given to every salesperson, showing how different kinds of sales checks are to be made out, how cash refunds are to be handled, how exchanges of different kinds are to be made, what must be done when merchandise is brought in for alteration or repair, discounts to which employes of the store are entitled, and so on.

Furthermore, the Lord & Taylor organization issues weekly bulletins to its salespeople, these dealing with such topics as dress regulations for salespeople; new heads of departments; employes' purchases; reduced magazine subscription rates offered to employes; invitations to visit novel departments of the store; information as to the kind of merchandise favored by fashion; information as to guaranteeing different fabrics against spotting, etc.; store rules, with quiz as to how these are being observed; reports of remarks made by customers; questions of loyalty to the store at all times during employment; information as to number of employes who were late during a given time; news of educational or inspirational value to the employes.

A specimen bulletin of the Lord & Taylor organization is reproduced in Exhibit 153. There is great variety in these, which is as it should be, for if they were all written according to some set program or arrangement they would not command the proper attention.

Lord & Taylor

Make the Bulletin yours! **Read and Contribute!**

Bulletin 104

LORD & TAYLOR MUST GIVE GOOD SERVICE: TO BE GOOD, SERVICE MUST BE HONEST, PROMPT, COURTEOUS AND COMPLETE.

Service to Employe-Customers
When an employe takes a shopping pass and goes about our store with the intention of buying merchandise, that employe becomes at once a customer, and it is with the courtesy which we extend to customers that he or she should be served. We cannot have a greater criticism passed on our organization than to have it reported that we fail to give good service to our own people. In the Lord & Taylor rules of etiquette there are no company manners, and among ourselves, in our own store family, we should have daily associations that are helpful and kindly. There is every reason why a fellow-employe should have your courteous attention. There are no reasons why he or she should not.

Winter Dress Regulation
The winter dress regulation will go into effect Monday October 16. On the selling floors, black or dark blue suits and dresses should be worn with shoes, hose and spats of either black or dark brown. In non-selling departments where employes do not meet the public, white waists may be worn. In both selling and non-selling departments it is requested that unnecessary jewelry be discarded during business hours and also that the use of cosmetics and perfumes should be limited. The woman of today who exacts the greatest admiration from us all is the woman whose dress is the least conspicuous and whose personal appearance is the most natural. Because we are business women, let us strive for the greatest simplicity.

Coal Conservation
Mr. Nevins of the tenth floor Sample Room has called attention to a recent newspaper appeal for city-wide cooperation in the efforts of the Mayor's Committee to conserve coal. Businesses like ours use large quantities of coal in the maintenance of their buildings, and it is very reasonable to suggest that we all help in such a time as

EXHIBIT 153.—Example of store bulletin for salespeople, issued by Lord & Taylor.

TRAINING THE SALES FORCE 341

this to reduce coal consumption by remembering that even the shutting off of one electric light may be a practical economy.

Merchandise News

The Radio Department has been re-installed on the seventh floor; the attractiveness of this service is greatly enhanced this fall by the fact that the World Series Baseball Games are to be broadcasted play by play.

The Cooking Demonstration Lectures which are under the supervision of Miss Thompson are also resumed on the seventh floor Mondays, Wednesdays and Fridays at 2 p.m.

Boys' first long trousers are carried on the fourth floor and not in the Man's Shop on the tenth.

Will employes whose furs are stored in our Fur Storage please give the department the benefit of one or two days' notice before asking for their delivery?

The routine of the department requires that much time before such articles can be released.

Lates

Tuesday morning, October 3, there were 246 employes who came to business late. 210 arrived between 8:50 and 9:00 o'clock and 36 arrived after 9:00 o'clock. This means that the first hour in the morning—one of the most valuable hours of the day—was shortened by at least one-quarter in the many departments where these late employes belonged. Multiplying the lost minutes by the 246 who were late, we can figure that Lord & Taylor lost through this means, many hours of valuable time. Our fall business is going to require of us all a full day's work each day, and we can claim credit for a successful season only in such proportion as we make our day actually 100 per cent efficient.

Absentees

Hereafter, will all Section Managers and Heads of Departments pass on to the Employment Office whatever word they may receive from absent employes? In this way, the Personnel Department will be informed of illness or misfortune, and the information will be valuable and very greatly appreciated.

Educational News

The first bracing days of the fall make us ready to plan our winter enthusiastically. We are not going to be fair to ourselves if we do not make plans that will include some mental food as well as physical and recreational stimulus. This year the Training Department finds that there is an unusually interesting field of opportunity for mental development. A splendid course in Home Furnishing is offered by New York University and given at the

EXHIBIT 153. *Continued*

Metropolitan Museum of Art. The Evening High School offers courses in General Textiles, English, Salesmanship, Advertising and Bookkeeping. The Textile High School gives classes in Cotton, Upholstery Fabrics, Woolens, Fabric Analysis and Textile Design which promise to be very interesting. There are many other courses offered which Miss Hall and her assistants will be glad to discuss with you if you will stop in the Training Office to inquire.

Lost

Miss Scanlon reports from the Package Room that two pieces of hand baggage have been left there uncalled-for and empty. They will be gladly restored to their owners upon proper identification.

The Man's Shop Not A Passage

Quite a number of employes are in the habit of using the Man's Shop on the tenth floor as a passageway to the stairs at the east end of the Cafeteria. In this way we are making use of one of our most attractive floors in a way which is not in keeping with its dignity and beauty. With this Bulletin number, notice is given that this custom must be discontinued and we believe that all employes will agree in the justice of this decision.

Mutual Benefit Evening

Tuesday night October 17, is the date of the first Mutual Benefit Euchre and Dance for the winter 1922–23. The attractions of the evening are very much worth-while and already there have been many donations of prizes. A Victrola will be given as the door prize. Supper will be served as usual at 5:30 p.m. and the regular Mutual Benefit brand of good snappy fun and music will last out the evening. The attendance has to be limited to employes only but preparations have been made for a large number.

Customers' Impressions

At 5:20 p.m. one day last month a customer telephoned the store. The person replying announced that no order could be taken as the store was about to close. Fortunately Miss Mahoney of our Telephone Department overheard the conversation in time to ring back the customer, get the details of the purchase she wished to make, and her name and address. This loyalty and readiness to serve on Miss Mahoney's part saved us in spite of another employe's indifference and in the ten minutes that remained of that business day, we were enabled to fulfill our obligation as a public servant. Whether we are in a selling or a non-selling department, let us not forget that our service to Lord & Taylor and to the public should not cease until the day's work is really done.

Saturday October 7, 1922

EXHIBIT 153. *Concluded.*

Schuster Company's Plan.—The Schuster Company of Milwaukee issues an employes' magazine, entitled *Keeping in Touch*, which contains much valuable information of the following classifications: goods handled and how to sell them; effective displays that have been made up by different departments; news as to department managers; health hints; news as to the different clubs of the Schuster Company, such as the baseball club, the swimming club; honor rolls of employes who have made the highest averages in sales for the month; also of those who have made no errors in sales checks for the month. Interspersed with the other material is information of a purely personal nature which goes a long way towards building up the *esprit de corps* of the organization.

The Schuster Company also has regular classes in salesmanship. These classes are conducted for new salespeople on the second morning of their employment. Further instruction is incidental, such as that given in interviews concerning shoppers' reports, interviews concerning low sales records, as the result of the observations of the work on a given floor or in a certain department or as the result of some poorly arranged display. All of this instruction is given during the regular working hours of the day. This store at one time held weekly classes in one of the departments, outside of working hours, but the plan was not particularly effective and was abandoned for the more satisfactory one here outlined.

Instruction is not confined to the lecture method, but is rather given along the line of the round table or discussion idea, as it has been demonstrated that the conference method is much more successful. In fact, this organization says, "We find that getting the salespeople to take part is essential to the success of the meetings."

The regular instruction work is in charge of a woman director. This is occasionally supplemented by having an outside salesman of some manufacturing concern speak to the different departments, emphasizing the important features of the merchandise he represents, so that the salespeople will be better qualified to handle the goods intelligently and successfully.

18   KEEPING IN TOUCH

SCHUSTER'S TRAINING DEPARTMENT

Have You Heard—
That Reading Classes Are Now Much in Vogue!

The Training Departments are holding what they designate as Reading Classes, although these are not held as formal classes in the stricter meaning of that word. As soon as it is decided that an individual is to be a regular in one certain department, she is called to the Training office to read material concerning the merchandise in her new department. The text books on these subjects are written by "men who know" and supplemented by samples and correlative materials compiled by the Training Departments. Nearly all of the departments have been covered.

It is hoped that everyone will take advantage of this opportunity and "read up" on his or her merchandise. Persons who have been in the department a long time are sure to find new lights on the subject that they have not seen before and it is not the object of the Training Department to limit the use of the compiled material in any way.

Let's get together and learn our stock even better than before. The Better Sales Campaign proved what an accurate knowledge of our own stock can mean. Here's our opportunity to do our own little "follow-up" and come out on top!

Honor Roll.

The following salespeople have had no errors in their cash during the month of April:

Third Street.
Ruby Weisner.
Ella Stein.
Louise Albrecht.
Cora Montey.
Martha Fiebrantz.
Alma Jahre.
Lucy Petersick.
Mitchell Street.
Mrs. Anna Hintz.
Emma Rosenthal.
Lillian Mueller.
Mrs. Margaret Funk.
Clara Griesel.
Mrs. E. Levenson.
Mayer Balkansky.
Mrs. P. Sheeran.
Mrs. Lillian Kanitz.
Elsie Leifer.
Selma Wartchow.
Mrs. Doris Peacock.
Elsie Schultz.
Otilia Schultz.
Mrs. Kate Mann.
Twelfth Street.
Mrs. P. Schellinger.
Mr. R. Reichardt.
Mrs. I. Schroenke.
Miss K. Harrington.
Miss M. Klinkert.
Miss L. Koester.
Miss E. Marquardt.
Miss C. Zassenhaus.

The following salespeople have had only one error in their cash during the month of April:

Third Street.
Lillie Ehlers.
Alice McMalion.
Josephine Luessman.
Minnie Seeger.
Mrs. G. Reimers.
Martha Dobratz.
Anna Lipperer.
Anna Weber.
Harold Gates.
Mitchell Street.
Marie Jeski.
Bertha Rollhagen.
Rose Gray.
Miss E. Thomas.
Anna Bartkowiak.
Mrs. G. Seyk.
Laura Abrahams.
Edward Zarnow.
Mrs. S. Klatt.
Mrs. E. Brawin.
Twelfth Street.
Mrs. M. Buth.
Miss I. Berner.
Mrs. A. Koeppen.
Miss E. Hellman.
Miss T. Marx.
Miss J. Stiles.
Miss M. Schmitz.
Miss C. Krueger.
Mrs. M. Weis.
Miss A. Borst.
Miss N. Marth.

The following cashiers have had no errors in their cash during the month of April:
Third Street.
Dorothy Vahl.   Norma Hahn.

The following cashiers have had only one error in their cash during the month of April:
Third Street.
Bessie Stein.   Georgie Brockel.   Eleanor Bellin.   Clara Mueller.

EXHIBIT 154.—Specimen page from a store magazine of decided educational value.

The training director of the Schuster Company makes the following comment:

> We have found that assigning a member of the training department to a certain section of the floor, making her responsible for the salesmanship and the personnel in her section, is the best method with which we have experimented, in raising the standard of salespeople's work.

Exhibit 154 shows a specimen page from the employes' magazine of this progressive store.

Strawbridge & Clothier's System.—This large department store, of Philadelphia, Pa., has a regularly organized training division, under the supervision of a woman educational director.

Two conference rooms have been placed at the disposal of the educational director and regular salesmanship courses are given to those needing such instruction. The classes are usually held in the early morning hours, this time having been chosen because the salespeople are fresher then and also because the store is less crowded in the early morning hours than later in the day.

It is the practice of this store to give what it calls "demonstration sales." That is, the educational director takes a certain article and demonstrates to the class the best method of selling that particular article. These demonstration sales are varied according to the need, and in the course of a season cover practically all departments of the store. The advantages of this method will be readily seen, for in giving a demonstration sale the instructor is not only appealing to her class through the sense of hearing but also through the sense of sight. Thus, the instruction is much more likely to be remembered and put into practice, even though it may have to be adapted to suit each particular case. In fact, this very point is brought out, for no sale could be a model to such an extent that it would fit every need. Individuals have to be approached and appealed to through different argument.

The Strawbridge & Clothier organization also maintains a sponsor association. This association is made up of represen-

STRAWBRIDGE & CLOTHIER STORE CHAT

Copyright applied for in 1920 by STRAWBRIDGE & CLOTHIER

VOLUME XV.   Philadelphia, June-July, 1922   NUMBER 6

EDITED BY AND IN THE INTEREST OF THE EMPLOYES OF STRAWBRIDGE & CLOTHIER AND PUBLISHED FOR THEM EACH MONTH, IN THE HOPE OF PROMOTING THE GENERAL WELFARE AND BRINGING EACH INTO CLOSER RELATION WITH ALL.

OPENING OF OUR BASEMENT STORE

A New Service for Strawbridge & Clothier Customers

As one stepped in from the subway on the morning of June 8 it almost seemed as if a magician had been at work over night. Gone were all traces of House Furnishings and China, so long occupying the basement Store, and in their place was a brand new Apparel Store for women and girls. New fixtures, soft rugs, ferns and potted plants furnished a pleasing setting for the new merchandise that was the centre of so much admiration and wonder.

It was no secret that the Basement Store was coming, but in the few days before its opening such wonders were accomplished in getting everything ready that it almost seemed as if someone waved a magic wand and said, "Come forth, Basement Store," and there it stood, challenging our delight and amazement.

Fills Definite Need

That the Basement Store is going to fill a definite need for the Philadelphia public is evident from the many exclamations of pleasure heard on and since the opening day. Old and new Customers expressed their satisfaction in this latest evidence of our Store's desire to be of the widest service to the community. Practically every large department Store in the country includes a lower-price Basement, and this Store is but answering a request that has been made hundreds, yes thousands, of times by our patrons.

Basement Managers

The general merchandising of the Basement is being directed by Mr. M. J. Comerford, who has been for over twenty years in charge of all the departments on the third floor of the West Store. Mr. Comerford is assisted by the following capable staff:—

Mr. M. W. Atwater, Executive Assistant.
Mr. H. C. Yaeger, in charge of Women's Apparel.
Miss Cosgrove, Assistant for Women's Apparel.
Miss L. Granitzer, Misses' Apparel
Mr. J. L. Curran, Shoes.
Mrs. M. Fitzpatrick, Infants' Wear.
Miss E. V. Jackson, Muslinwear and Waists, House Dresses, etc.
Mrs. Clara Sloan, Millinery.
Miss Mary Ward, Corsets.
Miss Carol Berkemeier, in charge of Office.

Excellent Sales Force

Completing the organization of the Basement Store is a selling force of one hundred and sixty persons, carefully chosen from hundreds of applicants. Their mettle was tried in the opening days when heavy business was supplemented by very hot weather, and yet only a half dozen "dropped out."

STORE CHAT extends a sincere welcome to all our new associates and wishes that our little sister, the new Basement Store, may grow greater every year.

EXHIBIT 155.—Title page of *Store Chat*, showing how newsy items about the store are featured.

tatives of the salespeople who have been especially trained, and it serves as a connecting link between the salespeople and the department of personnel.

The company also employs a librarian, who goes through the various trade papers carefully and clips articles. These are pasted on separate sheets and sent to the department or departments to which they would be of particular interest. It is left to the head of each department to see that such data is read and applied by the salespeople.

Store Chat, the official employes' organ of the Strawbridge & Clothier organization, is published monthly and serves to impart not only news of the store itself, such as is conveyed by the title page reproduced in Exhibit 155, but useful notes such as details of price contests, honor roll of employes, a page of clippings from other store papers, new features and improvements of the store, social notes, including store outings, and so on, as well as inspirational material, this appearing usually in the form of short, easily remembered paragraphs.

Exhibit 156 is a typical inside page of *Store Chat*.

Correspondence Course for J. C. Penney Company's Employes.—The J. C. Penney Company operates a chain of 371 stores, most of these being located in the West.

The educational department of this enterprise is located in New York City. From this working base the company sends out, at frequent intervals, a booklet containing two lessons, these being sent through the different store managers. Ten examination questions are scheduled for each lesson. These the salespeople answer and turn in to their manager, who, in turn, sends the examination to the New York headquarters. It is the duty of the store manager to distribute the lesson booklets to the salespeople and to see that the examinations are given proper attention. The examination papers are, however, all corrected in New York by the educational director and his staff. Great care is used in grading the papers, and it is the policy of the Penney Company to recognize ability and cause for commendation as readily as it does errors or misinformation. Each examination paper, showing comments in red ink, is returned to the student, with a typewritten comment on the work done. The work

STORE CHAT

Do You See What Is Wrong With This Sales Check?

The name and address is taken correctly on the BODY OF THE CHECK, but it is COPIED INCORRECTLY ON THE DELIVERY CARD.

A package went out the other day with the salescheck of which this is an exact copy. (We have changed the customer's name and the salesperson's number, of course, but that is all.)

Needless to say, the package was returned for wrong address and the customer was kept waiting while we hunted it up in the city directory and sent it out again on the next delivery trip.

MORAL

Always fill out the DELIVERY CARD first and then you will make no mistake because of having your hand over what you are copying.

TEN COMMANDMENTS OF HEALTH.

1. Walk in the open air.
2. Keep a contented mind.
3. Breathe deeply of pure air.
4. Enjoy innocent amusements.
5. Get plenty of sleep each night.
6. Give your body and soul plenty of sunlight.
7. Eat healthful, plain food—and just enough of it.
8. Associate with companions who will benefit you.
9. Give your body plenty of pure water, outside and inside.
10. Do unto others as you wish them to do unto you.

Are You Building Character and Success? If So—

You are not satisfied with mediocrity.

You are troubled by a poor day's work and a slighted job haunts you.

You are not satisfied to do a thing "just for now," but, instead, do everything to the best of your ability.

You are not willing to work in the midst of confused, systemless surroundings which you might remedy.

Commonness annoys you. Your ambition is ever apparent and you are continually raising your standard of excellence.

Adapted from Orison Swett Marden.

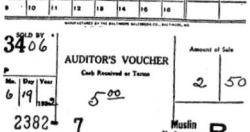

EMPLOYMENT ENJOYMENT
"THE WISE MAN is the one who gets enjoyment out of his work as he goes along—
who does not view happiness as a blessed state that will come only when he gets something he isn't getting now."

EXHIBIT 156.—Inside page from Strawbridge & Clothier's employes' magazine, showing how exhibits can be used to illustrate poor work or good work.

assigned in each booklet must be completely covered before another is taken up.

The lessons are based on general business training, with the idea of giving special instruction on the working principles of the Penney stores. From the more efficient, ambitious salespeople are chosen managers for new stores that are opened now and then, so that this, and the bonus system of the company, are the goals toward which the salespeople work. The course of instruction is supplied free of charge to the employes.

Educational Work of Titche-Goettinger Company.—Realizing that the salesperson is often denied the special training that is open for employes in other fields, the Dallas, Texas, store of Titche-Goettinger Company has established an educational department of its own, in charge of a woman director, where salespeople are given free instruction during the regular working hours of the store.

Classes in salesmanship and business systems are held daily, as well as continuation classes for boys and girls who have not had the opportunity of completing their grammar school education. The instruction given is made as practical as possible in order to fit the every-day needs of the students. Maps and bulletins put out by the Chamber of Commerce are used in these classes.

Reports of all errors made are sent to the educational director, and these are used, together with the sales record of each salesperson, in judging her ability and value to the store. A personal record file is kept, year by year, of each employe, and these record cards are a great help in reviewing the progress of the salespeople, and as a basis for recommendations for promotion or increase in salary.

It is also the duty of the educational director to see that each salesperson is placed in the position or department where she will be of the greatest value to the store. A recruit who might make a miserable record in the millinery department might prove perfectly capable in the shoe department. (Summarized from *Dry Goods Economist*).

Method of a Northwestern Store.—One of the most prominent stores of the Northwest holds classes for instruction in better salesmanship for all salespeople who show possibilities of development but who are not familiar with the principles of salesmanship as this store believes in applying them.

A series of six or eight classes is held once a week, each class lasting about an hour. The hour of meeting is from 9:15 to 10:15 in the morning.

The woman educational director of this store believes in getting as far away as possible from the lecture method and encouraging members of the classes to contribute toward the meeting. She proceeds on the well known theory that the more a person puts into a discussion, the more he gets out of it. Therefore, if the salespeople themselves can be induced to take part in the instruction, much more is accomplished than would be accomplished by the lecture method alone. At least one demonstration sale is held, and the class takes part in this also.

Outside speakers, such as men representing wholesalers and manufacturers, talk at the departmental meetings from time to time, explaining the outstanding features of the goods they represent and the best methods of selling them. The different departmental buyers arrange for these talks, and they always take place at the regular weekly meetings.

Suggestion Contests as an Incentive.—As a means of promoting interest in salesmanship generally, from time to time this department store holds what it calls "Suggestion Contests." For example, during a contest of this kind, the aim of each department is to see which can sell the highest number of articles by suggestion. Another prize is given for the largest total sales made through suggestion. This gives the department making few sales but selling more expensive merchandise an opportunity to make a showing as well as those departments selling a variety of small articles at low prices.

Quota Week.—Another contest that the retailer referred to in the preceding paragraph has held with good results was the "Quota Week Contest." A quota was set for each salesperson in the different departments, and during the quota week contest the object was to see how many of the individual salespeople in each department could reach or exceed the amount of sales that had been set.

Christmas Bonus.—It has been the custom of this store to give a 1 per cent commission bonus on all sales made during the two weeks preceding Christmas. This puts the salespeople on their mettle.

Method of S. Kann Sons Company.—This large department store, of Washington, D. C., believes strongly in classes for salesmanship instruction, but its management lays down no rule as to how or when the instruction is to be given. This store has a woman educational director in charge of the work. In the spring of 1922 two courses of instruction were given the salespeople, each covering a period of four weeks, with classes on Wednesday and Thursday mornings from 9:30 to 10:30. The lecture method was used entirely in these discussions, the idea being to get the salespeople to take an active part in the instruction work themselves by having them ask questions, submit problems, and so forth. Demonstration sales were also a feature of these classes.

Recently the educational director of this store held group meetings once a week on Wednesday mornings, the course to cover an eight-weeks' period. Four of the eight talks were given by superintendents and buyers of the store—two on service, two on merchandise knowledge and its value to the salesperson who expects to make a success of selling. The other four periods were given over to discussions, aided by the Graphic Service Charts, small merchandising books and salesmanship pamphlets put out by the Educational Department of the *Dry Goods Economist*, New York City.

As a reward for time and effort spent in these classes, the company provides some suitable entertainment for the class as a body at the conclusion of each session.

The employes of the S. Kann Sons Company also issue a little house organ or employes' magazine, entitled *The Kan-Sun*, which is published every two months. The educational director of the store is editor-in-chief of this publication. The issues are largely given over to inspirational material, merchandise information, salesmanship information, dress regulations, lists of departments and salespeople who have made perfect or nearly perfect records, lists of departments that have made no errors in addresses or given wrong addresses for delivery of goods as compared with those that have offended in this respect, with a plea for more "perfects," newsy items about store improvements, and notes of a social nature concerning both individual employes and group gatherings.

Jordan Marsh's Method of Eliminating Errors.—A real problem in any large retail store is that of having sales, billing and shipping slips made out in such a way as to prevent errors and misunderstandings.

A check of the slips from the salespeople of the Jordan Marsh Company, Boston, revealed the rather startling fact that there are fifteen trifling errors that can be made in filling out a sales slip that may cause much trouble and confusion in the shipping and credit departments; that there are fourteen omissions or errors in making out slips which cause trouble in the billing department, while the auditing department is constantly perplexed and handicapped on account of eight different errors or omissions on the part of salespeople in making out sales checks.

Having located the cause of most errors and misunderstandings, the educational director of the store determined, by the use of lantern slides, to show the salespeople how seemingly trifling omissions and errors on their part caused serious trouble and cost the store a tremendous amount of money, and in many cases even lost customers. After the salespeople had seen the harm that the errors did, another set of lantern slides showed them how to avoid such errors.

In order to further emphasize the importance of teamwork in this respect, the store went even further than the lantern slides and issued a bulletin to the salespeople, explaining why it was necessary to guard against inaccurate, incomplete or illegible entries.

Because the Jordan Marsh management took the employes into their confidence and showed them the "reason why," the plan was very successful.

(*Retail Ledger*, June 7, 1922).

Recent Practice of Jordan Marsh Company.—Among the recent methods adopted by this large Boston retailer for the improvement of salesmanship service are some playlets illustrating telephone service. These little dramas first show the ordinary way in which a telephone transaction is handled and then the better way.

The visualization of instruction of this kind seems to make a much better impression on employes than mere lecture work. Besides, there is a certain entertaining feature about a play.

The same idea could be carried out by the use of moving pictures, and, as a matter of fact, this has been done in other stores.

The Jordan Marsh Company now uses a questionnaire which is filled out by every new employe in the sales department. This enables the management to know the experience that the new employe has had and to get his or her views on certain subjects—all of which information opens the way for definite instruction.

The Jordan Marsh Company has regular Wednesday morning talks by department heads, either on service or merchandising.

FEATURES FROM OTHER EXPERIENCES

Use of Two House Organs by Louis Traxler Company.—The Louis Traxler Company, of Dayton, Ohio, finds use for two house organs. One is used primarily as a medium by which the management can address employes, while the other is an employes' house organ, operated by employes. *Traxology*, the publication created by employes, is published monthly. The other publication is issued twice a week. The frequent publication of the semi-weekly periodical gives the store an opportunity to bring in very timely topics. Such features as a page arranged in the form of a blank on which the salesmen and saleswomen can report a list of goods called for but which could not be furnished have been used.

Appealing to Cooperative Spirit of Employes.—In each issue of the house organ of the Jordan Marsh Company, Boston, Mass., there is published, under the title "The Open Door," a photograph of a wide-open door to the office of the president, George W. Mitton.

This indicates more graphically than mere words could do that the way is always open for members of the organization to bring matters personally to the attention of the chief executive of the store; that he is interested in all that goes on in the great establishment and that the cooperation and suggestions of the individual employes are welcomed at all times. The knowledge that direct access to the "Big Boss" is always available does much toward increasing the good-will and loyalty of the personnel of the store and in making the service of the salespeople of a higher order than is usually found.

Nothing saps the "spirit" or morale of an organization of any kind quicker and more effectively than the feeling that the men at the top are not interested in the ideas and welfare of the mass of employes; that employes are just cogs in a great human machine that grinds relentlessly, regardless of how the different members of the organization may feel about the way things are being carried on.

Suggestion Boxes.—Closely related to the idea of the "Open Door" as carried out by the Jordan Marsh Company is the idea of many large stores in having what they call a "suggestion box."

A good-sized box is fitted up attractively, with a slot in the top, through which any employe may drop suggestions or criticisms for the development of the store and its service. The salespeople are encouraged to make frequent contributions to this box. In some instances, prizes are offered each month for the most helpful suggestion or criticism. This stimulates a friendly rivalry that has been found to have a good effect all around.

While such an idea is certain to bring a measure of petty, unimportant things, the value of the plan as a whole is always good. Like the "Open Door," it creates among the salespeople a feeling of good fellowship toward those in authority, without which there can be no stable growth or development.

Ten Commandments of S. Kann Sons Company.—As a result of encouraging the workers to submit their ideas, one of the employes of S. Kann Sons Company, Washington, D. C., worked up the following ten commandments, which have been handed down by the firm to all of its workers as a means of stimulating effort and thus increasing sales:

1. Punctuality—Treat the time clock as your friend. Don't abuse it.

2. Appearance—See yourself as others see you. Let your mirror be your guide.

3. Fellowship—Do you treat your fellow worker as you would be treated? Start the day with a friendly spirit toward all.

4. Stock or Department—Know your stock well. Be able to tell your customer intelligently the merits of the particular merchandise being sold in your department.

5. Courtesy—A gift we all have in latent form, anxious to come to the surface with a little encouragement.

6. System—Start the day feeling that you will do everything possible to help give our patrons good service. Study the system of this establishment. Make it your business to become enlightened on the different departments that help to make our system as near perfect as the human mind can conceive.

7. Suggestions—Be not afraid to offer suggestions that may help this store to greater endeavor to please our patrons and our employes. We are all open to criticism and appreciate being told of our errors.

8. Cooperation—Maeterlinck says that "a single bee lacks the necessary intelligence to make honey; but a hive of bees develops a high order of intelligence. It is only when they work together that bees are productive." Let us be bees.

9. Employer—Is your position a one-sided bargain? On your side are you a clock-watcher? Do you realize that you are virtually a partner in this business; that you get out of it what you put in? Your desire to do your best will act as a boomerang. It will spur you on to greater efforts, which eventually spell "success."

10. Eventide—Leave this store at night knowing that through the day you have done your best. Have each person who comes in contact with you feel that in knowing you she has learned the meaning of "Love thy neighbor as thyself." Then and then only have you accomplished what life expects of you.

Converting Clerks into Temporary Customers.—As a means of educating his salespeople in the finer points of retail salesmanship, one merchant in a small-sized Pennsylvania town selects a time when the store is not overflowing with customers and takes a salesman aside and treats him as he would a customer.

In other words, he chooses an article on which he thinks the particular salesman may need coaching, and then proceeds to sell the article to the salesman, just as if the salesman were one of the most valued customers of the establishment. And he does not overlook the various good points of the article in question; these are all brought out and emphasized in such a way that they will always be remembered by the salesman when the tables are reversed and he is again the salesman instead of the customer.

This is a method that could not, of course, be carried out to advantage in a large organization, but it is particularly effective in small stores where it is not practical to employ a store instructor.

Centering the Sales Talk on Something Definite.—General talks on better salesmanship get about as far as general talks on anything else. The kind of instruction that has actually brought results in training for better retail salesmanship is the talk or demonstration that concentrates on some weak spot in the work, or on some related group of topics, or the talk that deals with one kind of merchandise.

Sometimes the New York, or some other big-city buyer for the firm is the man who can score on an important topic. Occasionally, a wholesale man or a manufacturer's representative is the helpful man in these meetings. While these are not necessarily more competent than the department head in the store itself, the general manager, or the person who is charged with the job of instructing, nevertheless the outsider has the advantage in that he specializes on a certain line of merchandise, and, furthermore, he often has had the opportunity of looking into the experience of various retailers and can pass along to a store the benefit of what others have done.

The following indicates the outline of a talk in a hardware store, where a conference was held on ways and means of selling more paint:

Go to our door and look around. How many buildings that you can see need painting? All that you see are prospects for paint of some kind. Not only outside paint but interior finishes offer a big market, too, for there is almost five times as much surface to paint on the interior.

In a town of 5,000 population there are approximately 1,000 homes. Town homes are painted on an average of once every four years.

A questionnaire to dealers shows that the average sale of paint for interior painting is ten gallons. Therefore, it requires 10,000 gallons of paint for all the houses in our town. As they are painted once every four years, that means there is a market of 2,500 gallons of outside house paint alone for some merchant to furnish every year. Why not get our share?

Then, think of the barns that require painting. Many farmers buy their barn paint by the barrel. Hundreds of gallons are used in every community—a big market. Barns need roof paint, too, as does every other building in town. Then, there are fences, wagons, implements, automobiles and an endless number of articles and surfaces that require paint. Consider the amount of paint used each season in the interiors. There are floors to be varnished and painted, walls and ceilings require flat wall paint, woodwork to be stained and varnished or enameled, screens, furniture and other inside surfaces. From the ridgepole to the foundation, there is hardly a single surface that does not require paint or varnish.

Nothing was discussed at this meeting but paint and painting materials—what the possibilities of sales were, how suggestions about paint could be most aptly made to all customers entering the store, how the stock of paint itself, the color charts, advertising matter, brushes, etc., could be arranged to the best advantage in the windows and inside the store to promote increase of sales.

Comparative Records in a Live Retail Store.—An enterprising Kansas retail store stimulates better salesmanship by prompt summarizing of all sales-records. The sales-slips are collected every afternoon and sorted before closing time and in the morning the remaining slips of the closing hours of the previous day are gathered. The additions, made on a special machine, are grouped by salespeople, and by departments. To show the net total sales for the day, the figures gotten on the adding machine are transferred to a large distribution sheet showing the total, the net sales, and the credits for each department and salesperson. From the total gross sales, the credits are subtracted. Thus, the sheet shows the net total sales for the day. The work on this sheet must be completed by two o'clock, because the audit clerk transfers the figures to salesperson-cards and department-cards carrying six months' record.

On the salesperson's card is his number and record of daily sales for every day in the six months' period. The card for the department carries the same information and is very valuable to the department manager as an index to show performance. These cards also afford opportunity for comparison with the previous year.

Each month the record shows whether the salesman has gone ahead, slowed up or fallen behind. He is aware that the management knows of his achievement, or lack of it, and he also knows that for extra business there is a bonus award at the end of the six months' period.

These reports furnish the basis for the plans at the weekly meetings of department heads.

Every Tuesday the audit clerk has ready a comparison of the previous week's business, by departments, with the same week of the previous year, and also a comparison of the month's business corresponding to the same month of the previous year. Total sales of departments to date are included and compared with the same period of the previous year. To emphasize the facts clearly, graphs are shown. Then, on Tuesday evening, after luncheon in the tea-room of the store, department heads meet to discuss business. All these reports are carefully studied, and departments weak in sales are provided for through advertising and other means.

(*System*, September, 1922).

Pointers from a Sales Instructor.—Ralph W. Kinsey has been associated for many years with the Dives, Pomeroy & Stewart system of stores. In an address before Rotary Clubs, Mr. Kinsey cites a number of points to be observed by employers and heads of departments in order to develop better salesmanship as well as improved morale.

Mr. Kinsey, in giving the following pointers, puts himself in the position of an employe and sets forth the kind of cooperation and consideration the typical retail employe expects or hopes for:

1. *Accessibility.*—The employer who does not make himself accessible—who shuts himself in tightly behind glass doors on the

top floor—must expect employes also to adopt this same attitude and build up a wall around themselves.

2. *Encouragement.*—Too often, the only words retail salespeople get from their bosses are criticisms of poor work. There is just as much need for encouraging comments.

3. *General Interest of Employers.*—Morale and improved effort are built up by kindness and interest of employers toward their helpers, especially in the case of illness or other misfortune. Some stores have found it a good plan to carry old employes on full pay during extended illness, and new employes on half pay.

4. *Increases on Merit.*—The retail salesman, like other workers, appreciates more the increase given voluntarily than the increase he has to ask for or to fight for.

5. *Promotion of Old Employes.*—Whenever possible, promote an old employe rather than bring in some one from the outside for an important position.

6. *Definite Plan for Employes.*—To develop the spirit of partnership, employes should be made to feel that there is a definite plan for them in the business—that they can advance if they develop the requisite ability. Such a consciousness on the part of employes has a tendency to eliminate restlessness and the disposition to change jobs.

7. *Social Atmosphere.*—Social organizations, athletic organizations, a club of the older employes, and so on, offer good possibilities. Such features are often real factors in the development of teamwork and *esprit de corps*. It is better to have such organizations either entirely self-supporting, or mostly self-supporting, so that the members will not feel that they are the objects of charity or the generosity of the firm. Some firms go so far as to put the house organ in the hands of employes and let those who receive it pay a nominal subscription price.

8. *Educational Work on Company Time.*—Employes are inclined to resent educational sessions unless these are conducted to a large extent on company time. Unless the store makes an effort to impart merchandising information and to train for better salesmanship and better managing, it can hardly hope to qualify employes to step into higher positions as vacancies occur.

Views of S. W. Straus & Company on Business Dress.—No store is operated by the firm of S. W. Straus & Company. The business of this firm is that of selling investments, and offices are maintained in the principal cities of the United States. Nevertheless, the views of this well known concern on business dress are interesting to all who employ salespeople or others who come into contact with the public.

The following are extracts from a Straus bulletin:

What is a Fine Appearance?

The frump in the office has become ancient history.

The day of the ear-ringed, bejewelled, made-up flapper is over. The best positions are won by women with real merit and ability, whose capability and competency are reflected in their dignified, businesslike appearance. They choose their clothes with discrimination, with a view to simplicity and suitability of occasion.

Neither do they neglect general attractiveness of appearance but realize the psychological effect of neatness and simplicity, not only upon themselves in their daily work, but upon their business associates and superiors. The healthy-looking, bright girl or woman who strikes the happy medium in personal attire is coming back in the business world and is meeting with the heartiest welcome.

SECTION XIII

COURSES AND MANUALS

Instruction for retail salespeople has appeared in a wide variety of forms, ranging from correspondence courses to chatty series of letters and small "manuals of instruction." Some of the more elaborate courses have had their origin with manufacturers and have reached men and women in the retail sales field through the cooperation of retail employers. On the other hand, some very comprehensive books of instruction, dealing not only with good selling practice, but with store forms and system, have been prepared by leading retail establishments.

The object in the review that follows in this Section is to bring out the leading features of these various types of text, so that any manufacturer, wholesaler, retailer or sales instructor, planning either a simple instruction book or a comprehensive salesmanship course, will not lack for constructive suggestions.

Instruction of Abraham & Straus to New Employes.—The large Brooklyn store of Abraham & Straus believes it is better to bring the new employe gradually to an understanding of good retail service. At the time of employment, the new salesman receives a booklet, entitled "Especially for the New Employe," this title on the front page being followed by:

We are desirous that our associates work *with* us, instead of *for* us. In so doing we all become partners in the success of this enterprise.

On the back cover is a little paneled display:

Cheerfulness is one kind of ability, a kind that is valuable in this business; so first, last and always be courteous, gracious and helpful, both to our public and your fellow-worker.

Exhibit 157 is a reproduction of the first article in this little twelve-page booklet. The facsimile signatures of the four members of the firm appear at the bottom of this introductory talk.

The remaining pages of the booklet deal with store regulations, such as working hours, the assignment of luncheon hours, permission for leaving department, sickness or unavoidable absences, dress regulations. Instruction is also given as to the accommodations provided for customers and the treatment to be accorded them. Employes' shopping regulations are made plain, as well as the privileges of employes. In each department of this big store there are especially selected employes, called "guides," whose duty it is to assist new employes in every possible way. The new employe is coached to seek assistance from these guides on anything about her work or the store rules and system that is not clear. New salespeople also have the privilege of attending, on store time, regular conferences, conducted for the betterment of merchandising and service generally.

Suggestion boxes are placed about the store, and once a month suggestions are collected and investigated by the "Suggestion Committee." Prizes are given for valuable ideas—first prize $10, second, $5. Other suggestions may receive honorable mention and win $2.50. The store says to its employes, "We need your ideas and like to have as many as possible presented each month."

Social Features Provided.—In an endeavor to build up goodwill and to provide for the needs of its employes, the Abraham & Straus organization maintains a cafeteria for employes, where food is served at cost. There are rest rooms, a smoking room for the men, a library and roof garden, all conducted exclusively for employes. The store also maintains a hospital for emergency use, and a dentist's office is located in the hospital, where dental work is done at a price approximating cost.

There are various social activities provided for employes. One of these is the annual outing, but even more popular are the frequent smaller gatherings, such as the choral society which meets every Monday evening, and the bowling team which meets Tuesday evenings. Free supper is served at both of these gatherings each week. When the weather permits, there are games and gymnastic performances almost daily on the roof.

INTRODUCTION

We, the managing directors of this company, feel that we should try to give you—our new employe—a short outline of a few of our general store policies in order that you may become "one of us" as quickly as possible; not only by reason of the fact that you are now employed here, but also that you may have toward the company, our customers, and your fellow-employes, the kind of attitude that has always distinguished employes of A. & S.

This business was founded by Abraham Abraham in 1865. That's a good many years ago, so you see that the policies of the business must have been very sound and just to have them survive and the store prosper over such a long period of years. This in itself places on you, who represent this company, an obligation to add lustre to its name in whatever way you can. It matters not what your position is, the work that you do will either add to or detract from the reputation of our company.

The store's policy toward its customers has always been that of unfailing courtesy; of just and fair treatment. We must make their shopping as easy as possible for them and any adjustments that they desire must be promptly and cheerfully given.

This company has always carried full stocks in every department which must be sold at a lower price, quality for quality, than any other store in Brooklyn. We maintain a large corps of shoppers to watch the prices of our competitors, but if you should hear from a customer that we are being undersold, it is your duty to inform your Aisle or Department Manager of the fact at once.

Toward its employes, this company has always endeavored to preserve a fair basis of treatment. There are many facilities afforded the employes in this store which are not found in other stores. Every effort will be made to see that your life under this roof is made as happy for you as possible.

In an organization as large as this, a certain amount of system is required. This system is made as simple as possible with as few rules as are absolutely necessary. These rules must be enforced. Familiarize yourself with the reason why they exist, then, if they appear irksome, suggest a remedy to your department head or through the suggestion boxes.

The management of this business is very anxious to secure ideas for the betterment of its present system, or on any subject whatsoever which will increase the progress of the business. Suggestion Boxes are placed about the store and prizes are awarded each month for the best suggestions. This competition is open to any employe.

EXHIBIT 157.—Introduction to booklet given to new employes of Abraham & Straus.

As an employe of A. & S., you hold a position worthy of the respect of your fellow-workers. If you desire them to recognize this, you must show that same respect to them. You are a preferred customer here; and during your shopping hours you should receive the utmost courtesy. If by chance anyone of our salespeople should fail to observe this courtesy, it would simply show that he or she does not hold the proper respect for himself or herself.

Our offices are always open to you, if for any reason you feel that you want to come to us for advice. We take a personal interest in everyone under our roof, and we want all of our employes to realize this.

In a large organization like this, promotions are being made constantly. There is a great opportunity for advancement, and that comes only to those who merit it by their earnest, whole-hearted effort and cooperation.

A. & S. will give you fair treatment, and expect the same from you in return.

S. F. Rothschild
Edward C. Blum
H. S. Straus
Wm. Rothschild

EXHIBIT 157. *Concluded.*

Joseph Horne Company's System Manual.

This prominent Pittsburgh retailer issues a thorough treatise known as a "System Manual for Floormen and Salespeople." This booklet is 8 by 9 inches, bound in attractive, stout paper covers and consists of forty-four pages, made up largely of illustrations. Many of the illustrations appear in the actual colors of the original subjects, so that the salespeople will have no difficulty in familiarizing themselves with the various forms to be used. A good proportion of the forms reproduced are shown properly filled out. A list of the forms is given on the final page of the manual, so that any employe may refer to the manual when in doubt as to what to do.

In Exhibit 158 is reproduced one of the pages of this manual, showing the "Merchandise Want Slip." Whenever a customer requests merchandise that cannot be supplied, the salesman makes out one of these slips. The slips are turned over to the buyers of the various sections and prove of considerable value to them.

The general instruction covers such points as dress regulations, requirements expected of all employes, employes' privileges, care of stock, showing of goods, and so on.

The manual is introduced to the employes in the following manner:

You all know the story of Bruce and the spider. How, when he lay wounded and despondent because his armies were scattered, he watched the tireless efforts of an insignificant spider spinning his web to reach a certain point. How curiosity grew into interest as the spider spun his fragile fiber and made persistent efforts to swing on it across to a given point and thus obtain the starting of his web. How from this homely incident Bruce took heart, called his armies, marched back into the fight and won his battles.

Merchandise Want Slip

№ 2156

Merchandise Want Slip

Salespeople are required to record immediately on want slips merchandise called for and not in stock, or that is not carried by Horne's.

A MERCHANDISE WANT SLIP MUST BE TURNED IN BY EACH SALESPERSON DAILY, with want, (if any), noted, or marked, "NO WANTS."

DATE	DEPT.	CLERK No.

INDICATE BELOW—ARTICLE, COLOR, SIZE AND PRICE

Voucher Envelope

VOUCHER ENVELOPE.

Date_____ Sales No._____ Dept._____

Salespeople are required to get back from the wrapper the stamped voucher for each delivered cash transaction, return until closing hour, then straighten out flat, enclose in this envelope and hand to floor man.

Failure to do so may result in the salesperson having to make good the amount of the transaction in case the original check does not reach the Auditing Department

JOSEPH HORNE CO.

Give careful attention each day to the following:

1. The INDEX ENVELOPE on which the amount of each sale is recorded, and in which the tissues are placed at the close of each day. Fill in your name, the date, department and clerk numbers. Record each sale on the index. Be sure that the amount of sale for each check is placed in the space correspondingly numbered on the index. Add your sales carefully before handing in your book and see that the serial number of the first and last saleschecks used are entered on the index.

2. The VOUCHER ENVELOPE, which is a small envelope in which to place your cash vouchers.

3. The WANT SLIP upon which a record is made each day of merchandise called for which was not in stock. A Buyer may be ever so good in judging value and knowing where to buy, yet salespeople actually selling goods can give many valuable suggestions as to "what to buy." If you have had no request for merchandise not in stock, write "No wants."

Sales Books, Index Envelopes containing tissues, **Voucher Envelope** containing vouchers, and **Want Slip** must be given to the Floorman or the person designated in your department to receive them at the close of each day.

EXHIBIT 158.—Specimen page from the manual of the Joseph Horne Company, showing how the various forms are pictured to the employes. In the manual itself, these are shown in the colors of the original forms.

Bruce might not have been king of Scotland had he not taken this lesson to heart.

We present you with this book, filled with little details of information with which you are expected to familiarize yourself. It will lend to your work an assurance, a certainty, a directness which will enable you, who come directly in contact with customers, to deal with almost any selling situation in a way that will be satisfactory to all. A satisfied customer, when handled with quickness, courtesy, and with an evident knowledge of knowing what you are doing, brings that customer back to you. We are interested in your cooperation not merely for our benefit but for the benefit you yourself will derive. To stimulate that cooperation, and thus mutually profit, is the object of this book.

Exhibit 159.—Index page and another page from the manual of Strawbridge & Clothier, showing the items covered and the kind of instruction given employes.

Strawbridge & Clothier's Manual.—These Philadelphia retailers furnish their employes with a "Manual of Practice," a paper-bound booklet 8½ by 4 inches, containing sixty-six pages.

```
    Errors recorded on this form, if reported in time on the
day the originial check is made out, will not be recorded on
your records.

                        Self-Correction Notice

                        For Service Betterment

    Examine PAID TAKE SALES immediately, as they cannot be cor-
rected after the customer has gone.

          EXAMINE CAREFULLY ALL TRIPLICATE SALES CHECKS
                           LOOK FOR:
```

- [ ] Error or Omissions in Name or Address
- [ ] Name or Address Missing
- [ ] Amounts Differ, Voucher and Check
- [ ] Dollars and Cents in Wrong Column
- [x] Calculations Wrong
- [ ] Carbon Copies Poor
- [ ] Check Made Out Wrong
- [ ] Wrong Color Check Used
- [ ] Price Per Article Omitted
- [ ] Purchaser's Name Omitted
- [ ] Tax Omitted Where Chargeable
- [ ] Value Omitted Where Required on Delivery Card

(Check Corrections you wish made and spare your record)

MONTH	DAY	YEAR	SALES NUMBER	CHECK NUMBER
6	15	1921	3751	40

CHARGE NAME AND ADDRESS

Mrs. L. K. Brown
1902 Chestnut St.
Phila.

EXPLANATION OF ERROR

Charged ff:
2 petticoats (672) at 5.50 = 12.00

SHOULD BE

2 petticoats (672) at 5.50 = 11.00

                                    Marion L. Day
                                    Salesperson's Signature

                    To Salesperson

    When an error is discovered, fill in this form AT ONCE and send
through the tube in a RED CARRIER.   Have Section Manager note correction on triplicate sales check which must be enclosed in the
Tally Envelope at night at usual.

                                    STRAWBRIDGE & CLOTHIER

EXHIBIT 160.—"Self-Correction" notice which the Strawbridge & Clothier organization encourages its employes to use and thus prevent errors from being registered against them.

No general salesmanship instruction is given, the entire booklet being taken up with reproductions of the different forms and records that the salespeople are called upon to fill out. Some of these are even reproduced in colors. Along with these reproductions are detailed instructions for the proper executing of these forms.

Two pages of the Strawbridge & Clothier manual are reproduced in Exhibit 159. One of these is the index page, giving a very good idea of just what is covered in the booklet and affording an easy reference for the new employe.

A feature of the Strawbridge & Clothier organization is the "self-correction" slip. All employes are furnished with these slips, which are printed in the style shown in Exhibit 160, on a canary-yellow paper, so that they stand out. The idea of using these forms is to encourage employes to check over the day's work, and assist in the adjusting and straightening out of errors. Errors reported on this slip are not recorded against the person making them. Not only is this form a good thing from the standpoint of the store; it is good psychology. Employes prefer to detect and correct their own errors rather than have them called to their attention by some one else.

In the back of the booklet are several blank pages for memoranda.

Method of Dives, Pomeroy & Stewart.—These progressive retailers of Reading, Pa., believe in starting early and then keeping at the job of educating and training employes and salespeople.

In Exhibit 161 are reproduced two pages from a little booklet issued by this firm to its very young employes—cash girls and messengers. The title of this booklet is "Getting Ahead." There are just 16 pages, and all of them are attractively and effectively illustrated, making the truths much more graphic to the young mind. All through the booklet, these young employes are made to feel their importance and place in the great organization. There is no talking down to them. This little introductory note is enough to make the chests of boys and girls swell with pride:

In a big engine, if a little bolt works loose, or the smallest cog-wheel slips, it stops the entire machine. So in this great store—if the least errand is done wrong or some other messenger duty is performed incorrectly, it may cause an enormous amount of damage.

So, you see, the position of messenger is a very responsible one. Remember this every time you have the least thing to do. Feel how important it is and be anxious and eager to do it right, so you will keep the great store machine working smoothly. Count yourself as important as the runners or message-carriers in our great army, without whose work the attacks and defenses could never have been carried out.

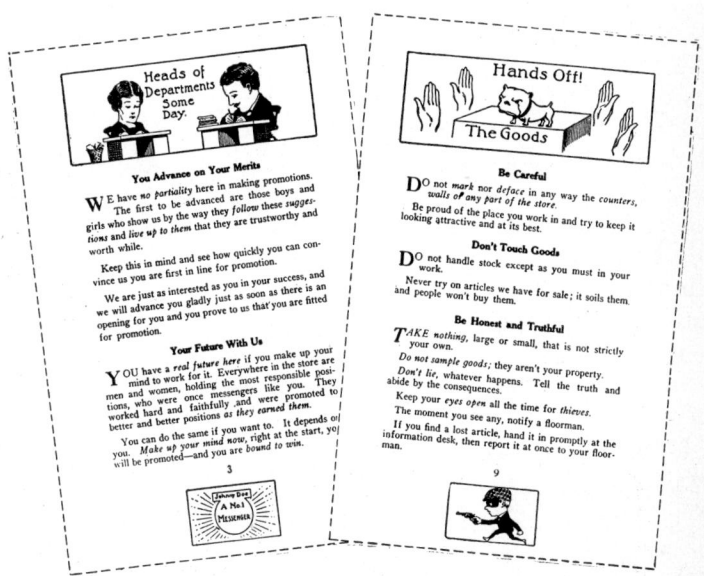

EXHIBIT 161.—Two pages of educational material for the younger employes.

Definite suggestions are made as to duties and unusual services that may be rendered, and these employes are made to feel that some day they may be heads of departments.

Exhibit 162 shows one page of a series of little 4-page bulletins issued by Dives, Pomeroy & Stewart from time to time to retail salespeople. Through a liberal use of cartoon pictures and a fair amount of readable text, this firm endeavors to drive home the fundamental truths of good retailing practice.

7. DAILY DUTIES.

Don't let Mrs. Customer know more than you.

(The ringing of the store gong indicates the opening of the store.)
- A. **Sell to the best of your ability**, making use of what you are told by your buyer, head of stock, the store instructor and what you have learned from experience.
- B. **Eliminate** anything which conflicts with the way the store wants things sold.
- C. Remember SERVICE is the great thing in selling—and give it.
- D. In order that you may wait on people quickly and satisfactorily, **know what goods you have in forward stock, reserve stock and on order,** their prices, sizes or colors and where you have them. You can't learn to play a piano till you know the keys. Neither can you learn to sell satisfactory till you know your stock.

8. SALE MAKING ACTIONS.
- A. **Don't criticise customers,** either by direct comment or by stare or laugh. It is the height of ill manners and a serious breach of business etiquette.
- B. **Be alert and wide awake.** Prove by your attitude you are eager to be of service to people. Therefore, to loll, sit, stand or lean on the counter while waiting on a customer will not be tolerated.

Helpful (?) Comment by the force

- C. **Give your customer complete attention.** Don't talk to other employees while serving a customer. It's ill bred and impolite, as the customer should come first at all times.
  If you must talk, modulate your tones and never talk across the aisle.
- D. **Don't "play" during working hours.** You are paid for so many hours of work. Be fair and use all of that time for business matters only. The usual ways of wasting time are:
  1. Reading anything not connected with business.
  2. Entertaining visitors at the counter.
  3. Doing fancy work or outside work in the department.
  4. Having personal mail sent to the store. (This is never delivered in the store, but re-mailed to your home address.)
  5. Using store telephones for personal business. (The store operator has orders to listen in and report any such conversation.)

The Customer wonders if she's gotten in a beauty parlor

- E. **Talk businesslike before customers.** Do not call fellow employees by their first name in front of customers. It sounds bad to say "Mamie," or "Jimmie," or "Lizzie," etc. The businesslike thing to do is to say "Miss Brown," "Mr. Jones," Mrs. Smith," etc.

- F. **Don't use messengers for personal business.** Messengers are hired to run store errands only. We have few enough as it is—don't weaken the force by sending one away on a personal errand.

EXHIBIT 162.—Dives, Pomeroy & Stewart's method of using cartoons to clarify the usual instruction about good selling service.

In addition, the Dives, Pomeroy & Stewart organization offers its employes a very thorough 3-year course. The following is an outline of this course:

STORE EDUCATIONAL SYSTEM.

In keeping with its broad-minded policy of offering you every inducement to improve yourself and to earn more money, the firm has established a very complete system of instruction so that you need not be held back through ignorance of either the store system or correct methods of selling. This system is divided as follows:

First Year.
- A. *Store System* (which you are now finishing)—4 weeks.
- B. *Salesmanship*—30 weeks.

  To encourage you in this work, you are offered a half day for good work.

Second Year.

  Manufacture of Merchandise—one year.

  Those who finish satisfactorily are counted as graduates, given a silver pin as a mark of honor, graduated at a public exercise, given a banquet and allowed to join the store alumni association.

Third Year.
- A. *Business Methods.*

  A course in business papers and business practice of greatest value to every business man or woman.
- B. *History of Costume.*

  Open to women only. A history of style and its development from the earliest days to the present.
- C. *Retailing.*

  A course especially for **ambitious men.** It covers the managing of a store in every detail and gives the employe who is looking ahead to some day becoming head of stock or buyer a splendid short cut.

  The graduates who take any of these classes are given a gold pin as a special mark of honor and admitted to the banquet of the graduating class of that year.

Summer Classes.

  During the warm weather, when most classes are discontinued, special classes are held in such subjects as French and Business English.

All these classes are held on the *store's time*, not yours, so that while you are learning how to better yourself in the store, the firm is paying you for your time.

Other features of the Dives, Pomeroy & Stewart organization are:

The Store Relief Association.

It is run by the employes for employes.

Absolutely reliable.

Divided into two classes—B and C.

To join you see Mr. Erb, and pay 60 cents to join B and $1 to join C. (Requirement to join C—a salary of $8 or more a week.) The dues are 13 cents a week for Class B and 25 cents a week for Class C.

If sick, B pays you $5 a week and Class C, $10 a week for eight weeks.

If you die, you get a death benefit that varies according to the number of members. (It is figured as follows: $1 for every Class C member and 50 cents for every Class B member.)

On July 1 all the money that is left, after paying out benefits, is redivided among the members in the form of a refund. Thus, in 1917 Class B members received back $4.46 out of the $6.50 they had paid in, while Class C members received $8.57 out of $13. This refund brings the cost per week in Class B down to 7.31 cents and in Class C, 8.91 cents a week.

In the time the association has been in existence there has never been a question of the honesty of its management. Not a cent is spent for salaries. The work is all done gratis by volunteer officers. *And there has never been a cent misappropriated.*

Store Saving Account.

All employes are entitled to open an account with Mr. Gehret, main office.

Any amount will open one.

Interest of 6 per cent is paid on deposits up to $100.

Interest on round sums of $100, 3 per cent.

The interest is paid semi-annually and on the exact number of days the money is deposited.

Money may be withdrawn at any time without preliminary notice.

Time Off.

Employees are allowed two days' sickness with pay.

Vacations of two weeks, one with pay, are given every summer, except to employes here 25 years or more, who receive two weeks vacation with pay.

Friday half holidays are also granted, as well as the usual legal holidays.

Turkeys are given every Thanksgiving to married men and messengers.

Blunder System.

This is installed to encourage accuracy and carefulness. You are marked for two things—time and carefulness in clerical work and store deportment.

The year is divided into four periods of three months each, starting January, April, July and October. At the beginning of each period you start with a score of 400. In the period every blunder that is counted costs you 4 points and every minute late costs you 1 point.

If, at the end of the period, you have left 350 points, or over, you are given a half day off. Thus, in a year's time you can get off two days.

Store Reading Room.

Established and run by the Educational Department. The books have been donated by employes and the firm gives us magazine subscriptions every year. Rules for taking out the books will be found on the door by the shelves.

"Store Booster."

This lively store paper, of which you will receive a copy of the next issue, is run by the employes. It covers our store life completely and no wide awake employe can hope to enjoy his life here without being a subscriber to it. It costs but 25 cents a year, the firm paying the difference in what we take in and what it costs to print our paper.

Social Organization.

The store has grown so large that the old-time social intercourse of employes in the store is much handicapped. To overcome this, the employes have established the following organizations:

Men's Club.

Open to any male employe of the store eighteen years old. It costs 25 cents a month and holds monthly smokers, at which the boys gather to play cards, pitch quoits and otherwise enjoy themselves in a social way.

One of the big features of our store life is the annual show which the club gives with the invaluable assistance of the girls of the store.

Alumni Association.

Composed of graduates of the store school. It meets once every two months and costs 10 cents a month in dues. The alumni asscciation does much to foster the school spirit, and so it gives the graduates a reception during the year and an outing in the summer. The alumni association does much good work in sending to our sick employes letters of remembrance and flowers and fruit. It also offers an annual prize to the salesmanship classes for the ones doing the best work in each class.

Quarter Century Club.

This is composed of the members of all our stores who have been in the employ of the firm twenty-five years or more.

They are given an annual banquet in April, the anniversary month of the store, at which the members who have reached the twenty-five-year mark are presented with a gold emblem and a purse of $25.

The other privileges of the organization include two weeks' vacation with pay.

New York Edison Company's Manual for Retail Salespeople.

—This manufacturer realizes that the maker of the goods should take part in training the people who come in contact with the actual consumers, so the company has issued a thirty-page manual for retailers in a size 5½ by 3½ inches. In this handy booklet good selling argument of a general nature is given, as well as specific information about electric household appliances and how to present them to the prospective buyer in the most appealing and pleasing way.

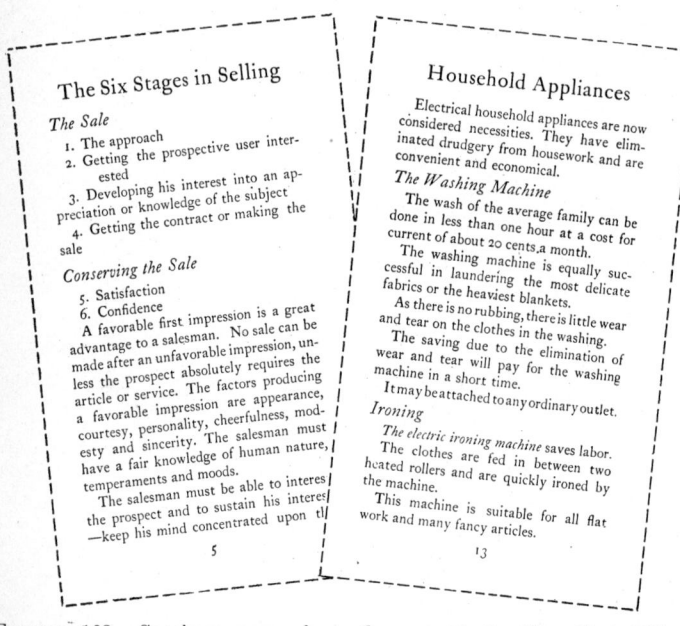

EXHIBIT 163.—Specimen pages from the manual the New York Edison Company furnishes its retailers.

In addition to this little manual, the company issues an employes' magazine and maintains a bureau of information, the duty of which is to gather interesting and newsy data from all sources and distribute the items to the proper departments.

Exhibit 163 is a reproduction of two of the inside pages of the manual, showing some of the general selling argument, as well as specific hints on the selling of electric washing machines and ironers. The typography of the pages is pleasing and readable.

Syndicated Manual for Retailers.—Exhibit 164 consists of two pages from a syndicated manual for retailers. This little booklet was called *Foundation Stones*. True to its name, the booklet treats of the fundamentals of good retail salesmanship. The booklet was freely illustrated and was issued

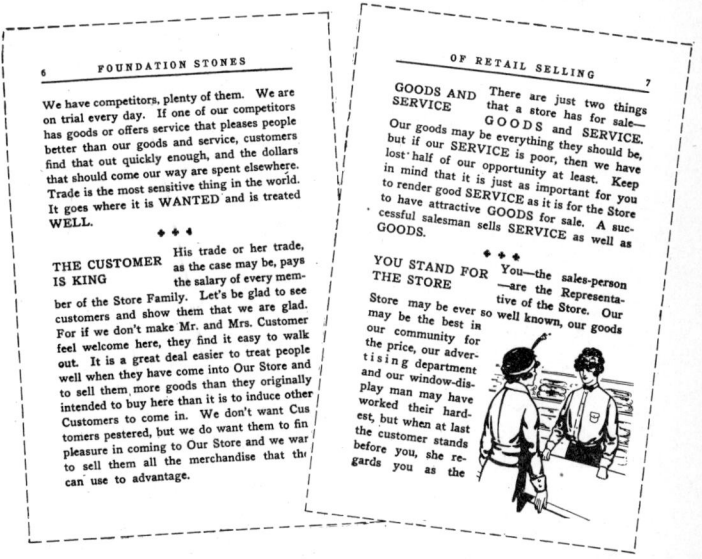

EXHIBIT 164.—Reproduction of two pages from a syndicated manual which was sold in varying quantities to the smaller retailers of the country.

in a convenient size—4 by 6 inches. It was sold in lots of from ten to several hundred to the smaller retailers, who passed the pamphlets around among the departments of their stores. Though there is not a great demand for such material, many retailers who would not undertake to get out a manual of their own are willing to subscribe to a syndicated aid of this kind.

Instruction Course of the Kuppenheimer Company.—The well known clothing firm of the House of Kuppenheimer, Chicago, concluded some years ago that manufacturers had been paying too little attention to salesmen in the retail store. It felt that far-reaching results could be obtained through more intimate contact and more intensive cooperation with the man who actually sells the goods.

Conspicuous among the many phases of cooperation that the House of Kuppenheimer has developed along this line is a complete course of retail clothing salesmanship covering the following topics:

Yourself
Awakening the customer's interest
The selling process
Leading the customer by suggestion and tact
Treatment of types
Studying the customer
Selecting the right merchandise
Selling more goods
Knowing the goods
In tune with the advertising
Service
Review

While these lectures constituted the backbone of the course, there were other articles and some exhibits sent along with the lectures, supplementing them and giving interesting and useful information on fabrics and other topics related to the selling of clothing.

The instruction in these lectures was not extremely elementary. The Kuppenheimer firm believed it was better to assume that a man selling clothing already had a fair fundamental knowledge of salesmanship. The instruction consisted of the most practical suggestions that could be assembled.

The fee charged for the course—$3—was asked merely to put the course on a better basis than it would stand if offered entirely free. Though it was suggested to the retail clothing merchants that it would be a good plan to refund the $3 to the salesman when he had completed the course satisfactorily, it was regarded as a better plan to have the salesman pay the $3 out of his own pocket at the beginning.

The Kuppenheimer people offered prizes ranging from $50 to $250 to the salesmen making the best records under the course, and dealers were urged to form salesmanship clubs and have their men meet regularly for systematic study and discussion, so that there would be a get-together spirit in connection with the course.

Over 3,000 copies of this course were sold to salesmen in representative Kuppenheimer stores and the firm has informed the author of this volume that its educational program has proved to be one of the most effective steps ever taken to further the sale of its product.

MERCHANDISING INFORMATION AND READING COURSES

A number of manufacturers, wholesalers, selling agents and trade associations have aided retailers in getting better salesmanship by furnishing single booklets, series of booklets, or series of bulletins giving useful merchandising information or hints on good salesmanship.

Some of this material is merely fundamental instruction, well illustrated by the talks on Better Selling which fill the succeeding Section of this volume.

Another group of such material is devoted entirely to merchandising information about a particular product or series of products, but in many cases the material serves a dual purpose —that of giving information about the goods, combined with suggestions on efficient selling.

Of course, it is first necessary for the dealer to agree with the manufacturer, wholesaler or association furnishing the information, on some good working plan so that some system may be followed. Frequently the method is first explained to the retailer by the manufacturer or wholesalers' traveling representative. The material itself may be sent in bulk and distributed by the merchants to his helpers, or it may be mailed in instalments by the week or by the month directly to the salespeople, addressing them either at the store or using their home addresses.

This type of work is in its early stages. Some of the helps sent to retailers are too technical, too historical, or too uninteresting to command any great amount of attention from the mass of salespeople. The manufacturer of kitchen cabinets is naturally interested most of all in having retail salespeople understand how to sell his particular make of kitchen cabinets, but he is more likely to get attention from retailers and their

378   RETAIL ADVERTISING AND SELLING

helpers by making his instruction broad in its application, so that any one who reads becomes not only a better salesman of kitchen cabinets but of all other merchandise.

BETTER SELLING BULLETIN

Clinching "Wear-Ever" Sales

Below are given a number of suggestions which have been found helpful in clinching sales of "Wear-Ever" Aluminum Cooking Utensils. The sale of equipments is mentioned, but the suggestions also apply to the sale of single utensils as well.

1. Ask a few Questions—

It is helpful to know a few facts concerning the kitchen equipment of your prospect. These facts greatly aid in clinching the order and usually can be secured by asking "Do you have much aluminum in your kitchen?" or "What pieces of 'Wear-Ever' do you have?"

The reply to such questions will open the way to further inquiry concerning just what pieces the prospect already possesses. With this knowledge you can center the sales talk on the pieces needed to complete the "Wear-Ever" equipment.

2. Place Utensils Aside—

It is advisable to have a space in the "Wear-Ever" display wherein you can place the utensils you are trying to sell. It's much harder for a prospect to make up her mind to purchase an equipment or even a few utensils if she can't see those utensils assembled together and separated from the others.

3. Be Ready to Suggest Model Equipments—

The real salesman is not the one who "forces" a sale but the one who helps the prospect make up her mind to purchase that which is being offered. It is much easier for the prospect to decide on an equipment if a model equipment is arranged on a table next to the general "Wear-Ever" display. If space permits, several different sized equipments can be arranged. The prospect probably will not decide to purchase the exact equipment offered, but that equipment will give her and the salesman something definite in the way of a suggestion. By substituting a utensil or two, or by changing the sizes a bit, it is much easier to fix up the very best equipment for the prospect's own personal use.

4. Help the Prospect Picture the Equipment in Her own Home—

Your aim is to place an equipment in the home of your prospect. That aim is more sure to be realized if you picture the convenience and satisfaction resulting from having a "Wear-Ever" equipment in her home.

In showing an equipment—or even a single utensil—let the prospect handle it. Tell her how *she* will use each utensil and combinations of utensils. Don't say "They use this roaster this way, Mrs. Jones", but, rather this:—"If *you* had this equipment, Mrs. Jones, you not only would use this piece as a roaster, but when it is canning season you would use it this way as a 'cold pack' canner." *In other words, make your talk personal.* Help your prospect visualize what a "Wear-Ever" equipment will mean to *her.* Help her imagine that the equipment you are showing her is not on the table of a store but in *her own home, being used by herself on her own stove.*

When you do this, then you have made it a whole lot easier for her to decide to purchase an equipment.

5. Securing the Definite Consent—

This brings us up to the critical part of the sales talk. However, this "stage" is passed more easily and successfully if you have been planning for it from the very first moment.

If you have driven home each point as you went along, you often-times are surprised at how easily the sale is made.

The prospect can best be brought to a definite decision, indirectly. You, for instance, can talk about the different sizes and thereby get the prospect to make a decision on the whole equipment. You can say:—"Mrs. Jones, in this 'Wear-Ever' equipment you can get different sizes of utensils if you prefer. For instance, you may prefer an eight-quart size of this kettle, to this six-quart one. However, I do believe that the six-quart size is large enough. I believe that this equipment as it now is, is just what you want. Isn't it?"

Or can you secure a decision by discussing the time of delivery:—"Mrs. Smith, we probably can have this equipment delivered at your home in time for preparing dinner. That would be fine, wouldn't it? Shall I have it sent up?"

6. Review the Main Points—

In case the prospect is not yet decided, review the main points in favor of "Wear-Ever". These points, as brought out in previous numbers of the BETTER SELLING BULLETINS can all be grouped under Saving, Service and Safety (or Sanitation). Get the prospect to see that in the purchase of an equipment she is purchasing—not just cooking utensils,—but the three "S's" Saving, Service and Safety. Then, sales will come much easier and purchasers will be much more appreciative of the real value of a "Wear-Ever" equipment.

EXHIBIT 165.—How the Aluminum Cooking Utensil Company put before retail salespeople points on clinching "Wear-Ever" cooking utensil sales.

Aluminum Cooking Utensil Company's Use of Selling Bulletins.—Proceeding on the plan outlined in preceding paragraphs, the promoters of "Wear-Ever" aluminum cooking utensils covered a list of more than 8,000 retail salespeople with a series of Better Selling Bulletins. These bulletins

BETTER SELLING BULLETIN

Ten "PAUL JONES" Selling Points

ON the back of "Dr. Crane's Ten Commandments of Salesmanship," it seems appropriate to give ten of the most outstanding selling points of the PAUL JONES middies and middy suits. By bringing these ten points to the attention of those of your customers who may be interested in middies or children's clothes, you will not only be doing them a real service but you will very likely add materially to your sales total for the year. Try it and see!

1. PAUL JONES middies are the original middy blouses, patterned after the regulation middies worn by the United States Midshipmen. Middy blouses were introduced to the girls of America about fifteen years ago by Mr. Morris, who made navy middies.

2. PAUL JONES middies and middy suits are guaranteed fast color. They will not fade no matter how often they are washed.

3. PAUL JONES middies are guaranteed as to workmanship, quality of material and fit. Nothing is too good for PAUL JONES middies. They are made in a spotlessly clean factory under the most hygienic working conditions by expert workers.

4. Even the buttons and tape on PAUL JONES middies are sewed on so as to be wear- and wash-proof. What a wonderful selling point to make to the busy mother who has her basket of mending more than running over.

5. PAUL JONES middies are almost everlasting. They out-wear any other make of middies on the market and are more suitable than any other style of clothes for romping children and athletic young women.

"Well Dressed Kiddies Wear PAUL JONES Middies."

6. There's a size and a style for every taste and every occasion—a price for every pocketbook. Sizes range from 2 to 14 years for children; 34 bust to 42 bust in misses' and women's sizes; the materials are cotton, serge and flannel. Prices range from $1.75 to $8.50 each.

7. Easy to launder and keep clean. All seams are double-stitched, so that there is no danger of fraying or pulling out, even under the most severe strain.

8. Comfortable and sensible for kindergarten, school, college, sports, gymnasium, picnics, mountain climbing, hikes, outings, seashore trips, housework, etc.

9. Retain their style and well-groomed appearance as long as they last, which is a long time. Repeated wearing and laundering does not seem to impair the shape, fit and style. They always look trim and attractive.

10. Their wonderful popularity. No other garment enjoys the wide range of usefulness and all-around wear as the PAUL JONES middies and middy suits. They are sought after and appreciated throughout America by discerning, sensible, thrifty mothers and young women. Those who have once used them know their wonderful value and that they are the most reasonable in the end.

Making new customers for PAUL JONES middies and middy suits is comparatively easy and something that not only brings satisfaction to you but to the customer as well. But customers are not likely to be as familiar with the good qualities of PAUL JONES middies as you are. Don't lose an opportunity to drive these ten points home wherever you can.

MORRIS & COMPANY, Inc., Baltimore, Md.

Keep your file of these BETTER SELLING BULLETINS complete. They will form a valuable reading course in Practical Salesmanship.

EXHIBIT 166.—"Merchandising information" side of a 2-page, loose-leaf bulletin supplied to dry goods stores by a clothing manufacturer.

were printed on both sides, one side containing general salesmanship instruction which would be useful in any kind of selling and the other containing the kind of merchandising information shown in Exhibit 165. The bulletins were sent out at the rate of one a month. The suggestions in this exhibit from the Aluminum Cooking Utensil Company were confined to "Clinching 'Wear-Ever' Sales," because the instruction on the other page of this bulletin (not shown here) was on the clinching of sales. Each one of this series sent out by the Aluminum Cooking Utensil Company contained material bearing on its own products in harmony with the general sales talk on the other page of the bulletin. If the

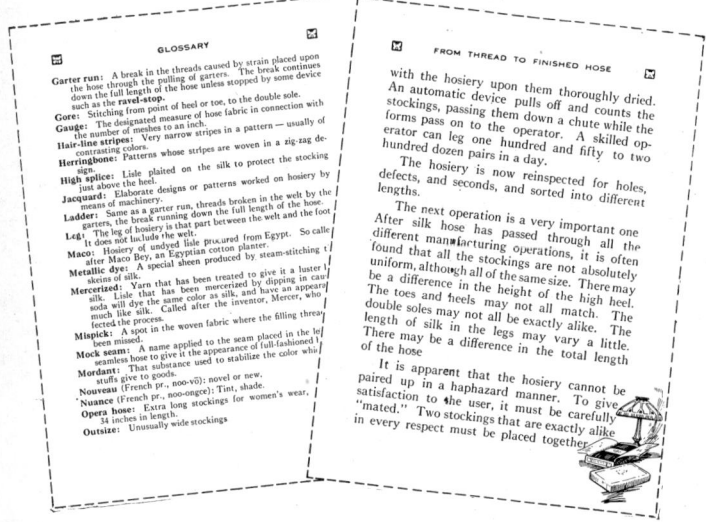

Exhibit 167.—Two pages from the Chipman Knitting Mills booklet, "From Raw Silk to Silk Hosiery."

subject of the general talk was that of "Getting Attention," then the special matter on page 2 was devoted to how to get attention for this manufacturer's products.

A number of other organizations have followed a similar plan but mailed their bulletins at more frequent intervals— once a week or every two weeks.

In the case of the bulletin of Morris & Company, reproduced in Exhibit 166, the first page consisted of Dr. Frank Crane's well known "Ten Commandments of Salesmanship." This practical general talk by a popular author was an appropriate prelude to the "Ten 'Paul Jones' Selling Points."

Aid from a Hosiery Manufacturer.—Exhibit 167 is a combination of two pages from an attractive booklet sent out by the Chipman Knitting Mills.

While intended primarily for the retail trade, this booklet is distributed through the jobbers. It is confined almost entirely to information about silk hosiery—the origin of raw materials, their treatment, methods of manufacture, packing, and so on. The book contains a number of attractive illustrations, to make the text clearer. Some of the illustrations show how stockings are examined for flaws after knitting; how double toes and heels are made; how the bleaching is done; how the stockings are dried on special machinery; how care is exercised in properly "pairing" the stockings, as well as folding and packing scenes.

Educational Booklets Sent Out by Jobbers.—Exhibit 168 shows four pages taken from a series of standardized booklets prepared by the Bronson & Townsend Company, of New Haven, Conn., with the cooperation of various manufacturers of hardware.

The Bronson & Townsend Company gives the following reason for getting out this series:

> Back of every one of the standard advertised lines there is a personality which, if properly presented to the buying public, will make the sale of these various lines much easier for the retail salesman. We believe that the personality of the developers of such lines as Disston Saws, Stanley Tools, Maydole Hammers, Nicholson Files, and other trade-marked goods is the kind of personality that appeals to the general public, when the facts are presented.
>
> With that end in view, we went to work, trying, through a system of booklets prepared by the individual manufacturers, to show up this personality in such form that the retail salesman would be interested in reading the story. Because he was interested in it, we have assumed that he would remember at least parts of it.

Being uniform in style and punched for binding, it was very easy for the retail salesman to keep his set of these little booklets intact. The booklets were small enough to be slipped into the pocket and read on the way to and from work.

This effort on the part of the Bronson & Townsend Company is significant, because it indicates a much-needed form of

EXHIBIT 168.—Specimen pages from a series of booklets furnished retailers by a hardware jobber in cooperation with the manufacturers whose goods he carries.

cooperation among manufacturers, wholesalers and retailers looking toward an intelligent dissemination of knowledge of the merits of merchandise and the proper methods of selling.

The Bronson & Townsend Company gives this information as to how a mailing-list for this series of booklets was secured:

> We first sent out a letter describing the series, and telling what we hoped would be accomplished by its distribution. We enclosed with this letter a postal card, asking our customers to check it if they wished the series sent to them direct, and left spaces on the card for them to write in the names of any of their salespeople to whom they would like it sent individually. After making up a list in this way we passed it out to our salesmen, and asked them to recheck it and add to it names which they felt ought to be on the list but had not been entered, due to carelessness on the part of the retail merchant. This has resulted in our getting together a list of approximately 500 names from a total of a little over 500 accounts. This does not mean that we are sending the series to all our customers, by any means, but we are making up for those we are not sending it to by sending it to several salespeople in some of the organizations.

Paper Manufacturer's Manual for Retailers.—Exhibit 169 is a reproduction of a page from *The White & Wyckoff Viewpoint*, a little booklet published by White & Wyckoff, manufacturers of high-grade stationery, with the idea of presenting in readable, story style hints for the better selling of stationery.

Because of the attractive, lively style of the text and a free use of cartoon illustrations, this little booklet probably commands considerably more attention and response than a dry treatment of the facts would bring from the retailer's salespeople.

How the Vanity Fair Silk Mills Train Retail Salespeople.—Several years ago the Vanity Fair Silk Mills, Reading, Pa., adopted the plan of sending out every five or six weeks a letter to the retail salespeople handling their products. These letters are on a sheet 5 by 6 when folded, with only the first and third pages printed—to simulate the note-size stationery used by women in their correspondence. The letters are signed "Barbara Wayne," a fictitious character of the sales manager's brain. The first sheet is attractively illustrated and the text starts with an initial. Exhibit 170 will give the

The White & Wyckoff Viewpoint

"Hustling Bill" discourses on burying the stationery department down "Gloom Lane"

"Howdy!" was Hustling Bill's* salutation, all smiles, as he breezed into James H. Lawson's Stationery store, Cor. Main and Randolph Streets, and the first person he glimpsed was Jimmy Lawson himself. The Distributor salesman spraddled out his feet, put his arms akimbo and looked around, now here, now there, with an expression of perplexed surprise.

"What's the matter?" demanded J. L.

"Oh, just a little astonished to find you have quit selling writing paper," was Bill's come back.

"Who said I'd quit?" gasped J. L.

"Well—I don't see the department anywhere," continued the Salesman, "where is it?"

"Right back here," and James L. led his companion to the rear of the store. The light was none too good and Bill was blinking. "There you are," resumed the Big Boss.

"So HERE it is!" Bill exclaimed, "bless its little heart—tucked away, down Gloom lane, eh? Where you have to get a guide to find it. Jimmy, I'm ashamed of you. This De-

"So HERE it is—bless its little heart"

---

*"Hustling Bill," of course, you know him. Previous stories, with his pithy come-backs, have given Bill quite a following. You'll agree that Bill is again right in his analysis of the merchants' problems and that his solutions are well worth while.

(7)

EXHIBIT 169.—Page from a manufacturer's booklet or manual mailed regularly to retail dealers. The "story style" of the appeal is effective, as well as the cartoon illustration.

reader a good idea of the general appearance of these little letters.

The Vanity Fair people keep their mailing-list up to date through reports sent in by the salesmen. In some cases the retail store manager asks that a certain quantity be sent to

"Dear Barbara Wayne: I enjoyed your letter telling me all about Vanity Fair's selling points, but to be perfectly frank, I haven't been able to use one! Customers don't stop nowadays to learn anything about the goods they buy—they fairly snatch things from us. Because they know it's hard to get sizes in silk underwear, they take what they can get when they can get it. I'd be glad to have the good old days back again, when we really 'sold' things instead of 'taking orders' like grocery clerks".

THIS discontented letter I received several months ago and, coming across it today, I could not help wondering how the little girl who wrote it is enjoying herself now.

There is no doubt that we're all glad to have normal buying with us again! To the person with real selling ability, there is no joy in a high sales book when it represents no effort or achievement on her part. From now on, real selling arguments can be used behind the counter and one's personal efforts recognized.

The hectic buying period just past did one thing for silk underwear—it increased the number of wearers! More women bought and wore silk underwear than ever before and we all know how hard it

EXHIBIT 170.—One of a series of letters sent to retail salesgirls by the Vanity Fair Silk Mills.

the buyer or manager direct, so that the literature may be distributed by him, but in most cases the letters are mailed to individual salespeople, home addresses being used wherever possible.

The value of this material probably lies in the fact that its appearance is very pleasing and the text is written in such a chatty, newsy way that one would hardly be conscious of the fact that it is salesmanship instruction.

From time to time the Vanity Fair Silk Mills offer prizes for the best letter of suggestions submitted. Exhibit 171 is a reproduction of one of the prize-winning letters.

This letter of Miss Hazel Soiseth has been awarded first prize in the Vanity Fair contest

---

The Vanity Fair Silk Mills,   Sioux City, Ia.,
    Reading, Pa.   February 13, 1920

Dear Miss Barbara Wayne:

After reading the interesting letters received from you I have learned many helpful points concerning my selling of Vanity Fair Silk Underwear. However the last letter from you reached here yesterday and I will answer your questions as best I can.

1. It is surprising to know how many people ask for Vanity Fair brand underwear. Within the past two months I have had more calls for Vanity Fair than for any other brand, although we carry a large line of Kayser and Van Raalte.

2. Some customers have referred to seeing advertisements in magazines, but have not specified which one, while others seeing our displays in our windows, cases, ledges, and shelves ask to see Vanity Fair underwear, and I gladly show our line and if they do not buy then, they eventually do buy Vanity Fair. I enjoy showing your line and knowing what I say about the goods can be relied upon, and selling the goods instead of merely handing them over the counter.

3. In no way can I criticize Vanity Fair.

4. It would be more convenient to have the size of the garment on the label or trade-mark as you may call it, as very few customers ever think of looking on the inside of the bloomer leg, for the size. Nine times out of ten they look on the label and say, "What size is this?"

EXHIBIT 171.—Prize-winning letter in a "suggestions contest" held by the Vanity Fair Silk Mills.

5. I think a gown made of Vanity Fair silk would be very practical. I was wondering about a gown with the top made similar to the top of chemise number 44010. I sell a great many garments number 44010 and everyone is very well pleased with them, I sold three to one customer one day. I should think this gown could retail for about $17.50 and know it would be a good seller. Another garment I'll suggest is a Vanity Fair combination. If one has ever tried glove silk, they always buy it, because it has such wonderful wearing qualities. Am enclosing a cut of second garment suggested.

6. These are Vanity Fair's best selling points.
1. The double back of the bloomer makes it a fine seller and is a fine talking point.
2. The reinforcement that runs clear down on the bloomer. The other brands only run part way down.
3. A good selling point on the bodice top vest is the neat hemstitched top. The extra length on vests and their good fit.
4. I think the one big point is that your garments are so moderately priced.
5. Your garments always look fresh and do not wrinkle so easily as others.

I think probably I have answered all your questions and I assure you that your letters are always welcomed.

Yours respectfully,
(Miss) Hazel Soiseth

Care of Davidson's

Exhibit 171. *Concluded.*

Other Forms of Instruction.—The moving picture has played a prominent part in the putting of proper selling information before retailers and their helpers. This form of instruction is of great advantage in the case of such products as machines, because the machines are not only pictured but operation is shown.

Other well known methods of disseminating merchandising information and good selling methods are through the lecturer and the skilled demonstrator. All have their proper place. The retailer who is disposed to utilize such forms of instruction will find many manufacturers more than willing to cooperate with him to any reasonable extent. Exhibit 172 is another example of a manufacturer's effort to improve retail selling.

Talks to Retail SalespeoplePage Seven

People may buy misrepresented goods once, but never a second time.

Be the kind of salesperson that people will learn to depend upon. The more you know about your goods, the more you'll be worth to the store.

Tell the truth about your goods.

The salesperson with a reputation for honesty will sell more than two salespeople with reputations for taking advantage when they have the opportunity.

Disloyalty is a form of dishonesty of the meanest sort.

Be loyal. Make the firm's interests yours, and many of your faults will be overlooked.

Push the line of goods they want pushed. It won't escape their notice.

A lie harms the business, but it does infinitely more harm to the salesperson who tells it.

Nothing truer ever was said than that "honesty is the best policy."

EXHIBIT 172.—Specimen page from a little manual entitled *Talks to Retail Salespeople*, sent out by the National Cash Register Company to retail dealers.

SECTION XIV

TALKS ON BETTER SELLING

The preachments that follow are reproduced here as illustrations of material that was originally published in loose-leaf bulletin form in the belief that salesmanship instruction submitted to retail salespeople is much more likely to be read and remembered when presented in attractive form in small units than if a whole course or big textbook is furnished at one time.

These preachments are representative illustrations of a course in salesmanship consisting of fifty or more loose-leaf "talks"—the word "talks" being used in a broad sense because of the conversational style of composition. In some cases, a binder for holding the sheets was furnished each subscriber or student. These bulletin talks in their original form were either handed out by the merchant who bought or received the material in bulk, or were mailed flat once every week, or once every two weeks, by some manufacturer or jobber cooperating with the retailer in the educational plan.

In some cases the subscribers or merchants used the bulletins in exactly the form in which they were received, passing them around among their salespeople and requiring each salesman to check off his name when he had read the bulletin. After the bulletins had gone the rounds, they were assembled in consecutive order in the binder for reference purposes.

Other merchants added some comments or special instruction on the backs of the bulletins, which were purposely left blank, thus linking up the general talk with some particular instance in the organization and making the application and timeliness of the talk more specific (see Exhibits 165 and 166).

Still other merchants made use of the material in their salesmanship classes, furnishing each member of the class with a copy of a certain bulletin and then basing the talk or discussion on the points which it emphasized.

In a few cases, the material was reproduced in employes' magazines, house organs, or a series of letters to employes.

The physical appearance of these bulletins was attractive, each one being printed on a sheet of good white bond paper, 8½ by 11 inches, with a green border around the text. The sheets were all round-cornered and punched for binding, and most of the topics were appropriately illustrated. It is the belief of the author that this attractive dress of the material was a big factor in its popularity as a syndicated service on better retail selling. These talks are no longer sold in loose-leaf form. Most of them are reproduced here in revised form so that they may be used as the basis, or starting point, of a series of lessons, should some reader of this volume be engaged in preparing a course for the improvement of retail selling. The explanation about their original form is given merely that any reader preparing a course may adopt every aid toward getting his instruction read and applied.

ATTENTION

There are a number of impressive things about military tactics—physical and mental exercises that make for the betterment of the man who has to practice them. But of all the things that men are

called on to do in this orderly, obedient life, nothing impresses me more than the transformation that takes place when an officer paces out in front of men standing at ease and calls out that meaning word "Attention!"

You know what happens. From a state of relaxation, every man stiffens to alertness. Any lapse from alertness for the next few seconds may mean making an awkward blunder and receiving a severe reprimand. The good soldier trains himself to concentrate as soon as he hears that word.

I am willing to go on record as saying that any one planning to make a success of selling would do well to go through a reasonable military training for the sake of learning how to take and carry out orders, which means, first and last, how to give attention. For without attention, no one can comprehend orders.

Attention is a big word generally. It is a particularly big word in selling practice. Every teacher of the art of selling puts down "getting attention" as the first requisite of selling. We advertise to get *attention*. We put goods on display in windows and on counters to get *attention*. We bring out goods and demonstrate them to get *attention*. We choose our opening remarks carefully to command *attention*. That is, we do these things if we try to make an art of the business of selling. But before we can master the art of "getting attention" from others we must learn how to "give attention" ourselves. If we fail to give attention to what our superiors say, we will fail to acquire much about goods, policies and practices that we should keep in mind. "Goes off half-cocked," "poor memory," "not thorough," "poor on details," "not dependable," "likely to say or do anything;" these and similar remarks are made daily about the great mass of salesmen who haven't learned to give attention, who have to be told things over and over again before they can be trusted.

And, then, there is another kind of attention-giving that is more important, perhaps, than the giving of attention to the customer, or rather the *prospective* customer, for many a prospective customer turns out in the end to be a customer of some other business firm rather than of ours.

Of course you have been in retail stores as a prospective customer and you have stood around waiting for some one to give you attention. How did you feel about it when there was an unreasonable or unnecessary delay in giving you attention? That's the way other people feel. There's no need of enlarging on this point. Even if a neglected customer stays, delay in giving attention will nearly always put him in a poor frame of mind.

The customer is KING. Don't forget that. His patronage pays everybody's salary. Therefore, put him first in attention-giving—in the retail store, over the telephone, in our letter-writing—even if some one else has to be slighted.

When we talk about the importance of giving attention, the reference is particularly, of course, to the forms of salesmanship that are practiced in those stores and offices to which customers come looking for goods or for information. The salesman who has the hard job of getting a hearing as he goes from house to house or from business place to business place is too appreciative of his opportunity to fail to give attention when he finally has the customer before him. But poor attention in the class of selling first referred to is responsible for an enormous loss of business. A sales manager desirous of getting distribution in a prominent store of a large city sent shoppers into that store to cover it thoroughly and find out just what the salesman and saleswomen of the store would try to sell outside of what the prospective customer would ask for. Two shoppers—a man and a woman—covered every department, strolling around and looking at goods. In only *one* case was there an effort to show merchandise other than that which the customer particularly asked about.

A Chicago store not so long ago had checks placed at all entrances and learned that approximately 200,000 people visited the building on one busy day. On that same day the store made 90,000 separate sales. Something like 110,000 people were interested enough to visit this famous store but went away without buying anything. Allowing for the fact that it is the policy of the store to encourage people "to come in and look around at your leisure," also for the fact that many people interested in buying could not find just what they wanted, it seems evident that there must still have been many thousands who came in with interest in some kind of merchandise or who at least needed certain merchandise and yet who went out without learning that the store was in a position to meet their needs acceptably.

It's all well enough to say that it is a hard job to give every one prompt and courteous attention. Maybe it is. But we have to deal with old Human Nature just as she is. When *we* go into a place of business to spend our money for merchandise, *we* feel important and entitled to the very best attention. We want everybody in that place who has anything to do with the business to be glad to see us and to extend every courtesy. We think that the store that falls down on this is not on to its job, and we are not far from the truth. I have stood around in stores scores of times and seen people neglected, while employes who were supposed to be selling goods "visited" with each other, talked with their friends, chatted over the telephone or gave their attention to other matters that should have been left until after the customer had received attention.

Getting attention goes further than the first greeting of the customer. We can't continue to hold a customer's attention in any kind of selling unless we, in turn, give attention to what he says or does. It is the finest kind of courtesy to listen attentively to the customer. That commands confidence, which is a tremendous factor in the closing of sales. Unless one gives close attention to the customer he can hardly size up that person's thoughts and tastes and appeal successfully to him.

When anything is to be offered for sale, whether the selling is to be done by advertisement, letter, or face-to-face solicitation, an all-important question is, "What is most likely to command attention, *favorable* attention?" Few salesmen seem to have asked themselves this question. Most of them start off weakly with openings of the "Don't you want to buy—" variety, instead of getting at the subject from the customer's point of view and inquiring into his need or appealing to his taste, his comfort, his pride, etc. "Buying" suggestions are usually resisted by the customer; the appeals to taste, comfort, pride, etc. are likely to command attention.

When we have solved the problem of how to give attention, how to get attention and how to hold attention, we have gone far in the interesting job of dealing successfully with mankind, whether we are selling goods or doing something else.

Business firms occasionally excuse their shortcomings in giving prompt and efficient attention by the plea of unusual conditions—shortage in stock, rush of work by the office force, and so on. A large automobile sales agency, for example, received a telephone inquiry at a time when it was very difficult to take care of new customers. The inquiry was answered with little show of interest and the promise made that the prospective customer would be informed later as to what might be done.

The man who begins house-to-house selling soon learns as much about the attention-commanding power of first words as the headline writer of a newspaper.

But the prospective customer never heard from the sales agency again. Eventually, he bought a new automobile from another agency.

A coal dealer, during the coal shortage of 1922–23, ignored letters from old customers. It was true that he could not supply one-third of those who applied for coal. This, nevertheless, did not excuse him from sending out a short explanation, which could have been a form, expressing his regret and promising service when it was possible to give it.

Courteous attention always makes a favorable impression. Failure to give it suggests a negligent or aloof attitude.

DO YOU GET A RUNNING START?

Not long ago there was a foot-race in which a crack runner who ran finely for nine-tenths of the distance lost the race by two yards. He finished strongly, too. His only trouble was that he didn't get a good start. Other runners in that race got a long lead in the first dozen yards and in spite of his fast pace afterwards, the crack runner lost.

Many contests are lost because of a poor start. Much is said about finishing well, and that *is* important. If one can always

Many a race has been lost because of a poor start.

finish contests and jobs strongly, the good finish may in some cases make up for a poor start. But it requires superhuman effort to make up for starting poorly, and often a poor start makes a failure certain. How much better it is to start well!

You know how it was when you met, for the first time, someone who dressed in bad taste, or who had dirty hands or nails, or whose voice or manner was disagreeable. Such things make a poor impression, and a poor first impression is very hard to remove, no matter how many excellent qualities are exhibited afterwards.

All of this leads up to the conclusion that it is highly important that the customer shall get a favorable first impression of our place of business, our appearance, our opening remarks, or our letter-writing. If one who goes into a retail store sees a disorderly counter, is neglected even for a few minutes, is greeted rudely or crudely, or is waited on by some one who is ignorant of the stock, an unfortunate first impression is made—an impression that is likely to cost good business.

There shouldn't be a moment's unnecessary delay in a store or an office in giving the incoming customer attention. He or she should be made to feel that the visit is welcomed and that the organization stands ready to give its most courteous and efficient service. That starts things moving the right way, creates confidence and receptiveness on the part of the customer instead of arousing a spirit of combativeness or defense. It enables the salesman, like the runner who gets a running start, to win without superhuman effort.

Look out for a good first impression—the running start—and the closing of sales will be made easy. Salesmanship isn't the complex thing that men sometimes make it out to be. He who knows his goods and who is imbued with the idea of giving customers his best service from the moment of first sight of the customer is likely to maintain a good pace in the selling of goods.

The importance of the running start goes further, however, than first impressions on customers. The man who begins every day, every week and every month with the determination to dig up new sources of business, to work toward extending his list of customers, to cut down dilly-dallying, time-wasting and the making of excuses to himself and his employer is also training himself to run a good race. Such a man comes within reach of his quota before the month is old. He is ahead of his program rather than behind. That in itself is a great stimulus.

COURTESY—THE WINNING QUALITY

One of the livest tributes to courtesy that I have ever read is the following, from *Drew's Imprint*:

Treating a customer like a rich uncle, so that you may extract his coin, is not courtesy—that's foresight.

Offering a seat to a man who enters your office is not courtesy—that's duty.

Listening to the grumblings, growlings and groanings of a bore without remonstrance is not courtesy—that's forbearance.

Helping a pretty girl across the street, holding her umbrella, carrying her poodle—none of these are courtesy. The first two are a pleasure, and the last is politeness.

Courtesy is doing that which nothing under the sun makes you do but human kindness. Courtesy springs from the heart; if the mind prompts the action, there is a reason; if there be a reason, it is not courtesy, for courtesy has no reason. Courtesy is good-will, and good-will is prompted by the heart full of love to be kind.

Only the generous man is truly courteous. He gives freely without a thought of receiving anything in return. The generous man has developed kindness to such an extent that he considers everyone as good as himself—treats others not as he should be treated (for generosity asks nothing) but as he ought to be treated.

All of us know that the kind of courtesy described in these paragraphs is all too rare.

It isn't that many of us really mean, or like, to be discourteous. The humdrum of our duties simply makes us indifferent. We become curt or impatient without realizing it. We forget that the fiftieth customer doesn't know that we have talked to forty-nine—that the one who asks the tiresome old questions doesn't realize that we have answered them hundreds of times.

A mere "Yes" or "No" when the customer expected some detail, some explanation; paying scant attention to what the customer says; criticizing the work of a fellow-employe in the presence of a customer; showing by a supercilious smile that we don't think much of the opinions of the customer—all these things show a salesman to be lacking in the fine art of courtesy.

The difference between courtesy and the lack of it is often a small thing. Once as I sat in a restaurant, a waiter from another table came up, and, without a word, "yanked" the sugar-bowl from my table in order that he might serve a customer across the room. In another restaurant another waiter wanted a bowl of sugar and came to the table at which I was sitting. With a bow that would have done credit to Lord Chesterfield, he picked up the sugar-bowl, offered it to me with "Have you had sugar, sir?" and then went off with it. These waiters were salespeople for the restaurant in which they worked, for what they did played as large a part in the impression that customers carried away as the food itself. One advertised his house badly; the other advertised it well and got more joy out of his work, at that.

One of the first things we notice about a stranger is his possession, or his lack, of good manners. We realize instinctively that the person who says, "Yes, Mr. Graham," instead of merely "Yes" is well bred.

If you have ever known intimately many educated persons of French or Spanish birth you have probably been impressed by their unfailing courtesy, and yet all of it seems perfectly natural. They have developed the courteous spirit until it has become a part of their lives.

Gushing, extravagant praise; flattery; agreeing with everything that other people may say; these things are not courtesy.

You may not be able to agree with a customer that a certain article is the best one for him to buy, but if he is interested in that, it is courtesy to show the goods and to do it with as much grace and interest as if it were the article you feel disposed to recommend.

Courtesy means putting customers first; means giving them immediate attention; taking interest in their needs; respecting their tastes and preferences; wishing everybody well and making them glad to be customers.

Courtesy means constant unselfishness—a regular habit of thinking about others and giving them every possible consideration. It means putting aside suspicion and giving people the benefit of the doubt until at least they have proved unworthy of our confidence. It means clothing our thoughts in language that bespeaks good breeding and graciousness. It means remembering the little things of life—speaking and writing the few words of condolence, congratulation, good wishes.

Courtesy, though not so long a word as politeness, is a bigger word. Politeness is the outward form. Courtesy is far-reaching; it goes down to the deep roots of character, includes politeness and much more.

Read this—from the *Talking Machine World:*

A salesman has to meet persons of all sorts. No artificial manner will suffice for the proper handling of them all. It is therefore the salesman's duty to learn to believe in his fellowmen, to realize that each of them has a right to exist in the world, and to get over the idea that any one is fundamentally better than any one else. Variety is indeed infinite. Men and women are not equal in respect of wealth, opportunity or culture, birth or breeding. But all men and women are nevertheless men and women, enrolled in the brotherhood of humanity and entitled, even when they are themselves bad mannered, to recognition as our fellows.

The external accompaniments and signs of the fine manner are, of course, to be found in that natural courtesy that radiates from men and women of fine, broad mentality. Courtesy is expressed in many ways. Courteous men and women do not raise their voices, because they know that a noisy voice usually distresses or disgusts. They do not tell funny stories to casual acquaintances, because they know that many men and women resent such familiarity. They are never effusive, for they realize that excessive politeness too easily degenerates into the manner of the second-hand clothing salesman. They, on the contrary, never refuse a request, are never too busy to stop and listen, never take advantage of the helplessness or ignorance of the aged or of foreigners, and, above all, never laugh at distress or trouble. They are kind to children, but they do not slobber over them. They are polite to all, but they never allow themselves to be known for their extreme politeness. They wait for the right opportunity to talk and when they talk they say what they mean, without falsehood or rudeness.

Nathaniel Fowler, Jr., one of America's best business writers, once said to a group of retail merchants: "Gentlemen, remember that you can have no monopoly of goods. The customer can always get the same goods, or very nearly the same goods, from other sources. The thing in the long run that will bring you success, if you earn success, is that which we call atmosphere or service, and that you can make distinctively your own."

Courtesy begets courtesy. The courteous person gets more out of life than most people. Every day he gives others pleasure and it is reflected back to him. If he is truly courteous, he isn't that way because it pays in money rewards, but just the same, courtesy is the greatest dividend-paying stock, year in and year out, that a man or a woman could own.

OURSELVES AS CUSTOMERS SEE US

Take a good look in the mirror now and then, in the quiet of your room, and answer honestly these questions: "Do I, when I go out to buy, like to be served by salesmen like myself? Would I engage helpers like myself if I were an employer seeking assistants who could attract and hold trade? Could I increase their pay, feeling that increases were merited?"

It will do you good to confess frankly to yourself, at intervals, whether or not you are really setting a proper standard for yourself and striving earnestly to live up to that standard.

I believe in these "mirror talks." One should not study himself to the point of self-depreciation. But most of us slight our standards. We know fairly well what we ought to be and do as salesmen if we are to render justice to our firms and to ourselves. It just takes eternal watchfulness and determination to live up to good standards. Because it is hard to discipline ourselves, we are inclined to slip back into the easy, happy-go-lucky, my-work-is-as-good-as-the-other-fellow's way of doing the day's duties.

The value of the quota system in selling is that it fixes a standard. The firm figures out an amount of business as a definite task or undertaking, and we set that as a mark. In our effort to measure up to the mark we have set, we achieve much more than we ordinarily would have done in the same time.

And so it is with character standards—mental quotas. Check yourself up. Set a standard and a high one. You may never reach it in 100 per cent completeness, but every time you set a worthy mark for yourself and dig in to reach that mark, you grow in power and control.

You could hardly beat old Ben Franklin's method of balancing the things for and against some problem he was trying to decide wisely. He wrote his points down in two lists. Somehow, the sight of written words helps to fix things in the mind as they are not fixed by unexpressed thoughts.

Here are some of the things that a "100 per cent salesman" possesses. The English language is so rich in synonyms that two people describing the same qualities or possessions would probably express themselves in different words, but the sum of salesmanship essentials would be about the same in every case.

Knowledge of Self
Knowledge of Other People
Knowledge of Your Goods
Knowledge of Similar or Competitive Goods
Knowledge of Business Generally
Knowledge of Selling in Particular
Personal Cleanliness
Attractive bearing or manner
Neat dress
Ability to listen well
Ability to talk well
Ability to get customer's view

Ability to concentrate
Good memory
Self-control
Tact
Patience
Loyalty to employer
Honesty
Energy
Courteous spirit
Broad-mindedness
Thoroughness
Persistence
Ambition
Confidence.

Now, then, suppose you take a sheet of paper and make up a personal chart. It can be a simple one. Just copy all these essentials of salesmanship in a single column. In machine shops when a thing is over a standard, they call it plus; when it is under the standard, they say it is minus. Opposite the items on your list on which you can honestly assure yourself that you measure up a to good standard, place a plus sign +. In the case of the other items write a minus sign −. The result is your mirror picture—your plus self and your minus self.

While the honest confession is good for the soul, it is only a starting point. Having a true picture of yourself, next draw in your mind the bigger and better self—yourself as you want to be—and as sure as the stars shine you have started on the road to that higher standard. Just as muscles grow by exercise, so the mental traits or qualities gain by effort, by practice.

WATCH YOURSELF

An observing saleswoman in a New England store relates an incident that carries a good lesson. She was in charge of the hosiery department and was giving attention to a woman who, for the moment, was looking over the display of hosiery. At the notion counter, a short distance away, there was another woman wearing a very peculiar hat. Says this saleswoman:

"Just about that time a salesgirl at an adjoining counter called to one of her fellow-workers and asked her to take a peep at the funny-looking hat on the woman at the notion counter. The two girls had a laugh over this. They did not know that the two women customers were friends. In a few minutes the woman at the notion counter joined her friend standing at my counter, who had heard the talk and laughter of the salesgirls. The latter immediately said to her friend: 'Now turn around slowly and let the girls here see your hat at close range and then they can have a better laugh over it.'

"After saying this she added: 'Now let's go to a store where the clerks are not likely to laugh and make fun of us.' And off they went.

"I am certain it was the means of the hosiery department losing a sale, and the chances are the store lost two customers at the same time."

Of course it is downright thoughtlessness and rudeness for store-employes to stare or snicker at the appearance of a customer. There is no excuse for such conduct. But it sometimes happens that customers take offense when salespeople really have no idea of being rude. Any side-remark made by one salesperson to another while in the presence of a customer is likely to be viewed with suspicion—to be taken either as a comment on the customer or as passing some confidential information about the goods that is not to be imparted to the customer, either of which creates an unfortunate impression. It is better, if something must be said to a fellow-employe, to say it openly or else ask the customer's pardon while you call the fellow-employe aside and give your message.

Over-familiarity of employes with one another is certain to make a poor impression. "I say, kid" may seem harmless to the one who utters it, but it is cheap and undignified.

S. A. Davis, Service Director of Buck & Ragner, a Chicago firm, gives some excellent cautions to retail salespeople about speech in a recent letter published in the *Retail Ledger*.

Mr. Davis deplores the use of what he terms "saloon expressions"—"What's yours?" "What'll you have?" and "Have I got yours?" He holds that much is to be gained by substituting such expressions as "Is your order taken, Sir?" or "Have you been served?"

Some of Mr. Davis' other suggestions are here presented in abbreviated form.

Don't refer to merchandise as "stuff" or use such words as "bunk," "junk," "dope," "fake," etc.

Instead of "dandy," "simply great," say "very serviceable," "well made," "an unusual article," "made of Swedish steel," etc.

"I'll show you something less expensive" is better than "I'll show you something cheaper."

"Yes, indeed" is to be preferred to "You bet," "I'll say so," "Sure thing."

"I beg your pardon: I don't understand," is superior to "How's that?" or "I don't get you?"

"You will be pleased with this, I am sure," has a little better sound than "You'll like this."

"Is there something you wanted?" and "What is it, lady?" are crude. Better say: "Can I serve you?" "Have you had attention, ma'am?" "Madam" is always to be preferred to "Lady"; the contraction "ma'am" is somewhat less formal than the precise "Madam" and is appropriate for most occasions.

Don't mutter "Thanks." Say "I thank you" or omit the thanking speech altogether.

Say "Have we?" not "Have we got?"

Never say "ain't got" or "ain't" anything else. Say "haven't," "isn't" or "aren't."

Finally, it is better to say "Is there something else that I can show you?" making specific suggestions connected with the merchandise the customer has already selected, than to say "Is that all?" or "Nothing else?" or even "Anything else?"

THE MATTER OF SPEECH

"Speech," says Plutarch, in his Life of Themistocles, "is like cloth of Arras opened and put abroad, whereby the imagery doth appear in figure; whereas in thoughts they lie but as in packs."

I can conceive of a dumb salesman and a dumb buyer managing to negotiate a sale, but that would be a tame performance compared with a transaction in which the salesperson and the customer have an opportunity to deal with each other through the glorious gift of speech, where they have the privilege of exchanging views, of learning from each other and finally doing each other a service. For the highest type of selling means a real service to the customer—as great a service as that which the customer renders the firm in giving it patronage.

There are several interesting viewpoints of speech.

1. The purely physical—the voice itself and one's manner of using it.

2. The skilful use of speech in leading the thoughts of others—reasoning ability.

3. Good command of English.

Not long ago a rough-looking salesman called on me. His voice was raspy and he had the unpleasant habit of sticking his face close to mine as he talked. He slobbered and sputtered, and his breath—well, the least you can say of it was that it was unpleasant. Whenever I drew back from him, he took a step nearer and seemed determined to make his speech-making machinery count against him as much as possible. I couldn't think much of what he was saying because my attention was centered on his speech-manners. Perhaps he sells his wares to some people. But he would have a hard time selling to me.

I confess myself unable to understand how people expect to make a success in dealing with other people when they have dirty teeth, decayed teeth, or anything else about their mouths, breath, or general appearance that gives offense or attracts unfavorable attention. Why do they wait until some friend has to shoulder the embarrassing job of speaking about it?

Not long ago I heard a clever speaker read a letter twice. This letter was from a boy at school writing to his father for more money. The first time the speaker read the letter, it made the impression of an impertinent, complaining epistle. The second time he read it, it was a pleading, courteous request. The difference lay entirely in the tones that the speaker used in his two readings. Never before had I realized how much of persuasion lies merely in the tones of one's voice.

The telephone companies, in employing new operators, search for young women whose voices are pleasant and who thereby play a large part in making the day's business run smoothly.

"I'd give every dollar I have for the silver of her voice," said a young actress of an older and very successful member of the profession. Not all of us are blessed with clear, silvery voices, but, after all, the impression we get from a voice is not so much from its mere pitch or physical quality as from the spirit behind the tone. In the case of the two letter-readings, the spirit behind the words made a world of difference in the impressions. People whose voices are somewhat gruff or sharp can put considerable graciousness into their voices when they make an effort to do so. Loud talking, over-rapid talking, mumbling—all can be corrected by effort. Just appreciate the value of a good voice and then make a persistent effort to correct the abuse of this sense. Few have really tried to improve their speech.

Voices reveal much about the people behind them. A voice may be vibrant and fairly radiant, or it may be dull, drab, and discouraging. The man who is in business has a decided asset if Nature has favored him with a melodious voice. If he hasn't such a characteristic by nature, it is a duty to cultivate it and to iron out all of the bumps and humps and wrinkles of annoyance, and irritability, and intolerance which it may show, for people are distinctly influenced by the voice of the person with whom they do business. You have met people whose tones immediately chill or irritate you.

Recall how quickly you recognize a voice over the telephone. It summons an immediate vision of the individual to whom it belongs. This is because it really *is* a vital and representative feature of that person's individuality.

Such a voice may not always be distinctly melodious. One of the great American orators has a voice that is none too pleasant. Yet great crowds are drawn and many lives influenced because that voice is *sincere, interested, earnest, kindly* and *never monotonous*.

The voice is a fair barometer, as it were, of disposition and mental attitude. It suggests at once whether the owner is a mere time-killer, a clock-server, a perfunctory worker, or one who is really interested in his task, and will, when occasion arises, put himself out to please.

If you are sincere and in earnest, giving the highest quality of service possible, your voice will glow with the joy of the opportunity. If you look upon your fellowmen and women as a mere mass of people, having no particular relation to you or you to them, except as you can get money out of them, your voice will portray the hardness and coldness of your nature, and, naturally, it will repel rather than attract.

On the other hand, if you are convinced that people, as you find them, are a good sort after all; that they are ready to meet you half way and to do their part if you will do yours, and if you are really anxious to make the world better because you have lived in it—then you are sure to own and operate a voice with its fair measure of winsome quality.

Good talking, as has been pointed out a number of times, means good listening—a courtesy to the other person that cannot be safely neglected. It means leading the thoughts of others rather than forcing, and this requires *tact*.

"Haven't you some other styles that you can show me?" I heard a customer in a retail store ask one day.

"I suppose so," was the cool reply. Compare the thoughts that this aroused in the customer's mind with the thoughts that would probably have been created by "With pleasure" or "Yes, indeed, I'll be glad to."

Very recently I received some favorable impressions of an employe serving a large corporation with which I do business, and then these impressions were marred by the young woman's invariably answering "Yeah" for "yes" and speaking to her fellow-workers as "Say, you."

Don't have your conversation abounding in such misused and overused words as *swell, grand, awfully, lovely, nifty*, etc. If the design is a graceful one, say *graceful*—not *grand*.

Don't talk about the "selling game," "putting through a deal," "getting by with a proposition," "one of our best sellers," "everybody's using it," and so on.

Be careful about the use of "cheap." "Low-priced" is a better description. Practice the use of varied expressions such as "High value for the price," "Best dollar pen on the market."

Mispronunciations grate on the ears. I remember how near I once came to laughing when a New York salesman referred to a Stuyvesant model of something as a "Stew-ves'-ant." The name is a local one and is pronounced as if it were "Sti'-ve-sant."

Use a good dictionary regularly or a list of "Words Frequently Mispronounced" in reviewing words that you are not sure of. The customer expects, with good reason, that you will know how to pronounce correctly the names of the commodities that you sell. The trade papers, trade associations and many of the manufacturers give valuable assistance in learning proper pronunciations of trade terms.

Selling is largely a personal performance. Here are two very personal questions: do your voice, your speech, your manner of talking, help or hinder you? If you could listen to a phonograph record of several hours of your daily conversation, wouldn't you be horrified by the proportion of inane, sloppy talk and by the lack of direction and good spirit in your speech?

SMILING INTO PEOPLE'S EARS

A telephone man says he is of the opinion that if a telephone receiver were a big imposing instrument people wouldn't be so impatient or careless in the way they talk into it. "But," he adds, "it is such an insignificant, defenseless-looking little device that most users seem to feel free to adopt a tone and to indulge in language that they wouldn't think of using were they talking face-to-face with the people who hear them."

The New York Telephone Company has this telling sentence in a recent advertisement: "Pleasing telephone manners bring generous-returns in good-will."

This expresses a big truth. Few people seem to realize the great possibilities of the telephone in the cultivation of good-will and in direct salesmanship. We are now

"What do yer want?"

so accustomed to the use of the telephone that we are likely to follow a routine style of talking. We answer "Yep" and bawl out "What do you want?" "Wait a minute" and "Naw, we can't do that" without thinking much of what sort of picture we are drawing in the mind of the one at the other end of the wire. This is not the style of talk that makes sales in the office or the store, when we face people, and it is not the kind of talk that will win business over the telephone. When a man is before you he can at least see your pleasant face—if you have a pleasant face—but over the telephone you can appeal to only one of his senses—that of hearing. His mind forms a picture from just what he hears.

We do not really mean to be curt, usually, but the person at the other end of the wire not being a mind-reader takes our manner as he gets it. A great deal of the time we could show an interest in our caller's message and perhaps offer some information that he will be grateful for. Such attention and service bring dollars.

Even when some one else is called for, it is time-saving as well as pleasing to the caller if we ask: "Couldn't I attend to it for you?" or "Will you give me your name and leave a message for Mr. Blank?" Frequently it will happen that you can attend to the matter as well as the person called for.

There is an office known to the writer where a young woman is paid several dollars a week over the usual compensation, because of the pleasing manner expressed by her voice. Her gracious, mellow greeting impresses you instantly with the thought that "Here is an office where they are glad to serve me." She is courtesy itself.

"The Smiling Voice."

If some one that you want to talk to is out, it is no trouble for her to put a note on his desk or to have him call you when he comes back. Calling that office on the telephone is a pleasant experience. Even if you haven't the natural charm of this young woman's voice, you can put courtesy and a smile into your words if you try.

Did you ever reflect over the fact that in telephoning, and otherwise, you can make your voice a distinct help or a positive hindrance, according to the way you put expression into it? "Good morning" can be uttered with a snarl or voiced with a halo of cheer and good-will that helps you and others to start the day right. Practice sometime with a simple sentence such as "No, we couldn't do that," and see how, with varying tones, you can change the spirit of these five words from outright rudeness to a smooth refusal that leaves no sting.

It's not all in the fact that your voice is naturally high or low, mellow or harsh. It's more what you try to put into your voice. Every telephone-user can be clear, courteous and businesslike if he has the right spirit.

True courtesy is of the heart and head rather than of the exterior manners, and our Friend of the Smiling Voice is essentially courteous.

We simply could not think of any one with *that* kind of a voice as rude, indifferent, or wilfully discourteous.

The Smiling Voice just naturally shapes itself into expressions of interest and desire to be of helpful service. Business today is worthwhile service for which money is paid in return, and of course the one who pays for the service is richer because of it, even if it has cost dollars and cents. Service is about the greatest thing in the world after all.

From how many places that you call up do you receive an agreeable impression immediately? The proportion is small, isn't it? This ought not to be so. Our sense of courtesy—our regard for the time, respect and good-will of the people we talk to—should not be any less because we happen to be carrying on the conversation over a wire.

"Must have a pleasing telephone voice" is seen with increasing frequency these days in the calls for new employes. It means something. Think about it when you pick up the "insignificant, defenseless" little receiver.

KNOW YOUR GOODS

There's one thing, above all others, perhaps, that the prospective customer expects, and that is that Mr. Salesman be well informed about the merchandise or service offered for sale.

If the man or the woman behind the goods isn't prepared to give the required information about them, merchants might almost as well put their merchandise on counters or out on the floors of exhibition rooms and let customers serve themselves in the style of the serve-self restaurants.

The customer needs hundreds of different kinds of merchandise. He hasn't had either time or opportunity to acquire detailed information about all of these things; but when he is ready to buy, it is usually the definite, detailed information that brings him to a decision as to whether he will take one article or another.

The salesman, on the other hand, is specializing—selling one product or one group of related products. If that happens to be rugs, then he ought to be almost an encyclopedia on the subject of rugs— the kind he is selling, as well as the kind he has to compete with. If the merchandise that affords him his daily bread is hats, toys, hardware, furniture, marine engines, or securities and he is not thoroughly informed on his wares, he is not "on his job" but sadly detached from it.

A customer in a high-class men's furnishings store stopped in front of a rack of handsome cravats. He felt one, reflectively and turned to the salesman with "What is it?" "Pure silk," answered the man behind the counter. "Is it wood-fiber silk?" queried the customer, detecting, as he thought, that the cravat had a somewhat different texture from those made of the product of the silkworm. "Pure silk," repeated the cravat salesman in exactly the tone he had used before.

The customer's question was a perfectly proper one. His reference to wood-fiber silk revealed that he was aware that cravats, hosiery and other goods are nowadays sometimes made of wood-fiber that looks much like silk, gives good service and is often spoken of as silk, artificial silk or wood-fiber silk. In this case he either knew more about the salesman's stock than the salesman knew or he was subjected to curt treatment in not having his question met.

When I bought my Victrola one of the first questions I asked was whether the case was genuine mahogany, or merely birch with a mahogany stain.

Hours invested in spare-time study pay big dividends.

The young woman showing the instrument said she guessed the wood was mahogany, but she wasn't sure. She obligingly found out, but she lost some prestige as a saleswoman right away by not having the definite information in her own head. Not only should she have known what I asked but she should have been able to explain, if need be, what advantage the veneered mahogany case has over the solid. I hesitated between two instruments, one priced at fifty dollars more than the other. I was willing to pay the fifty dollars extra if I could be shown in just what respect the higher-priced instrument was superior. Could she tell me? She could not. Her attempted explanation was vague and unconvincing, and when the manager of the store finally came to her rescue several of his statements were directly at variance with hers. Yes, I bought the Victrola and bought it in that store, but the sale was made only because I went there practically determined to buy an instrument, and only the crudest treatment could have killed the sale. But such faulty salesmanship isn't business. Few things are as nearly sold as Victrolas are when the customer walks in.

Why have mail-order houses built up enormous annual sales totals? Because mail-order men are past-masters in the art of giving information about goods, and even when deprived of face-to-face selling methods—a tremendous advantage enjoyed by the retail store—they tell people what they want to know.

There is a wealth of information on almost all classes of goods open to the salesman—books, trade magazines, catalogues and pamphlets to say nothing of the pointers that may be had from other salesmen, buyers, designers, inventors, expert mechanics, lecturers and demonstrators. Make this information your own and command the respect of buyers.

Years ago a National Cash Register salesman maintained such an extraordinary selling record that President Patterson had him come to Dayton, Ohio, to explain his "method." "Simple as daylight," said he, "they can't ask me anything about a cash register that I can't answer."

"SOMETHING JUST AS GOOD"

This old expression "something just as good" is a well-worn joke, and yet the problem of how to deal with the customer who asks for something that the store doesn't carry, or hasn't in stock at the time is a real one—something far from a joke.

In the first place, it is well-nigh impossible for any store, no matter how extensive its stock, to carry all of the goods for which it may possibly have calls. There are certain lines in which products more or less similar are made by dozens or scores of manufacturers, all advertising their wares to the customer and urging him to "ask the dealer" for their particular brands. From these various brands the wise dealer makes a selection and attempts to carry good stock of one, two, or maybe three of them. To carry all brands, even all of the well known ones, would, in many cases, be poor merchandising for him.

Let's agree, first of all, that it is the duty of the merchant and his helpers to be fair to the advertiser whose work and money have created interest in the article sought by the customer. A short time ago, I wanted some varnish for a porch floor that is exposed to rain. I asked for Valspar, "the varnish that doesn't turn white." I got it, but the salesman who finally supplied me that varnish suggested other varnishes, and ventured the opinion that there were half a dozen others, some costing less than Valspar, that would do the work just as well. Maybe so, but I had pinned my faith to Valspar and preferred that. The manufacturer of Valspar had practically made the sale in my case, and my only answer to the argument of the salesman that many other varnishes gave the same service was,

"Well, why don't their makers tell me about it?" This salesman was not obnoxious in his advising, but there was something about his suggestions that might in some cases create the suspicion that Valspar was merely higher-priced than some other varnishes because it is well advertised, and that, I thought, was not fair to a manufacturer who is undoubtedly making considerable business for retailers. There was another chance for suspicion, by the way—that the salesman was willing to sell a different varnish because the store made more on the substitute than it did on Valspar!

In another instance, I went into a retail store, named by a manufacturer, to buy some union suits that I had seen advertised. This retailer didn't have the goods but would place an order for me, he said. It would require two weeks, at least, to get the garments. And then, when I said I didn't want to wait that long, he handled the situation very well. He said "We have two other union suits, not exactly like the Blank suit, but with a cut very much like the one you describe. I'll be glad to show those, if you like." He was so nice about it that I asked to see the other garments, and, as a matter of fact, one of them pleased me *more than the style of the Blank suit*. In this case, the manufacturer who really started the sale was unfortunate, but the retailer actually did me a service by showing the other goods, while he was certainly fair to the manufacturer of the make that was first mentioned by the customer. This shows that there is a right way as well as a wrong way of putting forward other goods when you are unable to supply what the customer asks for.

As a matter of fact, stores often have in stock goods which are much better suited to the customer's needs than the particular article asked for. For a year or more, dealers in Victor Talking Machine records were out of stock of the "popular records" most of the time, but had records that in three cases out of four afford better music than the ones named by customers. In this, as in other cases, knowledge of stock and tact in handling the customer mean that the salesman can very often sell "something better" if not "something just as good."

Practice showing goods of other styles and sizes, when practicable. You can never lose anything by showing goods. But use great tact in commenting on the customer's preference.

When the article preferred by the customer will soon be in stock, offer to put one aside or to deliver it. Such service is appreciated and is a suggestion that paves the way to showing additional goods.

KNOW WHERE GOODS ARE

To be entitled to call himself a salesman, written with a capital S, a man must, of course, know the goods that he is trying to sell. The customer expects that and has a right to. But it is not enough to know what an article of merchandise is and what it will do. No one can reach the high mark of success in selling if he does not know where goods are —if he does not make a systematic effort to master the location of stock and to keep his stock in order.

It would be interesting if we could read the customer's thoughts when Bill shouts down to Fred—"Say have we any of that two-fifty stock?"

Take this matter of advertised goods, for example. The store puts goods in the windows or gives them special attention in the newspapers, maybe both. Interest is created in these particular goods. In comes a customer the next day: "Let me see the —— that you are advertising." What does the customer think when a blank expression spreads over Dorothy's face as she says, "I don't know anything about that," and then turns to Ethel with, "Are we advertising anything of that kind?"

When the call for advertised goods is met with "Right here, madam, and they are very good values at these special prices (or very attractive new models)," the salesman has secured a good running start toward making a sale.

The store has provided a way by which every employe may easily learn just what goods are being advertised *and where they are*. It is, therefore, inexcusable that anyone should neglect acquiring this important information. Even if the interests of the store did not suffer, it should certainly be a matter of pride with every salesman that he be thoroughly familiar with every item advertised from his own section of the store, if nothing more. In no other way can the store receive the full benefit of its advertising, and advertising costs a great deal. If the salespeople of the store seem utterly ignorant of the wonderful values that the advertising man has described, we can hardly blame the customer for concluding that perhaps the goods are not as represented. When goods are well worth buying it is perfectly reasonable to suppose that the people of the store will be familiar, both with the merchandise and its location.

Demonstration is easily half of the job of selling most things. You cannot demonstrate your goods effectively unless you can produce them quickly and confidently. Blundering and aimless searching are almost certain to cause suspicion or a lessening of the customer's interest.

No matter how busy you are, there are plenty of opportunities during a week's work to become familiar with stock, so that anything that either the customer may ask for or that seems to you to be something that the customer might like can be found instantly. When the salesman says, "We have something fine here that I think is likely to be exactly what you want" and is able to produce that merchandise instantly, the suggestion to the customer is that the goods are perhaps something out of the ordinary. Compare the suggestion conveyed by such salesmanship with: "We did have something else of that kind a while ago but I don't seem to be able to find it. Just wait a minute, will you, while I take another look."

Do you and your fellow-workers make a studied effort to so arrange your goods that everything can be conveniently found, no matter who has to take the stock out? There is an art in the arrangement of goods, but the best system in the world will not avail anything unless all those who have the right to take goods out for inspection are careful to replace everything in good order. The waste of time through goods being improperly placed is terriffic. Watch out for this and watch out also for the proper replacement of sizes. The mixing up of sizes causes considerable embarrassment.

Even when you are giving a good account of yourself in knowing the location of goods in your section of the store, you have still fallen short of the highest standard of salesmanship if you are not generally informed as to what other kind of goods the store has and in what departments or on what floors they may be found. The shoe salesman who knows that the store carries hosiery that matches certain shades of leather perfectly and who tactfully takes it upon himself to suggest that customers visit the hosiery section is on the road to super-salesmanship. This applies in greater or less degree to all departments, or sections, and to all stores. Compare: "I don't think we handle any goods of that class" with "We have a very good assortment of ———. You will find them on the fifth floor just to the right of the stairway."

Finding a way of selling something extra, in your own section of the store or elsewhere, that the customer didn't come in to buy has been appropriately called "suggestion selling." It calls for resourcefulness, tact and, obviously, a ready knowledge of stock and its location.

There are salespeople who have scored a success for themselves by even going so far as to suggest to customers that they call for Mr. Blank or Miss So-and-So when they visit another section of the store.

Perhaps you have not been instructed to do what you can to make sales of goods other than those in your own section. Will you wait for such a request? Are you not in this business of selling to make the largest possible success? It is something to carry out instructions faithfully, but it is more to do a little thinking and planning about better selling on your own account.

Pitch in and be the best informed salesman or saleswoman in the store—not only about goods themselves but where goods are. There are some fine jobs in the stores of this country of ours waiting for alert men and women who are working toward that ideal.

KNOW YOUR CUSTOMERS' NAMES

Recently I made a special trip to a little town up in the mountains of Pennsylvania for the purpose of talking with a firm of young men who have made a remarkable success as retail merchants—who have advertising and selling methods that enable them to meet not only the much-talked-of competition of the mail-order houses but the competition of the stores of nearby large cities as well.

Among the methods that these young men have worked out—and they have a number that afford good lessons to merchants in much larger places—is their campaign to get the names of customers and prospective customers, not only on classified mailing-lists so that they may be addressed readily but so that the salesmen may call people by name when they visit the store. These young men have even gone so far as to advertise the various members of the firm by their first names, so that the farmers of the surrounding community come in and call for "Bob," or "Jake."

You have been to hotels where, though it may have been months since you registered at the place, the man behind the desk calls you by name without apparent effort. I remember what a warm "home feeling" I had when I went back to an Atlantic City hotel after an absence of six years and had the clerk in charge say unhesitatingly "We are glad to see you, Mr. Hall."

To be able to call the customer by his name is to make a fine start. All of us like to deal with people who know us.

Enterprising hotel men make it a point to do this. When a guest is unknown to them, they at least refer to him by name as soon as he registers and his name can be learned. They know that it is finer courtesy to say, "Take Mr. Avery's bag up to Room 199" than to say, "Take this bag up to Room 199."

This matter of knowing customers' names is just as important to salesmen as it is to the hotel-keeper. Both are merchants, for that matter. It is not so much a matter of remarkable memory as it is a matter of effort. Most of us don't really try to remember names; that is, we don't concentrate on the undertaking.

I have had occasion to watch the work of one retail saleswoman who gives this part of her calling particular attention. She earns her living in a city of 150,000, and I am sure that it is within the truth to say that she can call the names of at least one-third of the people who come into her part of the store. One of my own relatives visited that store one day. She was addressed by name, and when she bought some linen goods this resourceful saleswoman said "I believe you would be interested in these initialed napkins." She brought them out as she spoke and, of course, showed the napkin that bore my relative's initial.

The first important step in remembering customers' names is, naturally, to be sure of the name. The hotel clerk gets this information from his register. The salesperson can get it from the sales-slip or the delivery card, and there is no reason why we should not ask people to spell their names for us when we are not sure of the spelling. Some such remark as "I want to be sure to get this right" and a smile always make this easy. Seeing the name written helps to impress it. Names of regular customers should be kept in a book or index so that they can be reviewed occasionally.

At the end of a day, run over in your mind the names of those customers whom you served. This review helps greatly. Memory, you know, is a matter of impression. Every impression makes the memory-dent or groove a little deeper. You couldn't forget the name of Woodrow Wilson, Lloyd George, Mary Pickford or Charlie Chaplin if you tried. Why? Because you see the names or hear them so often that the memory-dent or groove is kept deep.

Associating people with what they bought is another useful device for remembering names. "We have a fine little serving table here that would go well with the dining-table you bought from us" is a suggestion that is sure to bring consideration from the customer.

She brought out napkins bearing my relative's initial.

Finally, association may be used for fixing names in the mind. For example: suppose you have a customer whose name is Mrs. Carroll. She could be thought of as a singer—whether she is or not—a singer of "carols." This is what is meant by "association." A "Mr. Baker" might be fixed in the mind as a maker of bread, though his business might, in fact, be chemicals. "Mr. Jefferson" might be associated with Thomas Jefferson. Mr. Pierce might be recalled as the man of piercing eyes, if they are keen. A little ingenuity along this line will enable you to recall almost any name, no matter how odd. You can identify many people because of the similarity of their names to other names well fixed in your mind. Thus, I associate a Miss Dineen with a well known baseball umpire by the same name and a Mr. Turner with a boyhood acquaintance named Turner. Remembering names that are just like, or similar to, names of people you have known a long time is one of the best methods. It will enable you to recall all such familiar names as Jones, Smith, Brown, Wilson, and so on.

A memory-training specialist advises that humorous association be used when necessary—picturing, for example, Mr. Campbell riding on a camel. As a last resort, when other associations cannot be used, this specialist advises that the face of the person be visualized in the imagination with his name in large letters on his forehead. When the face is recalled, the mental image will very likely also produce the name. The important thing is to imprint in the imagination a picture of the face with some surrounding or association that will suggest the name.

GETTING INTO THE CUSTOMER'S SHOES

A successful saleswoman says that she marks the beginning of her greatest success and happiness in her work from the day she realized that salespeople are inclined to look at the matter of buying from their own point of view, whereas they should look at it from the customer's side of the counter—get into the customer's shoes, so to speak.

In her own words: "It came to me very forcefully one day when I was doing some shopping for myself and getting poor service. I was concerned, of course, about being perfectly suited with what I bought and with getting the best possible value for my money, and I resented, first, the indifferent attention and, finally, the effort of the salesman to press something on me that I didn't want.

"I saw then, as I had never seen before, why we who are in selling work all the time, making our living that way, regard customers as cranky, hard to please, expecting too much, etc. Every mother's son and daughter of us takes the customer-attitude when we go out to spend our hard-earned money. We like to have store-people welcome us, we expect them to show us their goods gladly and patiently, and we want plenty of time in which to do our selecting. When we don't conclude to buy, we don't like to be made uncomfortable by sour looks from some one who seems to be saying 'I've just wasted my time.'"

This saleswoman's frank statement of her experience and change of attitude makes clear a bed-rock principle of selling. Simple as it may seem, many people in selling work do not seem to have ever grasped the idea that the first thing to do in dealing with a customer is to get the measure of that customer, so as to understand his or her point of view. There is nothing wonderful or mysterious about this. Just ask yourself: "If I were this person, what would I expect in the way of service?" Then, do as you would be done by—the Golden Rule of Salesmanship as well as of life generally.

It is a big thing to get the correct mental attitude. When you have this you will get a good running start by dealing at the very outset with your prospective customer in a way that shows your desire to be of real service to him. You will listen courteously to what the customer has to say. You will take an interest in the purchase the customer has in mind and earnestly strive to show and sell the one article that above all others will please him permanently.

When you can take this attitude at the beginning of every day's work you will be able to sympathize with much that now very likely irritates you.

You will understand how a thing that may look small to your firm may be big in the eyes of a customer.

You will appreciate the importance of having every customer thoroughly satisfied, as far as that be possible. You know how you advertise among acquaintances the places that give you good service. Other people do the same thing.

The greatest asset a salesman can have among his customers is their belief that he is as much interested in seeing that they get satisfactory service as if the purchases were for his own use.

Getting into the customer's shoes, so to speak, will do another thing for you. It will prepare and protect you against the impatience or the unreasonableness of customers. You will see that a certain attitude of the customer is not assumed toward you as an individual and that, therefore, there is no reason why you should feel hurt or insulted personally. You are merely bearing it as a representative of your firm. So, just act your part as if you were an actor in a play. Preserve the appearance of patience and coolness. It is a principle of psychology that when we maintain the physical appearance of a state of mind it actually helps to create that state of mind. Thus, if you force yourself to smile, it is almost impossible to become angry.

WHAT'S A SALE?

A great deal of abstruse, "high-falutin'" advice has been written and uttered on the subject of "scientific salesmanship." To be sure, there is a science and an art of selling, just as with other occupations—science, the knowing; art, the doing. But there is nothing mysterious or profound about it—nothing that you cannot grasp in a few minutes. For that matter, you probably already know, unconsciously maybe, the steps of a sale and the principles, or factors, involved. Often, however, we are helped by restating what we know or by seeing such things illustrated or charted as the steps are shown in the accompanying illustration.

Legally, a sale is a transfer of ownership of something from one person to another. From a business or a mental point of view, a sale is a series of steps or stages from the point where we first get the attention of the customer to the climax where the prospective customer becomes finally convinced that the buying of the commodity is a desirable thing to do and acts on that decision.

The outdoor salesman or the traveling salesman finds the getting of attention, or the "approach," as he terms it, usually the most diffi-

cult part of his undertaking. He often has great difficulty in getting in to see his man or in inducing him to listen to a solicitation. The retail salesperson enjoys a great advantage in that the advertising of the store, its show-windows, or its local reputation, solves to a large extent the problem of getting attention. The very fact that people come in to look at goods means that they are in some degree interested. Don't forget, though, that it has cost money and effort —maybe a great deal of both—to create that attention or interest. Guard it with jealous care. And remember, also, that the firm having helped you toward a sale by creating within the customer a certain amount of interest, has left it to your selling ability to close the sale for that article, to sell allied merchandise and perhaps to secure, through your new customer, leads to other customers. *Attention* and *interest* are so closely interlocked that *interest* might appropriately be called *ripened attention*. Sometimes, indeed, all of the four steps of a sale are so close to each other and are so quickly made that it is hard to say where one begins and another ends.

The newsboy flashes a paper in front of you as you walk along. "Paper, Mister?" He has your attention and maybe your interest. "All about the Shaw Case!" He has developed your interest; you believe, or decide that you want a paper, and you act by reaching for the paper and passing him the price. He is greatly helped, of course, by his merchandise being of a familiar sort—something that you are already partly "sold on," so to speak. With purchases of greater cost and of less familiar merchandise the process is usually a more elaborate and deliberate one, requiring greater tact and skill on the part of the salesman.

Interest and *belief* are built up from *attention* by intelligent *explanation* and perhaps *demonstration*.

Action is induced by making out a complete case for the product and making it easy for the customer to *decide* to take it, without, at the same time, appearing to *press* or *force* him.

To guide the customer skilfully up the steps of a sale means that the salesman must have certain definite knowledge shown in the chart below.

The links that make a sale.

First of all, the salesman must know himself—must know what is required of him as a salesman, ascertain in what qualities he is weak and set to work to strengthen himself. Too much self-analysis, excessive introspection, is deplorable and often leads to self-consciousness and discouragement, but most salesmen err in the other direction and go through life half-way developed because they are indifferent as to what they need to make them measure up to the full stature of a salesman.

The real salesman must know his goods.

He must study and know people, so that he may understand his customer, not perfectly perhaps, but well enough to deal with him intelligently and helpfully.

And, finally, the salesman must study the *sale*—the fine science and art of selling; it is that, if you please. His education in selling methods is never complete. There is always something more to learn if one is alert and ambitious.

NOT "WHAT ELSE, PLEASE?" BUT "LOOK AT THESE!"

Once in my shopping experiences I walked into a men's furnishing store where I was unknown and asked a genial-looking salesman for some hose.

"Is this size about right for me?" I asked, when he had put some attractive hose out for my inspection. I recalled experiences when hose that were too short had cramped my toes.

"By George! Just the one other thing I need."

"Yes," he replied, "you will find that size just right. I looked at your foot before I came behind the counter. Very few men remember the size they wear."

I complimented him on his "service salesmanship," and then I suddenly remembered that I needed an extra union suit. He showed me something that suited me, and then he asked casually, "Now, I wonder if you don't need a pair of garters."

By George, I did! And it was the only other thing in "wearables" that I did need.

"Tell me," I said to this unusual salesman, "how you happened to mention the one additional thing that I did need? Why didn't you say 'Now, what else?' or rattle off a long list of things, as most salesmen do?"

Said he, smilingly, "There's no mystery about my method. You asked for hose first, and then remarked that you needed a union suit. So it seemed to me that if you needed anything else it would most likely be a pair of garters."

Simple, wasn't it—just studying the customer and the things he bought at the outset and then suggesting other merchandise that went well with what he bought. Yet this is one of those simple things that few salesmen concentrate on. They either rely on that general question "Anything else, please?" suggest too much, or fail to show the very goods that a customer would be likely to buy. Result: when Mr. Customer remembers about those extra items he is in front of somebody else's place, and Our Store has lost a sale that will never be recovered.

Out in Youngstown, Ohio, a thinking retailer resolved that he would have all of his salespeople stop asking such pointless questions as "Anything else today?" or "What else, please?" He urged them, also, to refrain from rattling off a long list of articles, because this seems to suggest to the customer that the store is anxious to unload a great deal on him, and instead of really considering the suggestions of the salesman he hastily answers, "Nothing else today" and retreats.

This Ohio merchant started a new system. Not only did he coach his helpers to be guided in their suggestions as to extra merchandise by what the customer called for when he came in, but he had each department decide, the first thing in the morning, on certain articles that would be brought to the attention of customers whenever opportunity afforded.

Instead of running aimlessly over a list of suggestions, the salesmen of this store schooled themselves to say in an easy, natural way, "Here is a very nice glove (or whatever the merchandise was) that we are offering." This drew attention to the merchandise itself, as if it were something likely to interest the customer, whether he needed such goods or not.

The plan of the Ohio merchant has resulted in a largely increased percentage of what he calls "suggestion sales." That language, "suggestion sales," is apt. He who is alert on "suggestion sales" soon learns where to draw the line between possibly boring or pressing the customer and that other extreme of simply handing out what people come to the store and ask for and not suggesting or showing anything else.

One of the greatest American shoe merchants rates the ability of his salesmen not by the number of pairs of shoes they sell but by the number of packages of polish. He holds that customers come into the store with the idea of buying shoes, and that, therefore, a shoe sale has already been started—that one's real ability as a salesman is shown in creating a demand for something that the customer did not come in to buy.

If the firm would figure out just how much it costs them in window-display and advertising expense to bring people into the store, the

It costs a lot to bring them in.

figure would probably astonish you. While the customer is in the store, in the humor to buy or to investigate, you have a golden opportunity. Don't let it go a-glimmering out the front door, lost beyond recovery. Look out for the "suggestion sales" and your sales record will take care of itself.

"CO-RELATED SALES"

I am indebted to the Burroughs Adding Machine Company for permission to reproduce in this *Bulletin* two of a series of charts of "Co-related Sales" that have proved their usefulness in one large field of retailing—drug stores—where the average purchase is small and where keen merchants are striving to sell the customer several articles rather than one, when they have been successful in getting him to call.

As the author of the charts, Otis R. Tyson, sets forth, there are two ways by which sales-cost may be decreased: (1) by selling the customer a large unit of the article in which he has expressed an interest—which may mean selling a larger quantity or an article of better quality than that asked for; (2) by selling him articles other than the one which was the specific object of his visit to the store.

Selling the customer a larger unit, or "trading up," as it is called, is especially useful where the customer can likely use a larger quantity of the article asked about and where the store can give an attractive price on a larger sized package or a number of articles. As all of us know from experience in making our personal purchases, we frequently feel indebted to the salesman who, while showing us the article asked for, helps us to select a more suitable one, though it does represent a larger investment.

But the "Co-related Sales Charts" relate to the skilful practice of bringing to the customer's attention articles that are related to the one which he or she came into the store to buy. The principle is an old one, but such charts as those shown help to visualize the possibilities.

Rarely are a customer's needs limited to one article. He just happened to think of something needed at once because his supply is exhausted, or he comes in for something that a member of his household asked him to purchase. There are many other things that would be just as useful as the one asked about, if only some alert salesman will take the trouble to suggest the article or to show it.

One of the first things likely to be said about this Co-related Sale principle is that customers may resent so much suggestion. But this will not be the case if the salesman does his work skilfully. Naturally, if all such suggesting is done in the attitude of forcing additional sales, it will harm rather than help the business of the store. But customers welcome helpful suggestions. They often cover things that they really need but had forgotten to ask about or didn't know existed.

Refer to such additional articles in a casual way, handing them to the customer for examination, if possible. For example: "Here is an unusually good brush if you happen to need one" or "This handy sharpener will pay for itself in a short time."

The chart illustrates the association of ideas. One thing in our minds suggests another closely connected with it. As has been well said, thoughts run in currents, flitting from one thing to another that lie in the channel of the original subject. "Mt. Vernon" suggests

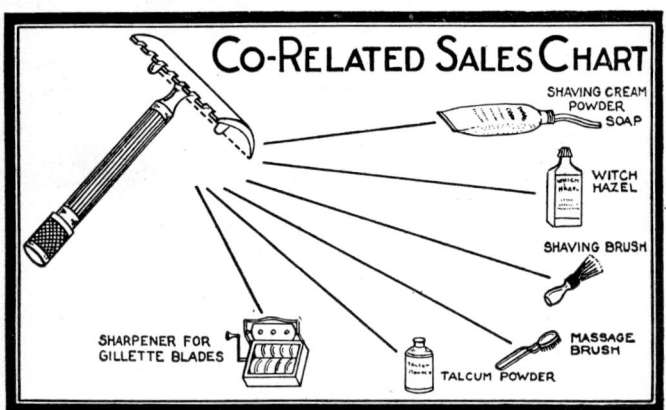

George Washington, "Wilbur Wright" suggests the aeroplane. The lawn-mower suggests summer, and so on. With every article of merchandise there are other articles closely connected, and the customer's mind will lead naturally and easily to a consideration of these things if an opportunity is afforded.

Such charts can be made up to apply to all lines of goods. Stockings, shoe-trees, polish, polishing brushes, extra laces, all are co-related to shoes. Collars and cravats are co-related to shirts. Porch furniture suggests grass rugs and screens. Filtered ink connects directly with the purchase of a fountain pen, so does fine stationery.

Some one is going to sell the customer things co-related to the first article he buys. Why shouldn't it be Our Store?

SELLING THROUGH SUGGESTION

Before the customer says "I will take this one" or "Send me that" his thoughts go through a certain course. Mingled with his sense of need or his interest is usually, in some degree at least, a tendency to resist the efforts of the salesman, especially if the salesman is too intent, too openly eager, to make the sale.

There is great need of ability to guide the customer's mind skilfully to the point of complete satisfaction with the goods under consideration and to decision and action. Here is where suggestion comes in.

Suggestion is defined by the dictionary as "the imparting or exciting of a notion or idea in an indirect or unobtrusive way—the calling up of an idea in the mind by a connected idea." If we say "You will have to hurry to get one," the full meaning is stated plainly and there is little left for the hearer to think out. If, however, we say, "These are going very rapidly and I doubt that we will have any left after this week" the language is such as to make the hearer think for

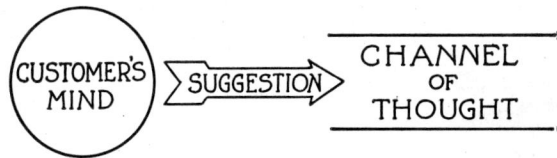

himself that if he wants the article in question he should hurry. He may resent the salesman's urging him to hurry but not the conclusion of his own mind that immediate action is desirable.

Think of the customer's thoughts as currents running in a number of directions, maybe with no decided trend. Just as by gentle direction—by providing an easy channel—a current of water, air or electricity may be so guided that it moves with power the way you want it, so may the current of thought be directed. Like water, air or electricity, thought can be drawn more easily than forced.

Reflect over your own attitude in buying. As soon as you feel that the salesman is too dictatorial, too positive, too pressing, your resistance is aroused. Let the salesman, however, quietly drop remarks that make you think things out for yourself and you are satisfied with your conclusions.

There are times, and there are types of customers, that require aggressive action, when the salesman must boldly and confidently state things completely and help the slow thinker and the indecisive person to select and act. But there are just as many cases when the subtle use of suggestion is the proper procedure.

Anything that has a tendency to lead the mind through the association of ideas is suggestion.

Let's suppose a salesman of fine domestic rugs that are remarkable copies of Orientals assures the customer that experienced rug buyers often cannot tell the difference between the domestic copies and the genuine Orientals. That statement may or may not be believed by the customer. Suppose, however, the salesman merely tells the customer of a case where an experienced buyer came in and looked at the domestic rugs, thought they were the genuine Orientals and asked where the domestic ones were. This is relating an actual occurrence of good suggestive value rather than making a bald assertion, and the customer pictures the incident in his mind.

Language which creates pictures in the buyer's mind is the kind that has the greatest leading or suggestive value. Therefore, try to illustrate your sales talk with incidents.

"Start your savings account today and before you realize it you will be driving your own car" is an attractive suggestion that has been used freely recently by Ford salesmen and in Ford automobile advertisements. The picture is appealing. It starts happy thoughts in many minds.

Study the suggestive power of even single words. "Smooth" suggests a slippery surface, while "even" brings up a picture of a level surface but not necessarily a slippery one. "Instalment plan" has an unagreeable association for many people; "Easy monthly payment plan" gets away from that association. Victrolas are always described as "instruments" rather than "machines" by their manufacturer.

Use the word "laundryman" in talking to the proprietor of a modern laundry and, without realizing it perhaps, you place him on a level with one of his ordinary helpers. Speak of him as a "laundry-owner" and you appeal to his sense of proprietorship. "Apartment" has a more agreeable sound than "flat." And so it goes. A careful regard for the picture-creating power of words shows in the monthly total of sales.

"All human action can be traced to some stimulation of one of the fundamental motives, such as Love, Pride, Fear, Caution, Sentiment, Religion, Justice, Hate, Reason, Gain, Ambition or Appetite," says a psychologist.

Suggestion can be used to reach a motive and to start some train of reflection that is at least not opposed to what the salesman is striving for, if not immediately favorable to it.

Until some response is awakened, the salesman is, as it were, shooting in the dark. He can only proceed in the faith that his solicitation has been effective before and will maintain its average. As he talks, he must study his man, his movements, his way of looking at things, his manner of talking, how he listens. If the prospective purchaser's attention wanders, the salesman must contrive to do or say something to fix attention; otherwise, the sales talk falls on empty air. On the other hand, some men are really paying attention while appearing, deliberately or unconsciously, not to pay attention. Sometimes this is done as a means of disconcerting the salesman.

An incident connected with the selling of gasoline and oil illustrates the force of suggestion. An attendant at one of these stations had the habit of asking, as automobiles drew up, "How much gasoline do you want?" The man in the automobile usually said, "Oh, about five gallons," or maybe he said "Ten gallons." Then the attendant would ask, "Any oil?" and the reply would likely be "Yes, put in a quart." A real salesman who was present one day said, "I will show you how to sell gasoline and oil," and when the next car drove up he asked, "Shall I fill her up with gasoline?" and the man said, "Yes." The salesman put in twelve gallons of gasoline. He then asked, "Shall I fill her up with oil?" and the man again said "Yes," and the salesman put in several quarts of oil. It worked just this way in nine cases out of ten and was a clear demonstration of the fact that intelligent selling could increase the average sale in that business from 25 to 50 per cent.

DEMONSTRATE!

If I were asked to utter one word that would contain the most valuable advice on the subject of salesmanship that I could give, that one word would be "Demonstrate."

If all customers had quick and fertile imaginations, and if every salesman had at his tongue's end the most graphic picture-painting language, demonstration might not be so important; but in selling goods we must reckon with the fact that many people have little imagination and we must also take into account that few of us have the ability to convey, by mere words, to every person we are called upon to serve, a true picture of what is in our own minds.

Most people are quicker to understand by the eye than through the ear. When they only hear about things, they are likely to miss much and to only half-way understand.

All of us have more or less natural curiosity about merchandise and in learning how things work. The street salesman understands this human tendency and makes use of it in holding his crowd.

James H. Collins, a well known business writer, tells of two salesmen who went out to sell a new model of a small mechanical device. One began talking to merchants in this way: "If you have a few minutes to spare I would like to tell you something about the new model that we are putting out." By the time he got this far, many of the merchants to whom he talked suddenly remembered that they had something else to attend to or interrupted him with the comment that they had all the stock they wanted in that line and couldn't possibly consider anything else just then.

The other salesman walked in quietly and with a mere word of greeting placed the new model in the prospective purchaser's hands, setting it in action as he did so. "This is our new model," he would say, after getting attention fixed on the device. His plan enabled him to get attention immediately, and he had no difficulty in making satisfactory sales.

Showing is always better than telling.

It is conceded that a large part of the success of the National Cash Register Company is due to the fact that all of its salesmen are trained to demonstrate skilfully. The N. C. R. man knows at just what point he ought to put cash in the drawer and record a transaction. He knows when it is effective to induce the prospective customer to "ring up a sale" himself and see himself, in imagination, owning this efficient store device.

I was once in a store where a customer was looking for bed springs. I was glad to see the salesman get right on a mattress and jump up and down vigorously to show the power of the springs. It was almost startling but his act showed something that no words could have made clear.

"Yes, demonstration is fine," says some one, "if you are selling a machine, but suppose you are selling something that can't be demonstrated?"

There is a way to demonstrate almost everything. Even breaking a bit of thread, to show strength, is demonstration.

Holding up thin cloth to the light, to show how it lets air through and keeps the body cool in hot weather, is demonstration.

Cutting paper with scissors to show the keen edge is demonstration. So is bending the sole of a shoe to show flexibility.

Bringing the ends of a collar together, manipulating a cravat to show its appearance as tied, thrusting your hand down into a stocking to show the design of the weave or the double strength of the heel—all this is in the realm of demonstration. Salesmen of Water-

Skilful demonstrators know the value of handing the prospective customer the easily operated article early in the interview.

man fountain pens have an impressive way of demonstrating the unfailing quality of the "spoon" feed by drawing long vertical lines for the customer's inspection. In this case, as is usual, oral explanation helps the demonstration but the actual performance visualizes the selling point as mere words could never do.

Snapping tightly woven goods to show its strength is demonstration. Draping it over the figure to give the effect of the finished garment is demonstration.

Every one knows the value of the "living model" demonstration, where the customer can stand off and see the suit or coat on another person. Not every article of merchandise can be demonstrated quite so effectively as that, but there is always some little act or example that can be performed to illustrate a strong selling point of the goods.

You may be a fine talker. If so, thank God for the gift, but don't try, by talk, to make a small boy feel the joys of having his velocipede. Demonstrate! Put him on the thing and roll him around.

LEARNING THE PRICE THAT THE CUSTOMER WILL PAY

There is one question that should never be asked a customer, and that is "What price do you want to pay?" The question is really discourteous and may be embarrassing to the customer. We can hardly blame the customer who answered such a question with the good-natured remark: "I have no particular sum of money in my pocket that I want to get rid of, and I am not a millionaire but, young man, I rather think I could buy anything in your store that

Show your goods, naming prices casually.

happens to strike my fancy. Suppose you show me what you have for sale and then I think I'll be able to decide how much money I want to leave with you."

The salesman is naturally desirous of finding out the class of goods that will meet the wishes of the customer, but the blunt question of "What price did you want to pay?" is not the salesmanlike way of getting guidance.

The salesman's general observation of the customer is the best preliminary guide as to what should be shown.

What the customer says is, of course, an even better guide, for he may have a fairly well defined idea as to what he wants, even if he does not choose to reveal this fully to the salesman at the outset.

One successful merchant advises his helpers: "Don't ask questions. Show goods. Just keep on showing goods and you will get all the leads you want as to the customer's likes and his ability to buy."

I do not, however, advise against preliminary questioning if it is tactful and leading. Such questions as "Are the chairs that you want to be used on the porch or in the living room?" "Do you care especially for mahogany?" enable the salesman to lead directly to what the customer is interested in seeing.

Suppose a woman customer is looking for shoes. She will usually indicate in a general way the kind of shoe she is thinking of buying. If a $10-shoe is brought out with some such remark as "This is a very nice walking shoe at ten dollars," mentioning the price naturally and casually with no hint that the customer may not be able to buy a $10 shoe, she will immediately ask for something lower in price if unwilling to pay as much as $10.

It is a safe rule to begin showing the better class of goods unless one is positive that the customer prefers the lower-priced merchandise. For one thing, the showing of the better goods gives the store standing. There is nothing in this plan that prevents the salesman from later showing lower-priced articles. For another thing, the showing of the higher-priced stock is a compliment to the customer. A man is usually pleased by being regarded as one who can buy a $60-suit, even if his limit is $30 or $40. Besides, he probably has a margin of $5, or more, over the limit he names.

Nothing that the store sells should be regarded as "cheap." The word is a dangerous one, for it conveys the idea of inferior quality. That an article is low-priced does not necessarily mean that it is inferior. The little hammer that sells at 10 cents is as good for the purpose it was meant to fill as the high-class mechanic's hammer selling for many times as much.

Millions have been made selling low-priced merchandise of good value.

Some stores have a rule, and it is a good one, that no goods carried by them may be referred to by the salespeople as cheap. The description "low-priced goods" is recommended. "Reasonably priced," "excellent value," "fine article for the price," "big value for a little money" are variations that may be used. Still other terms, conveying the same thought, will occur to every resourceful salesperson.

That the store carries an article in stock should be regarded generally as proof of the value of the article, though there may be times when the goods may have been disappointing and must be sold with a frank explanation of their shortcomings. But it is risky to depreciate your stock. A short time ago a customer walked into one of the largest rug stores of New York and asked to see a type of domestic rug that is rapidly winning favor. "You wouldn't want a rug like that," remarked the salesman at once. "Why not?" asked the customer, astonished to hear the salesman practically deny the advertised value of the goods. The salesman attempted an explanation of the superiority of higher-priced rugs but his remarks fell flat. He had disturbed the customer's confidence; the man walked out with little ceremony and bought his rug elsewhere.

WHAT LOST THE SALE?

Experience is a grand old teacher. Her lessons are often humiliating or bitter but none the less valuable because of that. The sales-

man who yearns for more power will reap all the profit he can from experience—his experience and the experiences of others, successful experiences and unsuccessful experiences.

There is a keen young business man in Philadelphia who arranges for regular conferences of his staff. At these conferences, he and his associates review, among other things, the mistakes of the previous week, and ask "What can we learn from this?" Thus do they make their slips and mishaps stepping-stones to better performance.

There are a certain number of sales lost in every store every week, and unless a store is very remarkable it is continually losing customers to other stores. Sometimes the reason for the loss of a customer is one that cannot be helped. Often the reason is something that could be corrected if the customer would only tell us frankly of his experience. Unfortunately, we cannot always, or even usually, have customers do this.

Recently two hundred people were asked why they stopped buying at one store and went to another. Here is the tabulation of their answers:

Indifference of salespeople	47
Errors in service	18
Forcing of substitutes	18
Tricky methods	18
Delays in delivery	17
Over-insistence of salespeople	16
Discourteous treatment	14
Delay in giving attention	13
Tactless handling of customer	11
Disorderly stock	9
Ignorance concerning goods	6
Unwillingness to exchange purchase	4
Dissatisfaction with quality	1

It is remarkable that so few of the cases have to do with the goods themselves—that nine-tenths of the dissatisfaction was with the service of the store in one way or another. This seems to suggest that if a store has a good assortment of reliable goods and can maintain a high standard of salesmanship and service, it runs small chance of losing customers. Surely this is a subject for thought.

It is easy enough to say that customers are over-critical, that they do not appreciate how hard it is to give perfect service to everybody, that they are often impatient and unreasonable, and so on. But we must take the situation as it is. Trade is sensitive. It is easily repelled. It goes naturally where it is handled well, where buying is made a pleasure. We can't afford to give ourselves the same consideration we give the customer. His trade pays your salary and mine and keeps the business running. He must be catered to. We must make that a study.

No business is on a proper basis unless it is continually raising the standard of its service; and "service" includes salesmanship, or salesmanship includes service, whichever you prefer. Every act of the representative of the store, from the time the customer enters to the delivery of the article, has its effect. The packer and the deliveryman play their part in making the impression that the customer has of us. Every letter, every treatment of a complaint, or a request for exchange, has its customer-holding or customer-losing effect.

Take this question of "What lost the sale?" to yourself. You frequently have the feeling that if a customer had been handled a little differently, had been given more attention or patience, a sale would have been made. Do you reflect, "Oh, what's the use of trying to please everybody?" or do you follow the plan of the Philadelphia business man and say "What can I learn from it?"

If you don't know what keeps you from being an unusually good salesman, have the courage to ask those who observe you in action what they think of your methods. It won't do you any harm even to ask your superior. You will always be respected for wanting to learn the weak spots in your work.

Review the tabulation of the reasons the two hundred people gave. Find how far they apply to our methods—our store—and do your part toward removing them. That's the kind of salesmanship that will win.

PEOPLE—THE GREATEST OF ALL STUDIES

In a previous talk it was pointed out that, in order to give the highest type of service, a salesman should, in addition to knowing himself, his goods and the art of selling, know the customer. Now, although we write and speak of "the customer" as if he or she were one person, we know that his "name is legion"—that there is an endless variety. As has been said, God abhors duplicates; He never made two people exactly alike, though he has bestowed certain traits so generally that we have become accustomed to them and can recognize them even in people whom we have not previously met or whom we know very slightly.

The study of mankind is, without question, the most complex that the salesman undertakes. He never gets quite to the end of this study. There is always something new and interesting about it. Merchandise can never be quite so developing.

The salesman represents in himself one type of mankind. He knows himself better than he knows any other person, and yet he finds himself sometimes puzzled in interpreting himself. He cannot always forecast exactly what action he will take under given circumstances. Indeed, he does many things that he never thought he would do—things that perhaps he has said he would not do. So if, with the opportunity to look into his own innermost being at will, the salesman does not always have perfect understanding of himself, he can hardly hope to have this perfect understanding of the thousands of people with whom he must deal, all having their own distinct personalities. But he can, from a study of well selected books and from his daily contact with humanity, greatly increase his knowledge of the laws and habits of thought, of how people receive impressions and come to conclusions. This brings us into the realm of psychology. If you are afraid of the word psychology, just call it the study of human nature.

Undoubtedly the most frequent and serious mistake that is made in dealing with other people is our inclination to look at things from our own point of view. It is a natural mistake, for in trying to judge what the customer would or should do, it is instinctive to ask ourselves "What would I do in this case?" The answer to "What would I do?" may be correct where the customer before you is of your type and tastes, your age, your walk in life, and so on. But age, education, nationality, sex, living conditions, temperament and still other factors play a tremendous part in shaping the likes and dislikes, the thoughts and the lives of people.

How successful would a man of 50 years and of conservative taste in the matter of dress be if he were selling clothing and furnishings to college boys and allowed himself to be guided entirely by his own individual tastes and preferences?

Suppose a salesman selling almost entirely to women persisted in looking at things from a man's point of view rather than a woman's?

What would happen if a city salesman went out to sell in the rural districts and made no effort to get the farmer's outlook on life?

You may not admire brilliant colors, but certain types of foreign-born customers do. To do business with them successfully, you must train yourself instinctively to adjust your point of view.

It is all very well to give customers the benefit of your judgment, but that judgment must be formed as the result of a study of the type of customer before you. If every one in the world had your individual preferences, we would all want the same hat, the same shoes, the same suit, the same home, and all would want to marry the same person, which, obviously, wouldn't do!

So add to your knowledge of types. Before long you will be acquainted with so many that when you deal with a new customer you will instinctively reflect that he or she reminds you of So-and-So and you will act accordingly. The next customer will correspond to still another type that you have in mind; you adapt yourself to that type, and so on.

All this, of course, means that to study human nature successfully, you must develop your powers of observation. All of us have the God-given power to see and understand other men and women with reasonable accuracy if we make an effort. But, in the words of John Calder, some people only *see*, while others *perceive* and still others *apperceive*. You may see, so far as physical sight goes, and still get nothing that helps you. When you go further and perceive, you are on the road toward making proper use of the power of observation. When you apperceive, you take in all that your eyes can give you, you appreciate the significance of the information, your mind connects the new material with what you knew before and you work out your plan of action.

Most "rules" about selling are useless just because there are so many exceptions to them that the rules aren't rules at all. But there are a few rules that always hold good, and though they are necessarily general, we are better salesmen by being reminded of them now and then.

Study the type of customer in hand and learn how to appeal to him.

I know that this simple rule that I am going to lay down is disregarded every day by salesmen of years of experience, because while I am in the business of selling I am also a buyer and it is most frequent for salesmen to make a poor impression on me by their neglect of this fundamental.

The fundamental is this: you must adapt your argument, your canvass, you presentation, or whatever you prefer to call your sales talk and demonstration, to the type of individual to whom you are trying to sell.

This means, of course, that before you can get very far in the process of selling, you must "size up" the customer as accurately as you can. If you do not, you will be like a novice who would try to shoot the guns of a battleship before he got the range of the target. Get this range or measure, and get it as quickly as you can. You don't have to stare at the customer. Just cultivate quick-wittedness with ears as well as eyes. As has been said so often we see but don't perceive or apperceive. We come before some one who is dressed conservatively and we offer something loud or flashy, or we do the reverse—try to sell conservative goods to those who obviously have been preferring more conspicuous merchandise. We talk about elementary facts to a man away up in technical knowledge maybe. We hear but we don't heed. The customer, unconsciously, perhaps, drops a hint with his first few remarks of what he is likely to buy. It often goes "in one ear and out of the other," and the salesman shoots wide of the mark by offering something that the customer doesn't want or advancing some argument that does not appeal and which probably only nettles him.

Observe, listen, and keep on observing and listening. By so doing you will sharpen wonderfully your power to "size up" customers and to adapt yourself to them.

Of late years some preposterous claims have been made for the so-called art of "reading character instantly." Only God has this instant and accurate insight. There is no good evidence that He has revealed the secret fully to mankind. To deceive ourselves into thinking that we can master a few things about races or types of people or study physiognomy a little and be sure of our judgment of every person we meet, with only a few minutes' observation, is to run the risk of most embarrassing errors. On the other hand, it has no doubt been made possible for us, by developing our powers of observation and the continual study of types, to constantly become more accurate in our judgments. There is nothing secret or mysterious about this. Before it can talk, the child knows those who like children and those who do not. It perceives this by undisguised study of our faces. We grown folks have just neglected this study, that's all. We have filled our minds with opinions, thought-habits, and set ways of doing things. All we need to do is to open our minds to new impressions and be guided accordingly.

Any attempt to form classifications or to define types of coloring, physical characteristics, etc., and to say that these call for certain procedure by the salesman, would be running the risk of becoming dogmatic and forgetting about the exceptions that are sure to come. Take, for example, the statement of one well known character-reader that persons of the blonde type are more fickle or changeable, as a rule, than those of the brunette type. It may possibly be true that in a thousand blondes there will be more fickle or variable people than in a thousand brunettes, but even if this could be demonstrated as an absolute, scientific fact, it does not help us in deciding whether any one blonde person that happens to be before us is of the fickle type or the opposite.

In a recent issue of the *Sample Case*, a magazine issued for experienced salesmen, a contributor gave the advice that the man having coarse hair responds favorably to profane and racy language. Such advice is not well founded. The coarseness of a man's hair is no reliable indication of his refinement or lack of it. Any one can review his acquaintances and prove this for himself.

And so it is with the study of head shapes, noses, eyes, mouths, chins, and skin. It is reasonable to suppose that the Creator intended our faces to be to some extent a reflection of the inside man, which is the real man. The heavy jaw instantly conveys to us the message that the person is determined. The weak, receding chin suggests indecision and pliability, but these are only suggestions. The heavily jawed person may be found, on close acquaintance, to be flabby in his mental make-up, and the person with some facial indication of a weak will may have developed a strong will.

Sometimes it takes us years to get a true measure of people's characters. Let's not, therefore, as salesmen flatter ourselves that we can be cocksure of the people with whom we deal when we have had only a few minutes in which to study them. Be ready to adapt yourself progressively, so to speak, as your acquaintance with the customer unfolds itself.

Fortunately, we do not have to go to a well equipped chemical laboratory to analyze and study humankind. We are daily in the midst of a great laboratory, in our contact with men, women and children of all types. If we are keen about adding to our knowledge of human nature and if we hold ourselves constantly open to fresh impressions, we can increase daily that big asset of every salesman—every business person, in fact—the ability to understand and to handle people.

The face of the customer is perhaps the best source of study, but the voice, too, tells a great deal. The well modulated tone at once suggests education and refinement. Harsh, boisterous talking indicates something else, the nervous, hesitating speech still something else.

It is obvious that what the customer says, thus revealing something of what is in his mind, is a fairly trustworthy guide in dealing with him. In no other way can you get so good a clue as to what is passing in his thoughts.

Finally, the dress and bearing of the customer must be studied. As all of us realize, it does not do to jump at conclusions about dress.

Awkward, shabbily dressed people may have considerable money to spend, while expensively dressed people who run around in fine automobiles are often penurious about certain kinds of purchases and go where they can save the last penny.

The lesson, therefore, is plain. Get all the guidance you can from all these sources. Though you will not be able to deal with your customers with perfect understanding in all cases, you will, by your eye and ear quick-wittedness, at least have a reasonable understanding of the person whom you want to guide to the point where he will gladly exchange his money for the thing you have to sell. When you adapt yourself you will be less likely to press to a decision the type of customer who declines to be pressed. On the other hand, you will not fail to throw out strong suggestions to the type who must really be persuaded or helped to take action.

While the variety in personality is endless, there are, at the same time, common characteristics seen so often as to make up familiar types.

The phlegmatic, slow-to-comprehend person is one familiar type. With such people the salesman must be unusually careful to make everything simple, and to repeat until he is sure that he is understood. Such a person is very likely to have little imagination. This means that the salesman must demonstrate the article before he can make its merits clear.

Then, there is the opposite type, the nervous, alert customer, quick to understand and likely to be impatient with laborious explanation. He thinks you should be smart enough to see when he understands. Such a person is likely to be pronounced in his likes and dislikes and not very open to suggestions as to what he should buy. At the same time, in his confidence and in his quickness, he is likely to overlook some really vital thing that the salesman can tell him. It is for the salesman to sense this and to lead the way skilfully back to the point or feature on which the attention of this customer can be concentrated. The discerning salesman understands that, in general, if there are no physical defects, a man's tongue keeps pace with his mind; that is, if he talks slowly he is thinking slowly. Hence, it is a mistake to rattle along at a rapid rate with a man of plodding, phlegmatic temperament. Take time to explain everything clearly. It may even be best to check up with some such question as, "I wonder if I have made that clear?"

On the other hand, the man of rapid thought becomes bored with detailed explanation of things that he can grasp quickly or information with which he has long ago become familiar. He is likely to become nettled if the salesman will not press on and give the exact information that he is looking for. If the salesman persists in sticking to deliberate explanation of familiar matters, the quick thinker will probably exercise his smartness by thinking ahead of the salesman and figuring out reasons against the salesman's conclusions.

Flattery is a rather dangerous tool but the vain customer exists and must be dealt with accordingly. When it is obvious that the type is one with which judicious compliment is the magic touch, use it.

But having succeeded with compliments, or even a little flattery with the vain customer, don't try it on the dignified or opinionated customer who may be quick to tell you, "I don't care what you like. I am the one to be satisfied."

Then, there is the skeptical or suspicious person who must be won by a show of frankness. Surprise him with some such statement as "You are exactly right about that. The goods won't give that service and we wouldn't want you or any one else to buy them thinking that they would."

The weak, irresolute type is also a common one. Such people have to be lead skilfully by suggestion to a preference and to the final act of taking the article. These require patience and often some of the familiar devices that salesmen use in closing a sale.

But by far the largest customer-type of all is the good average American man or woman, not of very pronounced characteristics but possessing a good variety of qualities. These are neither stingy nor extravagant. They are not stupid or slow, but, on the other hand, are not so keen or confident that they do not welcome information from capable salesmen. They are susceptible to the art of selling. They are square and good-natured when we treat them right.

No, no; you don't need rules for dealing with this every-day type of American man and woman. Just give them your best attention, do what your judgment dictates and your sales record will be satisfactory.

WANTED—TEAMWORK!

Some time ago, when I was in a hurry for an express shipment, I went around to the express office. Had a large box, sent on such-and-such a date from Philadelphia arrived?

"When was it shipped?" I was asked, and I gave the information.

"It may have come in this morning, but you will have to take that up with our Receiving Department," volunteered the young woman at the counter.

Oh, thought I, this is a self-serve business office. "Would you mind," I asked timidly, "leading me to your Receiving Department so that I can get this coveted information?"

"It isn't in this building. It is over at the P—— Railway station."

"Don't you have any information here as to what has been received?"

"No."

"You cannot tell a customer anything about what has arrived?"

"No, you will have to ask our Receiving Department about that."

"Do you have telephone connections?" I persisted. "Do you ever get this information for customers?"

"There's the telephone; you can use it. The number is———."

And so I stepped up to the telephone, got my number and gave a big express company an illustration of how a customer can learn for himself whether or not his merchandise has been received.

"Thanks awfully," I murmured when I had finished my telephoning. And then I added to this representative of the express company: "I serve a large corporation that ships many cars of merchandise daily. I wonder what a customer of ours would think of us if he called, asked about a shipment that we had made and we told him that he would have to apply to our Shipping Department for that information—that the business office did not have anything to do with shipping."

But I think that my irony was completely lost on the clerk. She was thinking about "my department" and caring nothing about the impression that a patron gets of a business as a whole when one employe passes along the trouble or responsibility to another without any attempt to cooperate or coordinate.

"Passing the buck" is rather commonplace slang, but it is expressive. There is a terrific amount of it in business offices, hotels, stores, factories, and everywhere else where many people are employed.

How often have you telephoned, told your story to some one who listened until you were through and then replied, "You will have to talk to Mr. B—— about that. Good-bye." No advice, no regret, no promise to take the matter up with the proper person.

Of course it is true that often something does come to an employe that he or she is not in a position to handle properly. But how much finer it is in such cases for the employe to say: "It is too bad that you had trouble. Rest assured we want everything to be right. I could take a memorandum of this but I believe you would find it more satisfactory to talk direct with Mr. X——. Just wait while I have Central connect you with him."

There is one thing in business life that I should like to swat with a club about the size of a telephone pole, and that is this narrow view of "my department" or "my work." Thousands of people seem to think it clever if they can dodge responsibility—especially if something has gone wrong—if they can show that the thing under discussion is none of their work and pass the customer along to the next fellow.

The customer does not give a rap about departments. When he thinks of a business he thinks of it as a whole. And the good-will of a business is wrapped up in it as a whole. If its packing or delivery is poor, the business as a whole suffers.

Therefore, every true salesman is jealously concerned about the reputation of the whole business. He is willing, more than willing,

to give every customer, every inquirer, earnest attention and to do what is required, if possible. If it turns out that he cannot attend to the customer fully, he will go out of his way to see that the customer gets prompt and proper service. He will not, by act, word, or expression, indicate that he is anxious to dodge—to "pass the buck." Nor will he reflect on other departments, other employes or the policies of the firm.

I like to hear salespeople say "we" and think "we," for that means that the individual has the interest of the business as a whole at heart.

The skilful football or baseball player is always ready to sacrifice his turn if by so doing his team can win. We call that "teamwork."

It means as much in business as it does on the ball field.

WHEN THE SHOPPER BRINGS A FRIEND

An earnest salesman confides in me that the most difficult situations he has to cope with are those occasions when the shopper brings a friend along to help her pick out the suit, the hat, the davenport or whatever else she may be thinking of buying.

"It happens right along," says he, "that I can please the customer but then the friend jumps in with 'Oh, I don't like that at all,' and away goes the good start I have made on my sale. Would that you or some wise adviser could tell us what to do with the pesky friend of the shopper."

Come, let us reason together.

Isn't it true that, after all, most sales have to please more than one person? Suppose the customer does come alone. The chances are that when she gets home, that suit, hat or davenport has to command the approval of some one else in the home circle or some outside

"She looks well in this, doesn't she?"

friend, or back it comes—if it is returnable merchandise. The people who check up returned merchandise can say something pointed on that.

May it not be better, in the long run, to have the customer bring her best friend along and that the salesman shall work for the approval of both while they are in the store and make a sale that stays sold?

It strikes me that too often we are inclined to forget that goods sent out are far from being sold unless all the conditions have been met. If the objections and criticisms come up in the home you will not be there to meet them, and when goods come back as being unsuitable it is then almost impossible to save the situation.

At any rate, I think my friend, Mr. Earnest Salesman, will agree that it is poor tactics to show by word, act, or expression that you are critical of the presence or the opinions of the friend. Start right with the friend by being agreeable and catering to her opinion and tastes.

I recall that once upon a time I went with a relative to a music store to aid in the selecting of a piano. The piano man, like the salesman first referred to, had two people to please, but he was a real strategist. When the selecting had narrowed down to two instruments, he played a little on both, and then asked for my opinion of the tones. I thought that one had a somewhat sweeter tone than the other, and I said so.

"You have a good ear," he remarked—not gushily but in a matter-of-fact way. Whether his remark was a real compliment or mere flattery, I have no way of telling. But I was pleased, and the piano that was finally purchased was the one that had appealed most to me. His method of conducting the sale was such that he had me working with him rather than against him.

So, I believe this problem of meeting the views of two people consists largely in showing a consideration for the second person—he or she who comes along not to buy but to pass critical opinions and to advise.

Try taking a positive rather than a neutral or negative attitude. By this I mean say to the friend: "She looks well in this, doesn't she?" rather than "Don't you like her in this?"

Go further, if you have to, and get the friend's view first, if the customer seems very much dependent on the opinions of her adviser. Say: "What is your choice between these two selections? Which is the better style for her, do you think? I know she wants this to meet the approval of her friends and I value your opinion." Such remarks must, of course, be made quietly and tactfully so as not to have the customer feel that you are reflecting on her ability to choose for herself. If you go too far in flattering the friend you will antagonize rather than win her. Real deference to her views and real compliments are safe.

Perhaps there are cases where it may seem advisable, finally, to oppose the advice of the customer's friend and say, pleasantly, "In spite of your friend's opinion, I believe this will be a most satisfactory selection for you. Different people have different views, of course. That's why we carry such a large selection, and, after all, you are the one who will wear the suit. You like it and if you are pleased, your pleasure means more than anything else."

But I am strongly inclined to the method first suggested. The orator, the politician, the preacher, all must appeal to a crowd. The lawyer has a jury of twelve to sway and one of these unconvinced can tie the verdict. Why should the capable salesman lack confidence in his ability to deal with a group of just two?

Get the range of both the buyer and the adviser. Start right with both. Don't forget that the friend is a possible buyer too. Maybe, with skillful handling, a double sale can be made. It has been done!

THOSE QUEER CUSTOMERS

These expressions are familiar ones: "I never could stand people of that type." "Don't that sort get on your nerves?" "What on earth do some people expect?"

They mean about the same thing—that some customers please us, and we get pleasure out of giving them service; that other types irritate us, and service to these is an unagreeable or disagreeable job—so much so that we show it whether we intend to or not.

Whenever I hear such remarks or see hostile or critical glances, my mind goes back to the greatest race of merchants that the world has ever known—the Hebrews, who are in business to do business and to whom we have to take off our hats, so far as salesmanship goes. These born merchants do not think any less of the dollar that comes from the pink-haired woman, or have any hesitancy about giving their best service to the man who wears purple socks or the one who talks noisily in the presence of those who like quiet conversation. They recognize that business is not the place for petty dislikes.

Now, if a salesman is so fortunate as to be able to choose just the people with whom he prefers to do business, that is quite another matter. This talk is not addressed to such exclusive mortals. It is for those men and women who go into selling as a business—one of the greatest in the world—prepared to study all of the one thousand and fifty-seven varieties of people and to give all of them ideal service, if that be possible.

What does it mean, anyhow, when we say we don't like certain types of people? Some are prejudiced against fat folks, for example. Why, I wonder? It will help all of us to study the psychology of likes and dislikes a little.

The first truth is that we allow ourselves to jump to conclusions. I have a business friend whose friendship means much to me. I am heartily ashamed of the fact that I allowed my first impressions of him to be so unfavorable and to sink so deep that my judgment was warped and for a year or more I did not give the man credit for what he was. Fortunately, we were so thrown together that we learned to know each other well. Despite his conspicuous faults, he is an admirable character, and I am glad to know him and to do business with him. At one time it irritated me merely to hear him talk. This experience taught me a great lesson.

If only we knew people well—knew their good points as well as the unfavorable side—we would be more charitable. Snap judgments are unfair.

The second truth is that some other salesman can get along smoothly with the people we don't like. This leads to the simple conclusion that the only reason we didn't get along with those people well was that *we did not try to get on a plane with them.* We stood aloof in our sacred exclusiveness. We did not do as the great Apostle Paul did, "become all things to all men."

We can't do business with Tony, the Italian; Susanna, the colored maid; the overworked, stinted housekeeper with her little brood of children; the crabbed old man in his dotage, unless we get down to business, broaden our point of view, try to get the viewpoint of such customers and deal patiently and sympathetically with them.

When we do all this we become bigger men and women. Every earnest effort to get on the plane with an unusual customer, to serve that person well and make a new business friend, is one more bit of development for Mr. Salesman or Miss Saleswoman.

Recently I heard a sales manager pass this comment on one of his men: "Fred isn't lazy but he works the same way with every customer—has no variety or flexibility in his style. His method is all right when it happens to fit but there are types of customers that he can't handle at all; he just irritates them. He can't seem to grasp the idea that the first thing a salesman, like a gunner, must do is to get the range." Does this comment cover you?

Who are we that we should set ourselves up as judges and put people down as cranks, curiosities, or "impossibles?" The business of selling is a service. The real manufacturer, the real merchant, the real salesman are in existence to serve all that need the goods produced, and serve them well.

THE "MONOSYLLABIC" SALESMAN

The name I am giving him isn't exactly accurate, for now and then he did get away from words of one syllable and say something more than "Yes" and "No," but he seemed determined to say as little as possible, and "monosyllabic" is a fair description of his sales talk.

I was out looking for some new fishing lines and possibly a better reel than any that I own. Of course, I realize right here that thousands of people who are selling dress goods, shoes, jewelry,

---

"No"—"Yes"

"Humph?"   "Um-humph"

"Anything Else?"

"That all?"   "Good-day"

(also Good-night!)

THE "HOW-NOT-TO-SELL" CHART

plows, washing machines or furniture will say when they read this: "Oh, that doesn't apply to my work. My merchandise isn't fishing tackle." Isn't it odd, though, that salesfolk will jump to the conclusion that a principle of salesmanship must be applied to the *identical thing* that they sell before it is of any value? One of the most valuable things that I ever applied to the sale of building material—a phase of selling that I know considerable about—was taken from the business of a manufacturer of cream separators.

The truth that is illustrated by this Better Selling Bulletin, and the truths of all Bulletins that have preceded, can be applied to almost any business in which a salesman is engaged. All we need to grasp is the knack of adaptation—of taking a lesson from the other man and applying it to our particular job.

I told Mr. Monosyllabic Salesman that I wanted a good fishing line. He set out a tray of them, and he also set his face. He was almost as uncommunicative as a wooden Indian. I was foolish enough to think that he might know a great deal about fishing lines, that presently he might ask me just what kind of fishing I was planning to do and make a recommendation. But he didn't. I might just as well have been in a Piggly-Wiggly store, looking at goods piled up in bins or on shelves and serving myself.

Finally, on the chance that this young man might be extremely modest and needed only a little encouragement to set his mind and tongue a-going, I picked up a spool of line that looked as if it might be something particularly good and asked a question about it. "It's a good line," he replied. I told him that I had guessed it was, and after he had lapsed into silence again, I did a little scouting and learned from the label on the spool that the line was Japanese silk thoroughly impregnated, not merely washed, with a waterproofing compound that made the line permanently waterproof. I also learned that running right down through the center of the line was a single, strong thread of silk on which the other silk was braided, which combination made an unusually strong line, though it was light in weight. The finest kind of selling points!

Then I asked if experience had shown that the waterproofing made the line stiff so that it would not reel out freely. "I guess not," he replied, "lots of 'em buy that line." He was frank, he was, for he said he "guessed." He didn't know anything about lines and apparently wasn't interested in knowing.

A salesman at another fishing-tackle store was just as frank when he showed me some reels. "Has this reel jeweled bearings?" I asked. "Hanged if I know," he answered, "truth is, mister, I know darned little about reels."

Again I thought of the Piggly-Wiggly stores where the customer goes in, wanders around among the exhibits of goods, learns what he can from labels, and gets along without the services of a salesman.

And then the next day I went into still another sporting goods store, where the man at the fishing tackle counter knew a lot about fishing, and fishing goods, a salesman who took great pleasure in finding out what the customer had in mind, the use he was going to make of his purchase, who could tell you all the little differences between various kinds of lines, reels, etc. It was a pleasure to buy from that fellow, and I went out with a lot of pride in the high-class goods that he helped me to select.

Not many buyers like the chatter-box type of salesman but there's no room in modern merchandising for the man or woman of the other extreme, who knows little or nothing about goods and doesn't want to know, who has to be quizzed by the customer as a lawyer quizzes a reluctant witness in order to pry out a little information.

It is perfectly true that there are staple goods that most customers are familiar with. It would be a waste of time to talk about them. But these are practically sold when the customer enters the store. They are well adapted to the Piggly-Wiggly system of selling, which uses a label instead of a salesman. Stores are full of other goods requiring intelligent salesmanship.

Know goods. Be enthusiastic about them. Cater to the customer's needs or interest. "Yes" and "No" conversation isn't salesmanship.

MAKING THINGS CLEAR

It's no easy thing—this job of making things so clear that the people we are dealing with cannot misunderstand. But if those with whom we are dealing don't understand us, our chances of exchanging our merchandise or service for their money is very slim.

An editor recently asked me what the Great War taught me, and after thinking a while I said I thought the biggest business lesson I got was the necessity for reducing things to the simplest possible explanations.

"Bond" is a little word of just four letters, and we thought that most people knew what it meant, but many thousands of people didn't know. Some thought, when they were buying government bonds, that they were giving the money to their government instead of buying the best security in the world and really *lending* money instead of *spending* it. What a job it was to drive home the lend idea! Others thought that the interest on the bonds was something that they paid to the government instead of something the government paid to them.

And so it was through the food conservation period, the War Chest campaigns, etc. Unless explanations were reduced to very simple terms and made over and over again, many of the people we were aiming at didn't understand.

It is so easy, when you are on the inside of a business, to get so familiar with what you sell and do that you imagine other people know what you know. Or maybe what you say about your products gets commonplace to you through so much repetition and you decide to eliminate the explanations.

Customers won't always tell you that they don't understand. Usually they have a little pride about confessing what may seem to be slowness or stupidity.

The other day I saw a dancing teacher instructing an adult pupil. She explained something that was very simple and easy to her and the pupil politely said "Yes," as if he understood. But she insisted, "Do you *really* understand it?" and he smilingly confessed that he didn't. The explanation had to be repeated again and again before he really understood. It wasn't because he was slow-minded or stupid, but because what she was showing him was thoroughly unfamiliar.

We can't, in selling goods, always come out with a frank, "Do you really understand me?" but in selling merchandise that is evidently unfamiliar to customers, we should be keen enough to sense that fact and take unusual pains to be clear. And we can ask very courteous questions, "Did you ever see this feature before?" and so on. That a customer may understand linens is no reason why she should be just as capable of judging rugs, camping outfits, garden hose, washing machines, or vacuum cleaners. Indeed, unless a salesman has good reason to believe that a prospective customer has a good understanding of a commodity, it is better to proceed with an explanation of the simplest points.

Just a few days ago a tailor showed me a piece of goods that he called "machine-made homespun," with a harder, closer weave than the hand-made article. He passed his hands over the goods to indicate the harder finish, and I followed him. But he didn't stop there. He detached a thread and showed me the hard twisting. He broke the thread to show its strength and passed part of the thread to me to break. He indicated with thumb and finger how hard it was to press the weave apart, and compared the weaving with that of a more loosely woven cloth. In short, he left nothing for me to guess about. Maybe I would have understood some of this anyhow, but he took no chances. He is the owner of his business and he has learned that it doesn't pay to take chances when a full explanation sells goods!

And then later I stood in a shop and heard a customer ask a question about the Corona Typewriter. That question was answered by the salesman but not a word was said about the weight of the handy little machine being only $6\frac{1}{2}$ pounds. Possibly that salesman has said "And it weighs only $6\frac{1}{2}$ pounds" so many times that he is tired of saying that or thinks that everybody ought to know it by this time. Not so. Five years from now the really keen salesmen of Corona Typewriters will say as impressively as they did last year, "And it weighs only $6\frac{1}{2}$ pounds."

Few things have been sold longer than shoe leather. It might be expected that most folks know what genuine oak-tanned leather is. But one of the world's greatest shoe-selling organizations makes it a point to explain just what "oak soles" are and takes the trouble to expose a small spot of space on the black soles of their shoes so that the tough yellow surface of genuine oak-tanned soles can be seen.

Many jokes and sneers have been directed at the book salesman, but the smart book salesman gives many other classes of salespeople a good lesson. He drills on a canvass that covers every essential point of his merchandise, and though he may vary his presentation to meet individual cases, he aims to cover the ground thoroughly in every case and will do so unless extraordinary conditions prevent him. He has learned that a complete canvass pays better, week in and week out, than haphazard procedure.

The customer's doubts and perplexities kill many a sale that is within easy reach. Anticipate them and apply the remedy—painstaking explanation of all the essential points.

THIS THING THAT WE CALL TACT

A young business acquaintance of mine is just now resigning a very good position—one full of opportunity. He admits frankly and sorrowfully that he is getting out and starting his career all over again with another concern just because he has not been tactful. He sees, when it is too late to help matters, that he has been tactless with employer, associates and customers.

At times, his lack of tact has made this young man disrespectful to his superiors. Among his associates, his inability to rule himself has bred distrust and jealousy. Talking too freely of matters he should have kept to himself put him in a position where others would not risk talking with him if it could be helped. He did not even keep to himself the amount of salary he received but talked about it and stirred up trouble with several employes receiving salaries smaller than his.

Over the telephone and in face-to-face talk, this acquaintance of mine was often "frank" with customers to the point of rudeness. Perhaps he didn't mean to be. Give him the benefit of the doubt. Just the same, he lacked tact—lacked control.

No matter how much speed he has or how wonderful an assortment of curves, no baseball pitcher can win games unless he has that essential thing that we call "control." And no man can win in the business game without control.

Tact may be defined as "saying (or doing) the right thing at the right time."

Being tactful is another of the fine arts. Of course it involves a study of the people we deal with, for what might be tactful with one person might be altogether the wrong thing with another.

It is fairly common to hear retail saleswomen address their women customers as "My dear." There are those who like being addressed this way, or who at least do not mind. In dealing with little girls it would not be out of order at any time, but generally speaking, such a term is entirely out of place with adult customers and may be resented. Use the name—"Mrs. Blank," or else "Madam" or "Ma'am." It is risky for the specialty salesman to leave off the "Mister" in addressing his customers and prospective customers until he is sure of his ground.

Time and again I have been urged by salesmen to buy some article just because "it is all the rage." I happen to be conservative in my tastes. Consequently, that a thing is "all the rage" is a very good reason why I would not buy it. This selling argument, used tactfully, however, might on occasion be effective.

A woman may be decidedly stout, but I question whether it is ever tactful to refer to her figure as a stout one. There are ways of getting around such a delicate situation. We can say that something is

"They always want something that we haven't got."

very suitable for "figures like yours," or "a woman of your style."

Those who like to follow the crowd will be impressed with the information that many of their friends and neighbors have bought what the salesman is showing. There is the other type of buyer with whom such procedure is untactful.

In a store not long ago I watched a salesman show a customer two different types of articles. Neither suited. When the customer asked if the store didn't have something else the salesman shrugged his shoulders and said, "Nothing else. You know, they always want something we haven't got." Of course the customer construed his "they" as referring to her. Perhaps it is the truth that customers are occasionally unreasonable in what they expect the store to handle, but it wasn't tactful to say so. The tactful thing is to be genuinely sorry that the establishment lacks just what the customer wants.

It is easy to snap back at the customer who wonders why the firm carries so many cheap things. The salesman of tact will explain graciously that the largest demand is for the popularly priced styles: "It is the exception rather than the rule that a customer wants the quality that you appreciate and are willing to pay for."

Being tactful means being broad in dealing with the almost unending variety of tastes and likes. No one can ever be a successful salesman or buyer who can't get away from the personal point of view and see things with the eyes of others.

"We don't carry the ordinary lines" may be uttered by a salesman without any intention of reflecting on the taste or buying ability of the customer but such a remark is untactful and might easily offend. It is unquestionably very difficult at times to refrain from a little curtness, sarcasm or irony, but these are not business-builders; be wise—cultivate instead courtesy, patience and tact.

The tactful salesman keeps clear of controversies on religion, politics and other dangerous subjects. He does not knock the goods and policies of his own firm or even those of his competitors.

Tact is a prime essential of successful salesmanship that must be instilled into salesmen. The sales manager of an insurance company illustrates this by citing the instance of how a wife objected to the husband's taking out a policy on the ground that the money she might receive at her husband's death would be "blood money." She could not, she declared, bear the thought of using such a fund.

The salesman paused a moment. He gave the woman credit for being entirely conscientious even if entertaining a notion based on false reasoning.

"Mrs. Blank," he said, "Don't think me impertinent if I ask if you have a savings account." She had, she replied.

"Well, now, you follow the plan of putting aside a certain amount every week or every month into that fund. You make certain sacrifices to do this, because you and your husband want to manage your affairs on a safe basis. If he happened to die before you did, you would use that money, wouldn't you? The fact that you and he saved it during his lifetime would not make you unwilling to use the money."

Of course her only answer to this argument was an affirmative one.

Then, the salesman built up skilfully the idea that insurance is just a cooperative form of saving and protection. This answer was effective. Had he combatted her original objection with merely a denial and had not used a good illustration tactfully the sale might have been lost.

Especially is tact required when it comes to the discussion of competitive products. Some sales executives argue that competition should be ignored altogether, as if it did not exist. "Talk your own goods," they argue, "and forget absolutely about competition."

While this may be the proper spirit on most occasions, it does not always work out in practice. But competitive claims must be met fairly and quietly and tactfully.

A buyer, describing in the *New York Times* the methods of a tactful salesman, told the following story of how a salesman by the name of Jones dealt with the claims of a rival product:

I had determined, before giving out the order you fellows got, to test out several kinds of the roof cement I wanted. I had had a trial barrel of your stuff delivered to me just a few days before Jones called. In the stock-room at the same time was another trial barrel that had recently come in from one of your competitors. These two had been the last to be tested, and because the others had not shown up as to quality the way I thought they should, it lay between your house and the other one to get the order. My way of testing showed the two to be apparently the same as to quality, which left it a matter of price, and on that basis there was no reason whatever for giving the order to Jones. I told him this and even went so far as to tell him the price the other house had quoted.

Instead of saying he was sorry and backing out gracefully, as many salesmen would have done, Jones asked if the two barrels were still in the stock-room. I told him they were and he asked to see them. Because he had been so pleasant about the whole affair, and apparently had accepted his defeat without a sign of grouchiness, I took him into the stock-room myself. Once there Jones looked at the head of the other house's barrel, and then drew a tape measure from his pocket. He measured the height and circumference of both barrels. He showed me each measurement as he took it and the two barrels proved to be identical in size.

I was trying to figure it all out when Jones quietly remarked that I would lose money if I bought the competing brand. This statement interested me, so I asked him to show me how. He first called my attention to the fact that although the two barrels were identical in size, the contents of the competitor's barrel weighed 150 pounds more than the stuff in yours. In other words, although the quantity in both barrels was equal, the 150-pound difference in the weights made your cost per barrel cheaper, despite the other fellow's lower price per pound. That was the first point Jones made. The second was that although the quality of the two cements appeared to be the same this was not actually the case. The greater weight of the cement in the competitor's barrel Jones said, meant that the stuff was weighted to cover a deficiency in its asbestos content. A retesting of the two cements showed this to be so, and Jones got my business.

THE SAVING QUALITY OF A SENSE OF HUMOR

Whether or not you were an admirer of the late Elbert Hubbard does not matter so far as the subject of this talk is concerned. If you followed his career you will concede that he was a wonderful salesman of what he created. Recently I had occasion to talk with a man who worked closely with Hubbard for a number of years, and I asked him for his impressions of the man who made East Aurora famous. One of his comments particularly impressed me. He said: "Hubbard had a keen sense of humor. *He could laugh at himself*, which is something that few men can do."

I have thought a great deal about that comment—"He could laugh at himself"—could make merry of his own mistakes, blunders, and perplexing situations.

Every one who undertakes to make up a list of the qualifications of a successful salesman or saleswoman puts down *confidence, optimism* and *good nature*. In the first place, the salesman, to a large extent, is an outsider in our affairs. When I say "our" and "we," I mean that for the time being we should put ourselves in the place of the customer, for all of us are buyers at one time or another and the viewpoint of the buyer is the one from which to judge the qualities of good salesmanship. We may seek the product we are thinking of buying and in this way come to the salesman rather than make him come to us, but, taking his work as a whole, the salesman is an outsider. His job is to give us goods or service—maybe both—in exchange for our money. And there is no getting away from the fact that in such transactions we like to deal with pleasant, good-natured people. The man of grim, glum expression, who comes to his daily work steeped in gloom or pessimism, whose talk with customers is cold, sour or pessimistic, who is quick to resent critical or idle remarks from the customer and to get vexed over a little "kidding" from the people who do business with him, is out of place in selling.

The people of Europe during the Great War remarked on the jovial nature of American soldiers. The disposition to joke, to banter, is an American characteristic. It comes into play continually in dealings with salesmen. The customer, feeling that as a buyer he has the advantage, is disposed to put the salesman on his mettle, to see how he can uphold the merchandise or the house he represents, to test his resourcefulness and try his self-control. The real salesman must school himself to stand the test. Of course there are customers who deliberately offer insults, but these are relatively few. The jokes and gibes of the general run of customers are not intended seriously.

I do not hold that because one is in selling work he or she should be servile or sacrifice any self-respect. But one may be reserved, dignified or self-controlled in the face of insolence or insult and stand on a higher plane than those who lose their tempers and descend to abuse or controversy. A courteous "I am sorry" may often be a "coal of fire" on the head of the unreasonable customer. Silence is often more potent than speech.

A. C. Dixon, a well known Baptist minister, used to say that he didn't allow people to hurt his feelings—that if they didn't mean to be unfair or insulting, he would not be so narrow as to put the wrong construction on their remarks, and that, on the other hand, if they really meant to hurt him he wouldn't give them the satisfaction of accomplishing their purpose.

Looking at the matter from another point of view: the man who takes himself or the world too seriously in these days of rapid action and tense living lowers his vitality. Nothing is better established than that anger, grievances, morbidness and the like take mental and physical force out of one's system. These negative moods soon become habits, like everything else that is indulged in frequently, and before long show their effects on the very faces of people—in their eyes, the dropping mouth, the lined face. Such a person is often in grave danger of sinking into a state of mind from which a long uphill fight has to be made.

On the other hand, the smooth, even temperament, the ability to take a little fun in good part, the knack of being cheerful when things don't look promising, to forget troubles and rest the mind by diverting it, is one of the secrets of real success. The troubles of the day are rarely ever as serious as they first appear to be.

No high-class firm prefers to have as its sales representatives the wearer of smirks and silly grins, the giggler, or the salesmen or saleswomen who take life so lightly that they are not the least concerned about their poor work or the success of their firms. But there is actual health and sales power in the laugh. Many a sale has been won through the sheer power of an even temperament and a cheerful smile.

A successful merchant died recently in the town where I make my home. He started in business with no advantages of the kind that are usually called "advantages." But he liked to deal with people and his good nature was unfailing. It was said of him when he passed out, at a ripe age: "He seemed to know every one who ever did business with him, and he had a smile for all."

DON'T JAR THE CUSTOMER WITH FAMILY JARS

Did you ever go into a store in the early morning and hear one salesman haul a fellow-worker over the coals with such remarks as "Where did you put those —— when you had them out yesterday? Yes, you did — no use trying to side-step now! How do you expect anybody else to find stock if you don't put it where you found it," and so on.

I had an experience like that recently. I had to stand by and hear the head of a department give a sharp lecture to a salesman on a matter that did not relate in any way to my call, and I felt much embarrassed. I was sorry not only for the salesman who was being humiliated in the presence of the customer but I was also sorry for the store. I finally ventured a good-natured remark to the effect that I had once heard that all good stores had a rule that family differences shouldn't be discussed in the presence of a customer. But my attempted humor met no response other than a look of annoyance. So I attended to my errand as quickly as possible and got out of the chilly atmosphere.

You have seen ball-playing where there is lack of team-play—where the catcher finds fault with the pitcher, where the second baseman and the short-stop wrangle and two out-fielders roast each other for interference, or supposed interference. The other side chortles with glee when this happens, for it means that they have a good chance to win. They know that no team can play its best when that feeling of shoulder-to-shoulder cooperation is lacking.

The *Dry Goods Economist* tells of an instance when one saleswoman could not find certain goods that the customer wanted and appealed to another saleswoman for information. "There they are right at your elbow," was the impatient response, "If the box was a snake it would bite you!"

Now, the plain fact is that not only is such nagging and bickering the worst sort of salesmanship but it is actually evidence of poor breeding.

When you go into a home you are astonished, besides being made to feel very uncomfortable, if the head of the household lectures his wife in your presence or the wife nags the husband or shows her temper. You do not feel that it is at all proper for a son or a daughter to be reprimanded while you are there as a guest. You feel—and you are right—that such unagreeable matters should be taken up in private, that all public evidences of them should be treated in dignified silence.

It should be the same way in a business family. It is too much, of course, to expect that a large group of employes can always be in perfect harmony. But differences that must come up should be discussed and settled in private. Don't let the store suffer.

Said a business man, when a general automobile agent began to discuss his complaint against the action of a sub-agent: "Please don't bring me into any quarrel that you may have. I have bought one of your automobiles after planning the purchase for about two years. I have a lot of pride in owning the machine. Don't spoil my fun by dragging me into your family fuss. Get together in the

Knocking, bickering and scolding turn the customer's thoughts away from buying, which should be made a pleasure.

back office and pull hair all you like, but leave me out. I'm your customer."

There is still another kind of jar or difference that should be kept away from customers, and that is disagreement with the policy of the firm. Just as soon as a salesman lets me know that he thinks his firm is acting small or unfair, he drops in my estimation. I honor him for saying, confidently, "This is the practice of the firm," and giving good reasons for the practice as far as he is able. He should believe that his employer is trying to do the right thing. If he doesn't think that, he ought not to be in the job. Even though the customer insists that some practice is wrong, and the salesman must say something, it is better to be non-committal and say: "Of course, there is something to that but the firm, after careful consideration, decided," etc.

Second-raters and third-raters blurt out their feelings, no matter who hears. The good salesman, like every other man or woman who practices self-control, knows that there are times when silence is golden.

LET THE LOOKER LOOK

Big rentals or big purchase-prices are paid by merchants for select corners in the "down-town shopping district." Why? The question almost answers itself. There's where the crowd is. There's where stores can be conveniently visited, and goods easily seen by people. To be where the public can't easily come in and look at what you have for sale is to court failure.

A tremendous yearly expense is incurred by all large stores for window space and for the services of expert merchandise-display men. Again why? For the obvious reason that the first important step in retail selling is placing goods so that people will be attracted by them.

If, then, it is so important to have a good location, where Our Store may get the attention of a large proportion of the passing crowd, and so vital to have Our Goods attractively displayed in the street windows and on racks, floors and counters inside, why in the name of common sense do we hear so much criticism of the "looker?"

Isn't it a fact that Our Advertising keeps impressing on people that we want them to feel free to come in and look around without the least obligation to buy unless they see what suits them? Aren't they warranted in believing, from almost everything that aggressive retail merchants do, that this is our state of mind?

Yet it is not uncommon to see some visitor to a store treated with scant consideration because he or she has been sized up as a "looker." Sometimes people are slighted or snickered at because they are queer looking.

Now the truth is that nobody is sufficiently skilled in "character reading" to pick out the best buyers invariably. And even if it were true that this could be done, it would be only plain courtesy and good business sense to give the less valuable class of trade just as high-grade service as we give to the so-called "better trade." Don't forget about the millions that have been made on profits from small sales and low-priced goods.

Nowadays it is more difficult than it ever was to tell who is the good buyer. Some very well dressed person may not have a bank balance of ten dollars, may, in fact, have hundreds of dollars of overdue debts, while some rough, illiterate customer may have been drawing extraordinary wages and have a bank-roll the size of a small muff.

We are prone to judge people from our first impressions of them. That is human, of course, but every one of us has made enough mistakes in this direction to teach us the lesson that it is never wise to jump to conclusions. An intimation that the customer before you is looking merely for cheap stuff may be insulting. On the other hand, you are never going to insult people by showing them better goods or more goods than they eventually buy.

There's another side to this subject that sometimes gets little thought—what the visitors to Our Store say to others about their experiences. Any keen merchant will tell you that he would give a great deal of money to have everybody who goes away from his store speak well to their friends of the way they were treated. It is the most valuable kind of advertising—the kind that money can't buy; it has to be won by service.

A new depositor in a large national bank who opened his account with an unusual balance was asked if he minded saying what brought him to the bank. He replied that his mother had wandered into the bank sometime before to ask for some information and had been treated so courteously that when "Father's insurance money came we thought we would deposit it here." What is good practice for a bank is good for a store.

It is human nature to like to look at attractive goods. And "a looker" sometimes likes to look goods over without being followed up or watched too closely by salespeople. Nobody can give you a rule about this but it really requires good judgment to give customers just enough attention and still let them feel perfectly at ease in looking over the goods of one section or wandering around the store. The salesperson who is alert will be able to tell from some little act or look of such a customer when he or she wants information or attention.

Some salesmen go even so far as to say that they make no outright effort to detain or dissuade shoppers when they indicate a desire to "look elsewhere before deciding." These salesmen recognize that the desire to look, to shop, is instinctive, particularly with women, and must be dealt with tactfully. Their attitude is: "All right, do that and satisfy yourself fully," and then having said this, they give a little parting canvass on the goods that seemed to have made the best

TALKS ON BETTER SELLING

impression. It frequently happens that the customer buys before looking elsewhere, or else soon returns to buy.

THE PLACE OF THE COMPLIMENT IN SELLING

It is held by some teachers of salesmanship that everybody can be flattered and that tactful flattery is often a powerful aid in making a sale. Perhaps so. Almost any device or expedient is sometimes a winner.

But it has never seemed to me that it should be necessary to resort to plain flattery any more than it should be to resort to lying. There are many of us who prefer to win our salesmanship victories with higher methods.

The trouble is that we don't watch for opportunities to give the deserved compliment or don't take advantage of the opportunities

"You are a good judge of values."

when we do see them. We are so eager to set forth our selling talk that we forget that the sale—if it takes place at all—must take place *in the customer's mind,* not in our minds or in our talk. Our conversation can only lead or encourage the purchaser's thinking. The buyer's mind must be brought from that half-interested stage, perhaps a defensive or even a suspicious state, to an attitude of confidence, then belief, before action, the final step of the selling process, takes place.

If we would pause just a moment now and then, let the customer talk a little and give him or her credit for what has been perceived or expressed, this confident or favorable state of mind may often be induced quickly.

If the customer is unusually keen, shows quick perception of some quality of the article, or exhibits considerable knowledge of it, it is not only within bounds but excellent salesmanship to comment on that.

Suppose, for example, you are selling drawing instruments and the prospective buyer makes a remark that shows acquaintance with such goods. You remark: "I see you know drawing instruments." You are not telling the customer anything that he does not know, but he will be pleased to have you sense his knowledge of the subject. You can then go on: "Then, here is something that you, as a draftsman, can appreciate, as one who does not draw cannot. This device in the joint absolutely removes all spring from the dividers. They stop exactly at the point where you take your measurement from the scale."

Suppose the customer points out the essential or distinctive feature of the article before you do. Such a comment from the salesman as "You have hit the nail right on the head, madam, when you say that the wear of a washing machine depends on............" would be pleasing and effective.

Quote the buyer when this can be done. "As you said a while ago, the main usefulness of a————— is ———————."

I was once in a rug department watching a salesman exhibit a lot of rugs. Following the customer's comment on a certain rug the salesman said, without gush, "You are a good judge of values. This rug is worth exactly $50 more than the other one you liked."

Mind you, he said "worth more," and he made the customer *acquainted with the higher price* while giving her a deserved compliment on her ability to judge values in rugs.

Compliments are often more effective when not too direct. There *are* times when it may be appropriate to say "That looks fine on you," "You have just the right proportions for that coat," but it is more often the case that the quiet, indirect or implied compliment is the more effective: "Few people see that point," "These appeal to every woman who has a finely appointed kitchen," "I was satisfied you would like that but I didn't want to express myself until you gave your opinion," "You maintain such a good standard throughout your office (or your shop) that I knew this would interest you," "You have had the experience in buying to enable you to appreciate the selling value of this garment," and so on.

The risk about the direct, open compliment is that the buyer may be "touchy" about the opinions of salesmen as to good style, what is most appropriate, what would sell best, and so on. He may think such remarks are fresh or presumptive, though they may not have been so intended. So it is best to pass the complimentary comment in the subtle way.

Mere flattery may be dangerous. Compliments given tactfully or when deserved, are always in order and always good salesmanship.

You like to receive credit for what you are, what you see and what you know. Other people are just as human.

APPEALING TO THE IMAGINATION

If you haven't read Lorin F. Deland's little book entitled *Imagination in Business*, do so. It will give you a refreshing and stimulating insight into how appeals to the imagination may help in selling.

People don't always, or even usually, spend their money for merchandise just for the sake of the merchandise itself. A handsome fur piece hanging in a closet means little to a woman. What really appeals to her is the pleasure she has in wearing the fur where other people are.

He who can see in a Thermos Bottle only a mechanical creation with a double wall that keeps the temperature of a liquid inside the bottle hot or cold for a long time is not destined to become a star salesman of Thermos Bottles. He must be able to picture in his own mind the use of the Thermos Bottle on picnics, automobile trips, and the like, and, when occasion requires, he must be able to suggest these pictures skilfully to prospective customers.

He who would sell me apple trees for my city back-yard should be able to picture what a joy a back-yard apple tree may be to a town man—its fragrant blossoms in the spring, its beauty in the fall when laden with juicy red apples, what it means for the children of the home to have such a tree, and so on. These things mean more than the dollar or two that a mere apple tree costs.

The salesman who markets correspondence or evening school courses would make little headway if he talked merely about studying or showed textbooks. To most young men the idea of studying is not attractive. The appealing thing is the future, the career, of the man of special training—the greater responsibility, bigger pay, more privileges that he has. So the salesman paints this bigger self and life as attractively as he can.

Likewise, the purchaser of the well-known "Five-Foot Shelf of Books" is impelled to purchase, as a rule, not so much by the actual value of the books as by the vision of himself as a man with a well rounded knowledge of classical literature. Very likely he is not a college graduate, and he regards this set of books as a way of making up for a cultural education that he did not receive in his younger days.

The Aluminum Cooking Utensil Company has spent considerable money appealing to the imagination of women with respect to their kitchens. The kitchen is represented as the housekeeper's workshop. She is reminded of the many hours she spends in it, and why it should be regarded as a real room of the house instead of something to be endured, of what fine cooking utensils—the tools with which the housewife does so much of her work—mean in satisfaction.

Many salesmen are afraid of the higher-priced goods. But when one draws a realistic picture of what an article of long-time service means it is not difficult to sell at good prices.

I have heard a real estate salesman describe to a prospective home-buyer what it means in the way of citizenship for a man to become a home-owner rather than a renter, how it helps him in business, the satisfaction that comes from getting rid of the mental bugaboo of moving, the real joy that comes to a man when he first sits down to a meal in a home that is his very own, and so on. Possibly the prospective buyer had seen some of these things dimly in his own reflecting, but the real estate man's suggestions gave him a true and pleasing picture that was largely new.

Review your own mental operations when you have had thoughts about purchasing something of real importance to you. You form imaginary pictures of yourself owning the article and perhaps a contrasting picture of yourself trying to get along without it. If you are considering the purchase of several things you picture yourself as owning each of them in turn and you weigh your different degrees of satisfaction. That is what your imagination is for—a frame in which to put pictures, as it were, where you can look at them and see whether or not you care to make a certain picture a reality. Prospective customers have this same imaginative power.

To create sales means creating ideas, and that means appealing to imaginations.

SELLING TO WOMEN

Women make up such a large body of purchasers and so many manufacturers and merchants cater particularly to the woman purchaser that special study and special consideration of her as a buyer and consumer is an important part of present-day merchandising.

Let not the feminine reader take exception to the fact that her sex is singled out for special attention. The merchant who aims to be successful in selling to farmers makes a special study of that large and distinctive group. Likewise, with the manufacturer or merchant who attempts to sell to dentists, doctors, mechanics, or musicians.

We gain something by concentrating study on any group of buyers. Let us not, however, jump to the conclusion, when we have singled out a group according to sex or occupation, that those making up this group are necessarily of similar tastes and temperament. There is a great variety of types among farmers, dentists, doctors, mechanics, musicians, and an even greater variety among such a broad group as women. Age, education, poverty and prosperity, nationality, general environment, etc., account for a great range in tastes and temperament.

Women generally, for example, are not regarded as capable in the investing of money as men. This is undoubtedly due to the fact that they have had less experience in investing. Yet there are women with ability for making judicious investments far beyond that of the "average man."

Women, likewise, are acknowledged to be less proficient in mechanical matters than men. Eleanor Gilbert, in a recent article entitled "The Fear of the Machine," comments on the fear or the reluctance women have about operating even office machines such as duplicating devices. "Few are the women," says she, "who can make simple adjustments on sewing machines, typewriters or household devices.

The possible exception is the automobile." This is largely due to the fact that mechanical work has not, in the past, fallen to women's lot to any great degree. Some "man of the house" adjusted things that went wrong fixed up broken furniture, etc. But the entry of women into factory work where they operate many kinds of machinery, the rate at which women are learning to operate automobiles, and so on, will probably bring about a great change in the proficiency of women in mechanical matters. But for the present it is well for a salesman to take extra pains to explain the mechanical operation of any machine or mechanical device that he may sell to women.

While facing the fact that womankind is of "infinite variety," there are, at the same time, enough distinctively feminine characteristics to afford considerable study.

Lest a "mere man" should overlook some important point of this big subject, I have drawn upon the views of two women very successful in appealing to other women, Mrs. Marion C. Rickert, of New York, formerly one of my assistants in the International Correspondence Schools of Advertising and Selling, and Marion C. Taylor, of Cleveland, a woman of large experience in the field of fashion and women's clothing, who recently gave the Association of National Advertisers a remarkable talk on "The Woman Appeal in Advertising" and who has kindly consented to answer a number of questions.

Mrs. Rickert's views form the greater part of the text under this topic. She quotes a number of Miss Taylor's observations.

The type that best describes the most characteristic American woman of today, whether she is working girl, debutante, business woman, or housewife, has been nicely summed up by Miss Marion C. Taylor, a recognized authority who is competent to speak from her wide experience.

"The so-called 'butterfly' type who rested content with a pretty face and a few gentle accomplishments is almost extinct, and in her place we have today a woman who prides herself upon being 'in the know.' Pride and ambition are the dominating characteristics.

"Your feminine audience today, therefore, whether rich or poor, in the class field or in the mass field, is a body of women keenly alive and interested in pretty much everything that is going on around them. I don't think you could ask for a more responsive audience and I don't think you could find a more critical one."

Miss Taylor has emphasized the point of "keeping pace" with the modern woman. In the small town where the woman hasn't the big shops and fashion exhibits, she has her newspapers and magazines with their abundance of first-hand information on all her interests. "Better to talk the language of your highest type," she says. A woman likes to be thought a notch higher than she is. It is subtle flattery. Failure to recognize her ideas and ideals and appealing to a type that is not representative of an aspiring up-to-date woman, is to risk losing prestige, which is almost the greatest thing a store can have in a woman's estimation.

Women demand quality more than they used to. Not primarily because real quality is economical, but because quality expresses the best style. It is merely the expression of the pace the ambitious modern woman has set for herself. I believe the sweeping statement can be made that in almost everything a woman buys, whether she be able to pay the price or is in moderate circumstances, the appearance of a thing, the beauty or correctness of its *style* count most. The woman *senses* far more than she reasons. She is impulsive, thinks quickly and decides on sight nine cases out of ten.

The modern woman is not so gullible as some merchants still believe. I don't think that anything can be gained by playing on a woman's

"Women are great 'lookers.' They like to browse."

gullibility—or her proverbial curiosity. If a firm advertises a sale of $100 suits for $59.75, which only recently a retailer of a certain town did, there are women credulous enough to "go and see," but I am positive that if the values were grossly exaggerated, as they must have been, this advertiser's statements will not be accepted the second time.

Woman's attitudes are seldom lukewarm. When she is displeased, when she receives a faulty article, or a blunder in service has been made, she is quick to condemn. It pays to gain her confidence, to make completely satisfactory adjustments, and to *take pains* to make them courteously. She not only condemns conclusively, but she commends good service with equal enthusiasm. She is a great propagandist. There are perhaps abundant cases of unreasonable feminine demands, but it does not pay to oppose her views. As Charles R. Wiers, formerly of the Larkin Company, says, "The woman must always be right; argument is futile." There probably always will be the woman to deal with who is a complex bundle of "whims, impulses and ultimatums" and if we cannot understand her, we had better agree with her. I have heard salesmen insist: "That shoe fits you perfectly, Madam!" The tactful, graceful thing to do is to get another shoe and try that—even if there is practically no difference in sizes.

The woman shopper is tremendously impressed by the *way* in which she is served. Sympathetic attention and courtesy put her in a buying mood. Most women are sensitive and proud and feel intensely a store spirit and atmosphere. To be waited upon helpfully and with *interest* is the subtlest kind of flattery. Even to be addressed by name is pleasing.

Your woman shopper is responsive to every influence created by the discerning manufacturer or merchant. Although she may appear to be hurrying, she is not likely to be hurried into a decision. She does not usually come into a store with her mind made up, or if she does, she is not likely to buy only the goods that she has in mind. Women are great "lookers." They like to browse. A browsing woman is in a buying mood.

When a woman is obviously interested as a looker, enter into the search for what she wants and volunteer some purely desire-creating suggestions. Do not hurry her. Do not emphasize the price or in any way try to rush her to the buying point.

One of the most effective ways to make the sale to the woman who is just looking is to *help* her look; to show an interest immediately and as much enthusiasm as you properly can without betraying your effort. In looking at a bargain pile of novelty underpretties one day, the salesgirl was on the job but she did not shadow me. When she saw that I had apparently found nothing suitable and was about to leave, she came up to me immediately: "Didn't you find anything suitable? Just a minute. I saw several especially good-looking styles here I think you'd like." And from the corner of the pile she produced two or three that were just what I wanted. I bought two of them. I was frankly pleased that she sized me up as the quality of the garments evidenced, and I felt that she had cleverly saved such pieces for just such emergencies.

If salesgirls would just use a little more of the knowledge they must have of their own sex, they would not only *sell* but they would enjoy selling. Do not praise everything a woman puts on. Women place great confidence in the opinion of another woman who seems to *know*. The vainest of feminines are not influenced by the flatteries of a saleswoman if she makes no honest effort to find and approve the *becoming* thing. It is a big thing for a saleswoman to build up a reputation for knowing what is correct and appropriate. Most women belong to a type in matters of dress. There can be nothing more interesting or profitable than giving intelligent thought and study to line, color and fabric, and using this interesting information to sell clothes that the wearer advertises every time she puts them on.

For do not forget that women continually advertise you among themselves—what you sell them and how you sell—and that such advertising is valuable enough to be sold right in the first place.

The following are some additional hints on selling to women, drawn from a number of sources.

There are extravagant women, of course, and there are penurious, close-buying men, especially among those men whose every-day work is that of buying, but taking the sexes as a class, women are more careful and more economical buyers of the types of goods sold by the large groups of retail stores. This is true, notwithstanding the apparent extravagance of women in these latter days with respect to the buying of certain classes of goods such as hosiery, shoes, furs, etc. Woman's susceptibility to the attractions of merchandise which has to do with personal adornment may be put down as the reason for her willingness to pay extraordinary prices for such articles.

As C. W. Post used to say, aptly, "There's a reason." Undoubtedly the percentage of women who have their own bank accounts or their fair allowances of the family funds has grown steadily during the past generation, but man still remains the money-earner to a very large extent, and he can be and is freer in the disposition of the family money. It is a truism that the wise woman of the household, when she is tempted to pay a larger price for household equipment than she feels may be justifiable, takes Mr. Man along with her to the store in order to give him the opportunity for saying, "Oh, if that is the thing we want, let's take it."

All of which leads up to the conclusion that with some exceptions—and all rules have exceptions—economy, good value for the price, an opportunity for real bargains, remain and will long remain good selling arguments with women customers. There is sound sense in the saying that women will go a block to save a penny.

Womankind's regard for style always makes it difficult for the salesman to sell to her goods that are out of style and always makes it easier for him to sell to her merchandise that is new, stylish or distinctive.

Styles in the kinds of goods and equipment that men buy do not undergo such rapid changes. The general run of women would almost prefer going without a coat than to have one that "is no longer worn."

It is worth while repeating that women are "born shoppers," and those who sell to them must reckon with that fact. "Why?" asks an experienced retailer, "do women think it is necessary to tell these little white fibs such as, 'I want to think over it,' when they ought to know that we know they mean when they say this that they are going up the street to see what our competitor has before deciding."

A research expert of national fame tells of a suburban general store near a large city that put in a good stock of suits and coats, believing that it was possible to build up a business in such goods. The new department was a failure. Nevertheless, a year later when a new store opened in this suburb, carrying coats and suits principally, the general store again put in a stock of these garments, and both began to do a good business! The secret was that when there was only one store in the community carrying suits and cloaks, women could not compare values—could not shop in a real sense—and they went to the nearby large city. When they could go to two stores, they were satisfied in many cases to make a selection in one or the other.

Those salesmen who have not learned to appeal to the mother instinct, to the housekeeper's pride in beautiful things for the home, have much to learn about the art of selling to women. "You will be proud to show this beautiful silver-like kitchen-ware to your friends," runs an advertisement. It suggests a good point of contact.

In selling by mail to women keep in mind their appreciation of detail. A study of the letters of women shows them to be proficient in describing merchandise that they have bought or seen. They are keen for happy combinations of color, for extra finishes and features, distinctive shapes and styles, and so on.

A woman's interest in the news of the community, what neighbors are buying and using, can be utilized sometimes as a stepping stone. A woman is hardest to deal with in house-to-house solicitation, because there she is constantly fencing against aggressive salesmanship. Nevertheless, remarks about orders taken from people that she knows, what others have said to the salesman about her interest, position, education or her good taste in certain kinds of commodities may be used as opening wedges.

Women are inclined to do a great deal of comparing and may change decisions several times before settling on a purchase, but business experience seems to indicate a keener responsibility on the part of women for their debts than is found in the case of men. A woman may decline to sign formidable-looking contracts or orders, but give her square treatment and she will pay, in a high percentage of cases. Make her happy over some purchase and she will go out of her way to help make additional sales.

There is a tendency on the part of women to exaggerate. The shipment of food supplies that arrived "all smashed up," as she is likely to write, probably had one corner knocked off with one can broken and another cracked. A garment that she may describe as "a horrible fit" can probably be adjusted by a simple alteration. The salesman who shows real interest and exercises patience will soon learn to overcome such situations.

PERSISTENCE PLUS PATIENCE PLUS PERSPICACITY

Once when I was responsible for a good-sized staff of helpers I employed a very intelligent girl. She made a fine impression on me at the outset—confident, clear-eyed, attractive and a good talker. I congratulated myself on having engaged such a "good find." But to my disappointment, this promising candidate, after a number of months, proved to be hopeless. She had brains of a certain kind but no desire to apply herself, no patience to work for improvement, no ability to look at her work and see its faults.

At about the same time I employed another young woman as a helper in the same class of work. This candidate was self-conscious

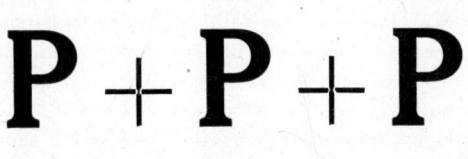

and not at all sure of herself. Only because it was rather difficult at that time to secure helpers did I conclude to give her a chance. This young woman was not brilliant and probably never will be. She never acquired a supreme self-confidence. But she did fall very much in love with her work, and oh, she was persistent, thorough and patient. And the exercise of her *Persistence* and *Patience* aided in the development of that other quality that we call *Perspicacity*. Look the word up if you aren't familiar with it. You will see that it means the knack of discerning clearly.

I have never been much of a chart-maker, nor am I overly fond of toying with words, but as I think of that experience of my own and of experiences I have observed in the work of other employers, I feel that a big business sermon could be preached on the P + P + P text.

Take, first, this matter of persistence. It calls for concentration. We fall short of many of the things of this world that we say we want, just because we don't go after them persistently enough. Did you know that the average young man or young woman is good for only two or three months when a course of spare-hour study is taken up? A brave start is made but the large majority lack persistence. It's the same way with jobs. Most people are drifters. Instead of making most of the opportunity they have, they grow discontented at about the time they have a chance to get ahead and jump into something else with the idea that the new field is a much better one. Sometimes it is. Often it isn't. The new field just looked better at a distance.

Persistence is a winning quality in selling. As I look back over the sales transactions in which I have played the part of buyer, I find that the salesmen who have secured most from me and my office are those who kept persistently and hopefully at their jobs, took my rebuffs and excuses smilingly, wished me well, but kept at the business of selling to me just the same.

Often when a prospective customer seems almost hopeless, a little further attention, a demonstration of some interesting point about the article or the service, will turn a near-sale into a real sale.

And, of course, Patience goes hand in hand with Persistence. One who is persistent but impatient will very likely lose all the force of his persistence. It is a common sight to see the persistent salesman grow nettled over the slow-mindedness or unwillingness of the prospective customer. This is easy to understand, too, but if salesmen would put themselves in the position of the customer and try to look at matters from that point of view it would be easier to be patient. It is only business to be sympathetic with people's whims and broad with respect to their narrow ideas or their ignorance. The biggest men I have ever known were those who were very tolerant with respect to the foibles of other folks. We might as well make up our minds that grown people are only children in a great deal of their thinking and talking and ought to be treated with as much skill and smoothness.

When we add Perspicacity to Persistence and Patience we have a strong combination. The ability to perceive and to apperceive comes only through concentration. You and I might walk for miles and miles and very likely, unless you have studied mushrooms, you would see none, while I would probably see half a dozen lots of them.

Why? Just because my eye, through concentration, has been trained to perceive mushrooms. It is no longer an effort with me.

There are other subjects to which you have probably given more attention than I have ever given. Here your alertness and keenness of understanding exceed mine. Let's not beguile or excuse ourselves by thinking that those who excel were endowed with extraordinary brains. The trouble with us is that we just don't exercise the brain-power that we have. You can't get development of either brain-power or muscle-power without persistent exercise.

It is a fair statement, I believe, to say that the general run of salesmen could easily double their efficiency by thinking of salesmanship as a profession and giving it their best thought.

Only yesterday a skilful salesman of fishing tackle sold me a new casting bait after laughingly telling me that he wanted to show me some new stuff but didn't want me to feel that he was trying to sell me. The clever rascal, with his nice questions and his interest in my collection of fishing tackle, learned what I already owned and what new devices I could use to advantage. He showed me these. I bought. He has perspicacity. He knows that putting out attractive bait means increasing his string of catches. And he sells a lot of fishing tackle.

NEGATIVE, NEUTRAL, AGREEABLE, OR AFFIRMATIVE

The older business men can recall days when, in certain sections of our larger cities, merchants of some of the smaller stores would stand out on the sidewalks and actually take hold of passers-by and pull them into the stores for the purpose of showing goods. There are instances related in which some prospective customers resented this practice to the extent of dealing a blow to the over-aggressive merchant.

The art of showing and selling goods has advanced considerably. It is generally recognized that we cannot take people by the collar, force them to look at goods and bluff, bully or nag them into buying. We have learned that leading is better than dragging, that "a good approach" in selling, whether we are calling on people at their homes or offices or having them come into our stores, means impressing them favorably at the outset, adapting ourselves to their views and thus being able to talk with them on their plane. Sometimes this is called "getting the point of contact" or "striking the responsive chord."

All business offices are familiar with the whirlwind type of salesman who comes prepared to override all obstacles and objections and who almost immediately advertises himself as a pest.

To go at prospective customers without any regard for their wishes or views, or to oppose their opinions bluntly, is what I am pleased to call negative salesmanship. You may possibly browbeat some people into buying, but you will fail in most cases and will do a poor day's work.

The negative sort of salesmanship may consist of mere words or facial expression. Judge the effect on the customer of such comments as: "You can buy that if you like, but it isn't the thing you ought to have and you'll be sorry you didn't take my advice."

"The model is wrong for your use, I tell you, but take it if it will make you happy."

"Sure, take it up with our competitor and see what he has, if you want to get stuck."

Then, there is the neutral, or passive, salesmanship. The salesman or saleswoman of this group maintains the frozen face, or the elevated chin, has no interest in what the customer wishes to see, hands out goods mechanically or leads the way to them wearily or with a bored air. You don't know whether the salesperson is ill, has had a recent love disappointment, thinks herself too good to be at the business of selling, or has a poor opinion of such small-fry customers as you are.

Agreeable salesmanship means getting started right by letting customers feel that it is a pleasure to serve them. There is no hint that the customer's want is too small or too peculiar to command the salesman's best attention.

There is no inclination on the part of the agreeable salesman to force views on the customer. If he or she doesn't like what is shown, there is no resentment or sneer, not even a superior smile. "You don't like that one; well now, let's see, I have another here that is even better quality and of an entirely different design. I'd like to show you that."

Agreeable salesmanship *leads* the mind of the customer. It anticipates what is passing in that mind and tries to adapt suggestions accordingly.

Affirmative salesmanship is all that agreeable salesmanship is and something more. The affirmative salesman is careful not to present his views offensively, but his knowledge of his products is strong, and he can talk with enthusiasm—confident enthusiasm. He is in a position to tell the customer just what service can be expected of a product. He is familiar with the results that other users have had. He doesn't try to show off his vast knowledge of goods, either, but does all this with the spirit of trying to give the purchaser the very best thing that can be had for the price.

He harmonizes, so to speak, with the buyer's views. When he can't agree, he says something like, "Yes, that is true in a way, but—." And his qualifications are expressed pleasantly.

And the affirmative salesman is a good closer. He starts out being agreeable and winds up by proving his case. He knows how to talk about the stock on hand, the market on such goods, the matter of delivery and all that. He is skilfully pressing for a sale, of course, but is careful not to show that. He knows that the customer is better satisfied if he feels that a decision was made without any pressure on the part of the salesman.

A slow, steady pull will move a ship that a quick jerk or shove will not budge. The brand of salesmanship that wins week in and week out, year after year, has that steady, sure influence to it.

MAKING BOOSTERS OUT OF COMPLAINERS

I recall vividly buying a two-piece suit of light material some years ago only to find when the suit was delivered that the trousers had pulled apart at the seam.

When I took the trousers back to the store, the salesman was offensively skeptical. The goods were most carefully inspected, he assured me, and it was practically impossible for a faulty garment like that to go out. Inferentially, he was making me out a liar and a piker. Naturally, I didn't like his attitude. "I know what I am talking about," I said, "I observed this as soon as I took the suit out of the box."

He finally agreed to give me a perfect pair of trousers, but he did it with poor grace and as he passed some other salesmen on the floor he showed the faulty garment and made a remark that I could guess from their smiles. I was much inclined to leave the store without waiting for the exchange.

This was poor work for the store. The faulty goods were replaced, and as long as the policy of the store permitted the replacement, the substitution should have been made willingly. I was more than irritated by the way my perfectly fair complaint had been handled, and it is hardly necessary to say that I never entered that store again.

Recently I was an interested observer when a woman brought back to a shoe store a pair of shoes with the soles in bad order. The salesman—he seemed to be the manager of the place—insisted that the shoes had been worn in wet weather and that such shoes were not made for that kind of wear. The customer insisted that this was not the case, and she seemed to be a good average type of American woman. The salesman finally became decidedly blunt: "You can't tell me anything about that—I know." The woman's face turned a nice rosy red, and with a "I-won't-argue-the-matter further," she stalked out, leaving the merchant in possession of the faulty shoes. I am no infallible judge of human nature, but my guess is that she was telling the truth and that the merchant regretted his attitude before she reached the door.

There's no getting away from the fact that both manufacturers and retailers in these days of liberal policies are imposed on a great deal, that there are customers who do not hesitate to misrepresent and take advantage. It is often difficult to draw the line. But this is certainly true—that if the firm will eventually adjust a certain kind of complaint it is only good sense to do it at once and with good spirit. Even if nothing can be done, the salesman and his firm have all to gain and nothing to lose by being courteous and forbearing.

No matter how well goods are made or how carefully they are inspected, some faulty merchandise will go out. Customers will be disappointed with some of the things they buy. And all of us like to change our minds now and then!

Once when I didn't like something that I had bought I took it back to the store with a little embarrassment. "With pleasure," said the salesman heartily when I asked for an exchange. "Whenever you get anything from us that you don't like when you get it home, fetch it right back or let us know. We want you satisfied."

I'm strong for that store!

A dry goods merchant tells me that he once had a customer bring back to his store a coat that she had bought almost a year previously. She explained why she had not worn the coat a single time, and the appearance of the coat bore out her claim. Styles had changed in the meantime and the garment was no longer salable as a stylish coat. She had the nerve (some women buyers have a lot of it) to ask that the coat be taken back and her account credited. It was a delicate situation. The merchant explained why he couldn't do what she asked but said he would take the coat, make an effort to sell it at a special price, with full explanation of the circumstances to the new buyer, and allow the original purchaser the full selling price received. I don't hold that this was the wisest thing to do. But it at least showed the merchant's resourcefulness in holding customers' good-will.

Give the complaining customer your most careful consideration. Your attitude should be that you are sincerely sorry that either your goods or your service have proved unsatisfactory and are willing—eager—to go to the limit to make the transaction right.

The thing complained of may seem small, even insignificant, to you. That is not the point. The point is that the customer—whose trade pays everybody's salary—is not satisfied. Be attentive and sympathetic. Sometimes a painstaking explanation adjusts a complaint.

Don't shut off the complaint too quickly. Some people feel better after they have expressed their views fully. Then, if you can't adjust the trouble, take it to some one who can, or promise the customer prompt attention. Give your most prompt and careful attention to letters that deal with faulty goods, missent shipments or mistakes in filling orders. Observe the large annual volume of business done by some national organizations that do business on the basis that the customer must be satisfied or the goods may be returned and the money will be instantly refunded.

A growing business must have new customers, of course, but it is just as important, perhaps more important, to retain old customers. Complaints call for much tact. He who can turn complainers into boosters has proved the mettle of his salesmanship.

LITTLE THINGS THAT HELP OR HINDER

Recently I heard an art director of many years' experience talk on the subject of "symbols"—of how a slight detail has a great deal of meaning to it and may play a strong part in turning a reader's or customer's thought into the desired channel. For instance, in a scene showing a married woman and an unmarried one, just the little detail of the wedding ring on the finger of one of the women was the needful thing to make the story suggested by the illustration entirely clear.

A play may be entirely spoiled because one bit of furniture on the stage does not correspond to the period in which the scene is supposed to be laid. A court-room act will be a farce if the court procedure is not conducted in strict accordance with legal custom. Often the effectiveness of a scene depends on a single gesture or facial expression.

All of which has its application to the fine art of selling. A judicious remark or "a fool comment" may make or unmake a sale.

Recently two women were examining some fine glassware in an Atlantic City shop. One of them was evidently in the mood to buy a certain piece, but she was in doubt as to which of two shapes she should select. Said the companion: "Both are pretty but I think the oval shape is probably the newer one." Whereupon the salesman remarked: "Neither one of them is new. Both of them have been here eight years." No comment is needed on such work. Whether it is from lack of power to think or just dowdy indifference does not matter. Certainly, unless one can say something to stimulate or direct the customer's thoughts toward desire and decision, absolute silence is advisable. But why let the wonderful gifts of sight and speech go unused?

Every line of selling, whether it has to do with automobile tires, china, books, kitchen equipment, wire nails, or with watches, affords its opportunity for keen study of merchandise, for keen observation of the people to be served. The following from the American Optical Company illustrates this thought.

It is morning and you look across your counter at an animated young person, all starched and tailored and eager for whatever the day may bring forth. In her eyes is the will to accomplish, and in every brisk movement a hint of the efficiency that is never offensively efficient. And you know at once what she will want. For her no heavy shell spectacles to cover half her face, no "varsities" with dangling ribbons to lasso the unwary by the way, nor yet a metal type frame to make itself conspicuous. She will want first of all, of course, what every woman wants—and every man, too, although we do not wish to be quoted as saying so—a becoming pair of glasses. But she wants more than that. She wants a pair of glasses which being "put" will "stay put," and which will not take it upon itself to fall off into her employer's letter file or her husband's morning coffee—and your mind turns at once to Fits-U mountings. She wants, too, glasses that are inconspicuous, and that at the time same will not interfere with her strenuous work and play—and you know that she must have a rimless mounting fitted with round lenses for a wider field of vision. And straightway you take from your case and lay before her the perfect tailored glass for perfectly tailored people—the Fits-U rimless eyeglass.

Or it is afternoon, and a lady-o'-dreams looks out at you from under her broad-brimmed hat. She, too, you know, will seek a pair of glasses which on shopping tour or at afternoon tea will know better than to embarrass her by falling awkwardly off. And you think again of the Fits-U mounting. One hand goes out toward the rimless tray again,—and then you draw it swiftly back; for you have remembered the new Windsor type in their dainty zylo rims. Deep wine-colored zylo it will be for dusky beauty, or the clearest of crystal for a lady fair. For Milady's glasses, like her fetching little gown, must be chosen not by rule of thumb, but by the many rules of type and occupation and the stern decree of fashion. And so when your hand comes out of your cabinet it sets upon the counter a tray of Fits-U Windsors, beautiful in every detail of design and workmanship.

"Now these——," you begin in your best professional manner.

But she interrupts.

"They're pretty, aren't they?" she says shyly.

And you know that your sale is made.

Here are some of the most common shortcomings on the part of salesmen:

Reflecting on the customer's judgment or taste: it is at times very desirable to guide or mold the customer's views, especially if a wrong notion is likely to lead to dissatisfaction with certain goods, but this must be attempted with much tact. Never say anything like

"You would do a very foolish thing" or "I know you won't be satisfied with that." Better say "I don't want to press you to take something that you don't like but I believe this would give you more satisfaction." It is well to keep always in mind that many different kinds of goods are made for many different kinds of people. It would not do for every one to like the same kind of clothes, shoes, furniture, office equipment or automobiles. Serve, but don't press personal views or tastes.

Dealing in generalities: "This is absolutely first-class quality," when the customer has asked for specific information. The remedy for this general weakness of selling practice is "Know your goods."

Reflecting on competitive firms or goods. The customer is naturally suspicious of all remarks made against competitive goods, because he expects you to be prepossessed in favor of your own firm and the class of goods it carries. It is better to be non-committal with respect to competitive lines, or, if you have to say anything, to show that you can be fair while emphasizing the reason why the customer should purchase what you offer. One can grant something and yet turn a customer's thoughts away from a competitive line: "It is a very nice looking article but it seems to have a poor record of service."

Failure to discover the objection or the obstacle in the way of buying: when prospective customers just don't like things, it is important to find the reason. Then maybe a little explanation of the article being shown or the showing of something entirely different will result in a sale. "Did you want this file for original filing or just for transferring old correspondence?" asked an office-supply salesman when the customer seemed to hesitate over the cost of stacks of well finished files. It turned out that an inexpensive transfer case filled the need exactly and the customer was pleased to be equipped at such a moderate cost. He had hesitated to say that he did not want to pay the cost of a new metal or quartered oak stack.

Often, just at the critical moment, there is a little detail to be pointed out, a well chosen comment to make, that will make the customer entirely satisfied to say "I'll take that."

I remember that once a salesman held my attention, when I was about to turn away, by pointing out a sensible feature about the neckband of a shirt. He made a sale where his chance seemed to be almost lost. He didn't take it for granted that I knew about the feature.

SALES AND NEAR-SALES THAT I HAVE SEEN

The store was one of those very exclusive jewelry places on Chestnut Street, Philadelphia. Maybe I should have had better sense than to go in there looking for a small, moderately priced clock on a wooden base. But I was adventurous that morning and rather tickled over having an excuse to enter this pretentious store.

The gentleman who stood behind the case toward which I advanced was middle-aged, stout and stiff. He was dressed in a severe and dignified style, something like a preacher or a bank president. As I caught his cold eye, it seemed to me that he read me through and knew that I wasn't looking for something high-priced. I told him my want before he made a remark and then he said simply, "We carry nothing below ———— dollars," and he did not move a finger to show me any of those precious higher-priced articles. The truth is that I probably wouldn't have bought one of his clocks, but then a little unbending might have made me feel like visiting that store again when I had something higher-priced in mind. Sometimes I get gay and blow myself to a really high-priced thing. I now feel somewhat timid about going into that Chestnut Street establishment again. It doesn't stand out in my mind as a friendly store.

I stood in another store—a Baltimore one—and watched a glove saleswoman give attention to a customer for certainly half an hour— maybe longer. The woman was of the type that may aptly be called "finnicky." She didn't seem to know what she wanted. In fact, she said so once or twice, but she hung at the counter and the saleswoman obligingly went back to her stock again and again in the hope of finding something that would suit. A number of pairs were tried on and inspected critically by the prospective customer, but invariably the gloves came off. "Somehow I don't just like that," was about all that she would say.

Finally the customer said she guessed she would go over to the B ——————— Store, naming a competitor. This was the last straw, but the pleasant saleswoman was apparently proof against all irritation. She smiled agreeably and said "I'm sorry I couldn't find just what you wanted, but we will have another good stock in next week. Come in again, won't you?"

My hat is off to you, Miss Extraordinary Saleswoman. You stood the test finely, and your ability grew by the test. We do like to buy from gracious people. They not only create pleasure for us but satisfaction for themselves. People who work by that standard don't find so much strain in the day's tasks.

He was only a youngster, probably not more than nineteen years old, but I give him credit for enterprise. I had ducked into a haberdashery hastily and asked if they carried belts for small boys.

"How old is he?" asked this young salesman.

"Only five."

He explained that belts for such young boys could be had only in children's-goods departments.

But the young fellow didn't let me get out without a suggestion. "We have a fine lot of shirts at very attractive special prices this week. Just look at this lot here," and the clever chap tried to lead the way. The only thing that killed his chance for a shirt sale was the lateness of the hour and my hurry. I told him I was well stocked up and couldn't stop then to look at even very attractive bargains. So he walked a few steps with me to the door and said pleasantly, "Come in to see us again when you have more time."

He will get along—that young fellow. I'd be willing to lay a small bet that some day he will be a proprietor or partner.

He has interest in his work, and enthusiasm and success usually go with interest.

I am a great admirer of the quiet preliminary suggestion by the salesman to the prospective customer who is just looking around. To come right out with "Did you want something?" "Wouldn't you like one of these?" is likely to repel some customers who don't want to commit themselves within a few seconds after looking at merchandise. Every salesman worthy of the name should make a study of the fine art of approaching the "looking customer" and making it easy for that person to talk or to inspect merchandise. Such remarks as the following, for example, applied to woolen scarfs are effective leads:

"These are very comfortable for the cold winter days when you are automobiling or out for a walk."

"We have these also in handsome black and white combinations. Here they are." (Placing them before customer.)

"These are the last of a large holiday stock and are being sold at a big reduction."

"Here is an especially good value. Is there any color that you particularly like?"

QUOTE THE QUANTITY PRICE

An Eastern city of moderate size recently asked my help in working out a buy-at-home campaign. The local merchants were concerned, as are the retailers of many of the smaller cities and towns, about the large volume of out-of-town purchases made by the home people, either from mail-order houses or the bigger stores of nearby large cities.

Searching around for the facts in the case I ran across this interesting situation: a large out-of-town food concern had a very capable salesman calling regularly on the housekeepers of the smaller city. He had a fine line of goods to offer, and he was a good demonstrator. He was more than a good demonstrator. *Whenever he had a quantity price that was attractive he named it*. If the customer could be interested in soap, he named the price for a box, and often by that method secured the housekeeper's entire soap business for months. On canned goods he would name the price by the dozen or by the case. The housekeeper frequently preferred to buy a dozen cans of some article, so as to have a supply handy. This traveling representative was accommodating and also very helpful in suggesting assortments.

You are suggesting economy for store and customer when you quote a quantity price.

The result of his call usually was that he went off with an order for more goods than a local grocery store would have sold to that home in a month.

Mind you, he didn't overwork his plan, either. He didn't press for a sale of a dozen or a case of something when it was obvious that the customer would be overbuying by purchasing that quantity, but he was free in naming his quantity prices, a thing that most retail-store salesmen seem to overlook.

It is undoubtedly true that the failure to keep in mind the quantity sale and the quantity price—when the class of goods is such that quantity prices are practicable—is a weak spot of most retail stores, a weakness that increases selling and delivery expense.

I made it my business to talk with a housekeeper who bought regularly from the food-store man of the

larger city, and I asked if she could remember how often in the last year or so a local store had taken the trouble to quote the price on a quantity of a given article. She could remember only one instance.

Perhaps you have heard the story, told many times, of the Italian fruit-vender who, when asked the price of bananas, put three in a paper bag, held them out toward the prospective purchaser and said: "Ten cents!" A trifle too aggressive, maybe, for most retail stores, but Tony recognized the merit of the quantity sale.

It isn't imposing on the customer and it doesn't take extra time worth mentioning, to say on the question of price: "Nine cents a can ma'am, or three cans for a quarter." Mrs. Sensible Housekeeper is very glad to save something on purchases of reasonable quantity if she can use the material, and she is a good judge of that—don't worry!

Don't be too sure that the goods you are selling don't afford opportunity for the quantity sale, if not for the quantity price. One of the most progressive clothing concerns in the country is coaching all of its salesmen to "talk two suits" to the man who comes in for clothing. Every man desiring to appear well dressed needs at least two suits of clothes in good order. One suit worn continuously becomes monotonous to him and his friends. If we are in the clothing business and he buys only one suit from us, he is very likely to buy a second suit soon from some other store.

The same thing applies to shoes. When the customer's tastes, size, etc., have been well determined, it is often easier to sell a second pair than it was to sell the first. If he or she is buying a walking shoe, the sale of another pair for dress occasions is possible.

Why not sell a box of hose or a half-dozen or a dozen collars instead of one or two? Get the wholesale habit!

"SUCH A LITTLE THING"

"It was such a little thing that we just couldn't get at it. We have a lot to do around here." So remarked a storekeeper, with a slight shrug of his shoulders, as if to say "Why bother me?"

He was talking to a customer who had complained that something she wanted attended to had been neglected although she had reminded the store once or twice.

Observe, please, that this proprietor is called a "storekeeper." He was not a merchant. No real merchant, no true salesman, ever tells a customer that anything he or she has a right to have attended to is a little thing—too little to have the earnest attention of the store.

With a real salesman a trifling request gets as respectful consideration as a big thing.

What customers ask about, and what they are often impatient and even unreasonable about, may be small things from the position of one in the store—but not from the customer's point of view. If you have the feeling, away back in your mind, that the customer's request is insignificant, at least have the sales sense not to say so. It is enough to know that the customer regards it as something we should attend to. To treat it as trifling is to insult or to irritate one whose good-will may be worth many dollars to the store.

Little things! Did you ever give much thought to the truth that it is attention to little things that gives one person or one store prominence over others? The big things in this world of ours are comparatively few; they don't come along every day. It is not given to every one to be a General Pershing or a Theodore Roosevelt. But our livee and days are full of little things that afford all a rich opportunity to give distinctive service—to be distinctive personalities. These little chances do not bring with them the inspiration and stimulation that attend great opportunities. Because they are of a routine nature they often require more resolution, more courtesy, more character.

It is a little thing for the Hotel Statler Company to have a paper put under the guest's door every morning, with the compliments of the hotel, but it has proved to be a big thing in cultivating good-will. That sort of policy has enabled the Statler people to do business on a large scale in four American cities. It gives them good publicity right here in this Bulletin, without cost.

It is a little thing for the Martinique Hotel, of New York, to close its letter about the return of an umbrella with the pleasant sentence, "We hope to have you as our guest again soon," but that friendly sxpression means much to the traveler.

It is a little thing for a store to instruct its salespeople that low-priced goods are never to be referred to as "cheap goods," but as long as the rule is observed by employes, no customer in the great Marshall Field store of Chicago is made to feel embarrassed because she wants popularly priced merchandise.

It is a little thing, apparently, to fail to listen for a minute to what the customer says. But that half-a-minute lapse from good selling methods may be just the weak link that loses the sale.

It was a little error for the subscription clerk in the office of a great newspaper to deposit a check but fail to order the paper sent to the subscriber. That slip meant the writing of several letters that should have been unnecessary and finally the hunting up of the paid check at the subscriber's bank. Result: a picture in the subscriber's mind of a carelessly conducted office.

It may seem a little and a harmless thing to be a bit fresh with the customer or to be over-familiar or sarcastic with a fellow-employe in the customer's presence, but such overstepping produces an impression on the customer that may not be erased for years.

It doesn't seem like such a vital thing, does it, for one to be late in the morning, to have dirty fingernails, to cough without turning the head, to make a few grammatical breaks, or to write a customer's name wrong?

But you judge your acquaintances by little things—the small courtesies, the little details of the day's work. That they are

"Men may rise on stepping stones * * to higher things."—*Tennyson.*

respectable and mean well does not save them from the loss of power that comes from not watching the little things. You have heard the old saying: "For the want of a nail, the shoe was lost; for the want of a shoe, the horse was lost; for the want of a horse, the rider was lost;" and so on. It's the daily doing of the little things well that prepares one for the big thing that may come along. He who despises the doing of small things well is not cultivating the character or the ability necessary for bigger deeds.

MORE ABOUT THE LITTLE THINGS OF SALESMANSHIP

One thing about shoe-selling methods makes a big impression on me. I refer to the practice of having the customer remove his old shoe and to the taking of an exact measure of his foot. It has been humorously explained that having the customer remove his old shoes promptly is an effective device for holding him in the store until he can be served. Be that as it may, the customer can hardly fail to be impressed by the careful measuring of his foot. It indicates to him, just when he is forming his first impressions of the store maybe, that the salesman is planning a thorough job. In other words, this preliminary act suggests *service*—that all-important thing that all

of us look for when we go out to spend our money, and which we don't always get.

It may seem a little thing. Maybe a shoe salesman of much experience could look at anyone's foot and guess the right size nine times out of ten. But the practice seems so much better than the usual "What size?" question. It strikes me that usually it is the skilful handling of these *little things* of selling that gladdens the heart of the customer and makes him happy to spend his money at Our Store.

It is so easy to do a little thing the wrong way. A small girl received a Christmas present of a pair of roller-skates and, childlike, soon lost her key. Her father went to the store where the purchase was made and asked if he could buy a duplicate key. "No, we don't sell them, that is, unless you wish to buy another pair of skates." The father—a business man—smiled. "Couldn't you get a key for me?" he asked. The saleswoman stepped back apparently for a conference with the head of her section and returned, saying with a shake of her handsome head, "No, we couldn't get it for you." "How shocking," replied the patron of the store, and then he leaned over the counter and whispered: "Don't tell it to any one else, Miss, but I belong to the Sherlock Holmes Detective Brotherhood, and we have wonderful ways of doing difficult things. Let me see a box containing a pair of those skates, please. Aha, I have it!—The Blinkety-Blink Skate Co., Blanktown, Ohio. I will write these good skate people for a key and in a few days I will return to this great establishment and explain how you can render this small service to the next customer whose little daughter has lost the key to her skates."

There was no money perhaps in ordering a new key for the customer in this case. But such an action would have given him an impression of the *service* of the store that would have been worth something. For a long time he will probably have a poor impression because of its unwillingness and lack of resourcefulness.

Said another customer in the toy section of a store: "I want something to take home to my youngster." "Boy or girl?" asked the bright-faced saleswoman instantly. "Boy," was the answer. "How old is he?" was the next leading question. "A little over two years." "Then you probably would like something in the unbreakable toys," said she, leading the way to that stock. Every question was to the point and the answers brought the interview quickly to where the saleswoman was in a position to give good service.

A prospective customer entered a store where the one man on duty was at the telephone. Evidently the store-representative was waiting for the person at the other end to look up some information. A word, or just a welcoming look, would have held the visitor who had done the store the honor of coming in to exchange his money for its merchandise, but the young man at the telephone simply stared at the wall until the telephone conversation could be renewed. Being completely ignored for a matter of several minutes, the prospective customer walked out.

"I like the style of this hat," said a man of good dress in a Broadway hat store, "but the quality is so poor." The quality was, in truth, poor, and the salesman was wise enough not to attempt the defense of quality that salesmen usually attempt in such situations. This salesman turned quietly to his stock and produced another hat of the same general style but obviously of superior quality. The sale was made instantly.

A customer was fingering some high-class cravats. "The colors are all so strong," he remarked finally. Now, you know, there is a rule laid down by some of the wise teachers of salesmanship to the effect that you must never disagree with the customer, but the salesman at this cravat counter was enough of a master of his job to know when the rules can be smashed. "Oh, no, sir," he replied pleasantly but confidently, "those colors are not strong for a cravat. You see, you are looking at the full length of the cravat. When it is tied, you see only about a third. The rest is under the vest. Strong colors are really required in cravats, sir." He picked up one of the cravats, knotted it skilfully, concealed the lower two-thirds and immediately added to the customer's knowledge of cravat-buying.

If you watch the little points of salesmanship the big ones will take care of themselves.

THE 66⅔ PER CENT SALESMAN

I recently read an article by a psychological and efficiency expert who declared that the average man is only 30 per cent efficient.

I don't take a great deal of stock in such exact statements. In the first place, dealing in averages is hazy. There is no such thing as "the average man" or "the average woman." Every one of us may be low in some quality and high in another, and who shall set himself up as a high judge to say just what the 100 per cent standard is?

On the other hand, it is safe to say that all of us are below the standard that we could maintain if all of our faculties were kept alert and active. It is extremely unlikely that any of us are close to "100 per cent," no matter what kind of work we are doing.

THINK

One rule of Salesmanship that always holds good.

I have taken the title of "The 66⅔ per cent salesman," not because I can measure efficiency with a fine gage, but because observation teaches that it is within bounds to say that most salesmen are using their brains and their physical energies to not more than two-thirds of their capacity. Putting it another way, if they were 6-cylinder engines, they are running on four most of the time and giving a lame or bumping performance that should be a smooth-running exhibition. Perhaps the real efficiency of most salespeople is away below 66⅔ per cent but the inefficiency is low enough anyhow, and the two-thirds basis will serve as well as any other for this discussion.

To illustrate: a display-window of gloves attracted me the other day and I walked in. A salesman was quick to observe my presence and he greeted me courteously. He gave me fine preliminary attention, which is something that a great many salespeople are not careful to do.

I said I wanted something in a dark shade of tan, or maybe a gray. He showed several pairs and then he produced a neat gray glove with the remark that if I wanted a good cheap glove they would suit me. Somehow, the word "cheap" grated on me. I wondered why he did not say "low priced," or "reasonably priced," in talking about a glove that sold for $3.50. "What's wrong with them?" I asked—the natural question when a salesman talks about something cheap. He then told me why the gloves were priced at $3.50, and his explanation offset the suspicion that the word "cheap" had aroused.

I bought a pair of the grays but fingered also a pair of dark tans. When, however, I passed my money to the young man, he gathered up all the gloves speedily, replaced them in stock and turned to me with the usual, trite "Now, what else?" As a matter of fact, I was debating buying two pairs of gloves—the gray ones for daily wear and the dark tans for special occasions. I might have bought the second pair had I been given half a chance.

Very likely this salesman concluded that by getting the other gloves out of my sight he clinched the sale of the $3.50 ones, but he wasn't studying his subject if he reached such a hasty conclusion. He probably has made no study of how to make extra sales, of how a little effort would greatly reduce the selling cost of his store. The purchase of two pairs of gloves while the stock was out would have saved his time and mine.

He just didn't think—that's all. A third of his brain cylinders weren't hitting! And yet he started well—was quick and courteous.

For years the National Cash Register Company carried, for the attention of its own representatives and for the people with whom these representatives do business, the one-word slogan *think*. Business men declined for years to buy cash registers because they had not been made to think about the necessity of accurate figures on sales. When the cash register was first produced it was regarded —not as part of a necessary business system adapted to all kinds of enterprises—but as a "contraption to catch light-fingered clerks." A history of the great N.C.R. business tells us that the early market for the register was mainly in saloons. The general run of merchant thought the introduction of such a device was a reflection on the honesty of his employes. He just was not thinking in the right direction, and before cash registers could be sold on a large scale the salesmen themselves had to *think* and to become competent to make other people *think*.

Cash registers and insurance are alike in one respect. Few people realize the need of the service of either until they are forced to think.

A factory owner or an office manager is entirely satisfied with the equipment he is using. He thinks it is entirely adequate. He tries to close his mind to suggestions that he change it and spend hundreds or thousands of dollars for new equipment. He must have the most impressive facts and figures put before him before his thinking machinery will admit the conclusion that the salesman desires. Sales organizations must have *thinkers* before they can change the currents of thought of such men.

You may not care for some of the things Henry Ford has said, but he said something when he remarked that "Thought will settle any problem."

Salesmen and saleswomen don't think enough. They are content to be "66⅔ per cent salespeople," when they could easily bring themselves up to an 85 per cent or maybe a 95 per cent standard.

SERVING WHILE SELLING

Dr. Frank Crane says that every man and woman who is happy in the work being done believes, down deep in the heart, that what he or she is doing is a real service to mankind.

Dr. Crane is right. We may fool ourselves into thinking that money or something else is the only thing we are working for, but if we get any happiness out of what we are doing, *we serve*, and we get satisfaction out of the knowledge that we are serving.

Serving in selling doesn't mean merely "waiting on people." You can go into a restaurant and be "served" and still go away feeling that your meal was an unsatisfactory one. If the napkin was soiled or limp, the plate dirty, the coffee sloppy and the waiter surly, the fact that you may have got everything that you ordered doesn't make the service something that you will remember with pleasure—something that will make you want to go back to that restaurant again.

No, *Serve*, *Serving* and *Service* have big meanings—bigger than they have ever had.

For one thing, you serve the customer by inquiring into his needs carefully and then earnestly helping him to fill them in the best possible way. Selling is an every-minute job with you, maybe, and one that at times becomes irksome and monotonous. Not so with the buyer. The purchase that he has planned to make is possibly one that has been thought over a good deal, and it may mean much to some home or office to have that sale satisfactory from the purchaser's point of view, to have him own something that will make him think well always of the firm or the salesman who made the sale.

People sometimes know exactly what they want or need. Very often they do not. To understand the customer's need, by careful and courteous inquiry, and then to endeavor to fill that need as conscientiously as if the customer were one of your own family may seem a high ideal, but it is the ideal that builds up good-will—that makes customers speak well of us, and that is the most valuable kind of advertising that can be had. It can't be bought. It comes only as the result of service.

A friend of mine about ready to leave town for a vacation in Florida went to a prominent shoe store in New York. Sometimes, you know, we hear it said that in these big buying centers the customer gets less than the usual consideration from salespeople. But just wait! My friend remarked that he was about to take his vacation and he wanted a pair of shoes for use on this trip.

"May I ask whether you are going North or South?" asked the salesman pleasantly. Immediately the information was forthcoming that my friend expected to spend most of his holiday tramping around on the sands of Florida.

"I see," said the salesman, "well, now, you don't want a heavy tramping shoe down there. You want something cool and light and I believe we have the very thing for you." And off he went to get it. What's more, he had it and he sold it. He talked of fishing, tramping, golf, and so forth, and showed other shoes. You can come close to guessing the rest. My friend saw another pair of shoes that he wanted and bought the second pair. He couldn't resist the inclination, as he went out, to compliment the shoe man on his interest in the customer's needs. "It's good business," said my friend.

"It is that," replied the salesman, "but it is more than that. I enjoy meeting people, finding out just what they need and then seeing how well I can fix them up."

If there is one thing that more than any other appeals to us when we are customers, it is the feeling that the salesman is taking a real interest in us, in our needs. So much of sales service, if it may be called that, is the other way—a bored, or fishy-eyed attitude on the part of salesmen, an air that says, "Oh well, here's the stuff. You know as much about it as I do. Take it or leave it, it's all the same to me." Just imagine how that attitude impresses the customer. You know how it impresses *you* when you are ready to spend your hard-earned money, whether for a can of shoe polish or a pair of non-skid tires. You want to be catered to. You expect interest shown in your visit or your inquiry even if your purchase is to be a small one. Your errand takes on added pleasure when the salesman starts off with a question that shows real interest, such as—"What is the style of the office in which the chair is to be used?" And your purchase means a lot more to you when you get that reception; shopping becomes a pleasant mission.

Other people are just as human as we are. When we are made to feel that a salesman is just trying to sell us something, we take the defensive and the transaction becomes a cold, commercial one. When it is apparent that the salesman has a genuine interest in seeing that we get the article that will give us the greatest satisfaction, salesmanship is turned into service—the greatest of all good-will builders. This holds true, whether the commodity is something for personal use or a purchase that we are making for our trade or our factory. In spite of all that may be said about this being a day of "cold-blooded business," there is plenty of sentiment and appreciation afloat.

You serve your employer, of course, when you serve the customer well. You reflect credit on his place of business. Never forget that when the customer stands before you, or you stand before him, you represent the firm as much as if you were the Big Boss—that all the fine features of the business, the convincing advertising and the attractive displays amount to nothing if, when the customer is in the humor to buy or to investigate, you do not deliver a service that backs up all that has gone before. You add to or take from the reputation of the firm at every sale.

Last but not least, when you serve every one else well, you serve yourself well. The motto of the Rotary Clubs is "He profits most who serves best," and it is not mere preaching. Look at it selfishly if you want—the cold truth is that you get your greatest development when you set yourself the job of day by day, week by week and month by month, serving other people well. That means personal discipline and efficiency that you can get in no other way. Money can never bring the happiness that comes from the consciousness of ability to give thorough service.

BE A GOOD SALESMAN OF YOURSELF

To get a job, to keep on holding a good job, to be constantly increasing your power and compensation, you have as much need of the science and the art of selling as you do when you deal with customers of your firm.

"Show me" says the keen buyer when you approach him and intimate that it would be greatly to his interests to do business with your firm. "Show me" also indicates the employer's state of mind when you undertake to put yourself on his payroll. He expects to see what you have for sale. You are expected to analyze your stock in trade, to "sell yourself," as it were—tell frankly, and without too much of the appearance of egotism, what you have done, what you feel sure you can do and why.

TALKS ON BETTER SELLING

As demonstration is one of the best methods of selling merchandise, so it is one of the best ways of selling services. The salesman who offers to prove to an employer, on any reasonable basis, what he can do is more than likely to have a fair chance.

"I can't use the goods unless they can make money for me," is another familiar state of mind of the keen buyer of merchandise. Likewise, the employer has little use for salesmen who can't make money for him. Unless the salesman can do real missionary work, the employer might as well use catalogues and letters, window-displays or other mere exhibitions of merchandise. He is losing money if salesmen merely do the clerical work of taking orders that would have come anyhow.

The buyer to whom you offer merchandise protests loud and long when you ask a higher price without giving more or better goods. Why, then, expect the employer, a buyer of service, to pay you more salary for this year's service than he paid for last year's service if the records don't indicate a substantial increase in the profit you make for the firm?

When the salesmen that you encounter think that they are bigger than the goods and service they sell, you know what your reflections are. You may create similar reflections when you begin to feel that you have the business of a firm of high standing tucked away in your vest-pocket and can divert it as you please.

Keen buyers like good-looking, dependable merchandise. You are a product to your employer, and more—for you are his representative. Why shouldn't he be just as desirous of having attractive-looking stock as the handler of hardware, shoes or automobile supplies?

If you are a wise salesman, you know that you don't own the patronage of many of your customers—that you have to be constantly alert to keep them away from competitors. Yet, how often a salesman thinks he is so solidly sold to his firm that he can take things easily, content himself with running along in the old route ("rut" often expresses it better), is deaf to hints, and neglects to try new methods that the management is so earnestly desirous of seeing tested in a thorough way. Then he wonders why he is regarded as one who is "slipping," or as a man who can be counted on to do only a certain kind of work acceptably.

"Fine talk," says the keen buyer, "but what will make me buy this apparatus is performance."

The same principle applies to you and to your job. Performance is the thing. Some men are wonderful salesmen in the conference. They are good talkers. But when it comes to hard work, day in and day out, week after week and month after month, when it is a question of the versatility and will power to use new methods and plans, then they do not perform.

In a number of organizations where the work of salesmen can be checked with fair accuracy, only one man in every three candidates actually "makes good" in the long run.

It may sound commonplace to once more remind every man who has something to sell that competition is keen in this day—that never before did people have so much opportunity to spend their money for so many different things. Never before was selling cost so high.

So is competition increasing among salesmen themselves. There are more good salesmen this year than existed last year and the number will be greater next year.

To sell himself on a satisfactory basis, and to stay sold, means that the salesman must be possessed of "the real goods."

SECTION XV

SALES IDEAS, PLANS AND EXPERIENCES

The following pages present a summary of a number of retail selling plans and methods that have proved effective in the building up of sales.

Some of these plans will be recognized as being those that have become more or less standardized or regarded as customs. Others are modifications or adaptations of old plans, some new feature having been added to give the plan the appearance of novelty or to provide a news flavor.

Still others of these plans are distinctly novel, some even sensational. Such plans would not, of course, adapt themselves well to every type of retail or local campaign. This qualification is just as fitting with respect to the older types of sales campaigns. Any kind of sales event calls for public interest and for enthusiasm on the part of the merchant and salespeople conducting it. Therefore, while a merchant or an educational director may draw his fundamental idea from a plan that has been carried out successfully by a fellow-merchant, he should endeavor to improve the plan, to bring it up to date, or to add some new and desirable feature.

Manufacturers' Interest in Retail Selling Plans and Methods.—While the summary here presented of retail selling plans and methods is assembled particularly as an aid to retailers, the fact is that manufacturers who sell goods through retail stores have almost as keen an interest in retail selling ideas as retailers themselves. Reflection will make it clear that it is difficult nowadays to draw the line between the interests of manufacturer and retail merchant, or between jobber and retail merchant.

Selling, in a broad sense, is not a complete job until the consumer has the product. Neither manufacturer nor jobber can long survive if, after making the sale to the retailer, the latter is unable to dispose of the product with reasonable success. Therefore, in modern merchandising the manufacturer whose goods reach the consumer through the retail-dealer outlet is, or should be, as much interested in effective retailing as the retailer himself.

Some of the plans here summarized are those that would of necessity have their origin with the retailer. Others are plans that might well be suggested by manufacturers or plans in which one or more manufacturers could cooperate.

An increasingly large number of manufacturers are today cooperating closely with the retailers of their goods, furnishing not only suggestions for sales plans but also valuable material in the form of window- and counter-displays, samples, newspaper and circular advertising, and so forth.

In this review, a number of business magazines are referred to specifically. The author wishes also to record the helpfulness of *Printers' Ink, Atlantic Coast Merchant, Dry Goods Merchants' Trade Journal, Merchants Record and Show-Window,* and *Walden's Stationer and Printer,* as a source of information or suggestion.

CHANGES THAT PUT NEW LIFE INTO BUSINESS

How an Analysis and General Change Helped.—A retail merchant who had come to the conclusion that his business was running in a groove without making much progress, referred to the young men of the store the problem of suggesting ways and means by which new life could be injected into the advertising and selling methods. Here are some of the suggestions made by employes that were carried out successfully.

1. A record was made daily of the number of sales by each employe of goods that the visitor to the store *did not call for*.

2. A study was made of the outstanding features of each article of merchandise that the store sold and the salesmen were encouraged to refer to these points at every opportunity rather than to assume that probably the prospective purchaser already knew the features of the goods.

3. The store changed its style of advertising temporarily and began a "question-and-answer" kind of copy. One week the advertising would tell how to take care of floors. A character known as "Aunt Priscilla" answered the household questions, and so on. Readers of the newspapers were encouraged to mail, or leave at the store, questions to be answered in succeeding advertisements.

In later issues, "Uncle Josh" handled questions about gardening, tools, etc. Still later, "The Autoist" and "The Vacationist" took up the job. The series made a most interesting appeal to the community.

Finally, encouraged by the success of this special kind of advertising, the store permanently abandoned its former stereotyped "announcements" and thereafter strove for newsy, entertaining messages.

4. Window- and interior-displays were arranged to harmonize with the newspaper publicity.

Display-Cases that Draw Attention to Related Goods.—An Indianapolis retailer has worked out an ingenious device for displaying his stock in a way that encourages additional sales. Small display-cases are built right into the fixtures and in these are arranged goods allied to the principal goods of the department. For example, in the hat department a display of gloves will be arranged in a supplementary case. When the customer has completed the first purchase the salesperson contrives to call her attention to, or induces her to step in front of, this small case. There is no attempt to force an extra sale but the salesperson is familiar with the glove stock and the prices and there is always the chance that the customer will be receptive to the remarks about the goods.

Bootblack Stand in Shoe Department.—A Los Angeles merchant, J. W. Robinson, concluded that the most propitious time to bring to a woman's mind the purchase of a new pair of shoes was when she was looking at her old shoes. Therefore he placed his bootblacking stand in convenient proximity to his shoe department. He also arranged a display of footwear just at the end of the corner of the settee where waiting customers of the shoe-shining department sit. Besides choosing this strategic point for the display, he arranges the shoes on

Oriental rugs, right on the floor so that the shoes are seen from the normal angle. The unusual exhibit attracts visitors from other departments and creates the desire for shoes.

Colored Boxes Get Concentration from Salespeople.—To clear out slow-moving merchandise a buyer of underwear put the goods in colored boxes as a means of attracting and holding the attention of the salespeople. The colors used were yellow and orange, in striking contrast to the usual colors of paper boxes, and the goods in these new containers were placed conspicuously in the department. As fast as these boxes were emptied, they were replaced by the ordinary boxes. Any yellow or orange box remaining stirred the saleswomen to extra effort, for a special credit was given for each sale of the slow-moving merchandise.

"Household Investment Club" Eliminates Uncertainty About Instalment Prices.—A Kansas City furniture store has done away with the uncertainty that often exists in the minds of many people in regard to the instalment plan—the idea that perhaps they are paying an exorbitant amount for the privilege of long-time payments. The store advertises furniture at the cash price only and, for those who desire to pay in instalments, maintains a "Household Investment Club," the dues of which are 4 per cent of the cash price of any article purchased. These dues entitle the purchaser to a certain length of time for payment. Thus the cash customer knows that he is gaining just 4 per cent by paying cash, and the instalment buyer knows that he will have to add only a reasonable interest charge to the advertised price if he wishes to use the credit system. This method enables the store to feature low price in its advertisements without any reference to cash price and credit price.

(Grand Rapids Furniture Record).

Using "Brick-Bats" and "Bouquets" to Increase Sales.—An Indianapolis grocer arranged in his window a big brown ham, a 15-pound package of sugar, and a 5-pound package of coffee. As a background, he put in a large basket of brickbats and a large jar of red roses. Then he put up a bulletin board with the following information on the next page:

SALES IDEAS, PLANS AND EXPERIENCES

BRICK-BATS AND BOUQUETS!

Send them in! We want them! The bouquets to cheer us up; the brick-bats to straighten us up.

To the customer sending in the best of either we will give a prize of one ten-pound ham; to the next best, five pounds of coffee, and to the third, fifteen pounds of sugar.

By "BEST" we do not mean the letter that contains the most blarney, or the most abuse, necessarily, but the one, which is, in our opinion, the fairest and most legitimate, and from which we are able to derive the most benefit.

A brick-bat may be of as much benefit as a bouquet in helping us to improve our business (maybe more!) and that's what we're looking for; help in making this the best store in the neighborhood.

These letters are to become our property, and will be displayed in this window, and also in the newspapers. Come on, now! Write us all about it!

The contest drew nearly one hundred complimentary letters. The prize-winning letters were displayed in frames in the window later and also published in the newspaper. One prize was won by a 9-year-old child whose letter brought out the idea that the salesmen in the store did not wait until all the grown people had been waited on before giving attention to youngsters. The merchant, Charles Marcus, also received a number of "brick-bats" which he displayed, with comments such as, "This is the first time that our attention has been called to this matter. We are glad to have a chance to adjust it." The "brick-bat" that won the prize was a letter reading, "I do not care to trade at your store because most of my purchases are necessarily made by telephone and the orders are seldom satisfactory unless I am there to inspect the goods."

Mr. Marcus, like a good advertiser, capitalized this letter. He put it on a large poster and answered it with a new feature in his business. Instead of dodging the "brick-bat" he met it squarely and commented as follows:

To the writer of this letter, Mrs. J. M. Boyle, goes the prize for the most effective brick-bat. We consider this letter the best of its type because it has been of the most help to us. Mrs. B. is a very desirable customer, and her complaint has opened our eyes to a real necessity in our store—a man who can take full charge of 'phone orders, to the exclusion of all other work. We realize that a great percentage of our patrons who need not necessarily order by 'phone would find it a great convenience, and we are therefore appointing Mr. Brookes to have full charge of this branch of the business in the future. He will endeavor to learn the particular choice in foods of those who are mainly 'phone customers, to memorize their numbers, and to cooperate in every way in making the 'phone-customer a satisfied customer.

Of course this "brick-bat" letter and the enterprising merchant's way of meeting the criticism were also featured in the newspaper advertising. Various letters furnished good, newsy advertising material for weeks.

Change in Store Policy.—The Pelletier store, of Sioux City, Iowa, began a new system of monthly sales with the following announcement in connection with advertising for the first sale:

It marks the inauguration of a new sales policy, that of clearing our stocks at the end of every month instead of just January and July. In our aim to best serve our patrons, this plan to "clean house" once a month will keep our stocks newer and fresher, more attractive for your selection, throughout the twelve months of the year.

In accordance with this policy, each department "cleans house" monthly and the goods selected for the sales are repriced as the occasion may warrant. A full-page advertisement is then made up with the goods listed as in a catalogue, those of each department being grouped together with only one line of description to each article. Two columns are used for prices, one for former price and one for the sale price, but often the former column is left blank if the reduction is not sufficient to attract attention or if the reduction, due to market conditions or other causes, has the appearance of being sensational. The arrangement of the advertisement is most convenient for customers after they have been attracted by the headline, which tells them of odd lots at special prices.

(*Retail Ledger*).

Gold Bond Guarantee to Purchasers of Nash Cars.—The L. A. D. Motor Corporation, Brooklyn, N. Y., distributors of Nash cars, assumes the maintenance and operating expenses of all Nash cars for the first 5,000 miles for an initial outlay of $50. This guarantees to purchasers a total running expense for this period of not more than 1 cent a mile and has worked out as an excellent selling feature.

The owner must agree to bring his car to the service station for periodic inspections. This enables the dealer to teach a new owner the value of making minor adjustments as soon as the need for them appears, and the value of proper lubrication—the two big causes for repair and replacement bills.

This plan has built up a large number of satisfied owners—the best basis on which to figure the sale of new cars. The fear of high operating expense is removed and the sales force does not have this argument to combat. Constant contact with the service station gives owners the best means of learning the proper use and care of cars and enables them to get the best value for the money invested.

Building Up a Quality and a Cash Business.—The business of Charles S. Haines in Sebetha, Kan., a town of about 2,000 population, affords a good example of how business on merchandise of excellent grade can be built up in a relatively small community. The experience of this store bears out the conclusion that the sale of a great deal of merchandise of high quality is not made in smaller towns and cities because merchants are too backward in catering to the needs of customers who want distinctive commodities. While caution in buying is a virtue, the caution of this group of merchants often means a broader opportunity for mail-order houses and the big stores of the larger cities.

Following the opening of a golf club in Sabetha, Haines put in a stock of golf clothes for both men and women and did well with it. According to an article in the *Business Magazine* on "Quality Goods on Main Street," this merchant achieved marked success in the selling of suits and dresses, ranging in price from $25 to $125, to farmers' daughters and wives.

The Haines store became convinced that the country-town store often errs in carrying too general a stock, thus losing the value of specialization and tying up its capital too tightly. Accordingly, the grocery department, the men's clothing department, carpets, rugs and upholstery, and, finally, the shoe department were dropped. The capital released by the elimination of these departments was used to enlarge and improve the remaining departments. Haines keeps in touch with the trend of suggestions in current periodicals and sees to it that his stocks will help the modern woman to carry out some of these ideas. Realizing further the influence of modern publications, Haines confines his stocks to goods that are nationally exploited, thus permitting the manufacturers to do the first and hardest part of his selling work.

This store occupies two floors and the steep staircase to the second floor was replaced by a gradual flight of stairs designed according to the proportions of the staircase in the Pennsylvania Station in New York City, which Haines had noted favorably on one of his buying trips. A space of about 10 feet, left by the erection of the new staircase, was used to display some of the most popularly priced toilet goods. This proved to be an excellent location for toilet goods.

The Haines store draws trade from surrounding territory of fifty or more miles in radius. There are no very large cities in this territory that offer decided competition, but this merchant is constantly building up his prestige throughout the territory by inserting advertisements weekly in nearby towns. His advertisements feature the quality of the merchandise carried and the service of the store. This newspaper advertising is supplemented by personal letters and folders that tell about new stock.

The salespeople are coached, whenever a sale is being made, to pick up information in their conversation with a customer that will enable them to learn of other people who are about to make purchases. Leads of this kind are followed up with personal letters that give information about the stock in which the prospective customer is interested. The return from 500 such letters sent out during one year showed the remarkable percentage of 250 direct sales.

After 44 years in business, this Kansas store changed its policy from a credit to a cash basis without any loss that could be traced. The trade was prepared for the change by the announcement of a sale to cover an entire week. In accordance with the usual custom, no prices were advertised, but the point that reductions would prevail on all merchandise was emphasized.

No requests for credit were made during the week and the store did a record business. At the end of the sale 480 of the 489 checks presented in payment for merchandise were found to have been signed by women. This fact showed that a large majority of the women had their own accounts.

The week following the close of the sale, page advertisements throughout the community announced the change of policy of the Haines Store from a credit to a cash basis. It was explained that this change would enable the store to offer high-grade goods at a reduction in price. This was followed by a direct-mail explanation to all persons that had done business recently with the Haines Store.

While this drastic change was being contemplated a merchandise expert expressed the opinion that Haines could not remain in the same town and do business successfully on this changed working basis. Nevertheless, the change was easily made. The cash plan enabled the merchant to reduce his prices from 3 to 10 per cent, and the business of 1922 showed an increase of 11 per cent over that of 1921.

SPECIAL SALE IDEAS AND EXPERIENCES

Special Sale Unit for the Business Girl.—The largest department store in a city of a million population recently turned its attention to the business girl with profitable results. An exhaustive survey was conducted—the sources of information ranging from United States government statistics to the store's own figures on sales of clothing to young women, and to talks with women themselves. The idea was to assemble an outfit for the business girl on the same principle as the bride's trousseau is planned and to sell various grades of outfits at various prices.

The store discovered that there are two broad divisions of customers among the business girls. There is the girl from seventeen to twenty-four years of age who spends a good percentage of her salary on clothes, and the older girl from twenty-four to beyond thirty who is inclined to spend more and to be rather a pace-maker in the matter of style and quality.

With these two groups in mind, the store selected outfits suitable in style and price for the younger and the older girl. Prices began at $15 for a unit of a hat, shirtwaist, skirt, stockings and shoes, and graded upward to $30. Complete units were displayed in the different departments and the higher-priced units offered a selection of various styles and colors.

Publicity for the sales included newspaper advertising, window-display and a style show in the store's display theater. The show portrayed familiar instances in the business girl's day from the time she began to dress for the office until she finally reached it and sat down at her typewriter.

The plan sold thousands of dollars' worth of goods and crowded the store with people for an entire week, resulting in a general increase of sales. The scheme has been repeated three times, which fact seems conclusive proof of its success.

(Summarized from *Dry Goods Economist*).

Spring Needlework Sale Draws Crowds.—An advertisement of a Washington, D. C., store which featured a special sale of art needlework, knitting yarns, stamped bed-spreads, towels, scarfs, etc., recently drew so many customers to the store that thirty extra saleswomen had to be employed for the special work. The sale was held near the notion section, which also benefited by the number of patrons, as did almost every other department of the store. Possibly the time of the year, early spring, had something to do with the success of the sale. The fancy-workers had recovered from the strain of making Christmas presents and were ready for summer front-porch work.

Homes Tagged with Coupons for Special Sale.—In featuring a coupon sale, a retail firm put on the front door-knob of every home in the city a tag bearing ten coupons, each good only on the day named. Thus, the customer had to call at the store one day for special prices on muslin, another day for special prices on pillow-cases, and so on.

The article featured for special sale was displayed in the window on the previous day.

A record of the amount of goods sold by coupon showed that the business on the days of the sale was double that for the same period of the previous year.

Departments Boost Each Others' Special Sales.—After a purchase is made in a Des Moines store, the salesman hands the customer a request card worded as follows:

> MAY I ASK YOU
> to present this card to any salesperson in the ......
> .... department, on the ...... floor,
> who will show you .... on special
> sale today.

These cards, with the blanks filled, are signed by the salesmen or saleswomen who present them. The system thus enables the store manager to determine to some extent if the salespeople in other departments are cooperating with those in whose department the sale is being held. As specially priced articles are featured in first one department and then in another, the salespeople throughout the store are made to feel that their friends in other departments will help them in turn.

"Surprise Sale" Brings Curious Buyers.—An Indianapolis dry goods store announced a novel sale in a two-page advertisement in the evening newspapers, describing and giving comparative values of staple articles from fifty-one sections of the store but printing a large question-mark in the space usually devoted to the prices. The word "surprise" was emphasized throughout the advertisement. In the store bright blue pasteboard interrogation points 3 feet high were hung from the ceiling in the fifty-one sections carrying the "surprise" goods.

This particular sale was not held as a money-maker but to increase the number of patrons. The prices were real surprises because of "lucky purchases" the buyer had been able to make and because on some of the items the prices were less than half the usual price. This "surprise sale" was successful enough on its first trial to take its place as a regular store event but the next time the store will profit by its experience and improve on the idea by displaying the merchandise in the windows several days before the sale. Also a restriction will be placed on the amount of merchandise a customer can buy, as in the first sale a number of the "surprises" were disposed of almost at the beginning.

$1 Off Any Unit of $5 or Over.—Howard's, of Mt. Vernon, N. Y., advertised that on a certain day any article in the store priced at $5 or over would be sold for $1 less. The "Dollar-Less Sale" was a success and after it was over the store found that the dollar off every $5 or more article worked out as only a 3 per cent discount. The discount on a $5 article alone was of course 20 per cent but on a $100 article it was only 1 per cent. The store had a little trouble in getting its employes to understand the discount system but the customers all understood clearly what a "dollar less" meant.

Saleswomen Wear Red Waists During Big Sale.—The Adler & Childs Department Store, of Dayton, Ohio, had been in the custom of holding a Loom End Sale annually, preceded by four page advertisements as well as by circulars mailed to a list of 25,000 or 30,000 people in the community. It was decided before a recent event of this kind to exploit the sale in only fourteen columns of space in the two Sunday newspapers. Red was chosen as the "sale color." The saleswomen wore red waists and the men had big red ribbons on the lapels of their coats. Red tags, banners, pennants and streamers were used as decorations. The store was advertised to open at 8:30 but the crowd began to assemble shortly after 7:30 and it became so large as to be almost unmanageable.

Two-hour Specials Bring Thousand New Customers.—A large food store in Topeka, Kan., planned 2-hour specials during one week, which was known as "New Customer Week." The advertisements featured free delivery service and included a shopping list. Certain specials were put on sale from 9 to 11 of each day and no telephone orders were accepted. The specials included such goods as red salmon, canned pears, corn, canned plums, high-class baking powder, etc. The store was arranged especially for these sales and demonstrations were also conducted on the goods featured. It is stated by a prominent trade magazine that this special drive for a thousand new customers was successful.

A "Bargain Booth" with a New Bargain Every Day.—The Lewis Dry Goods Company, of Denver, Col., is endeavoring to have its customers form the habit of visiting a certain booth in the store which is reserved for bargains. All other bargain counters have been discontinued and bargains are displayed only at the "bargain booth." The store's advertising promises new specials each day at lower prices than can be found elsewhere, and patrons are forming the habit of visiting the "booth" even when they have not read the day's advertisement, knowing that some sort of a bargain will be found there.

Two Articles for the Price of One.—As a variation from other bargain ideas, various retailers have exploited the plan of giving two articles of a certain class for the price of one. Or, to put it another way, "Buy one and we present you with another."

Sales through Cooperation with Charity Organizations.— A plan of enlisting the aid of charity organizations in increasing sales is that of offering to give such organizations a percentage of all sales during a given week. One store that has featured this plan makes the percentage 5 per cent. The preliminary newspaper advertising gives opportunity for each charity to make its claims known.

One day of the sale is usually set aside for each charity organization and on that particular day this organization receives some special newspaper notice. In conducting such a plan it is necessary for the merchant to get in touch with each organization weeks in advance and have committees appointed to cooperate. The larger the committees the better, and in doing their part of the work it has been found that special badges help matters. These committees not only buy goods themselves but influence their friends to do likewise.

One merchant who has had charity sales on his yearly program regularly offers the information that nearly five hundred women serve on the different committees appointed, many of them being present at the store. This is the type of sale about which a great deal of talk can be created if the merchant manages the affair properly.

Oral versus Printed Advertising.—To promote a general friendly feeling toward the store and to secure favorable talk, some well known stores in the smaller cities allow women to hold sales of their own of homemade baking, candy, etc., in their buildings. There is nearly always a group of women trying to raise money for local charities or for their churches or colleges. This type of woman is appreciative and anxious to reciprocate when she has been treated well. Moreover, she often has a wide circle of friends.

In spite of the constant need for window space, it may be good business to lend a window occasionally to displays of the local Needle-work Guild, the Y. W. C. A. Poster Contest, the Y. W. C. A. Basketry Class, and so on. These displays of the efforts of local talent not only attract attention but bring the valuable conversational advertising referred to.

Win the Alarm Clock When It Rings.—A furniture store in Shenandoah, Pa., used 100 alarm clocks to draw a crowd to a pre-spring sale. The clocks were set to ring at various hours of the day between opening and closing time and the store advertised that any person who happened to be nearest an alarm clock when it rang would become the owner of it. The clocks were, of course, distributed throughout the store.

The report is made that a crowd of good size lingered in the store hoping to win a free clock and the sales total for the day indicated a satisfactory result.

Another Alarm Clock Idea.—A small Southern store, during dull periods, holds a weekly "Silvery Chime Sale." Two alarm clocks are set by the store superintendent and paper is pasted over the faces so that nobody can tell when they are to go off. These clocks are placed in the department where a sale is to be held. When one alarm goes off the head of the department takes out a sign previously prepared telling the percentage reduction to be made on the goods and places it on the counter. Goods are sold according to the sign until the second alarm goes off, when the sign is removed and goods go back to their former price. As no one knows when the sale is to end, buying is brisk.

Women's Hose for Men to Buy as Presents.—An Eastern store at the opening of the holiday season advertised, in its men's department, boxes of women's stockings—silk, of course, for presents. A brief description of the hosiery was given, with the box-price, and this announcement: "In plain white boxes. Before December 18, boxes will be initialed in gold."

Customers gave the initials of the prospective recipient and the store pasted on the box gilt initials similar to those pasted in hat bands. Setting the date of December 18 for the initials brought about a large advance business. This idea seems to be one that might be worked the year round for birthday gifts on a variety of goods.

A Japanese Sale.—In towns having no Japanese or other Oriental stores, Japanese decorative effects will attract unusual attention. The store holding a Japanese sale should be decorated with various colors and sizes of Japanese lanterns, parasols, banners, strings of flags and cherry blossoms, for which Japan is famous. Having some, or all, of the saleswomen dressed in Japanese style adds to the picturesqueness. One store conducting such a sale had a small Japanese boy stationed at the door, giving to all who entered cards announcing free tea and coffee at a specially decorated booth. Souvenirs the first day of the sale were chrysanthemums with ribbons attached. All show-cards and price-tickets were done in the Japanese style and the entire store was perfumed with Japanese incense. This store managed to sell most of its decorations at a profit before the closing day of the sale.

A Quarter's Worth for 13 Cents.—In order to draw a little extra trade during a dull season, some stores advertise the small odd-figure sale, such as a 13-cent sale of many articles that are usually sold for as much as 25 cents. The merchant may lose money on some of these sales, but customers will not confine buying to the 13-cent articles and the sales account at the end of the day need not show a loss.

"Even change sales" are held on the same principle, an even price of 25 cents or 50 cents being placed on articles that usually sell for more. Customers do not have to wait for change.

Credit for the Old Hat.—A novel idea has been used by men's hat stores—that of advertising a credit of 25 cents allowed on an old hat brought in by a customer desiring a new hat. The old hats placed in the window make a queer-looking display that gets attention. After such sales, the old hats can be turned over to the Salvation Army or some other worthy organization.

"Dollar Day."—A number of towns have found the "Dollar Day" scheme a trade-bringer on days that are usually rather slow. Merchants cooperate in offering on a Monday or a Friday special bargains for one dollar. The more merchants there are joining in the plan, the more interest is aroused in attracting people to the town. In other words, the plan advertises the town as well as the stores taking part. Even if all the merchants will not cooperate, this "Dollar Day" idea can be used to advantage by two, or even by one, as the basis of a special sale.

Dollar Day Comparing Values in Different Years.—A Boston merchant used as a window feature a "dollar-sale day" by placing in the window two quantities of goods, showing what a dollar would buy under the higher prices that prevailed a few years previously and his current prices. The larger heap told graphically of the dollar's recovery as a buying unit.

Merchants in Shreveport, La., ran a "dollar week" on somewhat the same plan, using "Mr. 100-Cent Dollar" as an advertising feature during the week. Every merchant cooperating was urged to give as large a dollar value as possible so as to bring home to the public the fact that dollars were once more approaching pre-war purchasing value.

Housekeeper's Sale.—In order to arouse the enthusiasm of employes over a contemplated housekeeper's sale, a department store in a large Southern city offered prizes of $100, $50, $25, and several of $10 and $5 for the ten best suggestions that would make the sale a real event. Many worth-while suggestions were offered and almost 100 per cent of the employes signed the slip pledging hearty cooperation throughout the sale. This slip was attached to the mimeographed letter announcing the contest. Some of the suggestions carried out were the following:

All saleswomen wore bungalow aprons and dust-caps as a "dress feature" of this exploitation of housekeepers' supplies.

All the usual goods were removed from the first floor and replaced by household supplies. This was a change that could not fail to attract the attention of regular customers. The salespeople were instructed just where the removed goods had been placed so that customers could be easily directed.

A contest was held for customers. This was worked out by the store's advertising department and consisted of a series of pictures published at irregular intervals during the ten days of the sale. Each picture contained many articles the names of which began with one of the letters in the name of the store. Prizes were offered through the newspaper advertising for the longest list of names from the complete series of pictures. These prizes were valuable and were displayed in the store window during the contest period. Over 6,000 answers were sent in, showing that widespread interest had been taken in the contest.

This housekeeper's sale was not confined strictly to household equipment or clothing for the housekeeper but included almost every line of goods that the housekeeper requires for her family, from dress goods to gloves.

Employes' Sales Stimulate Interest.—In addition to the regular May White and August Clearance sales, the John Schoonmaker & Son store, of Newburgh, N. Y., holds four Employes' Sales during the year. Following the Employes' Sale in May a sale is held in June called the Employes' Vacation Fund Sale; and following the October Employes' Sale is the November Employes' Christmas Fund Sale. After the two Fund sales, the employes receive a bonus of 5 per cent of the gross sales for those two weeks, distributed among the employes on a percentage basis; the higher the salesmen's wages, the more bonus is received. Department heads and executives do not receive a bonus.

Though employes receive a bonus after but two of the sales, all four are called Employes' Sales because the employes stimulate interest in all these sales by writing letters and by personal selling talks. Some time ahead of each sale the advertising department collects from the salespeople names of customers to whom letters should be addressed. Cards are filled out by the salespeople with names and addresses and the name and department of the one filling out the card. These are filed alphabetically and in cases where the same name has been handed in by several salespeople, the extra cards are thrown out. This prevents the same person receiving half a dozen letters at one time. A general letter is then written by a girl in the advertising department who writes a legible and attractive longhand and a plate is made of it. No salutation nor signature appears on the plate. Five thousand letters are then printed and the girl who wrote the original letter takes the cards turned in by the sales force, fills in the names and addresses and signs the letter with the name of the salesperson who suggested the name. The letters are then sent out with booklets describing all items, prices and special attractions of the sale and giving the days when various articles will be placed on sale. In addition to these employes' letters to customers, complete descriptions of the merchandise to be offered during the sales are printed in the weekly *Store News* a twenty-page booklet, and 12,000 of these are mailed to regular customers outside the city. Space is also taken in twenty newspapers in the surrounding country during the week preceding the sales and also while the sales are in progress. In the city newspapers the advertising space is gradually cut down as the sales advance.

A novel method of advertising is worked out three days preceding the sales. A vacant room in the basement is set aside to receive samples of merchandise from every department that has anything special to offer during the sales. Each piece of merchandise is labeled with its price and the day it is to go on sale. A bright girl is put in charge of this "Inspection Room" to answer any questions put to her by people who come to look over the goods. During these three days of inspection the salespeople upstairs direct all customers to the "Inspection Room" and the popularity of the inspection indicates that most women feel the store is conferring a distinct favor on them in allowing them to look over the merchandise before it goes on sale.

(Summarized from *Dry Goods Economist*).

Special Three-Day Sales in a Three-Weeks Anniversary Sale.—The recent Anniversary Sale of a large Boston store lasted for three weeks and was subdivided into six sales of special related merchandise, such as the Sewing Sale, School and College Sale, Sale of Ready-to-wear Garments, and so forth.

All employes wore Booster Badges exhibiting the number of the anniversary, with colored ribbons, lettered according to the particular sale being held. The color of the ribbon, as well as the lettering, was changed with each special sale though the same badge was worn the entire three weeks.

ADVERTISING FEATURES

Advertises Recipes to Sell Cooking Utensils.—An enterprising California hardware dealer publishes a tempting recipe in his newspaper space every Wednesday morning, mentioning the kind of ovenware in which the food may be prepared and served (see Exhibit 173). Women coming in for the advertised piece see the assortment of ovenware as well as other utensils. Interest in better kitchen equipment is created by this type of advertising.

Competition between Department Managers.—In line with

EXHIBIT 173.—A pleasing advertisement that is likely to attract the attention of every housewife who does her own cooking and is therefore a possible customer.

Watch for our Wednesday recipe.

Apricot Cream Pie

YUM-YUM! It looks so good, and tastes even better than it looks. Easy to make, too.

Ingredients for Filling.

Juice from can of apricots.
Two eggs.
Tablespoon sugar.
Tablespoon butter.
Pinch of salt.
Two teaspoons flour.

To the beaten yolks of your eggs add the sugar, butter, salt, flour and a little water, then add to the apricot juice, which should be heating on your stove. Cook slowly until it is thick and creamy. Next place a layer of apricot halves in a pie crust baked golden brown, pour in your cream mixture, top with meringue, and set in hot oven a few moments until the meringue is set.

A "Pyrex" Pie Plate
makes it possible to serve your pie on the table in the same plate it was baked in. We also show a fine line of pie plates of tin, aluminum and enamel

VISIT OUR HELPFUL HOUSEWARES' DEPT.

Valley Hardware Co.

189 S. First St.

the growing tendency to personalize the store and make its employes known to the public, the holding of a competitive sale between managers of departments will sometimes be found helpful, especially in the smaller cities and towns. Advertisements can be made up showing photographs of the department managers and assistants, with something about the prizes offered to the departments that increase their sales. Each manager may be given space in the advertisement to describe articles his department has to offer at special prices. Advertising during the contest may be made newsy by reporting the standing of the various departments. The results of the contest and the awarding of prizes afford some opportunity for publicity.

One result of such contests is the discovering of talent and initiative among employes that on ordinary occasions do not come into the limelight.

Advertising the Salespeople.—Some stores that employ salesmen of special knowledge or experience and have reason to believe that these clerks will remain with them find it worth while to advertise their helpers. The following copy, according to *Good Hardware*, was used effectively by one store in connection with a half-tone portrait of the salesman referred to.

> Meet our authority on cutlery. Raised in the hardware business, he knows cutlery and takes a lot of pride in finding out what you want, and then showing you the proper article for your wants. Jake never buys an article without thinking how well it will please some customer or fill some need. If you want the best that money can buy, Jake will show you how to be sure you're getting it. If you want a pretty good pocketknife, let us say, and yet don't care to put much money into it, Jake is ready for you. He will show you one that fits your needs so well that you'll wonder if he wasn't reading your mind when he put it into stock. Our Old Rough and Ready, for instance, is a good example in a pocketknife at 75 cents. Incidentally, Jake is as patient in selling a quarter knife to a lad as he is in selling the father a gold-plated safety razor.

Salespeople's Photographs and Distinctive Letter-writing.—A men's clothing store in Indianapolis has its salespeople write their names across small photographs of themselves. Small half-tones are then made and prints from these are pasted at the bottom of letters sent to customers or prospective customers, the idea being that people will remember faces oftener than names, though the name is there for reference in case of correspondence with or regarding the salesperson.

This same store uses the method of writing letters and other appeals as if they were composed by the article for sale. A hat, for example, talks about itself and closes with "You can get me at ——" (naming that particular store).

In an effort to increase the number of charge accounts, this store sent out letters on blank pages torn from a ledger book, beginning "I am a ledger sheet. I want to be used."

Fur Show on "Fursday."—Because the Fur Fashion Show of the Fur Division of the National Garment Retailers' Association was scheduled for a Thursday, the committee in charge announced the event as "Fursday." The idea suggests adaptation by various retailers—"Bunday," "Shoesday," "Lensday," etc.

Exploiting Dress-making Service.—One retailer has found that an effective way of selling large quantities of wash goods is to exploit a dress-making service in connection with the goods, showing the typical styles in the store windows. Contracts were made with local dress-makers to take care of the work.

Sale of Aprons Advertised by Clerks Wearing Them.—A dry goods company in Fort Smith, Ark., equipped all its girls with aprons on the day before a big apron sale. Customers could not fail to notice the effect of the uniformly dressed saleswomen and cards were prominently displayed to advertise the sale. A similar plan was followed by the Kresge store in Philadelphia when the girls were provided with 10-cent dust-caps. The idea is one that may be carried out in many ways.

Big Sale Advertised by Letters to Buyers.—The Meyers Department Store, of Pasadena, Cal., used a novel method to drive home to patrons the fact that the "ten thousand bargains" advertised in celebration of its fifteenth anniversary were actually obtained by the store for the occasion and were not merely left-overs of store stock.

A circular was sent to the store's mailing-list in which was printed the following letter, which the store stated had been sent to 500 manufacturers and wholesalers:

Gentlemen:

For seven days, beginning May 13, we shall hold our fifteenth anniversary sale. We want to "bust" all sales records. Price only can do this. Please look around, dig hard, and let us know what you have to offer at a dead-loss price—something desirable that will just make 'em buy.

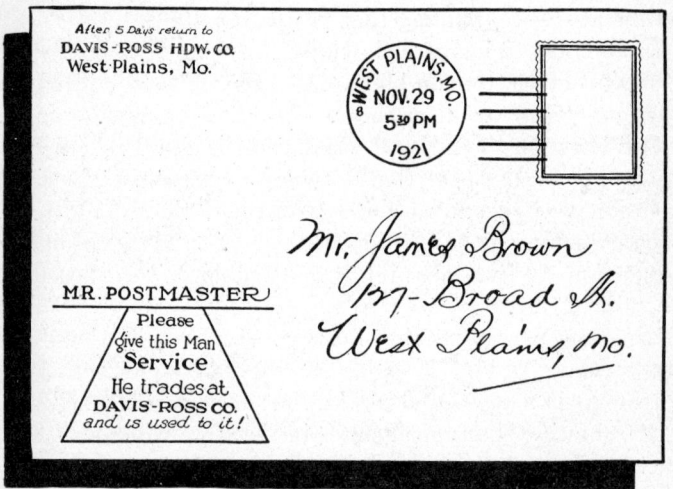

Exhibit 174.—An effective way of addressing envelops, used by a hardware store. This method of addressing commands the addressee's attention, even before he opens his letter.

If necessary, send sample, or wire (at our expense). We can't do big things without the help of our friends. Now its up to you.

The circular added: "Our friends got busy. Every express brought great lots of samples. From these we ordered. The bargains we bought are your bargains."

(*Retail Ledger*).

Advertisements on Bulletin Board at Entrance.—The L. Froug Department Store, of Pine Bluffs, Ark., maintains a small bulletin board at the store entrance, keeping posted on it the daily advertisements clipped from the newspapers.

Many department stores in the large cities keep their daily advertisements posted at the elevator entrances, where some also have the store directory.

Telegrams about the Old Straw Hat.—The Spines Company, of Wichita, Kan., telegraphed to fifty local business men at the end of summer, "Your straw hat is dead." The recipients of the telegrams were so taken with the idea that it got into the newspapers and the store received a little special publicity. A number of men answered the telegram in a way to carry on the idea—"Rushing undertaker to you immediately," or "Weather prevents my attending funeral, postpone it until tomorrow." Others called and bought their fall hats the same day.

Novel Method of Advertising Service.—Exhibit 174 shows a novel style of envelop which proclaims to all who see it that "service" is to be had by patrons of that store.

Capitalizing a Telephone Number.—An enterprising lumber retailer, of Springfield, Mo., was impressed one day with the difficulty one has in using a bulky telephone directory for looking up the business people in a given group. It occurred to him that a profitable kind of advertising would be some plan by which he could make his telephone number so well known that people would not have to finger a great many pages in order to get in touch with him.

His telephone number is 300 Green, and so he thought there would be no better way of emphasizing it than to literally make his business known as "green." With this plan in mind, he had his buildings and his delivery wagons painted green. There was green lettering on his letterheads, and in his billboard advertising he used the slogan "300 Green for Sudden Service," and of course this slogan was always painted in green on the billboards. Carrying the idea still further, he used green extensively in his own suits, shirts, hose, ties, etc. This was probably carrying the idea further than necessary, but through the careful working out of the idea this retailer has made himself known throughout his section as "Green," though his name is not Green. And he made it a rule to live up to his slogan with regard to service. He took no order that could not be delivered the same day.

There is a great deal to be gained in making a business distinctive. It may not always be possible to do this through the telephone number, or even through the name of the firm, but through some other means.

Prize Advertisement in Form of a Letter.—A department store in Los Angeles held a contest which indicated that either the women and girls of the city were well acquainted with the merchandise and service of the store or made it their business to become better acquainted. A prize was offered for the best advertisement about the store written by a high-school pupil and published in any of the school publications. The prize-winning advertisement later appeared in the newspaper space of the store. Besides creating a new type of interest, this prize-advertisement plan brought a fair volume of business to the girls' wearing-apparel department.

Following is the letter-advertisement that received the award:

Dear Polly:

I'm so thrilled! I've just been down to Bullock's on the girls' floor and oh the pretty clothes! You know they have a "high-school girls' section" and I think it's the loveliest kind of an idea.

There are such wonderful garments for the high-school girl, party frocks, school uniforms and such modish dresses of silk, velvet and wool!

And coats! The materials are velour, polo cloth and bolivia, in the most popular shades for autumn. The trimmings include fur collars, shawl collars, yoke effects, fancy stitching and patch pockets. And they're all fully lined! Can you imagine coats like that for $25! They're so durable and so charming. One of them of blue velour had an opossum collar! The minute I saw it I thought of you, for it's just the color of your eyes. I simply can't rest until I see that coat on you.

Did you ever see a jumper dress that was really chic? There is one beauty, of light brown serge, plaid with blue, brown and henna, that has a box-pleated skirt. And there's the dearest little henna crepe de chine waist that goes with it! When I first saw it I thought I'd have to be a millionaire to own such a rich-looking garment, but I found that the jumper was only $15, and the waist $6.95.

And such party frocks! They are of georgette, crepe de chine, satin, radium, net and taffeta, in apricot, green, pink, henna and blue. There are some darling models at $19.50.

I was surprised when I heard that Bullock's is offering uniform skirts at $5 and $6.95. Oh, yes, they have the regulation middies, with detachable collars and cuffs at $2.90, separate middies $1.95, separate collars and cuffs 95 cents and black taffeta ties at $1.25 and $1.50.

Can't you come in Saturday and go shopping with me? Remember, Bullock's closes at 1 o'clock. We could go to a show afterwards. Please come.

Loads of love,
Ruth

Exploiting Social Usages to Develop Engraving Business.—The J. K. Gill Company, of Portland, Ore., a firm selling books and stationery and also equipped for doing high-class engraving work, became aware of the disquieting fact that the amount of engraving business being done by the firm was relatively small.

The publicity manager decided that the most logical way of increasing the public's appreciation of this branch of service was to make capital of the fact that comparatively few people know the correct forms of the various social invitations and announcements. He forthwith created an attractive, modern American girl, naming her Harriet Louise Hewlitt. A series of small double-column newspaper advertisements was built up around this mythical character, telling about her engagement, her dinner parties, teas, luncheons, showers and finally her wedding. The correct form of engraving for each occasion featured was in some way woven into the advertisement, the series of advertisements forming a little serial story, entitled "Harriet's Romance—A Novelette in Eight Chapters." These advertisements were placed on the social page of the two Sunday newspapers for a period of eight weeks. People became interested in Harriet's round of gaiety and would watch for succeeding chapters of the "novelette." The advertisements were put on the social page because of the fact that women are always interested in this page and because of the fact that by far the larger portion of social engraving work is sold to women.

After the eight advertisements had appeared serially in the newspapers, the firm had them made up into an attractive booklet. Some one in the engraving department watched the daily social columns of the papers for announcements of engagements and other affairs. These items were used as leads, a copy of the booklet being mailed promptly, either to the young woman mentioned or to her mother.

EXHIBIT 175.—An advertisement that created engraving business by giving interesting information about social affairs.

EXHIBIT 176.—Another of the series of advertisements dealing in story style with social customs.

Exhibits 175 and 176 are reproductions of two of the advertisements used.

(Summarized from *Business*).

Successful Use of Pitcher as a Premium.—A furniture store in Knoxville, Tenn., drew many visitors by advertising an article to be given free to every person who made a purchase of $1 or more, or who paid an account in full. This present was a large glass pitcher with an ice-retaining lip. The advertisement showed a picture of the pitcher and the following appealing description:

> You can with safety hold it over the frailest tumbler and know that a piece of ice is not going to pour out and smash the glassware.
> (*Grand Rapids Furniture Record*).

CREATING AND EXPLOITING DISTINCTIVE SERVICE

A Gingham-gowned Hostess Receives Shoppers.—During National Gingham Week, Marshall Field & Company, Chicago, successfully stimulated interest in this material by featuring a Gingham House on the second floor of the store. A one-room house, presided over by an attractive young woman gowned in green and white gingham, showed the many possibilities of gingham in the way of draperies, cushions, counterpanes, etc.

The "hostess" explained to shoppers the many ways in which the material could be utilized in the country home, in children's rooms, for sun parlors, or for dresses and hats, and aided in deciding the number of yards necessary for any of these purposes. The concrete examples shown in the attractively arranged interior of the Gingham House appealed to every woman who saw them and made her an enthusiast over the possibilities of gingham, to the benefit of the store's sales account.

Helping the Male Shopper.—The male shopper is more or less of a joke in a department store but one manager has taken pity on his helpless estate and furnished the service of a woman "shopper's helper" to any man applying. The man explains his needs to this woman, perhaps gives her the samples his wife has sent him to match, and then reads his newspaper in the smoking room until a boy announces that his purchase has been completed. He returns to the desk of the "shopper's helper," inspects the purchases and, if satisfactory, pays for them.

The store manager reports that this service has gained many new friends for the store, the number requesting the assistance of the "shopper's helper" being surprisingly large.

Shoe Laces as a Follow-up.—A number of Walk-Over Shoe Stores have adopted the plan of sending out an extra pair of laces to each purchaser of a pair of shoes about a month after the purchase has been made. These laces go along in a mailing card, one side of which bears this copy:

Maybe you need 'em
Maybe you don't
Maybe you'll wear 'em
Maybe you won't
Just a minor part of "Footwear Equipment" for those Walk-Over shoes you bought recently.
We have your size on record.

The other side of the card bears this message:

Realizing that your shoes are the only part of your apparel that can cause you pain, we are using expert service to keep you comfortable.
If we have failed in any manner to properly fit or suit you, we will consider it a personal favor if you will return your recent purchase. We want to please you and make you feel that this is your shoe store.

Free Telephone Service to Encourage Orders.—Shopping by telephone is made easy for customers of the D. M. Read Company, Bridgeport, Conn. This company has established free telephone service with five adjoining cities and extended free delivery service to the same communities. The customer has only to call one of the numbers assigned to the store and connections will be made without charge. Of course this service feature is advertised consistently.

"Customers' Week."—A Minnesota retailer has found it worth while to have a "Customers' Week" as a yearly feature. Special announcements are sent to the entire customer list, expressing appreciation of the relationship and inviting the customers to come in, with their friends, and make themselves at home in "The Store that Friendship Built." The merchant, guarding against any appearance of egotism or self-glorifying, reminds customers of his desire to serve them, their children and their children's children in such an efficient, friendly manner that they will always feel like coming to the store.

Sends Operator as Well as Washing Machine.—A progressive household-supply store goes further than sending a washing machine to be tried at the home of a prospective customer. When a machine is delivered to a home the company also sends some one to do part of the family washing in the presence of the housekeeper. The working of the machine is carefully explained. This method of demonstration results in a greatly increased percentage of sales over the usual method of leaving the first operation of the machine largely to the prospective customer.

(Retail Ledger).

Specialists in Charge of Counters or Departments.—Some retailers have solved the problem of how to get more sales by putting the various counters or departments in charge of salesmen or saleswomen of real experience with the particular goods to be sold. Fishing tackle, for example, may be sold by a young man who is an ardent fisherman and can talk about the kinds of fishing tackle with enthusiasm and earnestness. The same principle applies to the athletic-goods department, carpenters' tools, etc. One store has scored a distinct success in supplying summer goods of various kinds to boys by employing high-school boys during the vacation season, by making the store the headquarters for the sale of tickets, by giving space to some of the advertising literature of the schools and athletic teams and by even devoting some of the store's advertising space to several of the school events. The result has been the cultivation of a substantial amount of school trade. In some lines of purchases, such as baseball and football goods, the total is a sizable one.

(Good Hardware).

Drug Store Gains Reputation for First Aid Service.—A drug salesman in a large store in the Middle West, after a number of attempts, persuaded his firm to urge, in its regular advertisements, that people in need of first aid service call on the telephone for him personally. By administering first aid in the case of serious burns, cuts, poisoning, sprains and other emergencies requiring instant and expert knowledge, this salesman soon built up a city-wide reputation for himself and the store, which naturally resulted in increased sales. He now has all the city's physicians charted according to office hours and addresses and is thus able to quickly summon further aid, which otherwise might be delayed because of the family's ignorance of the address of nearest doctor or his hours.

"Doctors' Directory" Service by Pharmacists.—To build up prescription business among doctors, two enterprising pharmacists established their store as a headquarters at which could always be found a record of the whereabouts of any doctor in the city at any time. By securing the cooperation of physicians through letters and personal interviews, this firm is notified by doctors when they leave their offices and when they return. In the city telephone directory, after the home or office address of every doctor cooperating in this plan, appears this statement, "If there is no answer, call Blank 223." Thus the patient or person calling the doctor is directed to the pharmacy where information can be secured. When calls are received at the store a form is filled in giving the name of the doctor, name of person calling, with address and telephone number and message, the time the call was made and the name of the clerk or salesperson receiving it. If the physician does not telephone or call at the store before returning to his office, these messages are delivered to him. This unusual service, according to the general manager of the firm, has caused the prescriptions to average 90 per cent of sales.

Special Attention to Children.—A study made by Armour & Company in one state revealed that, excepting Saturdays, 65 per cent of purchases are made by children. This indicates the importance, in certain types of stores, at least, of seeing that sales-service is pleasing to these young buyers.

A drug store has earned the good-will of children and their parents by having its salesmen pay particular attention to the children's errands and wait on them in turn instead of after all the grown people have been served. When a child has to take home change it is put into an envelop and the amount marked on the outside.

The Traveling Grocery Store.—There is nothing new about the door-to-door peddler but A. J. Porter, of Los

Angeles, Cal., has clothed him in a neat chauffeur's outfit and given him a grocery store on wheels to drive about the city, to the delight of housewives who are thus spared the necessity of dressing for a trip downtown. In announcing this plan, the following card was slipped under the doors of prospective customers:

Store-at-Your-Door

Starting tomorrow, we will have a truck working in your district with a complete line of the best standard brands of groceries. After the routes are established the truck will make regular calls. Our plan does away with extra expenses, such as store rent, clerks, lights, fixtures and many other things that go to make up general overhead of the store—all of which you pay for. With our plan we bring the things right to your door and you pick out just what you want and pay less. Give the Store-at-Your-Door a trial and in return we will give you good goods, service and low prices.

The truck has shelves inside and outside, the latter being protected when traveling, and contains a refrigerator for butter, eggs, cheese, etc. No fresh fruits or vegetables are carried. The firm's store and warehouse is used as the base of supplies, and by watching sales the truck is stocked with the quickest selling articles.

Opening the Store Just When Moving Picture Houses Close.—The "Extra Service Store" in Galena, Kan, earns its name by maintaining evening business hours when other grocery stores are closed. The proprietors used to close the store about 6 p. m. but one of them lived near the store and was often called on to serve customers after closing hour. He always opened the store because he disliked to disappoint people but he wondered why so many waited until after 6 o'clock to do their buying. By asking questions he found that the men did not get home in time to go to the store and their wives were too busy to go. Galena is a mining town, and in the evening most people go to the theater or the moving pictures. So this accommodating storekeeper decided to open in the evening after the shows closed. At first he and his partner waited on all customers but trade became so brisk that they offered double pay to any clerks who wished the extra work. This speaks for itself but in addition the originator of the scheme says:

> The result was astonishing. It was simply remarkable the amount of stuff people either had not time to get during the day or had forgotten what they needed. We always open now just as the first show is over and customers simply flock into the store. We actually sell more during that one hour than during any three hours of the day.
>
> This new scheme has not taken one cent away from our regular daily trade. It is still increasing. The hour at night has added at least 20 per cent to our sales.
>
> (*Progressive Grocer*).

Rental Bureau in House-furnishing Department.—L. S. Ayres & Company, one of the big downtown department stores, of Indianapolis, Ind., finds a Rental Bureau in its house-furnishing department a profitable institution. The Bureau is conducted as a clearing house for reliable information regarding rentable real estate in the city and has the cooperation of local real estate dealers and renting agents. No commission is accepted from the real estate dealer and no charge is made for the service to the customer. In cases where property listed with the bureau is in the hands of more than one real estate dealer, the young woman in charge of the bureau explains this to the inquirer and makes it clear that inspection of the property may be made through any agent, under no conditions making recommendation as to which man it would be preferable to deal with.

In order to have on hand the necessary data to carry on its work, the Rental Bureau uses the form shown in Exhibit 177. This is filled in by the real estate agent reporting property for rent.

As soon as a property is rented the agent telephones the Bureau and then sends in a confirmation card so the files can be kept up to date.

According to the advertising manager of the Ayres store, it is necessary that the store be somewhat of a public institution having the entire confidence of the community and of the local real estate board if the Rental Bureau is to be a success.

> # L. S. AYERS & CO.
> ## Rental Bureau
>
> Location *5108 E. North St.*
>
> | | | |
> |---|---|---|
> | Single............. | Basement............ | Bath *Yes* |
> | Double *Yes* | Heat *Furnace* | Electric Lights *Yes* |
> | Flat............... | Hdw'd Floors........ | Gas *Yes* |
> | Stories............ | Garage *No* | City Water *Yes* |
> | Duplex............ | Barn................ | Well............... |
> | Floor.............. | Porch............... | Cistern............ |
> | Rooms *4* | | |
> | Bedrooms *1* | | Rent *$32.50* |
>
> Rent includes..
>
> Remarks..
>
> Rental Agent *Gregory & Appel Inc.*

EXHIBIT 177.—Form used in the house-furnishings department of an Indianapolis store, on which to keep information about houses for rent. This information was maintained as a service feature for customers.

Aside from the general good-will gained for the store, he says:

We are also making the Rental Bureau pay in an immediate and practical way. We purposely located it on the fourth floor of our store, right in the midst of the house-furnishings. Every woman who comes to the bureau to inquire about a dwelling place must at least casually inspect a good part of our stock; and she sees these goods at exactly the right time. For we all know well enough that every time the family moves there is some new item of household furniture or furnishings to buy.

In addition, our Rental Bureau receives, each day, forms listing the names and addresses of all persons who have rented property listed with us. These are immediately turned over to our Home Service Department. The names listed are the finest kind of prospective customers for us, and they are followed up either by telephone or letter. A personal invitation is extended to them to come in and look over our stock. A splendid volume of business is secured in this way.

(*Retail Ledger*)

Handicraft Shop Utilizes Odds and Ends.—A progressive store of the Northwest, in an endeavor to take care of the customer who desires to make her own holiday gifts, established a department to teach people how to manufacture articles that would be acceptable Christmas presents. The company also had the idea that many odds and ends of merchandise might be disposed of in this way and, at the same time, good-will created for the store.

The Handicraft Shop, as this department is now called, has been in operation for 18 months and occupies a space of about 40 by 50 feet on the second floor, its success at the Christmas season making it evident that it could be kept busy the year round helping customers to make birthday, graduation, and wedding presents.

No merchandise is carried in the shop but customers are aided in their selection of materials and before beginning work must show a receipt slip identifying their materials as having been bought in the store. The woman who acts as hostess is an expert in transforming all sorts of unlikely objects into attractive gifts. "White elephants" in every department are turned over to her and transformed by customers into things they want. For instance, in the glassware department were a number of plain glass pieces of various sizes that were not selling. By the application of sealing-wax flowers and decorations, these plain glass pieces became such sellers that more had to be ordered.

The "hostess" presides over the Handicraft Shop all the year round, but has the aid of two or three helpers for the Christmas work. Customers are made to feel at home in this department and a special room is set aside for drying painted and glued articles, with a girl in charge whose duty it is to see that each thing is checked and returned to its maker. During holiday seasons tea is served to workers in the Handicraft Shop from four to five every afternoon. This is a pleasant little feature to draw visitors and create good-will conversation.

According to the publicity manager of the store, "The nub of the whole scheme is to get a woman of pleasing personality and original ideas to take charge, and have her make people feel as comfortable as possible. Also it is desirable to keep up with the new fads and introduce them as rapidly as they come along."

(Summarized in part from the *Dry Goods Economist*).

A Hat Manufacturer's Experience Gathered From a "Laboratory" Retail Store.—The John B. Stetson Company, well known hat manufacturers, maintains a retail store in Philadelphia as a kind of "laboratory" for the trying out of plans, satisfactory ones being later turned over to the retail hat trade. The seven standard recommendations listed below are results of this laboratory work.

To Increase Sales of Hats

1. *Avoid "flashy" stunts for quality goods.*
2. *Sell quality goods wherever your trade permits.*
3. *Feature one style, but carry a variety as well. The first gives rapid stockturn; the second, ability to satisfy all customers.*
4. *Sell hats in pairs, a derby with a soft hat.*
5. *Cultivate the courteously friendly attitude, which gives weight to your aid to the customer in selecting.*
6. *Size up the customer's style and show him but a few models that are suitable, instead of confusing him with many.*
7. *Remove all feminine atmosphere from the store or department.*

The Stetson Company offers the following explanatory details:

Stunts, while attracting the occasional customer—the transient trade—do not cultivate the steady buying, the class of customer who buys habitually at one place because he likes the service and the atmosphere of the store.

Emphasis is placed on the 2-hat sale plan. Suggestions by the salesman about the soft hat for day wear and a derby for the evening are regularly received well, as is also the question "How about your spring derby?"

It has been found well to feature pairs of hats in the displays.

Research work shows that department stores gain in hat sales not only by employing men exclusively in the sales work but by keeping this department away from the streams of women shoppers. While women buy large quantities of shirts, cravats, hose, etc., for their husbands, sons, and brothers, it seems that a man prefers to make his own selection of a hat. Another fact that research has brought out is that clothing helps the sales of hats more than ties, shirts and underwear.

The manufacturer gives retailers these suggestions as to color harmonies between clothing and hats, crediting the suggestions to the Kuppenheimer Company, manufacturers of clothing.

The dark gray hat goes with the blue suit, with the blue suit and blue overcoat, the blue suit and gray overcoat, the brown suit, the brown suit and gray overcoat, the gray suit, the gray suit and gray overcoat of contrasting shade, the gray suit of same shade as hat and the blue overcoat, the gray suit and black overcoat, the green suit, the green suit and black overcoat, the green suit and gray overcoat of contrasting shade, the black suit and black overcoat, the black suit and blue overcoat.

The light gray hat with a dark band goes best with the black suit and the blue overcoat.

The brown soft hat goes with the blue suit, the blue suit and blue or brown overcoat, the brown suit, the brown suit and brown, green or gray overcoat, the gray suit, the gray suit and green overcoat (if the hat is very dark brown), the green suit, the green suit and brown overcoat.

The tan hat goes with the blue suit, the blue suit and brown overcoat, the green suit, the green suit and brown overcoat.

The green hat goes with the brown suit, the brown suit and green overcoat, the gray suit, the gray suit and the green overcoat, the green suit, the green suit and the gray overcoat.

The gray-green hat looks well with the brown suit, the brown suit and green overcoat, gray suit, gray suit and green overcoat, green suit, green suit and dark blue overcoat.

The olive green soft hat goes with brown suit, brown suit and green overcoat, gray suit, gray suit and green overcoat.

The brown derby goes with the blue suit, blue suit and brown overcoat, or the brown suit of harmonious shade.

The black derby goes well with everything except perhaps the brown suit and green overcoat, the brown suit and gray overcoat, the gray suit and green overcoat, the green suit and gray overcoat.

It is particularly good with blue suit and black overcoat and the green suit and green overcoat.

(Summarized from *Retail Ledger*).

Free Camp Facilities for Motoring Tourists.— *The Automobile Trade Journal* outlines an interesting plan for the small-town automobile-service man as a means of directing the trade of tourists to his own station and, by a cooperative plan, to other stores in the same town.

A small tract of woodland a few miles out of town, owned by a dealer, was fitted up by him as a camp site. Platforms for tents, running water, lavatories, sinks—everything to add to the comfort of the traveling motorists, was included in the plan of the camp and offered to the tourists without charge. Arrows advertising the camp were placed along the roads, and a miniature reproduction of the camp in a department store window in the town gave tourists an inviting picture of what they were offered.

The service station maintained a supply of automobile accessories, oil and gasoline right at the camp and kept a capable man there constantly to take care of minor repair jobs. General overhauling and larger repair jobs were handled by the night force at the town station. Signs were placed about the camp telling of reliable town stores from which to obtain supplies, and a man at the service station in the town directed the tourists to the same stores. This enabled the owner of the camp site to call upon the town stores to share part of the expense of running the camp.

To the townspeople this dealer offers to furnish necessary information, routes, and so on, for taking motor trips to any part of the country.

Throughout the entire plan, this dealer features the car for which he holds the agency. In addition to the information which he gives to local people who contemplate touring is a list of service stations along their routes from which they can obtain proper service and supplies for the particular make of car sold by this dealer.

Capitalizing an Automobile-inspection Service.—An automobile-service station, realizing the need for conscientious, careful inspection and repair service, decided to create a real service for automobile owners and then base its advertising and selling campaign on that platform. The two brothers who operated this service station had already learned, from their experience with automobiles, that most tire trouble is due to neglect, ignorance or abuse. If tires are under- or over-inflated, if insignificant cuts are ignored or neglected, if the wheels are not properly set, the owner will sooner or later have trouble.

Accordingly, these brothers offered their customers and prospective customers free monthly inspections. Because the good-will of the firm was to be built up largely through this service, it was conscientious and painstaking, not just a service in name only. Every car brought in was gone over thoroughly and a written report made of just what the inspection revealed. A neat card form was used for these reports. It was left entirely with the owner of the car as to whether he would act on the information given him. And there was not the least obligation attached to the free inspection. The owner was at liberty to buy his tires from these brothers, if he felt so disposed, after looking over the report, but if he wanted to go elsewhere, nothing was said about the matter. Naturally, a great many inspections were made that brought no business, because no new tires or repair work were needed, but the business that did come from these free inspections was considerable. Many times the service man would find things that were not visible to any one except a tire expert.

While the business of this firm was especially to sell tires, it first started out to sell its service, letting the tire sales and repair work come as a natural result of the inspection service.

The stock of this concern is gone over daily, so that it may be kept complete always, even with respect to special and odd sizes of tires. Having started out to build their business on service, these brothers believe in giving it at all times and under all conditions. The shop is always open and the inspection card that is sent to the car-owner invites him to make use of the service regularly.

Only one make of tires is carried, at a standard price, and a record is kept of every purchase, so that if any question of failure to give proper mileage comes up, the record can be easily referred to. This has been found the best method of convincing customers that the firm's greatest concern is to keep tire-cost and troubles down to a minimum for all of its patrons.

Examples of Successful Self-serve Departments.—A Wilmington, N. C., department store has worked out an effective method of competing with the self-service stores by setting aside an entire department, 50×80 feet, that is operated regularly on a self-service plan. This store is one of a chain of thirty-one department stores located in North and South Carolina and Virginia. The name of the self-service department—"Pick-Take-Tote"—is appropriate because the word "Tote" is a colloquial expression throughout the section of country covered.

The layout of the department to which the self-service feature applies is unique in that different aisles radiate like spokes of a wheel from a central point where cashier and wrapping clerks sit. These radiating aisles bring the customer back to the central desk, no matter where he or she wanders, thus enabling the store to effect a saving in labor cost, for five people attend to the receiving of money and to wrapping. The goods are placed on flat and pyramid tables with prominent price tickets for each lot. Not only is the customer able to see all over the room from any point, but there is no obstruction from the cashier's desk and thus pilfering by dishonest customers is practically eliminated. The plan works very much as that of a cafeteria-restaurant where the patron puts on a tray the things selected and pays for them at point of exit. There is only one gate for the entrance and only one gate for exit. The aisles are wide, making it possible for a large number of customers to look around without crowding. The proprietors naturally put in this department a class of goods that to a large extent sell themselves on sight; such as house furnishings, tinware, crockery, glassware, etc. It is stated that sales have shown a gain of about 30 per cent since the department was installed a year ago.

A somewhat similar plan has been carried out by a Wilkes-Barre, Pa., store. Departments and goods are arranged for easy inspection and sales are made only for cash. Expenses have been reduced by eliminating various kinds of service: nevertheless, there are salesmen on hand to suggest purchases or to answer questions. This store carries the apt name of "Drygoodsteria," being operated much like a "self-serve restaurant."

(Summarized in part from the *Dry Goods Economist*).

Figures from a Michigan Experience.—The business of the Chase Mercantile Company, of Pontiac, Mich., affords still another instance of how a self-serve department can operate at low cost while at the same time serving the valuable purpose of a trade-bringer for the store as a whole.

According to *Business*, the Chase Mercantile Company formerly conducted a grocery department of the usual type, supervised by a manager, aided by a force of salespeople. Under this plan the department made sales of about $50,000 a year. After inspecting the self-serve departments of several other stores, the executives of the Chase Mercantile Company transformed their grocery department. Much of the old shelving was left in position but was divided by means of vertical partitions into sections for classified merchandise. An enclosure of meshed wire was put around the entire department. An attractive entrance and an exit were built, the entrance being fitted with a turnstile, and the exit split into three channels with island-like wrapping counters between the channels. Like good merchants, the Pontiac store executives laid out the exit of this grocery department so that it leads into another department in which meats was sold.

This self-serve department was filled with standard merchandise in packaged form. Small show-cards and price-tags were used liberally.

To reach the grocery department at all the customer must go through the main store. Referring to this feature, one of the firm says:

If we can't sell some of those 9,000 customers something besides groceries—if we can't avail ourselves of the opportunity of their presence in the store—then there's something wrong with our merchandise or with us.

The following figures are given as indicating the record of the newly arranged department:

> Floor space..................... 1,500 square feet
> Average investment in merchandise $6,500 to $7,500
> Annual sales..................... $220,000
> Weekly average of customers...... 9,000

The meat department shows a substantial increase in sales by reason of the proximity of the self-serve grocery department. The Pontiac firm announces the annual sales total of the meat department as $86,000 on an average investment of $1,400. It also gives the information that the basement dry-goods department, devoted largely to bargains and situated alongside of the grocery department, is turning its stock six times a year.

Referring particularly to the grocery department, the secretary and treasurer of the firm says further:

> It's paying its own way, carrying its own expense, including its salaries, rent, heat and light, and returning, besides, a net profit of 4 per cent on its sales—all on a margin of gross profit so narrow that the department is able to undersell competing grocery stores by an average of 20 per cent.

The department offers no specials and features no daily or weekly leaders. An article that sells at 8 cents when other grocery stores are selling it for 10 will be priced at 8 cents week after week, or as long as the cost to the store remains fixed.

APPEALS TO CHILDREN

Story-telling as a Feature for Children's Departments.—Many public libraries entertain children on Saturday afternoons with stories told by one of the children's librarians who has some special preparation for this work. These librarians visit schools during the week to arouse an interest in books and to invite the younger children to the story-hour. Department stores have found it worth while to adopt a similar plan to stimulate sales in the toy department at the opening of the holiday season A professional story-teller is employed. She visits primary schools and kindergartens, announcing her

Exhibit 178.—How Marshall Field & Company features its children's day programs.

program and inviting children to the store for the daily story-hour in the afternoon. The store features the story-hour in the newspaper advertising and invitations are also mailed to children. It has been found that most of the children drawn to these events are accompanied by grown-ups, which gives the store an excellent chance to sell attractive goods.

The plan may be made still more interesting to children by having the story-teller assume the role of "Mother Goose," the "Old Lady Who Lived in a Shoe" or any other character known to children.

(Summarized in part from *Dry Goods Economist*).

Jingle Contests for Children.—Young people are fond of taking part in contests for best names or jingles. A Midwestern store, recognizing this, carried out effectively a jingle contest connected with shoes. The contest was limited to boys and girls between 4 and 16. Cards giving the details of the contest were distributed to some extent direct to homes and also through school teachers. In covering homes the representatives of the store took along with them specimens of children's shoes which they showed to mothers. Prizes consisting partly of cash and partly of shoes were awarded. Special novelty banks filled with candy were given to the writers of twenty-five of the jingles that did not win prizes. Jingles that were not regarded as apt enough to win even the candy banks were returned to the writers with colored balloons as a token of the store's interest in the effort.

Of the 2,500 cards distributed, 2,000 were returned with jingles written on them. About 400 pairs of children's shoes alone were sold during the month.

Specially Decorated Room for the Sale of Children's Shoes.—Children are sometimes impatient over the purchase and fitting of new shoes. Often they look upon a trip to the shoe store as something to be endured rather than to be enjoyed and their mothers share this feeling. An enterprising New York firm, I. Miller & Company, has recognized this situation and met it successfully by providing a special room for the sale of children's shoes. Upon the walls of this room are nursery pictures and below the pictures, in glass cases guarded by large soldier-dolls, are artistic toy tableaux. Amusing silhouette figures chase each other around the lamp shades. Rows of small chairs are provided for the customers and shoes are fitted by pleasant saleswomen dressed in gray.

The appeal to children is continued in the artistically decorated shoe boxes and envelops for purchases of stockings. Happy, laughing children of various ages and sizes play around the sides of the box and another group adorns the lid. Sometimes the little customers are given souvenirs, such as balloons, with which they advertise the store all the way home.

(*Printers' Ink Monthly*).

A Doll Show.—To interest the children and, through them, their relatives and friends, a Rhode Island dry goods store held a doll show, offering prizes as follows:

For the best dressed doll, $5
For the second best dressed doll, $3
For the best home-made doll, $5
For the second best home-made doll, $3
For the funniest home-made doll, $3

The contest was limited to children under 12 years of age and the contestants had to present a statement by the parents that the work had been done by the child in whose name it was entered.

The show was advertised in the newspapers and by posters and cards displayed in the store and in the windows. Dolls entered in the contest were kept on exhibition in the store for a number of days. After the prizes had been awarded the winning dolls were displayed in one of the windows. Children not receiving prizes were given handsome souvenirs as a reward for their efforts.

Boy Customers' Pictures in House Organ for Boys.—Boy customers of the boys' department of Woolf Brothers, clothiers of Kansas City, receive copies of a house organ published especially for them. The little magazine is entitled *Knicker*, edited by "Tim," the store's publicity director, and always contains a comical cut of "Tim's Pup." One page is given to half-tone illustrations of boy patrons. Obtaining the good-will of the boys of today means obtaining the good-will of future heads of families as well.

Boys and Girls as Window-trimmers.—Here and there some live retailer in a moderate-sized city or town has excited the interest of townsfolk by holding a window-trimming contest for high school boys and girls. Where the school has an art department, it is well to call on the teacher to make up a team, picking those who possess artistic ability. A certain window should be reserved and the contestant allowed to use any articles in the store for his or her design. The displays may be kept in the window for three or four days, in turn, with a sign reading, "This window trimmed by Jack Smith for our contest." Prizes for the best displays will stimulate interest.

Boys' Club Helps Hardware Store.—A merchant in Wilmington, Del., employs a man 18 years old who got the idea —through waiting on boys in the store—of forming a boys' club. This young salesman made it a point to gather ten boys from 11 to 15 years of age and aid them in organizing a carpentry club. He explained that he would be glad to attend some meetings of the club and instruct them in the use of various tools. The result was an increased interest in tools and consequently increased patronage from the boys.

Stilts Help to Sell Boys' Shoes.—By placing a pair of stilts in the window with a card announcing that stilts would be given free with every pair of boys' oxfords sold, the Payne Shoe Company, Topeka, Kan., sold 144 pairs of a slow-moving line in two weeks and had to wire for another shipment of stilts and a new lot of oxfords to supply the demand.

EXPOSITIONS, DISPLAYS, DEMONSTRATIONS AND STYLE SHOWS

Murray Company's "Spring Party."—The Murray Company, a firm of brothers conducting a general farm supply store in Honesdale, Pa., make a feature every year of what is aptly called a "Big Spring Party." This firm arranges with a number of manufacturers to have special booths in charge of demonstrators or salesmen, provides for music, gives a bag of candy to every child, and free smokes to every man visitor. There are special assistants on hand to aid in showing folks through the store. As the town is a small one, this "Spring Party" proves to be an attractive feature to country residents for miles around and the number of orders taken for farm machinery and home supplies is sufficiently large to justify unusual expense for the event. It is advertised liberally by sending out broadsides to a comprehensive list of names. Special newspaper advertisements are inserted (Exhibit 179), also news items, in the Honesdale papers.

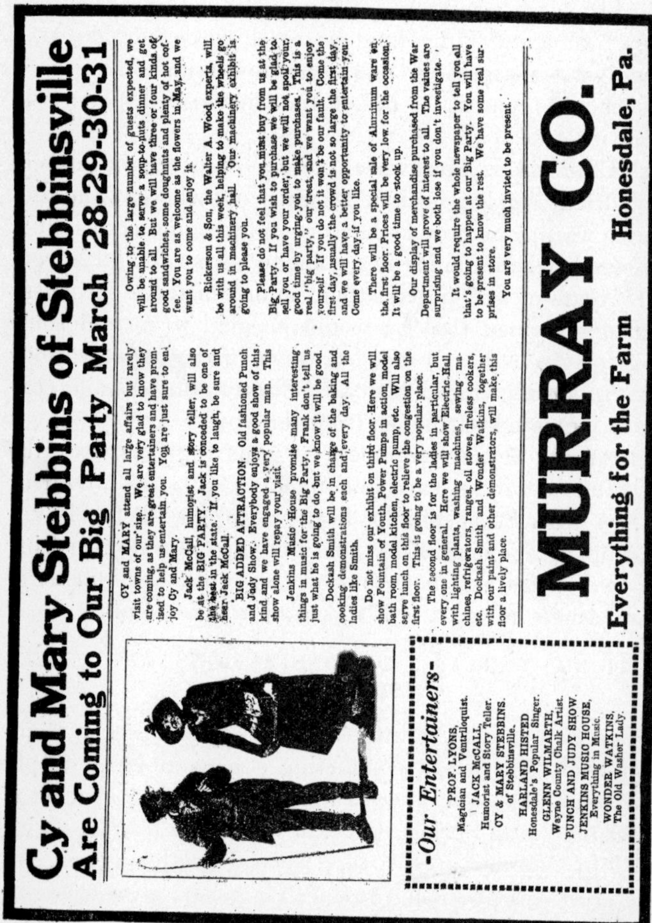

Exhibit 179.—How the Murray Company advertises a big annual event known as the "Spring Party."

Murray Company's recent party lasted four days. Some of the features were a full-sized silo erected in front of the store; a shed covered with three kinds of roofing handled by Murray Company on which water continually flowed without leaking through; a baking demonstration; an auditorium on the second floor seating 300 people and containing a regular stage on which there was a continuous performance throughout the four days. Professional talent was imported. Other features to hold the attention of visitors were four-minute talks by various demonstrators, music by local orchestras and the glee club, Punch and Judy show downstairs, exhibits of growing plants shown in connection with seeds, an electric hall showing the various lighting fixtures sold by the store, a radio outfit in operation, a picturesque pool of water in which real fish swam, a model bathroom, a model kitchen, special exhibits of carpenters' tools, and a free refreshment department that was kept working at full speed.

Sales Encouraged by Evening "Receptions."—The Taylor Carpet Company, of Indianapolis, Ind., has found that social evenings at the store, with a rule against the taking of orders, have paved the way for sales later on. Several "receptions" were held at the store with music provided, the stock arranged attractively and well lighted, and the public invited in to get acquainted with the store. No orders were solicited.

The idea back of the "reception" is to give the man of the family a chance to look over the carpets and housefurnishings. While his wife might be willing to take the responsibility of buying an article costing a few dollars, she probably would not risk $50 or more on an article he had not seen. As most men are employed during the day, and may be too far away to visit the shopping section during noon hours, the purchase would be put off indefinitely. The evening "reception" afforded an opportunity for families to look things over together and the sales account of the store showed that it resulted in decisions to purchase, as women returned the next day knowing just what they wanted. Soliciting sales during the evening would have caused people to feel less free to come into the store.

Saleless Furniture Exhibition.—During three days prior to the regular February sale the Bradford Furniture Company of New Orleans, La., held an exhibition with cash registers locked. The salesmen gave all their time to explaining and displaying the furniture in five completely furnished bungalows. Other stores cooperated with the furniture store by lending textile articles to be included in the exhibit. The newspaper advertisements created such curiosity that on the opening day the doors had to be closed early and only small groups admitted.

Expositions for Men and for Children.—Style shows are usually held in the spring and fall, with most of the stores' advertising directed to women. Window-displays are also made up to appeal especially to them. For this reason an exposition for men or one for children is something out of the ordinary. Experience has shown that such expositions attract much favorable attention. A large department store that holds semi-annual expositions for men sends out a few days beforehand formal invitations to a carefully selected list of men who have already been informed of the coming event by folders or personal letters.

The principal features of the exposition are displays of clothing arranged with accessories for every occasion. For instance, proper sports clothing is shown in connection with golf sticks, caddie bags, etc. Another exhibit shows how men's shirts, ties, and other apparel should be folded or arranged to the best advantage in wardrobes or trunks. All of the exhibits are marked by completeness and artistic arrangement, and salesmen are on hand to explain every detail.

The same store holds a children's exposition, turning the entire store over to children for three days. In addition to decorations and toys of every description, educational exhibits at one exposition showed a glass-blower at work, a potter at his wheel, a linotype operator, an Indian weaving blankets on a hand-loom, and many other interesting occupations. This exposition attracted many grown-ups, aside from those accompanying children.

Pure Food Exhibitions.—With the growing spirit of cooperation between manufacturer and retailer, a pure-food exhibition should be easy to arrange. It may be made to stimulate interest and sales in large grocery stores or in grocery sections of department stores. A store that makes an annual feature of this kind of a show constructs attractive booths and rents them to manufacturers for exhibiting and demonstrating their products. Unless a considerable variety of foods can be shown such an affair will not draw a general crowd.

Housekeepers' Exposition.—In these days when it seems that a new and indispensable device for the housewife is turned out every week, an exposition of utensils and equipment for housekeepers will attract a large attendance. If there is no store large enough, several stores can cooperate in renting a hall suitable for an exhibition of this kind and invite manufacturers to send their products and demonstrators for a certain number of days. The giving away of circulars, souvenirs, or samples of various products aids in drawing people.

"Made at Home" Display.—Few people in any community are familiar with most of the products that are made in the home town or the county. With this in mind the J. W. Knapp Company of Lansing, Mich., roused public interest by displaying in the windows and inside the store products from all the factories in Lansing.

This plan could be made still more interesting by enlisting the aid of members of an Industrial Department of some institution such as the Y.W.C.A. One such association holds industrial pageants for the purpose of interesting people in the work of the girls employed in local industries. In these pageants, after certain exercises by the industrial girls, the audience is conducted to an exhibition made up of decorated booths, where the girls from the factories display and explain the making of many articles. The manufacturers have been generous in supplying samples of the work at various stages of manufacture and, in some cases, samples to be given away.

Free Lunch at Five Grocery Stores.—Using the old attraction of something good to eat that costs the eater nothing, five grocers in an Illinois town combined in an effort to increase trade. A progressive luncheon of five courses, each course to be served by one of the stores, was planned for a certain Saturday and freely advertised during the previous days of the week.

The first store served an oyster cocktail with saltines. The occasion was used to feature a certain brand of crackers and a brand of sauce. The second course, at the next store mentioned in the advertisement, consisted of soup with crackers, a special brand of soups being featured. At the third store a tuna fish salad was served, demonstrating a particular brand of canned fish and a salad dressing. The fourth store served a slice of ham with mustard, a slice of bread and butter and a pickle, all certain brands which the store wished to advertise. Customers finished their lunches at the fifth store with a cup of coffee and cakes. In this cooperative plan most of the advertised goods were furnished by manufacturers who were interested. Such a plan need not necessarily be carried out in a cooperative way in order to be effective.

(Progressive Grocer).

Samples Make Satisfied Customers.—During an epidemic of colds and influenza an enterprising druggist provided a table in his store for displaying cough-drops. In front of packages of each brand he placed a small dish containing samples of that brand. Thus each customer could taste the cough-drops and be sure of getting a package that he would use instead of buying a box and perhaps throwing it away after trying one or two of the cough-drops.

(The Merchandising Co-Operator).

College Students Aid Stove Campaign.—The manager of a furniture company in Albuquerque, N. M., conducted a successful three-day stove demonstration with the aid of six young men from the State University and a number of young women from the domestic science department of the University. The young men made a canvass of the city, after college hours, compiling statistics on the number and conditions of stoves, and afterward aided in the store's display of new models of stoves. The young women prepared food on the stoves and served customers between the lectures, which were given by representatives of the various stove companies.

Coupons were printed in the store's newspaper advertisements which if clipped and brought to the store were good for a paper shopping bag. In addition to the actual stove-buying during the demonstration, the manager is confident that many visitors were turned into prospective patrons.

(*Retail Ledger*).

Demonstration Tour Sales Plan.—There is a good lesson for dealers in home-furnishing goods in the demonstration tour carried out in one of the Mid-western states under the supervision of the State College of Agriculture.

This home-furnishing demonstration tour was conducted in connection with an agricultural campaign to promote the raising of more clover. The campaign was made with a motor truck, which was fully equipped with demonstration material, such as small rugs, curtains, mantel (made of cardboard), bookcase or piano, and such small articles as vases, candlesticks, etc.

The agricultural part of the campaign was in charge of two experts from the State College, while the work of telling women how to make their homes attractive was left in charge of a woman expert on this subject. The object of the latter was to teach home decoration to women throughout the rural districts who had no opportunity of going to large stores and seeing model decorations and furnishings of all kinds. Some of the things the farmers' wives were told about were the choice and placing of furniture, the choice and placing of window-shades, curtains, hangings, the treatment of floors, the kinds of rugs to use, the things that should and should not be placed on a piano, bookcase, and so forth.

This demonstration truck was taken from one community to another and while the lectures were being given to the farmers on agricultural matters, their wives were being entertained in learning the always interesting art of making the home a cheerful and bright place in which to live.

The success of the campaign is indicated by the comment of A. J. Meyer, director of the extension work of the college, who says:

The report comes to me from every community in which meetings have been held that the women have been unusually enthusiastic. This is the first time that the college has attempted to carry this particular message to the women of the state—the story which our home economics department is telling to women. The story is one of home decoration, centering about a discussion of floor coverings, wall coverings and draperies. It was a subject concerning which we were very doubtful as to the reaction. We wondered whether farm women were thinking about these things that are not usually associated with the hard, practical problems of the home. Missouri women, however, are ready for the finer things of life. Homemaking has gone beyond the simple matter of cooking, baking, sweeping the floor and making beds. Making the home attractive by all the devices of which we have knowledge is a real problem to our farm women. They turned out in large crowds. They stayed through long meetings and then stopped to ask scores of questions at the close of every meeting.

Naturally, a plan of this sort, organized and forwarded by state employes, would be on a better basis for publicity than a private demonstration tour. Nevertheless, there is no reason why retail merchants should not cooperate with state and county officials in furnishing material and printed matter to make such a tour successful. And if there is no inclination on the part of state or county authorities to take charge of such an enterprise, the merchants might do something of this sort themselves through a merchants' association, a board of trade, or other cooperative effort on the part of a number of non-competing merchants.

As a matter of fact, an enterprising Victor dealer of Richmond, Ind., has a demonstration truck which he sends through the country, carrying an instrument and an exceptional selection of records. This "musical truck" never fails to receive a cordial welcome, and its sale of records has been a consistent one.

Child Models Exhibit Embroidery.—Living models for ready-to-wear garments are no novelty but a store in Sioux City, Ia., used the old idea in a new way by having children display the finished garments which could be made by customers who bought the stamped embroidery patterns offered by the store. Seeing how the garments would look when finished was a great incentive to buying the designs.

(Rural Trade).

Chorus Girls Models at Fashion Show.—When "Hitchy Koo" and Raymond Hitchcock arrived in Jacksonville, Fla., the owner of one of the largest department stores saw an opportunity to realize a lot of publicity for the store. Prominent posters were displayed in the windows and large space in the newspapers was devoted to advertising "Hitchy Koo" and "Sixteen Sweet Sixteens," the latter to be featured at the store in the garment salons at 3:30 p. m. Reservations were made for 200 in the improvised auditorium but the place was crowded long before the show began. These attractive young women of the chorus displayed evening gowns, street and afternoon dresses, and bathing suits. An orchestra was furnished by the store's music department and the show had all the atmosphere of the stage performance possible in the absence of Mr. Hitchcock. After the show the girls were rewarded with merchandise and an opportunity was extended to buy any pair of shoes at half price. The manager and his wife were given the chance to buy anything in the store at a 10 per cent reduction.

Style Show in Popular Restaurant.—The Oppenheim & Collins store, Brooklyn, N. Y., believes in going out after the type of patrons it desires rather than trying to entice them in to style shows in the store auditorium or theaters. Recently the store carried its style show into a popular restaurant and displayed on the stage in about an hour's time all the garments worn by the debutante through the day, from the morning negligee to the decollete gown for the evening. This afforded sufficient continuity for the show to receive good attention.

Living Models Show Kitchen Styles.—There is a large class of women to whom the style shows of evening gowns, wraps and "creations" do not appeal, the type of garment shown being one they have little or no use for or the prices being far out of their reach. The proprietors of a department store in Pottsville, Pa., realized this fact and originated a style show for the benefit of the woman who spends most of her time in the home. Living models were clad in becoming house dresses, intriguing bungalow aprons, dusting caps, boudoir attire, and other articles that the home-making woman needs. As it was a department store, the models were able to have for a background many articles of household furniture and kitchen equipment sold in the store. The result was that the firm made a number of substantial sales of up-to-date culinary contrivances in addition to sales of clothing.

All the advertising for this event was based on the idea that a woman should be as appropriately dressed for housework as for sports or parties.

CONTEST IDEAS

A Store-planning Contest.—A dry goods firm in Colorado altered and enlarged the store, adding two new departments. In addition to holding an "Alteration Sale" the proprietor offered prizes of $25 and $10 in gold to persons submitting the best plans for rearrangement of the store interior. A plan of the store as it was, including the floor space to be added to it, was shown in the advertisement offering the prizes. Prizes of a fine silk umbrella and a pair of shoes were offered to the ladies who made the best suggestions as to what the new departments should be and gave the best reasons for the suggestion. Many plans and suggestions were received, and people seemed to be eager to visit the store after the remodeling, in order to see how the winners' ideas had been carried out.

To Interest Farmers and Home Gardeners.—Stores in rural and suburban districts find contests of service in attracting and maintaining interest. Pumpkin contests are popular and have been conducted along many different plans. In the latter part of May one store mailed some pumpkin seeds in a letter to a large list of farmers in the vicinity, offering prizes from $25 down to $2 for the largest, second largest, etc., and $5 for the ugliest pumpkin grown from the seed. The date was set for the exhibition of pumpkins, judges were chosen, and the interest kept up during the summer by advertising in various ways.

The farmers especially took a great deal of interest in the contest and when the day arrived for judging, the store was flooded with pumpkins of all sizes, weighing from 50 to 116 pounds. All contestants entering pumpkins were given a free meal-ticket for dinner and after the pumpkins had been weighed and the prizes awarded another contest was announced. Prizes of merchandise were to be given to those guessing nearest to the correct number of seeds in the largest pumpkin.

This was not the end of the affair. One of the conditions had been that all pumpkins entered were to become property of the store. So with all the pumpkins on hand the store was able to hold a pumpkin pie contest for servant girls and maids, providing them with the main ingredient of the pie. These contests were given a good deal of publicity by the newspapers and served to extend the store's acquaintance among farmers within thirty and forty miles of the city.

Other stores distribute pumpkin seeds free and offer prizes of money or merchandise for the largest specimens brought in on a certain date. Sometimes stores cooperate in offering prizes and make the exhibition of pumpkins almost a town event, drawing farmers from miles around.

Another merchant conducts an annual corn-growing contest and finds the advertising received from it out of all proportion to the cost. He limits his contests to boys and offers $50 worth of merchandise in prizes. In the spring he makes up small packages of corn, enclosing a circular that sets forth the terms of the contest, and places these packages on display in his window. A package is given to any boy who asks for one and registers his name as a contestant. In the fall a window-display is made up showing the competing ears of corn. This contest interests the boys and through them the parents.

Other stores, without supplying the seed, offer prizes for the best ten or twenty ears of yellow or white corn, with no restrictions as to age or sex of contestants. There are many ways of varying the contests to appeal to different groups of customers.

"County Fair" to Attract Farmers.—For a store trying to draw rural trade, the scheme of a retailer in the state of Washington is one worthy of consideration. This retailer took the County Fair as a model and offered prizes of merchandise from his store for the best ears of corn, the largest pumpkins, the best pies, canned fruits and vegetables, etc.

The entries were, of course, shown in the store windows. Three farmers judged the men's entries and three farm women judged the home products. A nearby farm was lent for the purpose of providing a place for entries of cattle, colts and other livestock and after the committee had judged the animals, the prize-winners were decorated with their ribbons and paraded through the city. The fair interested farmers' households for miles around.

(*Dry Goods Economist*).

Prizes or Reductions for Finding Misspelled Words.—Only a store of the so-called popular class would adopt the plan of deliberately putting from one to half a dozen misspelled words in its advertisements, but some stores have carried out this feature, offering either a prize or a small reduction, 25 or 50 cents, from any purchase-price of a dollar or more. The method is a rather sensational one and yet it cannot be gainsaid that sensational methods are effectively used by stores of the popular type.

"Big Fish" Contest Brings Hardware Business.—A year's experience with a "Big Fish" contest has shown the proprietors of a hardware store in Hazleton, Pa., that arousing the interest of people in the community results in increased business. Prizes are awarded each month in the sporting department for the largest pike, trout, bass or other game fish caught that month. The only rule of the contest is that the fish must be registered after it is caught. It is not necessary to buy tackle at the store, and there are no restrictions in regard to age or sex of the contestants. The brown trout prize for May, 1922, was won by a man from Wilkes-Barre, thirty-one miles from Hazleton, showing that the interest in the store's contests is not confined to the home city. The managers of the sporting goods department report that the feature has paid for itself many times over and that new customers are increasing steadily in number. It is the aim of the store to become known as headquarters for fishermen all through the Hazleton and Pocono Mountains district.

Cinderella Slipper Contest.—An advertising scheme verging on the sensational was a "Cinderella Slipper Contest" held by a shoe store in Indiana. The firm had a pair of patent leather slippers, small size, made especially for the contest and advertised that the slippers would be given away on a certain Saturday evening to any woman whom they fitted perfectly, the only condition being that the trying on must be done in public.

Several days ahead of the contest the store window was appropriately decorated with a scene from the fairy tale, showing the entrance to a ballroom, the Cinderella slipper dropped on the top step, and the pumpkin coach drawn by mice, with a clock indicating midnight in a tower in the background. The advertising and the window-display attracted crowds of people to the store and when the time came to try on the slipper, contestants appeared for three hours until the slippers finally found an owner in a prominent young society matron whom they fitted perfectly. Much free advertising was given the store by articles in the newspapers and the contest was a subject of conversation for days.

Jingle Contest.—A Louisville, Ky., automobile sales office has used a jingle contest effectively in selling used cars. The used car problem is one of the automobile dealer's greatest concerns. When he is advertising the one or two makes of new cars he handles, his advertising has a cumulative effect. With the used car stock, the situation is different. This dealer found that it was better to tell the public that he maintained a used car department than it was to try to advertise each make of used car that he had for sale. His methods of keeping this department in people's minds are unusual and effective.

To acquaint the public with the location of the sales office, an arrangement was made with the best jazz band in town whereby the band practiced one evening a week in the showroom. Used cars, were of course, displayed effectively and an invitation was extended to the public to be present.

To attract the attention of many who perhaps would not come to hear the band, the dealer started a jingle contest as a regular feature of his newspaper advertising. Acceptable jingles about rebuilt cars were published and the writers each earned a dollar. In the case of a prize-winning jingle of more than ordinary advertising value, larger newspaper space is used. One of these was lately featured with a special border of comic Egyptian figures, as the jingle was headed "Old King Tut."

> Old King Tut did his merry strut
> Back in the chariot days.
> But if he lived now I'd venture to vow
> He'd modernize most of his ways.
>
> With autos so handy he'd be a Jim-dandy
> And, of course, in a Franklin he'd ride.
> Why, he'd give us the lilt in his Franklin rebuilt,
> With an added "Hoop La" on the side.
>
> Should he prepare to die, I know he would try
> To take in his tomb on the sand
> A rebuilt Franklin or two, and if that wouldn't do
> He'd take along Smart's River Band.
>
> But you know that old chappie was ever so happy
> With his chariots and banners afling;
> That's because he was "kilt" before Franklins were built
> So he died without missing a thing.

The "ballad" is signed C. R. Callis, 224 West Broadway, who composed the jingle and earned the prize. A panel in the advertisement describes the assortment of used cars as follows:

> Some splendid bargains in water-cooled cars, Ford, Dodge, Chalmers, Oldsmobile, Hupmobile, Hudson, Lexington, Packard, Cadillac, Peerless, Marmon, Stearns—all kinds—all prices, terms to suit. Come in and look them over. Open every evening this week. Joe Smart's Orchestra Thursday night.

Guessing Contests.—Guessing contests, if well conducted, attract attention. There are innumerable things which can be used as subjects for guessing, and the merchant conducting such a contest should strive to get away from old forms of this plan. The main object of such a contest is to draw people into a store. Sometimes sales are helped by allowing a guess with every sale, or with every sale of a certain amount or a certain article. Some merchants find it better to allow interested people to guess without buying. Prizes of merchandise are usually offered for the correct, or nearest to the correct, guess. The postal guide or the local postmaster should be consulted before any newspaper or any mail advertising is planned, for the postal laws forbid the transmitting through the mails of the details of any lottery or other contest unless the test is one calling for skill rather than luck. Names and addresses secured through contests may be used to build up mailing lists for direct advertising work.

A druggist placed a heap of empty photograph film spools in his window and offered a special photographic lens to the person guessing the correct number of spools in the heap. A guess was allowed with every purchase of photographic goods.

A clothing store offered prizes of two dozen and one dozen collars to the persons guessing nearest to the correct number of collars in a window-display. Every collar purchased allowed the customer one guess.

A grocery store offered a set of silver to the person guessing the nearest to the number of times the cash register was opened during a certain month.

A jeweler advertised that on a certain day at 9 o'clock he would wind a twenty-four-hour clock and place it in his window. A prize of $5 in gold was offered to the person guessing nearest to the number of minutes it would run. The prize for the second best guess was the clock itself. No one had to make a purchase in order to register a guess. A large box was placed inside the store and any one wishing to enter the contest was invited to take a blank card on which were spaces for name, address and guess. No one was allowed more than one guess.

Guessing the Dirt in the Carpet.—A severe and practical test, made in public of what a vacuum cleaner could do, was staged in a number of large centers by the manufacturer of the cleaner and resulted in greatly increased sales. Outside the hardware dealer's store a length of rug was spread on the sidewalk. In line with the center of this rug and immediately in front of the entrance to the store stood a cabinet on top of which was the cleaner.

Hundreds of pedestrians passing to and fro noticed the unaccustomed feel of the rug and had their attention directed to the cabinet with its specimen cleaner. On the cabinet were clearly printed posters announcing a guessing contest. It was stated that the rug was cleaned once a day, and a prize of a suction cleaner was offered to the person guessing the amount of dirt taken from the rug in one week. The plan was a complete success and attracted a large attendance at the store during the entire week of the contest.

(Marketing).

Contests for Salespeople.—For a number of years a prominent western dealer in music and muscial merchandise, Sherman, Clay & Company, of San Francisco, has carried out successfully contests based on the number of names of prospective purchasers turned in. It is believed by the management of this concern that the real mettle of the salesman is tested by a reward given for the number of prospective purchasers eventually sold from the list turned in rather than on the general total of the salesman's work.

To put it another way, the direct object of the contest is to make every employe feel that he is a part of the selling organization and spur him to an effort to bring in new customers.

While prizes are given for the largest number of prospective customers developed, this is not the only benefit that the employes receive from these contests. A certain commission is given on all sales made to these new customers, this commission going to the employes who turned in the names.

The cost of creating prospective buyers by this method is less than the cost through advertising or the usual means.

Cash-payment Contest.—A firm selling on the instalment plan has used to advantage a contest among salesmen for the largest initial or cash payment collected. This contest is worked out on the point system. For example, where a cash payment of 10 per cent is collected, the salesman is credited with one point; a 15 per cent cash payment gives him two points; a 20 per cent cash payment, three points, and so on. At the end of each month, the salesman scoring the highest total number of points receives a prize.

Contest to Increase Sales of Slow-sellers.—Every dealer is confronted with the problem of getting rid of slow-selling articles. One means that has been used with success is a lively contest. Recently, the Knabe Warerooms in New York conducted such a contest with pleasing results. An automobile was offered as a prize to the man who sold the largest number of moderately-priced Ampico upright models during a given period.

Terms of Contest Should Be Unmistakably Clear and Fair.— To be effective, the rules of a contest must be clearly and plainly stated. There should be no lowering of the credit standards of the firm, nor any departing from the regular rules laid down for the safe conduct of business.

MISCELLANEOUS PLANS THAT HAVE HELPED SALES

Revolving Tables Sell Goods.—A hardware dealer in Cazenovia, N. Y., has several slowly revolving tables in his window. He finds that articles placed on these tables will sell faster during the time they are in the window than any others in the store. Apparently the type of merchandise matters very little, for a great variety of articles, including some exceedingly slow movers, have had their sales speeded by this plan of revolving them in public view.

Use of Phonograph Record in Selling.—A number of enterprising retailers have made good use of a brief phonographic sales talk about heaters. The record was made by a well trained announcer. The novelty of the plan is striking, and the phonograph can be depended upon "to speak its piece." It will keep on working when the salesmen of the store may be busy. The manufacturer originating the records found that he could sell them at 75 cents apiece to his dealers.

Selling Goods on Approval to Suburban and Country Trade. An enterprising Indiana talking machine retailer experimented with this plan on a list of one-hundred prospects. The campaign resulted in the sale of sixty machines, considerable record, needle and accessories business, and twenty good prospects for future sales.

Taking a list of homes which had no talking machines, an energetic salesman visited each one, traveling in a Ford roadster and placing a talking machine in as many homes as possible, with argument of this kind:

"Good morning, Mrs............. I know just what you're thinking. You see my Ford out there and a phonograph on behind. You think I'm here to sell you that phonograph and you're all prepared to say 'No.'

"Not at all," he continues before Mrs.............. can interrupt. "That's a.............talking machine. The.......... Company is a big advertiser and they do things in a big way. Just now they are putting on the biggest advertising stunt you or I ever heard of. For one month, Mrs..................., they are going to lend one of the..................talking machines to every home in the country that hasn't already a talking machine of some kind.

"This is being done merely to advertise music. There is absolutely no obligation incurred by you to buy the machine at the end of the month. The company figures that by doing this in every home in the country without a talking machine they are going to sell the idea of music to the country. The more musical the country is, the better the company's business will be. You see the idea?

"Another thing, Mrs................... The................. Company is represented in this city by the..................Music Shop. The allotment of instruments for this city is limited, so the ....Shop people has had to cut down the list of homes to those in which they know the instrument will be well taken care of."

The experience of this firm showed that the family would either become enthusiastic over owning the instrument or some neighbor would come in and comment admiringly on it so that the family felt a little pride about giving up their new possession. The plan was to have the dealer call up the household in a few days to find out if the instrument worked well. No effort was made to sell in this telephone conversation but the head of the house was given to understand that it was perfectly all right for the machine to remain until the end of the month. In a day or so the salesman would make another call and tell what the terms of sale would be if Mrs. —— cared to keep the instrument.

It is stated that in the experience referred to, where good judgment was used in placing the instruments, 80 per cent of those called on were persuaded to keep the machine in the home for a trial.

Such a method could be adapted also to washing machines, vacuum cleaners, cream separators, etc.

(Summarized from *Talking Machine World*).

Outside Effort by an Inside Man.—"If business does not come to you, go out and find where it is and then direct it your way" is the idea of an enterprising hardware salesman in a West Virginia town. When this man finds business dull he takes an afternoon off and walks through some part of the town. As he walks he looks closely at every house or store to discover anything lacking that his store can supply. He may see a worn-out lawn-mower, a dilapidated swing, a window that needs an awning. He jots down this information with the name of the person, or the street address, and can then use his first-hand knowledge of the need as the basis of a solicitation from his firm. In cases where he knows the property-owner or the merchant, he does not wait to write a letter but gets an interview immediately. This latter method in one afternoon alone secured two hundred dollars' worth of business in awnings which under ordinary condition might not have come to the attention of this young salesman's firm.

(Summarized from *Good Hardware*).

Photographs of Homes of Users.—When a prospective customer wants to know where furnaces have been installed by a resourceful California hardware dealer he has put before him photographs of the homes with labels giving names and addresses of the owners. The photographs are mounted on a large board and displayed in the furnace department. This exhibit is occasionally placed in the window. Thus the prospective customer can see the types of homes possessing this dealer's furnaces, which is more impressive than a mere list of names, especially in the case of a newcomer to the city. This photograph plan could be used also in the case of water-heaters, electric-light fixtures, gas-ranges, and other articles that are likely to remain in a home when once installed. Photographs of homes in which a merchant places electric washers, vacuum cleaners, refrigerators, pianos, and other equipment or instruments, are excellent selling aids if a careful check is made now and then to see that the articles have not been moved from the homes photographed. Photographs are not only interesting in a newsy way; they aid the customer in visualizing the improvement or purchase under consideration.

Foot Specialist Talks to Saleswomen.—As a method of forwarding the sales of an orthopedic shoe, the buyer in the shoe department of a prominent department store induced a foot specialist, a regular medical practitioner, to give a talk to the employes on the construction of the foot, on foot troubles and how they could be remedied. Necessity for a correct shoe was of course emphasized, together with the fact that the store carried the right kind of orthopedic shoe. The lecture lasted less than half an hour.

Within two days of the lecture 5 per cent of the saleswomen of this store had purchased a pair of these shoes for themselves. This store has no men's department. It was not the buyer's intention to make the employes buy the shoes, but to impress upon them the fact that a shoe designed especially to relieve foot trouble was sold by the store and that they would be doing their friends a good turn by telling about it. The talk by the specialist caused much comment inside and outside of the establishment.

Numbering of Customers and Prospective Customers.—As a means of inducing regular visits to his store, a retailer of a medium-sized town has all customers and prospective customers numbered. Every working day one number is hung up prominently in the store, and if the person whose index card bears that number comes in that day he or she is entitled to an inexpensive but useful gift.

Selling to the Newly-weds.—Many merchants dealing with various kinds of housekeeping merchandise make it a point to list newly married couples as early as possible. It usually requires very little trouble to get this information through the recorder of marriages or the city or county official who has the responsibility of issuing marriage licenses. If the community is such that it is possible for the merchant to gage the social status of the newly married couple and their probable purchasing tendencies, he can adapt his solicitation accordingly. The amount of merchandise needed to equip a new home is such that a merchant is warranted in making a special effort to get this business, even if he secures only a part of the patronage of the new home. One Illinois merchant who previously had given no attention to this source of business reports that the first year he concentrated on it he increased his sales 25 per cent and attributed the increase largely to his special effort.

Telephone Calls to Aid in Selling Real Estate.—Through the chance experiment of a cub salesman with a telephone book as a possible source of prospects, a real estate firm has hit upon the most profitable method of obtaining sales leads that it has ever used. This experiment was developed by the company into a regular scheme for canvassing by telephone. A group of well coached employes do this work in the evening. Names of those who show interest are turned over to the salesmen. The idea is to call people when they are at home and comfortable, not subject to the distractions of the business day; and the purchase of real estate being a family matter, it is desirable to telephone when the family is assembled. The telephone book as a resource is never exhausted, because it is never possible to tell who may be interested. A person not at all interested one time may suddenly acquire more money and be really interested; another changes his mind; a third is unwell at the time of the salesman's first call and in no mood to discuss purchase of real estate, but at the next call may be ready to listen attentively.

(*System*, September, 1922).

Tips from Moving Men.—A number of retailers selling house outfitting goods have found cooperation with moving concerns and van-drivers profitable. The plan is for the moving man to telephone the store promptly after a moving job, which gives an opportunity to send a salesman with specimens of upholstery, etc.

Teachers as News Bureaus.—Teachers have been found very useful as merchants' representatives to report marriages, births, deaths, removals, contemplated improvements, etc. An inducement to the teacher for this cooperation may be a small discount on all her purchases at the store.

Tactics That Enable One Man to Sell $500 Worth of Clothing Daily.—Wallace N. Moyer, of Jacob Reed's Sons, Philadelphia, is said to be one of the best retail salesman of clothing in the United States. The fundamental reasons for his success are given by a close observer as follows:

1. His ability to classify men as to type and to select without hesitation a model exactly suitable to the customer's desires, physique and color requirements.

2. His knowledge of the store's merchandise which makes for facility and speed in handling customers, because almost invariably he chooses the right garment, thereby avoiding the embarrassment of confusing and befuddling the patron.

3. His power of tactful persuasion and the use of suggestion, which enable him to sell a man the suit or coat that becomes him best.

In Mr. Moyer's judgment, "Most clothing salesmen do not realize the importance of knowing just how clothes should fit a man." He adds, I never allow a man to go out of our store dissatisfied or wearing a suit that would not measure up to my own personal standards.

"This attention to the details of proper fitting has helped me get the confidence of my customers. It has also brought hundreds of resales and the kind of advertising that is worth thousands of dollars in new business."

This enterprising salesman keeps a list of the names and addresses of his patrons and when the store offers special values in suits or coats and he has time to do it, he calls up customers that he believes would be interested. He also stimulates business by writing letters, for he has many customers at a distance, some of them former residents of Philadelphia and others who visited the city, met and liked him and send him orders from their home towns. The story is told that one of his customers who sells vacuum cleaners copied one of Moyer's selling letters and used it to sell fifty cleaners in one day.

(Summarized from *Retail Ledger*).

Selling Musical Instruments to Farmers.—In a recent editorial, *The Talking Machine World* tells of a musical instrument salesman who recently won a trip to New York as a first prize in a salesmanship contest conducted by a Middlewest music house. As it was the second time this man had carried off the honors, he was asked how he managed it. He attributes his success to an intelligent and systematic effort to get farm trade. It is his opinion that the farmer makes the best kind of prospective customer for musical instruments. His reasons for this were that the farmer spends more time in his home than the city man and that he consequently has a greater appreciation of the home. Also, that the farmer does not suffer from industrial fluctuations as city dwellers do, and that he is usually prepared to pay cash for what he buys.

But this salesman reiterates that in order to sell the farmer the salesman must approach him like a human being and there must be an entire absence of "that patronizing air" that so many salesmen unfortunately seem to think it necessary to adopt when approaching people who live in the rural districts.

Cooperative Market Day.—To draw trade from surrounding counties, the merchants of a Minnesota city cooperated in a community welfare program during the summer of 1922, with unusually good results. The general plan, briefly, was to designate the first Wednesday of each summer month as Market Day. From one Market Day to another merchants gave out tickets with each dollar's worth of goods sold. These tickets were perforated so that the recipient, after writing his name and address on one half, could tear it off and place it in a box in the store, keeping the other half until Market Day when the drawing took place and prizes were given to the persons whose names were drawn.

Before each Market Day large circulars, about 2 by 3 feet, were mailed to farm homes and the people in nearby towns. These circulars contained advertisements of over thirty merchants describing the three or four selections of their merchandise. They also contained a list of the prizes and rules of the contest. It was necessary to have a ruling as to residence, for at a drawing of a similar kind in another city the prize automobile had been won by a member of a passing automobile party, to the great disgust and disappointment of the townspeople. Other features advertised in the circulars were a big community auction, moving pictures, a band, and other entertainments, all of which varied each Market Day.

The expense of the tickets and the various entertainments was paid by the merchants according to the number of tickets actually given out, which was fair, as the man who gave out the most tickets had taken in the most dollars. The percentage of expense was determined by dividing the total expense by the number of tickets used, after the unused tickets returned by merchants had been deducted. In one month this expense amounted to $8/10$ of 1 per cent, and in another month only $7/10$ of 1 per cent.

Ready-packed Candy Sells Easily.—Within eight months J. G. Patton, founder of the L'Aiglon Shop, built up a candy business which ranks second to none in Philadelphia. The space for sale and display of candy is not more than 40 square feet but the location is an ideal one for candy-selling as the shop is next to the high-class L'Aiglon Café. However, location alone is not responsible for the phenomenal success of the shop. During Christmas week over thirteen tons of candy were sold. Mr. Patton says the enormous sales "were due to the definite establishment of a unique and individual position in the retail candy trade, brought about through concentration upon two kinds of candy which experience and analysis demonstrated the buying public wanted." He explains further:

Formerly we gave our patrons a large variety of candy to select from. A study of comparative sales of leading and popular sellers led me to believe that the public would forego selection if a standard variety of chocolates and fudge which did not vary as to quality— but which was broad enough to suit the majority of tastes—was packed ready to be sold over the counter without delay.

If the reasons for our success and growth could be briefly summarized, they might be put down as follows:

Standard and high quality.

Concentration upon two particular assortments.

Ability to serve patrons quickly by having our candy wrapped and ready to sell.

Low prices due to our policy of small profit and large volume. Special reduction in all our prices on Friday and Saturday of each week and giving patrons two pounds of our usual grade of candy for one dollar.

(*Retail Ledger*).

A Variation of the Coupon Idea.—Dealers in commodities such as teas and coffees have found an effective method of keeping track of purchases, where premiums are offered, to be that of furnishing the housekeeper with a card that is punched for every pound purchased. The premium is avail-

Through courtesy of Printers' Ink Monthly and Alex. Taylor & Company, Inc.
EXHIBIT 180.—The Taylor baseball outfit for boys.

able when the sales total runs to a certain amount. These cards might carry illustrations of the premiums offered, as well as the slogan of the dealer. This is only a variation of the certificate or coupon plan.

Displaying Kitchen Utensils in Sets.—Magazine and newspaper readers have become familiar with the exhibits and charts of domestic science schools indicating the articles of food necessary for a meal for a family of four or more. Guy Hubbart, in a recent issue of the *Dry Goods Economist*, advances a similar idea as a means of selling kitchen utensils. He suggests, for example, placing on display all the utensils, from paring-knife to ice-cream freezer, that would be needed to prepare a given menu for a family of six. Cards showing the price of each item should be attached and a central card may show the price for the complete outfit. Outfits will vary with menus selected and can be made up in different sets, as a "breakfast kitchen set," a "luncheon kitchen set," etc. While many sets probably will not be sold as a unit, the display calls to the attention of the housewife the need of having complete equipment. Such a display is also in order for a window.

Example of the Combination Sale.—Exhibit 180 shows the Taylor baseball outfit for boys. The exhibit is reproduced in this volume through the courtesy of *Printers' Ink Monthly* and Alex. Taylor & Company, Inc. The advertiser writes:

Although we started the exploiting of this outfit rather late in the season and the competition was very keen, we found our plan to be successful. It is almost trite to say that packaged goods receive the greatest recognition and also permit the most economical form of publicity.

INDEX

A

Abraham & Straus' instruction to new employes, 361
  prizes for errors found in advertising, 30
  social features for employes, 362
Adaptation, value of, 1
Address of store given in advertisements, 178
Addressograph Company's mailing-list chart, 214
Adler & Childs' use of color in special annual sale, 508
Admonitions in advertisements, 329
Advertised goods, knowledge of, by salespeople, 411
Advertisements, address given in, 178
  aids to reading of, 161
  arrangement of, 149
  arrangement of signatures in, 162
  contest for best, written by customers, 520
  examples of syndicated, 187
  featuring a character in series of, 521
  from newspapers used as circulars, 252, 253
  layout of newspaper, 163
  parts that make up, 149
  position of signature in, 175
  posting on bulletin board at entrance of store, 518
  presenting too great variety of articles in, 281
  prizes for errors found in, 30, 552
  problem of small, 180
  size of, 140
Advertisements, story form of, 140
  style card for setting of, 170
  suggested layouts of small, 181
  syndicated, furnished building-material dealers, 189
  type faces suitable for, 171
  typographical arrangement of, 148
  value of illustration in, 144
Advertising agency view of concentrating on few brands, 47
Advertising and selling, organizing for, 12
Advertising appeals to children, 537
Advertising appropriation, review of methods of determining, 16
Advertising, bargain type of, 289
Advertising budget, value of, 17
Advertising, calendars, novelties and specialties in, 269
  coupons used in, 546
  direct methods of, 202
  distinctive, 309
  distinctive styles of, 309
  distribution sheet for, 21
  does it influence women?, 6
Advertising expense, distribution of, 20
  form for monthly, 19
Advertising expenditure, monthly index of, 19
Advertising, exploiting of imaginary characters in, 490
  final purpose of, 326
  good, formula for, 272
  how to furnish copy for, 179
  humor and sprightliness in, 277
Advertising ideas, plans and experiences, review of, 515
Advertising illustrations, syndicated, 195

INDEX

Advertising, increasing effectiveness of, 25
  institutional style of, 305
  keeping salespeople informed of, 29
Advertising language, reform in, 291
Advertising layouts, 162
  Lord & Taylor's method of furnishing, 180
  R. H. Macy & Company's practice in furnishing, 179
Advertising, manufacturers' syndicated and cooperative, 186
Advertising message, importance of "meaty," 184
  Chas. R. Mears' views on, 184
Advertising, newsiness in, 284
Advertising novelties, useful, 256
Advertising on delivery wagons, 269
Advertising, planning and managing newspaper, 139
  prizes for errors found in, 30, 552
  question-and-answer style of, 490
  reading notice form of, 143
  research to determine aid of, 8
Advertising salespeople, 516
Advertising series, 140
Advertising scrap-books, usefulness of, 33
Advertising space, judicious use of, 140
Advertising, street-car, outdoor and specialty, 257
Advertising to women, survey of, 5
Advertising, value of, to retailer, 139
  view of expert planner of, 146
  views on good newspaper, 185
  what direct, is and does, 202
Aggressiveness, danger of too much, 473
Agricultural State Colleges, cooperation with, 547

Aitchison & Co. advertisement, 296
Alarm clocks, use of to increase sales, 510
Alpha Cement syndicated advertisement, 189
Aluminum Cooking Utensil Co. selling bulletin, 378
American Optical Co., view on studying customers and merchandise, 479
Analysis of methods, value of, 498
Analyzing lost sales, 432
Analyzing the customer, 434, 451, 460
Animals, use of for display purposes, 122
Animated displays sell goods, 557
Anniversary sale idea, 514
Appeals to women in advertising clothing, 5
Appearance, S. W. Straus & Co. views, 359
Approval selling plan of talking machine dealer, 557
Apron sale idea, 517
Armour & Company's view of children customers, 526
Armstrong Cork Company's turnover chart, 49
Arnold, Constable & Co. advertisement, 305
Arrangement of stock, 412
Associated Advertising Clubs' effort for language reform, 291
Associated Retail Advertisers, division of, language reform, 291
Associations of retailers, material furnished by, 198
Associations, salesmanship instruction by, 332, 335
Attention, importance of good, 390
Automobile bumpers, window-display of, 129
Automobile dealer's contest idea, 553
Automobile dealer's operating guarantee increases sales, 502

INDEX

Automobile dealers' service salesmanship, 533

Automobile dealers, syndicated advertisement for, 197

Automobile display room, view of, 96

Ayer, N. W. & Son's view of concentrating on few brands, 47

Ayres, L. S. & Company's rental bureau in house-furnishings department, 528

B

Babson Statistical Organization, chart of stock, turnover and monthly sales compared with purchasing power of city, 76

Background treatment for show-windows, 124

Bailey & Brown grocery layout, 168

Baker, Murray & Imbrie sporting goods advertisement, 154

Bamberger, L., & Co. departmental and seasonable direct-mail booklets, 232, 233, 234
  letter used in direct mail solicitation, 222
  mailing card used by, 228

Bank billboard, example of, 267

Bankers' classified mailing-lists, compiling of, 205

Bankers Trust Company layout and advertisement, 165, 166

Banks, turnover statistics from, 66

Bank's welcoming letter to newcomers, 216

Barbara Wayne letters of Vanity Fair Silk Mills, 385

Bargain advertising, 289
  reform in language of, 292

Bargain basements, view of, 100

"Bargain Booth" sales, 508

Barlow's Baby Grand Piano billboard, 264

Baseball outfit for boys, 565

Better selling talks, 389

Billboard advertising, argument for, 265
  road signs giving merchant's location, 268

Billboards, 262
  amount of copy for, 262, 263
  color and pictorial treatment of, 262, 268
  de luxe type of, 264, 265

Biltmore Hat street-car card, 260

Blakely Laundry billboard, 264

Bloomingdale Brothers' Shopper advertising, 324

Boggs & Buhl, view of advertising, 185

Bond Brothers, window-display of, 131

Bonus, methods of paying, in grocery and coffee-roasting businesses, 88
  on slow-moving goods, 78

Booklets and folders appropriate as enclosures, 226
  imprinting of dealer's name on, 238

Booklets, bulletins and meetings to inform salespeople of advertising, 28

Bootblack stand in shoe store helps sales, 490

Borders around advertisements, purposes of, 150
  example of harmonious, 152
  fish, for advertising sporting goods, 154
  inappropriate, 174
  novel, 153
  wasteful, 175

Boren, Richard M., views on advertising, 147

Boys' club, hardware store's, 541

Boys, special house organ for, 540
  special outfits for, 565

Brands, concentration on few, 46
  turnover slowed up by too many, 46

Brett, Ralph U., view of advertising, 185
Brill Brothers' advertisement, 318
Bronson & Townsend, booklets sent out by, 381
Brooklyn Trust Co. advertisement, 297
Brown's Grocery advertising layout, 167
Brown-Umlandt Co. advertisements, 294
Budget, value of, in advertising, 17
Builders and contractors, syndicated advertisements for, 199
Building materials dealers, letter suggested for direct solicitation of, 219
Bulletin, example of employes', 340
Bulletin on selling "Wear-Ever" cooking utensils, 378
Bulletin, selling, Morris & Co. (Paul Jones Blouses), 379
Bulletins to keep salespeople informed of advertising, 31
Bureau of Business Research of N. Y. University, report of compensation methods in grocery business, 87
Burroughs Adding Machine Co., advice on turnover, 48
  mark-up table, 61
  turnover table, 52
Business women, special outfits for, increase sales, 505
Butter-Nut Bread billboard, 266
Buying at home, inducing, 244–248
Buying of stock, questionnaires aid in, 6
Buying, what influences?, 4

C

Cabinets that facilitate selling, 115
Calendars and advertising novelties, 269
Calendars in specialty advertising, 270
Callis, C. R., contest jingle of, 554
Campbell's Soup advertisement analyzed, 275
Candy, packaging of, increases sales, 564
Cantilever Shoes street-car card, 258
Card for keeping tabs on customers' buying, 236
Cards used in special sales, 507
  use of, in direct advertising, 227, 228
Carrying expense, 59
Cartoons used by Dives, Pomeroy & Stewart, 369, 370
Cass, Helen Landon, on "column" or "shopper" advertising, 325
Catalogue advertising, insuring attention for, 237
  attitude of merchants toward, 230
  of Duffy-Powers Company, 231
  of Marshall Field & Company, 230
  unfair method used by Western retailer, 237
Catalogues for specialty stores, 229
  type of merchandise to be listed in, 229
  used in direct advertising, 229
Chain-store house organs, 238, 244
Changes that helped sell more goods, 498
Character reading, place of, in selling, 437
Characters, exploiting of imaginary, in advertising, 490
Charge customers, mailing-list of, 210
Charity organizations, cooperating with, as sales feature, 509
Chart for rating employes, 82
  of correlated sales, 423, 424
  of cost and profit percentages in different retail lines, 35
  of mailing-list sources, 213

INDEX

Chart of sales by months in various lines, 67
  of stock, turnover, yearly sale and purchasing power of city, compared, 77
  of turnover, 49
  organization, of Duffy-Powers Co., 14
  showing how customers are influenced in buying, 4
Chase Mercantile Company's self-serve department, 536
Checking results of direct advertising, 236
Chestnut Street Association advertising, 324
Children, appeals to, in advertising, 537
  and men, expositions for, 544
  as models, 548
  contests among, 539
  doll show to interest, 540
  mailing-list of, 208
  percentage of sales made by, 526
  special attention to, increases sales, 526
  special house organ for, 540
Chipman Knitting Mills, manual on silk hosiery, 380
"Cinderella slipper" contest, 552
Circularizing with newspaper-advertisement reprints, 252, 253
Clarke Brothers' style card, 170
Classified mailing-lists for bankers, compiling of, 205
Clothing store, view of front of, 97
Club plan of instalment selling, 500
Coal dealers, syndicated advertisements for, 189
Coal dealer's timely advertising, 317
Coffee and tea dealer's premium and coupon method, 565
Coffee-roasting business, compensation methods of, 87
  methods of paying bonus in, 88

Coffee window-display, 134
College students as demonstrators, 546
Collins, Harry, advertisement of, 174
Color and pictorial treatment in billboard advertising, 262, 268
Color harmony as aid in selling hats and clothing, 532
  in displaying merchandise, 119
Color in street-car cards, 260
  use of in moving slow-sellers, 500
"Column" advertisements, 321, 325
Combination sales, 565
Comments of customers, prizes to secure, 501
Commission form of compensating salespeople, 85
Comparative records in stimulating salesmanship, 357
Comparative-price advertising, 290
Compensation, 78
  chain-store plan of, 80
  commission form of, 85
  examples of, 81
  methods and percentages in grocery business, 87
  N. Y. University Bureau's Business Research recommendations on, 89
Competition, example of unfair, 237
Competitive goods, reflecting on, 480
Competitive products, tactful reference to, 454
Competitive sales among different departments, 516
Complaining customers, how to treat, 485
Complaints, capitalizing, 500
  how to deal with, 475
  place of, in selling, 461, 468
Contests among children, 539
  featuring of, in window-display 127

Contests featuring of manufacturers, 127
  for arrangement of store interior, 550
  for best advertisements written by customers, 520
  for salespeople, 556
  ideas for, 550
  rules and terms of, 557
  to attract farmers, 550, 551
  to stimulate sales, 84
  use of, during special sales, 512
  use of, in training salespeople, 350
  window-trimming, among boys and girls, 540
Contractors and builders, syndicated advertisements for, 199
"Convenience goods," definition of, 3
  extending territory for sale of, 248
Cooking utensils, advertising recipes sell, 515
Cooking utensil dealer's, plan for building up mailing-list, 211
Cooperating with state colleges, 546
Cooperation between departments, 440
Cooperative and syndicated advertising, 186, 201
Cooperative delivery reduces expense, 41
Cooperative effort of local merchants to combat mail-order buying, 248
Cooperative marketing plan, 563
Copy about tests, 288
  bargain style of, 289
  billboard, 262, 263, 268
  common faults of, 272
  comparative-price style of, 290
  distinctive styles of, 309
  importance of effective, 184
  institutional style of, 305
  language reform in, 291
  place of humor, sprightliness, and punch in, 277

Copy, service style of, 308
  "snappy" style of, 277
  specific statement in, 278
  street-car card, 257
  the writing of, 272
  typewriting of, 179
  using news and style in, 284
  value of curiosity appeal in, 295
Corelated sales chart, 423, 424
Corn Exchange Bank advertisement, 306
Correction notice style of copy, 307
Correction system of Strawbridge & Clothier, 367
Correspondence course used by J. C. Penney Co., 347
Corticelli Silk Mills silk-worm window-display, 133
Costs of postage in direct advertising, 224, 225
Costs of selling, comparative, 34
  percentages in different lines, 79
Cotrell and Leonard advertisement, 322
Counter containers for small goods, 111
Counteracting mail-order buying, methods used by local merchants, 244, 246, 247
County agents, cooperating with, 546
"County fair" contest to attract farmers, 551
Coupon idea, variation of, 565
Coupons, use of in newspaper advertising, 546
  use of in special sales, 506
Courses and manuals, 361
Courses of reading and merchandising information, 377
Courses, salesmanship, average amount of work done in, 336
Courtesy as a winning quality, 395, 400
  avoiding scolding or bickering in presence of customer, 457

INDEX

Courtesy as getting along with different types of customers, 445
    need for, in dealing with women, 468
    respecting the customer's preference, 410, 411
Crane, Dr. Frank, on happiness in work, 492
Crane, R. W., view of enclosed window-displays, 123
Crating, 39
Curiosity-exciting copy, 295
Customers, announcing special sale by letters to, 517
    card for keeping tabs on buying of, 236
    comments, using, to increase sales, 500
    contest for best advertisements written by, 520
    examples of letters to, 217
    gaining new, through special sales, 508
    getting viewpoint of, 416, 430, 435, 465
    hardware store's method of addressing letters to, 517
    how to deal with complaining, 475, 485
    how to deal with the "looker" type of, 459, 468
    keeping in touch with, 560
    letters to, by salespeople, 516
    names, how to remember, 415
    names in copy, 385
    names, value of knowing, 413, 414
    serving the particular or peculiar type of, 445
    study of, important, 479
    studying the type of, 434, 435, 436, 445, 460
Customers, taking an interest in, 390, 493,
"Customers' Week" as annual feature, 524
Customers, what influences, chart of, 4
    when to agree with, 475

D

Dairy company's advertising, 146
Dale, Joan, "Shopper" advertising, 324
Dartnell Corporation chart of sales by months in various retail lines, 67
Davis, S. A., suggestions on speech in selling, 401
D'Andrea Brothers, letter used in direct solicitations, 217
Delivery, cooperative, decreases expense, 41
    expense, 39
    saving in, 38
    wagons, advertising on, 269
De luxe type of billboard sign, 264, 265
Demand for products determines turnover rate, 43
Demand, study of, 72
Demonstrating as instruction method, 387
    stoves, 546
Demonstration as a means of making explanations clear, 450
    need for, in selling, 412, 427
    of washing machines, 525
Demonstrations, style shows, displays, etc., 541
Demonstration-tour sales plan, 547
Demonstrators, college students used as, 546
Departments, competitive sales among, 516
    cooperation between, 440
Departments or counters, specialists in charge of, 525
Department store advertising layout, 163
    organization, chart of, 14
    trend of, 15

Department store range of mark-up and profit in, 64
  review of average sales per salesperson, 65
  self-serve department in, 535
  table of gross profit and stock turn, 65
  table of turnover in, 69
  tendencies in layout of, 99
  view of front of, 96
Description, essentials of good, 274
Direct advertising, advice on, by National Retail Dry Goods Association, 202
  by department store, 203
  cooperation of manufacturers with dealers, 219, 220
  definition and purpose of, 202
  departmental and seasonable solicitations, 232, 233
  envelop enclosures, 224
  imprinting dealer's names on manufacturers' folders and booklets, 238
  method of checking results of, 236
  miscellaneous methods of, 251
  need for distinctive letter-writing, 215
  need for timeliness in, 252
  specimen folders and booklets, 226
  type of, for farmer, 237, 238
  tying up with newspaper announcements, 252
  use of mailing cards in, 228
  use of single and double postal cards, 227, 228
  useful forms for, 256
  waste in, 214, 225, 226, 227
  weaknesses of, 225, 226, 227
Direct-mail campaign by service station, 255
Direct-mail solicitations, seasonable, 232
Display, additional suggestions on, 172

Display, animated, 557
  examples of poor, 174, 176
  excessive, 175
  unit type of, 124
Display advertising, unusual size of type in, 315
Display of products made in home town, 545
Display types, distinctive, 173
Display-cards or posters, 130
Display-cases draw attention to related goods, 490
Displaying merchandise, 118
  color harmony in, 119
  homemade racks for, 112
  related merchandise, 119
Display-windows, lending space in, to charity organizations, 510
Disston Saw booklet, 382
  contest, 127
Distribution, cooperative plan of, 563
Dives, Pomeroy & Stewart methods, 358, 368
  store bulletin, 31
Doll show to interest children, 540
"Dollar Day" sales ideas, 508, 512
  window-display feature for, 512
Dollar, idle, cuts down profits, 71
Domestic science schools, cooperating with, 546
Donahoe & Donahoe's survey work, 11
Donaldson, Co., L. S., plan of catalogue advertising, 231
Donaldson-Lithographic Co., examples of attractive billboards, 266, 267
Dress of salespeople, special, for special occasions, 508
Dress-making service, exploiting of, sells yard goods, 517
Drug store, building up business of, 525, 526
  floor plan of, 23
  lemonade well, 117

Drug store, method of apportioning expense, 22
   range of mark-up and profit in, 64
Dry Goods Association, advice of National Retail, on direct advertising, 202
   comments of, on turnover, 66
   statistics from, on average sales per salesperson, 65
Dry Goods Economist's view of retail sales manager of future, 15
Dry goods, review of, with respect to brands, 47
Duffy-Powers Company's attitude toward catalogue advertising, 231
   organization chart, 14

E

Eastman Kodak Co., syndicated advertisement of, 192
Easton Oyster & Lunch House advertisement and rearrangement of, 183
Eckles, Mrs. L. E., result of questionnaire to women buyers, 7
Edison Co., New York, manual, 374
Editorial style of copy, 305
Educational displays, 133, 135
Electrical products, turnover table of, 43
Employes, chart for rating, 82
   part-time, 37
   special sales for, 513
Enclosures, appropriate, 226
English, use of good, 401, 402, 404
Engraving business, exploiting social events to develop, 521
Envelop enclosures in direct advertising, 224
Equipment and layout of store, 90

Errors in advertisements, prizes for, 30, 552
   Jordan Marsh Co. method of dealing with, 352
"Essay" style of copy-writing, 273
"Even change" sales, 511
Evening selling, Kansas merchant's experience with, 527
"Event" advertising, 325
Expense, items of, in principal branches of retailing, 79
   methods of reducing general, 37
   overhead or carrying, 59
Experiences and ideas, effective, 497
Expositions, displays, demonstrations and style shows, 541
   for housekeepers, 545
   for men and children, 544

F

Farmers and gardeners, contests among, 550, 551
Farmers, cooperating with, 268
   selling musical instruments to, 563
   type of direct advertising for, 237, 238
Federal Reserve Banks, turnover statistics from, 66
Field, Marshall, & Co. advertisements, 313, 314
   children's day programs, 537
   consumer house organ, 241
   "gingham sale" idea, 523
   types of catalogue merchandising used, 230
Fifth Avenue Shop advertisement, 176, 177, 178
Filene's, Wm., Sons Company, 4-page letter, 220, 221
Financial advertisement, layout of, 165
First aid service, exploiting of, aids sales, 525

INDEX

First National Bank, Madison, Wis., letter used in direct solicitation, 216

Fish border for sporting goods store, 154

Fixed expense, range of, 62

Fixtures and show-cases, 102

Fixtures, panel or background type of, 125

Flashlight batteries, cabinet for, 115

Fletcher, Frank Irving, views on copy, 282

Folders and booklets appropriate as enclosures, 226

Food concern's tactics in getting quantity orders, 483

Food exhibitions increase sales, 544

Force in selling, 473

Foreigners, names of, for mailing-lists, 214

Form letters, use of, by J. L. Hudson in advertising general store, 253

Fowler, National, Jr., advice to retailers, 398

Frederick Piano Company advertisement, 158

Froug, L., Department Store's method of posting advertisements at store's entrance, 518

Furniture exhibition, "Saleless," 543

Furniture store's use of alarm clocks to increase sales, 510
  use of premiums as advertising feature, 522

Fyfe, R. H., & Company, comments on making up specialized mailing-lists, 223

G

Garber, D. A., view of advertising, 185

Gas Association salesmanship course, 335

Gill, J. K., Company "character" advertising series and advertisements, 521–522

Glove saleswoman's tactics, 481

Gold & Company's novel display of infants' clothing, 133

Good nature in selling, 455

Good-will, cultivating through charity sales, 509

Goods, give location of, in large stores, 179
  how to display, advantageously, 118
  know location of, 411
  knowledge of, by salesmen, 407, 446

Government and educational reports, use of, by retailers, 3

Gramana Dairy Co. advertisement, 146

Grand Rapids Show Case Company show-cases, 109, 110

Grocery advertisement, layout of, 167, 168

Grocery business, compensation methods in, 87
  range of mark-up and profit in, 63

Grocery stores' free lunch idea, 545
  methods of paying bonus in, 88
  tactics in getting quantity orders, 483

Guarantee, featuring, increases sales, 502

Guessing contests, 554, 555

Gummed tape, usefulness of, 38

H

Haberdasher's advertising, 145

Haberdasher's window-display, 131

Haberdashery salesman, tactics of, 482, 489

Habits of women buyers, result of questionnaire on, 6

Habits on buying staples, 43

Hafner, G. W., explanation of turnover, 50
Haines, Charles S., view of building up business, 503
Hamburger, A., & Son's questionnaire to women, 7
Hardware contest idea, 552
Hardware dealer's display-window, 133
Hardware display-cases, 113
Hardware, range of mark-up and profit on, 63
Hardware store's boys' carpentry club increases sales, 541
  method of addressing letters to customers, 517
  method of creating business, 559
  remodeling of, 91
  suggestion for ideal arrangement of, 97, 100
  view of front of, 93
"Harriet's Romance" advertisements of J. K. Gill Co., 521
Harvard Bureau of Business Research, table of selling costs in principal branches of retailing, 79
Hat manufacturer's experience with retail "laboratory" store, 531
Hat manufacturer's recommendations for sales of hats, 531
Hat sale, use of telegrams in, 519
Hat store's idea of giving credit for old hat, 511
Headline construction, 295
Headlines of advertisements, purposes of, 153
  division of, 156
Henning shoe advertisement, 151
Hess Brothers' advertisement, 305
High-school pupils, advertisements written by, 520
Historical events, featuring in window-displays, 130
Holiday selling, ideas for, 510, 530

Home demonstration agents, co-operating with, 546
Home-town products, display of, 545
Honor roll, method of publishing, 344
Horne, Joseph, & Co. manual and methods, 364
Hosiery, silk, manual on, 380
Hour, or two-hour special sales, 508
House-furnishing department, rental bureau in, 528
Housekeepers, expositions for, 545
House organs, 253
  consumer, Marshall Field & Company's, 241
  for group of local stores, 244
  special, for boy customers, 540
  use of, by Louis Traxler Co., 353
Howard's "dollar-less" sale, 508
Hubbard, Guy, on selling in sets, 565
Hudson, L. A., use of form letters in advertising general store, 253
Human element versus bargain advertising, 293
Human figures, use of for display purposes, 122
Humor and sprightliness in copy, 277
Humor in selling, 455

I

Illustration and text of advertising, 156
Illustrations, syndicated, 195
  value of, in advertisements, 144
Imagination, appealing to, 463
Imaginary characters, exploiting of, in advertising, 490
Impression, value of good first, 394
Imprinting dealers' names on direct-mail literature, 238
Individuality in advertising, 312
Infants' wear, displaying of, 133

Information about goods, making explanations clear, 449
  sources of open to salesmen, 409
Instalment selling, club plan of handling, 500
  contests used in, 556
Institutional style of copy, 305
Instruction, miscellaneous forms of, 387
Interior show-cases and windows, 102
Introductions, place of, in copy-writing, 273
Iowa State University's survey of retail outlets, 3
"Island" arrangement of store front, 98
Iver Johnson booklet, 382

J

Japanese decorations for sale, 511
Jewelry, range of mark-up and profit on, 63
Jewelry store, bad tactics of, 481
Jingle contests, 553
  for children, 539
Jobbers, booklets sent out by, 381
Joint Coffee Trade Publicity Committee window-display, 134
Jones, Paul, selling bulletin for retailers, 379
Jordan Marsh Co. method of training, 352

K

Kann, S., Sons Company's method of compensating, 84
  method of training, 351, 354
"K. C. B." style of copy, 311
King Brothers Co. unusual methods of adding names to mailing-list, 207
Kinsey, Ralph W., pointers as a sales instructor, 358
Kitchen equipment, display of, 121

Kitchen styles shown by living models, 549
Kitchen utensils sold in sets, 565
Knapp, J. W., Company's display of products made in home town, 545
Knowledge of products, importance of, 407, 446
Kodak supplies, syndicated advertisement of, 192
Kuppenheimer Company's course, 375
  suggestions on color harmony as an aid in selling, 532

L

L'Aiglon shop's method of increasing candy sales, 564
Landers, Frary & Clark's syndicated service to rug-cleaners, 186
Langley advertisements analyzed, 278
  newiness in, 287
Language in copy-writing, range of, 272
  reform in, 291
  value of correct, 401, 402, 404
  value of simple, in copy-writing, 274
Laundry, plan for building up mailing-list for, 211
Layout and equipment of store, 90
Layouts as aid to effective advertisements, 162
  of financial advertisement, 165
  of grocery store advertisement, 167, 168
  methods of furnishing, 179
Layouts of large stores, tendencies in, 99
Leads, hardware merchant's plan of creating, 559
  newspapers as source of, 214
Lecturing as instruction method, 387

INDEX

Lefax chart of sales by months in different lines, 67
Lemonade well for soda fountain, 117
Letters, cooperation of manufacturers with dealers in preparing, 219
  mimeographed, used by J. L. Hudson in advertising general store, 253
  multigraphed, used in direct advertising, 253
  to customers announcing special sale, 517
    examples of, 217
    method of addressing, 517
  to salespeople from Vanity Fair Silk Mills, 383
  used by Wm. Filene's Sons Co., L. Bamberger & Co., First National Bank, Madison, Wis., and D'Andrea Bros. Co. in direct advertising, 216, 217, 220, 221, 222
  writing of, by salespeople, 516
Letter-writing in direct advertising, 215
Lewis, A.T., & Son Dry Goods Company's attitude toward catalogue advertising, 231
  "Bargain Booth" feature, 508
  bulletins and circulars used in direct advertising, 232
  letter of solicitation, 218
Library Bureau advertisement, 315
Liggett Stores' method of charging for display space, 137
  method of checking results from window-displays, 126
Lighting of displays, National Electric Light Association's suggestions on, 125
Lighting of show-windows and cases, 118, 125
Lighting system of clothing store, 97
  importance of proper, 101

Lingerie, novel display of, 132
Little things, value of attending to, properly, 485
Living models, children used as, 548
  chorus girls used as, 548
  show kitchen styles, 549
Local events, capitalizing, 549
  featuring of in window-displays, 123
Local products, display of, 545
Long-distance mail-order buying, offsetting, 244
Lord & Taylor advertising layout and finished advertisement, 163, 164
  chart for rating employes, 82
  method of furnishing advertising layouts, 180
  method of training, 339
  system of compensating, 82
Loss, definition of, 59
  speeding up of turnover may eliminate, 74
Loss of sales, reasons for, 432, 433
Loyalty of employes to store policy, 458
Luckey, Platt & Company's plan of direct advertising, 231
Luggage dealer's plan for building up mailing-list, 212
Lumber dealer's plan of capitalizing telephone number, 519
Lyon Automobile Bumper window-display, 129

M

McCreery, James, & Company's view of advertising, 185
McPhee & McGinnity's service advertising, 308
Macy, R. H., & Co. advertising layouts, 179
  advertisements, 305, 307
  novel display of umbrellas, 132

Macy, R. H., & Co. window-display of modern kitchen, 121
Magazines and papers for stores, 238
Mailing cards, use of in direct advertising, 228
Mailing-lists, chart showing various sources of, 213
  classification methods, 211, 212
  classified, for bankers, 205
  controlled by, 203
  getting names for, 251
  importance of keeping, up to date, 214
  method of compiling special, 560
  miscellaneous suggestions on, 210, 214
  names for, supplied by salespeople, 208, 253
  names for, supplied by teachers, 253
  names secured for, by department store, 232
  of charge account customers, 210
  of children's names, 208
  of foreigners, 214
  organizing of, 203
  out-of-town customers having purchases sent, 212
  responsibility for, 203
  rug-and-carpet cleaners' methods of building up, 202
  specializing in making up, 204, 205
  unusual methods of adding names to, 207
  value of news items in building up, 214
Mail-order buying, cooperative effort of local merchants to combat, 248
  offsetting of, by local merchants, 244, 246, 247
Manuals and courses, 361
  sent out by jobbers, 381
  syndicated, for retailers, 375

Manufacturers' advertising, cooperating with, 26
Manufacturers' cooperation with dealers in preparing direct-mail literature, 219, 225
Manufacturer's folders and booklets, imprinting dealer's name on, 238
Manufacturers, interest of, in retailers' methods, 497
Manufacturers' plates to retailers, 188
Marcus, Charles, plan of using comments from customers, 501
Mark-downs, avoidance of, 69
  definition of, 59
Market tendencies, study of, 72
Marketing, cooperative plan of, 563
Marking goods, 62
Mark-up and profit, examples of range of, 62
  definition of, 59
  examples of figuring, 59
  how to figure, 58
  methods of arriving at, 45
  table, 60
Maxwell, H. C., Company, examples of de luxe billboards, 264
Mayer's Shoe Store, street-car card on Cantilever Shoes, 258
Mears, Chars. R., views on advertising messages, 184
Meat market, view of front of, 94
Meats, range of mark-up and profit on, 63
Men and children, expositions for, 544
Men shoppers, department stores' aid to, 523
Men's clothing, how to sell successfully, 562
  range of mark-up and profit on, 63
Mercantile Trust Co. advertisement, 301

Merchandise, displaying of, 118
  featuring outstanding merits of, 498
  knowledge of, important, 479
  resourcefulness in exploiting, 27
  suitable for direct advertising, 202, 203
Merchandise want slip, example of, 365
Merchandising aids, 113
  information and reading courses, 377
Meyers, A. J., view of traveling demonstration, 547
Meyers Department Store's method of advertising special sale by letters, 517
Miller, I., & Company's method of selling to children, 539
Miller Lock booklet, 382
Mirrors, use of, aid in selling, 117
Mitchell-Fletcher Company's direct advertising methods, 233, 235, 236
Models, Children as, 548
  chorus girls used as, 549
Moffats advertisement, 298
  novel electric border, 153
Montague, Charles J., street-car card, 259
Morris & Co. selling bulletin, 379
Motives, research and questionnaires to determine, 9
Moving men, cooperating with, 561
Moving pictures as instruction aids, 387
Moyer, Wallace N., selling tactics of, 561
Multigraphed letters, use of, 252, 253
Murray Company's methods of counteracting mail-order buying, 246
  "Spring Party," 541
Music company's advertisement, 158
  sales tactics, 557, 563

Music company's survey to increase buying, 10
Musical instruments, selling, to farmers, 563

N

Names as headlines, 298
  as newsy items in copy, 285
  of customers, how to remember, 415
  of customers, value of knowing, 413, 414
Namm, A. I., & Son's historical window-display, 130
  organization, 12
Nash automobile maintenance guarantee increases sales, 502
National Cash Register Company, demonstration in selling, 428
  pointers on sales training, 338
  salary-calculating chart, 80
  talks to retail salespeople, 381
  view of value of increased turnover, 73
National Commercial Gas Association course, 335
National Electric light Association's suggestions on lighting displays, 125
National Retail Dry Goods Association, advice of, on direct advertising, 202
  comments on turnover, 66
  review of advertising as aid in selling, 8
  review of miscellaneous methods used in direct advertising, 251
Nature scenes in displays, 129
Needlework sales, featuring of, 506
Neighborhood store, advertising of, 248
  house organ for, 248
  problem of, 248
Net profit, multiplying turnover increases, 49

Newcomers, bank's welcoming letter to, 216
"New Customer Week" special sale, 508
New employes, example of instruction of, 361
New England store's announcements of purchases mailed from Paris and New York, 252
Newly-weds, selling to, 560
News element in advertising, 284
Newsiness in advertising, examples of, 286
Newspaper advertising combined with street-car advertising, 260, 262
  planning and managing, 139
  tying up with direct advertising, 252
  used as circulars, 252, 253
  use of, in direct advertising, 241
  views on, 185
Newspapers as source of leads, 214
Newton, George B., Coal Co., timely advertising of, 317
New York Edison Co. manual, 374
N. Y. Times' view of mark-up and profit, 58
Night selling, Kansas merchant's experience with, 527
Novel displays, 122
Novelties in specialty advertising, 270
  useful, 256
Novelty in headlines, 299
Novelty special sales ideas, 505
Novel window-displays, 132

O

Oakland Motor Co. advertisement, 317
"Observing Shopper" advertisement, 323
Odds and ends, how to utilize, 530
Oilcloth display rack, 112
Old stock, resourcefulness in exploiting, 27
One-cent sale, variation of, 509
Oppenheim, Collins & Co. advertisement, 305
  novel style show, 549
Operating expense, 44
  distribution of, 22
Organization, functional, 12
Organizing for sales, 1
Organizing mailing-list work, 203
Ourselves as customers see us, 398
Outdoor advertising signs, 262, 268
  trucks and wagons as mediums for, 268
Outfits, featuring of special, 505, 565
Out-of-town customers, cultivating, 557, 563
  free telephone service for, 524
  getting names of, 212, 251
Overhead and selling expenses, 44
Overhead, fixed, or carrying expense, 59
Ovington advertisements, 152, 327

P

Packaging of candy increases sales, 564
Packing and wrapping, saving in, 38
Paint, how sales talk was centered on, 356
Panel or background fixtures, 125
Panelling, use of, in advertising, 155
Paper manufacturer's manual for retailers, 383
Papers or magazines for stores, 238
Patience, need of, in selling, 471
Pelletier Store's change in policy increases sales, 502
  method of increasing turnover, 75
Penney Dry Goods Stores compensation methods, 82
Penney, J. C., Co., method of training, 347

People, need for study of different types of, 434
Percentages of profit, table of, 61
Percy, Carl, view of price on displayed articles, 138
Permanent Builder, syndicated advertisement furnished by, 200
Persistence, need for, in selling, 471
Personal names in copy, 385
Pettis Dry Goods Company's auction plan of apportioning advertising space, 25
Photographs of salespeople used in letters to customers, 516
Photographer's plan for building up mailing-list, 211
Photographs, use of, in selling, 559
Physicians, drug stores' service to, increases sales, 526
Pillows, novel display of, 132
Plates, examples of syndicated, 187
Plays and playlets as instruction methods, 352
Plumb, Fayette R., examples of syndicated advertisements of, 191
Pogue, H. & S., Company, street-car card, 261
Policy of store, change in, increases sales, 502
  loyalty to, by employes, 458
Politeness, value of, 395, 400
Porter, A. J., traveling grocery store idea, 526
Postal cards, use of single and double, in direct advertising, 227, 228
Postal regulations affecting envelop enclosures in direct advertising, 224
Posters and painted boards, use of, 262
Posters or display-cards, 130
  easy method of making, 135
Premiums, use of as advertising feature, 522
Preparation for selling, 1

Price, common terms in figuring, 59
  comparative, use of, 290
  how, featured in advertising, 162
  learning what, the customer will pay, 430
  quoting of quantity, makes extra sales, 483
Price-figuring and turnover, 42
  overhead considered in, 45
Price tickets on displayed articles, 136
Prince School of Salesmanship, 331
Prize advertisements, 520
Prizes for contests, 551, 552, 554
  for errors found in advertisements, 30, 552
  offering for sales suggestions, 512
  to secure customers' comments, 501
  use of, in cooperative marketing plan, 563
Profit and mark-up, examples of range of, 62
  how to figure, 58
Profit, comparison of large and small, 42
  definition of, 59
  increasing, by use of modern equipment, 90
  small percentages or rapid turnover increases, 70
Profit-maker, essentials of, 45
Profit percentages, table of, 61
  turnover determines, 50
Prospective customers, examples of letters to, 217
  how to find, 213
Publicity, increasing effectiveness of, 25
"Punch" in copy-writing, 277
Pure food exhibitions, 544

Q

Qualities of successful salesman, 399
Quantity price, quoting of, makes extra sales, 483

Question-and-answer style of advertising, 490
Questionnaire methods as aids to buying, 6
 on catalogue advertising, review of, 230
 on habits of women buyers, result of, 6
 result of Iowa State University's, 3
Questions as headlines, 297
 value of, in copy-writing, 283
Quota week contests, 350

R

Read, D. M., Company's free telephone service to out-of-town shoppers, 524
Readers, getting viewpoint of, 303
Reading courses for salespeople, 377
Reading notice form of advertising, 143
Real estate, selling, through aid of telephone, 561
Reasons for buying, analysis of, 5
Reed, Jacob, Sons, advertisement, 316
Records of salespeople as aids in stimulating staff, 357
Related goods, drawing attention to, 490
Related sales, 412, 420, 422
Remarks likely to be misconstrued by customer, 400
Remodeling store, hardware merchant's plan of, 91
Rental bureau service increases sales of house-furnishings, 528
Research to determine aid of advertising, 8
Research work for retailers, 3
"Retail," definition of, 1
Retailers' Associations, cooperative material furnished by, 198
Retailers' Association, National, review of advertising as aid to selling, 8
Retailers, prominent, methods of training sales staffs, 339
Retail Ledger's expense and profit chart, with comments, 35
 review of range of mark-up, fixed expense and net profit in retailing, 62
Retail Research Association's review of tendencies in layouts of large stores, 99
Retail selling, requisites of good, 16
Retail Shoe Salesman's Institute course, 332
Returned goods, how to deal with complaints about, 475
Revolving show-cases, 109, 116
Rexall Magazine, plan of publication and distribution, 238, 239, 240
Road signs giving merchant's location, 268
 as sales bulletins for farmers, 268
Roberts, John M., & Sons, advertisement of, analyzed, 282
Roosevelt Military Academy advertisement, 155
Rotary Clubs, service motto of, 494
Roundup, Mont., merchant, methods of counteracting mail-order buying, 246
Rural trade, cultivating, 557, 563
Rush's Garage, advertisement of, featuring used cars, 197

S

Salaries of salespeople, chart for calculating, 80
 fixing, according to sales total, 79
Salary-calculating chart of National Cash Register Co., 80
Sales and near sales, how made or killed, 481

Sales, average, per salesperson, review of, 65
corelated, 412, 420, 422
little things that help or hinder, 478
reasons for failure to make, 432, 433
review of plans that have helped, 557
special, review of ideas and experiences, 505
the steps of, 418, 419
through combination of goods, 565
Sales ideas, plans and experiences, 497
Sales manager of future, view of, 15
Salesmanship courses, average amount of work done in, 336
Salesmanship, qualities that make up good, 399
Salesmanship schools, state and private, 331
Salespeople, advertising, 516
as customers see them, 398
Business Research Bureau's recommendations on compensating, 89
chart for rating, 82
contests for, 556
dress of, for special sales, 508
efficiency of, 489
essential qualities of, 399
keeping, informed of advertising, 28
letters to, by manufacturers, 383
little things that help or hinder, 478
methods of securing mailing-list from, 208, 212, 253
must "sell" themselves, 494
need for knowledge about advertised goods, 411
S. Kann Sons Co. ten commandments for, 354
special sales for, 513

Salespeople, talks to, by National Cash Register Co., 381
thoughtlessness of, 489
training of, 331
Sales suggestions, offering prizes for, 512
Sales tactics, examples of effective, 481
learning the price that the customer will pay, 430
offering substitute for goods asked for by customer, 409
reasons for loss of sales, 432, 433
respecting the customer's preference, 410, 411
studying the customer's needs, 473
Sales talk, advantage of centering, on something definite, 356
Sales total, determining salary according to, 79
monthly variation in, 66
Sample drawer, 113
Samples, druggist's method of using, 546
Sanford, Harry, Drug Store, floor plan of, and method of apportioning expense, 22, 23
School children, window-trimming contests among, 540
School teachers, cooperating with, 561
Schoonmaker, John, & Son's employes' sales, 513
Schroeder, John, Lumber Company, street-car card, 261
Scolding, avoiding, in presence of customer, 457
Scrap-books, usefulness of, to retail advertisers, 33
Schuster, Ed., & Company's method of compensating, 85
method of training, 343
Seasonable advertising, 325
Seasonable merchandise, displaying of, 120

INDEX

Sebetha, Kan., merchant's plan of building up business, 502
Self-correction system of Strawbridge & Clothier, 367
Self-serve department of department store, 535
Selling and operating expense, distribution of, 22
Selling and overhead expenses, 44
Selling costs, comparative, 34
    table of, in different lines, 79
Selling expense, what is included in, 59
Selling percentages in different retail lines, chart of, 35
Selling price, table to determine, 60
Selling methods, effective, 497
Selling, organizing for, 12
    preparation for, 1
    related sales in, 412, 420, 422
Selling, talks on better, 389
    to women, 465
Service, creating and exploiting distinctive, 523
    in selling, 492
    novel method of advertising, 519
    style of advertising, 308
Service record form of Milwaukee store, 86
Service salesmanship increases sales, 560
Service station's direct-mail campaign during dull season, 255
Sets, kitchen utensils sold in, 565
Sharpe, George B., comments of, on mail for farmers, 237
Sharples Cream Separator Co., example of syndicated advertisement of, 192
Sherman, Clay & Co. advertisements, 284
    contest for salespeople, 556
Shoe advertisement, 151
Shoe business, research data on, 64
    review of, with respect to brands, 47
Shoe dealer's classification of mailing-lists, 223
    orthopedic service increases sales, 560
"Shopper" advertising, 321
Shopper, how to deal with the "looker" type of, 459, 468
"Shopper's helper," exploiting of, for male shoppers, 523
"Shopping lines," definition of, 3
Shoe salesmanship, example of good, 493
    institute course on, 332
Shoe salesman's tactics, 487
Shoe store, bootblack stand in, helps sales, 490
    contest idea of, 552
    plan of selling to children, 539
    view of front of, 95
Shoes, range of mark-up and profit on, 63, 64
Shoes, stilts help to sell boys', 541
Show-cards and posters, easy method of making, 135
    lettering of, 122
Show-cases as aids in selling, 103
    and cabinets for tools, 113
    and windows, interior, 102
    for small articles, 111
    revolving, for tools or knives, 116
    tables, 108
    wardrobe revolving type of, 109
Show-windows, background treatment for, 124
    charging for, 137
    enclosed or open-backed?, 123
    lighting of, 118, 125
Signatures, arrangement of, in advertisements, 162
    position of, in advertisements, 175
Signs, outdoor, 262, 268
Silhouette displays, 132
Slogans, usefulness of, 302
Slow-moving goods, bonus on selling of, 78
    contest to increase sales of, 556

Slow-moving goods, method of disposing of, 500
Small advertisements, careful planing of, with suggested layouts, 180, 181
Small-town merchant's plan of building up business, 502
"Snappy" style of copy, 277
Social features of Abraham & Straus, 362
of Dives, Pomeroy & Stewart, 372
Social usages, exploiting, to develop engraving business, 521
Soda fountain, lemonade well for, 117
Solicitations, seasonable direct-mail, 232
Special offerings, give location of, in advertisements, 179
Special outfits, featuring of, increase sales, 505
Special sales, cards used in, 506
coupons used in, 506
ideas and experiences, review of, 505
novelty features of, 507
Special service, exploiting of, aids sales, 524, 525, 526, 528, 530, 533
Specialists, employment of, 525
Specialties and novelties in advertising, 269
Specialty advertising, arguments for, 269
creating interest in article offered, 271
distribution problem in, 271
forms of, 269
selecting article adapted to business, 270
suggested announcement to create demand for article offered, 271
Specific statement, value of, 278
Speech in selling, 401, 402, 404
Spines Company's use of telegrams in hat sale, 519

Sporting goods advertisement, 154
Sporting goods contest idea, 552
Sporting goods dealers, syndicated plate for, 196
Sporting-goods merchant, plan for building up mailing-list, 211
Standards of salesmanship, 399
Staples, habits of people in buying, 43
Start, value of good, for salesmen, 394
State colleges, cooperating with, 546
State education in salesmanship, 331
Stationery, window-display of, 128
Steps of sale, 418, 419
Stetson, John B., Company's retail "laboratory" store, 531
window-display, 131
Stock arrangement of, 412
knowing location of, 411
knowledge of, 407
questionnaires aid in buying of, 6
Stock control, card form for, 56
U. S. Chamber of Commerce recommendations on, 54
Store address in advertisements, 178
Store arrangement, contest for, 550
Store bulletins, 31, 340
Store fixtures and equipment, 102
Store-front construction, features of, 92
Store-front views of Connecticut hardware store, 93
Store mailing-lists, 204
Store paper, 238, 253
Store policy, change in, increases sales, 502
Store policy, loyalty to, by employes, 458
Stores, large, training methods of, 339
Story form of advertising, 141

Straus, S. W., & Co. on business dress, 359
Strawbridge & Clothier's manual, 366
  method of training, 345
Street-car advertising combined with newspaper advertising, 260, 262
Street-car cards, amount of copy needed for, 257
  color treatment of, 260
  cooperation of companies controlling space in obtaining designs for advertisers, 257
  examples of, 258, 259, 260, 261
  typography of, 260
  value of, 257
Students of salesmanship, amount of work done by, 336
Style as news in copy, 284
Style card for composing room, 170
Style in copy-language, 272
Style, novel and unexpected statements in copy, 302
Style show in popular restaurant, 549
Sub-headings, purposes of, 155
Substitute article offered in place of article asked for by customer, 409
Suburban and country trade, cultivating, 557, 563
Suggestion boxes, use of, 354
Suggestion contests among salespeople, 350
Suggestion, directing the customer's channel of thought, 424
  negative, in selling, 474
  use of, in making related sales, 412, 420, 422, 424, 425
Survey or research work, value of, to retailer, 3
Surveys, special, *Dry Goods Economist's* view of, 5
Syndicated advertising of cement manufacturer to dealers, 189

Syndicated advertising, example of, furnished sporting goods dealers, 196
  examples of, 187
  extent of, 186
Syndicated and cooperative advertising, 186
Syndicated illustrations, 195
Syndicated manual for retail stores, 375
Syndicated plates for sporting goods dealers, 196
System manual of Joseph Horne Co., 364

T

Tact in selling, 451
Tact, when to use compliments, 461
Tactics, meeting the approval of the shopper's friend, 443
  place of imagination in selling, 463
  suggesting related articles, 412, 420, 422
Tactless talk in presence of customer, 400
Tailor, men's, letter from, 217
Talk, tactless, in presence of customer, 400
Talking machine dealer's approval selling plan, 557
Talking Machine World's view of surveys, 10
Talks on better selling, 389
Taylor, Alex., & Company's baseball outfit for boys, 565
Taylor Carpet Company's evening receptions increase sales, 543
Teachers, cooperating with, 561
Teamwork in selling, 440
Teaser advertising, 295
Telegrams, use of, in hat sale, 519
Telephone as an aid in selling, 561
Telephone number, capitalizing, 519

Telephone salesmanship, need for courtesy and pleasing voice in, 402, 406
Telephone shopping made easy for out-of-town customers, 524
Ten commandments of S. Kann Sons Co., 354
Testimonials in advertising, 144, 288
in sales work, 500
Tests as items for copy, 288
Tetley's Tea advertisement, 329
Text and illustration of advertising, 156
Text of advertisements, type suitable for, 171
Text, relation of type to, 157
Three-panel displays, 128, 129
Tire-dealer's road signs, 268
Titche-Goettinger Co., method of training, 349
Tools, display of small, 113
Toy store's sales tactics, 489
Trade associations, assistance of in making displays, 134
Trade bulletins, use of, in training salespeople, 333
Trade tendencies, study of important, 72
Training for sales force, 331
Training methods of representative stores, 339
Traveling demonstrations, 547
Traveling grocery store, 526
Traxler, Louis, Co. method of training, 353
Trucks and wagons, possibilities of, as outdoor advertising mediums, 268
Turnover and price-figuring, 42
comments of National Retail Dry Goods Association on, 66
demand for product determines, 43
explanation of, 50
foe to, 71

Turnover, golden rules of, 48
how department store increased, 75
multiplying, increases net profit, 49
part played by concentration in, 46
rate of, how to determine, 51
rate of, in different department stores, 69
speeding up of, may eliminate loss, 74
table, 52
table of different electrical products, 43
U. S. Chamber of Commerce recommendations on, 54
variation of, 43
Type faces suitable for advertisements, 171
for display purposes, distinctive, 173
relation of, to text of advertisement, 157
Typographical style card, 170
Typography, distinctive, 172
for street-car cards, 260
in advertising, 148

U

Umbrellas, novel display of, 132
U. S. Chamber of Commerce recommendations on turnover and stock control, 54
stock control card, 56
United Cigar Stores' compensation methods, 80
United Drug Company's store paper, 238
Used-car advertisement, 197

V

Vacuum cleaner contest idea, 555
Valley Hardware Co. advertisement featuring recipes, 515
Vanity Fair Silk Mills' letters to retail salespeople, 383

Van Sciver, J. B., Company's billboard advertising, 263
  method of overcoming neighborhood store problem, 248
Victor dealer's survey work, 11
Victrola advertisements by Sherman, Clay & Co., 284
View of salespeople by customers, 398
Viewpoint of reader, getting the, 303
Viewpoint, value of, change in copy, 304
Voice, the, how it reveals character, 403, 404
  in selling, 402
Voucher envelop, example of, 365

W

Wagons and trucks, possibilities of, as outdoor advertising mediums, 268
Walk-Over Shoe Stores' plan of using shoe laces as follow-up, 524
Wanamaker, John, distribution of advertising expense, 20
"Want slip," merchandise, example of, 365
Washing machines, demonstrating of, 525
Wayne, Barbara, letters of, 385
"Wear-Ever" selling bulletin, 378
Weber & Heilbroner advertisement of clothing, 145
Westinghouse Electric & Mfg. Co. plan of furnishing syndicated advertisements, 193
Weyerhaeuser Forest Products' suggestion on crating and packing, 39
White lettering, use of, 158
White space, use of, in advertisements, 149
White & Wyckoff manual, 383
  three-panel display, 128
Wholesalers, distribution of booklets, by 381
Windows and show-cases, lighting of, 125
Window-display merchandising, 118
Window-displays, animated, 557
  checking up results from, 126
  educational, 133, 135
  example of poor, 119
  featuring contests in, 127
  featuring historical events, 130
  ideas for novel, 132
  linking up, with local events, 123
  money value of, 130
  nature scenes in, 129
  of home-town products, 545
  percentage of sales attributed to, 130
  points on, 118
  seasonableness in, 120
  three-panel types of, 128, 129
  timeliness in, 127
  variety in, 120
Window-space, charging for, 137
Window-trimming contest among school children, 540
Winter campaign of service station, 255
Women buyers, advertising to influence, 6
Women, exhibitions for, 545
  how to deal with, 465
  style shows for, 548
  what kind of articles they demand, 465
Women-appeals, survey of, 5
Women's Advertising Club of Los Angeles, result of questionnaire to women, 6
Woolley, Edward Mott, advice on making up bank mailing-lists, 205
Woolworth compensation methods, 80
Wrapping and packing, saving in, 38

Y

Yourself, how to sell, 494

RET